Appendix D

NIC Details

The proposed changes to Employers' NICs were announced by the Secretary of State for Social Security on 30 November 1998 and take effect from 6 April 1999. Please insert this page in the relevant section in the Payroll Management Handbook 1998/99.

Class 1 Not Contracted-out

	1999/2000		
	Employee (%)		Employer (%)
	Standard	**Reduced*	
Total Earnings			
£0.00 to £66.00 weekly	Nil	*Nil*	Nil
(£0.00 to £286.00 monthly)			
£66.01 to £83.00 weekly	10	*3.85*	Nil
(£286.01 to £361.00 monthly)			
£83.01 to £500.00 weekly	10	*3.85*	12.2
(£361.01 to £2,167.00 monthly)			
Over £500.00 weekly	10 to UEL	*3.85 to UEL*	12.2
(Over £2,167.00 monthly)	thereafter Nil	*thereafter Nil*	

* Reduced rate for married women and widow optants

Class 1 Contracted-out money purchase (COMP) scheme

	1999/2000		
	Employee (%)		Employer (%)
	Standard	**Reduced*	
Total Earnings			
£0.00 to £66.00 weekly	Nil	*Nil*	Nil
(£0.00 to £286.00 monthly)			
£66.01 to £83.00 weekly	8.4	*3.85*	(0.6)
(£286.01 to £361.00 monthly)			
£83.01 to £500.00 weekly	8.4	*3.85*	11.6
(£361.01 to £2,167.00 monthly)			
Over £500.00 weekly	8.4 to UEL	*3.85 to UEL*	12.2
(Over £2,167.00 monthly)	thereafter Nil	*thereafter Nil*	

* Reduced rate for married women and widow optants

Class 1 Contracted-out salary related (COSR) scheme

	1999/2000		
	Employee (%)		Employer (%)
	Standard	*Reduced	
Total Earnings			
£0.00 to £66.00 weekly	Nil	Nil	Nil
(£0.00 to £286.00 monthly)			
£66.01 to £83.00 weekly	8.4	3.85	(3.0)
(£286.01 to £361.00 monthly)			
£83.01to £500.00 weekly	8.4	3.85	9.2
(£361.01 to £2,167.00 monthly)			
Over £500.00 weekly	8.4 to UEL	3.85 to UEL	12.2
(Over £2,167.00 monthly)	thereafter Nil	thereafter Nil	

* Reduced rate for married women and widow optants

NIC Class 1 earnings limits

	1999/2000		
	Week £	Month £	Year £
Lower earnings limit (LEL)	66	286	3,432
Earnings threshold (ET)	83	361	4,335
Upper earnings limit (UEL)	500	2,167	26,000

Note: Employee NICs are payable only on earnings above the LEL. Employer's NICs are payable only on earnings above the ET.

Tolley's Payroll Management Handbook 1998–99

Editor
Lyn Hirst

Publishing Manager
Mike Nicholas

Tolley Publishing Company Limited
A member of the Reed Elsevier plc group

First published 1987
Second edition 1988
Third edition 1989
Fourth edition 1990
Fifth edition 1991
Sixth edition 1992
Seventh edition 1993
Eighth edition 1994
Ninth edition 1995
Tenth edition 1996
Eleventh edition 1997
Twelfth edition 1998

Published by
Tolley Publishing Company Ltd,
Tolley House, 2 Addiscombe Road,
Croydon, Surrey CR9 5AF, England
0181-686 9141

Typeset by
Letterpart Limited,
Reigate, Surrey

Printed and bound in Great Britain by
The Bath Press, Bath

Preface

The aim of this book is to provide payroll practitioners with a complete survey of the theory and practice of payroll administration. The 1998–99 edition contains extensively revised and updated comment on the key topics of PAYE, National Insurance, pensions, computerisation, office automation and the expanding field of employment law. All these topics, and others such as banking, impinge on the operation of payroll. New legislation, work-practices and developments and innovations in technology, to mention just a few, have a direct impact on payroll procedures which the payroll administrator will need to assimilate and implement.

Although payroll administration historically has always held some degree of esteem in most organisations (not least because the payroll office 'paid' the wages) it is only over the last decade or so that the role of payroll has begun to receive wide recognition. This can be attributed to several reasons. The monitoring and control of employment costs is essential in every business. The spread of automation and computerisation has produced efficiencies in the payroll function, but also served to improve availability of accurate and up-to-the-minute management information. The increased policing of PAYE and National Insurance by the Inland Revenue and DSS, coupled with the application of penalties, has focused employers' attention. The work of associations and organisations, such as the Institute of Payroll and Pensions Management (IPPM) and the Payroll Alliance has served to raise the standing of the payroll professional.

It is surprising that some employers are still unaware of the importance of their payroll function beyond simply 'paying the wages'. This relates back to the fact that the costs incurred in staffing and equipping payroll offices are seen as an unavoidable overhead. But failure by a company to invest in skilled payroll staff, and in suitable modern equipment and software, may prove over time an expensive misconception. There needs to be investment in equipment, information and skills in the payroll function. The visible return may be reduced payroll staffing levels, but there will be other less visible savings, such as lower error rates, reduced liability for undeducted income tax and NICs, improved management information, etc.

The role of the payroll function continues to evolve. Historically, payroll was labour intensive. Today the modern payroll office is highly efficient and a source of vast amounts of invaluable management information. It interfaces with many other functions and accounts for possibly the biggest single expenditure item of the business. Today's payroll administrator safeguards assets by applying management skills and legislation and contributes indirectly to the success of the business. Accordingly, the payroll function should no longer be seen as just an unavoidable overhead but as a cornerstone of a modern and successful business structure.

This twelfth edition includes as many changes as possible across the entire spectrum of payroll work, up to 31 October 1998. Wherever possible other significant changes which will affect payroll administration at some point in the next twelve months have been identified and incorporated into the text.

Tolley is pleased to contribute to raising the profile of the payroll function and providing a valued source of information by the publication of the *Payroll Management Handbook*.

Comments on this annual publication and suggestions for improvements are always welcomed.

TOLLEY PUBLISHING CO LTD

Contents

Contents

Contents

Contents

Abbreviations

GENERAL

ACAS	=	Advisory, Conciliation and Arbitration Service
ACH	=	Automated Clearing House
AEO	=	Attachment of Earnings Order
APACS	=	Association for Payment Clearing Services
APP	=	Appropriate Personal Pension
APR	=	Annual Percentage Rate
APSA	=	Association of Payroll and Superannuation Administrators
APM	=	Alternative Payment Method for Class 1A NICs
APP	=	Appropriate Personal Pension (Scheme)
APT&C	=	Administrative Professional Technical and Clerical
ATM	=	Automated Teller Machine
AVC(s)	=	Additional Voluntary Contribution(s)
BA	=	Benefits Agency
BACS	=	Bankers Automated Clearing Service
BACSTEL	=	BACS Telecommunication (Service)
BASIC	=	Beginner's All-purpose Symbolic Instruction Code
bn	=	Billion (American = One thousand million)
BPMA	=	British Payroll Managers Association
BUPA	=	British United Provident Association
CA	=	Contributions Agency; Certified Amount; Court of Appeal
CAC	=	Central Arbitration Committee
CAO	=	Conjoined Arrestment Order
CASE	=	Computer Aided System Engineering
CCAEO	=	Community Charge AEO
CCT	=	Compulsory Competitive Tendering
CEP	=	Contributions Equivalent Premium
CGT	=	Capital Gains Tax
Ch	=	Chapter (of Act)
CHAPS	=	Clearing House Automated Payment System
CIMP(s)	=	Contracted-In Money Purchase Scheme(s) (a misnomer)
COBOL	=	Common Business Oriented Language
CODA	=	Computerisation of Schedule D Assessment
COEG	=	Contracted-Out Employment Group
COMB	=	Contracted-Out Mixed Benefit
COMP(s)	=	Contracted-Out Money Purchase Scheme(s)
COP	=	Computerisation of PAYE
COSR	=	Contracted-Out Salary Related Scheme
CRU	=	Compensation Recovery Unit
CSA	=	Child Support Agency
CSR	=	Company Secretary's Review
CTAEO	=	Council Tax AEO
DfEE	=	Department for Education and Employment
DEC	=	Digital Equipment Corporation
DEO	=	Deduction from Earnings Order (Child Support)
DHSS	=	Department of Health and Social Security (now split into Department of Health, and DSS)

DIP	=	Document Image Processing
DMS	=	Document Management Systems
DOB	=	Date of Birth
DoE	=	Department of the Environment
DSS	=	Department of Social Security; Decision Support System
DTR	=	Double Taxation Relief
DTI	=	Department of Trade and Industry
EAT	=	Employment Appeal Tribunal
EC	=	European Community; European Communities
ECON	=	Employment Contracted-Out Number
ECSC	=	European Coal and Steel Community
EEC	=	European Economic Community
EFT	=	Electronic Funds Transfer
EDI	=	Electronic Data Interchange
EIS	=	Executive Information System
EMU	=	Economic and Monetary Union
ESOP(s)	=	Employee Share (or Stock) Ownership Plan(s)
Euratom	=	European Atomic Energy Community
EWC	=	Expected Week of Confinement
FMS	=	File Management System
FPCS	=	Fixed Profit Car Scheme (now known as IRAMARs – *see above*)
FRS(s)	=	Financial Reporting Standard(s)
FSA	=	Financial Services Authority (formerly known as the Securities and Investments Board)
FSAVC(s)	=	Free-standing AVC(s)
FURBS	=	Funded Unapproved Retirement Benefit Schemes
GAYE	=	Give As You Earn (charitable giving)
GCL	=	Graded Contribution Limit
4GL	=	4th Generation Language
GMP	=	Guaranteed Minimum Pension
GUI	=	Graphical User Interface
HL	=	House of Lords
HM	=	Her Majesty's
HRM	=	Human Resource Management
HSA	=	Hospital Savings Association
IBM	=	International Business Machines
IBPM	=	Institute of British Payroll Management (now IPPM *see below*)
ICL	=	International Computers Limited
IPD	=	Institute of Personnel and Development (formerly known as IPM)
IPM	=	Institute of Personnel Management (now known as IPD – *see above*)
IPPM	=	Institute of Payroll and Pensions Management (formerly IBPM)
IPR	=	Intellectual Property Rights
IRAMAR(s)	=	Inland Revenue Authorised Mileage Rates (formerly known as FPCS rates)
IS	=	Information Systems
ISDN	=	Income Support Deduction Notice

ISDN	=	Integrated Services Digital Network
ISO	=	International Standards Organisation
IT	=	Information Technology
ITIP	=	Income Tax Instalment Payments System (Isle of Man)
ITO	=	Information Technology Office
JENI	=	Judgment Enforcement Northern Ireland AEO
LACSAB	=	Local Authority Conditions of Service Advisory Board
LAN(s)	=	Local Area Network(s)
LCD	=	Lord Chancellor's Department
LEL	=	Lower Earnings Limit
LPI	=	Limited Price Indexation
Ltd	=	Limited (A private limited company)
Max	=	Maximum
MCA	=	Married Couple's Allowance
MCNI	=	Magistrates' Courts Northern Ireland AEO
MFR	=	Minimum Funding Requirements
Min	=	Minimum
MIS	=	Management Information System
MLP	=	Manufacturer's List Price
MOSES	=	Modernisation of Schedule E Systems
MPP	=	Maternity Pay Period
NALGO	=	National Association of Local Government Officers
NAPF	=	National Association of Pension Funds
NATFHE	=	National Association of Teachers in Further and Higher Education
NBPI	=	National Board for Prices and Incomes
NCC	=	National Computing Centre
NCR	=	National Cash Register; No Carbon Required
NHS	=	National Health Service
NI	=	National Insurance
NICs	=	National Insurance Contributions
NINO	=	National Insurance Number
NIRS	=	National Insurance Recording System
NJC	=	National Joint Council
NMB	=	National Maritime Board
NMW	=	National Minimum Wage
NTS	=	National Tracing System
OCR	=	Optical Character Recognition
OIR	=	Official Interest Rate
OMP	=	Occupational Maternity Pay
OPAS	=	Pension Advisory Service
OPB	=	Occupational Pensions Board
OPRA	=	Occupational Pensions Regulatory Authority
OSP	=	Occupational Sick Pay
p	=	paragraph (of Act, booklet etc.)
PAYE	=	Pay As You Earn
PBR	=	Payment By Results
PC	=	Personal Computer
PCB	=	Pensions Compensation Board
PE	=	Phase Encoded

PHI	=	Permanent Health Insurance (also known as Salary Continuance Schemes)
PIA	=	Personal Investment Authority
PIW	=	Period of Incapacity for Work
PLC	=	Public Limited Company
PMI	=	Pensions Management Institute
PMR	=	Payroll Manager's Review
PRP	=	Profit-Related Pay (sometimes used for Performance-Related Pay)
PP	=	Personal Pension
PSA	=	PAYE Settlement Agreement
PSO	=	Pensions Schemes Office
PSPF	=	Public Sector Payroll Forum
PSPG	=	Private Sector Payrolls Group
Pt	=	Part (of Act)
PTS	=	Percentage Threshold Scheme
PUP	=	Paid Up Pension
PRs	=	Protected Rights
QA	=	Quality Assurance
QW	=	Qualifying Week
REP	=	Regional Employment Premium
RPI	=	Retail Prices Index
rpi	=	Rows per inch
s	=	Section (of Act)
SAS	=	Statements of Auditing Standards
SAYE	=	Save As You Earn
SEA	=	Scottish Earnings Arrestment
SCAO	=	Scottish Conjoined Arrestment Orders
SCMA	=	Scottish Current Maintenance Arrestment
SCON	=	Scheme Contracted-out Number
Sch	=	Schedule
SERP	=	State Earnings-Related Pension
SERPS	=	State Earnings-Related Pension Scheme
SET	=	Selective Employment Tax
SFO	=	Superannuation Funds Office
SI	=	Statutory Instrument
SMP	=	Statutory Maternity Pay
SO	=	Stationery Office (formerly HMSO)
SORP	=	Statement of Recommended Practice
SPA	=	State Pension Age
SSADM	=	Structured Systems and Design Methodology
SSAP(s)	=	Statement(s) of Standard Accounting Practice
SSP	=	Statutory Sick Pay
SWIFT	=	Society for Worldwide Interbank Financial Telecommunications
T&A	=	Time and Attendance System
TRP	=	Total Remuneration Package
UEL	=	Upper Earnings Limit
UK	=	United Kingdom
URL	=	Universal Resource Locator
USA	=	United States of America

VAT	=	Value Added Tax
VDU	=	Visual Display Unit
YOP	=	Youth Opportunities Programme
YTS	=	Youth Training Scheme

LAW REPORTS

AC	=	Appeal Cases
AER	=	All England Law Reports
Ch	=	Chancery Division
ER	=	English Reports
HL	=	House of Lords
ICR	=	Industrial Cases Reports
IRLB	=	Industrial Relations Law Bulletin
IRLR	=	Industrial Relations Law Reports
LJKB	=	Law Journal King's Bench
QB/KB	=	Queen's Bench/King's Bench
STC	=	Simon's Tax Cases
TC	=	Taxation Cases
TLR	=	Times Law Reports
WLR	=	Weekly Law Reports

STATUTES

AA 1814	=	Apprentices Act 1814
AA 1950	=	Arbitration Act 1950
AJAA 1934	=	Administration of Justice (Appeals) Act 1934
AEA 1971	=	Attachment of Earnings Act 1971
AF(C)A 1917	=	Air Force (Constitution) Act 1917
BEA 1882	=	Bills of Exchange Act 1882
CA 1985	=	Companies Act 1985
CA 1989	=	Companies Act 1989
CAA 1981	=	Criminal Attempts Act 1981
CBNA 1954	=	Currency and Bank Notes Act 1954
CCA 1984	=	County Courts Act 1984
CgA 1971	=	Coinage Act 1971
CLSA 1990	=	Courts and Legal Services Act 1990
CTGA 1979	=	Capital Gains Tax Act 1979
ChA 1957	=	Cheques Act 1957
CMA 1990	=	Computer Misuse Act 1990
CPA 1947	=	Crown Proceedings Act 1947
CSA 1991	=	Child Support Act 1991
CuA 1983	=	Currency Act 1983
CYPA 1933	=	Children and Young Persons Act 1933
DDA 1995	=	Disability Discrimination Act 1995
DPA 1984	=	Data Protection Act 1984
DPA 1998	=	Data Protection Act 1998
DSA 1987	=	Debtors (Scotland) Act 1987
EA 1982	=	Employment Act 1982
EA 1989	=	Employment Act 1989
ECA 1972	=	European Communities Act 1972

ECA 1973	=	Employment of Children Act 1973
EdA 1944	=	Education Act 1944
EmPA 1975	=	Employment Protection Act 1975
EPCA 1978	=	Employment Protection (Consolidation) Act 1978
EqPA 1970	=	Equal Pay Act 1970
ERA 1996	=	Employment Rights Act 1996
ER(DR)A 1998	=	Employment Rights (Dispute Resolution) Act 1998
ETA 1996	=	Employment Tribunals Act 1996
EWYPCA 1920	=	Employment of Women, Young Persons and Children Act 1920
FA 1961	=	Finance Act 1961
FA 1970	=	Finance Act 1970
FA 1973	=	Finance Act 1973
FA 1976	=	Finance Act 1976
FA 1978	=	Finance Act 1978
FA 1980	=	Finance Act 1980
FA 1981	=	Finance Act 1981
FA 1986	=	Finance Act 1986
FA 1987	=	Finance Act 1987
F(No 2)A 1975	=	Finance (No 2) Act 1975
F(No 2)A 1987	=	Finance (No 2) Act 1987
FA 1988	=	Finance Act 1988
FA 1989	=	Finance Act 1989
FA 1990	=	Finance Act 1990
FA 1992	=	Finance Act 1992
FA 1993	=	Finance Act 1993
FA 1994	=	Finance Act 1994
FA 1995	=	Finance Act 1995
FA 1998	=	Finance Act 1998
FB	=	Finance Bill
FCA 1981	=	Forgery and Counterfeiting Act 1981
FgA 1913	=	Forgery Act 1913
FSA 1986	=	Financial Services Act 1986
FyA 1961	=	Factories Act 1961
HSWA 1974	=	Health and Safety at Work etc. Act 1974
IA 1986	=	Insolvency Act 1986
ICTA 1970	=	Income and Corporation Taxes Act 1970 (Repealed)
ICTA 1988	=	Income and Corporation Taxes Act 1988
IhTA 1984	=	Inheritance Tax Act 1984
InA 1978	=	Interpretation Act 1978
ITA 1918	=	Income Tax Act 1918 (Repealed)
ITA 1952	=	Income Tax Act 1952 (Repealed)
ITA 1996	=	Industrial Tribunals Act 1996
IT(E)A 1943	=	Income Tax (Employment) Act 1943
LA 1980	=	Limitation Act 1980
LGA 1972	=	Local Government Act 1972
LGFA 1988	=	Local Government Finance Act 1988
LGFA 1992	=	Local Government Finance Act 1992
LR(CN)A 1945	=	Law Reform (Contributory Negligence) Act 1945
MSA 1970	=	Merchant Shipping Act 1970

NMPPA 1865	=	Naval and Marine Pay and Pensions Act 1865
NIA 1911	=	National Insurance Act 1911
NIA 1946	=	National Insurance Act 1946
PA 1964	=	Police Act 1964
PA 1969	=	Police Act 1969
PA 1995	=	Pensions Act 1995
PAA 1971	=	Powers of Attorney Act 1971
PHA 1936	=	Public Health Act 1936
PIA 1971	=	Pensions Increase Act 1971
PjA 1911	=	Perjury Act 1911
POA 1969	=	Post Office Act 1969
PSA 1993	=	Pensions Schemes Act 1993
PYPA 1884	=	Pensions and Yeomanry Pay Act 1884
PWA 1960	=	Payment of Wages Act 1960 (Repealed)
RFA 1980	=	Reserve Forces Act 1980
RRA 1976	=	Race Relations Act 1976
SA 1950	=	Shops Act 1950
SA 1972	=	Superannuation Act 1972
SDA 1975	=	Sex Discrimination Act 1975
SDA 1986	=	Sex Discrimination Act 1986
SSA 1975	=	Social Security Act 1975
SSA 1986	=	Social Security Act 1986
SSA 1989	=	Social Security Act 1989
SSA 1990	=	Social Security Act 1990
SSA 1998	=	Social Security Act 1998
SSAA 1992	=	Social Security Administration Act 1992
SSCBA 1992	=	Social Security Contributions and Benefits Act 1992
SSHBA 1982	=	Social Security Housing Benefits Act 1982
SSPA 1975	=	Social Security Pensions Act 1975
SSPA 1994	=	Statutory Sick Pay Act 1994
St. SPA 1991	=	Statutory Sick Pay Act 1991
TAs 1831–1940	=	Truck Acts 1831–1940 (Repealed)
ThA 1968	=	Theft Act 1968
TMA 1970	=	Taxes Management Act 1970
TUA 1984	=	Trade Union Act 1984
TULRCA 1992	=	Trade Union and Labour Relations (Consolidation) Act 1992
TURERA 1993	=	Trade Union Reform and Employment Rights Act 1993
WA 1986	=	Wages Act 1986
WAL(S)A 1880	=	Wages Arrestment Limitation (Scotland) Act 1880
YP(E)A 1938	=	Young Persons (Employment) Act 1938

Acknowledgements

The publishers acknowledge the ready co-operation of Her Majesty's Stationery Office (SO) in permitting the reproduction of the Inland Revenue and DSS material published in this Handbook. All the forms are subject to Crown copyright.

The following chapters have been originated or updated by the following authors.

1	Introduction	*Edmund P Moynihan* MBCS, ACIS,
26	Payroll Technology	*APMI, MIPPM, Reader in Business Administration and Information Technology, Liverpool John Moores University*
2	Outline of Payroll Administration	*Philip Bird* FIPPM, MInstAM
3	Legal Framework	*Richard Hendry* LLM, Associate Director,
4	Payee Status	*Collinson Grant Consultants Ltd*
5	Payroll Law	
6	Background to Pay and Benefits	*Simon Garrett*, Managing Director, BDO Stoy Hayward Ltd, Benefit Consulting
7	Pay Schemes	
8	Disability and Maternity Benefits	*Roger Self* BA, Editor of Tolley's Pensions Administration
10	Pension Schemes	
14	Pension Contributions	
21	Pension Payroll Procedures	
9	Benefits, Expenses and Termination Payments	*Alan Lowrey*, Senior Tax Manager, Williams Jeffery Barber
11	Income Tax	
12	National Insurance Contributions	*Jim Yuill*, Director of Social Security Services, Ernst & Young

13	**Attachment of Earnings Orders**	*Norman Green BSc (Hons), GIMA, MIPPMdip, MBCS.CEng, CMG UK Ltd*
30	**Future Developments Affecting Payroll Administration**	
15	**Voluntary Deductions**	*Sarah Semple BA (Hons), freelance editor and writer*
19	**Payroll Accounting**	
25	**Manual Calculation Methods**	
16	**Payroll Organisation**	*Ian Whyteside FMAAT, MIPPM, Exchequer Services Manager at Slough Borough Council*
17	**Management Skills**	*Paul McCallion CPsychol, FIMC, Management Consultant at TDS Northern Ireland Ltd*
18	**Employee Payroll Procedures**	*Yvette Lamidey, Group Payroll Manager at WH Smith Ltd*
20	**PAYE Procedures**	*Mike Evans, Remuneration and Benefits Consultant at Pannell Kerr Forster*
23	**Security and Administrative Controls**	*Paul Sheehan, MIPPMdip, Service Manager within Managed Payroll at CMG*
24	**Payroll Audits**	*John McAloon BA(Hons), FCA, Internal Audit Manager, BICC Cables Ltd*
22	**Payment Methods**	*P Simon Parsons PG Cert, MIPPMdip, Chief Analyst / Millennium Manager at Centrefile Ltd*
27	**Computerising Your System**	
28	**Selecting a Computer System**	
29	**Implementation of Your Computer System**	

The publishers wish to thank the several authors who assisted in the updating of this book in 1998.

1 Introduction

Scope of this chapter

1.1   Payroll administration is concerned with the calculation and payment of wages, salaries, pensions, and other disbursements such as employee expenses. State social security and charitable payments are specialised branches of the same subject, although this handbook concentrates on employed earnings and occupational pensions. Initially a reader unfamiliar with the subject may suppose this to be a straightforward matter and merely a question of handling a large volume of periodic payments. In practice, however, numerous complications arise. These are the result of the interaction of major factors such as employment law, the design of employee incentive schemes, the design of sickness and pension arrangements, taxation, social security regulations, the banking services available and the technology of business automation. These factors are, of course, constantly changing. They represent no more than the current embodiment of the somewhat fickle views of business executives, trade unionists, governments and individual employees expressing their preferences through the labour market. This has been true since at least the early 19th century, although the pace of change and complexity of all aspects of payroll have markedly increased over the last 50 years. As a result, large-scale payroll operations many years ago reached the stage of being impractical without computers and other forms of office automation. Some people in fact suggest, that as regards pay and benefits, the legislation and the rules made by employers have reached the point of self-defeating complexity. There is, however, no doubt that the current period of complexity and rapid change will extend well into the future.

The payroll administrator can make a practical contribution to the formation of the employer's rules governing pay and benefits. However, his primary function is to incorporate these internal rules and legislation into an effective payroll service. In addition to paying wages and pensions he must also carry out his employer's statutory duty to act as a tax collector and social security officer.

(For convenience the references in this book to payroll administrators and payees are often grammatically masculine. The legal position is contained in the *Interpretation Act 1978, s 6* which states that: 'unless the contrary intention appears words importing the masculine gender include the feminine'. However, from a more practical point of view, with both administrators and payees, the percentage of women is usually quite high. The sex ratio depends on factors like the traditions of the employing industry, e.g. women payees are in a majority in retailing. Furthermore, administrators or payees may be organisations rather than people. For example, trade unions are frequently payees, and often receive their membership subscriptions from employers, who deduct them from employees via the payroll.)

In large undertakings there is no standard division of duties between payroll, personnel, pensions and financial administration. A close liaison, however, is always found between these functions on payroll and related matters irrespective of the organisational structure.

Purpose of this handbook

1.2   This handbook seeks to provide a wide survey of the whole of payroll administration. As there are already many excellent books on particular aspects of payroll work, such as income tax or maternity benefits, these subjects have been dealt with in outline and references have been given. Indeed, the vast amount of knowledge required by the modern payroll administrator is such that most chapters can be no more than a basic introduction to a particular topic. Also, the treatment of associated business functions such as pensions and computing has been mainly restricted to the payroll aspects. There is inevitably some overlap between chapters so that they can be read independently for the sake of convenience. Besides the payroll administrator other business professionals may find this handbook helpful. Pensions administrators, personnel officers, company secretaries and accountants will find it of practical use. Computer systems analysts and industrial engineers who are involved with payroll and incentive schemes will also find it valuable.

The handbook's perspective is that of the large employer in the UK with hundreds, thousands or tens of thousands of staff. The background implied is often that of a large manufacturing company, retail chain, financial institution or local authority. The small company with 50 or 100 employees cannot afford specialists like the payroll manager or systems analyst and many of the individual rôles will be the responsibility of a single person. There is still a payroll to be supervised by the company secretary, accountant or office manager. Hopefully much of the handbook can still be of use to them, as the principles are the same irrespective of scale.

Limitations of this handbook

1.3   The figures, legislation and regulations used here are those for the 1998/99 tax year unless stated otherwise. The payroll environment is always changing and this handbook reflects the situation as at 3 August 1998. There is some limited coverage of special types of employee such as armed forces personnel, mariners and directors of companies. There are not many differences in principle between employee payrolls and pensioner payrolls, so much of what is said about employees also applies to pensioners. However, Chapter 21 (Pension Payroll Procedures) explains the differences. The legal regime assumed throughout the book is that of England and Wales, although the other parts of the UK are subject to similar payroll legislation.

Neglect of the payroll function

1.4   For many years payroll administration was a 'Cinderella' occupation in large British organisations. This theme is contained in comments about the wages office published in the 1930s.

> 'Here we have an offshoot, originally, of the cashier's department which has developed along its own lines, often without adequate supervision. The scope of its duties has been widened somewhat by modern legislation as well as by increasing demands, both internal and external, for wages information and records. In a large works it often serves so many masters that it seems to be the immediate concern of no one in particular to investigate its methods — hence its neglect, notwithstanding the important functions it performs'.

(See Reference (1) in 1.12 below.)

It is strange, given the accelerating complexity of payroll work over the last 50 years, that this quotation was true, until perhaps the early 1980s. Payroll staff were often forced to pick up their skills rather haphazardly 'on the job'. Accounts staff have tended to regard payroll as obviously important, but a routine backwater. Personnel people used to show little interest in the field except for specific purposes such as a source of data on earnings. Amongst IT staff payroll work has been seen as a critical application where it is only too easy to make an expensive and embarrassing mistake when changing payroll software. Thus, some IT staff try to avoid payroll work because of its dangerous nature, and because it is not regarded by the management of an ordinary organisation as a core computer application.

However, there have been marked changes over the last decade with the development of payroll professional and trade organisations, and successful qualifications assessed by examination and coursework in payroll practice administration. Futhermore, an MSc has recently been introduced in payroll management. All this provides a strong indication that payroll practice is at last being recognised as a demanding profession. Another indication is the significant number of national conferences and journals devoted to payroll matters.

National payroll statistics

1.5   Payroll administration is, of course, a subject of the greatest economic importance. The following UK statistics give a broad indication of this. Approximate and round figures are used in some cases.

3

(*a*)   **UK workforce (1998)**

UK workforce (1998)	Millions of people
Employed	24
Self-employed	3
Unemployed	1
Total economically active	28
Economically inactive	8

(The economically inactive are those people between 16 and State retirement age who are not employed or self-employed, and who are not actively seeking paid work.)

Note that most of the above figures are fairly stable, changing by relatively small percentage amounts over the years. However, the unemployment figure is of considerable political importance. Fortunately the number unemployed is usually only a small proportion of the working age population, but the number does fluctuate considerably from year to year. The method of calculating this figure can also be challenged. As a broad indication the number of unemployed people had fallen below 1.4 million by mid-1998.

(*b*)   The number of people over 65 years of age will be about 9 million by the year 2000. (The economically inactive are those people aged between 16 and state retirement age who are not employed or self-employed, and who are not actively seeking paid work.)

(*c*)   **Financial statistics (1996)**

UK financial statistics (1996)	£ billion
Gross national product (at market prices)	752
Employed earnings	400
Self-employed earnings	70
Income tax	67
Total National Insurance contributions	41

(*d*)   As an indication of the level of employee payroll payments, an adult worker's average earnings were estimated to be about £368 per week in 1997. Price inflation was just over four per cent in mid-1998.

(*e*)   **Typical pay levels**

The following table gives a broad indication of current wage and salary levels for a few occupations. It should be remembered that the pay for the same occupation varies significantly for many reasons. These reasons include geographical location within the UK and the level of responsibility or skill required which is sometimes indicated by a prefix, for example chief accountant or senior clerk. Also, scales, on which pay progresses according to years of service, are common in occupations like teaching. Of course, the whole 'reward package' needs to be considered. The reward package includes not only pay but also benefits like a company car and pension scheme which may be worth an extra 20 or 30 per cent on top of basic earnings.

Occupation	Representative basic pay (£s per week in 1997)
Fork-lift truck driver	170
Payroll clerk	200
Firefighter (experienced)	350
Teacher	400
Senior computer programmer	450
Medical doctor (in general practice)	900

The details of pay in various occupations are published in surveys. An example is Reference (6) in 1.12 below.

(*f*)   To indicate the level of pension payments, in 1998/99 the basic State pension is £64.70 for a single person and £103.40 for a married couple. Of course, pensioners frequently have other sources of income, particularly occupational pensions. On average, though, occupational pensions are probably smaller than the basic State pension.

Many social security benefits, e.g. income support, are at a lower level than State pensions. (See Reference (5) in 1.12 below and Appendix D for the details of social security rates.)

(For general economic and pay statistics see References (2) and (6) in 1.12 below.)

Main payroll functions

1.6   As already stated, there are no clear-cut divisions between the payroll, personnel, pensions and accounts functions. There is also no universally agreed approach to sharing the responsibility for payroll computer systems with the information technology department. The main payroll functions are usually:

(*a*)   calculating gross pay and deductions such as income tax and pension contributions;

(*b*)   keeping payroll records;

(*c*)   payment of net wages and salaries;

(*d*)   payment of deductions to the Inland Revenue, charities etc;

(*e*)   preparation of annual returns to employees, Inland Revenue etc;

(*f*)   preparation of pay statistics and reports.

Other areas which are commonly administered either partially or fully by payroll administrators include:

 (i)   time and attendance records;

 (ii)   sickness and maternity leave;

 (iii)   holidays;

 (iv)   employee benefits such as loans and luncheon vouchers;

 (v)   employee expenses;

 (vi)   the preparation of the P11D tax returns associated with employee benefits and expenses;

 (vii)   assisting with some pension functions, e.g. collecting pension contributions and membership data;

(viii)   pension payroll.

There is often an overlap with the cashier's function because of the need to handle large volumes of cash and cheques in many payroll departments. Sometimes the two functions are merged or, alternatively, payment of cash wages is hived off to a separate cashier's department.

Main payroll objectives

1.7   The main objective of payroll administration is the prompt and accurate payment of all payees. Payees are, of course, not just employees or pensioners. They include, as already indicated, organisations such as charities or medical insurers which receive deductions from pay. The payroll process requires the collection of data and accurately completing all the pay calculations for hundreds or thousands of payees within a period as short as a week. All the payslips have to be distributed and payments made within the same time scale. The calculations taken as a whole are quite complex. It is a tribute to payroll administrators that this whole process is taken for granted and that it is an ongoing weekly or monthly success.

Another major objective of payroll work is, of course, the operation of the income tax and National Insurance contribution deduction schemes under the Pay As You Earn scheme. PAYE is, in fact, an extremely effective integrated tax collection system involving the Inland Revenue, the Contributions Agency (control of the Contributions Agency is due to pass from the Department of Social Security to the Inland Revenue), the employer and the employee.

Organisation of payroll administration

1.8   Payroll administration falls uncomfortably between the personnel and accounting functions of business. In many organisations it is seen primarily as a financial function and the payroll manager reports to a senior accountant. In some organisations the chief payroll administrator reports to the personnel director while in a small organisation a part-time administrator may be responsible to the company secretary.

An old idea which has become popular in recent times is outsourcing. This means that the whole or part of a business activity is performed for a fee by an outside organisation. Many business activities, including the payroll function, can be partially, or almost wholly outsourced.

As already indicated, payroll staff may only cover part of the payroll function or alternatively have additional duties. This makes it difficult to set out any hard and fast rules on payroll staffing. The situation is further compounded by the effects of pay frequency and the complexities of the pay structure. However, a guarded view is that one payroll person is required for every 400 employees, assuming a good quality computer payroll system and two or three thousand employees in total. (See 16.7 below for an examination of relevant considerations.) As payroll administration can benefit from the economies of scale, better staffing figures can be obtained in very large organisations.

Links with other departments

1.9   In whatever way the payroll and related functions are organised, there is a need in both public and private sector organisations for regular communication between departments. The primary link is with the personnel department, as it handles both joiners and leavers and conditions of service.

The other main link is with the accounting function, as labour represents a major cost for most businesses. With regard to the pensions department, virtually all their basic data, such as contributions and salary changes, emanate from the payroll system. The payroll department also often acts as a local pensions representative. The payroll administrator also needs to collect information from an employee's own department. For instance he could require authorised details on expenses, overtime, incentive payments and sickness. The payroll department has contact with the employee or pensioner and the queries and small problems have to be treated sympathetically.

It should be noted that some modern management ideas such as business re-engineering seek new methods of organising a business. These ideas challenge the traditional concept of a department with a specific function employing a set of people doing defined related jobs, for example in payroll administration.

Where a central computer or bureau service is used there is a continual two-way communication between computer and payroll staff. Payee data must be fed into the computer and the results given back as print-outs, payslips, computer-printed cheques, etc. Behind the scenes the computer staff regularly revise the computer system in line with new business and statutory requirements. This requires close co-operation with the payroll department. The auditors also continually check both the manual and computer systems.

Payroll technology

1.10   In the early 20th century, payroll administrators used primitive office automation, for example mechanical time recorders and calculators. Today most payrolls are computerised. Traditional mainframe computer systems are still common, but many payroll administrators use personal computers. These may be free-standing. However, they are frequently linked to other personal computers as part of a local area network, or linked to a central mainframe computer, or both. Personal computers can also act as terminals for a large computer payroll system. They are frequently used for other office work such as word processing. In both large and small businesses the payroll administrator may rely on standard payroll software packages. Payroll systems programmed entirely for one organisation are less common these days. This is due to the increasing costs of maintaining these systems and the ease with which modern packages can be enhanced to meet the special requirements of a particular organisation. Because computers play such a vital part in the payroll operation it is essential that payroll and related staff fully understand their use. The payroll staff must actively participate with computer staff in the design, testing and implementation of new computer systems. They must similarly participate in the updating of computer systems, which is frequently required in the current era of business and statutory change. In a small organisation payroll staff may find that they have to do a lot of the computer work themselves, perhaps with a little help from a computer consultant. Both large and small organisations can use a computer bureau for their payroll work in preference to using their own computer system. Computers tend to eclipse other more mundane office equipment such as the photocopier and telephone. Such devices are, needless to say, vital in modern payroll administration. Payroll administration can still rely on the modern form of time-and-attendance systems where employees 'clock on' using swipe cards and electronic terminals. Payroll staff also use more recent forms of information technology such as electronic mail and the Internet.

An outline history of payroll administration

1.11   A few key dates in the history of payroll administration are shown in the panel Figure 1A below.

Figure 1A

Some key dates in the history of payroll administration

- 1799 – Income tax introduced in the UK.
- 1831 – The first *Truck Act* requires that manual workers are paid in cash.
- 1834 – The Civil service pension scheme given a modern form.
- 1894 – The Simplex time recorder produces printed output as employees 'clock' in and out of work.
- 1909 – The start of UK State pensions.
- – Statutory minimum wages introduced for specific 'sweated' industries, e.g. tailoring.
- 1911 – Scientific management firmly established.
- 1912 – The commencement of National Insurance.
- 1920 – Automatic payrolls based on primitive office equipment – 'push the button and the machine does the rest'.
- – The modern form of personnel management established in the USA.
- 1944 – PAYE commences.
- 1948 – The Welfare State and the modern social security system established.
- 1954 – The first computerised payroll system, operating on LEO, the first British business computer.
- 1961 – Graduated Insurance introduces the earnings-related principle for contributions and State benefits.
- 1975 – The abolition of National Insurance stamps and the Graduated Insurance scheme.
- – The *Employment Protection Act* introduces extensive rights for employees.
- 1978 – The start of SERPS (the State Earnings Related Pension Scheme), and contracting-out.
- 1980 – The formation of APSA, the Association of Payroll and Superannuation Administrators, the first payroll professional body.
- 1983 – Statutory Sick Pay commences.
- 1985 – The formation of the BPMA, the British Payroll Managers Association; the name is later changed to the IBPM, the Institute of British Payroll Managers. The IBPM merges with APSA by 1998 to form the IPPM, the Institute of Payroll and Pensions Management.
- 1986 – The *Wages Act* repeals the *Truck Acts* and allows cashless pay for manual workers. It also regulates deductions from pay.
- 1987 – Statutory Maternity Pay commences.
- 1988 – The consolidation of previous tax legislation into the *Income and Corporation Taxes Act*.
- – Personal pensions in the modern form.
- 1990 – During the 1990s there are many minor changes e.g. Statutory Sick Pay can no longer be recovered, and contributions must be paid to a pension fund within two weeks of the tax month end.
- 1998 – A national minimum wage to be introduced.

Payroll administration is believed to have grown out of the cashier's function. During the 19th century, however, there was relatively little statutory control of payroll activities. Most of the employment legislation in this era had social objectives, for example, regulating the employment of children in factories. However, the *Truck Act 1831*, which was extended by following legislation, insisted on cash wages for manual employees to prevent the abuses of payment-in-kind. For decades this legislation frustrated the ambition of employers to use cashless methods of payment such as cheques for manual workers. Benefits have always been provided to employees, for example, accommodation and food for servants. In the 19th century modern-style pension schemes had begun to emerge for some employees, for instance those in the civil service and railway companies. Ideas like profit-sharing were also proposed in this era.

By the beginning of the 20th century payroll administration could be difficult. For instance, the piecework schemes in the textile mills of the era could be complex, and payment by the hour implied all the problems of time recording. All this made gross pay calculations tedious. However, there were no statutory deductions from pay such as National Insurance contributions. The word 'payroll' then merely signified a formal list of names and payment details.

It is probably true to say that by the early 20th century payroll work in the UK existed as a business function rather a single department. Thus payroll work in an Edwardian factory would be scattered across the jobs of the time-keeper, the wages clerk in the accounts office, the cashier, and the cost clerk. Most of the early descriptions of payroll work emphasise wages administration rather than paying salaries. This is partly due to the greater complexity of wages administration and the fact that salaried staff are a small minority in establishments like factories and coal mines. Personnel management would have barely existed, except as a few dispersed activities like the recording of employee addresses and basic welfare provision. For a view of early 20th century payroll administration and its supporting information technology see Reference (4) in 1.12 below.

Relevant 20th century developments up to 1945 were as follows.

(*a*)   **Scientific management** — This was developed at the end of the 19th century. One aspect was an emphasis on employee incentive schemes carefully established through work study.

(*b*)   **Management accounting** — Today this embraces topics like investment appraisal and budgeting, as well as costing. Even in the 19th and early 20th century companies used payroll data for calculating the labour costs of, say, manufactured items. The need for data on earnings for costing, budgetary control, and management purposes, increased the burden on payroll systems.

(c) **National Insurance** — The *National Insurance Act 1911* brought in the complications of stamping employee cards to record payments for health insurance. This was later followed by unemployment insurance stamps.

(d) **Personnel management** — Personnel management began to develop during the early part of the 20th century. By the 1920s and 1930s it had almost reached its modern form in the USA. For example, it covered matters like employment, health and safety, training, and trade unions. In the UK, personnel management emerged more slowly from welfare work and the practical demands of employment matters. Personnel management and human resource management (HRM), the contemporary version of personnel management, have frequently had significant effects on payroll work by changing the nature of the employment environment, e.g. through new pay structures.

(e) **PAYE** — The *Income Tax (Employment) Act 1943* introduced Pay As You Earn in 1944. The intention, which has been very successful, was to collect tax every pay period from employees via the employer's payroll system. (See Reference (3) in 1.12 below.) The authority to operate PAYE is now contained in the *Income and Corporation Taxes Act 1988*.

(f) **Payroll technology** — The full panoply of early 20th century office machines was used in payroll work. Mechanical time-recording clocks were regarded as a great step forward at this time. Mechanical calculators and various printing machines all had their role. Punched card equipment, the precursor of computers, was used by large employers prior to the Second World War.

After 1945 there were several major developments.

(i) **The Welfare State** — The current social security system commenced with the *National Insurance Act 1946* and has become increasingly more complicated. During this period a supplement to the system of State pensions, called graduated pensions, was introduced in 1961 and abolished in 1975. The State Earnings-Related Pension Scheme (SERPS) was introduced by the *Social Security Pensions Act 1975* and came into force in 1978. The SERPS was nearly abolished in 1986 but was eventually retained in a modified form. There were, of course, numerous other changes in State benefits. These changes impinged on the payroll department directly when collecting National Insurance and graduated pension contributions. The current system of variable contributions collected through PAYE replaced National Insurance stamps in 1975. Statutory sick pay (SSP) was introduced in 1983 with major changes for payroll and personnel practice. Statutory maternity pay (SMP) was introduced in 1987.

(ii) **Pensions** — Some occupational pension schemes, notably the Civil Service scheme, go back to the 19th century. However, there was a considerable expansion in the post-war era. The payroll office collected

11

contributions and often ran the pension payroll. The *Social Security Act 1986* has introduced many pension changes, including personal pensions from 1988 as a rival to occupational pension schemes. Again there were payroll implications in this change. The *Pensions Act 1995*, which has many changes for pensions administration, also contains further payroll implications.

(iii) **Employment law** — The 1960s, 1970s and 1980s brought in extensive changes in employment and industrial law. Some of this affects payroll practice. For instance, the *Wages Act 1986* abolished the right of a manual worker to insist on cash pay. Much of contemporary employment legislation has been consolidated into the *Employment Rights Act 1996*.

(iv) **Pay structures** — There have been many attempts to revise pay structures as a contribution to improving the overall performance of organisations. For instance, there was productivity bargaining in the 1960s. Some of these developments have been encouraged by the Government, for example the tax incentives for profit-related pay. Also performance-related pay for white-collar staff has become increasingly popular over the last few years, particularly amongst large public and private sector employers.

(v) **Benefits** — Besides pay structures, employee benefits such as sick pay, medical insurance, company share schemes and company cars have attracted considerable attention. This is partly because of the intrinsic merit of the benefits and also because of the significant tax and NIC savings associated with them. However, tax, NIC and social security regulations can make benefits administration complex. Also, unjustified tax advantages, such as those on company cars, have been gradually eroded. There is currently increasing interest in flexible benefit schemes where the employee chooses, within limits, his own benefits and their level.

(vi) **Computers** — Computers were first used for payroll work in 1954 by Lyons, the catering firm. Lyons, remarkably, designed, built and programmed its own computer called LEO (Lyons Electronic Office), initially for both sales order processing and payroll administration. Lyons later started its own computer manufacturing company, and used LEO to offer a payroll bureau service.

Since the 1950s computers have gradually replaced other types of office equipment. The systems have become increasingly sophisticated, covering not only payroll but also related business applications such as personnel. The introduction of the Bankers' Automated Clearing Service (BACS) in 1968 enabled wages, salaries, and pensions to be paid directly into the employees' bank accounts by electronic funds transfer. BACS links the employer and bank computers. Twenty years ago most computerised payroll systems were based on central mainframes where data was transferred from forms onto punched cards or punched tape so that it could be fed into the computer. Today there are other options besides mainframes. For instance personal computers can be used for small office-based payroll systems. Continuing advances in electronics, computing and telecommunications have continuing implications for payroll administration, for example the use of optical disks to store historical payroll data and 'reporting tools' that allow non-computer staff to report on payroll data.

(vii) **Publishing** — Given the economic importance and dynamic nature of payroll work, it is surprising that payroll publishing was minor and sporadic until the mid-1980s. Since then, however, publishing has become vigorous in payroll-related matters.

(viii) **Continuing developments** — Payroll is a very dynamic field. There are continual legal, business and technological changes which have a marked effect on payroll administration, virtually every year. An example is the change to Statutory Sick Pay (SSP) introduced in 1994. This transferred the liability to pay SSP, which was supposedly a social security benefit, from the Government onto most employers. See Chapter 30 (Future Developments Affecting Payroll Administration) for further details of impending and possible changes.

References

1.12   Some aspects of payroll administration, such as taxation, have an extensive literature. References to such specialist topics are contained in the appropriate chapter of this handbook. References (1), (3) and (4) below contain historical views of the payroll function. There are several current journals devoted to payroll administration, for example, *Payroll Manager's Review* (PMR). However, many administrative, financial and legal publications occasionally publish articles which are relevant to payroll matters. The Institute of Payroll and Pensions Management (IPPM) also circulates literature on payroll topics. The Payroll Alliance and other organisations also provide payroll information. (See Appendix F for the addresses of relevant organisations.)

(1)   Garden D J, 'Time-keeping and Wages Office Work', Pitman, 1934.

(2)   Beadle J, 'United Kingdom National Accounts', The Stationery Office, 1997.

(3)   Miles P, 'PAYE: Fifty Years of Age and Going On . . .', PMR, April 1994.

(4)   Moynihan E, 'Payroll Matters: Past, Present, and Future', Peterborough Software, 1994.

(5)   'Social Security Benefit Rates for 1998/99', PMR, March 1998. (These rates are published by PMR annually in advance of the relevant year.)

(6)   'New Earnings Survey', Office for National Statistics, September 1997.

2 Outline of Payroll Administration

Scope of this chapter

2.1 Payroll administration is often presented as a series of fragmented specialist subjects such as income tax, statutory sick pay and employment law. In practice these legal requirements are often applied simultaneously to the problem of paying employees or pensioners. The main functions and organisation of payroll work have already been described in 1.6 to 1.9 above. This chapter uses the example of a typical employee and employer to illustrate the main day-to-day work together with some background considerations. It is designed to provide an elementary overview for trainees and others unfamiliar with payroll work.

Reward management

2.2 The process of determining and controlling both the structure and level of employee pay and benefits is the main part of reward management. This is typically a personnel department function with some involvement from financial specialists. Once pay schemes are established it is the job of the payroll department to ensure that employees are paid, and to carry out various other aspects of pay and benefits administration such as collecting tax.

For the employee, reward management and payroll administration appear relatively straightforward. Take the case of Richard, a trainee accountant, who applies for a post with United Widgets PLC. The company manufactures car and other machine components. It has 4,500 employees in total of whom 1,200 work at its main factory. The number employed by the company has shrunk markedly in recent years. The payroll staff on this site now consists of three people.

Richard's job application is handled by the personnel department. His pay and other employee benefits, such as pensions, are his 'reward' for working at United Widgets. They are broadly determined by his occupation and status. The annual salary range might be £13,500 p.a. to £19,000. At the interview, the salary offered is determined by his qualifications, experience, pay from his previous employer, and, to a small extent, by his bargaining skill. Thereafter he depends on annual pay rises.

In the past, part of the annual rise was guaranteed by a scale which incrementally increased the rate of pay with the employee's years of service up to a maximum. There were also general increases which uplifted the pay rates in the scale, broadly in line with inflation. A person at the top of a scale would only receive cost of living increases until promoted onto a new scale.

At United Widgets, this scheme, which was commonly found amongst other employers, has recently been replaced. In line with modern ideas United Widgets introduced performance-related pay for its administrative employees. Under the new scheme an employee's salary progress is not guaranteed, but depends totally on the employee's performance throughout the year. Typically, an employee who performs badly has no pay rise; a barely satisfactory employee receives a cost of living increase only; a mediocre employee gets 1 per cent on top of the cost of living; a good employee receives the cost of living plus 2.5 per cent; and an excellent performer is rewarded with 4 per cent in addition to the cost of living.

Pay details

2.3   Once the pay details are established, United Widgets' personnel department send them to the payroll department. When Richard joins the company at its main factory, he hands over a Form P45. This contains income tax details from his previous employment for the information of his new payroll department. (See Appendix C below for an example of Form P45.) He also provides information about his bank account so that he can be paid by automated credit transfer. The National Insurance contribution requirements are established from his employment details by the payroll staff. Any special deductions to be made from his pay, such as charitable donations, require Richard's written authorisation.

Payroll procedures

2.4   The payroll procedures are dealt with under the headings listed below.

(*a*)   ***Paying employees*** — The payroll department store all the details of new employees on their computer. This calculates the gross pay and all the various deductions, such as income tax, to arrive at Richard's net pay. Every month his net pay is transferred directly from United Widgets to his bank's computer. This is done via a telecommunications line using EFT (electronic funds transfer) to BACS (Bankers Automated Clearing Service). Richard receives a computer printed payslip confirming that his bank account has been credited with his pay. (See Figure 22A below for a payslip example.) The manual workers in the United Widgets factory used to receive cash wages weekly which required more effort to prepare and involved greater security risks, such as armed robbery and theft.

However, cash pay for manual workers has now been replaced by the automated bank credit transfer system.

(*b*)   ***Variations*** — Overtime, holidays, sickness, expenses and any other 'variations' from normal hours or pay rates are notified on a standard form by Richard's own department. This is sent to the payroll department and then entered into the computer. The manual workers have no annual salary in the sense that Richard has. They are paid by the hour for attendance and receive incentive payments based on the amount they produce. All the relevant data must then be checked and entered into the computer by the payroll staff every week.

(*c*)   ***Pay changes*** — As regards manual staff, annual general increases and other changes in the pay structure are negotiated with the trade unions recognised by the company. The details are notified to the payroll department and applied to all relevant employees. If the negotiations with trade unions are protracted, the increase may be backdated. Implementing a backdated pay award requires careful calculation for all employees. One complication is that some may have joined, and others have been promoted or have left, during the relevant period. A more alarming possibility from an administrative viewpoint is a change in the pay structure itself rather than increasing the actual pay rates. This usually means reprogramming the computer as well as changing the pay rates stored inside it.

The administrative staff have a performance-related pay scheme. So for Richard, his departmental manager scores his work performance throughout the year. A formula is used to convert the score into a pay rise and the payroll department is notified. The payroll department are also notified of changes such as promotions. The trade unions representing the salaried staff are unhappy about performance-related pay, but they have been pragmatic and monitor the scheme, and try to negotiate improvements.

(*d*)   ***Other benefits*** — The payroll department has to administer other benefits such as holidays, sick pay and maternity pay. Each of these benefits has its own 'scheme' or rules and requires additional records.

In the case of sick pay and maternity pay, United Widgets has to comply with the statutory schemes. It has, however, decided to supplement the statutory sick pay scheme with its own scheme – usually referred to as company sick pay or occupational sick pay (OSP). This means, for instance, that when Richard falls sick it must operate two sets of rules simultaneously. Both schemes require the careful recording of periods of sickness to check that Richard's sick pay entitlement is not exceeded, and this requires the use of a mixture of government and company forms.

There are still separate company sick pay arrangements for manual and salaried staff. For instance, manual workers at United Widgets do not receive any sick pay until they have been ill for three days, whilst office staff receive sick pay from the first day of illness.

In some businesses the personnel or HR department control all benefits related to attendance or absence, suc has holidays and maternity pay. In these cases the payroll department is just notified of the amounts payable and the periods for which they are due.

A few employee benefits, such as company cars and employee share schemes, are administered by the company secretary. The pension scheme is administered by a separate department (see (*f*) below), but the payroll department plays an important role in deducting, recording and reporting pension contributions.

(*e*)   ***Leaving*** — When Richard decides to leave United Widgets after a few years, the payroll department is notified by the personnel department and his pay is terminated at the appropriate date. He is given a Form P45 which notifies his tax details to his next employer. The Form P45 is also used by Richard for the purpose of self-assessment of his income tax liability.

The pensions department is also informed of his departure so that his pension rights can be calculated. The pension entitlement can be claimed from United Widgets' pension trust fund when Richard finally retires many years hence. Alternatively, the pension rights can be transferred to a personal pension policy or to another company's pension fund on his joining that company.

(*f*)   ***Pensions*** — The word 'pensions' actually covers a set of different benefits, for example retirement pensions, widows' pensions, disability pensions, life assurance etc. These benefits are paid out of an investment fund created from contributions collected via the payroll. At United Widgets, pensions are administered by a separate department. However, there is regular liaison on many matters with the payroll department. It is also the payroll department at United Widgets who actually pay pensions according to instructions received from the pensions department. In some other companies the pensions department operates its own pension payroll and other companies outsource the administration of their pensions.

Information technology

2.5   The payroll department enters payee data into the central computer through a visual display unit (VDU). When instructed by the operator the computer performs all the pay, tax and other calculations. It then produces a series of printed reports and forms, for instance an employment costing report and the payslips. It then uses the BACS telecommunication service (BACSTEL) to send an electronic message containing employee pay details for processing by the banks. (See 22.10 below for an outline of credit transfers using BACSTEL.) If Richard has a query the payroll staff can use the VDU to check his records.

For shop floor workers there are time and attendance terminals which record the times of starting and finishing for each person. The employee inserts a plastic card in the terminal to 'clock' in and out. The terminals are connected directly to a micro-computer which is itself connected to the payroll system main computer. This allows direct entry of the attendance data for wage calculations. Previously, old-fashioned mechanical time-recorders were used to establish attendance. These machines stamped the worker's entry or exit time on his 'clock card'.

United Widgets uses a large central mainframe computer for all the payroll work at its main factory. The mainframe does work for other departments, such as finance, as well. The payroll programs were purchased from a specialist software house as a 'package'. As the programs are flexible they can be adjusted to meet the unique features of United Widgets' payroll administration.

United Widgets is considering changing its payroll IT system. One option is a modern computer bureau service like that used by a neighbouring company. Another is to outsource the payroll function in its entirety. However, United Widgets' favoured approach is to use a small network of personal computers in the payroll office. The software would be a reputable payroll package and the network would be devoted entirely to payroll activities. The networked personal computers would also offer other facilities such as word processing and a spreadsheet system.

The payroll department does, of course, use other common forms of office automation, such as a photocopier. New types of office automation, for instance DIP (Document Image Processing), are being considered for other areas of administration at United Widgets. Using current technology DIP may not yet be cost effective in the payroll department, though doubtless it will be attractive in the future.

Pay calculations

2.6   Richard's pay, as calculated by the computer every month, can be illustrated in round figures as follows for 1998/99:

Build-up to gross		£	£
(a)	Basic pay	1,350	
(b)	Overtime pay	210	
(c)	Total gross pay		1,560

Gross-to-net		£	£
(a)	Income tax	219	
(b)	National Insurance contributions (NICs)	134	
(c)	Savings	60	
(d)	Total deductions		413
Net pay			1,147

Note: Figures rounded for purposes of illustration.

Each of the various pay elements above, e.g. the overtime pay and income tax may itself have to be calculated. The tax and NIC (national insurance contributions) calculations are complicated by variable rates on different parts of the employee's earnings. In this case there are no pension contribution deductions as Richard has yet to join the pension scheme. When he does join after a waiting period of one year, contributions are calculated at five per cent of 'pensionable pay' each month. In the United Widgets' scheme pensionable pay is defined as basic pay less a fixed amount, which is currently £420 per month. This deduction is meant to allow for the basic pension which Richard will receive from the State on retirement.

The employer has extra financial liabilities over and above the gross pay for each employee. These are sometimes referred to as 'on-costs'. The main extras are the employer's NICs and the employer's pension contributions for those in the pension scheme. These liabilities are calculated for each employee before being totalled and printed by the computer. In Richard's case the company has to pay each month £156 as employer's NICs. Furthermore when Richard joins the pension scheme United Widgets might typically pay £94 (ten per cent of pensionable pay) as the employer's pension contributions, and this is in addition to Richard's own employee contributions. The NICs and pension contributions together give an extra monthly employment cost of £250 on top of his gross pay of £1,560. Extra benefits such as sick pay and holdiay entitlement are a further cost to the company.

Pay As You Earn

2.7   The Pay As You Earn (PAYE) system is an effective method of collecting income tax and NICs. The employer is responsible for collecting the tax and contributions every pay period from employees and paying the money over to the Inland Revenue. In principle PAYE is a relatively straightforward administrative system. However, the regulations have to allow for numerous special situations such as strikes, multiple employments and the employee's death.

Most common situations are covered by special PAYE forms (see Appendix C for a list of them). For example if Richard, our trainee accountant, had joined United Widgets straight from college, then he will not usually possess a PAYE Form P45 issued by a previous employer. In this case a Form P46 is prepared and sent to the local tax office. It is, in effect, a request for the employee's tax details.

Under PAYE the statutory deductions (usually income tax and NICs due) do not just depend on the level of pay. Tax due from each employee is calculated according to his level of earnings, the tax already paid in the current year and his tax code, e.g. 419L. The tax code is calculated by the Inland Revenue to recover the correct amount of tax evenly over a year. NICs are also calculated according to the amount of earnings and a category called a 'table letter'. The table letter (e.g. A or D), unlike the tax code, is determined by the employer according to the employee's circumstances. For example, an employee over State pensionable age has a table letter C which indicates that the employee is not liable for NICs, but the employer must contribute up to ten per cent of earnings. (Figure 25A below shows how the statutory deductions can be calculated manually.) In practice, of course, they are invariably calculated by the computer for large payrolls.

At the end of the year the payroll department must prepare a series of PAYE documents for the Inland Revenue. The department must also issue Form P60 to each employee. (See Appendix C below for an example.) This contains a statement of the total taxable pay earned and the total tax and NICs collected during the year. A 'year' in this context is, of course, always a 'tax year' beginning on 6 April and ending on the following 5 April.

The operation of PAYE and associated requirements such as SMP (statutory maternity pay) is defined by regulations made under Acts of Parliament. In practice, payroll staff usually work from practical guides issued by the Inland Revenue and the Contributions Agency. Updated copies of these guides, the various tax tables, and tax forms, are issued almost every year. As an example, Booklet 480 (1998) gives information on the tax treatment of employee expenses and benefits, and is usually updated annually.

Pay and benefit schemes

2.8   A manufacturing employer such as United Widgets has a diverse labour force. For example, it could contain cleaners, production operatives, electricians, clerks, sales representatives and directors. It must, therefore, devise a series of pay schemes and employee benefits such as pensions suitable for each type of employee. These 'reward packages' have to serve a series of major business objectives in a cost-effective manner.

The company objectives can include attracting and retaining the right staff, providing incentives for good job performance and promoting the company image. There are, of course, many other objectives and considerations when designing employee pay and benefit schemes. There is also some doubt as to whether most employers actually do achieve the optimum balance between their various objectives which could clash, for example recruiting the best staff, an affordable cost for total pay and benefits and a responsible image.

As already mentioned the process of monitoring and revising employee pay and benefits is a primary part of reward management. Organisations must regularly revise their 'reward packages' to try to meet the requirements of both the employer and employee more effectively. This is, to some extent, forced on all parties by a rapidly changing business environment, e.g. changes in taxation, new jobs created by new technologies and competition.

The personnel department at United Widgets has a major role in making changes to pay and benefits. The personnel department is also concerned with wider issues. These could include, for instance, the relationship between changes in employee reward structures and matters such as industrial relations, career development and recruitment. Other specialists, including payroll staff, are often involved in pay and benefit changes. The nature of the changes determines which specialists participate. A further complication at United Widgets is that changes in employee pay and benefits can lead to protracted negotiations with trade unions.

Some businesses, such as United Widgets, employ industrial engineers and management services officers. They apply work study techniques to improve the methods of working and pay schemes, particularly for manual workers. A basic concept of work study is to be scientific about improving business processes, measuring work, and designing pay schemes. This should remove unreliable intuition and guesswork. Work study can be used to devise incentive schemes, usually based on the idea that greater output is objectively rewarded with greater pay. The work study approach is perhaps seen as old-fashioned today and only applicable in limited circumstances. However, the idea of linking pay to performance is, if anything, more popular, though the current modern approach is usually more subjective.

Other specialists involved in pay and benefit changes include the pensions manager, the company secretary, and the accountants. The latter are particularly concerned about the financial implications of any changes. Consultants are sometimes engaged to advise on matters such as establishing employee share schemes.

United Widgets, like many similar companies, is continually reviewing and changing its employee pay and benefit arrangements and associated conditions of employment such as working hours. Recent and possible changes, which could affect payroll operations, include the following:

(*a*) cashless pay, i.e. paying manual workers by automated credit transfer rather than cash;

(*b*) revised pension arrangements, e.g. a COMP (Contracted-Out Money Purchase scheme);

(*c*) single status, which means that manual workers receive similar benefits to staff employees, such as full sick pay;

(*d*) revised incentives for all grades of staff, e.g. bonuses for the quality as well as the quantity of production, to be earned by manufacturing workers; profit-related pay for office staff; and new commission arrangements for sales representatives;

(*e*) new methods of organising work, e.g. an 'annual hours' system where employees are paid a steady weekly wage for a varying number of hours each week. The weekly hours vary within a fixed annual total to match the expected pattern of the workload throughout the year;

(*f*) further refinements to its performance-related pay scheme for salaried staff and the possible abolition of pay scales;

(*g*) alterations to its computer systems, e.g. improvements to the system for monitoring labour costs.

Many of the above ideas are promoted by current business thinking, especially HRM (Human Resource Management), the modern form of personnel management.

Many pay and benefit schemes are extensive and complicated. They are recorded in special handbooks which usually have a restricted circulation. In the case of United Widgets, this handbook would describe in detail such matters as salary and grading, working hours, holidays, sick pay, maternity pay and expenses. Many of these details must be also held in the computer so that it can perform all the payroll calculations. The complexity is justified on the grounds that the schemes must cover thousands of employees with differing skills, responsibilities and working conditions. In terms of legal formality each individual employee usually has the relevant parts of the pay and benefits schemes incorporated into his own contract of employment. This is usually stated in their letter of appointment along with their position on the relevant pay scale.

Obviously some 'reward packages' are secret and negotiated directly between the employer and employee without any trade union acting as a 'bargaining agent'. The senior executive pay and benefit schemes are the most obvious example. To preserve confidentiality, the senior executives are paid by a special and separate payroll system which is administered by the company secretary of United Widgets. The role of a company secretary may best be described as the chief administrative officer of a company.

The impact of legislation on pay

2.9   The payment of employees and pensioners is constrained by many legal factors, for instance, employment protection legislation insists that employees are given itemised payslips. Employment law thus has a major influence. Social security laws have a major impact on the design and operation of pension schemes. An illustration of the effect of law is provided by tax and NICs which take a large proportion of both the employees' earnings and the employer's profits. There is thus a strong mutual incentive to try to minimise the Government's share. Historically, many employee benefits, such as company car schemes, have been used partly for their tax-avoidance advantages. However, the Government has progressively restricted the tax advantages of such benefits. For instance, the taxable benefit of the provision of company cars has been steadily increased with the tax due now calculated on the list price of the vehicle. Another example is the effect of redundancy legislation. The scale of redundancy payments laid down by law provides a starting point for management or trade unions to seek better terms. (See 9.17 below for details of redundancy payments.) The result is that large employers often offer redundancy payments increasing with service in a similar way to the statutory scale. The benefits are, however, superior.

On a day-to-day basis the payroll department at United Widgets has a good working knowledge of payroll law, particularly on matters such as SSP (statutory sick pay). However, they refer to the regulations or other sources such as the personnel department or local tax office when dealing with uncommon situations. As previously mentioned, there are many booklets issued by the Government which are used in payroll or related work, e.g. CA 28, 'The Employer's Manual on National Insurance Contributions'. The auditors, when checking the payroll procedures, also look for any failure to follow legal requirements.

3   The Legal Framework

Scope of this chapter

3.1   The law has a significant role in payroll administration, yet there is no readily available package which can be called 'payroll law'. Payroll law is in fact a mixture of the relevant law covering employment, tax, social security, banking, etc. The legal rights and duties outlined in this book are drawn from different formal sources and areas of law and are applied by various enforcement systems. It is therefore desirable, if not necessary, that the payroll administrator should possess a working familiarity with the framework of rule-making and enforcement within which payroll administration activities must be conducted. The practical importance of all this can be illustrated by tracing the effect of government proposals. For example, SMP was proposed with several other social security and pension changes in the White Paper 'Reform of Social Security' (Cmnd 9691). Some proposals eventually become part of an Act of Parliament: the *Social Security Act 1986, s 46* (now contained in *Social Security Contributions and Benefits Act 1992*) in the case of SMP. This particular Act also included pensions legislation, some of which affected payroll operations. Further regulations are then often made under an Act, e.g. the *Statutory Maternity Pay (Medical Evidence) Regulations 1987 (SI 1987 No 235)*. The Acts and regulations are then often summarised in booklets issued by government departments

To demonstrate the diverse nature of payroll legislation SMP is also taxable under the PAYE regulations, but not subject to court orders under the *Attachment of Earnings Act 1971*. Obviously this kind of legislation must be understood in terms of its day-to-day application. In addition, however, by following it through its various stages the administrator and computer systems designer can plan for the effects of the legislation well in advance of it coming into force. Regarding enforcement a payroll problem may involve legal action of some kind with the employer opposing a payee, a government department or another party such as a bank. Non-compliance with SMP regulations can result in fines. A further complication for some administrators and payroll software designers is a payroll system that must operate under a non-English legal regime, for example the Channel Islands.

This chapter surveys the general legal framework which forms a background to the work of the UK payroll administrator.

Key points of the legal framework

3.2   These features are summarised below.

(*a*)   The law regulating payroll administration is drawn from many different areas and sources and subject to constant change. It thus demands extra vigilance from the payroll administrator and related staff.

(*b*)   Guidance on new developments should be sought from the publications of professional bodies or other relevant literature such as DSS booklets etc.

(*c*)   The legislative and judicial systems of Scotland, Northern Ireland, the Channel Islands, the Isle of Man and Eire, although having similarities, often differ to a material extent from those applicable to England and Wales.

Sources of law

3.3   The payroll administrator seeking a concise statement of relevant law is confronted with difficulties which are compounded by the fact that the various legal rules are derived from different sources. A basic explanation of the primary sources of law and their inter-relationship is essential before any detailed examination of the substance of the law. The statutory references in this chapter and in the rest of the handbook are abbreviated (see Appendix A (Table of Statutes)).

The sources of law are summarised below.

(*a*)   ***Acts of Parliament*** — Bills approved by both Houses of Parliament and accorded the Royal Assent have, unless and until repealed by a subsequent Act, legal effect and, in the event of conflict with rules derived from any other source, have priority. The legislation of the European Community (EC), formerly known as the European Economic Community (EEC), is an exception to this rule. (See 3.3(*d*) below.) The Acts of Parliament are generally called statutes or primary legislation.

(*b*)   ***Delegated legislation*** — This type of legislation usually takes the form of a Statutory Instrument (SI). Delegated legislation is issued by a Minister of the Crown, e.g. the Secretary of State for Employment, under powers conferred and limited by a particular statute (the 'enabling' Act). It is subject to various forms of 'laying procedure' which enable scrutiny and possible rejection by Parliament. The purpose of delegated legislation is to supplement and substantiate an item of primary legislation and, since it effectively emanates from Parliament, it prevails, in the case of conflict, over rules derived from other sources. This type of legislation is also termed secondary legislation.

(c) **Case law** — Cases coming before the courts can be concerned either with the application of the common law principles and/or the interpretation of relevant statutory provisions according to the facts of each individual case. The common law is a system of law essentially based on previously decided cases and not on legislation, for example, the law of contract, the law of negligence.

In either situation, in addition to being binding on the particular parties involved (subject to the possibility of reversal on appeal), a decision in a case can have far-reaching legal effects in establishing a rule of law to be followed by the courts in subsequent cases involving the same issue. (See also Appendix B (Table of Cases).)

There exists a hierarchy of courts in England and Wales which enables a principle of law established by certain higher courts in reaching a particular decision to create, if new, a precedent which becomes binding on all inferior courts or tribunals for the purpose of deciding future cases. This precedent, which is called a *ratio decidendi*, remains unless and until it is subsequently overruled by a superior court or by subsequent legislation. A judgment may also contain an interpretation of the law which does not relate to the facts of the case but which is stated by way of an aside to elaborate on the law. These statements are termed *obiter dicta* and have a persuasive effect when future cases are decided. A description of the hierarchy of courts in England and Wales is given in 3.5–3.7 below.

(d) **Legislation of the European Community** — The UK is a member State of the European Communities. These are the European Coal and Steel Community (ECSC), the European Atomic Energy Community (Euratom), and, most importantly, the European Community (EC).

The EC issues various forms of legislation through the Commission and the Council. The EC treaty stipulates that EC legislation shall be incorporated into national law and can be given legal effect in the member States without national legislation. This is called 'directly effective' Community legislation. *European Communities Act 1972 (ECA 1972), s 2(1)* applies this in the case of the UK. It should be noted that the EC legislation must also be 'directly applicable' before this incorporation occurs. In other words it must confer rights and duties on individual legal persons and not merely impose obligations upon the State. 'Directly effective' EC legislation prevails over any conflicting national law. Further, not all EC legislation is 'directly effective'. 'Regulations' have this quality, but it is not usually the case with Directives or decisions of the Commission and Council, which require implementation by the passing of a specific statute or a SI by a member State in order to become legally enforceable in national courts. [*ECA 1972, s 2(2)*]. But if a Directive is clear and unqualified in its terms, it may become directly effective in national courts once the deadline for implementation in national legislation has passed without the member State taking the necessary action.

Even then, however, Directives themselves are only enforceable in the courts against the State or its organs. This differs from some provisions of the EC treaty itself, for example *Article 119* (see below), which are also enforceable between private individuals and employers.

The influence of EC legislation in the UK courts can be seen in the area of sex discrimination, particularly in cases involving equal pay. For instance, *Pickstone v Freemans plc [1988] IRLR 357* concerned the interpretation of the UK *EqPA 1970* in accordance with *Article 119* of the *EC Treaty* and the associated Equal Pay Directive 75/117, as did *Rainey v Greater Glasgow Health Board [1987] ICR 129* and *Barber v Guardian Royal Exchange Assurance Group [1990] IRLR 240 (ECJ)*. (See 5.8 below.)

The national courts of the member States are required to give legislation passed as a result of an EC Directive a 'purposive' meaning, i.e. to construe domestic legislation in a way which conforms with relevant EC provisions regardless of when the national law came into existence. This means that, for example, the *SDA 1975* must be interpreted in the light of the Equal Treatment Directive adopted in 1977. However, sometimes, an Act and an EC Directive may conflict so blatantly that the former will have to be amended in order to be consistent with the latter. For example, until November 1993, the *SDA 1975* specified a limit on the amount of compensation which can be awarded to a successful complainant. In *Marshall v Southampton and South West Hampshire Area Health Authority (No 2) [1993] IRLR 445 ECJ*, it was held that the Equal Treatment Directive contemplates no such restriction. Therefore, the *Sex Discrimination and Equal Pay (Remedies) Regulations 1993, SI 1993 No 2798* abolished it. Whilst not required for compliance with the *Marshall* decision, a similar change has been made to the *Race Relations Act 1976*. Another example of the need to amend UK legislation in the light of EC provisions is provided by the decision in *R v Secretary of State for Employment ex parte Equal Opportunities Commission and another [1994] IRLR 176 HL*. This directly concerned the incompatability, with *Article 119* and the Equal Treatment Directive, of statutory restrictions on those working under 16 hours per week claiming redundancy payments and compensation for unfair dismissal. In response to this decision, 1995 regulations removed, with effect from February 1995, all qualifications based on hours worked from these and other employment rights. (See 4.6(*h*) below.)

The adoption of the *Single European Act 1987*, which deals with the free movement of goods and peoples within the European Community, has hastened the process of integration. This has resulted in two developments. Firstly, in 1989, the Community Charter of the Fundamental Social Rights of Workers (the 'Social Charter') was adopted, under which various Directives on employment matters have since been developed and discussed. Secondly, the *Maastricht Treaty on European Union* was signed in February 1992 and became effective on 1 November 1993.

A protocol to the *Maastricht Treaty*, regarding development of certain principles laid out in the 'Social Charter', was signed by the (then) other eleven member States of the EU. In 1997, the United Kingdom, which had opted-out for five years, chose to become a signatory. This will lead to domestic measures to implement a number of directives: of particular relevance to payroll practitioners will be new laws on parental leave and part-time workers.

Another significant EU instrument, although not derived from the 'Social Charter' itself, is the *Working Time Directive*. This covers maximum hours, rest periods and breaks and minimum holidays (see 5.9 and 5.20 below). United Kingdom legislation to implement its requirements came into force in October 1998.

Legislative process

3.4   Given the contemporary significance of legislation (see 3.3 above) as a source of payroll law rules, it is important to outline the salient features of the procedures leading to the passage of new legislation.

Legislation is generally introduced in Parliament by the government of the day. Measures introduced by individual members of Parliament generally require government support in order to be successful. Therefore, specific pieces of legislation tend to have their gestation within a particular political party and its policies, frequently those portrayed in the manifesto for the previous general election. The general proposals stated in the manifesto then result in a process of detailed development.

Detailed consultation is usual on new legislation both between Whitehall departments and with interested parties in the private sector. For major legislation the normal practice is to issue a consultative document known as a 'Green Paper', which formally outlines the options being considered by government.

Once a Minister decides to legislate he must gain approval from the Cabinet's new legislation committee which allocates Parliamentary time and supervises the drafting of the Bill by Parliamentary counsel. For major legislation, departments usually issue a 'White Paper', which outlines the case for legislation and describes the proposed contents of the Bill. White Papers leave some detail to be decided in the drafting stage and may have 'Green Edges' in that some aspects of the Bill may remain open for discussion. Interested parties and professional organisations can be consulted on the wording of the draft Bill although it is very rare for any group outside Whitehall to see the whole Bill.

Broadly, the Parliamentary procedure relating to the scrutiny and approval of Bills depends on whether the Bill is public, i.e. altering the general law, or private, i.e. concerned with the interests of named groups, individuals, and corporations. The procedure for public Bills, which would contain matters relevant to payroll law, can be illustrated by the use of the *Wages Act 1986* (the surviving provisions of which are contained in the *Employment Rights Act 1996, Part II*) as an example:

House of Commons	*1986 dates*
First reading (formal introduction and publication)	30 January
Second reading (debate of principles)	11 February
Committee stage (discussion of detail)	12 February – 29 April
Report stage (debate on Committee amendments)	14 May
Third reading (final discussion)	15 May
House of Lords	
First reading	16 May
Second reading	5 June
Committee stage	24/26 June
Report stage	8 July
Third reading	22 July
House of Commons	
Lords amendments considered	23 July
House of Lords	
Commons amendments considered	24 July
Royal Assent	
Wages Act 1986 becomes law on receiving the Royal Assent	1 August

Although assent by both Houses of Parliament is constitutionally required in normal circumstances, clear majority control of the House of Commons is the ultimate key to the passage of a Bill. This is because the *Parliament Acts 1911–1949* provide that Bills can, if necessary, receive the Royal Assent after having been approved only by the Commons. In effect, the Lords can now only delay and not prevent legislation.

Delegated legislation (see 3.3 above) is regulated by the *Statutory Instruments Act 1946* in relation to the matters of numbering, printing and publishing. Where such legislation is required, by its 'parent' Act, to be laid before Parliament, the laying procedure may take one of two basic forms. The 'positive' form involves the need for the delegated legislation to be approved by resolution of both Houses before taking effect. The 'negative' form provides that the legislation will have effect subject to cancellation by a resolution within 40 sitting days. In order to assist Parliamentary scrutiny of the vast number of measures in the form of delegated legislation, all Statutory Instruments (SIs) are subject to surveillance by the Joint Committee (Lords and Commons) on Statutory

Instruments, which can object to procedural or substantive deficiencies. Since Parliament does not have the time to achieve perfect scrutiny, delegated legislation is also subject to judicial review by the courts (see 3.6 below), which may declare SIs *ultra vires* or procedurally deficient.

Government departments such as the Inland Revenue summarise the provisions of Acts of Parliament and their associated SI regulations in convenient booklets, for example, Booklet 480, 'Expenses and Benenfits – A Tax Guide', which is issued to employers and explains the treatment of various benefits and expenses. These booklets are for general guidance only and do not usually have legal force.

Enforcement of payroll law in England and Wales

3.5   Enforcement of payroll law obligations depends on more than one system. Many matters, civil and criminal, are resolved by recourse to the 'ordinary' common law courts. This is so in any subject which has a common law origin, even though the application of a statute may be involved. For instance, in discussing the common law subject of negligence, a court may consider the *Law Reform (Contributory Negligence) Act 1945*. This also applies to cases where a statutory scheme has expressly conferred jurisdiction on those courts. For instance, the various offences under the *CA 1985* are triable in a magistrates' court. [*CA 1985, s 731*]. Nevertheless, some statutory systems relating to the Welfare State, for example, employment rights and social security, are so distinct and widespread in their effects that special 'courts' for enforcement of rights and determination of entitlements have been set up in the form of tribunals. Having highlighted the 'ordinary' and 'specialist' systems of enforcement, it should be noted that a breach of law can be subject to both. Employment law is a prime example. Whilst most modern statutory rights of the employee are enforced through the system of employment tribunals (see 3.8 below), any questions of 'pure' contract, for example, 'Is this a term of my contract?' or 'Is this in breach of my contract?', have, historically, been resolved by the 'ordinary' courts (although this situation has recently changed – see 3.8 below). Further, the different systems are unified, at the higher level of appeal, in that a definitive ruling, if needed, can be obtained from the House of Lords. (See 3.6 and 3.8 below.)

Finally, it should be remembered that, apart from legal enforcement, there are other methods for the resolution of legal disputes. Most notably these include the process of arbitration, and also that of conciliation. (See 3.9 and 3.10 below.)

Civil courts

3.6   These cover matters relating to the law of contract or of tort, for instance negligence, defamation etc., and associated subjects such as agency and restitution. Proceedings must be commenced either in the High Court (usually the Queen's Bench Division) or, county court. The former venue will normally be appropriate for claims of £50,000 or more, the latter for claims of less than £25,000. Between these two amounts and even outside them, there is a wide discretion for one court to order the transfer of proceedings to the other. Apart from financial substance,relevant factors for the exercise of this discretion include a case's broader or public importance, its complexity and the likelihood of a speedy trial. [*CCA 1984, s 2, CLSA 1990* and *High Court and County Courts (Jurisdiction) Order 1991, (SI 1991 No 724)*]. The basic hierarchy of relevant courts is illustrated in Figure 3A, which gives a simplified view of the relationship between civil courts.

An appeal from a decision of either the County Court or a division of the High Court lies to the Court of Appeal (Civil Division) and thereafter to the House of Lords. Whilst the appeal to the Court of Appeal is normally available as of right, an appeal to the House of Lords is only available with the leave of that court or the Court of Appeal. [*AJAA 1934, s 1*]. The usual grounds of appeal are that the lower court has made an error of law in coming to its decision, i.e. that it has misapplied or overlooked a relevant statute or case law authority which might affect that decision. Other commonly encountered bases of appeal are that judicial discretion (e.g. in relation to the costs to be awarded), has been exercised wrongly or that an award of damages is either excessive or diminutive. Binding precedents (see 3.3 above) can only be created by decisions of the House of Lords (binding on all lower courts) and the Court of Appeal (binding on all lower courts but not on the House of Lords). Other courts are only capable of creating persuasive precedents.

In relation to matters within the sphere of the *EC Treaty*, it is possible for an English court or tribunal to request the Court of Justice of the European Communities to give a preliminary ruling on the interpretation of the Treaty itself or of directives and regulations (*EC Treaty, Article 177*). This facility only relates to questions of EC law and is applicable only where an interpretation is necessary to enable the English court or tribunal to give a judgment. The system of reference has produced some notable decisions on sex discrimination and equal pay, such as *Marshall v Southampton and South West Hampshire Area Health Authority [1986] ICR 335* and *Barber v Guardian Royal Exchange Assurance Group [1990] IRLR 240*. (See 5.8 below.) The courts listed in Figures 3A and 3B may seek a preliminary ruling on a point of European law from the Court of Justice of the European Communities.

Criminal courts

3.7   The criminal law, resting largely upon public rather than private enforcement, is of marginal direct significance for payroll staff. Therefore the court hierarchy is not analysed in detail. Proceedings commence either in the Magistrates' Court (summary offences) or Crown Court (indictable offences).

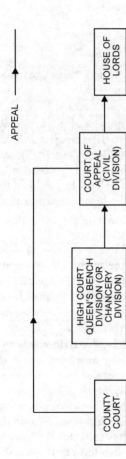

Illustration of a simplified view of the relationship between civil courts

Figure 3A

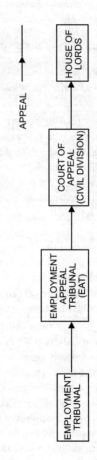

Illustration of a simplified view of the relationship between an industrial tribunal and the higher courts

Figure 3B

Employment tribunals system

3.8   Industrial tribunals, renamed 'employment tribunals' by *ER(DR)A 1998* since 1 August 1998, have jurisdiction to hear the following as well as numerous other statutory matters.

(*a*)   References concerning itemised pay statements. (See 5.13 below.) [*ERA 1996, s 11*].

(*b*)   Complaints and applications concerning equal pay. (see 5.8 below.) [*EqPA 1970, s 2*].

(*c*)   Complaints of unfair dismissal. [*ERA 1996, s 111*].

(*d*)   Complaints concerning deductions from pay. (See 5.12 below.) [*ERA 1996, s 23*].

Proceedings relating to any of the above must be commenced in an employment tribunal which, under *ETA 1996, s 3(1)*, and the *Industrial Tribunals Extension of Jurisdiction (England and Wales) Order 1994 (SI 1994 No 1623)*, also has jurisdiction to hear some claims regarding breach of a contract of employment or sums due under it. (See 5.3 below.) The basic hierarchy of the relationship between an employment tribunal and the higher courts is illustrated in Figure 3B.

An appeal from a decision of an employment tribunal lies, as a matter of right, to the EAT (Employment Appeal Tribunal), provided the appeal is based upon a point of law. An appeal from the EAT can be made to the Court of Appeal with the leave of either court, and from the Court of Appeal to the House of Lords with the leave of either of those courts.

Employment tribunals sit under the chairmanship of a legal practitioner with a minimum of seven years' experience, and with two lay members, one from either side of industry and both drawn from a list maintained by the Secretary of State for Employment. The chairman of the EAT, which is equivalent in status to the High Court, is a High Court judge. There are usually two, but sometimes four, lay members. Therefore, since majority decisions are, as in the Court of Appeal and House of Lords, acceptable, it is possible for the 'lawyer' chairman to be out-voted by the lay members, although this rarely occurs in practice. There is scope for cases concerning deductions from pay (see 5.12 below), insolvency (see 5.34 below), itemised pay statements (see 5.13 below), guarantee payments (see 5.26 below) and certain other matters to be heard by an Employment Tribunal chairman alone or accompanied by one lay member only.

As with the civil court hierarchy (see 3.6 above), only the Court of Appeal and House of Lords can create binding precedents to be followed by employment tribunals and the EAT.

Arbitration

3.9   Arbitration involves the settlement of a dispute by an independent third party in preference to recourse to the courts. It is often the subject of an express term in a contract, although this is more likely in a commercial contract than in a contract of employment.

However, ACAS (The Advisory, Conciliation and Arbitration Service) may refer an actual or potential employment dispute to arbitration to be determined by an appointed specialist or the Central Arbitration Committee (CAC) with the consent of both parties to the dispute. [*Trade Union and Labour Relations (Consolidation) Act 1992, s 212*]. The CAC is composed of persons experienced in employment relations and who include both employer and worker representatives. Any decision reached by the arbitrator in these circumstances is not subject to *AA 1950, Pt I* and is therefore not binding on the parties. But, the parties' initial consent generates a strong practical pressure to accept the decision. In this way the process of voluntary, but statutorily encouraged, arbitration can affect pay rates and the terms of the contract of employment.

The *ER(DR)A 1998* lays the foundation for ACAS to offer binding voluntary arbitration, as an alternative (with the parties' consent) to recourse to the employment tribunals, in some individual employment disputes . The precise scope of the scheme is, as yet, unclear.

Conciliation

3.10   The function of conciliation given to ACAS is authorised by *TULRCA 1992, s 210*, and covers disputes relating to pay and conditions. However, since conciliation is little more than the provision of a forum for the discussion and possible settlement of an existing or imminent dispute, it has no legal effect until agreement is reached.

The role of ACAS in conciliating is particularly important in disputes regarding the alleged infringement of statutory rights under *ERA 1996* and other Acts. 'Private' agreements supposedly settling such disputes do not always prevent a complaint to an employment tribunal: only a settlement conciliated by ACAS and recorded on its Form COT 3 or a written 'compromise agreement', entered into after the employee has received independent legal advice from a qualified lawyer (or, when *ER(DR)A 1998* is implemented, some other 'independent adviser'), are effective for this purpose. [*ERA 1996, s 203; SDA 1975, s 77; RRA 1976, s 72; DDA 1995, s 9*].

Differing legal systems within the British Isles

3.11   This chapter and the two following chapters are almost exclusively concerned with the legal regime and rules applicable to England and Wales.

The systems applicable to other parts of the British Isles, although worthy of separate detailed treatment, are summarised below.

(*a*)   **Scotland** — Acts of Parliament presumptively extend throughout the UK, but Scotland may be the subject of specific exclusion, sometimes additionally receiving legislative attention by means of a separate part of an Act or even a separate Act. (See 13.12 and 13.13 below for an example of specifically Scottish legislation in the payroll context.)

The system for the administration of civil justice is headed by the House of Lords (Scotland) and the Court of Session, preceded by the EAT and employment tribunals (statutory employment jurisdictions — see 3.8 above) or the Lord Ordinary (non-statutory jurisdiction).

(*b*)   **Northern Ireland** — As in the case of Scotland, Northern Ireland is often the subject of separate legislative treatment, frequently similar in form to that applicable in England and Wales. The system of civil adjudication culminates in the House of Lords (Northern Ireland) and the Northern Ireland Court of Appeal, preceded by the High Court (common law jurisdictions) and industrial tribunals (statutory employment jurisdictions).

(*c*)   **Offshore Islands** — The Isle of Man and the Channel Islands possess their own legislative and judicial systems. For instance, the Isle of Man legislates for itself through the Court of Tynwald (House of Keys and Legislative Council), each piece of legislation requiring the Royal Assent. Acts of the UK Parliament can be extended, either expressly or by Order in Council, to the Isle of Man. But this is only done after prior consultation with, or in the case of tax provisions, the consent of the Isle of Man government.

This court hierarchy is capped by the Judicial Committee of the Privy Council (in common with many other dominions), preceded by the Staff of Government Division and the High Court in relation to common law matters. There is a separate Employment Tribunal, against whose decisions there is currently no appeal, to adjudicate upon certain statutory employment rights.

The Isle of Man social security benefits and contributions are similar to those in the UK. Employers must also deduct income tax from employee's pay and pensions under the Income Tax Instalment Payments System (ITIP).

(*d*)   **Eire** — The Irish Republic is, of course, an independent sovereign State with its own legislature (the Oireochtas) and courts (Supreme Court and High Court in relation to common law matters, the Employment Appeals Tribunal concerning statutory employment rights). The only formal legal link with the UK lies in those Acts of the UK Parliament passed before independence in 1922, which still remain in force.

There is a series of Irish employment Acts, for example, the *Payment of Wages Act 1991* concerns payslips. A PAYE income tax system is in operation and social insurance contributions are paid by the employee and employer.

Similarity of rules

3.12 Notwithstanding differences of legal system and origin, a significant community of history and culture between the above regions has resulted in a frequent similarity in the wording or effect of many legal rules. However, similarity or identity should not be presumed in any given case, and the payroll administrator of an employer in England or Wales with payees in those other areas should seek to establish the detailed nature of applicable provisions.

Main areas of relevant payroll law

3.13 As indicated previously, payroll law is drawn from various legal fields which have their own titles. For the purposes of this handbook, the main areas concerned are as follows.

(*a*)   ***Employment law*** — Employment law revolves around the contract of employment which exists between employer and employee and also embraces the modern employment protection rights which are conferred by statute and are now mostly contained in *ERA 1996*, e.g. the right not to be unfairly dismissed. [*ERA 1996, s 94*]. It is central to payroll administration in that levels of pay are fixed primarily or initially by a term in the contract of employment and also because certain statutory rights are clearly important, e.g. the right of an employee to receive an itemised pay statement in a certain form. [*ERA 1996, s 8*].

(*b*)   ***Industrial relations law*** — This is a wide-ranging area of law covering such matters as legal liability for industrial action and internal trade union organisation. The main payroll law input arises from the fact that rates of pay and other matters collectively agreed between employers and trade unions can become the subject of a term in the individual contracts of employment by various methods of legal incorporation. Also, such statutory institutions as wages councils (see 5.6 below), ACAS (see 3.9 and 3.10 above) and the CAC (see 3.9 above) may, by virtue of their powers and duties, influence pay rates.

(*c*)   ***The law concerning discrimination and equal pay*** — Discrimination against individuals on the grounds of their sex, race, disability or trade union activities is policed by statute. Sex discrimination in relation to pay is a significant area of legislative concern which is governed by the *EqPA 1970* (as amended in 1975 and 1983).

(*d*) **The law relating to banking** — This branch of the law is concerned with the legal relationships between banker and client and, to a lesser extent, between banker and third party payees. Its importance for payroll practice arises simply from the fact that cheques, credit transfers on paper or via the Bankers' Automated Clearing Service (BACS) are often used to pay employees. Thus inevitably questions arise as to the effect on the employee and employer of errors made by the bank.

(*e*) **The law of agency** — Agency is a situation whereby an individual or institution (the agent) is engaged by another (the principal) to bring about a contract between the principal and a third party. In the present context, employees, particularly payroll staff, can be seen as agents of the employer (the principal) with possible authority to bind the employer in pay transactions with other employees. This can be so even where the agent exceeds, deliberately or inadvertently, the authority which the principal has conferred on him. There is also an overlap here with banking law, in that the bank can, in some circumstances, be operating as the agent of its customer.

(*f*) **Wages Councils** — In existence since 1909, Wages Councils regulated minimum pay in industries, or sectors thereof, where there was 'no adequate (voluntary collective bargaining) machinery' for regulating pay. An order made by a Wages Council was binding on employers within the relevant industry, any breach of such orders resulting in the imposition of fines. Wages Councils were abolished from September 1993. However, in the case of employees within the ambit of a Wages Order before that time, the specified rate of pay will be a term of his or her contract.

(*g*) **The Truck Acts 1831–1940 and the Wages Act 1986** — The *TAs 1831–1940* regulated two areas of payroll practice. The application of fines or other deductions from an employee's net pay and, in conjunction with *PWA 1960*, the form in which payment is made (see Chapter 21 (Payment Methods)). In particular, these Acts allowed manual workers to insist on cash payments. Due to problems experienced in the contemporary application of the *TAs 1831–1940*, the *WA 1986* repealed them and introduced a new regime furthering the concept of 'cashless pay' and imposing more specific restrictions on the making of deductions. The *WA 1986* is now *ERA 1996, Part II*.

Until January 1987, when the *Truck Acts* were repealed, employees had the right to payment of wages in cash unless an employee requested that his wages be paid by some other method, for example, by cheque or by direct transfer to a bank account. Contracts of employment dated before the repeal of the *Truck Acts* which specify payments in cash remain in force until new agreements are negotiated.

(*h*) **The law of contract** — The legal principles which underpin the enforcement of agreements between individuals as well as institutions

38

are important to payroll law, but these principles tend to appear in other forms. The rules of the law of contract are integral to some of the areas already discussed, particularly employment and agency law. Also, payments may be made by the employer on the basis of some mistake or misrepresentation, and in some instances the law of contract (or of restitution) invalidates the payment or the underlying agreement so as to enable the payment to be recovered.

(j) **Criminal law** — Criminal law results in legal punishment, for example, imprisonment or a fine, being imposed by the State via the criminal courts when its rules are infringed. Some very incidental criminal law matters have already been encountered in this section, for instance, enforcement of wages council orders by fines. The most likely link between the 'mainstream' criminal law and payroll concerns is that relating to various offences of dishonesty. For instance, an employee may claim or receive wages or expenses to which he knows he is not entitled. Fraudulent overtime or incentive scheme returns are common examples.

(k) **The law concerning injury at work** — Both under statute [*HSWA 1974*] and at common law the employer is under a duty to take reasonable care for the safety of his employees. This is particularly relevant in the case of payroll staff who are required to carry cash and are exposed to the risk of robbery with violence.

(l) **Corporate law** — Although not a subject of major significance to payroll procedures, company law may have some incidental implications for the payroll manager. For instance, the requirement in the *CA 1985* for a company's annual report to shareholders to specify the average 'weekly' number of employees etc. usually requires reference being made to payroll records. Other types of organisation such as local authorities can also be subject to payroll-dependent legal provisions.

(m) **Income tax and NICs** — The deduction from pay of income tax and social security contributions via the PAYE system is a major payroll responsibility.

(n) **Attachment of earnings** — The collection from employees of payments due to a court of law is a minor payroll responsibility, although likely to increase dramatically on account of non-payment of the Community Charge as a result of the implementation of the *Community Charges (Administration and Enforcement) Regulations 1989 (SI 1989 No 438)* and on account of child support by absent parents under enforcement provisions of the *Child Support Act 1991*.

(p) **Data Protection** — The *DPA 1998* imposes restrictions on the holding and use of personal data (see 5.37 and 23.16 below).

References

3.14   The following books contain a general introduction to the legal and constitutional framework of the UK and other regimes within the British Isles. The taxation books include some notes on the legal and administrative framework as well as tax details.

(1)   Padfield C F, 'British Constitution', Heinemann, Seventh Edition, 1987. (A standard introductory textbook which includes an overview of the English legal system.)

(2)   Boulding J, 'Taxation in the Channel Islands and Isle of Man 1998–1999', Tolley Publishing Co Ltd, 1998.

(3)   Saunders G, 'Taxation in the Republic of Ireland 1998–1999', Tolley Publishing Co Ltd, 1998. (Includes some brief notes on the Irish social security system.)

(4)   Keenan D and Riches S, 'Business Law', Pitman, Fourth Edition, 1995. (A student's introduction to English business law.)

(5)   John G, 'A New Resolution', PMR, July 1998.

4 Payee Status

Scope of this chapter

4.1   Each type of payee has his own separate legal status which governs such matters as his pay-related rights and tax position. Thus, the situation of the employee, self-employed and pensioner are markedly different in this respect. Some employees also have a unique legal position, for instance, agency workers and policemen. Even 'ordinary' employees have small differences in legal status, for instance company directors are subject to different rules for benefits-in-kind. Many differences in status are only significant in terms of the employer's own contract of employment, for example, it is still common for businesses to offer better sick pay to 'white-collar' staff than to 'manual' workers. This chapter can only outline the position of some important occupational groups and common variations in payee status. It concentrates on the statutory aspects such as the effect of status on NICs. However, it is essential that the payroll administrator and computer software designer take into account all the differences as they can significantly affect the calculation of pay and related matters. In a minority of cases the status of some payees may not be clear, but nevertheless it must be correctly determined. Taking the example of a shipping company, the payroll administrators may have to identify and respond correctly to the differing legal status of pensioners, directors, merchant seamen, government trainees, ordinary employees, etc. Ignoring the details of particular employment contracts the main general areas of interest are the effect of payee status on employment rights, income tax and NICs. In addition, payee status has a bearing on industry or occupation-wide features of employment such as membership of a national pension scheme. For the purposes of this chapter an 'industry' is considered to be any national economic function and not just a particular type of physical productive activity such as a motor car manufacturing. So local government and education are also viewed as 'industries' with their own legal framework and employment custom and practice.

Key points of payee status

4.2   The main aspects of payee status can be summarised as follows.

(*a*)   The determination of a payee's legal status is an essential payroll task.

41

(*b*) Employees can have special status, e.g. they may be youngsters, which could affect liability to NICs. Different aspects of payee status can also apply simultaneously, e.g. an employee can be higher paid and over SPA, both of which affect payroll procedures.

(*c*) Certain occupations are subject to special payroll legislation, e.g. members of HM Forces.

(*d*) Non-employees commonly covered by payroll administration include the self-employed, pensioners and government trainees.

(*e*) Besides employment rights the primary effect of payee status is on statutory deductions and pension scheme membership.

(*f*) Failure to identify a payee's status correctly could lead to incorrect pay calculations and procedures. This could cause an employer considerable problems particularly with the Inland Revenue and DSS. Rigorous administrative procedures are essential to avoid these difficulties.

Importance of distinguishing an employee from other payees

4.3 This handbook is mostly concerned with issues which typically arise during an employment relationship, i.e. that existing between employer and employee. Some of the legal matters discussed can and do extend to other forms of pay relationship, but nevertheless the central concern with employees is maintained. This focus arises for two main reasons. First, most basic individual rights contained in *ERA 1996* and *TULRCA 1992* are only available to an 'employee' (contrast *EqPA 1970, SDA 1975, RRA 1976* or *DDA 1995*, which also cover those working under contracts personally to execute any work or labour). Secondly, the vast majority of those performing work, and therefore the majority of payees for the purposes of a payroll department, are undoubtedly employees. This latter point is important to bear in mind. Whilst the distinction between an 'employee' and other types of 'payee', for example a contractor or a pension beneficiary, is significant for legal reasons, it is in relatively few situations that there is any real doubt as to the legal status of the payee. Nevertheless, a dispute concerning the rights of one class of payees can have serious consequences for the payer, particularly because it may be a 'test case' for other similar payees.

The area which causes the most problems is the distinction between an employee and a self-employed person. There are, of course, advantages in classifying a worker as self-employed. The employer avoids all the extra legal responsibilities owed to an employee, e.g. redundancy and maternity rights, and there are income tax benefits accorded to a worker who is categorised as self- employed under Schedule D rather than as an 'employed earner' falling within Schedule E. (See 11.6 and 11.8 below.) The self-employed classification also involves mutual NIC advantages. (See 12.20 below.) However, employees receive superior social security benefits in return for the greater NIC liability. Needless to say, it is difficult to persuade the relevant authorities to accept doubtful 'self-employed' classifications. (See 4.4 below.)

Notwithstanding the clear similarity between the terms 'employee' and 'employed earner' it should be noted that the latter category embraces 'office holders' such as Members of Parliament, whereas members of this group are not 'employees' for the purpose of employment protection rights. The term 'office' was defined by Rowlatt J in *Great Western Railway Co v Bater [1920] 3 KB 266; [1922] 2 AC 1* as 'a subsisting, permanent, substantive position which had an existence independent of the person who filled it, which went on and was filled in succession by successive holders'. 'Office' has been held to include the position of a director of a company registered in the UK whether public or private and irrespective of where he resides or his degree of involvement. See also *McMillan v Guest [1942] AC 561*, and, in *Mitchell and Edon (Inspectors of Taxes) v Ross [1962] AC 813* relating to the part-time health service appointments of medical specialists. The term 'employment' was held by Rowlatt J in *Davies (HM Inspector of Taxes) v Braithwaite [1933] 2 KB 628; 18 TC 198* to mean 'something analogous to an office which is conveniently amenable to the scheme of taxation which is applied to offices'.

Definitions of 'employee', 'casual worker' and 'home worker'

4.4   If the distinction between employees and others is, of necessity, significant, it is not legally precise. The central, statutory definition of an 'employee' is 'an individual who has entered into or works under (or, where the employment has ceased, worked under) a contract of employment', i.e. a contract *of* service or apprenticeship. [*ERA 1996, s 230; TULRCA 1992, s 295(1)*]. This type of contract should be distinguished from a contract for services undertaken by an independent contractor. However, beyond this linkage of 'employee' with the 'contract *of* employment' the statutes have not defined precisely the term 'employee'. Thus, the job of defining, and in doubtful cases of determining status, has been left to the courts and tribunals. The most popular expression of the current legal approach to establishing status is 'Is the person who has engaged himself to perform these services performing them as a person in business on his own account?' (*Market Investigations Ltd v Minister of Social Security [1969] 2 QB 173*) or, more directly, 'Are you your own boss?' (*Withers v Flackwell Heath Football Supporters Club [1981] IRLR 307*). If it is answered in the affirmative, then the worker concerned is not an 'employee'. It should be noted that the existence of a formally constituted business, run by the worker, is not necessary for such an answer to be given. Issues which are relevant to a conclusion include the following.

(*a*)   Who provides the work equipment and materials?

(b)   What is the extent of the employer's control over the worker and what scope is there for the worker to manage his own work and to generate his own profit or loss?

(c)   To what extent is the individual skill and personality of the worker relevant to the performance of the work?

(d)   Are there obligations to offer work over a period of time and what are the consequences of a refusal?

The answers and facts revealed by consideration of these, and other issues, are weighed by a court or tribunal in order to reach a conclusion as to status. The significance of a particular fact or issue may vary case by case (*Hall (HM Inspector of Taxes) v Lorimer [1992] ICR 739*). For instance, in the *Market Investigations* case above it was held that a market research interviewer was an 'employee', despite having some discretion and independence in performing the work, because the company's ultimate control over her manner of work was considered to be the overriding factor. The factor of control, evidenced by a stipulated hourly rate of pay and regulation of timekeeping, attendance and conduct, was sufficient in *McMeechan v Secretary of State for Employment [1997] IRLR 353*, to make an agency worker an employee of the agency for the purposes of a particular assignment in respect of which he was owed payment. (Contrast *Wickens v Champion Employment [1984] ICR 365*, *Ironmonger v Movefield Limited [1988] IRLR 461* and *Knights v Anglian Industrial Services [1996] EAT 640/96*.) But in *Hitchcock v The Post Office [1980] ICR 100* a sub-postmaster was found not to be an 'employee' of the Post Office because the concerns of his own retail business outweighed the supervision and control to which he was exposed whilst fulfilling his official duties. The same conclusion was reached, in *Duke v Martin Retail Group PLC [1994] IRLB 496*, in respect of the manager of a newsagents shop. Although subject to corporate control on such matters as goods sold, fixtures, fittings, cleanliness and opening hours, the manager's personal responsibility for employees' remuneration and liability insurance, as well as the freedoms to delegate performance of duties and to carry on other business, meant that he was an independent contractor.

Particular problems of classification arise in relation to casual, intermittent workers and to those who perform their work at home. With the former, the perceived legal objection to being classified as 'employees' has been that it is difficult to find a continuous or 'umbrella' contractual relationship which links the various periods of work done for the same employer and which would be based upon a future reliance by the parties on each other (*O'Kelly v Trusthouse Forte plc [1984] QB 90*, *Clark v Oxfordshire Health Authority [1998] IRLR 125*). Nevertheless, construction of the requisite 'mutuality' is possible. In *Nethermere (St Neots) Ltd v Gardiner & Taverna [1984] ICR 612*, homeworkers with no fixed hours, who had some capacity to determine the amount of work they were given and performed, were held to have an overriding contract of employment: this was said to be based on their continuing expectation of, and reliance on, further work from a particular employer. A similar outcome occurred in

Carmichael & Leese v National Power plc [1998] IRLR 301, in relation to tour guides engaged on a 'casual as required' basis. However, it should be noted that, even where such workers are considered to be 'employees', access to statutory rights is likely to be limited because of the frequent need to have a certain period of continuous employment.

The main problem for the payroll administrator is, as in the *Hall* case, the distinction drawn between Schedule D, Cases I and II income, and Schedule E, Cases I, II and III income. The former covers effectively the income of a self-employed person and the latter that of an employee. There are no statutory definitions of these two categories for taxation purposes so that one has to resort to the case authorities for a definition. As already discussed the distinction between people liable for tax under Schedule D and Schedule E is largely based on that between persons with a contract *for* services and those with a contract *of* service, and one main criterion is the degree of control exercised by one party to the contract over the other. Thus a contract for services entered into by a professional person (Schedule D, Case II) would give that person a great deal more discretion over how he fulfilled his part of the contract than would be available to an employee under a contract of service. In *O'Kelly's* case above the Court of Appeal held that the test of whether a contract was a contract of employment or a contract for services was a pure question of law. However, the application of the test depended so much on the finding and assessment of the available facts and the precise quality to be attributed to them, that the primary question was one of fact and degree.

In the *Davies* case above an actress had appeared on stage, in films, in radio plays and had made records all under separate contracts. It was held that all her engagements were part of one profession carried on by her and she was assessable under Schedule D, Case II. In *Fall (H M Inspector of Taxes) v Hitchen [1973] 1 AER 368; [1973] STC 66*, a ballet dancer was engaged under a standard contract to Sadler's Wells Trust Ltd for a minimum period and thereafter at two weeks' notice. He was required to work full time for a regular salary and to undertake no outside engagements. He was held to be correctly assessed under Schedule E, Case I. A distinction may have to be made between the various classes of income received by the taxpayer. Thus in *Blackburn (HM Inspector of Taxes) v Close Bros Ltd [1960] 39 TC 164* it was conceded by the Crown that merchant bankers who received fees and allowances for performing managerial and secretarial services for companies could be assessed under Schedule E, Case I in respect of these fees and allowances alone, although their ordinary profits were assessed under Schedule D, Case I.

In determining status, courts and tribunals, as well as the Inland Revenue and the DSS, are loth to accept without question, a declaration in the relevant contract concerning that status, or to treat a contractual stipulation as to the method of discharging income tax and NIC liabilities as conclusive of status. Their reluctance is based largely upon a concern that a worker might be compelled into accepting, or unwittingly adopt, a particular status and thereby be deprived of important statutory rights and protections. Therefore, whilst a declaration may happen to support the conclusion derived from other indicators (as in the *Duke* case above), it will be ignored by a court if it does not reflect the reality of the work relationship (*Ferguson v John Dawson and Partners (Contractors) Ltd [1976] 3 AER 817*) and is only significant if, after consideration of other relevant factors, the worker's status is ambiguous (*Massey v Crown Life Assurance Co [1978] 1 WLR 676*). Such an approach can produce the anomalous situation that a worker who has been operating as self-employed for income tax and NIC purposes is suddenly declared to be, for those purposes, an 'employed earner'. This opens up the following two possibilities which could occur together for the worker and his employer.

(i)   They may be prosecuted for defrauding the Inland Revenue and DSS where the contractual declaration was utilised for this purpose.

(ii) Their tax and NIC affairs may need to be adjusted retrospectively. This is often done by means of a private and informal settlement with the Inland Revenue.

Also, employment rights, previously assumed to be unavailable to the individual, may come within reach. For example, in *Plant Movements Ltd v Long [1992]*, the EAT found that a person, who had changed from 'employee' to 'self-employed' status and enjoyed the benefits of the latter for almost a year before his contract was ended, was able to present a complaint of unfair dismissal.

The legal test to establish whether or not a worker is an 'employee' is of a very general nature. It is, therefore, not always easy for an employer to determine the legal category into which a worker falls. Where there is doubt concerning status, in addition to seeking advice or a ruling from the Inland Revenue, the DSS or professional advisers, it may be advisable to accord a worker the day-to-day legal rights and facilities which are available to an 'employee'. So, for instance, the use of a standard itemised pay statement (see 5.13 and Figure 22A below) for all individual workers eradicates the possibility of a worker, previously perceived as self-employed and not accorded the facility, establishing that he is an 'employee' and complaining that he has not received such a statement. Also, this approach is more likely to avoid problems with the Inland Revenue and DSS. The income tax and NIC regime adopted for a specific worker in practice often dictates whether or not various other legal provisions are considered to be applicable. But it should be remembered that assumed status is not conclusive of the legal status.

Finally, notwithstanding the legal distinction between an 'employee' and other payees, it should be remembered that the same individual may operate as both an employed and a self-employed worker, e.g. an employee who also has his own part-time business as a paying hobby.

The Inland Revenue and the DSS have taken steps to ensure that they take a consistent view of any employment status problems and have brought out a joint booklet on the subject. (See Reference (1) in 4.9 below for further details.) They have also appointed individual officers in each office to deal with employment status matters.

Special occupations

4.5   Many occupations have a special legal status. For instance *CA 1985, s 285* recommends that only a qualified accountant, lawyer or chartered secretary is appointed as company secretary to a public company. *CA 1989, s 25* specifies that only a person who is a member of a recognised supervisory body, and is eligible for the appointment under the rules of that body can be appointed a registered auditor for a company. A further example is the *Merchant Seamen (Certification of Deck Officers) Regulations, (SI 1980 No 2026)* which specify the number and certification of officers on different types of ship. Of course, this handbook is primarily concerned with those matters which affect pay and benefits. One example of this is employed divers who in some cases are taxed under Schedule D. [*ICTA 1988, s 314*]. Another case is members of visiting foreign armed forces who are exempt from income tax. [*ICTA 1988, s 323*].

One important feature of some 'industries' is the importance of national pay and conditions agreements which cover large numbers of employees in specified occupations. In the public sector there are 'Whitley Councils' where employer and employee representatives negotiate these national agreements (see 16.10 below), or pay review bodies where recommendations are made to the Government. Currently, however, there is a move towards local pay bargaining in both the public and private sectors.

The examples below briefly illustrate the special payroll features of some important occupational groups.

(*a*)   ***Crown employees*** — Crown servants can be defined as persons 'directly or indirectly appointed by the Crown' and paid out of money provided by Parliament. [*CPA 1947, s 2(6)*]. Thus, most obviously, members of the Civil Service, whether working in Whitehall or elsewhere, come within this category. At common law, a Crown servant is traditionally viewed as not possessing a contract of employment and as holding office at the pleasure of the Crown. Whilst this view has been modified to permit contractual claims for pay already earned (*Kodeeswaran v A-G for Ceylon [1970] 2 WLR 456*), it still prevails in relation to dismissal and has been codified with regard to changes in terms and conditions of service. [*Civil Service Order in Council 1982, Article 4*].

However, Crown servants have access to the employment protection rights contained within *ERA 1996*, with the exception of redundancy payments. (See 9.17 below.) [*ERA 1996, s 191*]. The redundancy payment exclusion is nullified by the existence of a separate and more generous scheme. The other statutory protections may be removed from Crown servants (or groups thereof) if necessary in the interests of national security. Equal pay and discrimination legislation (see Chapter 5 (Payroll Law)) also applies to Crown service (*EqPA 1970, s 1; SDA 1975, s 85; RRA 1976, s 75*) as do the SSP and SMP schemes. [*SSCBA 1992, ss 161, 169*].

Finally, a Crown servant is an 'employed earner' for income tax and NIC purposes.

(b)   **Local authority employees** — Local authorities are statutory corporations established and regulated according to various local government Acts, primarily *LGA 1972*. Their powers and duties to perform various functions derive from specific Acts such as the *Public Health Act 1936* and the *Education Act 1944*. Local authorities are only empowered to pay their employees at a 'reasonable' rate (*Roberts v Hopwood [1925] AC 578*). However, their employees present no unusual requirements from a payroll viewpoint. Most of the unique features of local authority payrolls are a result of history and business traditions and the legal aspects are incidental. Thus, one noticeable feature is the use of similar terms and conditions of employment across the country. This is the result of Whitley Council national negotiations covering all authorities and wide categories of employees such as manual workers. The national agreement may be supplemented by local agreements although these tend to cover such matters as bonuses and working hours rather than basic rates of pay. Standard pay rates are contained in documents with names like the 'Purple' or 'White' Book (for white-collar and manual workers respectively). The local government superannuation scheme is also a standard national scheme covering local government officers and manual workers. The scheme has a statutory basis in the *Local Government Superannuation Regulations 1986 (SI 1986 No 24)*, made under *SA 1972, ss 7, 12*. It should be remembered that local authority payroll departments can also be responsible for teachers, police, and firemen and that each of these groups has different terms and conditions of employment from ordinary local government staff. Pension payments can also be another responsibility of the payroll department.

Elected local authority members (councillors) are office holders who receive payments for 'approved duties', e.g. attendance at council meetings. [*LGA 1972, ss 173–177*]. The allowances paid are usually subject to income tax and NICs, except for those payments which cover prescribed expenses. Councillors can also receive SSP.

(c)   **National Health Service workers** — Persons employed in the National Health Service are, without statutory intervention, considered to be Crown servants (*Wood v Leeds Area Health Authority [1974] ICR 535*). Health workers are accorded exactly the same employment rights as 'normal' Crown servants. (See 4.5(*a*) above.)

Terms and conditions of employment are determined through the negotiating machinery of the Whitley Council system and pay review bodies, and are then usually confirmed and made binding by order of the Secretary of State.

Pension arrangements for those working in the National Health Service are contained in the *National Health Service (Superannuation) Regulations 1980 (SI 1980 No 362)*, issued by the Secretary of State for Social Services under *SA 1972, s 10*.

(d) **Workers of statutory corporations** — Although statutory corporations, for instance British Coal and the BBC, are in fact ultimately controlled by the Government, they are not regarded as Crown organisations and therefore their employees are not Crown servants (*Tamlin v Hannaford [1950] 1 KB 18*). Consequently these employees have 'normal' contractual status and potential access to the full range of statutory employment rights.

(e) **Armed forces** — Members of the armed forces are subject to the rules of military law which vary in precise content according to which arm of the services is involved. Regular members of the armed forces have access to some statutory employment rights, including those to:

(i) an itemised pay statement (see 5.13 below);

(ii) written particulars of employment (see 5.4 below);

(iii) paid time off for ante-natal care (see 5.21 below); and

(iv) pay during suspension on maternity grounds (see 5.21 below).

[*ERA 1996, s 192*].

Pay and pensions are covered by various provisions which are briefly summarised as follows:

(A) in the case of the Army, Royal Warrants are promulgated in Army orders made under prerogative powers or under *PYPA 1884, s 2* for soldiers' pensions;

(B) in the case of the Navy, Orders in Council are made under *NMPPA 1865, s 3*;

(C) in the case of the Air Force, Orders in Council are made under *AF(C)A 1917, s 2*;

(D) in the case of the Reservists, Orders in Council are made under *RFA 1980*.

Pensions due to death or disablement in war are covered by the *Naval Military and Air Forces etc. (Disablement and Death) Service Pensions Order 1983 (SI 1983 No 883)*.

Serving members of the armed forces are only eligible for a restricted range of social security benefits and pay-reduced Class 1 NICs in recognition of this. [*Social Security Contributions Regulations 1979 (SI 1979 No 591), reg 115*].

(*f*) **Merchant seamen** — Merchant seamen in British ships are a special class of employee whose employment rights are partly covered by *ERA 1996*, e.g. unfair dismissal. In addition they are also governed by *MSA 1970* and regulations made thereunder as amended by *MSA 1974* and *MSA 1979*. The personnel aspects of the Acts and regulations made under them are important, covering aspects of marine employment such as the repatriation of seamen shipwrecked abroad and misconduct endangering a ship. Industry-wide terms and conditions of employment are set by the National Maritime Board (NMB). As regards payroll operations there are some small legal differences between merchant seamen and other employees. Payment of wages is governed by *MSA 1970*. *Section 9* provides powers for making regulations concerning deductions, the manner in which wages are paid and the format of an 'account of seaman's wages' (payslip) etc. However, merchant seamen are also covered by separate NIC regulations. The secondary NIC rates are lower than normal where a seaman is registered as a foreign going mariner and this reflects the fact that when abroad he is entitled to a restricted range of social security benefits and does not use the NHS facilities so that different table letters are used to indicate this. (See *Social Security (Contributions) Regulations 1979 (SI 1979 No 591), reg 89*.)

There are, of course, several practical differences related to mariners' work, e.g. payslips may be posted to them. Another practical difference is that seamen are often members of the two industry-wide pension schemes covering the shipping industry (the Merchant Navy Ratings and Merchant Navy Officers' Pension Funds).

(*g*) **Voluntary workers** — People often work without remuneration, e.g. for a sports and social club, charity, trade union or professional body. As the work is performed on a gratuitous basis the only payments should be legitimate expenses. The 'contractual' position of such people, when members of the association concerned, is defined by the rules, e.g. the constitution of a club or a union rule-book. Non-members, e.g. the spouse of a member who is 'helping out', have no contractual position other than perhaps an implied right to expenses. If there is an element of remuneration in any payment, e.g. an honorarium, then normal PAYE practice applies as the individual is operating as either an employee or office-holder of the association, e.g. club secretary or treasurer. An individual could also possibly be self-employed in some circumstances.

Special types of employee

4.6   Some payees are in a special legal position for reasons other than their occupation, for example because of their age. As far as payroll operations are concerned the main effect is on income tax and NICs.

(*a*) **Minors** — The employment of children aged under 14 is largely prohibited and the employment of children over 14 is confined to 'light work' which does not endanger health, safety development or attendance at school (*CYPA 1933* and *1963*, as amended by the *Children (Protection at Work) Regulations 1998 (SI 1998 No 276)*).

There is less regulation of young persons or adolescents (those above minimum school leaving age but under 18. The regulations implementing the *Working Time Directive* (see 3.3 above and 5.9 and 5.20 below) will not treat adolescent workers separately from others when they introduce a maximum 48-hour working week, although they will make specific provision on a number of other issues.

Where minors are employed, the employer is contractually bound to fulfil obligations, most obviously to pay the agreed wage or salary for work done. However, the contract of service is not legally enforceable against the minor unless it is, as a whole, beneficial to him (*Clements v LNWR [1894] 2 QB 482*). Nevertheless, a contract can be beneficial notwithstanding the existence within it of some terms detrimental to the minor and it will be deemed beneficial if it only contains terms upon which a minor could reasonably expect employment.

Employees receiving remuneration when aged under 16 are also not subject to NICs, but can pay tax if their income is sufficient.

(*b*) **Apprentices** — Being primarily for educational purposes, a contract of apprenticeship is not strictly a contract of service. But most statutory employment rights are extended to apprentices who are treated as working under a form of 'contract of employment'. [*ERA 1996, s 230; TULRCA 1992, s 295; EqPA 1970, s 1; SDA 1975, s 82; RRA 1976, s 78*].

Although the absence of the normal written apprenticeship agreement, signed by both parties, is, therefore, not fatal to the availability of these rights, it denies the 'apprentice' the rights to enforce the usual obligations of an employer under an apprenticeship agreement. [*AA 1814, s 2*]. Most important here is the obligation to teach an apprentice the relevant skill or trade.

Given that apprentices are usually minors when commencing their training, the law of contract concerning minors applies. (See 4.6(*a*) above.) Thus, the apprenticeship contract is only binding on the apprentice if it is of an overall beneficial nature. One way of avoiding possible disputes about enforcement against a minor is to include the minor's parents as parties to the apprenticeship contract.

(*c*) **Students** — To the payroll administrator students are usually one type of part-time, casual or temporary labour, e.g. Saturday work in a shop or full-time vacation work as holiday relief in a warehouse. As such their terms of employment are similar to others in the same category, i.e. they have very limited employment rights and PAYE etc. applies. Where the student works only a few hours a week earnings are often not sufficient for tax and NICs to apply (see 19.9(*b*) below for further details). However, during a vacation period only the student may avoid tax by completing a P38(S) Form and the employer must follow the appropriate PAYE procedures in these circumstances. (See Inland Revenue Booklet CWG2, Chapter 4 for further details.) As regards NICs the normal rules apply.

(*d*)   **Senior citizens** — If employees are over a certain retiring age they are, or may be, excepted from the following:

   (i)   certain employment rights, e.g. protection from unfair dismissal (non-discriminatory retirement age below 65 or, otherwise, 65);

   (ii)   SSP (State pension age);

   (iii)   employee's NICs (State pension age);

   (iv)   pension scheme contributions, but this depends on the rules of the employer's scheme.

Special tax codes often apply to people over SPA, because those on lower incomes are entitled to the extra tax relief of an age allowance. (See 25.7 below.)

(*e*)   **Women** — Some married women or widows are still eligible for reduced NICs. For this to apply they must produce a 'certificate of election' (Form CF383 from the DSS). The right to reduced NICs is either deliberately surrendered by a woman or lost on divorce and cannot be renewed on remarriage. The DSS appear to take the view that the employer must revoke the certificate on quite casual evidence of an end to a woman's marriage. The right can also sometimes be lost through widowhood or insufficient earnings. (See DSS leaflet CWG 2, Employer's Further Guide to PAYE and NICs, paragraphs 81 to 86 and Reference (8) in 4.9 below for further details.)

Prior to 1989 there were several protective restrictions on the employment of women. The *EA 1989* reduced their scope, for example, by allowing women to work underground in mines, but still not permitting their employment in factories within four weeks of childbirth.

(*f*)   **Multiple employments** — In principle multiple employments present no special problems as each employment is treated separately. A common case would be a full-time teacher taking on part-time night school work sometimes with the same employer, e.g. a local authority. From a practical payroll viewpoint the most common complication is with regard to NICs. Where the employee's earnings exceed the UEL with his main employer then he can request that the DSS send a RD 950 Form to his other employers exempting him from paying employee's NICs on the minor employments. The other employers are still liable for their share of the NICs in this case. Where the employee has two or more jobs with one employer, earnings from both employments must be aggregated for NIC purposes. (See DSS leaflet CWG 2, paragraphs 65–71 for further details and paragraphs 74–79 in the same document for the contracting-out complications. Reference (9) in 4.9 below is also useful.)

(g)   **Casuals** — Casual employees have no special status or exemptions from PAYE etc. merely because they are employed for short periods of time. Naturally their contractual and statutory rights are rather basic. However, the PAYE requirements are less stringent if the weekly earnings do not exceed the LEL which is often the case where the employment is only for a few hours per week. In this case only the employee's name, address and pay need be recorded. If the total yearly earnings for a casual exceed £100 a Form P38A must be completed at the tax year-end. (See 20.9(*d*) below.)

(h)   **Part-time employees** — Part-timers, however defined, pose no special contractual problems. Further, the rights contained within the *SDA 1975, EqPA 1975, RRA 1976* and *ERA 1996, Part II* have always been available to these employees. However, since the decision in *R v Secretary of State for Employment ex parte Equal Opportunities Commission and Another* and the resultant regulations amending the law (see 3.3 above), 'thresholds' requiring a minimum of sixteen or eight hours work per week have been removed from all statutory employment rights under *ERA 1996* and *TULRCA 1992*, including those to time off (see 5.21 below), guarantee payment (see 5.26 below), redundancy payments and compensation for unfair dismissal.

(j)   **'Higher paid' employees** — It should be clear that most employees have some special statutory status which affects payroll and related operations. One of the most important is the classification of employees as 'higher paid', i.e. those whose remuneration (including benefits-in-kind) is £8,500 p.a. or more. These employees together with company directors are subject to more severe taxation on benefits-in-kind. (See 9.3 below for further details and 20.16 below which discusses the PAYE aspects.) The *FA 1989* has officially replaced the somewhat archaic term 'higher paid employees' with the phrase 'employees earning £8,500 or more'.

(k)   **Company directors** — Company directors have special duties and responsibilities which are defined in the *CA 1985* and the Articles of Association of each particular company. The word 'director' is often used in the public sector to designate important managerial posts, but the term so used has no special legal significance. A company director's terms and conditions of employment are laid out in his contract, which may be a full service contract and in the Articles of Association. Usually he is both an office-holder and employee, particularly for tax and NIC purposes. One key aspect of a director's status is that his tax and NIC regime is more strict. He is treated as a 'higher paid' employee when taxing benefits-in-kind and also his NICs are calculated cumulatively.

(See 20.16 and 12.16 below for further details on the tax and NIC details.) However, the fact that a director pays Class 1 NICs and is taxed under PAYE is not conclusive of his status for the purpose of employment legislation. For example in *Buchan and Ivey v Secretary of State for Employment [1997] IRLR 80* the EAT held that directors who were also controlling shareholders were able to prevent their own dismissal and, therefore, were not 'employees' entitled to a redundancy payment. (See also *McLean v Secretary of State for Employment [1992] EAT* and *Fleming v Secretary of State for Trade and Industry [1997] IRLR 682* (Court of Session).) Nevertheless, in *Secretary of State for Trade and Industry v Bottrill [1998] IRLR 120*, the EAT stressed that having the sole or controlling shareholding is only one (albeit an important) factor in deciding status. There is no rule of law that an individual in such a situation cannot be an employee, especially where, as in *Bottrill* itself, the individual's control over the company is theoretical and outweighed by other indicators of employment.

(*l*)   **Foreign employees** — This is obviously a complex area because of the possibility of two or more legal regimes being involved, particularly with an employee whose stay in any one country is transient. Income tax and NICs are, of course, the main practical concern. Double Taxation Relief (DTR) is often used to prevent or reduce double taxation of the same income by two governments. The employment rights in *ERA 1996* and allied legislation do not extend outside the UK. The payroll consequences of employing foreigners are very briefly discussed below.

   (i)   In most cases foreign employees permanently based abroad are paid through local payroll operations and subject to overseas laws. Occasionally foreign employees are paid through payroll systems located in Britain, for example employees based in the Isle of Man are paid from England. In this case the employer must follow local regulations.

   (ii)   Where foreign employees working in the UK are working for a UK employer then they are often ordinary employees for PAYE purposes etc. A UK employer can sometimes benefit from the services of a foreign employee, e.g. by secondment. Even if the foreign employee is remunerated by his overseas employer the UK 'intermediate employer' must apply PAYE provided the foreign employee is under his control. (For further details see 11.9 and 12.19 below as well as Reference (14) and (34) in 4.9 below which outline the main tax and NIC complications. DSS leaflet CWG 2, paragraphs 117–124 is also helpful.)

(*m*)   **Expatriate employees** — Most employment protection rights contained in *ERA 1996* and *TULRCA 1992* (see Chapter 5 (Payroll Law)) are not available to an employee ordinarily working outside the UK. A potential exception to this can be found in the insolvency provisions (see 5.34 below) which cover any employee normally working within the EC. [*ERA*

1996, s 196]. For those rights which require a qualifying period of continuous employment, past work abroad for the employer cannot be counted unless a secondary Class 1 NIC was payable. However, 'surrounding' periods of employment in Great Britain can be joined to calculate continuous employment. *[ERA 1996, ss 210–219]*. Other legislation relating to employment rights (see Chapter 5 (Payroll Law)) is also confined to employees working within Great Britain. *[EqPA 1970, s 1; SDA 1975, s 6; RRA 1976, s 4]*.

Whilst 'expatriate' employees are excluded from the right to written particulars (see 5.4(*p*) below), employees 'temporarily' posted abroad for a minimum of one month are entitled, as an item in their particulars, to information on:

(i)   the duration of the work outside the UK;

(ii)   the currency for the payment of remuneration;

(iii)   any additional pay or benefits due as a result of working abroad; and

(iv)   any terms and conditions regarding return to the UK.

The NIC position of employees working abroad for an employer resident in Great Britain depends upon the location of the foreign employment and in some cases the expected duration of that employment. (See 12.19 below.) A UK resident's earnings from overseas employments are not subject to UK tax and are subject to the tax regime of the country concerned provided that the individual concerned is officially absent from the UK for at least a year. (See 11.9 below and also References (15)–(18) in 4.9 below.)

Non-employees

4.7   The following categories of payee are not employees, but are often the responsibility of the payroll administrator. Sometimes another department may be responsible, for example the pensions department may operate a pension payroll.

(*a*)   ***Trainees under government-funded schemes*** — YT trainees do not normally have a legally binding contract, of any form, with their 'employers' (or managing agents) (*Daley v Allied Suppliers Ltd [1983] ICR 90*). Although a training agreement is issued to the trainee by the 'employer' and contains the basis of the relationship, the specimen agreement states that it is not to be legally enforceable. Therefore, there can be no direct legal enforcement of the agreement's contents nor any statutory employment protection for the trainee.

However, there can be indirect enforcement of the contents of the agreement by the State (previously in the guise of the Training Agency, and now the Training, Enterprise and Education Directorate of the

Department of Employment and Education, which operates through local Training and Enterprise Councils) which does have a contract with the 'employer'. Thus the contents of the agreement relating to trainee allowances (upon which income tax and NICs are not payable), travel allowances, hours of work (a weekly maximum of 40), holiday entitlement (18 days plus public holidays) and sick pay (up to four weeks) can be made available to the trainee. Normally the 'employer' makes the payments and then recovers the money from the managing agent. Further, trainees are expressly accorded protection under the *HSWA 1974, FA 1961* and the *Health and Safety (Youth Training Scheme) Regulations (SI 1983 No 1919)* and are not to be discriminated against in relation to denial of access to training, the terms of such access or termination of training. [*SDA 1975, s 14; RRA 1976, s 13*].

A full range of statutory rights can become available if a contract of service comes into being. In some cases, a YT trainee is explicitly taken on as an employee. Alternatively, this outcome might occur merely by the 'managing agent' omitting from the training agreement the clause concerning non-enforceability. Alternatively the trainee might do work in excess of that required by the training arrangement. However, although a contract of service might well exist in respect of this excess work, there would be problems associated with the hours. (See 4.6(*h*) above.)

Although other types of government trainees have not been a frequent subject of litigation, such trainees are likely to possess the same legal status as YT trainees. Again some have also been classed as 'employees' with contracts of service with normal employment rights. Needless to say the situation is very changeable with new training and employment schemes continually coming into existence and old ones disappearing.

(*b*) **Self-employed people** — As well as being subject to different income tax and NIC regimes such individuals are excluded from many statutory employment rights. (See Chapter 5 (Payroll Law), also 11.3 and 12.5 below and Reference (1) in 4.9 below for further details on the income tax and NIC position of the self-employed.) However, certain statutes cover persons working under contracts for services provided the work is performed personally. [*ERA 1996, s 230* (for *Part II*); *EqPA 1970, s 1; SDA 1975, s 82; RRA 1976, s 78*].

(*c*) **Self-employed construction workers** — Under *ICTA 1988, Pt XIII Ch IV* where a business carrying out construction work makes a payment to a subcontractor or his nominee then the payer must deduct basic rate income tax in respect of that part of the payment which represents the labour cost. The subcontractor may apply to the Inland Revenue for a tax certificate, often called an 'exemption' or a '714' certificate. This exempts the payer from the need to make this tax deduction. (For further details see References (21) and (22) in 4.9 below.) It should always be kept in mind that a '714' certificate has no relevance to NICs.

It should also be noted that current draft Regulations may affect the way in which the scheme is administered and policed by the Inland Revenue. These Regulations will take effect from August 1999.

(*d*)   ***Pensioners*** — There are four broad categories of pensions for the purposes of this handbook. The rights of the pensioner depend on the source of the pension. These four categories are as follows.

   (i)   Social security pensions of some sort are available to most of the working population and their dependants. Their rights are defined in the Act of Parliament governing the particular pension concerned.

  (ii)   State occupational schemes are available to employees of local and the national government of their dependants. They obtain their pension rights from superannuation schemes established directly or indirectly under an Act of Parliament.

 (iii)   Private sector schemes are normally established as trusts. The pensioners' rights are contained in the trust deed and rules. In addition, there is also significant statutory regulations.

 (iv)   Annuities arise where a pension is purchased from an insurance company and an annuity is a contractual right. The contract may be with the annuitant or the trustees of a pension scheme who purchased the pension for him.

See Chapter 10 (Pensions) for a more detailed account of pension arrangements.

Practical implications

4.8   This chapter has by no means exhausted the less usual payroll cases, for example, ministers of religion, hospital doctors, share fishermen, sub-postmasters, entertainers etc. Often, however, payroll administrators who are responsible for special types of payee such as civil servants have ready access to the relevant regulations and are drilled in their use. However, even experienced payroll administrators can initially find the work very demanding when they change 'industries'. This is often due to the sheer volume of pay and benefit regulations unique to their new employer which must be mastered quickly. Also the relevant documentation is sometimes less than perfect.

Some payroll software packages may not provide the requisite facilities for less common types of payee such as merchant seamen. Even if the tax and NIC aspects can be handled, special types of labour often require special facilities and different types of management reports from the computer systems. Another area which can cause difficulty is using computer systems to report conveniently all expenses and benefits for the annual Forms P9D and P11D. (See 20.16 below.)

One common difficulty is the use of casual, temporary, contract and self-employed staff. A major problem is that the personnel or payroll departments may never even know of their existence. Departmental managers may employ them directly without realising the PAYE and other implications. A simple but incomplete precaution is the issue of regular circulars reminding managers that they must notify the payroll office of all temporary labour used.

Problems in actually determining payee status are rare except from distinguishing validly between the employed and self-employed. It is, for instance, usually obvious that a person is a local government officer rather than a policeman. However, borderline cases between various categories can arise. Errors though are more likely to occur because someone has failed to collect the basic details or failed to respond correctly to an employee's status, for example operating cumulative NICs for company directors.

A final point which applies to all areas of payroll work is that staff must be trained to handle correctly all payee status issues. Regular management checks and internal audits can identify and correct any procedural errors before they become serious.

References

4.9   The essential starting-point for all payroll work is DSS leaflets CWG2 'Employer's Further Guide to PAYE and NICs' and CWG1 'Employer's Quick Guide to PAYE and NICs'. These briefly discuss the tax and NIC treatment of the more common exceptions to normal full-time employment. The introductory guides to the payroll treatment of special types of payee are the general references of Chapters 5 (Payroll Law), 10 (Pension Schemes), 11 (Income Tax) and 12 (National Insurance Contributions). Specialist publications, often with a restricted circulation, exist for particular industries and occupations. In some cases the DSS and Inland Revenue produce booklets devoted to the tax and NI position of particular types of payee, examples of which are given below.

(1)   IR 56/NI 39, 'Employed or Self-Employed? A Guide for Tax and National Insurance', Inland Revenue and DSS.

(2)   'Guidance Note: Crown Servants and Statutory Employees', Industrial Relations Legal Information Bulletin No 331, June 1987.

(3)   Gaskell N J J, Debattista C and Swatton R J, 'Chorley and Giles' Shipping Law', Pitman, Ninth Edition, 1992.

(4)   CA 23, 'National Insurance for Mariners', DSS.

(5)   CA 24, 'National Insurance for Masters and Employers of Mariners', DSS.

(6) IR 46, 'Income Tax and Corporation Tax: Clubs, Societies and Associations', Inland Revenue.

(7) IR 121, 'Income Tax and Pensioners', Inland Revenue.

(8) CA 13, 'National Insurance Contributions for Married Women', CA.

(9) CA 01, 'National Insurance for Employees', CA.

(10) Smith F, 'Summer Casuals', PMR, August 1987.

(11) CA 25, 'National Insurance for Agencies and People Finding Work Through Agencies', CA.

(12) Souster P, 'Directors' Responsibilities & Liability', Accountancy Books, 1990.

(13) CA 44, 'National Insurance for Company Directors', CA.

(14) Faichney R, 'Foreign Employees', PMR, June 1987.

(15) Faichney R, 'Going Abroad', PMR, July 1987.

(16) NI 38, 'Social Security Abroad', CA.

(17) NI 132, 'National Insurance for Employers of People Working Abroad', CA.

(18) IR 6, 'Double Taxation Relief for companies', Inland Revenue.

(19) FB 30, 'Self-Employed', BA.

(20) CA 02, 'National Insurance Contributions for Self-Employed People with Small Earnings', CA.

(21) IR 14/15, 'Construction Industry Tax Deduction Scheme', Inland Revenue.

(22) 'Employment Law Problems: Who Is An Employee?', Incomes Data Services, Brief No 510, February 1994 (Part 1), and No 511 February 1994 (Part 2).

(23) CA 65 'National Insurance for People Working for Embassies, Consulates and Overseas Employers', CA.

(24) FB 26, 'Voluntary and Part-time Workers', CA.

(25) 'Guidance Note: Working Overseas', Industrial Relations Legal Information Bulletin No 454 August 1992.

(26) Talbot R, 'Transfer of Employees To and From the United Kingdom', PMR, January 1996.

(27) Dugdale H, 'Employment or Self-Employment', PMR, February 1996.

(28) 'Guidance Note: Employment Status 1 — General Principles', Industrial Relations Law Bulletin No 533, November 1995.

(29) 'Guidance Note: Employment Status 2 — Specific Categories', Industrial Relations Law Bulletin No 534, December 1995.

(30) 'Guidance Note: Part-Time Workers 1 — Extension of Employment Protection Rights', Industrial Relations Law Bulletin No 524, July 1995.

(31) 'Guidance Note: Part-Time Workers — Contractual Rights', Indutrial Relations Law Bulletin No 525, July 1995.

(32) 'Contracts of Employment: Company Directors — Whether Employees', Incomes Data Services Brief No 573, September 1996.

(33) 'Employment Law Problems: Part-time Workers', Incomes Data Services Brief No 578, December 1996.

(34) 'What You Should Know About International Assignments', PMR, August 1996.

(35) Clarke A. 'Children at Work', PMR, May 1998.

(36) 'Guidance Note: Trainees', Industrial Relations Law Bulletin No 592, May 1998.

(37) 'Children at Work', PMR, May 1998.

(38) 'Abusing the FED', PMR, May 1998 (foreign earnings deductions).

(39) 'Building Regulations', PMR, May 1998 (construction workers).

(40) 'We're all Going on a . . .', PMR, July 1998 (student workers).

(41) 'Satisfaction for Foreign Workers', PMR, September 1998 (the abolition of foreign earnings deductions).

5 Payroll Law

Scope of this chapter

5.1   As previously discussed in Chapter 3 (Legal Framework) payroll law is drawn from disparate legal sources. Major areas of involvement are the law concerning employment and the rules regulating income tax and NICs under the PAYE system. But the boundaries of payroll law spread much further to encompass areas such as criminal law, company law, the law of agency and the law of trusts and banking. More recently it has extended to cover data protection. This chapter adopts a broadly sequential approach to the topic of payroll law. Starting with the establishment of basic entitlements, primarily through the medium of the contract of employment, it examines possible modes of variation of entitlement; it then discusses the issues relating to the act of payment and finally covers the various eventualities which may befall the payer and payee.

Some areas of payroll law are treated separately, such as income tax and data protection, in Chapter 11 (Income Tax) and 23.16 below.

One vital aspect of payroll law is the status of the payee. The employed, self-employed and pensioner are subject to different legal rules. Also some employees, for example children, are subject to special legislation. These important issues and related matters are discussed in Chapter 4 (Payee Status). This chapter concentrates mainly on ordinary employees.

Key points of payroll law

5.2   The salient features of payroll law are summarised below.

(*a*)   The extensive nature of payroll legislation demands extra vigilance from the payroll administrator and other relevant staff.

(*b*)   The training of staff in elementary principles of payroll law increases the likelihood of legal problems being recognised early and resolved.

(*c*)   Employment law has many practical implications for the payroll function.

(*d*)   Where unusual or complex legal problems arise, or are envisaged, advice should be sought from solicitors, auditors, professional bodies or government departments, or guidance obtained from the relevant literature such as booklets from the Department of Employment.

(*e*)   An audit of current payroll administration practices should be conducted at regular intervals to ensure compliance with those aspects of the law touching on the day-to-day administration.

(*f*)   Computer payroll systems can facilitate compliance with legal requirements.

Contract of employment

5.3   This topic can be conveniently dealt with under the following headings.

(*a*)   ***Immediate effect*** — It has already been stated that the relationship of employer and employee is governed initially by the contract of employment which represents the agreement between them and which comes into effect on the day stated in the contract.

(*b*)   ***Nature of the contract of employment*** — The contract of employment differs from many other contracts which operate in the business sphere in two significant respects. First, it is often not produced in a comprehensive written form. It is occasionally supplemented by an oral agreement. The written components are frequently not in a purpose-built format but are contained in letters of appointment, employment handbooks, memoranda and union agreements (but see 5.4 below). Second, the contract of employment tends to rely, to a greater extent than other contracts, on terms and duties which are implied rather than those which are expressly agreed upon by employer and employee. Some terms are implied by the law in all employment contracts because their content is deemed to be essential to any employment relationship, for example the obligations of co-operation and faithful service. Others are implied in a specific employment relationship because of its nature, the conduct of the parties or the customs of the relevant industry. For instance, in *Sagar v Ridehalgh and Son Ltd [1931] 1 Ch 310*, an employer was found to be entitled to make deductions from an employee's wages for bad workmanship on the basis of accepted trade custom despite the employee's ignorance of that custom (but see 5.11, 5.15 and 5.16 below). An implied term cannot, in the event of a conflict, override an express term in a contract.

(*c*)   ***Express and implied terms concerning pay*** — It is rare for the matter of pay itself not to be the subject of an express agreement. Occasionally, however, this situation may arise, especially where a person has been engaged to perform a short-term or 'one-off' function. In such circumstances the employee has an implied right to reasonable remuneration (*Way v Latilla [1937] 3 AER 759*) which can only be excluded by an express term to the contrary which indicates that the employer had an absolute discretion in the matter of payment. There are also situations where, despite express agreement on the basic issues of the amount and period of payment, unusual or unforeseen circumstances cast doubt on the applicability of that agreement. For instance, where an employee is absent from work due to sickness or injury (see 5.22–5.24 below) or where he is laid-off due to a lack of work (see 5.25–5.28 below). In such circumstances, if there is no express term to cater for the eventuality, the courts are required to imply a term into the contract. However, it should be remembered that an implied term cannot override an express term.

(d)   ***Determining the content of the pay obligation*** — The precise content of a term on pay, particularly concerning the amount, can often be derived from other sources. For instance, the contract may 'adopt' relevant collective agreements negotiated between employer and trade unions (see 5.5 below) or statutory agencies may impose compulsory minimum rates (see 5.6 and 5.8 below).

(e)   ***Failure to pay*** — Where an employer fails to pay an employee the agreed amount, he is in breach of the contract of employment unless there are good reasons for his failure. Such reasons include the making of agreed deductions (see 5.11 below), or the employee's failure to attend for work or to do acceptable work (see 5.11, 5.12 and 5.22–5.28 below). If the employer does commit a breach of contract in this way, the employee can recover the pay due by suing him for breach of contract in a court or employment tribunal, or by making an application to a tribunal under *ERA 1996, Part II*. (See 5.12 below.)

The facility to complain to an employment tribunal of a breach of contract, or that sums due under the contract have not been paid, was introduced by the *Industrial Tribunals Extension of Jurisdiction (England and Wales) Order 1994, SI 1994 No 1623*. Its main limitations are that the claim must arise or be outstanding on the termination of employment and the maximum compensation is £25,000. An employer faced with such a claim is permitted to submit a counterclaim against the employee.

It should be noted, however, that any contract deliberately to defraud the Inland Revenue is void and therefore unenforceable by a party to it (*Tomlinson v Dick Evans 'U' Drive Ltd [1978] ICR 639*). Indeed, a Scots case, *Salvesen v Simons [1994] IRLR 52*, has gone further and held that the parties' ignorance of the illegal character of their agreement will not save it from being unenforceable.

Written particulars of employment

5.4   An employee is entitled to be given by his employer a written statement of his major terms and conditions of employment. It must be provided within two months of the beginning of employment. [*ERA 1996, s 1(1) and (2)*]. The details to be specified are:

(a)   identification of the parties;

(b)   the date of commencement of employment and continuous employment;

(c)   the scale/rate of pay or method of calculating pay and the pay interval;

(d)   any terms and conditions relating to hours of work;

(e)   any terms and conditions relating to holidays;

(f)   the employee's job title or a brief description of the work;

(g)   the place of work or an indication that work is or could be at various locations;

(h)   disciplinary rules and procedure (not required from employers of less than 20 employees);

(j)   grievance procedure;

(k)   the length of notice the employee is entitled to receive and give;

(l)   any terms and conditions regarding sickness, sick pay and pensions;

(m)   the expiry date of a fixed term contract or the expected duration of any other contract intended to be 'temporary';

(n)   any collective agreement directly affecting terms and conditions; and

(p)   information in the case of a posting abroad (see 4.6(m) above).

[*ERA 1996, s 1(3) and (4)*].

Items (a) to (g) must be supplied in a single document (the 'principal statement'). [*ERA 1996, s 2(4)*]. But, subject to the two-month time limit, other items *may* be supplied by subsequent instalments.

It is permissible, in relation to items (h) to (l) only, to refer the employee to other documents which are reasonably accessible to him. However, on item (k), reference can only be made to applicable legislation or collective agreements. [*ERA 1996, s 2(2) and (3)*]. If there are no details to be given under any heading, that fact must be stated.

The written statement or particulars issued by the employer, whilst reducing uncertainty and being useful for evidential purposes, is not a contractual document nor is it conclusive evidence of the contents of the contract (*System Floors (UK) Ltd v Daniel [1982] ICR 54*). Therefore, it is possible for the details given to be overridden by conflicting evidence. For instance, in *Robertson and Jackson v British Gas Corporation [1983] ICR 351*, employees established a contractual entitlement to an incentive bonus scheme by reference to letters of appointment, the court ignoring the relevant part of the statutory written particulars which indicated that, in the circumstances which prevailed, no such bonus would be payable. Reference may be made to an employment tribunal concerning non- existent or allegedly deficient particulars. The tribunal has powers of amendment or substitution of particulars [*ERA 1996, s 11*], but this does not extend to inventing terms on a subject on which no evidence of agreement between the parties can be found. (*Eagland v British Telecommunications PLC [1992] IRLR 323*).

Negotiation and agreement between employer and trade unions

5.5   There is no doubt that in practice collective negotiation and agreement have a significant effect upon pay rates of individual employees. The main question is how, in legal terms, an agreement between employer and union comes to take its place as part of the separate agreement (the contract of employment) between employer and employee. In view of the law's unwillingness to accept that a union bargains as a legal agent of its members (*Burton Group Ltd v Smith [1977] IRLR 351*), the two most acceptable answers are as follows.

(a)   *Express incorporation into the contract of employment* — This is achieved by the simple and tidy device of a clause in the contract of employment which clearly states that the contract is, on specific matters such as pay, subject to, for instance, 'agreements for the time being in force between Y Ltd and Z trade union'. In this way it is the contract of employment which itself establishes how the pay rate is settled, albeit by adopting the results of negotiation elsewhere. The process of expressly linking the collective agreement and the contract of employment is further encouraged by the possibility that an employee is referred to a collective agreement document for the details of the written particulars (see 5.4 above).

(b)   *Implied incorporation into the contract of employment* — Even where there is no express clause in the contract, the relevant provisions of a collective agreement may become impliedly incorporated, either because corresponding provisions in previous agreements have been observed by employer and employees (*Arthur H Wilton Ltd v Peebles [1994] EAT 835/93*), or because the employer and particular employee have already started to observe the provision in question. The employee can provide consideration sufficient to enforce the employer's commitment on pay simply by continuing in employment thereafter (*Lee v GEC Plessey Telecommunications [1993] IRLR 383*). However, it should be remembered (see 5.3 above) that an express term prevails over any implied obligation in the case of conflict.

Minimum rates of pay

5.6   There were two dozen or so Wages Councils who were empowered to make orders with an impact upon one-tenth of the UK workforce, mainly covering those employees in the retail, catering and clothing manufacture trades. Wages Councils were controlled by the *Wages Act 1986* which enabled the Councils to make orders fixing the basic rates of pay, overtime rates and amounts deductible for living accommodation. The effect of a Wages Council order was to substitute its pay level for that contained in relevant contracts of employment where the contractual level was less than that stipulated in the order.

Whilst Wages Councils have not existed since 31 August 1993 (see 3.13(*f*)), the applicable pay rates from their most recent Orders are already incorporated into the contracts of employees in employment on that date. Therefore, a unilateral reduction of pay to a level below these rates by an employer would normally amount to a breach of contract.

In the agriculture industry there remains the Agricultural Wages Board constituted under the *Agricultural Wages Act 1948*, which makes orders regarding the rates of pay, holiday entitlements and other terms and conditions of employment within the agricultural sector.

By mid-1999 the provisions within the National Minimum Wage Bill should be in force. The Bill stipulates that all 'workers' (including agency and homeworkers) who are over compulsory school age have the right to be paid the national minimum wage (NMW). An individual who receives less than the NMW will have the right to recover the underpayment by way of an application to an employment tribunal under *ERA 1996* (see 5.12 below) or a court action for breach of contract. Further, it will be unlawful to discriminate against or, in the case of an employee, dismiss a person because they have taken steps to secure their right to the NMW. Additional powers, such as enforcement notices and penalty notices (requiring payment of twice the NMW for a specified period) are envisaged as exercisable by officers appointed by the Secretary of State. Finally, the Bill features prosecutions for failures to comply with the NMW or associated record-keeping provisions and for obstructing enforcement officers: conviction will attract a maximum fine of £5,000 for a single offence. The NMW, expressed as an hourly rate, will be fixed by the Secretary of State after consultation with the Low Pay Commission .

Variation of the contract of employment with regard to pay

5.7   Given that the contract of employment is the starting point for establishing pay levels, it is also the usual base for their variation or the variation of related matters, e.g. the introduction of cashless pay. (See 6.12 and 22.17 below.) Lawful contractual variation may arise by any one of three basic methods, which are summarised below.

(*a*)   ***An existing express clause permitting variation*** — There can be a clause in the original contract which gives the employer the power to increase, not necessarily annually, the employee's pay. Whilst the scope and, perhaps, the necessity for any amendment is at the discretion of the employer, this discretion exercised by the employer has been contractually agreed between the parties.

A second type of clause in this category is that which expressly incorporates the pay provision of a collective agreement into the contract of employment. (See 5.5 above.) For example, in *Higgins v Cables Montague Contracts Ltd. [1995] IRLR 535*, a pay cut of 20 per cent was validated by a collective agreement permitting it and a clause in the contracts of employment which incorporated, as contractual terms, 'the relevant provisions of the collective agreements currently in force'. In *Airlie v City of Edinburgh District Council [1996] IRLR 516 (EAT)*, a similar position prevailed in relation to the employer's alteration of an incentive bonus scheme.

(b) **Specific agreement to vary** — It is, of course, possible for the parties actually to agree, in written or oral form, to a particular change in pay even without the existence of an express permissive clause. The objection to this form of agreement is that the parties must agree each variation, whereas the express clause secures an overriding agreement applicable to all variations.

(c) **Variation by conduct and practice** — It is possible, although perhaps relatively unlikely, that, without overt agreement, the employer will commence paying and the employee will accept increased rates of pay. In such circumstances this conduct of paying and accepting can operate to vary the previously agreed pay levels. This type of conduct tends to be binding in this manner only when it has been pursued consistently for some period of time and the circumstances support an intention to create a legal obligation (*Young v Canadian Northern Railway Company [1931] AC 83*). Thus, even a management policy on payments, although applied in the past, may not generate a contractual entitlement enforceable by an employee (*Quinn v Calder Industrial Materials Limited [1996] IRLR 126*). Certainly one increased payment by the employer, particularly if made in error (see 5.14–5.18 below), would not vary the contractual rate of pay.

In relation to variation of pay generally, it is necessary for the employee's written particulars (see 5.4 above) to be amended so as to reflect the change. This is done by means of a written notice of the variation given to the employee within a maximum of one month of it taking effect. [*ERA 1996, s 4(1)*]. Such a notice may be provided by the pay slip.

Direct reduction of the contractual rate of pay without agreement will be a breach of contract by the employer. As there is no necessity for the employee to resign and the simple fact of continuing to work does not mean the employee has accepted such a unilateral change (*Rigby v Ferodo Ltd [1988] ICR 29*), this can result in a claim for damages covering a lengthy period. But if the employee does resign in response, damages for the breach will only cover the notice period to which the employee would have been entitled if dismissed (*Boyo v London Borough of Lambeth [1995] IRLR 50*). Also, if the reduction is substantial, the breach of contract will be sufficient to entitle the employee to resign as 'constructively' dismissed [*ERA 1996, s 95*] and allege unfair dismissal. It may be possible for an employer to show that the action was fair provided there was a good reason, for example survival of the business, behind the change and it was preceded by reasonable consultation. (*Hollister v National Farmers Union [1979] ICR 542*.) However, where a pay reduction is imposed by the purchaser of a business, any resulting 'constructive' dismissal will usually be unfair under *Transfer of Undertakings (Protection of Employment) Regulations 1981 (SI 1981 No 1794), reg 8* (*Delabole Slate Ltd v Berriman [1985] IRLR 305*).

Even maintenance of the existing rate of pay, by the unreasonable refusal of increases on review dates, may constitute a breach which goes to the root of the contract (*Clark v BET plc [1997] IRLR 348*) and lead to a 'constructive' dismissal (*GEC Avionics v Sparham [1993] EAT 714/91; 494 IRLB 10*). Of course, pay reduction may also be the consequence of a change in another aspect of the contract, for example hours or duties. Change of these matters is more likely to be the subject of an express clause giving the employer freedom to do so. Nevertheless, whatever the particular subject, such an express power to alter content must be exercised reasonably, otherwise the employer's implied obligation to maintain trust and confidence may well be breached (*St. Budeaux Royal British Legion Club Ltd. v Cropper [1995] EAT 39/94*; *Star Newspapers Ltd v Jordan [1993] EAT 344/93*).

Discrimination and pay rates

5.8   The following statutes confer rights on sections of a workforce to obtain fair and just treatment in pay and other conditions of employment.

(*a*)   **The Equal Pay Act 1970** — This Act (*EqPA 1970*) came into force on 29 December 1975. It implements the United Kingdom's obligations under *Article 119* of the *Treaty of Rome*, which provides that 'each member State shall . . . ensure and . . . maintain the application of the principle that men and women should receive equal pay for equal work'. If there is any conflict between *Article 119* and *EqPA 1970*, or any doubt as to the latter's scope, the interpretation (by the European Court of Justice) of the *Article* prevails.

As subsequently amended, *EqPA 1970* operates by means of a statutorily implied 'equality clause' to eradicate pay inequalities between male and female employees who are in the 'same employment'. The term 'pay inequalities' used here refers merely to an imbalance in any single term of employment, not imbalance in the overall 'remuneration packages' of the employees concerned (*Hayward v Cammell Laird Shipbuilders Ltd [1988] 2 WLR 1134*). Thus an applicant's basic rate might be improved to the level of her male comparator, notwithstanding that her overtime rates and paid holiday entitlements were more beneficial.

In *Barber v Guardian Royal Exchange Assurance Group [1990] IRLR 240 (ECJ)* it was held that benefits under 'contracted-out' pension schemes are 'pay' under *Article 119*. Therefore, the principle of equal pay is breached if, on a compulsory redundancy, a man is only entitled to a deferred pension whereas a woman of the same age (and doing equal work) is entitled to an immediate pension as a result of an age condition varying according to sex. This is so even if the age differential is derived from the basic State pension scheme. The principle in *Barber* was subsequently extended to cover also pension schemes which supplement and are directly linked to the State scheme (*Moroni v Firma Collo GmbH [1994] IRLR 130 ECJ*) and, further, to the very right to join a pension scheme (*Vroege v NCIV Instituut Voor Volkshuisvesting BV & Stichting Pensioenfonds NCIV [1994] IRLR 651*).

In *Ten Oever v Stichting Bedrijfspensioenfonds Voor Het Glazenwassers – en Schoonmaakbeorijf [1993] IRLR 601*, the European Court decided that such equalisation of benefits in occupational pensions (including the value of transfer benefits and lump sum options – *Neath v Hugh Steeper Limited [1994] IRLR 91 ECJ*) is normally confined to those benefits payable in respect of employment after the date of the *Barber* judgment, 17 May 1990. The only exception to this rule is for those individuals who had started proceedings, or made an equivalent claim, under national law before that date.

The *Pensions Act 1995* now implements *Article 119* in relation to pensions by providing that all occupational schemes are deemed to include an 'equal treatment rule'. It covers the terms on which persons become members and those on which members are treated in respect of the accrual of benefits after 17 May 1990. The means by which the rule is activated and defeated mirror those for pay equality under *EqPA 1970* (which are described below). The normal remedy on a successful application to an employment tribunal under *PA 1995* is a simple declaration of the applicant's rights. The employer then comes under a duty to provide to the pension scheme the necessary resources to secure those rights, but no sum is payable to the applicant.

Under *EqPA 1970* itself, pay equality requires that the compared employees, who may occupy a single job consecutively rather than contemporaneously (*MacCarthy's Ltd v Smith [1980] IRLR 210 (ECJ)*), are employed on 'like work', i.e. the same or broadly similar work, 'work rated as equivalent' (under a valid job evaluation study) or 'work of equal value' (under a study conducted by an independent expert appointed by an employment tribunal. [*EqPA 1970, s 1(1), (2)*].

Even where an employee can establish that one or other of these situations applies, the employer can prevent the requirement of equal pay by showing that the discrepancy in the pay of the employees concerned is not the result of the man's terms and conditions of employment being in any respect more favourable than the woman's, but that it is genuinely due to a material factor which is not the difference of sex between the two cases. [*EqPA 1970, s 1(3)*]. This provision allows the employer to plead such factors as the differing skill, experience, qualifications, productivity or labour market values of the employees in question as the reasons for their differing pay levels (*Rainey v Greater Glasgow Health Board [1987] ICR 129*). However, it is clear that an employer cannot defeat the employee's equal pay claim by arguing that, for instance, men tend to have certain abilities or characteristics and therefore the man in question should receive more pay (*Shields v E Coomes (Holdings) Ltd [1978] 1 WLR 1408*).

Separate pay bargaining structures, themselves each non-discriminatory, do not amount to a genuine material factor justifying unequal pay (*Enderby v Frenchay Health Authority [1993] IRLR 591 ECJ*). It was also held in the *Enderby* case that the state of the employment market, causing an employer to increase the pay of a particular job to attract applicants, could be objective justification for a difference in pay between that job and one of equal value. But the European Court also stated that it may be that only part of the difference can be so justified and, therefore, that the lower rate of pay would have to be increased to the extent that it was not defensible. This is known as 'proportionality'. In *Ratcliffe v North Yorkshire County Council [1995] IRLR 439*, the reduction of the pay applicable to a predominantly female job in order to secure a contract under compulsory competitive tendering was found to be a material factor but one due to the difference of sex. Therefore, the employees affected were entitled to equal pay with their male comparators who occupied a job unaffected by the process.

Whilst the *EqPA 1970* largely depends for its effect upon the making of applications to employment tribunals by individual employees, its potential consequences are greatly increased by the 'equal value' form of claim. This allows an employee to instigate a comparability study with an employee performing a very different job even where there are employees of the opposite sex performing the same work and being paid at the same level as the applicant employee (*Pickstone v Freemans PLC [1988] IRLR 357*). So, for instance, in *Hayward's* case above a female canteen cook was held to be employed on work of equal value to that of male employees working variously as painters, joiners and insulation engineers. The independent expert reached this conclusion by giving 'low', 'moderate', or 'high' assessments of the different jobs under the headings of physical demand, environmental demand, planning and decision-making, skill/knowledge and responsibility. It can be seen that if the study produces a finding of equal value which is adopted by the employment tribunal, hitherto unforeseen consequences can follow for grading systems and pay structures. The most effective preparation which can be made against this possibility is to ensure that all jobs within the undertaking have been graded properly and fairly and the gradings used as the basis of pay structures. This is effective because 'equal value' claims are inadmissible where the jobs to be compared have already been accorded different values on a non-discriminatory basis in the study. [*EqPA 1970, s 2A(2)*]. However, in order to come within this 'defence', the study in question must be of an analytical type (*Bromley v H & J Quick Ltd [1988] IRLR 249*).

An employer can introduce in evidence results of a job evaluation study in an attempt to show that there are 'no reasonable grounds' for an equal value claim even though the study was undertaken after the initiation of the equal value proceedings (*Dibro Limited v Hore [1990] IRLR 129 (EAT)*). But it is a matter for the discretion of the tribunal as to whether the proceedings are stayed to allow an employer to conduct a study (*Avon County Council v Foxall and Webb [1989] IRLR 435 (EAT)*).

A claim under the *EqPA 1970* must be brought during employment or within six months of it ending (*EqPA 1970, s 2(4)*) and, if successful, may be backdated for a maximum of two years preceding the initiation of proceedings (*EqPA 1970, s 2(5)*). The second limitation is under attack as being contrary to *Article 119* (which contains no limitation whatsoever), particularly in relation to pension cases brought by part-timers (see above). In *Dietz v Stichting Thuiszorg Rotterdam [1996] IRLR 692*, the ECJ ruled that *Article 119* itself permits the backdating of equalised benefits in 'pension access' cases to 1976 rather than May 1990 (the date of the *Barber* decision): it also stated that limitations under national laws are only valid if comparable with those for similar employment actions and if they do not make claims under *Article 119* impossible or excessively difficult. In *Magorrian and Cunningham v Eastern Health and Social Services Board and Department of Health and Social Services [1998] IRLR 86*, the ECJ declared that the application of *section 2(5)* would contravene *Article 119* in a case where access to enhanced benefits depended on having 20 years' service. Whilst this clearly undermined *section 2(5)* in relation to applications by part-timers excluded from pension schemes, the position remains sufficiently unclear for the House of Lords to have referred the question of the provision's validity to the ECJ in *Preston v Wolverhampton Healthcare NHS Trust, Fletcher v Midland Bank plc [1998] IRLR 197*. In the meantime, the Advocate General of the ECJ has delivered a preliminary opinion in *Levez v T H Jennings (Harlow Pools) Ltd [1996] IRLR 499*, a case which does not concern pensions at all. Relying, in part, on the comments in the *Dietz* case and partly on the lack of any discretion for courts and tribunals to extend the *EqPA*'s limitation period (even where there has been a justification for the delay in instigating proceedings), he favours invalidating *section 2(5)*. It remains to be seen whether the ECJ itself will adopt this stance.

(b)　**Race Relations Act 1976** — It is unlawful for an employer, on racial grounds, to treat a person less favourably than he treats or would treat other persons with regard to the terms of employment, including pay, which he affords that person. [*RRA 1976, ss 1(1), 4(2)*].

(c)   **Trade Union and Labour Relations (Consolidation) Act 1992** — An employee has the right not to be discriminated against on the grounds of his actual or potential union membership or activity or because of his unwillingness to become a union member. [*TULRCA 1992, s 146(1)*]. However, inducements, e.g. personal or individual contracts with higher rates of pay, are lawful when offered to employees to 'opt-out' of collective bargaining or leave a trade union provided they are clearly part of an employer's policy to change the employee relations system operating for all employees or a particular class of employees. [*TULRCA 1992, s 148(3)*].

(d)   **Employment Rights Act 1996** — Those designated as 'protected' or 'opted-out' shop workers, or betting workers, have the right not to be subjected to a 'detriment' on the ground that they refuse to do Sunday work. However, if an employer offers financial or other incentives to those willing to do such work, there is no 'detriment' for those not offered or not accepting the incentive. [*ERA 1996, s 45*].

(e)   **Disability Discrimination Act 1995** — It is unlawful for an employer, for a reason related to a person's 'disability' (which is widely defined), to treat that person less favourably without justification than he treats or would treat others with regard to the terms of employment, including pay, which he affords that person. [*DDA 1995, ss 4(2), 5(1)*].

Establishment of entitlement to fringe benefits

5.9   Almost exclusively, fringe benefits are within the domain of the particular contract of employment concerned. Although there are statutory income tax considerations concerning benefits such as cars, expense accounts and clothing allowances (see Chapter 9 below), these matters only arise once the benefit is conferred by agreement between employer and employee.

With the exception of employments covered by the Agricultural Wages Board, which may direct what holidays are permitted and rates of pay for time off, the specification of holiday entitlements has been almost exclusively a matter for determination within the contract of employment. The only statutory intervention has been to require communication, by the written particulars of employment (see 5.4 above), of the detail of any entitlement to holidays and holiday pay.

However, the *Working Time Regulations (SI 1998 No 1833)*, implementing the EU's *Working Time Directive (93/104)* and taking effect in October 1998, alter this situation (see 5.20 below).

Variation of entitlement to fringe benefits

5.10   A variation is most likely to be effected by way of mutual agreement between employer and employee or through existing contractual authority (see 5.7 above). Even where considerable freedom to vary is available, the relevant term, as interpreted by the courts, must be complied with. For example, in *Bainbridge v Circuit Foil UK Ltd [1997] IRLR 305*, a contract of employment contained the right for the employer to amend or terminate a permanent health insurance scheme 'without prior notice' to employee members. It was held that, whilst these words meant that advance notice of a change was not necessary, 'notice' or notification ultimately was. Therefore, as the employer had never got round to telling the employees that the scheme had been terminated, the equivalent of its benefits remained a contractual entitlement.

There is, however, a possible statutory ground for intervention in that it is unlawful to discriminate on the grounds of sex or race in relation to 'access to benefits, facilities or services'. [*SDA 1975, ss 1,6(2); RRA 1976, ss 1, 4(2)*]. Where there is such unlawful discrimination an employment tribunal may, as an alternative or in addition to awarding compensation to the employee, recommend that the employer rectify the discriminatory situation. [*SDA 1975, s 65; RRA 1976, s 56*]. The effect of such a recommendation is to put the employer under pressure to equalise benefits as between relevant employees in order to avoid an award of compensation or further awards being made.

A pregnant employee is entitled to a 14-week maternity leave period. [*ERA 1996, s 71*]. During this time, she is entitled to the 'benefit of the terms and conditions of employment which would have been applicable if she had not been absent', excluding any right to 'remuneration'. Therefore, withdrawal or reduction of contractual benefits other than pay will be a breach of contract which may justify a claim of 'constructive' dismissal. Further, even if it was argued that pension benefits were 'remuneration' and therefore need not be continued, a specific statutory intervention provides otherwise. A period of 'paid maternity absence' (which includes an absence covered only by SMP) must be treated, for pension purposes, as if it were a period of normal working with normal pay. [*SSA 1989, 5 Sch*]. The right to a maternity leave period, which does not depend on length of service, co-exists with the current statutory right to return to work after pregnancy and confinement, which is available to those with two or more years' service. The latter, which contemplates an employee being absent for approximately 40 weeks, does not confer any express entitlement to the maintenance of contractual benefits. Therefore, provided the contract is not deemed to have continued due to the employer's words or actions (see *Crouch v Kidsons Impey [1996] IRLR 79*), it may be possible to discontinue benefits, other than pension benefits whilst an employee is still receiving SMP or occupational maternity pay (see above), from the fifteenth week of the longer maternity absence.

Establishment of the employer's authority for deductions from pay

5.11   As the employment relationship is based on contract, the initial source of authority (apart from overriding legislation) for making deductions from pay is that contract. So the right to deduct might be derived from an express term, be implied from custom and practice (see *Sagar v Ridehalgh and Son Ltd [1931] 1 CL 310* (see 5.3 above)) or arise simply from the employee's failure to work as promised (see 5.29 below).

Statutory regulation of deductions from pay

5.12   However, since 1986, statute has regulated more stringently most types of deduction. In general a deduction is only permissible where required by statute or where the 'worker' has agreed to it. Examples of the statutory requirement would be regarding income tax *[ICTA 1988, ss 203–205]* and NICs *[SSCBA 1992, 1 Sch]* or, as in *Reynolds v Cornwall County Council [1996] EAT 1189/95* pursuant to an order served by the Child Support Agency. Agreement may take the form of a term in the contract of employment, either in writing or with written notification (which must have been given individually to the employee concerned — *Kerr v The Sweater Shop (Scotland) Ltd [1996] IRLR 424 (EAT)*) of its effect or may be by specific written consent in advance of the deduction. *[ERA 1996, s 13(1)(5)(6)]*. Such consent must also be prior to the event which gives rise to a particular deduction (*Discount Tobacco & Confectionery Ltd v Williamson [1993] IRLR 327*).

A collective agreement varying an employee's contract need not itself have been reduced to writing at the time a deduction is made, provided the employee has received direct and personal written notification of the effect of the collective agreement (*York City and District Travel Ltd v Smith [1990] IRLR 213*).

In the case of a deduction to recoup a loan or advance payment, a written clause simply regarding the employee's obligation to repay is insufficient to provide the authority required under *ERA 1996, s 13(1)*: it must refer specifically to deduction from pay as the, or a, method of recoupment (*Potter v Hunt's Contracts Ltd [1992] IRLR 108*).

In the case of workers in retail employment, there is an additional statutory requirement in some cases. Deductions in respect of cash or stock shortages may not exceed ten per cent of the wages payable on any one pay day. Although where the total loss to the employer exceeds ten per cent of the wages further deductions can be made in relation to subsequent wage payments. This ten per cent limit does not apply to the final payment, e.g. prior to dismissal or resignation. *[ERA 1996, ss 17–22]*. In the cases of other reasons for deductions, as well as other types of employee, it is necessary to comply only with *ERA 1996, s 13*.

Whilst the statute refers to deductions from 'wages', this expression includes salary and also covers:

(*a*)   any fee, bonus, commission, holiday pay or 'other emolument' referable to employment 'whether payable under contract or otherwise'. This last phrase means that it is possible to use *ERA 1996* to challenge deductions from, for example, bonus or commission payments to which an employee has only an expectation rather than an entitlement (*Kent Management Services Ltd v Butterfield [1992] IRLR 394*);

(*b*)   SSP (see Chapter 8);

(*c*)   SMP (see Chapter 8);

(*d*)   various payments due under *ERA 1996* and *TULRCA 1992*. [*ERA 1996, s 27(1)*].

The following types of payment are not 'wages':

(*a*)   loans or advances of wages;

(*b*)   expenses;

(*c*)   any pension, allowance or gratuity in connection with retirement or as compensation for loss of office;

(*d*)   redundancy payments;

(*e*)   any payment to a worker not made in his capacity as a worker. [*ERA 1996, s 27(2)*].

Pay in lieu of notice is not 'wages' (*Delaney v Staples t/a De Montfort Recruitment [1992] IRLR 191*). Therefore, any deduction from these excluded forms of payment can only be challenged under *ERA 1996*.

A 'deduction' occurs 'where the total amount of any wages that are paid on any occasion . . . is less than the total amount . . . properly payable', except if the deficiency is caused by an 'error of computation'. [*ERA 1996, s 13(3)*]. A complete non-payment is capable of constituting a 'deduction' (*Delaney v Staples t/a De Montfort Recruitment [1991] IRLR 112*). The term also covers the situation where a lesser sum is paid after the employer has unilaterally reduced the contractual rate of pay (*Bruce v Wiggins Teape (Stationery) Ltd [1994] IRLR 536, McRuary v Washington Irvine Ltd [1994] EAT 857/93*) unless that action flows from a change, the employer is entitled, by the terms of the contract, to introduce without the employee's specific consent (for example, a change of shift as in *Hussman Manufacturing Ltd v Weir [1998] IRLR 288 EAT*). In *Chiltern House Ltd v Chambers [1990] IRLR 88*, an employee left without giving due notice. The employer responded by withholding, from wages owed, an amount as damages for breach of contract. The EAT rejected the employer's argument that there was no 'deduction' under *ERA 1996* as the full wages were not 'properly payable' to the employee on this occasion: retaining part of wages due to satisfy a claim for breach of contract is a 'deduction' and, unless authorised in writing, unlawful.

An 'error of computation' is literally construed and does not cover an employer's decision not to pay because he believes he is contractually entitled not to (*Yemm v British Steel Plc [1994] IRLR 117*). Similarly, where an employer reduced an employee's salary under the mistaken belief that this, along with demotion, was within the terms of the disciplinary procedure, there was no 'error of computation' (*Morgan v West Glamorgan County Council [1995] IRLR 68*).

Deductions for some purposes are exempt, wholly or partly, from the requirements of *ERA 1996, s 13(1)*. Under *ERA 1996, s 14*, these are the following:

(*a*)   deductions to recover an overpayment of wages or expenses. For the non-statutory position on recovering overpayments, see 5.14 to 5.19 below. A deduction on termination to recover an advance of wages or commission made at the outset of employment is not, apparently, protected by this exemption: nevertheless, it is lawful, under *ERA 1996, s 25(3)*, as its purpose is to recover money already paid in respect of future wages (*Robertson v Blackstone Franks Investment Management Ltd [1998] IRLR 376*);

(*b*)   deductions as a consequence of disciplinary proceedings held by virtue of a statutory provision. This is very specific, covering proceedings in, for example, the police and fire services;

(*c*)   deductions, in pursuance of a statutory provision, as a result of a demand from a public authority. Typical examples here would be demands by the Inland Revenue for outstanding tax or attachment of earnings orders under *AEA 1971* (see Chapter 13);

(*d*)   deductions made in accordance with the demand of a third party to whom a worker has initially agreed in writing that payments should be made. This covers deductions made for payments such as pension contributions or trade union subscriptions, where the amount due might change with time or fluctuations in an individual's earnings: fresh written consent is not needed every time (see 15.3 below).

However, separate legislation states that an employer's deduction of union subscriptions from an employee's pay will be unlawful unless the employee has, in the preceding three years, given written authorisation which has not been withdrawn subsequently. If there is an increase in the subscriptions deductible from pay (other than one arising only because of a pay rise), deduction of the additional amount will only be lawful if the employer has given the employee one month's advance notification and included a reminder that the employee may withdraw the authority for deductions. [*TULRCA 1992, s 68*]. (See 15.3 below.)

Further, a worker can cancel the political levy component of union dues simply by serving a form of written notification on his employer. [*TULRCA 1992, s 86*]. If he does so, the initial written authority to deduct union dues ceases to have effect in relation to that component (see 15.3 below);

(*e*)   deductions as a result of a worker having participated in a strike or other industrial action. For the contractual position regarding industrial action and pay, see 5.29 below;

(*f*)   deductions to satisfy an order of a court or tribunal requiring payment by a worker to his employer (but only with the initial written agreement of the worker).

Once it is found that a deduction falls within one of these excluded categories, *ERA 1996* ceases to apply, even if it is alleged that the deduction was not justified (*SIP (Industrial Products) Ltd v Swinn [1994] IRLR 323*). Of course, the employee may have an alternative claim in law, for breach of contract or non-payment of sums due, and, sometimes, such a claim may be heard by an employment tribunal. (See 3.8 and 5.3 above.)

A worker must complain to an employment tribunal, within three months of the alleged infringement (in the case of a series of deductions, the last in that series), that his employer has made a deduction which breaches *ERA 1996, ss 13 or 17–22*. The three months run from the last date on which the disputed payment could be made, rather than from the actual date on which it was (or, in the case of complete non-payment, was not) made (*Group 4 Nightspeed Ltd v Gilbert [1997] IRLR 398*). The tribunal must consider not only whether the type of deduction is authorised but also if the deduction was justified in the particular circumstances (*Fairfield Ltd v Skinner [1992] IRLR 4*). If the complaint succeeds the tribunal must order the employer to repay that part of the deduction which amounted to the infringement and the employer is precluded from recovering that amount again, even though it might actually be owed to the employer as a debt or contractual obligation. [*ERA 1996, s 24*]. It is, however, possible that a settlement may be reached between the parties since the services of an ACAS conciliation officer are available in relation to any complaint.

Itemised payslip as required by law

5.13   Every employee has the right, at or before the time of payment, to be given by his employer a written itemised pay statement. This statement should contain particulars of, *inter alia*, the following:

(*a*)   the gross amount of wages or salary;

(*b*)   the amounts of each variable and each fixed deduction from the gross amount with a note of its purpose;

(c)   the net amount of wages or salary;

(d)   if different parts of the net amount are paid in different ways, the amount and method of each part payment.

[*ERA 1996, s 8*].

For the purposes of this provision tips earned by the employee are not 'wages' (*Cofone v Spaghetti House Ltd [1980] ICR 155*). It should be stressed that the employee's right to a pay statement is absolute and does not depend upon a request by him that the employer provide an appropriate statement (*Coales v John Wood and Co [1986] ICR 71*).

There is no need for the employer to specify individual deductions of a fixed amount if he has provided the employee with a written statement of individual fixed deductions which are to be made. This statement must be reissued, with any amendments, at least every twelve months. [*ERA 1996, s 9*]. Where a statement of this type is issued, the regular itemised statement need only display a cumulative total of all fixed deductions.

A reference can be made to an employment tribunal to determine the nature of particulars which ought to have been provided in any statement. If the tribunal finds that the particulars were deficient it makes a declaration to that effect. Further, where the employer made un-notified deductions from pay during the thirteen weeks preceding the reference, it may order repayment to the employee of a sum not exceeding the amount of those deductions. [*ERA 1996, s 12*].

Types of payment error

5.14   A basic principle of contract and restitution is that money cannot be recovered if it was paid due to a mistake of law rather than due to a mistake of fact. The former can be categorised as a misapprehension as to the existence or meaning of relevant legislation, other laws or as to the meaning of some private legal document, e.g. a contract. For instance, in *Ord v Ord [1923] 2 KB 432*, a husband paid his estranged wife money without deducting income tax because he thought he was prevented from making the deduction by a term of their contract. He was unable to recover from his wife the amount of tax due when made personally liable for it. The overpayment arose due to a mistake of law, i.e. the misinterpretation of the contract. In contrast, a mistake of fact, normally allowing recovery (but see 5.16 below), is represented by errors such as those relating to the identity of the payee, the details which determine a payment and the actual amount payable. Wrongly transcribing pay details from one document to another is an example of a mistake of fact. The distinction between a mistake of law and a mistake of fact can sometimes be rather fine in modern payroll situations such as administering SSP.

The distinction is, as stated above, very difficult to make in practice. Where an incorrect overtime payment has been made it may be difficult to recover the overpayment, but not impossible. This is a question of practicalities. If, however, the mistake was due to a misinterpretation of legislation and an overpayment arises, it can only be recovered if the employee consents to it. Very often in a large payroll operation the costs of correction exceed the amount overpaid and, in such cases, the overpayment is allowed to stand.

Possible mistakes of fact in making payments

5.15   There are two possible types of mistake which are as follows.

(a)   *Mistake as to the identity of the payee* — In the absence of fraud by an employee mistakes of identity can be caused by simple clerical errors. (See 5.18 and 5.19 below.) For instance, overtime pay can be credited to the wrong person when input to a computer payroll system. Also, wages and salaries are occasionally paid to the wrong person by mistake. Where control procedures (see 22.14 below) fail to prevent a genuine error arising, recovery by the employer would normally be permitted (but see 5.16 below).

(b)   *Mistake as to the amount payable* — Where the employer calculates a gross pay entitlement, which ultimately produces an inaccurate net payment, there is a mistake of fact which enables recovery of the overpayment. In *Larner v London County Council [1949] 2 KB 683* the employer made up the difference between service and civilian pay for employees joining the forces during the War. Overpayments, caused by the employee's inadvertent omission to notify the employer of service pay increases, could be recovered by the employer. Where an overpayment arises as the result of erroneous tax and National Insurance deductions, the entitlement to recover for payment to the Inland Revenue or DSS depends on the reason for that error and when it was discovered. A clerical or administrative oversight would amount to a mistake of fact allowing the employer to recover the overpayment. For instance, in *Avon County Council v Howlett [1983] 1 AER 1073*, a computer input error led to erroneous extra sickness payments amounting to a sum of £1,007. This was held to constitute a mistake of fact. But a misunderstanding of the legislative provisions underlying PAYE would be a mistake of law. Thus, the employer could not recover resulting overpayments (although the Inland Revenue and DSS could still recover their 'lost' deductions).

Factors preventing recovery of money overpaid

5.16   There are two main factors which hinder the recovery of overpayments. These factors are as follows.

(a) **Reckless overpayment** — Money paid under a mistake of fact is not recoverable if it 'is intentionally paid without reference to the truth or falsehood of the fact, the [payer] meaning to waive all inquiry into it' (*Kelly v Solari [1941] 152 ER 4*).

(b) **Estoppel** — A person may be estopped, i.e. prevented, from denying or seeking to recover something where that person has, by words or conduct, made a representation of fact to another which was intended to be, and was, acted upon by the other to the latter's detriment. Although this may seem to be of advantage to an employee who has been mistakenly overpaid, its use is restricted by the operation of the following rules.

   (i) An effective representation of fact involves something more than mere overpayment (*R E Jones Ltd v Waring and Gillow Ltd [1926] AC 670*). The extra ingredient here could be supplied by the employer's failure to seek repayment, particularly after a query from the employee or where the failure is compounded by the employer's confirmation that the correct amount has been paid.

   (ii) The payee must have relied on the representation by altering his position in such a way that it would be unjust to require repayment (*Lipkin Gorman (a firm) v Karpnale Ltd [1991] 3 WLR 10*).

   (iii) The payee must not, due to his fault, have caused or significantly contributed to the relevant mistake. This was a reason for allowing the employer to recover in the *Larner* case. (See 5.15 above.)

Banking errors and fraud in paying wages

5.17 Very many wage and salary payments use the banking system in some way. Even cash for wages is usually drawn from a bank. The liability for banking errors and fraud can potentially be assigned to the employer, employee, or bank. Other parties such as a computer bureau could also be implicated. (See 5.41 below for further details.)

Criminal law consequences of theft, fraud or dishonesty by the employee

5.18 These acts of an employee can be classified as follows.

(a) **Theft** — Theft is committed where a person 'dishonestly appropriates property belonging to another with the intention of permanently depriving the other of it'. [*ThA 1968, s 1(1)*].

(b) **Obtaining property by deception** — This offence arises if a person 'by any deception dishonestly obtains property belonging to another, with the intention of permanently depriving the other of it'. [*ThA 1968, s 15(1)*]. Frequently an employee who dishonestly makes a financial gain, whether at the expense of the employer, another employee or both, commits offences under both *sections 1* and *15* of the *ThA 1968*, but there are situations where only one offence is involved. For instance, an employee who innocently takes the pay belonging to another but later decides to keep it can only be guilty under *section 1* of *ThA 1986*. The pay of the other employee was not obtained by any deception.

(c) **Obtaining a pecuniary advantage by deception** — A 'pecuniary advantage' includes 'the opportunity to earn remuneration or greater remuneration in . . . employment', and to obtain such advantage by deception is an offence. [*ThA 1968, s 16*]. In principle, therefore, an interviewee or applicant who lies about his previous qualifications, experience, earnings or other material fact commits this offence.

(d) **Forgery** — This offence occurs where a person makes a 'false instrument' with the intention that it be used to induce somebody to accept it as genuine and, by so accepting it, to commit some act or omission to his or another's detriment. [*FCA 1981, s 1*]. It is also an offence, with the same intention, to use an instrument which is false and known or believed to be such. [*FCA 1981, s 3*]. Under these provisions, the preparation or use of falsified time sheets, expense forms etc. would be an offence. Further, if the forger's intention is actually achieved, offences under *ThA 1968* may be committed.

(e) **Attempts to commit an offence** — If, with intent to commit any of the above offences, a person commits an act which is more than merely preparatory to its commission, he is guilty of attempting to commit the offence. [*CAA 1981, s 1(1)*].

(f) **Recovery of money obtained by theft, fraud and/or dishonesty** — Where a payer has paid or overpaid an individual as a result of the latter's dishonesty, the question of restoration can arise. Although there has never been any problem attached to 'tracing' and recovering specific 'earmarked' cash or cheques which remain uncashed or unmixed with a dishonest individual's other funds, the common law was less certain in following cash *per se*, or the proceeds of a cheque, once it became mixed with other funds. Essentially, this related to a practical problem of identification. However, the rules have been equitably modified to the extent that, even if the money is mixed, tracing is permissible into any sums within or emanating from the mixed fund (*Banque Belge pour L'Etranger v Hambrouck [1921] 1 KB 321*). Where a dishonest individual has passed on money received to an innocent third party without consideration, the owner can normally still recover, subject to requirements of identification. However, where the dishonesty renders the original transaction voidable rather than void, e.g. a case of misrepresented identity, the owner is unable to recover if no avoidance steps, e.g. informing the police and banks, have been taken by the time the third party acquires the money.

Other consequences of false representations

5.19   Where a person, by words or conduct, makes a representation of fact which is, and which he knows to be, false and which is intended to be acted upon by another, he is liable for damages in the tort of deceit if that other suffers loss by acting upon it (*Bradford Third Equitable Benefit Building Society v Borders [1941] 2 AER 205*). In order to prove deceit, it is not necessary to show that the falsity was the only or prime influence on the payer's decision to pay. It need only be shown that it had a real or significant effect on his mind (*JEB Fasteners Ltd v Marks Bloom & Co [1983] 1 AER 583*). Thus where an employee's false representation as to his identity, hours worked, expenses etc. caused a payment or overpayment to be made, the employer can recover damages to restore him to the financial position he would have been in if the representation had not been made. A victim of the tort of deceit has the alternative of bringing an action in restitution to recover any overpayment (*Refuge Assurance Co Ltd v Kettlewell [1909] AC 243*). However, there is little contemporary practical advantage in adopting this alternative.

The employee's dishonesty, whether in relation to particular payments or to the contract of employment as a whole, for example, false statements of material fact on application or interview, usually provides the employer with good grounds for dismissal. But where the dishonesty is of the latter type, the employer has probably already paid a number of wage or salary instalments prior to dismissal and may wish to recover these amounts from the employee as a loss caused by the latter's deceit. This is usually barred for two reasons which are as follows.

(*a*)   The relevant payments, under a 'back pay' system, were made for work done by the employee and, whilst the employee may have lied about a particular fact, such payment would indicate no fundamental dissatisfaction with that work on the employer's part and, therefore, no loss has been suffered by the employer as a result of the deceit.

(*b*)   In practical terms, the employee would not usually have the resources to meet any significant claim by the employer for damages or repayment. This is, of course, a pragmatic and not a legal reason.

It should nevertheless be added that where an 'advance pay' system operates, dismissal at the beginning of the payment period would allow the employer to sue for recovery of payment already made for that period, since no work would yet have been performed by the employee in relation to the period. By a similar process, dismissal at the mid-point of the period would, in theory, permit recovery of 50 per cent of the amount paid.

Entitlement to holiday pay

5.20   Historically, there has been very little direct legal regulation of the holiday pay aspect of the employment relationship. Primarily any entitlement has been a matter for contractual agreement, perhaps by way of a term incorporated from a collective agreement (see 5.5 above). Where there is express agreement between employer and employee, the relevant statute requires that the written particulars contain details of the entitlement. (See 5.4 above.) In the absence of express agreement, it has hitherto been necessary for the employee to establish an implied term, derived from custom or conduct (see 5.3 above), granting holiday pay. However, the *Working Time Regulations* (see 5.9 above) provide for a minimum annual leave entitlement of three weeks (four weeks from November 1999) for each worker with three months' service. Payment in lieu of this allowance is specifically precluded, except on the termination of employment, as is its deferral (in whole or in part) until another holiday year. An employer is able to require all or any of the leave to be taken (or not taken) on specified dates, provided a minimum of four weeks' notice is given to the worker. A worker desiring to take leave on particular days must give similar notice to his employer, who may serve counter-notice within seven days to prevent the leave being validly taken on one or more of those days. The current order of the Agricultural Wages Board (see 5.9 above) will continue to apply to workers within its ambit with regard to arrangements for taking leave and operating leave years. The rate of holiday pay for an agricultural worker will be the higher of that specified in the wages order and that due by reference to the Regulations.

Despite this basic entitlement being introduced by legislation, some principles derived from judicial decisions under the common law are still relevant. It has been suggested that, in the absence of contrary indications, an hourly-paid employee is impliedly entitled to be paid when absent on recognised public holidays (*Tucker v British Leyland Motor Corporation Ltd [1978] IRLR 493*). Of course, where there is an entitlement to paid holidays it may be contractually linked to the employee taking holidays during stipulated periods, e.g. factory shutdowns. If so, an employee can lose his right to accrued holiday pay by failing to take his holiday during these periods (*Hurt v Sheffield Corporation [1916] 85 LJKB 1684*). There are specific provisions covering holidays taken when notice of termination has been given. (See 5.32 and 5.33 below.)

Notwithstanding the permissive provision in the *Working Time Regulations* (see above), there is no general legal right, on resignation or dismissal, to payment in lieu of holidays accrued but not taken (*Morley v Heritage plc [1993] IRLR 400 – CA*). Any right to such payment will arise, expressly or impliedly (*Janes Solicitors v Lamb-Simpson [1995] EAT 323/94*) from the particular contract and may be limited. For example, no payment might be due if a dismissal was for gross misconduct.

Where there is a right to pay for accrued holidays, the daily rate for a salaried employee is calculated by dividing the annual salary by 365 (*Thames Water Utilities v Reynolds [1996] IRLR 186*). Further, accrual continues during a notice period while an employee is on 'garden leave': the subsistence of the contract of employment is the vital factor (*Whittle Contractors Ltd v Smith [1994] EAT 842/94*).

Other paid time off from work

5.21   Employees in certain categories or situations are entitled to be paid for time off from work for certain purposes including, *inter alia*, the following circumstances.

(a)   *Officials of independent, recognised trade unions* —These people are to be given reasonable paid time off in order to carry out their duties and to undergo relevant training approved by the trade union or TUC. [*TULRCA 1992, s 168*]. Trade union 'duties' are restricted to those concerning negotiations with an employer on matters in relation to which a trade union is recognised by that employer, or other functions which the employer has agreed may be performed by the union. Approved training can only be related to this range of duties.

(b)   *Those under notice of redundancy* — Employees under notice of redundancy who have two or more years' continuous employment are to be allowed reasonable paid time off in order to look for new work or to arrange training. This is subject to a maximum of two-fifths of a week's pay. [*ERA 1996, s 52*].

(c)   *Pregnant employees* — An employee who is pregnant cannot be unreasonably refused paid time off to attend ante-natal care appointments. However, a precondition of this right is the employer's entitlement, except in the case of the employee's first appointment, to require the production of a certificate of pregnancy and/or an appointment card. [*ERA 1996, s 55*]. It should be noted that an employee who is absent from work due to pregnancy and confinement may also be entitled to limited maternity pay. (See 8.12 and 8.16 below.) However, apart from statutory maternity pay (which is a Social Security benefit payable by employers but thereafter recoverable from the State), there is no general legal obligation on an employer to pay employees during maternity absence. Although there is an entitlement to a basic 14-week maternity leave period during which the contract continues, 'remuneration', unlike pension benefits (see 5.10 above), is excluded from the 'benefits' which must be maintained during that time. [*ERA 1996, s 71*]. In *Gillespie v Northern Health and Social Services Board [1996] IRLR 214*, the ECJ held that the principles of equal pay (see 5.8 above) and equal treatment (see 3.3 above) did not require full pay to be maintained during maternity absence and that it was for national legislation to establish the amount of any benefit payable to an employee in such circumstances. However, it also decided that an employee absent on maternity leave was entitled to the benefit of any relevant pay rise during her absence. Consequently, the SMP rules now require an employer to adjust the higher, earnings-related element of SMP if a pay review is backdated and thereby alters an employee's salary in the period used to calculate that element.

Also an employee who is pregnant, has recently given birth or is breast-feeding has had the right to a period of paid leave or 'suspension', on 'maternity grounds', if:

(i)   her normal work is a threat to her health or safety (under designated health and safety laws); and

(ii) there is no suitable alternative work available.

[*ERA 1996, ss 66–68*].

(*d*) **Trustees of occupational pension schemes** — Employees who are pension scheme trustees are to be given reasonable paid time off to perform appropriate duties or undergo relevant training. [*ERA 1996, ss 58–59*].

(*e*) **Employee representatives** — An employee representative under the consultation provisions of *TULRCA 1992* or the *Transfer of Undertakings (Protection of Employment) Regulations 1981*, or a candidate for such a position, is entitled to reasonable paid time off to perform his functions. [*ERA 1996, ss 61–62*].

A complaint can be made to an employment tribunal where there are alleged violations of any of the above rights.

Statutory entitlement to pay during absence due to sickness or injury

5.22   Broadly speaking, under *SSCBA 1992* an employer is usually liable to pay an employee's SSP at the appropriate rate for up to 28 weeks. Once this liability is discharged, the employee transfers to State benefits claimed directly from the DSS. (See 8.17 below.) Given that the appropriate weekly rate is subject to a statutory maximum (see Appendix D), it becomes important, in relation to any employee normally earning a weekly amount in excess of that maximum, to determine whether or not he is also entitled to sick pay under his contract of employment.

Contractual entitlement to pay during absence due to sickness or injury

5.23   There is relatively little problem if the contract expressly states whether or not there is a sick pay entitlement. Legislation requires that, where there is such an entitlement, details should be given in the written particulars. (See 5.4 above.) It is possible that the contract confers an entitlement that is restricted, either in terms of duration, amount or both. For instance, the entitlement may be for three months on full pay and three months on half pay before the entitlement is extinguished in relation to any one period of absence.

If there is no express term, a dispute as to entitlement can only be resolved finally by a court's decision as to the content of an implied term. The decision in *Mears v Safecar Security Ltd [1982] 3WLR 366* states that, in relation to implied terms on sick pay, there is no presumption in favour of the employee being entitled to payment and the content of the term depends totally upon the particular facts of the case. In this case, the employee was not entitled to contractual sick pay because the evidence indicated that it was the employer's established practice not to pay, that the employee had never asked for pay when actually absent, which in this case was for over six months, and that the employee did not seek to claim sick pay for some time after finally leaving that employment.

Whether the basic right to sick pay is express or implied, a term may still need to be implied as to the duration of any entitlement. The period of the duration is that which is reasonable in the circumstances of each case (*Howman and Son v Blyth [1983] ICR 416*). The most relevant factor in determining what is reasonable in any given case is the practice adopted in the particular trade, industry or organisation in question.

Many employers provide permanent health insurance cover, sometimes linked to pension scheme membership, to indemnify employees against loss of earnings once any entitlement to occupational sick pay has expired and a period (often 26 or 52 weeks) of disablement from work has elapsed. Usually, eligibility for receipt of such benefits depends upon an employee remaining as such, at least until the 26 or 52 week 'gate' is reached. However, it is not uncommon for employers, often after obtaining a medical report, to dismiss, with notice or pay in lieu thereof, a long-term sickness absentee. Two decisions, English and Scottish respectively, have emphasised that to take this action, and thereby remove permanent health insurance protection, will amount to a breach of contract despite the employer's express power, in other circumstances, to terminate the contract with notice (*Aspden v Webbs Poultry and Meat Group (Holdings) Ltd [1996] IRLR 521, Adin v Sedco Forex International Resources Ltd [1997] IRLR 280*). Consequently, in order to avoid potentially significant claims for damages from employees dismissed before the point of eligibility for permanent health insurance, it is necessary for the contract of employment expressly to make the availability of the protection subject to the employer's right to terminate in accordance with the contract's provisions.

Relationship of SSP and contractual sick pay

5.24   Where the employee receiving SSP is also entitled to sick pay under his contract of employment, he does not usually gain financially as compared with a period when he is working normally. Any contractual payment made by the employer for a day for which SSP is payable would normally count towards the satisfaction of his statutory liability. [*SSCBA 1992, 12 Sch*]. Thus the employee can typically only receive, in relation to any week, a maximum amount corresponding to his normal weekly pay which is composed of SSP and that portion of his contractual sick pay entitlement necessary to make up that amount.

Pay during 'lay-off'

5.25   It should be noted that 'lay-off' is used to denote a situation where the employee is not given, or admitted to, work because of circumstances affecting the employer but where the contract of employment continues to exist. Where there is termination of the contract by the employer at the time of 'lay-off' there is a dismissal, however temporary it is or is intended to be. The provisions to be discussed below do not apply to these cases.

Statutory entitlement to pay where work is not provided

5.26   An employee who has been continuously employed for at least one month is entitled to a 'guarantee payment' when he is not provided with work by his employer, on a day on which he would normally be required to work, where the lack of work is caused by:

(*a*)   a decline in the employer's requirements for the work which the employee does; or

(*b*)   any other event affecting the normal working of the business in relation to that work.

[*ERA 1996, ss 28(1)(2)(3), 29(1)*].

Relevant events for the purposes of the second part of this provision would include fires, floods or power failures interrupting work, but would not extend to the annual works closure so as to allow payment to an employee not entitled to holiday pay (*North v Pavleigh Ltd [1977] IRLR 461*). Where the lack of work occurs because of a strike or other industrial action involving any employee, of the employer in question or an associated employer, there is no right to a guarantee payment. [*ERA 1996, s 29(3)*]. Nor is there any entitlement to a payment for a particular day if:

(i)   the employer has offered to provide suitable alternative work for that day and the employee has unreasonably refused the offer; or

(ii)   the employer has imposed reasonable requirements to ensure that the employee's services are available and the employee has not complied with them.

[*ERA 1996, s 29(4)(5)*].

Where an employee has a right to a guarantee payment for a particular day, the amount is calculated by multiplying the number of normal, i.e. contractual, working hours on that day by the guaranteed or basic hourly rate. [*ERA 1996, s 30*]. However, this is subject to a statutory maximum payment variable by SI, currently set at £15.35, for any day and to a limitation of availability of five days in any three-month period. [*ERA 1996, s 31*]. A three-month period starts with the employee's first workless day and the period's end is not notionally extended by the fact that the employee returns to paid work with the employer within three months of that workless day (*Jones v Squire's Garage and Road Transport Ltd [1994] EAT 752/92; 515 IRLB 16*). An employee may complain to an employment tribunal in relation to his employer's failure to pay all or part of a guarantee payment and, if the complaint is upheld, the tribunal orders the payment to be made. [*ERA 1996, s 34*].

Where an employee does receive a guarantee payment in relation to a day on which he was not offered work, he is not entitled to unemployment benefit for that day. [*Social Security (Unemployment, Sickness and Invalidity Benefit) Regulations 1983, SI 1983 No 1598*]. The relatively limited amount and duration of the statutory guarantee payment mean that it is still important to establish if an employee has a contractual right to payment when laid off. (See 5.27 below.) In this context, and particularly in relation to the incorporation of provisions from collective agreements (see 5.5 above), it should be noted that the Secretary of State for Employment has the power to exempt from the statutory scheme employers who are parties to collective agreements which cover the guarantee payment issue satisfactorily. [*ERA 1996, s 35*].

Contractual entitlement to pay where work is not provided

5.27   Contractual terms which give the employee a right to pay if there is no work can be more flexible than the statutory provisions discussed above. These terms mainly cater for the situation where the employee works every day but on short time, whereas the statute relates only to whole days when there is no work. As already indicated (see 5.26 above) many instances of lay-off are covered by an express term in the contract of employment frequently derived from a collective agreement provision on the subject. In the absence of an express term, there is no general implied right for an employer to lay off without pay (*Neads v CAV Ltd [1983] IRLR 360*). The content of the implied term depends on the circumstances of the case.

In *Browning v Crumlin Valley Collieries [1926] 1 KB 522* miners who were laid off without pay whilst necessary repairs to the mine were undertaken were considered to have no legal right to payment. It was decided that the parties had implicitly agreed, when the contract of employment commenced, to share the loss arising from interruptions which were beyond the employer's control. The employees' 'share' was loss of wages. But an earlier decision in *Devonald v*

Rosser and Sons [1906] 2 KB 728 permitted pieceworkers to recover wages for a period of lay-off caused by a slump in the fortunes of the employer's business. The latter approach is preferred in the absence of an express or clear implied term to the contrary, any such contrary implication usually being derived from trade custom or usage. In this context, the courts require that the relevant custom be 'reasonable, certain and notorious' amongst employers and employees of the trade concerned ('notorious' means 'well-known' in this context). The employer's allegation that there was a custom permitting unpaid lay-off failed in both the *Devonald* and *Neads* cases. There is one notable exception to the apparently accepted principle that the employee has an implied right to pay when laid off. It arises where an employee is engaged, as in *Puttick v John Wright and Sons (Blackwall) Ltd [1972] ICR 457*, on the understanding that he does, and is paid for, specific jobs but is to be laid off in the intervening periods.

Relationship of statutory and contractual entitlements

5.28   Where an employee has a contractual right to a payment which is more advantageous than his statutory entitlement, he is entitled to receive the full sum due under contract. *[ERA 1996, s 32(1)]*. Where a contractual payment is made in relation to a particular workless day, it 'goes towards' discharging the employer's liability to make up the guarantee payment for that day, and *vice versa*. *[ERA 1996, s 32(2)]*. Thus, if the contractual payment is less than the guarantee pay entitlement, which would be unusual, the employer would only be liable for the balance of the guarantee payment due. Conversely, where the contractual payment exceeds the statutory guarantee pay entitlement, the employer has no further liability in relation to the day concerned. An employee who receives payment under contract, in excess of his guarantee pay entitlement, for five or more workless days falls within the exclusion in *ERA 1996, s 31(2)(3)(4)(5)* (see 5.26 above) and is, therefore, not entitled to claim a guarantee payment during the relevant three-month period (*Cartwright v G Clancey Ltd [1983] ICR 552*).

Contractual entitlement to continued payment during industrial action

5.29   Whether an employee participating in industrial action is entitled to continued payment of wages depends upon the nature of the industrial action involved. Deductions from pay on account of a worker having participated in industrial action are not regulated by *ERA 1996*. (See 5.11 and 5.12 above.) *[ERA 1996, s 14]*. The right to continued payment of an employee laid off due to the industrial action of others depends on matters already discussed (see 5.26–5.28 above) and is not dealt with here.

The common law rule is that the employee earns his wages by being ready and willing to do his work (*Henthorn and Taylor v CEGB [1980] IRLR 361*). Thus an employee is unable to claim pay for days when he is not so ready and willing because he is on strike. In this context, a day's pay is ⅟ₓ of gross annual pay, where x is the number of days in a year on which the employee is contractually obliged to work (*Smith and others v London Borough of Bexley [1991] IDS Brief p 448*). Work to rule involves continued working but with strict observance of terms, conditions and works rules. Given that the employee is performing his duties, and thus must be considered ready and willing to perform his work, he is normally entitled to be paid for the work done. There is the legal possibility that such industrial action amounts to a breach by the employee of the implied term of co-operation contained in the contract of employment (*Secretary of State for Employment v ASLEF (No 2) [1972] 2 QB 455*). It would be difficult for the employer to translate this into action on the employee's pay, partly because of legal problems concerning quantification of the damage suffered by the employer, and partly because on practical grounds any such action would tend to exacerbate the employer's problems by causing the industrial action to escalate.

A ban in relation to compulsory (required under contract) or voluntary overtime raises the same issues as the work to rule. If the employer still permits the employee to work his normal hours and the employee is so working, then the latter is normally entitled to pay for the hours worked. Again, although such industrial action might be a breach of the duty to co-operate at work, it is often difficult for the employer to do anything beyond, obviously, not paying for any overtime. However, an employer is not obliged to accept part- performance of the contract by an employee. So if an employee conducts a limited form of industrial action or withdraws goodwill, so that the full range of contractual duties are not being done, the employer may exclude him and pay nothing at all while the situation continues (*Ticehurst and Thompson v British Telecommunications Plc [1992] IRLR 219*).

For a further discussion on recent developments concerning both industrial action and deductions generally, see Reference (11) in 5.42 below.

Entitlement to accrued pay in the event of industrial action

5.30   Any entitlement to money already earned is not affected by subsequent industrial action of any type. However, the employer is under no obligation to facilitate its payment. Thus, for instance, where a personal collection system operates, the employer would not be obliged to post or otherwise deliver a cheque or pay packet to a striking employee's home address. Similarly, tax refunds, in effect being accrued pay, are not lost by subsequent industrial action, but the employer is under no obligation to facilitate their collection. (See 19.19 for details on the legal restrictions on refunds during a strike.)

National Insurance and social security implications

5.31   Since both primary and secondary Class 1 NICs are basically percentages of 'earnings paid' [*SSCBA 1992, s 8*], there is no liability on employer or employee to contribute in respect of periods where there were no earnings due to industrial action. In certain circumstances an employee may wish to pay voluntary contributions to safeguard his rights to a retirement pension.

Pay obligations during the notice period

5.32   Where an employee gives, or is given, notice to terminate the contract of employment, provisions of *ERA 1996* govern the employee's rights during the statutorily required minimum periods of that notice provided that:

(*a*)   the employee has at least one month's continuous employment; and

(*b*)   the employer's notice required by the contract does not exceed the statutory minimum notice (which rises with service up to a maximum of twelve weeks after twelve or more years) by more than one week.

[*ERA 1996, s 87*].

If these conditions are satisfied the employer is liable to pay the employee at the average hourly rate where:

  (i)   the employee is ready and willing to work but no work is provided; or

 (ii)   the employee is incapable of work through sickness or injury; or

(iii)   the employee is absent from work wholly or partly because of pregnancy or childbirth; or

(iv)   the employee is absent in accordance with a contractual holiday entitlement.

[*ERA 1996, ss 88, 89*].

The two situations in which these obligations do not apply are as follows:

(1)   payment for any period when, at the employee's request, he is absent with the permission of the employer, including statutory time off (see 5.22 above);

(2)   payment of any part of a period of notice given by the employee where, subsequently, he takes part in a strike.

[*ERA 1996, s 91(1)(2)*].

Pay obligations when the employee leaves his employment

5.33   Where *ERA 1996* regulates the employer's obligations during the notice period, it provides that if an employee has given notice, the employer's liability for notice period pay does not arise unless, and until, the employee actually leaves. [*ERA 1996, ss 88, 89*]. Also, it should be noted that the normal statutory limitation on the extent of deductions for cash and stock shortages does not apply in relation to final pay instalments (see 5.11 above).

Where *ERA 1996* does not apply, the manner in which pay for the notice period, if any, is paid will depend upon the terms of the contract. Regardless of the application of the statutory rules, an agreement that an employee need not work a notice period, but will nevertheless be paid in the normal way for it, means that the contract will continue for the duration of the notice. In *Hutchings v Coinseed Ltd [1998] IRLR 190*, it was held that an employee who, in such circumstances, takes up other employment before the notice elapses is neither guilty of repudiation, invalidating the right to salary, nor subject to the duty of mitigation. Therefore, full notice pay is due from the original employer, without allowance for the employee's earnings elsewhere.

Again, regardless of the application of statutory rules and irrespective of whether notice is given at all (if it is not, pay in lieu of notice will normally be necessary), the employer is contractually obliged to pay to the employee any additional accrued pay at the relevant date.

Apart from possible accrued holiday pay (see 5.20 above), this will usually comprise wages or salary for work done to that time. In *Ali v Christian Salvesen Food Services Ltd [1997] IRLR 17 (CA)*, a case on deductions from wages (see 5.12 above), consideration was given to payments due under an 'annualised hours' system, based on a notional standard working week with overtime only being payable for hours worked in excess of the annualised total. It was held that pay for work done to the termination date should be based only upon the notional weekly hours and should not take account of any hours actually worked over and above that weekly standard.

Statutory provisions relating to the insolvency of the employer

5.34   If an employer becomes bankrupt or insolvent, the employee is a preferential creditor in relation to pay due for the four months preceding the bankruptcy or insolvency subject to a maximum (presently £800) and accrued holiday pay. [*IA 1986, s 386, 6 Sch 9, 10*]. Statutory guaranteed payments (see 5.26 above), time off payments (see 5.25 above) and SSP (see 5.22 above and 8.4 below) are treated as pay due. [*IA 1986, 6 Sch 13, 15*].

It is also worth noting that certain payments due from the employer can be paid to the employee by the Secretary of State [*ERA 1996, s 182*] and that the Secretary of State may also discharge the employer's unpaid contributions to an occupational pension scheme. [*PSA 1993, s 124*]. If either type of payment is made to, or on behalf of, the employee, his creditor's rights against the employer are transferred to the Secretary of State. [*ERA 1996, s 189*].

Other considerations relating to the insolvency of the employer

5.35   Money owed but not categorised as a secured debt or sums in excess of the statutory maximum can possibly be recovered as unsecured debts of the employer. However, some of the employer's debts which are recoverable from the Secretary of State (see 5.34 above) are not secured. Thus, it is in the employee's interest to recover such debts from the Secretary of State, leaving the latter to recover an unsecured debt which has been transferred to him.

Representatives of payer and payee

5.36   It may be that a member of the payroll department has, or is deemed to have, authority to reach pay agreements or settlements on behalf of the employer. In other words, in law he is the agent of the employer (or principal) with the ability to bring about a contract, or variation of an existing contract (see 5.7 above) between the employer and a third party, the employee. This result might occur either where an agreement is reached with the individual employee concerned, or if the provisions of collective agreements are incorporated into the relevant contracts of employment. (See 5.5 above.) As already indicated, it is usually necessary for the member of the payroll staff to have been given, by the employer, the requisite express authority to negotiate with the employee. However, it is possible for an employer to be bound by the terms of an agreement made by payroll staff who do not have express authority. This arises where:

(*a*)   the employer represents, by words or conduct, to the employee that the payroll staff have authority to reach agreements;

(*b*)   the employee relies on the representation;

(*c*)   the employee 'alters his position' in relying on the representation.

In these circumstances the payroll staff would be said to have 'apparent authority' to contract with the employee, and the employer would be estopped (see 5.16 above) from denying it unless the employee knew, or should have known, of the absence of true authority. For example, in a Scottish case, *Hoogerbeets v British Coal Corporation [1991] 434 IRLB 6*, a redundancy scheme counsellor's alleged assurance to an employee that he would receive enhanced benefits was not enforceable against the employer. The counsellor did not have actual authority to make such an agreement and the employer had not indicated or represented that she had such authority.

However, it is quite usual for payroll staff to agree to make 'adjustments', for instance, in relation to back pay or previous alleged underpayments. Evidence of such authority to bind the employer may well be found in the common practice of referring all pay queries to the payroll department. In order to exclude this possibility and consequent estoppel, it is advisable for the employer to warn all employees, by means of written notices, that the payroll staff do not have the power to reach binding agreements. However, the employer then has to state who does have this power. Finally, where payroll staff do exceed their authority, if any, in reaching a purported agreement, the employer can, if he chooses, adopt or ratify that agreement, thus retrospectively conferring the required authority on the staff concerned and being bound by the terms of the agreement.

The payee might wish to appoint a representative to collect or receive payments, for instance, if he is sick. In the case of the collection of cash pay, the employer is advised to seek written evidence of the alleged representative's authority prior to delivering the cash to the latter. Whilst money paid to a fraudulent third party is, in principle, recoverable by the payer (see 5.18 above), problems of identification and tracing the offender mean that, in practice, the employer is unable to recover these payments and remains liable to the true payee.

Occasionally, pension beneficiaries or annuitants may request payments to be made to the bank account of an agent or a representative. If so, the payee should notify the payer of the agent's authority to receive payment either by a formal deed conferring a power of attorney [*PAA 1971, s 10*], or in writing.

Payroll records

5.37   Documentation and records which are not required to be sent to the Inland Revenue are to be retained by the employer for at least three years after the end of the tax year to which they relate. [*Income Tax (Employments) Regulations 1993 (SI 1993 No 744), reg 55(12)*].

The *DPA 1984* already prohibits certain disclosures of information which are 'automatically processed'. Contravention of these provisions constitutes a criminal offence and may also require the payment of compensation to the individual who was the subject of the disclosure. The *DPA 1998*, which repeals and replaces the 1984 Act from Spring 1999, will regulate the holding and disclosure of paper-based personal data as well. (See 23.16 below.) It is also possible that unauthorised disclosure of pay information relating to an individual which causes loss might amount to a tort at common law, requiring compensation to be paid to the individual. Of course, this would not be the case where disclosure of earnings was required by law, for instance for income tax or NIC purposes. Where inaccurate data concerning an individual is provided to a third party and, as a result, loss is suffered by the former, the party making the inaccurate statement could conceivably be liable for negligence and be required to compensate that individual. Such a situation might arise, for instance, where an employer understates an employee's salary to a financial institution which then refuses a loan of money to the employee.

Safety of the payroll staff

5.38   The employer is under a duty to ensure, so far as is reasonably practicable, the health, safety and welfare at work of all his employees. [*HSWA 1974, s 2*]. It should be noted that 'at work' is not confined to work on the employer's premises. Rather it connotes anything done by an employee in the course of employment. Whilst the above duty is delimited by the idea of 'reasonable practicability', an employer may breach the duty by, for instance, providing inadequate physical security measures in a payroll office where cash is handled, or by failing to adopt obvious protective measures in relation to an employee who is sent to the bank to collect cash (see 23.12 below). A wide range of offences may be committed under the *HSWA 1974*. Upon conviction in summary proceedings in a magistrates' court the maximum fine for many offences is £20,000. On indictment in a crown court the penalty may be an unlimited fine and up to two years' imprisonment.

Where an employee actually suffers injury in the performance of his payroll duties, the employer may be liable for damages in negligence for failing to take reasonable care to provide a safe system of working (*Wilsons and Clyde Coal Co Ltd v English [1938] AC 57*). Further, the duty to provide a safe system of work extends to protection of an employee's mental well-being (*Walker v Northumberland County Council [1995] IRLR 35*). Therefore, it is possible, as in the *Walker* case, that an employee suffering a nervous breakdown due to the circumstances under which he is required to work will recover damages for this if the employer should have reasonably foreseen its occurrence.

An employee may complain to an employment tribunal regarding dismissal or detrimental action taken by the employer because of certain health and safety functions or actions undertaken by the employee. [*ERA 1996, ss 44, 100*]. In the case of a complaint of unfair dismissal, there is no continuous employment qualification.

'Headcounts'

5.39   Briefly the notes accompanying a company's annual accounts must provide details of:

(*a*)   the average number of persons employed by the company in each week during the financial year;

95

(b)   the aggregate of wages and salaries paid or payable in that year together with social security and pension costs.

[*CA 1985, 4 Sch 56, 94*].

Further, the notes must reveal earnings and pensions of directors. [*CA 1985, s 232, 6 Sch 1, 2*]. Small companies are exempt from these requirements. [*CA 1985, s 246, 8 Sch 2*]. These provisions impose no direct legal obligation on the payroll department, but those compiling the accounts are only able to obtain the relevant information from the payroll or personnel departments. (See 24.20(e) below for a more detailed description of the 'payroll' requirements under *CA 1985*.)

As a result of the amendments introduced by the *CA 1989, s 13* information regarding the salary levels of employees as distinct from the salary levels of directors need not be disclosed.

Disputes over pay and pay elements

5.40   There is little direct legal regulation of this issue. Any dispute over pay would require to be resolved either by the courts (see 3.5 above), arbitration (see 3.9 above) or by discussion, negotiation and agreement. However, there is limited statutory involvement in relation to deductions (see 5.11 and 5.12 above) and concerning the content of itemised pay statements (see 5.13 above). (For disputes concerning income tax and NIC deductions, see 11.6 and 12.7 below respectively.)

Banking and payment methods

5.41   Space does not permit a full discussion of the law of banking and payment matters, which is an extensive subject. However, a brief summary relevant to payroll and pension administrators is given below. The relationship between a bank and its customers, both payer and payees in the payroll context includes, *inter alia*, the following legal and contractual aspects.

(a)   *The general law of contract* — Banks provide services for a considera-
      tion on express and implied terms. In particular, they operate bank
      accounts for their customers, and operate payment services. There has
      been considerable criticism of banking practices and the Office of Fair
      Trading has criticised the more arbitrary actions of the banks *vis-a-vis*
      their customers. It is likely that codes of practice will be issued soon.

(b)   *The rules of agency* — A bank acts as the agent of its customer, for
      example, by paying a standing order.

(c)   *Banking practice* — This covers matters such as confidentiality and a
      duty to keep an accurate record of transactions.

(*d*) **Statutes** — Special statutes regulate some aspects of banking, for instance the *Bills of Exchange Act 1882* which covers cheques.

Each payment method has its own legal status and a brief description is given below.

(i) **Cash** — This is covered by the rules for legal tender. Providing there are no contractual provisions to the contrary, a payee cannot refuse to accept cash which complies with these rules. The rules merely limit the number of coins of the realm which must be accepted (see *CgA 1971*, as amended by *CuA 1983*). Any number of Bank of England notes are legal tender. [*CBNA 1954, s 1*]. In law, all forms of cash are regarded as 'negotiable chattels'. This means that the title to coins and notes passes with delivery provided the transferee takes it in good faith and for valuable consideration. Where the transfer is without good faith or valuable consideration the money can be recovered if it can be identified as specific coins or notes. However, assuming good faith and valuable consideration the transferee can get good title even though the transferor, for example, the original thief, had none. But the practical effect of this legal rule is reduced considerably by the nature of the rules on tracing.

(ii) **Cheques** — These are 'negotiable instruments' covered by *BEA 1882* and the *ChA 1957*. A cheque is statutorily defined as 'a bill of exchange drawn on a banker payable on demand'. [*BEA 1882, s 73*]. A cheque which is negotiable can be validly transferred from one person to another by the payee endorsing on the back of the cheque. This grants full ownership to the transferee even where the immediate transferor has stolen the cheque. The cheque must, however, be accepted in good faith for valuable consideration. Because of the dangers of stolen and fraudulently endorsed cheques, this facility may be restricted or eliminated by crossing the cheque, for instance by entering the words 'not negotiable' between parallel lines. (See 21.8 below.) The legal effect of this move is to deny a transferee a better title to the cheque than that possessed by the transferor. [*BEA 1882, s 81*].

(iii) **Credit transfers** — These instructions are mandates to the recipient bank requesting that arrangements are made to debit the customer's account and credit the payee's account.

(iv) **Electronic funds transfer, e.g. BACS** — A technological and centralised refinement of the credit transfer system is the BACS service which now processes a large proportion of wage and salary payments in the United Kingdom. (See 21.10 below.) The payers ('users'), or their bankers, input payment data to BACS (via magnetic tape, floppy disc, cassette or telephone link) which sorts the inputs and transmits them to the bank accounts of the various payees. The user's direct contractual relationship under this system is with his own bankers (the 'sponsoring bank') since BACS is, in effect, only another clearing facility provided by those bankers (in conjunction with all other major clearing banks). To this extent, the duties of banker and customer would be those stipulated by the general law of banking.

(v) *Other payment methods* — Other payment methods such as postal orders also have their own legal status which is quite different from cheques or credit transfers. (For more detail, see Chapter 22 (Payment Methods)).

A banker who over-credits a customer's account may not be able to recover the excess (*United Overseas Bank v Jiwani [1976] WLR 964*).

Here the conditions to defeat a bank's claim were outlined and are as follows:

- a misrepresentation of the state of the account by the bank must have occurred;

- the customer must be misled by the misrepresentation;

- the customer must have acted on this reliance in such a way that it would be inequitable to require repayment.

In payroll work this is much more likely to work in favour of the payee than the payer. Whenever an account is incorrectly debited a bank is obliged to refund the amount whatever the reason. It should be noted that a customer has no obligation to check his bank account statements and inform the bank of any inaccuracies (*Tai Hing Cotton Mill Ltd v Liu Chong Hing Bank Ltd [1985] 3 WLR 317*). A bank is often responsible to its customers for incorrectly paying on the presentation of cheques. However, there are exceptions. For instance, a bank may debit a customer's account where cheques have been negligently drawn permitting alteration (*London Joint Stock Bank v Macmillan and Arthur [1918] AC 777*). It can also enjoy some statutory protection, for example, when a cheque is paid which is drawn on the bank and bears a forged or irregular endorsement or no endorsement. This is provided the payment is in the ordinary course of business and in good faith. [*BEA 1882, s 60; ChA 1957, s 1*]. These examples emphasise the importance of care in handling and preparing cheques if the customer is to avoid liability. The use of special crossings and cheque protection machines are examples of possible precautions.

References

5.42 The reference material for this chapter is as follows:

(1) Slade E, 'Tolley's Employment Handbook', Tolley Publishing Co Ltd, Twelfth Edition, 1998.

(2) 'Tolley's Employment Law', a looseleaf service, Tolley Publishing Co Ltd.

(3)   Selwyn N M, 'Selwyn's Law of Employment', Butterworths, Tenth Edition, 1998.

(4)   Department of Employment and Education Booklets
      – 'Written Statement of Main Terms and Conditions of Employment', Employment Legislation Booklet PL 700, Employment Department.
      – 'Itemised Pay Statement', Employment Legislation Booklet PL 704, Employment Department.
      – 'Employee's Rights on Insolvency of Employer', Employment Legislation Booklet PL 718, Employment Department.
      – 'Guarantee Payments', Employment Legislation Booklet PL 724, Department of Employment.
      – 'The Law on the Payment of Wages and Deductions: A Guide to Part I of the Wages Act 1986', Employment Legislation Booklet PL 810, Department for Education and Employment.

(5)   'Equal Pay — A Guide to the Equal Pay Act', Department for Education and Employment, (PL 743).

(6)   'Equal Pay for Work of Equal Value — A Guide to the Amended Equal Pay Act', Equal Opportunities Commission.

(7)   'Job Evaluation Schemes Free of Sex Bias', Equal Opportunities Commission.

(8)   'Code of Practice on Equal Pay', Equal Opportunities Commission.

(9)   'Race Relations Code of Practice', Commission for Racial Equality.

(10) 'Guidance Note: Holidays 1 — Contractual Issues', Industrial Relations Law Bulletin No 544, May 1996.

(11) 'Employment Law Problems: Time Off for Public Duties', Incomes Data Services Brief No 586, April 1997.

(12) 'Employment Law Problems: Contracts of Employment and Implied Terms', Incomes Data Services Brief No 562, April 1996 (Part 1) and No 563, April 1996 (Part 2).

(13) 'Guidance Note: Written Particulars of Employment', Industrial Relations Legal Information Bulletin No 491, February 1994.

(14) 'Guidance Note: Sex Equality in Occupational Pensions', Industrial Relations Law Bulletin No 508, November 1994.

(15) 'Employment Law Problems: Pensions and Sex Equality', Incomes Data Services Brief No 534, February 1995.

(16) 'Guidance Note: Wages Act 1986 — The Story So Far', Industrial Relations Law Bulletin No 504, September 1994.

(17) 'Employment Law Problems: Guarantee Payments', Incomes Data Services Brief No 509, January 1994.

(18) 'Guidance Note: Maternity Rights 1 — Maternity Leave', Industrial Relations Law Bulletin No 509, November 1994.

(19) 'Guidance Note: Maternity Rights 3 — Health and Safety', Industrial Relations Law Bulletin No 511, December 1994.

(20) 'Employment Law Problems: Maternity Questions and Answers', Incomes Data Services Brief Nos 564 and 565, May 1996.

(21) 'Guidance Note: Changing Terms and Conditions 1 — Ways of Implementing Changes', Industrial Relations Law Bulletin No 539, February 1996.

(22) 'Guidance Note: Changing Terms and Conditions 2 — Consequences of Unilateral Changes', Industrial Relations Law Bulletin No 540, March 1996.

(23) 'Guidance Note: Changing Terms and Conditions 3 — Specific Changes', Industrial Relations Law Bulletin No 541, March 1996.

(24) 'Employment Law Problems: Notice Rights — Questions and Answers', Incomes Data Services Brief Nos 566 and 567, June 1996.

(25) 'Employment Law Problems: Statutory Sick Pay', Incomes Data Services Brief No 585, March 1997.

(26) 'Implementing the Working Time Directive', Incomes Data Services Brief No 612, May 1998.

(27) 'The Draft Working Time Regulations', Industrial Relations Law Bulletin No 593, May 1998.

(28) Prime V, 'Minimum Requirements', PMR, March 1998.

(29) 'The National Minimum Wage Bill', Incomes Data Services Brief No 603, December 1997.

(30) 'National Minimum Wage Bill', Industrial Relations Law Bulletin No 585, January 1998.

(31) 'Guidance Note: Equal Pay 1 — Legal Framework and Preliminary Issues', Industrial Relations Law Bulletin No 575, August 1997.

(32) 'Guidance Note: Equal Pay 2 — Unequal Pay for Equal Work', Industrial Relations Law Bulletin No 576, September 1997.

(33) 'Guidance Note: Equal Pay 3 — Defences and Remedies', Industrial Relations Law Bulletin No 578, October 1997.

(34) 'Employment Law Problems: Equal Pay — The Material Factor Defence', Incomes Data Services Brief No 589, May 1997.

6 Background to Pay and Benefits

Scope of this chapter

6.1　　Employees not only receive immediate cash benefits from their work. The 'fringe benefits' and 'perks' such as luncheon vouchers, holidays, company cars and pensions are all part of the total remuneration 'package' (TRP). All these benefits have to be administered and they have income tax and, in some cases, National Insurance implications. Payroll, pensions and personnel departments are all involved. Some benefits may also be administered by the company secretary or finance director, for instance employee share or car schemes.

Both modern and traditional management ideas see pay and benefit schemes as making an important contribution to achieving business objectives. For example, the modern emphasis on team-working leads to group bonuses to motivate and reward collective performance. By way of contrast, traditional management inclines towards using individual bonuses. This is to encourage each separate employee to maximise his or her own performance. (For a more detailed discussion of traditional and modern personnel management ideas, and their effect on payroll administration, see Reference (18) in 6.13 below.)

Americans tend to use the word 'compensation' in place of the terms 'pay and benefits' or 'remuneration'. They describe the whole process of designing and controlling pay and benefits as 'compensation management' which is sometimes called 'reward management' in the UK. It must be admitted, however, that in the UK this practice often appears to be a piecemeal rather than an integrated process. When considering reward management it is impossible to neglect the conditions of employment. Thus pay or benefits may compensate for undesirable conditions, e.g. shift working. In other cases the conditions of employment, e.g. part-time flexible hours, may be considered a benefit to some employees. In theory, and sometimes in practice, controlling the less tangible aspects of employment may be considered part of reward management. These other aspects might include, for example, a pleasant environment, training, and prospects for promotion. However, classifying these things as 'rewards' would be doubted by many people.

Employee fringe benefits can amount to over 50 per cent of gross pay. Effective design and management of benefit schemes is, therefore, an important consideration. It is not only the benefits themselves that are significant but also their 'structure'. These are the rules which determine who receives the benefits, how much is given and when. A particular 'scheme' incorporates a benefit structure and other matters such as administration and finance. Employee benefit structures are extremely varied and there is little consistency between employers and different types of employment. In particular, the detailed rules governing holiday or sick pay arrangements differ markedly.

From the practical administrator's viewpoint, written copies of explicitly authorised benefit rules are essential. Sometimes, particularly in the less significant areas, the unwritten rules of 'custom and practice' apply. The rules are often stored in the computer, usually for the calculation of pay and benefit elements such as overtime. Pay and benefit rules can be stored as 'parameters' for standard calculations which have local variations. For instance, these parameters could contain factors such as overtime pay rates, or the percentage amounts by which a pension is reduced for early retirement. Pay and benefit rules can also be programmed directly into the software.

This chapter considers the theory behind pay and benefits. It can be a controversial topic. However, a broad understanding of the issues helps explain current pay and benefit structures and their future development. This whole area is very much the province of the personnel officer, trade union official and employee benefits consultant. As described in 16.9 below the payroll administrator can have an essential role in ensuring that pay and benefit schemes are capable of efficient administration.

Overall the emphasis in this chapter is on the economic aspects of employment. Of course, non-economic rewards such as job satisfaction and social status can also be important. Chapter 7 (Pay Schemes) concentrates on pay structures and related issues such as job evaluation. The common complicated benefits of disability pay and pensions are considered in separate chapters (see Chapters 8 (Disability and Maternity Benefits) and 10 (Pension Schemes)). Chapter 9 (Benefits, Expenses and Termination Payments) considers common miscellaneous benefits such as holidays and cars. *Payroll Manager's Review* often carries case studies on the administration and structure of pay and benefits in particular industries or companies. See for instance Reference (6) in 6.13 below which considers the payroll aspects of operating the Channel Tunnel. As another example, Reference (7) describes the pay and benefits function in HMV, the record store group.

Key points of the background to pay and benefits

6.2   The main aspects of employee pay and benefit schemes are listed below.

(*a*)   The aggregate of an employee's pay and benefits is called a 'total remuneration package' (TRP).

(*b*)   Fringe benefits can be expensive and they can exceed 50 per cent of basic pay. This is particularly true for senior managers.

(*c*)   Pay and benefit packages need careful integrated planning if they are to be appropriate, effective and allow for complications such as income tax and NICs.

(*d*)   Most pay and benefit structures are complex, so clear and comprehensive documentation is essential for administration and computer systems.

(*e*)   Pay structure details stored in computers must be carefully checked.

(*f*)   There is a considerable amount of social science which may be relevant to pay and benefit issues.

(*g*)   The effectiveness of employee pay and benefit schemes is often unclear and it can be difficult to justify the details scientifically.

(*h*)   Monitoring and regular reviews of pay and benefit levels are essential to allow for factors like inflation and industry changes.

(*j*)   Pay and benefits also need to be reviewed regularly to maintain rational structures which meet the changing needs of the employer and employee.

(*k*)   Modern computer systems ease the work involved in monitoring and revising pay and benefits.

(*l*)   The administrative complications of pay and benefit schemes should always be considered.

Illustration of a pay and benefits scheme

6.3   A simple example of the scale and range of employee pay and benefits is shown below.

Example — Peter works as an analyst-programmer in the information technology department of a large financial institution in outer-London. His notional basic pay is £20,000 p.a., but his true annual employee pay and benefits package in round figures is itemised below.

		£	£
(a)	Basic Pay (for working 44.4 weeks)	17,077	
(b)	Holiday pay (5 weeks)	1,923	
(c)	Sick pay (for 2.6 weeks, includes SSP)	1,000	
(d)	*Notional basic pay*		20,000
(e)	London weighting	2,000	
(f)	Overtime (about 91 hours at time-and-a-half)	1,500	
(g)	*Total of additional payments*		3,500
(h)	Mortgage subsidy (2% subsidy on a £50,000 loan)	1,000	
(j)	Professional examinations (British Computer Society examination fees plus correspondence course)	500	
(k)	Subsidised meals (two hundred meals in the head office canteen at £1 subsidy each)	200	
(l)	Value of interest on season ticket loan, granted interest-free to employees (valued at 7.75% p.a. on a £1,000 average loan paid back over one year)	78	
(m)	*Total of above employee benefits*		1,778
(n)	Employer's pension fund contributions (10% of Peter's pensionable salary of £15,242. Pensionable salary, as defined in the pension scheme rules, is basic pay less a deduction of £4,758 to allow for the basic State pension).	1,524	
(p)	*Total remuneration package*		£26,802

Depending on the pattern of sickness, Peter's employer must pay up to £144.82 as SSP (statutory sick pay) for the 2.6 weeks of sickness. Prior to 6 April 1994, 80 per cent of the SSP could be recovered from the Government by a corresponding reduction in the amount of NICs paid. From April 1995, total SSP payments can only be recovered to the extent that they exceed 13 per cent of the total liability for NICs for both the employees and the employer during a particular month. (See 8.4 below.) In Peter's case SSP acts only as a minimum which is normally included within the far greater amount of OSP (occupational sick pay) – £1,000 above. Obviously this situation is common with many salaried staff.

The value of all the employee benefits compared with basic pay, excluding overtime is:

$$\frac{£(26,802 - 17,077 - 1,500) \times 100}{£17,017} = 48\%$$

If the less common benefits of the London weighting, mortgage subsidy and season ticket loan are ignored, Peter still has 'fringe' benefits worth £5,147 which represent 30 per cent of basic pay.

It should be noted that the employer is also liable for NICs on all cash earnings, which in this case are £23,500. Assuming the pension scheme is contracted out of the SERPS this amounts to a further cost of about £1,760 for the employer. Peter himself is, of course, liable for NICs on pay up to the upper earnings limit (UEL) of £25,220 but not on the additional benefits. Most benefits including 'benefits in kind' are, however, taxable but until recently free from NICs. There are still significant benefits which do not attract NICs but increasingly statutes have been introduced to specifically charge NICs on benefits, for example, secondary Class 1A contributions on company cars and car fuel. (See Chapter 9 (Benefits, Expenses and Termination Payments) below for a discussion of the tax and NIC position of benefits.)

A further point worth noting is that 'white-collar' jobs such as that of a computer analyst-programmer usually have a straightforward employee pay and benefits structure. There are none of the administrative complications as in the case of factory shift allowances, piecework or incentive schemes.

Complexity of pay and benefit schemes

6.4   Employee pay and benefits is an area of considerable administrative complexity. There are several factors that contribute to this complexity, and some are listed below.

(*a*)   ***Inherent complexity*** — Some pay and benefit rules are by their very nature complex. An example is a GMP (guaranteed minimum pension). As the name implies this is a statutory minimum benefit found in many occupational pension schemes. The calculation for this benefit is tedious and the data required is the whole of the annual earnings history of an employee. Yet a GMP is only one benefit, and one calculation, amongst the many found in a typical pension scheme. See Chapter 10 (Pension Schemes) for further details.

(*b*)   ***A variety of rates*** — Even where the pay and benefit rules are apparently simple for any one employee, there are many different rates covering the employees as a whole. For example within one organisation there may be numerous separate pay grades, each with their own set of annual increments. See Chapter 7 (Pay Schemes) for information on pay structures.

(*c*)   ***A multiplicity of pay and benefit elements*** — Several different types of reward apply, or potentially apply, to each employee. This is illustrated in the simple example of Peter, the computer analyst-programmer, in 6.3 above. The number of reward elements for the workforce as a whole may be large. A list of common pay elements and benefits is given in 6.10

below. Each extra pay element or benefit then has its own rules, for instance, occupational sick pay and shift allowances.

(*d*)   **State requirements** — Government regulations, usually for tax and NICs, add a further level of administrative complexity, such as for company car benefits.

One consequence of the large variety of employee benefits is the extensive specialist vocabulary used. Examples of these specialised terms are 'lead-in pay' (interim pay used when a new incentive pay scheme is being developed), 'retained benefits' (an employee's preserved pension benefits in previous pension schemes), and 'golden parachute' (a generous payment when an employee leaves). (Reference (3) in 6.13 below is a dictionary of such terms.)

Effectiveness of pay and benefit schemes

6.5   The general impression is that employees have a good intuitive appreciation of pay structures and immediate fringe benefits. However, it is a matter of common experience that many people find it difficult to assess the worth of the less tangible benefits. The value of a £1 luncheon voucher is obvious, even if perceived as being worth slightly less than £1 cash. But what is the value of a good pension in 30 years' time? Clearly one option is to pay employees extra cash and not provide benefits like luncheon vouchers and pensions. This may not be sensible or effective. Continuing with the examples, the luncheon voucher is not taxed on the first 15p per day and not subject to employee or employer NICs. The contributions to a pension scheme are tax-free and if the employee were to opt out he could lose important disability, retirement and death benefits for himself and his family.

As the example in 6.3 above shows, employee benefits are expensive. Pay and other employment costs approach two-thirds of the UK gross domestic product. Given this high cost of pay and related benefits it is clearly sensible to design total remuneration packages which have maximum effectiveness. However, a definition of the effectiveness of employee benefits is inevitably complex and depends on one's viewpoint. Clearly the perspective of employers, employees, trade unions and governments are not identical. Only the employer and employee viewpoints are briefly described below.

Employer's viewpoint of pay and benefit schemes

6.6   There has been comparatively little research into the employer's motives and objectives in designing employee pay and benefit structures. Clearly many alternative reward structures can be designed for the same overall cost. However, presumably for the employer the most effective pay and benefit structure is one which makes a maximum contribution to the success of the organisation at a minimum cost. This is obviously an ideal which is difficult to achieve or to assess precisely.

With regard to pay and benefits, major considerations for the employer are discussed below.

(*a*) **External associations** — Trade unions, employers' federations and national joint councils have traditionally played a major role in negotiating pay and conditions in many organisations. Thus pay and benefits have often been set nationally between the representatives of a group of employers and trade unions. Local agreements could then supplement national agreements. This is less true today, and there is a move in favour of employment units agreeing or settling their own local pay and benefits.

Law and government can sometimes be a factor in determining pay and benefits, for instance in the past through Wages Councils and pay restraint legislation and in the future through the anticipated minimum wage legislation which is due to come into force from April 1999. (See Chapters 3 (Legal Framework), 5 (Payroll Law) and 29 (Government) where the role of law and government in payroll administration is examined.)

(*b*) **Competition** — The pay and benefit packages offered by other employers set a competitive standard for recruiting and retaining labour. See Figure 6A below for the standard economic theory on the determination of pay rates in a perfect labour market. Skills shortages (or surpluses) and demographics will often impinge on the degree of competition an employer will face for a particular type of employee. A good deal of pay and benefits information is available in the form of surveys and reports. (Reference (1) in 6.13 below regularly provide some good examples.

(*c*) **Incentives** — A traditional purpose of pay structures is to motivate people to work hard and effectively. This often involves performance-related payments on top of flat rates of pay. Some incentives, such as public recognition of achievement or long service awards, may primarily have a non-economic value.

(*d*) **Fiscal and administrative efficiency** — It is often said that employees are motivated to work for their benefits net of deductions and that they particularly resent tax and NIC 'stoppages'. Accepting this viewpoint employers can try to maximise the net benefits received by their employees. This can be done by exploiting oversights, concessions and incentives in the tax and social security system. An astute employer can use these opportunities to offer his employees greater net benefits for the same total cash cost, for example, pension funds can currently invest £100 in employee contributions at a net pay cost of £77 to the employee at the basic rate of income tax (see 14.10 below for further details). Also, some benefits-in-kind are taxed, but they are not subject to NICs. This distinction is being eroded in view of the Contributions Agency's trend to extend the scope of its levy.

It is sometimes possible and sensible to 'contract-out' of State benefits. This is common in the pensions field where the State pension benefits must be replaced by an equivalent occupational benefit and reduced NICs are granted in return. Contracting-out avoids the double provision of social security and occupational benefits.

Many benefits provided by the employer also require specialist skills and effective administration. The employee cannot match this himself nor obtain discounts in the financial services and other markets.

(e)   **Image and prestige** — The acceptance of a moral obligation to provide welfare benefits such as good pensions and sick pay clearly can enhance an employer's standing in the labour market. Also many employees do not obtain necessary welfare benefits for themselves or their families unless they are offered conveniently and preferably 'free' by the employer. Good employment conditions can improve an employer's general business image. Conversely, any widely-reported deficiency in the employee benefit structure can damage the employer's image.

(f)   **Equity** — It is commonly accepted that there is an underlying 'fair' rate for each job and that employee pay and benefit differentials should be objectively justified. This is one of the motives for introducing job evaluation which is explained in 7.15 below. Equity also leads to a vast range of 'plusages' to compensate for variations in conditions and duties. Examples of these are allowances for being on call, providing instruction to trainees, fire-fighting duties and so on. Some plusages may be in the form of time allowances or benefits-in-kind rather than cash, for instance 'wash-up' time for dirty work or the provision of special clothing such as uniforms. There has been a tendency to seek a simplification of pay structures in recent years, possibly at the expense of equity.

One problem with equity is that pay and benefit comparisons may be made both inside and outside an organisation with conflicting results. For example, the high pay of some computer staff may be unjustified according to an internal job evaluation scheme but justified in the external labour market (see 7.15 below). Of course, the whole subject of reward differentials between groups is a notorious cause of disputes.

(g)   **Control** — A well-constructed pay and benefits package is one of the tools of management control of a business. For instance, overtime and bonus payments can be used to quickly expand business activity. Redundancy and early retirement provisions can be used to ease the pain of contraction.

(h)   **Revision** — Pay and benefit levels need revising regularly to allow for the effects of inflation as well as changes in labour market rates. Traditionally this is one of the main driving forces behind the annual general increase in pay and trade union negotiations. In practice, of course, changes in pay and benefit levels are often combined with small adjustments to the structure. It should be noted that historically

Figure 6A

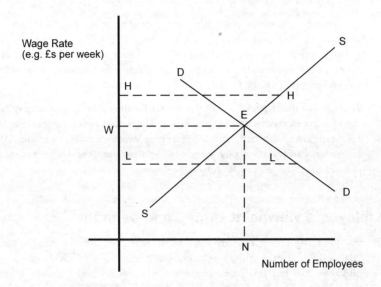

Illustration of the standard economic theory concerning pay rates in a perfectly competitive labour market.

Line DD shows how the demand for labour, in terms of the number of people that can be employed, increases as the pay rate falls. Line SS shows how the supply of labour, in terms of the number of employees available, increases as the pay rate rises. The lines refer to the total labour market, i.e. to all employers of a particular occupation.

If pay rates are low (line LL), the graph shows that employers find the low supply of labour inadequate to meet the high demand. They must increase pay rates to obtain staff. This both reduces their own demand for staff and increases the supply. If pay rates are high (line HH) there is a high supply of labour in excess of the low demand. Employers can then reduce pay rates, which increases their demand for staff, and reduces the number of applicants for jobs. Thus market forces drive pay rates and the number employed towards an equilibrium position, Point E. This represents the point, at a pay rate of W and total number employed of N, where supply and demand are equal.

This is a very simplified view of how the general level of pay is determined, but the assumptions of a perfect market are sometimes approximately true. Unfortunately lines SS and DD are never static! DD will move in response to economic conditions, for example, and SS will move in response to training or demographics, for example.

employee earnings have generally increased slightly faster than the RPI (Retail Price Index). Over the years this difference leads to significant increases in real earnings.

The employer must occasionally be prepared to make radical structural changes to pay and benefits when business conditions change. The reasons for revising pay and benefit structures are discussed in more depth in 6.8 below. The practical administrative implications of revision are considered in 6.11 below.

(j)   *Foreign complications* — All the above considerations apply to pay and benefits connected with overseas work. This could cover placements for UK employees abroad, or foreign employees working in the UK. However, careful allowance needs to be made for the special circumstances involved, e.g. different tax regimes.

Employee's viewpoint of pay and benefits

6.7   What attracts an employee to an organisation and encourages good performance? To answer this question, work motivation has been much researched over the last 100 years. However, most of the theories and research conclusions appear to be no more than commonsense views expressed in technical language. One of the most popular of these numerous theories is Maslow's 'hierarchy of needs'. Figure 6B below illustrates the theory. Maslow suggests that the lower levels of need must be satisfied before a higher need is considered. The theory suggests that only the lowest unsatisfied need can act as a motivator. With a slight adjustment of terminology Maslow's hierarchy of needs, in terms of employment, can be summarised as follows, starting with the lowest needs first.

(a)   *Basic needs* — good pay and good working conditions.

(b)   *Security* — a stable work environment with little prospect of redundancy or adverse change. The provision of sick pay and an old age pension.

(c)   *Affiliation* — work companionship.

(d)   *Esteem* — self-respect, the respect of colleagues and status. Status symbols, e.g. company cars.

(e)   *Self-fulfilment* — the development of skills and responsibility and the achievement of goals or ambitions.

Cynics have remarked that the theory's popularity with management is because it de-emphasises the importance of cash pay as a motivator. For instance, promoting work companionship through a sports and social club may be a cheaper and more effective way of attracting and holding staff than a rise in pay. For this to be so, Maslow would require pay and job security to be adequate and existing work companionship to be unsatisfactory. One practical limitation

Figure 6B

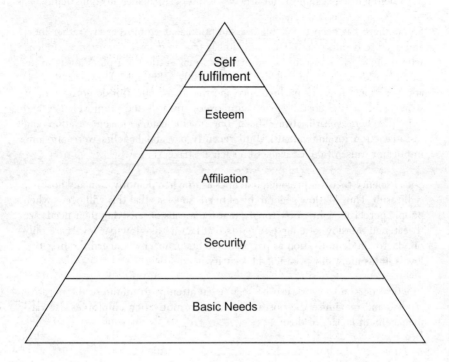

Illustration of Maslow's hierarchy of need

is that Maslow's theory applies to the whole of an individual's life. Some needs can therefore be satisfied at work and some in the employee's private life. Latter theorists such as Porter and Lawlor focus on the importance of employee 'expectations', for example, staff are only likely to work hard and . co-operate if they believe that this leads to significant rewards.

Perhaps the most realistic and despairing theory is rather pompously known as 'Schein's complex man' theory. In a nutshell, Schein propounds the view that an employee's motives are complex and change from time-to-time. People will respond differently to different managerial strategies, including pay and benefit structures. No single management strategy to motivate employees can succeed for all employees at all times. One way of partially meeting this problem is to provide employees with a choice of pay and benefits within some kind of total. This can be done using cafeteria schemes which are discussed briefly in 6.8 below.

(See Reference (3) in 6.13 below for a further discussion on the design of employee pay and benefit schemes and the various factors involved. Much of

Chapter 7 (Pay Schemes) outlines incentive arrangements. Reference (3) in 6.13 below discusses the wider aspects of job performance in some depth.)

So far there has been the implicit assumption that employees are rather inert and need to be motivated. This is obviously true in many circumstances. Indeed where the work is routine some managers may settle for a plodding unmotivated workforce as being all that is realistically achievable. However, there is another aspect to work performance and that is the effect of demotivation, or worse still, active hostility from employees towards the employer. Pay and benefit schemes have always been one major cause of demotivation and dissatisfaction for individuals. Until recently pay and benefits were also one important cause of collective action such as strikes.

Social science theories provide guidelines as to when demotivation and hostility will result. Thus Maslow's hierarchy of needs suggests that this will occur when people perceive, rightly or wrongly, that the means of satisfying their needs are threatened. Maslow of course suggests that factors like low pay levels are only one factor in demotivation as pay and benefits primarily concern the first two levels in his hierarchy – basic and security needs.

Practical personnel work can be seen as an attempt to minimise the negative aspects and maximise the positive features in motivating employees. Reward management is part of this.

Conclusions on the design of employee pay and benefit schemes

6.8   Do employee benefit structures achieve their supposed objectives? Do incentive schemes motivate employees to work hard? Do pensions and sickness schemes give security? Do share schemes create a feeling of common purpose and commitment to the employer? It is questionable whether they are efficient in most cases either from the employer's or employee's point of view. However, even if the 'scientific' approach provides little more than a few useful ideas, a systematic evaluation of remuneration packages is always useful.

Underlying any discussion on employee pay and benefit schemes are two opposing philosophies. The first approach is to provide simple 'rational' pay and benefit structures which give the employees good steady earnings and assured benefits. According to this view a stable co-operative environment has then been created for high economic performance. Complex structures are seen as self-defeating because they are difficult to comprehend and control, and lead to discord and discontent. The second approach stresses both the complexity of work, human motivation and all the other factors that pay and benefit structures must address. According to this view the search for simple structures is illusory, as any acceptable structures must match the almost endlessly varied needs of the employment world. This view also tends to emphasise the importance of incentives for both individual and collective performance. It usually implies fluctuating non-guaranteed earnings.

It is obviously easy to adopt an intermediate stance between these two approaches. However, with persistent concern about the performance of the UK economy and individual industries, it is certain that benefit structures will continue to be seen as one major way of improving employee productivity and commitment. There will always be an interest in performance-related pay systems for all types of staff.

As mentioned, there is a possible way of dealing with 'Schein's complex man' theory, that is the view that, amongst other things, people are all different in their needs and responses to pay and benefit structures. This is to design 'cafeteria' or 'a la carte' schemes where employees choose a combination of pay and benefits which suit their own personal circumstances. Such benefits are valued and the employees can make their choice within a total ceiling value. Clearly this leads to greater administrative complexity but may achieve worthwhile results. A simple method of bringing the employee's attention to the value of a remuneration package is issuing annual benefit statements. These list all the benefits available and can provide estimates of their cash value. They are mostly confined to pension rights but can be extended to other employee pay and benefit details. (See 10.24 below for further details.)

It is doubtful whether employee pay and benefit structures as a whole are scientifically designed, even in new organisations. Yet clearly most structures have a crude rationale. Aside from the impact of general inflation, pay and benefit structures need to be reviewed for several reasons, which include the following.

(*a*) **Decay** — Most benefit and incentive schemes 'decay'. Basically schemes get more and more out of line with the real world as conditions change, for example, a manual workers' bonus scheme may need revision to reflect improvements in technology. The type and volume of work also slowly change over the years. The employees may also find weaknesses and loopholes which can be exploited to the detriment of the organisation.

(*b*) **New opportunities** — New technology, new business ideas and changes in the tax and social security regimes offer new opportunities and close off old ones. For instance, in the last decade share schemes have been encouraged by favourable tax legislation but certain 'reward by asset transfer' schemes have been made liable to NICs.

(*c*) **Business fashion** — There is no doubt that particular pay and benefit structure ideas become fashionable. Usually, of course, there is some underlying justification. Contemporary examples include staff status for manual workers and performance-related pay for managers.

(d)   ***Equity*** — Few jobs remain the same over the years. Some grow in their demands, others decline. Fair dealing between job-holders demands some kind of revision. Equity can also lead to the more delicate and subtle considerations of such matters as implicit sex discrimination. As already mentioned, one of the main reasons for job evaluation is rationalising and formalising the concept of equity within an organisation. Recent hostile commentary on the high pay of some company directors, particularly in utility companies, indicates that the idea of equity is a consideration outside an organisation.

The current and future situation with regard to reward management is very fluid. To give a flavour of this a few points are outlined below.

 (i) Pay and benefits can be seen as a key part of the human resources strategy for an organisation.

 (ii) Traditional pay and benefit arrangements are under attack from several quarters. For instance, personal pensions introduced in 1988 have been promoted, sometimes excessively, as replacing membership of employer pension schemes (many employers are fighting back, however, with group personal pension schemes).

(iii) White-collar pay scales with annual increments are seen as out- of-date with modern performance-related pay schemes as the alternative. These modern schemes tend to award increases mainly on performance ('merit') as opposed to the employee's pay progressing up a salary scale or giving an increase to compensate for inflation. Performance is appraised, usually annually, by assessing each employee's progress towards agreed targets.

(iv) Many new ideas and schemes are being introduced, such as annual- hours working.

 (v) Reward management is becoming extensively computerised, for example, in areas like job evaluation as well as traditional payroll administration.

(vi) There is a certain amount of confusion as to what is the best way to proceed given doubts about both traditional and modern ideas on reward management. The plethora of ideas and schemes, compounded by administrative complexity, makes the situation worse.

(vii) There is social and political concern about high-levels of senior management remuneration. Some of this concern comes not only from left-wing groups, but also from customers, other employees and shareholders.

(viii) There is also the opposite concern about the low-levels of pay and benefits received by some categories of worker. Such workers include those previously covered by Wages Councils (now abolished), for instance, people in clothing manufacture. Other groups that often receive low rewards are those in part-time and casual employment. The expansion of insecure employment is also perturbing, as are long or irregular working hours. A more general worry is the suggestion that the UK economy is becoming the 'sweatshop of Europe' and that it cannot sustain enough well-paid secure work. These concerns are leading the Government to introduce a national minimum hourly wage which some commentators believe may damage employment prospects and security for low paid workers.

(ix) Now that the UK has signed the Social Chapter, new mechanisms (such as Worker's Councils) will influence the process of reward management both directly and indirectly. It remains to be seen how far European practices will filter into the UK, however.

Further aspects of the current and future situation with regard to pay and benefits are mentioned in Chapter 30 (Future Developments Affecting Payroll Administration).

Range of pay and benefits and their rules

6.9   It is worth considering the whole range of pay and benefits available to an employee. As mentioned above it is possible to contract-out of certain National Insurance pension benefits to avoid providing two sets of independent benefits, one from the employer and one from the State. The examples stated in 6.10 below only cover the more common cases met in employee benefit administration. There are many different benefits available and several variations of each. The majority of these benefits affect payroll administration in some way. Behind each pay and benefit element should be a set of rules covering entitlement, calculations, method of payment or delivery of the benefit, and exceptions. A familiar example is the payment scale and rules governing employee travelling expenses. In this case the employer's rules must, of course, be harmonised with the requirements for tax administration contained in Inland Revenue Booklet 480 (1997). Some details of the major pay and benefit schemes and their rules are given in Chapters 7 (Pay Schemes), 8 (Disability and Maternity Benefits), 9 (Benefits, Expenses and Termination Payments) and 10 (Pension Schemes).

Important aspects of pay and benefits are found in some general conditions of employment. These may be a benefit, such as flexitime, or something requiring compensation through allowances, for instance, shift working. In either case they involve administration by personnel or payroll departments.

List of main employee pay elements and benefits

6.10   Some pay and benefit elements are from external sources, such as State social security payments. Some of these additional pay and benefit elements are legitimately taken into account when rewarding employees, for instance occupational pensions are often reduced to allow for the basic State pension. In other cases the reduction of an employee's total reward to allow for other sources of pay or benefits is of a more dubious nature. For example, the pay and benefits of part-timers may be deliberately reduced to allow for the fact that the average part-timer is a married woman with a working husband or a semi-retired man with a small occupational pension. A list of the more commonly met pay and benefit elements earned or received by employees is given below.

(a)   ***National Insurance benefits*** — National Insurance benefits form part of the overall UK social security system. The original insurance principle has been eroded somewhat since the enactment of the *National Insurance Act 1911*. Today National Insurance is seen as mainly a form of taxation and only partly an employment insurance system. The benefits are small compared to national average earnings. (See Appendix D for a list of the main social security rates.

The main NI benefits from April 1997 are:

(i)   SSP (for short-term employee sickness – now mostly employer-funded);

(ii)   maternity allowance and statutory maternity pay (SMP);

(iii)   incapacity benefit (for short-term sickness where SSP does not apply, and long-term sickness);

(iv)   disablement benefit;

(v)   unemployment benefit;

(vi)   widow's benefits;

(vii)   the basic State pension and the additional State Earnings-Related Pension (SERP).

The above benefits usually depend on an adequate history of NICs. It should also be remembered that employees and pensioners are also able to receive many non-contributory social security benefits such as family credit or child benefit. (See Reference (4) in 6.13 below for a comprehensive description of the UK social security benefits.)

SSP and SMP are both administered by the employer through his payroll system. Contracted-out pension schemes are responsible for paying the guaranteed minimum pension (GMP) or an annuity based on protected rights (PRs). The GMP or PRs are the contracted-out equivalent of the SERP.

(b)   ***Additional State benefits*** — These include:

(i)   non-contributory social security benefits, e.g. child benefit, family credit, and council tax benefit;

(ii) other State benefits, e.g. travel-to-work expenses under the Work Trial Scheme.

(c) ***Earnings*** — The main components consist of:

(i) *Fixed pay elements*

- basic pay;

- plusages, e.g. special additions for extra responsibilities or qualifications, for example first aid duties or welding certificates;

- premia, e.g. shift allowances;

- increments, e.g. scale increases linked to age and service.

(ii) *Variable pay elements*

- overtime;

- modern performance-related pay or traditional incentive payments covering individuals or groups;

- bonus, e.g. profit sharing or a discretionary sum.

(d) ***Security benefits*** — The main examples comprise:

(i) occupational sick pay and occupational maternity pay;

(ii) redundancy and lay-off pay;

(iii) disability pension;

(iv) lump sum death benefits and widow's pension;

(v) retirement pension.

(e) ***Welfare benefits*** — Typical benefits are:

(i) holidays and special leave, e.g. for maternity or paternity;

(ii) canteen services or luncheon vouchers;

(iii) medical services and insurance, e.g. BUPA;

(iv) special clothing;

(v) sports and social clubs;

(vi) child-care provision either in the form of facilities or vouchers;

(vii) redundancy counselling;

(viii) pre-retirement counselling.

(f) ***Additional pay and benefits*** — These include:

(i) company car and fuel schemes;

(ii) share schemes;

(iii)   housing finance, e.g. mortgage subsidies and relocation expenses, or the provision of accommodation;

(iv)   discounted employer products and services;

(v)   assisted travel or season ticket loans;

(vi)   home or mobile telephone costs paid;

(vii)   professional association fees;

(viii)   study and examination expenses for professional qualifications;

(ix)   interest-free or reduced rate loans;

(x)   incentive prizes, e.g. holiday costs paid by the employer for a successful salesman;

(xi)   suggestion scheme prizes;

(xii)   long-service awards;

(xiii)   outings and parties for employees and their families;

(xiv)   services, e.g. collecting premiums through the payroll for employee insurance policies;

(xv)   education and training not related to the employer's needs;

(xvi)   London allowances;

(xvii)   payment of school fees;

(xviii)   Christmas gifts.

(g)   ***External pay and benefits derived from other sources*** — These benefits can affect an employee's tax and NIC position as well as his claim to social security benefits and include:

(i)   other regular employment or receipt of pension;

(ii)   union strike pay;

(iii)   earnings from subsidiary employments (moonlighting) are sometimes restricted or forbidden by the main contract of employment. Occasionally subsidiary employment or earnings may be actively encouraged by the employer, e.g. consultancy work by college lecturers or the tipping of restaurant waiters;

(iv)   incentives from the employer's suppliers (typical in some retail operations) which can be cash, vouchers or benefits-in-kind;

(v)   recoveries in respect of jury service;

(vi)   wages from part-time military service, e.g. with the Territorial Army;

(vii)   family support, e.g. with young workers.

Administrative considerations

6.11   An older term for the monitoring, control and maintenance of pay schemes is 'wages and salaries' administration. This somewhat ambiguous term does not refer to payroll administration, i.e. matters like calculating and paying wages and salaries. As already explained the broader and less confusing modern term for the control of pay and benefit schemes is reward management. In the textbooks it is often presented as a human resource management function, but in the author's experience the situation is more complicated. For example, general management are actively involved in making reward management decisions and need information on which to make these decisions. Also the role of the accountant, and consultants such as actuaries, is crucial with regard to the costing and financial implications of reward management. Furthermore accounting systems should continually monitor the actual costs of pay and benefit schemes.

Employee pay and benefit schemes are not always designed for administrative simplicity. Often a small change in the benefit rules can make a major difference to administrative convenience. This can have a significant effect on running costs and the quality of service offered. So a not contracted-out pension scheme whose rules demand precise integration with all the State benefits accrued in one particular employment is inevitably complex. Approximate integration can be much more practical even if less theoretically correct. Even if genuine attempts are made to eliminate unnecessary complexity, most benefit schemes still remain far from simple. This is merely a reflection of the variety of circumstances to be covered by the rules.

Employee pay and benefits are usually part of the employee's contract of employment unless they are discretionary. Therefore, given their legal status and complexity clear authorised documentation is essential. This documentation is the basis for planning administrative and computer systems as well as day-to-day running of the benefits service. It is also required in order to enable an employer to comply with his statutory obligations to report pay and benefits to the tax and NIC authorities. Deficiencies in documentation can cause considerable problems for both the administrators and supporting personnel such as computer staff. The administration of most employee benefits, for example company cars and pensions, requires special records and procedures, which are often computerised. When pay and benefit rules are incorporated in a computer system it is essential that the system is thoroughly tested after every change. Sufficient notice must be provided for the computer staff to make any necessary changes. The computer is also useful to investigate the effect of proposed pay and benefit changes, such as the effect on the employer's costs or employee's gross and net pay. This computerised investigation of the effects of different changes is variously called modelling, simulation or 'what if' analysis, and spreadsheet software is commonly used. The rapid production of graphs, diagrams and tables adds to the advantages over manual methods. Special software packages are also used.

Employee benefits administration often requires specialist staff and departments, such as pensions. However, external expertise is often required, for instance the advice of an actuary should be sought when changing pension and sickness benefits. The services provided by other types of employee benefit consultants may also be useful, e.g. in the case of share schemes.

Introducing new or changed employee pay and benefit schemes

6.12   Concentrating on the administrative aspects, the following procedure is suggested when changing pay or benefit schemes:

(*a*)   consider the use of an employee benefits consultant;

(*b*)   examine all proposed changes for their effectiveness from the employer's and employee's viewpoint;

(*c*)   consider the administrative and legal complications;

(*d*)   discuss the changes with the employees or their representatives;

(*e*)   formally document the new pay and benefit scheme;

(*f*)   give adequate notice of the changes to all the administrative staff concerned;

(*g*)   design and document new administrative procedures and computer systems;

(*h*)   consult the internal auditor;

(*j*)   plan the implementation of the new office procedures and supporting computer systems;

(*k*)   train all relevant staff;

(*l*)   test new computer systems thoroughly;

(*m*)   implement and monitor the new scheme;

(*n*)   review the effectiveness of the new pay or benefit arrangements in the light of the original reasons for the changes.

References

6.13   There are many general and specialist sources of information on employee benefits. Those given below refer to the areas covered by this chapter. They also include material relevant to other chapters.

(1)   Income Data Services, Monks and Reward publish a whole series of surveys, reports and studies covering many detailed aspects of employee pay and benefit structures.

(2)   Moynihan E, 'Pay and Benefits Dictionary', Peterborough Software, 1991.

(3)   Taylor S, 'Employee Resourcing', Institute of Personnel and Development, 1998. (A standard student's introduction to personnel management including motivation, pay and benefits.)

(4)   Matthewman J, 'Tolley's Social Security and State Benefits 1998–99', Tolley Publishing Co Ltd, 1998.

(5)   'Tolley's Payroll, Remuneration and Benefits', (a looseleaf) Tolley Publishing Co Ltd, 1998.

(6)   'The French Connection', PMR, January 1995. (A discussion of conditions of employment at Eurotunnel Services Ltd, the Channel Tunnel company.)

(7)   'HMV on Record', PMR, February 1996. (A case-study including pay and benefits administration.)

(8)   Moynihan E, 'Payroll and Human Resource Management', PMR, September 1995.

(9)   'Tolley's Employer's Payroll Health Check', Tolley Publishing Co Ltd, 1998. (Includes a day-to-day guide on tax and NIC treatment on benefits.)

(10)   'Income Tax, NICs and the NHS', PMR, July 1998.

(11)   'LA Law', PMR, September 1998. (Pay and benefits in local authorities.)

7 Pay Schemes

Scope of this chapter

7.1   The method by which the employees' pay is calculated constitutes a 'pay scheme'. The term 'payment scheme' is often used which confuses the two terms. In this handbook the word payment is confined to the process of paying people, for example with cash or bank credit transfers.

Chapter 6 (Background to Pay and Benefits) outlines the general background and theory of pay schemes. This chapter considers their design with the emphasis on the pay of typical employees, for example, an office manager, a clerk, or a factory operative. As discussed previously the development and control of pay schemes is part of reward management. Various familiar words are loosely used to describe an employee's pay, each with their own nuance, for instance, remuneration, wage, and salary. The concept of total remuneration was also discussed in Chapter 6. This basically implies considering the total value of the pay and benefits an employee receives from employment, such as a salary, subsidised canteen meals and free medical insurance. Looking at this another way, pay elements should not be examined in isolation. However, employees in particular are reputed to have a tendency to concentrate on pay (and often net pay) without regard to the value of benefits. One of the purposes of the comprehensive benefit statements discussed in 10.24 below is to counteract this tendency.

The illustration of pay and benefits for a typical employee in 6.3 above shows that the bulk of an employee's 'reward' is usually paid in money. Typical frequencies of payment are weekly for wages, and monthly for salaries. Other payment frequencies are sometimes met for normal pay, for example fortnightly. Bonuses and the like may be paid less frequently, for example yearly.

The design of pay and benefits is often considered as part of Human Resource Management (HRM). However, as implied in Chapter 6, the determination and control of pay and benefits are also part of financial management. There are several reasons for this, but the most obvious is that pay and benefits are a large part of the operating costs of a business. Furthermore pay schemes have always been of concern to operational

> management. For example, sales and production managers often regard
> pay schemes as being of considerable importance for controlling and
> motivating their staff.

Key points of pay schemes

7.2   The main points of pay schemes can be summarised as follows:

(a)   pay schemes should meet business objectives which are clearly defined;

(b)   the influence of other employee benefits, e.g. share schemes, should not
be forgotten;

(c)   the wage and salary structures should provide adequate differentials to
provide incentives and reward different levels of productivity, skill and
responsibility;

(d)   the wage and salary schemes should be appropriate to the type of work
and the circumstances of the organisation;

(e)   there should be established procedures for reviewing, updating and
controlling the pay scheme;

(f)   job evaluation provides some important techniques for designing
'rational' pay schemes;

(g)   there is a growing tendency towards performance-related pay, and
towards pay arrangements which reward factors like flexible working,
quality, skill and competency acquisition, and teamwork.

Objectives of pay schemes

7.3   Pay schemes cannot be avoided although they may evolve by means of
ad hoc decisions rather than by conscious design. Although a broad rationale is
usually discernible, pay schemes often appear complex and confusing in their
detail. This can be due to several reasons, for example, multiple small and *ad
hoc* changes over a period of time which weaken the initial logic of a scheme.
But as mentioned in 1.1 above the primary role of the payroll administrator is
to administer pay schemes and not be too concerned about their design.
However when pay schemes are revised, or need to be explained to employees
and others, it is helpful to understand the rationale underlying their design.
Schemes are documented, perhaps in a somewhat piecemeal fashion, in a series
of internal documents. External documents can also be important, for
instance, where pay is set nationally.

Pay schemes have always been an important consideration in what is now called
Human Resource Management (HRM). Modern HRM appears to contain a
shift in emphasis compared to personnel management which was its predeces-
sor. Thus HRM in general can place an emphasis on controlling the individual

via performance-related pay rather than using collective bargaining with trade unions to set pay rates for whole groups of employees. (See Reference (1) in 7.21 below for discussion of HRM and its relationship with pay.)

Although the general nature of HRM is influential, payroll administrators are most concerned with the human resource policies and objectives of their own employer, especially with regard to pay, benefits, and conditions of service. Pay policies and schemes should contribute to overall business objectives. Some typical objectives and the ways in which they are met, at least partly by pay schemes, are laid out below.

Pay scheme objective	Example of means
(a) To obtain suitable applicants	Wage and salary surveys of local, national and international labour markets to determine competitive pay rates for comparable jobs.
(b) To retain employees	Pay rates which fairly reflect the worth of the job by recognition of skill, experience, responsibility, physical demands and working conditions.
(c) To motivate employees to a high level of job performance	Rewards which positively reinforce good performance. Other types of incentives can be offered.
(d) Flexibility	Rewards which encourage flexible working and relevant training and education.
(e) To comply with government legislation	Personnel policies which incorporate all legal requirements, e.g. equal treatment legislation. Payroll systems designed for compliance, e.g. by meeting PAYE requirements.

The employer's motivation and objectives are also discussed in 6.6 above. As Chapter 6 (Background to Pay and Benefits) explains, the pay scheme is the major part of the employee's remuneration package and it is designed to meet objectives such as those above. However, employee benefits such as cars, medical insurance and pensions have their place in supporting pay scheme objectives and also affect the payroll administration. Conditions of service such as shift arrangements, holidays and flexi-time can also be a factor. Needless to say, it is almost impossible to design pay and benefit structures which are free from any practical or theoretical objections.

Labour market surveys

7.4   Data on labour markets is available from various sources.

(*a*)   National surveys are published, *inter alia*, by Computer Economics, Incomes Data Services, the New Earnings Survey (the Department for Education and Employment), Marks and the Reward Group.

(*b*)   Professional and other bodies publish earnings data. Examples include salary surveys from the Engineering Council and the Chartered Institute of Marketing.

(*c*)   Reports of pay settlements are published by Incomes Data Services and Industrial Relations Review and Report.

(*d*)   Management consultancy companies and some universities carry out commercial surveys of international, national and local labour markets. Employee benefit consultancies may also provide information.

(*e*)   International surveys are more difficult to obtain from published sources. Some embassies, however, provide data on pay levels in their countries.

(*f*)   Other methods may be less formal but equally relevant, such as using job advertisements and employers' clubs covering a locality or industry for information on pay and conditions of employment.

Pay schemes for different groups of employees

7.5   It is a matter of management philosophy as to whether or not to make distinctions between the methods of paying groups of employees. It has been common to have several different pay structures in an organisation to reflect the different occupational groupings comprising the workforce, although there is an increasing trend towards integrated pay structures. These groups can be classified as follows:

(*a*)   senior and middle management, consisting of directors, senior executives, heads of major departments and immediate subordinate managers;

(*b*)   technical and professional, consisting of non-managerial personnel with specialist skills and qualifications, such as engineers, systems analysts and legal advisers;

(*c*)   junior management and supervisors;

(*d*)   clerical;

(*e*)   skilled manual, consisting of trained direct labour used in production;

(*f*)   miscellaneous manual, consisting of semi-skilled and unskilled labour;

(*g*)   some occupations, particularly selling, do not fit easily into the above structure. This can be handled by having special pay and conditions for such occupations. For example, some life assurance sales people have been paid attractive commissions with little or no guaranteed pay;

(*h*)   part-timers, temporary staff, casuals, the self-employed, subcontractors etc. are quite important in certain trades and occupations. They are often outside the arrangements for the above groups. However, there is a vast range of pay schemes and pay levels for such people whose occupation can range from teenagers still at school who work on Saturdays in a local supermarket to subcontracted builders and computer consultants. Such people may be better paid than the equivalent employee, but usually receive limited benefits or none at all and have less security of employment. There is evidence, however, that short or fixed term employees (perhaps on contracts lasting three years or so) and multiple employments (where one employee legitimately works for more than one employer) are on the increase.

The pay schemes for the above groups do not usually form a single wage and salary hierarchy. Overlaps occur between occupational groups reflecting such considerations as the influences of collective bargaining, the external labour market, the structural design of the organisation and the need to provide opportunities for promotion. Most of the pay schemes discussed below require careful administration and involve extensive paperwork or its electronic equivalent. For many employers there are still national pay and benefit schemes covering a whole group of associated organisations, a particular set of occupations or a whole industry, for example, employers in the construction industry. These schemes are formally documented in handbooks. There may be further supplementary local agreements.

Types of pay structure

7.6   As discussed in 6.8 above there are, with regard to pay structures, two main opposing philosophies, which are given again below.

(*a*)   A simple structure which gives a steady predictable pay.

(*b*)   A complicated structure which leads to variable pay. The variations may be due to factors like employee performance, allowances for special circumstances, and fluctuations in the overall economic scene.

These two opposing philosophies make many assumptions. One view is that they can both be right (or wrong) depending on the nature of the employees and circumstances of an organisation. Needless to say many organisations take an intermediate stance, and try to combine steady basic pay with fluctuating pay elements. The approach adopted also varies according to the type of employee. This leads to the familiar and complicated pay structures often met by payroll practitioners. These pay structures must cover all the occupations and employment grades in a large workforce. For example, semi-skilled manual workers may be paid for timework with a supplementary incentive scheme. The office staff in the same organisation may be on service-linked pay scales with some performance-related pay. Both types of employee may qualify for overtime pay and profit-related pay.

In the past, any discussion of pay structures would have made a strong distinction between manual (waged) and white-collar (salaried) employees. Before the 1980s it was common for manual workers to have more insecure pay, e.g. they were more vulnerable to lay-offs, and often had no sick pay or pension benefits from the employer. Although manual and white-collar workers are commonly distinguished in payroll administration there is a modern trend for the differences to become blurred. This tendency reaches its extreme form in 'single-status' employees where every employee, no matter what their occupation, is covered by common pay and benefit schemes.

The main types of pay arrangement, several of which may be combined together, are listed below.

(i)   *Fixed pay* — A fixed amount of pay is given irrespective of factors like hours worked or performance. This is rare as the main source of income from employment, but see the discussion on honoraria in 7.7(*a*) below. Fixed pay is common with allowances, which can be a minor source of pay. These are discussed separately below.

(ii) *Timework* — There are predetermined rates of pay, usually for the hour, day, week or month. Monthly pay is often expressed in an annual form, e.g. £20,820 p.a. instead of £1,735 per month.

(iii) *Pay for output* — This is basically payment by results (PBR), and it covers most incentive schemes. Piecework for manual workers is a common example. Figure 7A below illustrates a more complicated PBR scheme.

(iv) *Pay for input* — An example is extra pay on acquiring a skill or competence, e.g. in first aid.

(v)   *Allowances* — These are paid to cover special circumstances or compensate employees for some extra inconvenience or hardship, e.g. a dirt allowance or shift allowance.

(vi) *'Negative' pay* — For example employees may be fined. This is explained further in 7.7 (*l*) (vi) below.

(vii) *Tipping* — This can be regarded as an arbitrary incentive scheme operated by customers rather than the employer. Interestingly there may be PAYE consequences. (See CWG2 1998 'Employer's Further Guide to PAYE and NICs'.)

Of course, in practice, most income is earned via timework or PBR schemes. The other types of pay arrangement like allowances are usually supplementary.

The design of any type of pay scheme can become complicated, with detailed rules covering the various circumstances and exceptions. Also, tables of pay rates are often required.

The following sections outline some common approaches to designing pay structures for individuals. There is then a section on group pay schemes. (See Reference (3) in 7.21 below for details on the various types of individual and group pay scheme.) In most cases pay schemes refer to employees, but in life assurance, for example, incentive schemes can apply to self-employed sales people. Numerous variants of each idea are met in practice. The arguments for and against the use of each concept depend on the circumstances.

Virtually all forms of 'pay' are, of course, subject to income tax and NICs. Expense allowances are exempt to the extent they are used to meet genuine business expenses. Pay elements may or may not be pensionable depending on the relevant pension scheme rules.

Individual pay arrangements

7.7   Common terms and schemes for individual pay arrangements are given below. The terminology is rather loose, but what really matters is the definition of a particular employer's scheme contained in his documentation. Note that some of the terms used such as 'payment by results' and 'incentive pay' have a similar or overlapping meaning.

(*a*)   *Honoraria* — Strictly these are payments made without any legal obligation. An honorarium can be a fixed method of pay whereby the fee, which may be quite modest, is not directly linked to the hours of work or results achieved. Ordinary employees are unlikely to meet such systems of pay. However they may be used, say, for the secretary or treasurer of a club. This arrangement is meant as limited compensation for the extra duties (usually quite heavy) performed by these officers compared to other officers such as the vice-chairman. Honoraria may be paid to part-time trade union officials for the same reasons.

(*b*)   *Lumpwork* — Payment is a lump sum for a few hours or days of work, or a job done. The term is used with contract or casual employees, e.g. in building work.

(*c*)   *Spot rates* — These are roughly the current market rates for anything, and in the pay context the term usually refers to time rates. Spot rates are commonly used with contract or casual staff taken on for a few days or weeks, and sometimes for permanent staff. The important feature of employment spot rates is that there is only one rate for a job, and not a band or scale of rates.

(*d*)   *Timework* — This is used for some types of manual work, e.g. for toolmakers where quality is an important consideration. They are also common for retail and clerical staff. The need to measure hourly or daily

Figure 7A

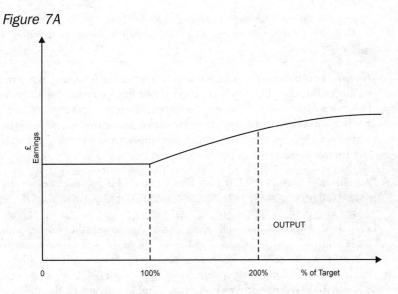

Illustration of the Rowan incentive scheme

The scheme formula is shown below and its graph above. This old scheme is based on the time saved to complete a job with respect to the time allowed.

The Rowan formula:

$$Earnings = \left(Time\ taken + \frac{Time\ saved \times Time\ taken}{Time\ allowed} \right) \times \frac{Rate\ per}{hour}$$

Figure 7B

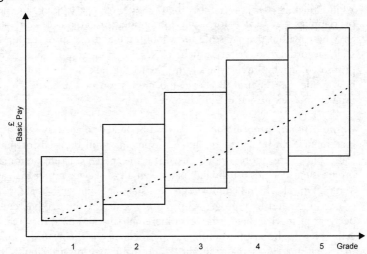

Illustration of a graded salary structure with a varying overlap between the grades

attendance for pay purposes combined with the need to control absences has led to a strong demand for time and attendance systems for over a century.

(*e*)   ***Incentive schemes*** — There are many variations. The basic idea is to give employees an incentive to do as much as possible by rewarding them in line with their performance. Piecework, bonuses, commission and performance-related pay are all examples of 'incentive' schemes in the widest sense of the word. Because of their importance incentive schemes are discussed separately below.

(*f*)   ***Measured day work (MDW)*** — This was used for manual work in the motor industry in the 1970s, but has not proved popular in the UK. It was seen, perhaps optimistically, as solving some of the problems associated with incentive schemes. It involved paying the worker at a fixed rate for a predetermined and agreed level of performance established by work study methods. It is sometimes known as the high-day rate or controlled daywork system. With stepped MDW there are several different levels of performance and pay. Employees contract to achieve a particular level of performance and receive its associated rate of pay.

(*g*)   ***Pay progression*** — Salaried staff traditionally expect some kind of pay progression over and above the rate of inflation. In the past annual pay progression, especially in public services, was almost automatic, at least within a particular job grade. Movement between grades was often based on a combination of merit and service. Today pay progression can depend more on performance. See 7.8(*b*) below.

(*h*)   ***Grades*** — Linked to job grades there are pay grades (often for salaried white-collar staff). There are then a set of overlapping or non-overlapping pay scales for each job grade. An employee can start anywhere within the pay scale for a job grade and may progress up the scale according to criteria such as service and competence. When promoted an employee typically moves to the next highest rate in the new grade. See Figure 7B above. Job grades can be established by job evaluation as explained in 7.15 below.

(*j*)   ***Automatic pay progression*** — Pay can be linked to age, say with a pay increment each birthday. Age-linked scales may still be used for junior staff, but were more widely used in the past. Current automatic progression schemes usually link pay to length of service rather than age. With a typical scheme employees have a starting point on a 'scale' (a set of pay rates) and they progress up the pay scales by one pay increment per year of service (hence the term incremental scale) until they reach a ceiling level. The justification is that performance is theoretically linked to experience. As already implied, automatic pay progression is less popular today than in the recent past. However, automatic pay progression is still used, for example in education. See Figure 7C below.

Figure 7C

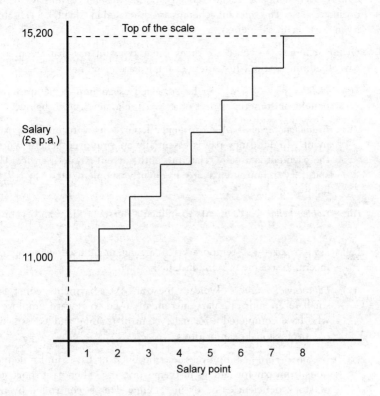

A graphical illustration of a pay scale for a particular job grade

The number of salary points can vary considerably. Traditionally progression is automatic and one pay point per year of service, though personal performance may be a factor. It is more usual to give pay scales as tables rather than graphs, for example:

Salary point	Salary scale (£s p.a. from 1/4/98)
1	11,000
2	11,600
3	12,200
4	12,800
5	13,400
6	14,000
7	14,600
8	15,200

(*k*)   **Disability pay** — Remuneration like OSP, SSP and SMP is seen as an employee benefit or social security benefit rather than pay in the ordinary sense. The relevant schemes are discussed in Chapter 8 (Disability and Maternity Benefits).

(*l*)   **Other schemes** — There are many other types of pay that are met in payroll administration. Just a few examples are given below.

   (i)   *Holiday pay* — This can be regarded as an important employee benefit or sometimes part of a saving scheme. See 9.5 below.

   (ii)   *Redundancy pay* — A more general phrase is a 'termination payment'. Redundancy pay is essentially an employee benefit where the payment is usually related to both current pay and service. The statutory requirements are frequently supplemented. See 9.17 below.

   (iii)   *Golden hellos* — Payments to induce a person to join an organisation.

   (iv)   *Lead-in pay* — A temporary pay arrangement used when a new incentive scheme is being installed.

   (v)   *Educational awards* — Typically these are extra payments, either as a small lump sum or salary increment, used to reward employees who have completed a formal system of training and assessment, e.g. professional examinations.

   (vi)   *'Negative' pay* — Employees may be fined or have similar deductions from pay for failings in their work, e.g. when cash shortages or stock deficiencies occur in retailing. This is controlled by the *Wages Act 1986* and discussed in 5.12 above. Fines should of course be distinguished from normal deductions, many of which are voluntary and in the interest of the employee, for example, regular savings, or made under statute, such as a deduction made according to a court order. Another type of fine is 'quartering', that is rounding a manual worker's attendance down to the nearest quarter of an hour if he is a little late. A further example of negative pay is a 'pay-or-stay' arrangement for training. Basically, employees must refund the costs of recent training if they leave the employer.

Incentive schemes

7.8   Incentive schemes are very common and there are many types. The general principles and some examples are discussed below.

(*a*)   **Background** — The idea of an incentive scheme is to motivate employees to work well by rewarding them in line with performance. Piecework (discussed below) is one example of an 'incentive' scheme.

Historically, incentive schemes have been common, such as in mining and textile manufacturing in the nineteenth century.

A key requirement for an incentive scheme is a strong link between effort and results. A reasonably stable environment is also required as it can be difficult to make changes. One common objective in designing incentive schemes is that they should be self-financing, i.e. that the extra pay given to employees must be financed out of the extra output. This may not always be the case as the employer can seek intangible benefits from the scheme.

The methods used to assess and reward 'performance' can be complicated. Thus incentive pay is often related to performance, as measured in terms of the number of items made in a factory, the time taken to do a job, or the value sold by a salesperson.

(b) ***Performance-related pay*** — Literally this implies any pay scheme which takes performance into account. In practice the term tends to imply modern schemes, particularly for white-collar workers. Performance-related pay has become so important that it is considered separately in 7.9 below.

(c) ***Work study*** — Manual incentive pay schemes often attempt to be objective ('scientific') by using work study techniques. Work study is sometimes known by the misleading term 'industrial engineering'. This involves measuring aspects of the work such as the time required for an employee to perform machine operations in a factory. (For an interesting early discussion of the 'scientific' approach to designing incentive schemes see Reference (2) in 7.21 below, which is a classic text.)

The Rowan Scheme illustrated in Figure 7A above is an early 20th century example of the work study approach. It proceeds by establishing the standard time allowed for completing a particular job. The employee has an incentive to work harder, and do the job in less than the allowed time. Pay is determined, via the formula, and in this case it depends on the time saved by the employee. In recent times the popularity of such schemes has declined.

The Rowan scheme is a traditional example of an 'efficiency' or 'productivity' scheme, i.e. an incentive scheme which rewards employees according to the savings resulting from more efficient working.

(d) ***Piecework*** — This is usually associated with some form of manufacturing or manual work. The employee (or contractor) is paid for each item (piece) produced. Pure piecework is not all that common as employees often have guaranteed minimum earnings. This is necessary, for instance, to protect employees against interruptions in the production process, like machine breakdowns, which are beyond their control.

(e) ***Bonuses*** — This word is used very loosely, but it often denotes some kind of uncertain or infrequent pay element for an individual or group.

In some situations the word merely implies an ordinary incentive pay scheme with pay varying in line with performance or output, for instance, a regular factory production bonus. In other cases a bonus may be paid where a particularly good job has been done. An example of this would be in a software house where a team of analyst-programmers may exert themselves to complete a profitable job on time to the satisfaction of an important customer. The management may then wish to express both its appreciation and provide encouragement via a bonus. The bonus payment may be entirely at the discretion of the management, i.e. there is no formal scheme.

Attendance bonuses are a pay element, usually fairly small, that reward good time-keeping.

A Christmas bonus is designed to create goodwill. It may be related to pay, for example, one week's extra pay. It may only depend on the employee having a minimum amount of service and being in employment at Christmas. It should be noted that some Christmas bonuses are given in kind, such as a turkey or a bottle of wine, or holidays for top performance by sales staff.

(*f*)   *Commission* — The word usually implies a scheme for sales personnel whereby the reward is directly linked to sales value. A flat rate per item sold or a percentage of the total sales value are the simplest approaches. The rate of commission may be variable. For instance, it may increase over a certain range of sales values (an 'accelerator') and decline over another range of values (a 'decelerator'). Accelerators are used to provide an extra incentive once a particular sales level is reached. Decelerators are used to control 'windfalls', i.e. very good sales due to luck. Some schemes are not simply linked to sales value but also take account of margin achieved when the salesman is responsible for selling a range of products at different margins. Sales pay schemes may use basic pay with commission. Commission-only schemes are associated with selling life assurance and double glazing.

Note that where an employer's objectives are more complicated then a bonus scheme may be designed for sales staff. For example, there may be group bonus schemes or non-cash incentives such as luxury goods for good sales performance.

(*g*)   *Multi-factor incentive schemes* — These measure performance and hence give a reward based on two or more factors, for example, the amount produced and its quality. Incentive schemes for directors and senior employees will typically take a multi-factor form.

Performance-related pay

7.9   Performance-related pay is part of modern employee performance management. The abbreviation for performance-related pay is PRP, although the same abbreviation also stands for profit-related pay. In theory performance management involves all aspects of an employee's performance, e.g. counselling, training and discipline. Pay may or may not be part of this. But today, performance is often linked to reward management, i.e. pay and benefits. Crudely, if people perform well with respect to their objectives they will be rewarded. Merit pay is a similar but older idea than performance-related pay.

Performance management is much more than a traditional incentive or bonus scheme. In the past, such schemes have only affected a minority of white-collar workers such as sales staff. Over the last few years performance management schemes have spread rapidly amongst large white-collar employers. Such schemes are common for managers, and they can also be designed for blue-collar workers. Perhaps over 80 per cent of large employers have some kind of formal performance management scheme.

In outline, pay-linked modern performance management can operate as follows on a regular cycle (say six-monthly or yearly). The steps are listed below from a management perspective:

(a)   translate corporate objectives into departmental and individual objectives;

(b)   agree individual objectives with the employee;

(c)   continuously review objectives and performance;

(d)   prepare for the formal review. The preparation is done separately by both the manager and individual employees;

(e)   typically a special form is completed which asks the employee to assess his or her performance in the period concerned. Managers may also record their initial views on an employee's performance;

(f)   review formally with the employee actual performance against individual objectives. These meetings should involve full and frank discussions between the manager and the individual concerned;

(g)   devise a personal improvement plan to be part of the next set of individual objectives;

(h)   record the conclusions on a form and rate or score the employee's performance over the review period, e.g. on a scale which goes from bad to excellent. This should be done in a fair and logical way;

(j)   determine performance-related pay on the basis of the employee's rating.

The last step above is, of course, omitted where the performance management process is not linked to pay. For further discussion on appraisals and reviews see Chapter 17 (Management Skills).

The details of performance management schemes are very varied. Schemes can try to assess an employee's social and personal qualities, but most tend to concentrate on work results. Typically a scheme assesses each employee under a set of headings, like quality of work, initiative and meeting personal targets such as installing a new computer payroll system on time. The score under each heading is totalled to give an overall rating.

Where a pay-linked scheme is used then there are numerous ways of calculating the extra pay. One common method is to turn an employee's performance rating into a permanent pay rise. This rise may actually be a mixture of true performance pay and a cost of living increase. However the guaranteed cost of living element may be entirely eliminated. Thus in a period of 3 per cent inflation a scheme might use a scale which awards nothing for unsatisfactory performance, 3 per cent for barely satisfactory performance, 4 per cent for a mediocre rating, 5.5 per cent for a good appraisal, and 7 per cent for excellent performance. Alternatively, performance pay may be paid as variable one-off bonuses on top of a cost of living increase. Some performance pay schemes exploit incremental scales by stopping the progression of poor performers. Good performers can receive extra increments. Some schemes may concentrate performance rewards on a few employees with top performance ratings. This involves using a set of rules which mean money is received on an all-or-nothing basis. Group and team PRP are also sometimes met. It should be noted that some pay review arrangements are only partially performance linked. For example factors like management discretion and the length of time since the last increase may also be used to help determine the pay increase. See References (4) to (6) in 7.21 below for further details.

Group pay arrangements

7.10   It has already been mentioned that some incentive pay arrangements may exist in either an individual or group form. There are many incentive pay arrangements which affect large groups of employees and in some cases virtually all employees, for example, company-wide profit-sharing schemes.

(*a*)   ***Group incentive pay*** — By inference the group is usually 'small', for example, a team. Usually the idea is to divide the incentive rewards either equally or according to a formal scheme amongst the group members. Group incentive schemes are used to encourage co-operation and where, for instance, it is not possible to attribute the performance of the production process to an individual.

(*b*)   ***Unit-wide incentive schemes*** — The business unit concerned could be a factory, say. Scanlon and Rucker schemes are examples of American origin. With Scanlon plans the idea is to seek improvements in the ratio of total wages to total sales turnover. The Rucker plan looks for improvements in total labour costs compared to total added value (basically sales revenue less the cost of externally purchased goods and services). In both cases a reduction in relative labour costs is used to calculate a bonus for all the workers involved. This is similar to the concept of 'gain sharing' where the benefits of productivity improvements or other cost savings are shared with the unit's employees.

(c) **Profit sharing** — Basically a formula is used to share the profits of a company with its employees. Profit-related pay schemes have increased considerably in popularity due to the tax relief granted to registered schemes. (See 9.14 below for details, and also see Reference (11) in 7.21 below.) It remains to be seen how many such schemes will survive the withdrawal of tax relief.

(d) **Employee share schemes** — Profit-sharing schemes which use a share of profits to buy shares in a company for its employees. Executive share option schemes are effectively bonus schemes linked to the increase in value of the employing company's shares. See 9.14 below.

Allowances

7.11 Allowances are usually given to allow for special circumstances or to compensate employees for some inconvenience or extra cost. Pay allowances should not be confused with income tax allowances. Another point is that some allowances are in reality expense allowances, for instance, mileage allowances for car travel. Some common examples of allowances are listed below.

(a) **Geographic allowances** — The most common example is the London allowance to compensate employees for the greater cost of living in this area. Such allowances may be an addition to hourly, weekly, or monthly pay. With banks there is often a scale with the allowance varying. In the London area it may vary according to the distance a branch is located away from the centre of the city. The allowance may be around £3,000 per annum in central London. Allowances are sometimes given for other areas, such as the South East of England.

(b) **Overtime pay** — This is probably better described as timework or premium pay rather than an allowance. Practice is very variable. For example, employees may be paid by the hour at various rates according to the period worked, e.g. evenings, weekends and public holidays. Typical rates are the basic rate of pay, or an enhanced rate of 'time and a half' (basic pay plus a half). Working public holidays may qualify for 'double time' (twice the basic rate). Paid overtime is sometimes unpopular with modern management. Overtime pay can be restrained by arrangements like annualised hours (working a variable number of hours per week within an annual total).

(c) **Shift allowances** — Allowances are frequently offered for working 'antisocial' hours on a regular basis. The allowance may vary according to the shift worked (early, day, or late shifts, or a rotating shift pattern). For instance, a late or evening shift may qualify for 15 per cent above normal rates.

(d)   ***Special allowances*** — Allowances may be paid for tools, clothing, poor working conditions and additional duties such as being willing to fight fires in factories or do first-aid work.

(e)   ***Stand-by pay*** — An allowance for an employee who can be called into work at short notice. A related allowance can be given to an employee for answering queries over the phone when off duty.

(f)   ***Short-time pay*** — This is a reduced rate of pay used where there is insufficient work for an employee, for example, there may be no working, say, for one day a week. Lay-off pay is similar except that it usually implies pay for a period without any work. See 5.26 above for the legal implications.

(g)   ***Round-sum allowances*** — These are meant to cover normal employee expenses. An estimated amount is given to the employee whatever the actual level of expenditure. Some of the special allowances above may actually be expense allowances, such as tool allowances. See 9.18 below for the tax problems.

(h)   ***Pay in lieu*** — This is made where the employee forgoes some normal rights.

Pay increases

7.12   Employees may receive pay increases for several reasons. These reasons include an increase in the cost of living, automatic progression up a pay scale, greater performance under a PBR scheme, promotion, and further increases which represent their share of greater prosperity. This section, however, focuses on increases in pay rates, and not on pay increases due to other factors such as progression up a pay scale.

Typically employees expect a regular increase in pay rates to cover the rise in the cost of living (inflation) plus a little extra. This expectation is historically justified. For the economy as a whole, employee earnings have increased slightly faster than prices (by under one per cent per annum recently). Increases in pay rates are usually annual.

Pay increases are of considerable concern to the Government, because of their (debatable) effect on inflation. This has lead to several direct and indirect attempts at government control of wage increases. (See 7.18 below.)

From an employer's viewpoint a prime consideration is the cost of any type of increase and how this cost may be recouped, for example, via improved productivity, or by passing the extra charge onto customers, or a reduction in profits. The employer also has to consider other factors with regard to increases, like being competitive with other employers. Such factors are discussed in 6.6 above.

Real pay increases (i.e. increases after allowing for inflation) can occur as planned under a pay scheme. For example, employees can receive pay additions with service according to an incremental scheme. However, as discussed in 7.13 and 7.14 below, some real increases in pay may not be anticipated by the employer. In general terms real pay increases in the economy as a whole must be funded by increased productivity, i.e. greater production of wealth per unit of labour. This broad concept must allow for complications. For example, over the last century, not only has real gross pay increased markedly, but so have fringe benefits. Also the hours worked per week have declined. (It remains to be seen whether the recent increase in hours worked per week is a blip or a reversal of this trend.)

With an individual employer it may be difficult to distinguish between a cost of living increase and any additional increase. This is illustrated with the performance-related pay scheme in 7.9 above where the two are merged together. Also employers often try to gain changes to conditions of service, pay schemes and working practices in return for an increase in pay which might only cover the increased cost of living. Conversely trade unions may seek, and employers may give, increases above the cost of living with the employees giving little or nothing in return. (Arguably, it is this sort of increase that could be regarded as inflation.) In some cases cost of living increases may be almost automatic, for instance where sales commission increases in line with the price of the goods or services sold.

Pay reductions sometimes occur. For instance if a business is in difficult financial circumstances reduced pay rates may be imposed on employees, or negotiated with them. Indeed the purpose of some pay schemes, such as profit sharing schemes, is partly to share both gains and losses between the employer and employees. Some schemes automatically reduce earnings. Using a previous illustration, commission schemes can produce reduced earnings because of weak sales in a poor economic environment.

Pay structure considerations and problems

7.13   There are many considerations when designing a pay scheme, e.g. competition with other employers and equity. Some of these main points have already been discussed in 6.6 above.

It is difficult to evaluate modern approaches to pay structures compared to the old ideas. The old ideas persist in various forms, perhaps with new names like 'performance-related pay' rather than 'merit pay'. However, there are general changes in the nature of pay and benefit schemes. These partly reflect the changing nature of work, and partly reflect a change of emphasis in tackling pay issues. Old approaches to pay schemes are sometimes seen as being divisive, inflexible, ineffective and linked to collective bargaining. Modern approaches to pay are supposed to reinforce factors like treating people as individuals, team work, flexible working, quality, and the acquisition of relevant skills and knowledge.

There is also a whole series of problems with pay schemes. These are familiar to most people with business experience. They are even more familiar to personnel officers, work study officers, business managers and trade union officials. They must seek to cope with these problems, or at least mitigate their effects. Some of the common problem areas are listed below. They can usually be overcome, at least partially.

(*a*)   *Cost* — As in many areas of life this is usually a major consideration with a pay or benefit scheme. Shortage of finance may lead to less than ideal schemes and rates of pay. This can, of course, lead to further problems like the resignation of good employees.

(*b*)   ***Differentials*** — Words with related meanings are often used. For example 'relativities' are similar to reward differentials, i.e. the differences between the employee rewards for different jobs either within an organisation or outside it. 'Comparability' refers to the idea that the rewards for similar jobs amongst different employers or industries should be similar.

Pay differentials in particular can cause many problems. Differentials between internal jobs can be seen as unjustified and may lead to disquiet. Pay differentials can also lead to 'leap-frogging', which is discussed in 7.14 (*e*) below. Discrepancies between market rates and internal rates for the same occupation are discussed in the next paragraph. Job evaluation is one solution offered for the problems caused by *ad hoc* pay differentials.

(*c*)   ***Market rates*** — The simplified economic theory of how the market determines wages and salaries is shown in Figure 6A above. Market forces can however cause problems. For example, the going rate for certain specialists may be too high compared with internal pay scales for the appropriate job grades. One partial solution to this problem is to give a special pay allowance to bring the internal rate up to the market rate. Some organisations do, of course, pay above the average market rate to attract and retain the best people, others take a more radical view and outsource the function concerned.

(*d*)   ***Pay 'drift'*** — Where pay increases faster than planned. This is discussed in 7.14 below.

(*e*)   ***Senior executive rewards*** — The details of this subject are outside the scope of this book, which concentrates on the pay and benefits of ordinary employees. However the rewards of senior executive employment have special considerations. For example, the higher rate of tax and employer NICs encourages benefits like share options and enhanced pension schemes. Also, as recent events at utility companies have demonstrated, there can be public relations difficulties. This is because senior executive pay is partly exposed in the accounts of an organisation and the subject of media reporting leading to hostile reactions from shareholders, consumers, the public and politicians. Partly to address these problems all public companies have established remuneration committees staffed primarily by non-executive directors. Remuneration committees determine the contracts of service and emoluments of executive directors and senior executives. It is the responsibility of such committees to ensure that the rewards of executive directors and senior executives aligns their interests with those of the company's shareholders. Published company accounts, for example those of ICI for 1996 and later years, contain details of the remuneration packages of these senior staff. (See 24.20 below for the details that must be disclosed under *CA 1985*.)

(*f*) **Administration** — Some pay schemes are difficult to administer. This can lead to delays in payment, errors and unnecessary expense, resulting in loss of confidence by both employees and employer. One sensible defence against this is to ensure that payroll staff are involved in the design of schemes to ensure that they are workable. Where appropriate computer staff should be involved for the same reason.

(*g*) **Subjectivity** — Performance-related pay for white-collar staff in particular may include 'soft' (subjective or vague) criteria. Even with 'hard' (objective and measurable) targets, the assessment of achievements or failings may be modified by a subjective allowance for the circumstances. For example a manager may have failed to meet his or her targets because of staff sickness in the department. It may be difficult to assess whether this is a valid explanation or a pretext concealing ineptitude. The subjectivity may also include personal bias either unjustifiably in favour of or against particular employees.

(*h*) **Lack of motivation** — For instance, incremental pay scales with automatic progress provide no motivation to increase productivity (though they may have advantages also, such as encouraging staff to stay with the employer).

(*j*) **Distrust** — Payment by results and performance-related pay schemes can be divisive. They can create a hostile, distrustful environment, both between employees and management and between the employees themselves. Historically this has often been a problem with incentive schemes in manufacturing and is part of the rationale behind team-based rewards in such circumstances.

(*k*) **Restriction of output** — Cohesive groups of employees may manipulate output in undesirable ways. Ironically this can occur particularly where incentive schemes (group or individual) are operating. For example, output may be kept to artificially low levels to persuade management to raise incentives.

(*l*)   ***Rate-cutting*** — Where employees earn more under a pay scheme than management expect, believe acceptable, or can afford, then the rates may be reduced. Fear of rate-cutting is one of the reasons why employees may restrict output (and hence their own earnings).

(*m*)   ***Loss of quality*** — This is a classic example of sub-optimisation (the management theorist's term for improving one aspect of a system at the expense of another part). Thus the work may be rushed to meet the quantity targets of a bonus scheme, but the quality may be poor.

(*n*)   ***Changes*** — Changing a pay scheme to reflect new conditions can be a problem. For example, trade unions are likely to see the need for changes as a negotiating opportunity. Insensitive or inept changes may create more problems than they solve, in as much as they may result in employee demotivation. See also 7.14 (*b*) below.

(*p*)   ***Abuse*** — Pay schemes can be abused in many ways. One common practice in the past was to work slowly during the day. The uncompleted work then ensured that overtime at premium rates was available in the evening or at weekends.

Pay drift

7.14   Pay 'drift' is sometimes known as pay creep. This occurs when pay increases faster than planned. It may happen for several reasons, some of which are listed below.

(*a*)   ***Wrong assumptions*** — For instance, incremental pay scales are sometimes costed on the assumption that there will be a net loss of staff paid at the higher rates who will be replaced by staff on lower rates. Thus staff turnover should maintain a reasonable average cost. Attempts may be made to impose this. For example, a common ploy is to insist that only junior lower paid staff are recruited. Strategies such as this can antagonise departmental managers who want experienced staff. However, even with recruitment and other restrictions, the number of staff in the upper areas of the pay scales may increase more than anticipated, particularly in periods of recession when staff turnover is low.

(*b*)   ***Work changes*** — Changes in the method of work or environment make good performance easier or more difficult or just different. This is an important special case of the assumptions underlying a pay structure being invalidated. In some cases the changes may be rapid and in other cases slow and gradual and hence more difficult to perceive. The changes may be various, e.g. economic or technical. Using a more specific example, changes in interest rates and tax rates can affect sales. As another illustration, changes in the methods and equipment used in a factory may increase output without any extra effort from the employees. In both of these examples an incentive scheme linked to performance needs changing, but this takes time both to detect, negotiate and implement. Employees are reluctant to accept a new pay structure where, say, technical and economic changes have been to their benefit under the old pay scheme.

(c) *Rate and grade creep* — Managers may buy or reward co-operation and performance by increasing pay rates or giving higher job grades in an *ad hoc* way. The result is that the average rate of pay increases faster than anticipated. In the previous example the increase in average incremental pay is an automatic consequence of circumstances. With rate or grade creep the increases are ostensibly under the control of managers and personnel officers.

(d) *The ratchet effect* — This is where old or unjustified rates and restrictive practices are bought out by the management, perhaps under the pretext of a 'productivity deal'. This usually means including extra pay and benefits, or improved conditions, over and above what is normally justified. New unsatisfactory practices gradually appear which again have to be 'bought out', and so the process continues.

(e) *Leap-frogging* — This is where one group of workers use the rewards of another group to justify increases for themselves. This process can then be used by another group of workers and so on. Leap-frogging can occur on a local, organisation-wide, industry-wide, or national level.

Job evaluation

7.15   Job evaluation is undertaken to value different types of job relative to each other. Although mainly used for setting pay and benefit levels it can be useful for other purposes, for example, employee performance management, career development and recruitment. The various methods used to value jobs are explained below. They are based on a mixture of subjective views, objective data, and estimates. These methods are of course 'proven' to some extent by their use in numerous organisations.

Job evaluation attempts to provide a relative valuation of jobs which incorporates the views of managers, workforce and to some extent society as a whole. These views include ideas like 'equity' and the 'contribution' each job makes to an organisation. Because subjective views are such an important part of job evaluation it is spurious to claim that it is a 'scientific' process. However, it can claim to be a rational approach. For example, it attempts to be systematic and consistent, and the methods used are amenable to computer support. Theoretically, a pay scheme based on job evaluation should reduce the grievances of employees on matters like the pay differentials between jobs.

There are three broad types of job evaluation scheme which are outlined below with a brief example.

(a) *Non-analytical schemes* — These work by examining and comparing whole jobs. For example all the jobs in an organisation are simply ranked in order of perceived value. Though it is easy to place a finance director ahead of a factory operative there can be problems in ranking, say, a clerical office supervisor and a chemical laboratory technician.

(b)   ***Analytical schemes*** — These assess jobs by breaking them down into a number of different factors and scoring the factors. For example, the factors for a job might include the required level of education and training, responsibility for the work of other people, and any exposure to adverse physical conditions. Each factor for a particular job can be rated on a points scale. The factor ratings can be combined to give a total score for each job. It is usual to weight the factors before totalling them.

(c)   ***Competency based schemes*** — A modern approach in which jobs are analysed into groups of competencies. The concept of 'competence' has recently become important in practical training and education, though there appears to be a little confusion regarding its abstract definition. 'Competence' is broadly the ability to apply a combination of knowledge, skill and personal qualities to handle successfully a particular task or feature of a job. Alternatively, it can be seen as a characteristic which is linked with good performance in a job. Thus, for instance, a mainframe computer salesperson should be competent in 'presentation' and 'negotiation'. These competencies need, of course, to be analysed further, for example, part of competence in negotiation is identifying and developing areas of mutual agreement. Jobs can be graded in terms of competencies.

Some schemes (usually focused on managers and senior employees) are also designed to recognise any special skills outside the norm for the job that a particular employee is able to apply for the benefit of his employer. For example, the production director may have a particular flair for strategic planning which compliments the managing director's own skills. Such schemes seek to recognise the positive impact of these special skills by evaluating the individual as well as the job.

There are many proprietary methods which are broadly based on the above ideas, such as the Hay Guide Chart Profile method and the PE International Pay Points Method.

Job evaluation is essentially comparative. Thus whatever job evaluation scheme is used there is the further step of converting the results into job grades and pay. For example the rank of a job, or its number of points scored, needs to be related to pay. Objective pay data, e.g. internal and external rates for particular jobs, is important for this exercise, but it is based on judgement rather than science.

Job evaluation should provide a method of grading jobs and arriving at pay differentials which is acceptable to both management and current employees. It should also be helpful when recruiting. A proper scheme is also useful in avoiding any problems with sex discrimination where different groups of workers are predominantly male or female. (See 5.8 above for a discussion of the legal aspects of job evaluation and sex discrimination.)

(See References (7) and (8) in 7.21 below for further details on job evaluation.)

Collective bargaining

7.16   Collective bargaining about wages and salaries (and other employee benefits) may take place at a number of levels.

(*a*)   ***Workplace (or plant)*** — Employee representatives, i.e. shop stewards and plant management negotiate pay levels and structures. This is typical of the industries which operate PBR systems.

(*b*)   ***Organisation*** — Negotiations between union and management cover most employees in the organisation, e.g. the construction industry and some banks and insurance companies.

(*c*)   ***Industry*** — Unions or a federation of unions and the employers' association negotiate on pay and benefit matters. Some come together on an '*ad hoc*' basis while others act as a result of standing arrangements usually based on the model devised by the Whitley Committee during World War I known as Joint Industrial Councils or Whitley Councils. Local authority staff terms are negotiated by such Whitley Councils called NJCs (National Joint Councils).

(*d*)   ***National or regional*** — Wages agreed with an employer are applied throughout the country or on a region by region basis. Different rates are applied to regions as opposed to a national rate (see 16.10 below).

The role of trade unions and collective bargaining has been weakened over the last 15 years or so due to political, legal, economic and social changes. Decentralised bargaining has also become more popular with employers.

Wages Councils

7.17   Wages Councils which were established by law to fix minimum pay for low-paid industries were abolished by *TURERA 1993*. Only the Agricultural Wages Board remains in operation. They featured the characteristics of voluntary collective bargaining with the addition of independent members whose votes could settle a disagreement between the main parties. A statutory minimum wage will be re-introduced in April 1999.

Incomes policy

7.18   This relates to government intervention to control incomes by statutory legislation, by other devices or voluntary agreement with organisations like the Trades Union Congress. An incomes policy is generally disliked by management and unions alike because it interferes with collective bargaining and sets maximum pay increases below employee expectations. Employees often perceive a maximum increase as an entitlement. Organisations with an informal pay system are able to circumvent an incomes policy, for instance by sham promotions to higher pay levels or by introducing new or improving existing benefits such as company cars.

Direct incomes policies were not used by the last Conservative government, which remained in power until May 1997. However, it did use indirect methods of controlling incomes, for example, broad financial restrictions on public sector services which indirectly restrained the pay of employees. It seems unlikely that the present Labour government will reintroduce direct incomes policies as it neither favours their use nor needs to adopt such policies to combat inflation. (See 28.6 below for further details on government incomes policies.)

Developing pay schemes

7.19   The typical steps in developing and implementing a pay scheme are:

(*a*)   define the objectives and investigate management and employee views concerning pay schemes;

(*b*)   analyse the existing situation to assess the extent to which objectives are being achieved;

(*c*)   evaluate alternative pay methods in relation to the objectives and the circumstances of the organisation and the labour market, and assess any cost implications;

(*d*)   consult and negotiate with employee representatives, if any, when developing the scheme;

(*e*)   consider the use of pilot schemes prior to full implementation;

(*f*)   monitor the effectiveness of any new scheme and modify when appropriate.

(See also 6.12 above.)

Wage and salary control

7.20   Administrative procedures should be designed to monitor the scheme and to control wage and salary costs against budgets. Historical control compares actual cost with the budgeted cost, analyses any variances and takes appropriate corrective action. Regular ongoing controls are necessary to ensure prompt action. Computer-based payroll and personnel systems provide information on such aspects as:

(*a*)   salary increases inconsistent with planned progression within and between grades;

(*b*)   direct and indirect labour costs in relation to output and performance;

(*c*)   the proportion of overtime, shift pay and other allowances in relation to total pay;

(*d*)   total pay levels of departments, areas, and individual jobs.

Payroll and personnel IT systems can provide links to spreadsheet and statistical software. This makes graphical and mathematical analyses of pay data much easier than in the past.

References

7.21   The references and further reading in 6.13 above mostly apply to this chapter as well. Reference (1) in 6.13 is particularly useful for details of current pay schemes and their rates.

(1)   Beardwell I and Holden L (Eds), 'Human Resource Management', Pitman, 1994. (A good modern discussion of the HRM background together with an introduction to pay schemes.)

(2)   Taylor F W, 'The Principles of Scientific Management', Harper, 1911. (A classic management text with an emphasis on PBR schemes.)

(3)   'Introduction to Payment Systems', ACAS.

(4)   Armstrong M and Baron A, 'Performance Management', Institute of Personnel and Development, 1998.

(5)   'Appraisal-Related Pay', ACAS.

(6)   Moynihan E, 'Performance-Related Pay', PMR, August 1993.

(7)   Neathy F, 'Job Evaluation in the 1990s', Industrial Relations Services, 1994.

(8)   'Job Evaluation — An Introduction', ACAS.

(9)   Biggs M, 'Operating Profit-Related Pay', PMR, February 1996.

(10)   'The Benefits of Flexibility', PMR, November 1997.

Note that PMR often carries articles which discuss various aspects of pay schemes as well as related matters such as benefits and employee conditions of service.

8 Disability, Maternity and Family Benefits

Scope of this chapter

8.1   This chapter covers the payroll treatment of both disability and maternity benefits provided by the employer and their inter-relationship with benefits provided by the State. It also covers family benefits in the light of developments such as paternity leave and leave when adopting a child as set out in the Government's recent White Paper, 'Fairness at Work'.

It is striking that it is useful to deal with disability and maternity benefits in the same chapter when, from a broader social and philosophical point of view, one can question whether it is right to regard pregnancy, childbirth and the early days of motherhood as a form of disability. It is true, of course, that the employee's situation is that temporarily she cannot work – but, the same could be said of an employee who is called to perform jury service for a lengthy trial.

The reason that from a payroll point of view it is convenient to deal with disability and maternity benefits together lies with the historical similarity between statutory sick pay (SSP) and statutory maternity pay (SMP). This should not disguise the fact that there are now important differences between SSP and SMP: for example, in the normal course of events an employer cannot recover any of the cost of paying SSP to an employee but in the case of SMP payments, the greater part of the cost can be recovered from the State – and, under certain circumstances, the complete cost.

There are other distinctions. If employees are provided with an occupational sick pay (OSP) scheme which, say, provides full pay in the case of sickness for up to six months, then it is clear that it would be unlawful to treat a sick female employee any differently from a sick male employee. If both a male and a female employee were hospitalised for a serious medical condition for six months, then, *prima facie* both would continue to be paid their salary for those six months. However, if an employee, working under that same contract of employment, is unable to work in the latter stages of her pregnancy and for several weeks after giving birth, she will not normally receive full pay under the OSP scheme. Instead it is common for her to be excluded from the terms of the OSP scheme and to receive six weeks pay set at the rate of 90 per cent of her average pay, followed by twelve weeks at a relatively low flat-rate (£57.70 pw 1998/99), followed by a period of unpaid leave but with a right to return to work.

Clearly, therefore, it is important on legal grounds to distinguish between disability and maternity benefits, despite payroll similarities.

One element that the two statutory disability benefits, SSP and SMP have in common is that they are complicated to administer. An investigation published back in 1993 by the National Audit Office found consistently high levels of errors in a sample of investigated cases of SSP and SMP examined during the 1990/91 tax year. The proportion of SSP and SMP cases with errors were 25 per cent and 29 per cent respectively (see Reference (13) at 8.20 below). Attempts at deregulation and the increasing availability of good payroll software may have helped reduce the error rate although there is no evidence to hand to demonstrate this. It is also the case that, while most cases of entitlement to either SSP and SMP are straightforward, there will from time to time be individual cases of simply mind-boggling complexity.

The complexity, to be fair on the parliamentary draftsmen, can, in part be simply seen as the inevitable result of seeking to establish a universal level of minimum earnings for employees at times when they are sick or around the time they are to have a baby, while at the same time trying to be flexible to different working situations and the legitimate need of employers to exercise absence control.

The disability, maternity and family leave benefits dealt with in this chapter can be classified under the following headings:

(*a*)   ***Short-term sickness*** — Occupational sick pay (OSP) schemes, which form part of the contract of employment, are usually financed completely by the employer, although there are some OSP schemes to which the employee will contribute on a quasi-self insured basis. OSP schemes are practically always short-term, meaning that the payments will normally cease after a specified continuous period of entitlement, say, six months or so. Payments made under OSP schemes offset the employers' liability to pay SSP. Of course, where an employer makes OSP provision, SSP acts as the statutory, default short-term sickness benefit.

In practice, it is important from an absence control point of view to distinguish between an employee who has frequent, but short periods, of sickness absence and an employee who has had very few days of sickness absence in the past but who then becomes ill for an extended period. SSP attempts to distinguish between the two sickness patterns by not giving any entitlement until an employee has been sick for four working days, although once a four day period of incapacity for work (PIW) has been established, payment will be due for any subsequent days of incapacity for work falling within the eight weeks of the end of the first PIW. It is rare, however, to find OSP schemes which distinguish between the two patterns.

(b) **Long-term disability** — There are three basic approaches taken by employers when an employee is long-term sick or disabled and payments under the OSP or SSP provision have been exhausted. The employee's contract can be terminated — sickness absence is potentially grounds for a fair dismissal at any time provided proper consultation and consideration of the medical evidence has been carried out.

A second option is that the employer may provide, on either an insured or a self-insured basis, a Group Permanent Health Insurance (PHI) provision, a scheme to provide salary continuance to those who are long-term sick or disabled. The individual who is long-term sick continues to be an employee on the employer's payroll. For this reason, Group PHI schemes are sometimes known as 'salary continuance schemes'. If the Group PHI scheme is insured, the insurer will assess whether or not a benefit becomes payable under the insurance contract whatever the employer may have promised to the employee under the contract of employment. This could result in an employer having a liability to pay salary continuance to a long-term sick employee but being refused reimbursement from the insurance company.

A third possibility is that the employee may be a member of an occupational pension scheme sponsored by the employer. In which case the trustees of the scheme may have discretion under the trust deed and rules of the scheme to pay an early retirement pension. In this situation the long-term sick person retires and ceases to be on the employer's payroll.

(c) **Maternity benefits** — An employer may provide a contractual maternity pay scheme, or indeed, may provide contractual maternity pay under the same terms as the occupational sick pay scheme. In such cases, payments made under the employer's scheme will offset any liability to pay the employee SMP. However, it is common to find that the only pay benefits to be made are those required by the SMP scheme. In considering maternity benefits it is important to draw a distinction between the statutory requirement to make, in most cases, payments to the employee under the SMP social security scheme and the separate statutory requirements under the employment legislation to grant the employee a period of maternity leave. In fact, any employee who is about to give birth has a right to a period of maternity leave but there will be some employees who do not have the right to receive payments under the SMP scheme i.e. there is a universal right to maternity leave but not to paid maternity leave.

The fact that maternity leave comes under the employment legislation while maternity pay comes under the social legislation has given rise to a number of anomalies – some of which will be removed under the proposals contained in the Government's *'Fairness at Work'* White Paper. An example is that all employees who are expecting a baby have a right under the employment legislation to a period of at least 14 week's unpaid maternity leave. Employees who have two years' continuous employment as at the 11th week before their baby is expected have a right to an extended leave period running for 29 weeks from the start of the week in which their baby is born. Employees who have 26 weeks' continuous employment as at the 15th week before the week their baby is expected have the right to 18 weeks' SSP from their employer provided they have stopped working for that employer. As a result, those employees who have a right to SMP but not to an extended leave period must sacrifice four weeks' SMP entitlement if they wish to ensure their right to continued employment with their employer. It is proposed that the minimum 14 weeks' maternity leave period will be extended to 18 weeks.

(*d*)   *Family leave* — The Government's recent White Paper 'Fairness at Work' sets out a series of measures that will implement in domestic legislation the requirements of the *European Parental Leave Directive*. These include:

- three months' parental leave for men and women when they have a baby or adopt a child, plus protection from dismissal for exercising this right;

- time off for urgent family reasons to help employees look after a sick child or deal with a crisis at home.

The White Paper indicates that domestic legislation will be introduced by December 1999. However, the White Paper also emphasises that the Government wishes to achieve a coherent package, including existing maternity rights, which both support employees who are parents but also supports employers' competitiveness.

The *Parental Leave Directive* is flexible about how family leave should be taken:

- in a single block or as an annual allowance;

- full or part-time;

> - at any time up to the child's eight birthday or a lower age, or with some required to be taken at the time of birth or adoption; or
>
> - under individual arrangements agreed between the employer and the employee.

Income tax and National Insurance treatment of the benefit

8.2   Occupational sick pay (OSP) schemes, statutory sick pay (SSP), contractual maternity pay and statutory maternity pay (SMP) are all paid by the employer's payroll department through the PAYE system. All these payments count as taxable pay and also as gross pay for National Insurance contributions purposes. (There is an exception in the case of any OSP or contractual maternity pay scheme where a proportion of the benefit paid derives from contributions paid by the employee to fund against the eventuality. In such cases, the proportion of the benefit derived from the employee's own contributions is payable free of income tax and National Insurance contributions.)

It should be noted that the weekly rate of SSP and the flat weekly rate of SMP payable after the first six weeks are both set at less than the current lower earnings limit (LEL) for National Insurance purposes. As a result, if the employee does not receive any other payments in excess of these minimum statutory payments, there will be no liability to pay National Insurance contributions. Although for earnings less than the LEL, for social security benefit purposes, the DSS will credit the employee with earnings equal to the LEL while in receipt of either SSP or SMP.

In the case of a Group Permanent Health Insurance (PHI) policy, any premiums paid by the employer to the insurance company are not regarded as a benefit-in-kind for the employees covered by the scheme. As a result, the employees face no income tax liability on the value of the premiums paid. Nor is there any National Insurance contributions liability on the value of the premiums. In the event that an employee becomes long-term sick or disabled, he or she will normally remain on the employer's payroll. Any PHI benefit is paid by the insurance company direct to the employer. The employer will then pay the benefit to the employee through PAYE so that income tax and National Insurance contributions are deducted in the normal way. If the individual subsequently ceases to be an employee but remains entitled to the PHI benefit, the insurance company will normally assume responsibility for paying the benefit directly to the employee via the PAYE system.

In cases where ill-health leads to the early retirement of an employee, and a pension comes into payment from the occupational pension scheme, the PAYE procedure is the same as in any retirement – see Chapter 21 (Pension Payroll

Procedures). At retirement the individual has ceased to be an employee and comes off the company payroll. Pensions payable by an exempt approved occupational pension scheme are taxable but no National Insurance contributions are payable.

Where the long-term ill are no longer in employment and so are not paying National Insurance contributions, the DSS will credit them with earnings at the LEL for social security benefit credit purposes provided they are entitled to receive the State incapacity benefit.

Ex gratia lump sum payments not exceeding £30,000 made by an employer to an employee to compensate for loss of employment through disability, injury or ill health are not liable to income tax or National Insurance contributions (see 8.18 below).

Controlling absenteeism

8.3   The levels of absence through sickness vary particularly between different types of business. A survey by the CBI suggested that on average one million workers are absent sick on any given day. As this is both disruptive and expensive, employers need to monitor and control sickness along with other types of absence. The withdrawal of employers' reimbursement of 80 per cent SSP back in April 1994 has accentuated this need and there are many manual and computer systems available both for benefits administration and absence monitoring.

Sickness, injuries and industrial diseases must be recorded and notified in accordance with the statutory requirements. Departmental inspectors have powers of entry, to require interviews, view records, etc. and compel disclosures as stated in Chapter 12 (National Insurance Contributions). Employers also sometimes define their own notification requirements for their OSP scheme to operate in parallel to the statutory requirements. However, procedures such as notification requirements for an OSP scheme may be more rigorous than those acceptable for SSP, for instance a medical statement from a GP (General Practitioner) must be provided by the employee after seven days in a period of sickness absence.

SSP has proved costly because of extra administration and employment costs. There have, of course, been some positive benefits to employers in that it has focused attention on the problems of absenteeism and forced them to be more effective in controlling and monitoring their sickness procedures. An absence rate of five per cent in the case of a company with 3,000 employees is the equivalent of employing an extra 150 employees. Based on a modest average annual pay per head of £12,000, sickness costs £1.8 million per annum on this basis, excluding all other costs.

With some restrictions the employer decides what rules should apply for SSP regarding notification of sickness, either by telephone or in writing or both. The employer must take reasonable steps to make the rules known to its employees, e.g. including them as part of the terms and conditions of employment. In addition the employer cannot demand notification before the first qualifying day, nor can it require notification using any particular document such as a medical certificate or an in-house form. However, if no rules exist, then an employee is still entitled to SSP providing the employer is notified no later than the seventh calendar day after a qualifying day of absence. If the employee is late in notifying his absence for one or more qualifying days, and the employer is not satisfied as to the reason given for the lateness, the employer may withhold SSP for the same number of qualifying days.

The employer can ask its employees to provide reasonable evidence of incapacity, for instance a 'self-certificate' for periods of one to seven days (or longer) or a doctor's statement for spells of more than seven days. A self-certificate is a form signed by an employee giving details of his or her sickness. It is for the employer to decide whether the employee is incapable of work or not. The employer can refuse to pay SSP if it has good reason not to pay. The employee can then have recourse to the new appeal system established by the *Social Security Act 1998*. The onus is on the employer to control sickness absence.

There are a number of key elements in any effective policy to control sickness absence:

(*a*)   the effective recording of each sickness absence;

(*b*)   the effective analysis of absence statistics to identify where particular absence problems are developing;

(*c*)   the involvement of middle management and line managers in monitoring sickness absences;

(*d*)   clearly communicating any absence policy to all employees;

(*e*)   providing an occupational health service for periodic general checks to prevent illness and for the examination of employees who are often sick;

(*f*)   conducting return to work interviews with employees after a period of sickness;

(*g*)   the proper enforcement of disciplinary procedures in cases where absence becomes a disciplinary matter;

(*h*)   more effective recruitment checks before a new employee is hired.

It should be emphasised, of course, these tasks fall first and foremost a personnel and line management issue rather than a task for the payroll department. But because of the payroll in operating the SSP sickness, or an OSP scheme that ensures that the SSP requirements are always met, it may well be the case that the payroll department will sometimes have the primary role in recording sickness absences and carrying out the effective analysis of sickness absences.

In some OSP schemes, the individual is allowed a specified number of days of sickness absence on full pay in any pre-defined period of time. Once that threshold is passed, the individual will only receive his or her SSP entitlement. In some OSP schemes, both individual and general limiting thresholds are in place. For example, each employee might be able to receive full pay for up to 14 days sickness absence in any calendar year but after 14 days the individual will only receive his or her SSP entitlement. However, this entitlement can be subject to an overall absenteeism control that would mean that all sick pay cover in excess of the SSP entitlement would discontinue if the total number of sickness absences in any one month ever exceeded three per cent of all attendances.

For any such OSP systems to work, it is vital that sickness absences can be correctly monitored. There are three main measures in common use:

(i)   lost time rate;

(ii)   frequency rate;

(iii)   individual frequency rate.

The lost time rate is defined as:

$$\frac{\text{Total absence (hours or days) in the period}}{\text{Possible total hours or days available}} \times 100$$

The frequency rate is useful in showing the average number of spells of absence per employee irrespective of the length of each spell. It is defined as:

$$\frac{\text{Number of spells of absence in the period}}{\text{Number of employees in the period}} \times 100$$

The individual frequency rate shows the number of employees absent at all during a period of time. It is defined as:

$$\frac{\text{Number of employees having one or more spells of absence}}{\text{Number of employees}} \times 100$$

It may be thought important, in the application of an OPP system, to be able to distinguish between an employee who has many frequent, short periods of sickness absence and an employee who has a good attendance record until a more lengthy period of sickness ensures. Of course, it would be unjustifiable automatically to describe the first employee as a malingerer. Proper investigation would be required – for example, the frequent short periods of sickness absence may be because the employee has a medical condition that requires frequent periods of treatment such as kidney dialysis.

A team at Bradford University have suggested a measure, known as the 'Bradford Factor' which measures an employee's irregularity of attendance. The formula is given by:

$$P = S^2 \times D$$

where:

P = the number of absence points marked up by the employee;

S = the number of spells of absence in, say, the last 52 weeks;

D = the number of days absence during the same period.

Employee A who has been sick for one spell lasting ten days during the last 52 weeks – Employee A only notches up $1 \times 10 = 10$ absence points.

Employee B has been sick for two spells each lasting five days during the last 52 weeks – Employee B notches up $(2 \times 2) \times 10 = 40$ absence points.

Employee C has been sick for five spells each lasting two days during the last 52 weeks – Employee C notches up $(5 \times 5) \times 10 = 250$ absence points.

Employee D has been sick for ten spells, each last one day during the last 52 weeks – Employee D notches up $(10 \times 10) \times 10 = 1,000$ absence points.

An employer may wish to implement an OSP system which reduces an individual's entitlement to full pay during sickness, subject to the flexibility to respond to extenuating circumstances and the need to observe the SSP requirements, when that individual's number of absence points exceeds a predetermined level.

Statutory sick pay

8.4   In April 1983 the Government shifted much of the onus for the payment of State sickness pay from the DHSS (as the DSS was then) onto employers. From then on employers had to pay statutory sick pay on behalf of the State under *SSHBA 1982*, the amending legislation and associated regulations. The principal regulations are the *Statutory Sick Pay (General) Regulations 1982 (SI 1982 No 894)*, which have been substantially amended over the years.

Employers have the responsibility for administering and paying SSP for the first 28 weeks of qualifying illness. They are normally unable to recover any of the SSP payment from the Government. However, since 6 April 1995 when the percentage threshold scheme (PTS) came into operation, employers have been able in certain circumstances to recover a proportion of SSP in a tax month. (See 8.14 below.)

SSP is payable on a daily basis by the employer to most employees who have earnings which attract liability for Class 1 NICs. Certain employees are excluded from the SSP scheme, such as people who are on small earnings below the National Insurance lower earnings limit and those aged over 65. A list of employees who are not eligible for SSP is given in 8.5 below. State incapacity benefit may be payable to employees who do not qualify for SSP. SSP daily rates are very low and are shown in the current issue of DSS leaflet CA35/36. (See also Appendix D.)

Example — Mary, who works part-time, earns £70.00 per week and is eligible for SSP. After the first three qualifying days of sickness, for which she receives no SSP, she is then entitled to £57.70 for each week of sickness. If her average weekly earnings had been less than £64.00 she would not have been entitled to SSP.

SSP is payable for a maximum of 28 weeks in any one period of entitlement.

Only where the SSP paid exceeds 13 per cent of total NIC liability in the tax month can recovery in part be made from the NICs paid to the Inland Revenue under PAYE procedures by virtue of the percentage threshold scheme (PTS). (See 8.11 and 20.12 below.) Details of any amounts of SSP recovered from tax and NICs payable to the Inland Revenue Accounts Office must be recorded on Form P14 (or substitute) and Form P35 (or substitute).

If SSP is due for a particular day, any other payment made for that day (and which is earnings for NIC purposes) will count towards the employer's liability to pay SSP for that day. Conversely, a payment of SSP for a day goes towards the employer's liability to make a contractual payment for that day. [*SSCBA 1992, 12 Sch*]. The most frequent situation is where the employee is entitled to OSP for the day, but the same principle can be applied to other payments due under the contract of employment, for example, in respect of bank, public or annual holidays.

Example — Mark is absent sick over the Christmas period. His employer pays him under his contract of employment for Christmas Day, Boxing Day, New Year's Day and the in-between company 'shutdown' days (which had been designated as part of the annual holiday entitlement). Mark is also entitled to SSP throughout the period. The contractual payments in respect of the annual and public holidays can meet in part or full the employer's duty to pay SSP for those days.

OSP due under the contract of employment is sometimes specified as additional to SSP. The total sick pay (SSP plus OSP) is often made up to a defined level, i.e. full or half basic pay. In the example above Mary's SSP might be supplemented under her OSP scheme to give her the basic pay of £70.00 per week as total sick pay.

Applying the SSP rules

8.5   Since 6 April 1997, an employer may choose whether or not to operate all the rules of the SSP scheme provided the employer pays contractual remuneration to an employee for the days he or she qualifies for SSP at a rate which is at or above the SSP pay rate. The contractual remuneration can take the form of the normal rate of salary or wages or any other form of OSP provision which meets the minimum SSP entitlement. However, the employer must still keep basic records of sickness absence and amounts paid so that a National Insurance Inspector can check that any employee has received his or her full entitlement. Furthermore, the employer must also still keep sufficient records to complete the following forms:

(*a*)   Form SSP1 (or an in-house computerised version of it) so that employees can claim the State incapacity benefit when they have received 28 weeks' entitlement to SSP or, if earlier, they have exhausted their entitlement to OSP and for some reason they were not entitled to SSP – see 8.6 below.

(*b*)   Form SSP1(L) if asked to do so by an employee who is leaving that employment – see below.

This means that in practice, an employer's payroll department must still always record the following details even if the employer provides an OSP scheme that is more generous than SSP:

  (i)   the first day for which SSP liability arises (note that this is not necessarily the same as the first recorded day of sickness because of the effect of waiting days – see below);

 (ii)   the last day for which SSP liability arises (note again that this is not necessarily the same as the last recorded day of sickness);

(iii)   the number of weeks and days of SSP entitlement;

(iv)   the number and pattern of qualifying days for SSP purposes (see 8.6 below).

The operation of the Percentage Threshold Scheme (see 8.14 below) is unaffected by whether or not the employer can be said to be operating all the rules of the SSP scheme.

Employers remain liable to pay SSP to any employee if that employee satisfies the qualifying conditions for any day of incapacity where contractual remuneration is not paid for that day or paid at less than the SSP rate for that day. Given this requirement, it is difficult to know exactly what it intended by the phrase used by the DSS, 'freedom from operating the SSP scheme'.

SSP has many complications and this goes some way to explain the high error rate in dealing with the scheme. Figure 8A contains a summary of the SSP entitlement rules, the main features of which are explained below. Many of these SSP rules and procedures are, of course, often integrated with those for OSP to avoid duplication. However, as explained above, an employer cannot impose conditions for SSP which are stricter than the law requires.

Before SSP is due there must be a period of four or more days' sickness in a row. All days including weekends and holidays are counted. This is called a PIW. Shorter periods of sickness do not count for SSP as they are not PIWs. SSP is not paid for the first three qualifying days in a PIW or two or more 'linked' PIWs. These first three days are called 'waiting days'. 'Qualifying days' are usually working days and are explained below. A period of entitlement to SSP can be defined as either one continuous PIW or a series of 'linked' PIWs. PIWs are considered linked if there are not more than eight weeks between them. PIWs which are linked together count as one PIW. Linking also provides a method of measuring the total period of SSP entitlement to ensure that it does not exceed 28 weeks. PIWs with different employers are not usually linked. Figure 8B below contains examples of linked periods.

In rare cases the linking periods could be such that the PIWs span a period of four or more years. To avoid employers having to keep records for this period of time, there is a cut-off period at the end of three years. For example, if a PIW begins on 22 July 1996, and maximum entitlement still has not been reached by 22 July 1999, SSP liability in that PIW ends. Such a situation could arise if there is a series of linked PIWs, each lasting only a few days and never separated by more than eight weeks. SSP liability only restarts when there is a subsequent unlinked PIW. A period of entitlement could also be terminated by other events, such as the expiry of the contract of employment.

8.6   An employer must determine which days qualify for sickness. In most instances qualifying days are normal working days under the contract of employment, but they do not have to be so defined. The employer can, however, agree with its employees any pattern of qualifying days subject to two rules. First, there must be at least one qualifying day in each week beginning with a Sunday, and second, qualifying days must not be defined by reference to the days of an employee's sickness. Thus, for instance, where staff work on a shift basis, certain days of the week may be designated as qualifying days irrespective of the days actually worked in any one week.

Certain employees are automatically excluded, and they are:

(*a*)   members of HM Forces; and

(*b*)   foreign-going mariners.

Figure 8A

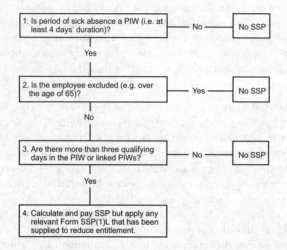

Illustration of a simplified summary of SSP entitlement rules

Figure 8B

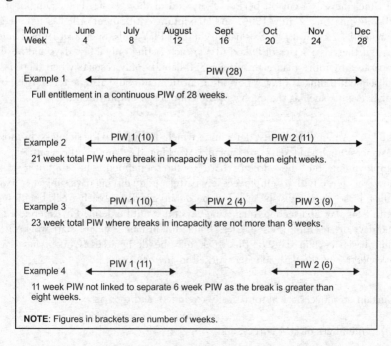

Illustration of linking periods of incapacity for work (PIWs)

As already mentioned some employees are excluded from the SSP scheme and may be able to claim incapacity benefit from the DSS. In essence, an employee is excluded from SSP if on the first day of the PIW, linked or unlinked:

   (i) he or she is over age 65;

  (ii) the contract of service is for three months or less;

 (iii) he or she has average weekly earnings less than the LEL in force on the first day of the PIW;

  (iv) he or she is within 57 days of receiving a relevant State benefit;

   (v) no work has been done under the contract of service;

  (vi) he or she is involved in a strike;

 (vii) he or she has already been due 28 weeks of SSP from previous employers and an SSP1(L) Form is operative;

(viii) he or she is in legal custody;

  (ix) in the case of a woman, in addition, she can be disqualified from SSP due to pregnancy. This normally happens when the employee receives SMP or State maternity allowance (MA). If a pregnant employee is absent from work with a pregnancy-related illness in the six weeks before the EWC (expected week of confinement), SSP is not payable;

   (x) he or she is under 16 years of age;

  (xi) either the employee or the employer is outside the jurisdictional limits of the scheme.

In addition, employees who were sick and had a PIW which began before 6 April 1996 and were, or subsequently went, outside the European Economic Area are not entitled to SSP during that or any subsequent linked PIW. This exclusion does not apply in the case of employees whose PIW began on or after 6 April 1996.

8.7   It is important to note that the application of the exclusion depends usually on the situation at the beginning of the first linked PIW with the current employer. Some exclusions can have effect during a PIW and apply from that date. The employer is legally obliged to complete a Form SSP1 or an equivalent in-house version for each PIW where an exclusion applies. The form gives the reasons for not paying SSP as one or more of the above exclusion conditions. Figure 8C below is an illustration of the Form SSP1 issued to employees who are excluded from SSP or who are about to exhaust their SSP entitlement. The SSP1 'change-over' form is used both to explain to an employee why he or she is excluded from SSP and also to facilitate the transfer to State benefits. The form (or an in-house equivalent) should normally be handed or sent to the employee not later than seven days after the employer was notified that the employee's sickness would last at least four days.

Alternatively, the time limit is the first pay day in the tax month following the one in which the reason for issuing the form arose but only if the employer's payroll arrangements are such that it is impracticable to issue the form within seven days. However, the time limits are stricter in the case where the employee's entitlement to SSP is ending because he or she is due 28 weeks' SSP in a PIW. (See 8.11 below).

SSP is not paid for the first three qualifying days in a period of entitlement. These three days are deemed to be 'waiting days', and hence payment of SSP commences from and includes the fourth qualifying day. In many instances there are less than four qualifying days and therefore no SSP is payable.

Three simple cases which illustrate the significance of qualifying days and PIWs are shown below (Monday to Friday are qualifying days).

Case 1

August 1998								September 1998						
Su	M	T	W	Th	F	S	Su	Su	M	T	W	Th	F	S
2	3	4	5	6	7	8	9	6	7	8	9	10	11	12
S	S	S	S	S	S	S	S		S	S	S			
	W	W	W	P	P			(no PIW)						

Case 2

July 1998															
Su	M	T	W	Th	F	S	Su	M	T	W	Th	F	S	Su	M
5	6	7	8	9	10	11	12	13	14	15	16	17	18	19	20
	S	S	S	S	S	S	S	S			S	S	S	S	
	W	W	W	P				P	P		P	P			

Case 3

July 1998											
F	S	Su	M	T	W	Th	F	S	Su	M	T
10	11	12	13	14	15	16	17	18	19	20	21
S	S	S	S				S	S	S	S	
W			W			W				P	

Note: The symbols are as follows:
S = Sick   W = Waiting day   P = SSP payable

Case 1 — The second period of sickness is not long enough to make a PIW.

Case 2 — The second period of sickness is long enough to make a PIW and links to the first PIW. Hence they are regarded as one PIW and no further waiting days occur.

Case 3 — Both periods are long enough to make a PIW, and link together. In each period there are two qualifying days. The Friday and Monday of the first PIW and the Friday of the second PIW are treated as the three waiting days.

8.8   Incapacity for work can be demonstrated in a number of ways. The most common instance will be where a doctor or other medical practitioner, such as an osteopath or chiropractor, certifies that an individual is incapable of, or should refrain from, work. An individual does not have to be sick to be entitled to SSP. For example, an employee could have broken her glasses or misplaced his contact lenses, damaged an artificial limb, be convalescing, carrying an infectious disease or refraining from work on doctor's orders as a medical precaution.

An employer decides if SSP is payable on the basis of the evidence available. If the employer decides not to pay, the employee can request a written statement. The employee has the right to challenge the decision through the appeal procedure established by the *Social Security Act 1998*. A Form SSP1 must be given to those people who are excluded from the SSP provisions, for instance, employees working under a contract for a specified period of three months or less.

8.9   A single weekly rate of SSP has applied since 6 April 1995. (See Appendix D for the current rate.) No SSP is payable to employees whose average earnings are below the LEL. The daily rate of SSP is the weekly rate divided by the number of qualifying days in the week concerned. For example, if the weekly rate is £57.70 and a week contains five qualifying days, then the daily rate is £57.70 ÷ 5 = £11.54. Note that the daily rate will vary between weeks in a period of absence if the number of qualifying days varies, say, because of shift rota working.

SSP is subject to income tax, NICs and attachment of earnings orders. Voluntary deductions, e.g. trade union dues and overpayments, may also be deducted/recovered from SSP. There are no additional payments for dependants.

The calculation of average weekly earnings for SSP is described in the Contributions Agency's Manual CA30. The main situations are outlined below.

(a)   ***Weekly-paid employees (including fortnightly and four-weekly)*** — The gross earnings are totalled, in most cases, over the last eight pay periods ending with the last normal pay day before the PIW, unlinked or linked, began and divided by eight. In making the calculation, earnings must include SSP, OSP, SMP, bonuses, overtime etc.

Under new arrangements adopted from April 1998, the payments can be divided by the number of weeks covered by the payments, rather than the number of weeks in the period, provided that:

(i)   the employee is paid weekly (or in multiples of a week); *and*

(ii)   a normal payment has been made so that the 'relevant period' contains more, or less than, eight weeks' pay or is not an exact number of weeks.

Guidance is given in the CA30 supplement dated April 1998 issued by the Contributions Agency.

(b)   ***Monthly-paid employees*** — The calculation of average weekly earnings for monthly paid employees has been the subject of some controversy. Paragraph 49 of the April 1997 issue of the Contributions Agency's Statutory Sick Pay Manual CA30 gives revised guidance.

Average weekly earnings for monthly paid employees are calculated as follows.

First it is important to work out the period over which to average earnings. This period ends with the last normal payday before the PIW began and starts with the day after the last normal payday which was at least eight weeks before that.

All the gross payments made to the employee in that period should be added together and the sum divided by the nearest number of calendar months in that period. The result should be multiplied by 12 and divided by 52.

Example — The Contributions Agency gives the following example.

An employee is sick from 22 December 1997 to 3 January 1998. Her contract does not specify when she is to be paid. It is her employer's practice to pay employees their December salary early but, apart from that, employees are paid on the last working day of each month.

The last normal payday before the PIW is 20 December 1997 since the December salary is paid early. The last payday at least eight weeks before that is 30 September 1997. The period over which to average the employee's earnings is 1 October–20 December 1997. In that period, the employer paid the employee in question £1,254.16 on 31 October, £1,254.16 on 30 November and £1,254.16 on 20 December.

Total earnings in the period   =   £3,762.48

The payment covers 3 months (2 months and 20 days is rounded up)
$$((£3,762.48 \div 3) \times 12) \div 15$$

=   £289.42154 average weekly
earnings

(See Reference (20) in 8.20 below for a discussion of how to determine the number of calendar months in the 'eight week' period before a PIW.)

Special calculations are required to identify the level of average earnings for both new employees who become entitled to SSP but for whom either insufficient or no pay days are available, and for those employees who are paid monthly in multiples of weeks, for example, four weeks one month, five weeks in another month.

Figure 8C

SSP1–9/97

Claim form

Statutory Sick Pay (SSP) and Incapacity Benefit

About this form

There are **4** sections in this form.

Section 1
is for the employer to give information about Statutory Sick Pay (SSP). Notes for the employer about when to fill in this form are on **page 2** of this form.

Sections 2, 3 and **4**
are for the employee to claim Incapacity Benefit.

Statutory Sick Pay is money paid by employers to employees who are away from work for 4 days or more in a row because they are sick.

Incapacity Benefit is a social security benefit you may be able to get if you are still sick when your SSP ends or if you cannot get SSP.

Section 1

About SSP and your employee

About your employee

Please tell us about your employee

Surname

Other names

National Insurance (NI) number

Letters   Numbers   Letter

Clock or payroll number

Tax reference number

1

Illustration of Form SSP 1

165

Why you cannot get Statutory Sick Pay

I am filling in this form because

☐ I cannot pay you SSP

☐ I cannot pay you SSP after [/ /]

I have ticked a box to tell you why you cannot get SSP. The notes on **pages 4** and **5** explain the reasons in more detail.

I cannot pay you SSP because

A ☐ You claimed Incapacity Benefit, Severe Disablement Allowance or Maternity Allowance during the last 8 weeks, so you may be able to get Incapacity Benefit instead of SSP.

B ☐ Your contract of employment has expired.

C ☐ Your contract of employment has been brought to an end.

D ☐ You will soon have been getting SSP for 28 weeks or you have already had SSP for 28 weeks.

E ☐ You have not earned enough money.

F ☐ You are only going to work for me for 3 months or less.

G ☐ You are aged 65 or over.

H ☐ You are expecting a baby soon or you have just had a baby.

J ☐ You have already been sick on and off for 3 years.

K ☐ You were away from work because of a trade dispute on the first day you were sick.

L ☐ You were in legal custody or you were serving a term of imprisonment when you became sick.
Or you are now in legal custody or sentenced to a term of imprisonment.

M ☐ You were not in the European Economic Area (EEA) on the first day you were sick or you are not in the EEA now. But if you are sick on or after 6 April 1996 see **page 5** *Changes to SSP from 6 April 1996 – outside the EEA.*

N ☐ You have not started working for me yet.

3

Illustration of Form SSP 1 (continued)

More information we need

The employee's first day of sickness

To work out this date you will need to check
- your sick records for this employee, and
- any form **SSP1(L)** *Leaver's statement of SSP* from a previous employer.

If your employee has a form **SSP1(L)** from a previous employer and has been off work sick for 4 days or more within 8 weeks and one day of **date 2** on their **SSP1(L)**, the first day of sickness is **date 1** on form **SSP1(L)**.

If your employee has had 2 or more spells of sickness of 4 days or more in a row which were 8 weeks or less apart, the first day of sickness is the first day they were off work sick at the beginning of these spells of sickness.

For all other employees who have been off work sick for 4 days or more in a row, the first day of sickness is the first day they were off work sick.

The first day of sickness is [/   /   ]

About the SSP you have paid

How many weeks and days of SSP will have been paid to this employee when SSP ends?
Count from the first day you have paid SSP up to and including the date you have written on **page 3** of this form. If you are including any SSP paid by a previous employer, count from **date 1** on their form **SSP1(L)**.

[weeks   days]

How many qualifying days are there in the last week that SSP is due?
Count the number of qualifying days in the full week, not just the number of days they can get SSP for. Remember, for most employees qualifying days are the days of the week that they normally work.

[days]

6

Illustration of Form SSP 1 (continued)

Employer's declaration

I declare
that the information I have given is correct and complete.

I understand
that if this employee has been getting SSP, I must continue to pay SSP until the
date I have written on **page 3** of this form.

Employer's name

Signature

Date   /   /

Position in firm

Phone number and extension   extension

Fax number

Address

                    Postcode

Business stamp

SPECIMEN

What to do next

Please place this form and the notes sheet in the wallet which
came with this claim pack. Send the wallet to your employee
with any medical certificates that cover a period you cannot pay
SSP for.
Medical certificates are also called sick notes or doctor's
statements.

7

Illustration of Form SSP 1 (continued)

8.10   A new employee need no longer be asked for the DSS Form SSP1(L) which may be issued by the former employer. This form contains details of the SSP entitlement claimed by the employee in his or her previous employment. However, since 6 April 1996 an employer is only required to complete form SSP1(L) if asked to do so by the employee and the new employer is not required to ask a new employee if he or she had been given form SSP1(L) by a previous employer. As part of the general procedures for dealing with new employees, a form similar to that shown in Figure 8D below can be issued. Manual CA 30 provides, at paragraph 52, advice to employers of new employees.

Figure 8D

The Polygon Toy Company Ltd

The following information is required for SSP purposes. Please tick the relevant items.

Have you been receiving any of the following State benefits during the past eight weeks?

(*a*)   Incapacity benefit.

(*b*)   Maternity allowance.

(*c*)   Severe disablement allowance.

My benefit was stopped on the .... and I enclose a DSS 'linking letter'.

I declare that I have not received any of the above benefits during the past eight weeks.

I have obtained a SSP1(L) Form from a previous employer.

Signature of employee .... Date ....

An illustration of a simple internal form requesting SSP details from a new employee

Where the gap between the last day on which SSP was payable with the previous employer and the first day of a PIW with the new employer is less than 57 days, then any Form SSP1(L) is operative. The new employer's SSP liability is reduced by the number of weeks shown on the Form. For example, where a Form SSP1(L) in such circumstances shows seven weeks' SSP was paid by the previous employer the new employer's SSP liability is reduced from 28 to 21 weeks. Where the Form is not operative because the time gap is too wide the new employer's SSP liability remains at 28 weeks. But the two PIWs do not otherwise link – i.e. the PIW with the new employer begins with three 'waiting days'.

When an employee is ill at the beginning of the twenty-third week of SSP entitlement, the employer must provide that employee with a Form SSP1 (or in-house equivalent) which eases the transfer from SSP to DSS paid benefit at the expiry of the twenty-eighth week. The employee may return to work between receiving the Form SSP1 and the expiry of the 28 weeks. In that event the employer should at once issue a further Form SSP1 if there is another linking period. Where the liability is due to end before the twenty-third week of SSP, for example, because the contract of employment is due to end, a Form SSP1 should be issued two weeks before the liability is due to end. It should also be issued where the liability ends unexpectedly before the twenty-third week of SSP as soon as it is known it will end or has ended. If the employee's contract of service is ending the employer may also be asked by the employee to issue a leaver's statement Form SSP1(L).

8.11   Since the inception of the SSP scheme, the amount of SSP that employers can recover from the State has been subject to review and change. The full amounts paid and a percentage of those amounts (being NIC compensation) used to be recoverable from the monthly (or quarterly) remittances of PAYE income tax and NICs to the Inland Revenue. However, there have been significant changes to employers' rights to recover SSP in recent years.

(*a*)   The enactment of the *Statutory Sick Pay Act 1991* on 12 February 1991 brought about the following changes to the statutory sick pay scheme:

   (i)   recovery of SSP was restricted to 80 per cent of the amount of the SSP paid;

   (ii)   the NIC compensation based on the amount of SSP paid was abolished;

   (iii)   relief for small employers was introduced. Small employers were able to recover 100 per cent of the SSP paid in a PIW, after there had been liability to pay six weeks' SSP. SSP could only be recovered for the days beyond the six weeks mark. A small employer was one whose total NICs (primary and secondary contributions) in the qualifying tax year were not more than £16,000.

(*b*)   The enactment of the *Statutory Sick Pay Act 1994* on 6 April 1994 brought about the following changes:

   (i)   recovery of SSP was abolished;

   (ii)   small employers were able to recover 100 per cent of SSP paid in a PIW, after there had been liability to pay four weeks' SSP. SSP could only be recovered for the days beyond the four weeks mark. The definition of 'small employer' was changed, to be those whose total NICs in the qualifying tax year were not more than £20,000.

(c) The enactment of the *Statutory Sick Pay Act 1994* also provided for a new SSP compensation scheme to apply from 6 April 1995. The following changes were introduced by the *Statutory Sick Pay Percentage Threshold Order 1995 (SI 1995 No 512)*:

  (i) the small employer's relief scheme, was abolished;

  (ii) a new SSP compensation scheme, the Percentage Threshold Scheme (PTS), was made available to all employers.

The position in the 1998/99 tax year for SSP is as follows:

The employer may be able to recover a portion of the SSP by means of the percentage threshold scheme (PTS). The PTS allows an employer to recover the amount of SSP paid in a tax month which exceeds a specified percentage (13 per cent for the 1998/99 tax year) of gross (primary and secondary) Class 1 NIC liability in the same tax month. For example, if gross Class 1 NIC liability is £1,000, and the SSP paid is £210.00, then an amount of £80 (calculated as: £210 – £130 (£1,000 × 13%) can be recovered.

There are two features which should be considered when making calculations to identify the amount, if any, of SSP to be recovered. First, where there is more than one PAYE reference for the employer, then the amounts of gross Class 1 NIC liability and SSP for the separate payrolls are to be aggregated for the purposes of PTS calculations (*Statutory Sick Pay Percentage Threshold Order 1995 (Consequential) Regulations 1995 (SI 1995 No 513)*). Secondly, where SSP is paid later than the month following the month in which the incapacity for work occurred, the relevant amount of SSP is required by legislation to be excluded from the PTS calculations (*Statutory Sick Pay Percentage Threshold Order 1995 (SI 1995 No 512)*).

Statutory maternity pay

8.12 SMP replaced the previous maternity pay scheme with effect from 6 April 1987. [*SSA 1986, ss 46–50, 4 Sch*]. It is payable by the employer. State maternity allowance may still be payable to those women who do not qualify for SMP. Full details are given in the Contributions Agency SMP Manual CA29 issued in April 1997, but a brief outline of the SMP is given below. Significant changes to SMP (and the State maternity allowance) were introduced for pregnant employees with an expected week of confinement (EWC) commencing on or after 16 October 1994. These changes transpose *EC Directive 92/85/EEC* (the 'pregnant workers' Directive) into UK law.

(a) For SMP purposes, an employee is a woman over the age of 16 whose normal average weekly earnings for the period of eight weeks ending with the week immediately preceding the 14th week before the expected week of confinement (EWC) are not less than the LEL in force before the start of the 14th week. The employer is defined as whoever is liable to pay the employer's share of NICs and could, in certain cases, include a previous employer or concurrent second employer.

(b)   SMP has two elements: an earnings-related amount of 90 per cent of average earnings payable for up to six weeks, and a flat rate amount payable for the remainder of the maternity pay period (MPP).

Earnings-related SMP is payable to an employee in the latter stages of pregnancy and/or after giving birth provided she has worked for the same liable employer for a continuous period of at least 26 weeks continuing into the week (the qualifying week) immediately preceding the 14th week before the EWC.

Flat-rate SMP (sometimes referred to as the 'standard rate') is payable for up to twelve weeks in addition to the six weeks at the higher rate or for up to 18 weeks where the higher rate is calculated as less than the standard rate. The flat rate is the same as the standard weekly SSP rate.

(c)   A woman who has worked for her employer for less than the required period or who is self-employed may be able to claim a maternity allowance from the DSS.

(d)   There is flexibility in choosing the date for the full 18-week entitlement. The first week in the MPP can be any of the eleven weeks before the EWC but the MPP must start at the beginning of any week on or after the 6th week before the EWC during which the employee is absent for a pregnancy related illness. At the latest, the EWC must begin with the week immediately following the week in which the baby was born.

(e)   If the employee returns to work for her employer in a week for which SMP would have been payable (i.e. one of the 18 weeks) she is disqualified from entitlement to that week's SMP. The maternity pay period (MPP) is not extended to take account of any weeks lost but any SMP lost will always be at the lower rate first.

(f)   A married woman paying reduced rate NICs is eligible for SMP.

(g)   SMP is subject to tax, NICs and normal voluntary deductions. However, it is excluded from being attachable earnings for the purpose of an Attachment of Earnings Order.

8.13   Like SSP, the detailed rules of SMP are quite complicated and leave some discretion to the employer and employee. Some further important points are summarised below.

(a)   SMP and SSP are mutually exclusive. Furthermore, SSP cannot be paid during the 18 week 'disqualifying period' whether or not the employee receives SMP or maternity allowance. However, provided she qualifies under the normal rules, a woman can receive SSP before or after the disqualifying period but SSP cannot be paid for a period of sickness absence which is pregnancy-related and falls in the six weeks before the EWC. The Benefits Agency has published a leaflet, NI 200, 'Pregnancy, Related Illness', as a guide to help employers decide whether an illness is or is not pregnancy-related.

(b)   SMP cannot be paid whilst a woman works for any other employer considered associated with the main employer for NIC purposes. The liability of the employer to pay SMP ceases on the Saturday of the week before the week in which the woman, after confinement, starts work for another employer with whom she was not in employment at the qualifying week. She can return to work after her baby is born to work for a second employer who also employed her during the 15th week before the EWC without affecting the liability of her first employer to continue to pay her SMP.

(c)   SMP is payable for a maximum of 18 weeks. The period for which it is paid is called the maternity pay period (MPP). SMP cannot start earlier than the eleventh week before the EWC unless childbirth is earlier, but as already mentioned, the employee has some flexibility as to when it does start. The MPP can be shorter than 18 weeks, for example because the employee chooses to return to work. The MPP will end if the employee dies. It should be noted that if there is a stillbirth then SMP is paid in the normal way, provided the stillbirth occurs after the start of the sixteenth week before the EWC. SMP does not cease just because the employee's contract comes to an end within the MPP.

(d)   An employer can decide on any suitable method for the employee to give notice of maternity leave and can refuse to pay SMP if notice is not received at least 21 days in advance without a good reason. The employer needs medical evidence of the date the baby is due, as entitlement is based on the EWC. Normally this evidence is a Form Mat B1 issued by a doctor or midwife. The MAT B1 cannot be issued earlier than the beginning of the 14th week before the EWC. It should be noted that all calculations, entitlements etc. are based on the expected week of confinement, not the actual week. The actual date of confinement has little effect on SMP except that SMP must come into payment for the week immediately following the week in which the employee gives birth.

(e)   Although some women will fail to satisfy the benefit conditions, very few women are automatically excluded from the scheme at the outset. However, those who are excluded are girls under the age of 16 and foreign-going mariners, e.g. stewardesses. Serving members of HM Forces are, however, included in the scheme.

(f)   Payment of the full amount of SMP as a lump sum is sometimes made by employers. However, this may lead to difficulties of recovery from the employee and the DSS were the employee to die or return to work during the MPP.

8.14   Employers are able to recover the greater part of the SMP payments they make from the State – and in some cases, more than 100 per cent of the payments made can be recovered. The position in the 1998/99 tax year for SMP is as follows below.

The level of reimbursement of SMP depends on whether the employer is a 'small employer'. Small employers are defined as those whose total NICs in the qualifying year are not more than £20,000. The qualifying year is the last complete tax year before the beginning of the employee's qualifying week.

(*a*)   Employers (other than small employers) can recover 92 per cent of the SMP.

(*b*)   Small employers can recover 100 per cent of the SMP and a further seven per cent of SMP as the NIC compensation.

Short-term sickness and maternity benefits

8.15   Occupational sick pay (OSP) is a common employee benefit. It is usually paid in total by the employer and forms part of the employee remuneration 'package'. Depending on the contract of employment, OSP usually brings the employee's entitlement to SSP up to a guaranteed level, i.e. a percentage of basic pay. OSP is often payable for a period related to the employee's service, sometimes at the full rate of the employee's basic pay and in some cases half pay is available for a further period. Sick pay arrangements differ greatly between employers. For instance, the OSP scheme year may vary between employers and, in some cases, will not be a fixed twelve-month period but instead will be a rolling twelve months for each employee. In the latter instance, entitlement to OSP is by reference to absence in the twelve months preceding the first day of the current period of absence. The following scheme illustrates the principles:

Service	Allowance
During first year	25 days' full pay and, after completing 4 months' service, 50 days at half pay.
During second year	50 days' full pay and 50 days' half pay.
During third year	75 days' full pay and 75 days' half pay.
During fourth and successive years of service	100 days' full pay and 100 days' half pay.

Note: All days referred to above are 'working days'.

This scheme provides that the sick pay allowance is granted for the year beginning 1 April. When an employee is absent due to sickness on 31 March the new entitlement to sick pay does not commence until he or she has returned to work. The period of sickness from 1 April is then deemed part of the previous sickness year.

OSP schemes may have exclusions. Typical examples include:

(*a*)   sickness during holidays;

(*b*)   illness during industrial action;

(*c*)   injury resulting from dangerous sports;

(*d*)   absence due to pregnancy or maternity (since contractual or statutory maternity pay is payable instead);

(*e*)   the first few days of any illness;

(*f*)   insufficient service.

Any practice of excluding part-time staff from OSP schemes could well give rise to a claim for indirect sex discrimination (and in any case the employer would have to fulfil its SSP obligations provided the part-time employee had average earnings at least at the level of the Lower Earnings Limit).

OSP scheme rules should define such matters as which employees are included or excluded from benefits, the entitlement periods, amounts payable, waiting days etc. Sometimes additional sick pay is given at the discretion of the employer when the formal OSP has expired. In many OSP schemes, particularly staff schemes, there are no waiting days as there are for SSP. In some cases, e.g. where the employee does not qualify for OSP, payment of SSP may be due. Funding for OSP schemes is by direct financing from the employer on a pay-as-you-go basis or by effecting a group insurance or by operating a separate sick pay fund with contributions by employees and the employer. Note, however, that an employee cannot be required to contribute to cover by the SSP scheme.

Contractual maternity pay schemes usually supplement statutory maternity benefits (SMP or DSS maternity allowance) and such schemes cover large numbers of employees in the public sector, for example teachers and local government employees. The scheme rules govern all the usual matters such as eligibility, the amount payable and period of payment. One feature is that any element of contractual maternity pay in excess of the employee's SMP entitlement may be refundable if the employee elects not to return to work. Where the employee does not return to work then, in certain circumstances, the employer may recover the secondary NICs paid in respect of contractual maternity pay. [*SSCBA 1992, s 167*]. An alternative approach to the design of a contractual maternity pay scheme is in fact to delay the payment of any contractual pay in excess of the SMP entitlement until the employee has returned to work for a defined minimum period. A woman may, of course, qualify for contractual maternity pay and not the statutory benefits or *vice versa* according to the rules of the various schemes.

Contractual maternity pay schemes typically aim at total benefit levels varying from full to half pay for, say, 18 weeks. A typical contractual maternity pay scheme may top up the SMP entitlement so that the employee receives full pay for the first six weeks and then half pay for a further 12 weeks. These schemes do not usually cover the full period of entitlement to maternity leave as defined by the *Employment Rights Act 1996 (ERA 1996)*.

8.16   A number of points should be noted in connection with pregnancy and maternity leave. The UK Government transposed *EC Directive 92/85/EEC* into UK law by including provisions in *TURERA 1993* which amended the *Employment Protection (Consolidation) Act 1978* and which is now consolidated in *ERA 1996*.

Firstly, there are employment law considerations. These include an employee's entitlement to time off with pay for ante-natal care, the right to return to work and prohibition of dismissal because of pregnancy. Employment rights relating to the contract of employment must be ensured in circumstances where either action has been taken under health and safety requirements or the employee is on maternity leave. For example, holiday entitlement and pension rights must be maintained. The scope of these provisions may lead to test cases where pregnant workers contest that their employers have not complied with the legislation.

There are also health and safety at work requirements. For example, new or expectant mothers cannot be obliged to perform night work where a certificate is received showing this is necessary for the safety or health of the worker concerned.

Another consideration is that all pregnant workers are entitled to fourteen weeks' maternity leave. The employee must notify her employer of pregnancy, the expected week of confinement and the commencing date of her absence at least 21 days before it starts. Two weeks' maternity leave must be taken following childbirth (*Maternity (Compulsory Leave) Regulations 1994 (SI 1994 No 2479)*).

The following covers some important practical points concerning disability administration.

(*a*)   ***Notification and authorisation*** — Entitlement to all disability benefits requires timely notification to the employer supported with evidence. Clearly this can be difficult in some cases, for example, a sick employee living alone without a telephone. For prolonged illness regular reports are usually required. With maternity leave a woman must notify her employer of when she intends to commence maternity leave. Many schemes specify that employees jeopardise receipt of the benefit if they do not notify the employer correctly without good reason.

In most cases the payroll office require no special authority to pay a disability benefit. It is sufficient that the notification and evidence are in good order and that the employee qualifies under the rules. Indeed in these circumstances they would look for special authorisation to with-hold benefit. In some circumstances, however, particularly a 'hardship case', the employer may at its discretion make *ex gratia* disability payments to employees who do not qualify under the normal rules. In this case again specific written authorisation would be sought.

(*b*)   ***Payment*** — With bank transfers there is no particular problem in paying sick employees or women on maternity leave. Cash payments can present problems particularly where the absence is more than a few days. Methods used in these circumstances can include giving pay packets to a representative authorised by the employee, retaining pay packets for later collection by the employee, sending pay packets by registered mail and by posting cheques. With SMP a lump sum payment can be paid covering the whole of the MPP but this has certain risks as identified in 8.13(*f*) above. The inconvenience and security risks of cash disability payments for both the employer and employee are two arguments in favour of cashless methods.

(*c*)   ***Recording*** — Sickness schemes are expensive and open to abuse. There is also considerable scope for interpretation, for example when is a person fit or not fit for work? Good records are not only a statutory requirement but an administrative necessity. Certain records in relation to SSP and SMP must be retained by employers for a period of at least three years. They also provide statistical evidence of fair and reasonable use of a scheme by both individuals and groups. There is, of course, considerable scope for integrating disability recording procedures with other types of absence recording systems, such as holidays and unauthorised leave.

(*d*)   ***Official forms*** — A list of SSP and SMP official forms used by the employer is given below (substitutes can now generally be used for the SSP forms):

   (i)   SSP1 is issued to employees excluded from SSP or transferring to State benefits (see Figure 8C above);

   (ii)   SSP1(L) is a leaver's statement which reduces the next employer's SSP liability;

   (iii)   SSP2 is a sheet for recording absences etc;

   (iv)   SSP33 is a form which enables the employer to comply with legislation while calculating the employee's SSP entitlement. Its use is optional;

(v)   SMP1 is issued to women excluded from SMP;

(vi)   SMP2 is a sheet for recording SMP details;

(vii)   SMP3 is a checklist and worksheet – its use is not compulsory.

In addition, every employer finds it necessary to use additional forms to cover its own disability schemes.

The question of whether Form P45 should be issued to a woman on maternity leave has been simplified to the extent that all women enjoy a general right to a minimum of 14 weeks' maternity leave. There is also the right to an extended period of maternity leave where the employee has a right to return to work at any time during the period beginning at the end of her minimum maternity leave period and ending 29 weeks after the beginning of the week in which childbirth occurs. This right is granted to those who can be treated as having been 'continuously employed' for at least two years at the beginning of the eleventh week before the EWC. Where a woman does not have a right to return, the P45 is to be issued either upon making the final payment of SMP and showing the date of the final payment of SMP, or immediately upon receiving a request from the woman for her Form P45, in which instance the date of leaving to be shown will be the date on which the most recent payment of SMP was made. Where the woman has a right to return she remains an employee until employment ceases, for instance if she fails to return to work on the appointed day (without having medical grounds for a four-week postponement), at which time the Form P45 is to be issued. Throughout the maternity leave the normal PAYE procedures are to operate, which may allow the employee to benefit from a tax refund. After the issue of the Form P45 any further payments are subject to tax at the basic rate of tax in the usual way.

(e)   ***Errors*** — In general, if it is found that errors have occurred in disability administration, adjustments must be made and the records corrected in the same way as for any other payroll mistakes. Where SSP or SMP are involved, the situation can require contacting the local social security office if State benefits are affected or the mistake occurred in a previous tax year. Underpayments should be made good, where appropriate, by paying the employee the arrears. In the case of SSP due to an employee who has left employment actual payment may not be necessary as the employee may have already received, for instance, OSP for the particular period involved. (The same principle may extend to SMP/contractual maternity pay.) However, in these circumstances adjustments need to be made to the totals of SSP paid (for example, on the employee's records and perhaps in respect of remittances to the Inland Revenue). Where overpayments have occurred then the employer may be required to repay an amount to the DSS where the amount involved has been recovered from remittances to the Inland Revenue. This will be the case regardless of whether or not the employer seeks recovery of the overpayment from the employee (see 5.16 above for the legal aspects). The SSP compensation scheme which came into effect on 6 April 1995 provides for calculation of the amount of SSP which can be recovered by reference to the NIC liability for the tax month. (See 8.11 above.) Where the NIC liability for a month is subsequently adjusted, this might affect the SSP recoverable under the PTS.

Long-term disability

8.17   An employee who becomes long-term sick or disabled and is unable to work may become entitled to one or more of the State benefits designed to support disabled people. Many of these benefits have figured large in the Government's recent Green Paper, 'New Ambitions for our Country: A New Contract for Welfare', announced by the Minister for Welfare Reform on 26 March 1998. In particular, the Government has announced that it will fundamentally reform incapacity benefit for future claimants. From a relatively minor part of the benefit system 20 years ago, incapacity benefit now costs £7.8 billion a year – almost one-tenth of the entire social security budget. It is received by 1.75 million people, three times as many as in 1979. The Green Paper states: 'Over this period, [incapacity benefit] has proved a simple, but costly escape route for government to keep unemployment numbers down. In some cases [incapacity benefit] has taken on the characteristics of a more generous form of unemployment relief. That was never the intention. It is an insurance benefit for those incapable of working'.

The main State benefits payable to long-term sick and disabled people of working age are:

- incapacity benefit;
- severe disablement allowance;
- disability living allowance;
- disability working allowance;
- industrial injuries disablement benefit.

These benefits are fully described in 'Tolley's Social Security and State Benefits Handbook 1998–99', but a short summary is given for each of them below.

(*a*)   ***Incapacity benefit*** — Incapacity benefit is a contributory (i.e. depends on the employee having paid sufficient National Insurance contributions), non-means-tested benefit. It replaced the former sickness benefit and invalidity benefit with effect from 13 April 1995. Incapacity is assessed during the first 28 weeks of incapacity using the 'own occupation' test – the ability of the employee or self-employed person to carry out their own job. After 29 weeks the test for incapacity is based on the 'all work test' which assesses the person's ability to carry out a range of work-related activities.

Incapacity benefit is paid at the short-term, lower rate for the first 28 weeks of incapacity. In 1998/99 the weekly rate is £48.80 and is not taxable. It is not paid to employees who are entitled to SSP from their employer. See also Appendix D for a Table of Rates.

Incapacity benefit is paid at the short-term, higher rate to an eligible claimant for weeks 29 to 52 of incapacity. In 1998/99 the weekly rate is £57.70 and is taxable, i.e. it is the same as the SSP rate. Non-taxable increases for children may also be payable with the short-term higher rate.

Incapacity benefit is paid at the long-term rate to those under State pension age who have been sick for more than a year (although those who are terminally ill or who receive the higher rate care component of disability living allowance receive the long-term rate of incapacity benefit from week 29 of the incapacity). An age addition is paid with the long-term rate provided the claimant was less than age 45 when the incapacity began – there are two rates of the age addition depending on the age of the claimant when the incapacity began. Increases may be payable for an adult dependant who is caring for a child or who is aged 60 or over. All these benefits are taxable. Non-taxable increases for children may also be payable. In 1998/99 the basic weekly rate of long-term incapacity is £64.70. If the claimant was aged 35 to 44 inclusive when the incapacity began, an age addition of £6.60 is also paid. If the claimant was aged under 35 when the incapacity began, an age addition of £13.15 is also paid.

(b) ***Severe disablement allowance*** — Severe disablement allowance is a non-contributory, non-means-tested, non-taxable benefit payable to those who are incapable of work and who do not satisfy the contribution tests for incapacity benefit. Claimants must have been incapable of work for at least 28 weeks. Those who became incapable of work after age 20 must demonstrate that they have been 80 per cent disabled for at least 28 weeks. Age additions are payable depending on the age at which the claimant became incapable of work. Increases may also be payable for dependants. In 1998/99 the basic weekly rate of severe disablement allowance is £39.10 with weekly age additions of £13.60, £8.60 and £4.30 depending respectively on whether the claimant on first becoming incapable of work was aged respectively under 40, between 40 and 50, and between 50 and 60.

(c) ***Disability living allowance*** — Disability living allowance is a non-contributory, non-means-tested, non-taxable benefit payable to those who become disabled before age 65, replacing from April 1992 the former attendance and mobility allowances. It is payable to disabled people who need personal care (the care component) and/or need help in getting around (the mobility component). The claimant must have needed help for three months and be expected to need help for at least a further six months (unless it is recognised that the claimant is terminally ill when it is immediately payable). There are three rates of the care component and two rates of the mobility component depending on the level of help needed. In 1998/99 the three weekly care component rates are £51.30, £34.30 and £13.60; and the two weekly mobility component rates are £35.85 and £13.60.

(d) **Disability working allowance** — Disability working allowance is a non-contributory, means-tested, non-taxable benefit designed to top up the earnings of disabled people who are in low paid work. The allowance is aimed at those on long-term incapacity benefit or severe disablement allowance who have a limited earning capacity. A claimant must work an average of 16 hours or more a week. Entitlement depends on parallel entitlement to other social security benefits. Being means tested, the amount of disability working allowance received depends on the claimant's income, capital and the claimant's family type.

(e) **Industrial injuries disablement benefit** — Industrial injuries disablement benefit is a non-contributory, non-means-tested, non-taxable benefit which was first introduced in July 1948. It is payable to those who have been disabled because of an industrial accident or prescribed industrial disease. The claimant cannot receive the benefit until 90 days after the date of the accident or the date of the onset of the prescribed disease. To be entitled the claimant needs to be medically assessed on the degree of his or her disablement. The degree of disablement also determines the weekly rate of disablement pension that is paid. Constant attendance allowance and exceptionally severe disablement allowance may also be payable to a claimant who is in receipt of industrial injuries disablement benefit and who needs constant care and attention because of the effects of the industrial injury or disease. In 1998/99 the weekly rate payable to a person assessed at 100 per cent disabled is £104.70. If also entitled to exceptionally severe disablement allowance and the highest level of constant attendance allowance, the claimant would receive a further £126.00 a week.

8.18   Long-term disability pay can be provided through the workplace in the following ways:

(a) ill-health early retirement pensions;

(b) permanent health insurance;

(c) accident and sickness insurance.

The level of any ill-health early retirement pension depends on the rules of the pension scheme. If the scheme is a defined benefit scheme (such as in the case of a typical final salary scheme), it is common to find that the ill-health pension is calculated on the current level of the employee's pensionable earnings and the full prospective service which the member could have achieved if he or she had remained in pensionable service until the scheme's normal retirement date

(NRD). In some cases, this more generous level of ill-health early retirement pension is reserved for employees who are unable to carry out any work as a result of their illness or disability. Where the employee is prevented from carrying out his or her own job but could undertake other, lighter work for another employer, the ill-health early retirement pension may be calculated on the members' current level of pensionable earnings and only on his or her actual pensionable service.

Early retirement pensions, paid on the grounds of ill-health, can be paid to scheme members at any age. Such pensions are, of course, subject to PAYE and paid in the same way as retirement pensions. (See Chapter 20 (Pensions Payroll Procedures).)

Ill-health early retirement pensions are invariably more generous than other forms of early retirement pension where the amount of accrued pension rights is frequently subject to a reduction if it has to come into payment before the scheme's NRD. An example of the contrast between the terms of a pension paid early on the grounds of ill-health with one paid is through early retirement given below.

Example — Charlie develops a mild heart condition which stops him from carrying out his normal work although he would still be capable of clerical work. He is aged 55 and currently has final pensionable earnings of £14,000 a year. He is a member of a final salary scheme where pension builds up at the rate of 1/60th for each complete year of service. Normal retirement date is age 65. Charlie had joined the pension scheme when he was 40.

If he were taking early retirement at age 55 and was still enjoying good health, his pension would be reduced under the rules of his particular scheme by four per cent for each year taken before NRD:

i.e. $15/60 \times £14,000 \times ((100 - (4 \times 10))/100) = £2,100$ p.a.

If he were so ill that he were completely unable to work, then under the scheme rules his pension would be based on his full prospective service to NRD:

i.e. $25/60 \times £14,000 = £5,834$ p.a.

However, since he is genuinely suffering from a condition that prevents him from carrying out his own work but could undertake lighter work for another employer, then under the scheme rules, his pension is based on actual pensionable service but with no reduction for early payment:

i.e. $15/60 \times £14,000 = £3,500$ p.a.

Long-term disability can also be insured against by the employer taking out a group permanent health policy. Like all forms of insurance similar policies contain different terms. Typically, however, a claim for 75 per cent of an employee's salary to be paid until retirement age or return to health may come into payment after six months of disability. The definitions of 'disability' are not always generous and there are usually exclusions, for example, incapacity resulting from alcohol or drug abuse, dangerous sports or travel to certain parts of the world. Many insurers also impose exclusion clauses if the employee is shown to be HIV positive. Policy benefits payable are frequently reduced by the amount of long-term incapacity benefit payable by the State (even if the individual concerned fails to qualify to the benefit). Generally the insurance money is paid gross in arrears to the employer every month, who then pays the employee under the PAYE system. Group accident and sickness schemes broadly differ from permanent health insurance schemes in that lump sum benefits are typically offered for loss of limbs, sight, or on death. Sickness payments are also only available for a limited period, for example for 52 weeks.

If an employer compensates an employee for the loss of his or her job following an accident by awarding the employee an *ex gratia* lump sum payment, the first £30,000 of any such payment is free of income tax by virtue of the *Income and Corporation Taxes Act 1988, ss 148* and *188*. The lump sum is not included in gross pay for National Insurance contributions purposes. This tax treatment is unaffected by the payment of early retirement benefits under a tax approved pension scheme. Where any lump sum payable in these circumstances does exceed £30,000, the employer is advised by the Contributions Agency's Manual CWG2, 'Employer's Further Guide to PAYE and NICs', to contact the local PAE Tax Office.

Treatment of damages of compensation awards

8.19   Employees who are injured as a result of an accident that occurs at the work place or is otherwise work related and employees are suffering from a disease resulting from their work may be able to bring a successful claim for compensation against their employers. If so, there are a number of payroll-related aspects that can arise.

(a)   ***Recovery by the State*** — The *Social Security (Recovery of Benefits) Act 1997* has introduced a new Compensation Recovery Scheme for the recovery by the State of social security benefits in cases where the courts award compensation. The scheme is administered by the Compensation Recovery Unit (CRU), part of the Benefits Agency and came into operation in October 1997.

The Act applies where one person makes a payment to another in respect of an accident, injury or disease and certain State benefits have also been, or are likely to be, paid to the other person during a specified period. The person making the compensation payment must apply for a certificate of recoverable benefits showing the State benefits payable to the injured person. The compensator must then pay to the Secretary of State an amount equal to these State benefits. However, the compensation payments can be reduced to allow the compensator to recover some or all of the payments made to the Secretary of State. If part of a compensation payment is attributable to a head of compensation listed in column 1 of *Schedule 2* to the Act, and if State benefits corresponding to that head, as indicated in column 2 of the Schedule, have been paid to the injured person, the compensator can reduce that part of the compensation payment by the amount of the benefits so paid.

The following example shows how the new scheme works. A person who receives a compensation payment for illness or injury of £23,000, of which £18,000 is specifically awarded for pain and suffering and has received State benefits of £26,000, he will receive the full amount of £18,000 from his compensation. Payment of the £26,000 benefit will be the responsibility of the negligent party or his representative.

Regulations to supplement the provisions of the Act were laid on 15 September 1997. These are the *Social Security (Recovery of Benefits) Regulations 1997 (SI 1997 No 2205)* which covers the main workings of the scheme and the *Social Security (Appeals) Regulations 1997 (SI 1997 No 2237)* which set out matters relating to the making and hearing of appeals against certificates of recoverable benefits.

(b)   **Inter-relationship with ill-health pension** — A number of court cases have dealt with the issue of whether an employee who has been injured by the actionable negligence of the employer should have any damages received from the employer reduced to take account of any occupational pension benefits which result from the accident. In the lead case, *Parry v Cleaver [1970] AC 1 HL*, the House of Lords held that pension benefits payable to the former employee as a result of an accident should *not* be brought into account to reduce the damages payable by the employer. The pension benefits were similar to insurance and to require the pensioner to bring them into account would be to deprive the pensioner of the benefit of part of the wages which he had earned from the employer.

(c)   **OSP treated as a loan** — Some OSP schemes carry provisions to the effect that where the employee has suffered an injury the sick pay paid in respect of the related absence from work is to be treated as a 'loan' which is repayable upon damages or compensation being awarded against a third party or the employer. The value of the loan repayable in such circumstances is the net pay (i.e. after deductions of tax and NICs) (*British Railways Board v Franklin [1993] IRLR 441 – CA*). An employer can apply to the Inland Revenue and DSS for a refund of the income tax and both the employee's and employer's NICs.

(*d*) **Tax and National Insurance contributions** — Damages or similar payments made to an employee injured at work are not subject to income tax or National Insurance contributions provided there is no contractual liability on the employer to make the payment.

References

8.20   A list of reading and details of DSS leaflets are given below.

(1) 'Tolley's Payroll, Remuneration and Benefits — Statutory Maternity Pay and Statutory Sick Pay', Tolley Publishing Co Ltd, 1998.

(2) Matthewman J and other expert contributors, 'Tolley's Social Security and State Benefits 1998–99', Tolley Publishing Co Ltd, 1998.

(3) FB28, 'Sick or Disabled?'.

(4) Contributions Agency and Benefits Agency employer guides consisting of the following:

  (*a*) CWG1, 'Employer's Quick Guide to PAYE and NICs', covering Class 1 NICs, Class 1A NICs, SSP and SMP.

  (*b*) CWG2, 'Employer's Further Guide to PAYE and NICs'.

  (*c*) CA30, 'Employer's Manual — Statutory Sick Pay'.

  (*d*) CA29, 'Employer's Manual — Statutory Maternity Pay'.

  (*e*) CA35/36, 'Statutory Sick Pay and Statutory Maternity Pay Tables'.

(5) NI 252, 'Severe Disablement Allowance'.

(6) NI 244, 'Statutory Sick Pay — Check Your Rights'.

(7) IB 202, IB 214, 'Incapacity Benefit'.

(8) NI 6, 'Industrial Injuries Disablement Benefit'.

(9) DS703, 'Disability Working Allowance'.

(10) NI 2, 'If You Have an Industrial Disease'.

(11) FB8, 'Babies and Benefits'.

(12) NI 17A, 'A Guide to Maternity Benefits'.

(13) National Audit Office, Report by the Comptroller and Auditor General, 'Statutory Sick Pay and Statutory Maternity Pay', HMSO, January 1993.

(14) FB2, 'Which Benefit?'

(15) NI 196, 'Social Security Benefit Rates'.

(16) PL 958, 'Maternity Rights', issued by the Employment Department.

(17) 'Reducing the Burden of SSP (& SMP)', PMR, December 1995.

(18) 'SSP Exemption Proposals', PMR, February 1996.

(19) 'It's All Relevant', PMR, May 1996.

(20) 'Sense and Common Sense', PMR, March 1996.

(21) Self R, series of six articles on SSP in PMR, November 1996 – April 1997.

(22) 'Challenging the Lower Earnings Limit', PMR, October 1997.

(23) 'Average Weekly Earnings for SSP and SMP', PMR, November 1997.

(24) 'Happy Returns', PMR, December 1997 (the right to return to work after maternity leave).

(25) 'Finding the Key to SMP', PMR, July 1998.

(26) 'Keeping the Baby Blues at Bay', PMR, August 1998 (maternity leave).

(27) 'Who is Entitled to SMP?', PMR, August 1998.

(28) 'Paying SMP', PMR, September 1998.

9 Benefits, Expenses and Termination Payments

Scope of this chapter

9.1   Chapter 6 (Background to Pay and Benefits) discussed the role which benefits can play in an employee's remuneration package. In many cases, the total value of the benefits provided for employees may be a considerable proportion of an employer's total employment costs (wages, salaries, bonuses etc).

Some benefits, such as a company car which is provided for both private and business use, are recognised as being significant 'perks' to employees and, as such, are highly appreciated. Other benefits however are not so immediately apparent as such. For example, the provision of a subsidised canteen, sick pay or paid holidays, often tend to be taken for granted and may not be considered to be benefits at all by those who receive them.

It should be noted too that certain benefits can be of as much value to the employer who provides them as to the employee who receives them. For example, a benefit such as the provision of free or cheap medical insurance (BUPA, PPP etc.) can be used to help a key employee to regain his/her health (and thereby return to work so much more quickly) or to choose the time at which any necessary medical treatment is obtained.

This chapter outlines typical common benefit schemes such as those which offer cars, shares in the employing company, redundancy pay etc. Some cash benefits, such as profit related pay, are covered in this chapter because they involve special administration outside the normal payroll routine. However, such schemes are now considered to have outlived the purpose for which they were originally introduced and are in the process of being phased out.

Other schemes, such as those involving disability and pensions, are full subjects in their own right and are covered in Chapter 8 (Disability, Maternity and Family Benefits) and Chapter 10 (Pension Schemes).

Certain benefits may only be available to specific employees within an organisation. For example, a loan for the purposes of buying a car, upon which either no interest or a low rate of interest is charged, might only be available to those employees who are required to travel regularly by car in the performance of their duties. In other cases, the seniority, status or grade of an employee within an organisation may determine the size, type or value of any company car which may be provided to him.

Some benefits will often be administered by people other than payroll staff – share schemes are a good example. However, there will normally be some form of payroll involvement by way of, for instance, the collection of savings from participating employees to purchase the shares.

Certain types of benefits carry special income tax or NICs concessions. In the case of profit-related pay schemes, there are strict conditions which must be met if the scheme is to receive Inland Revenue approval.

Key points and general observations on benefits, expenses and termination payments

9.2   Expenses paid to employees are grouped together with benefits for tax purposes and the Inland Revenue can be expected to pay close attention to the method by which employers pay expenses to employees. In the event of a Schedule E compliance visit or a PAYE audit taking place, both Inspectors of Taxes and PAYE auditors will examine a sample of the expenses claims submitted by employees.

The purpose of such an examination is to determine whether the expenses are 'reasonable and justified'. In other words:

(a)   is the level at which expenses are paid consistent with the level of expenditure which the employee might reasonably have been expected to incur in performing his duties? and

(b)   did the employee need to make the business journey or incur the expense in question in order to perform his duties?

If either the Inspector or the PAYE auditor considers that one or other of these tests is not met, he may argue that the expenses are 'excessive' or 'unjustified' and is likely to seek recovery of any additional PAYE and NICs which may be due in connection with them from the employer.

Less frequently, where it is clear that the employer has sought deliberately to pay excessive and unjustified expenses to employees as a means of increasing their tax free remuneration, the Inland Revenue may take legal proceedings against the employer or, at the very least, impose a significant financial penalty.

As in many areas of payroll and allied work, it is essential that the *minutiae*, not only of the Government's regulations, but also those of the employer himself are followed carefully. However, the administration of expenses and benefits procedures is one which has possibly more 'grey' areas than elsewhere and especially careful treatment is necessary.

It is necessary to identify every type of benefit and expense payment which may exist within the employing organisation and to determine how each should be dealt with from the point of view of PAYE, NICs or the reporting of benefits. As will be appreciated, such an exercise can represent a mammoth task, particularly in a large organisation which may have many different departments, paying locations or a variety of business activities.

This notwithstanding, the Inland Revenue will insist that the exercise be undertaken and can be expected to grant little by way of concession to the employer who gets it wrong.

For most practical purposes, the payroll administrator can resolve any tax and/or NICs uncertainties concerning benefits and expenses by reference to standard sources. Inland Revenue Booklets 480 and CWG2 (Employer's Further Guide to PAYE and NICs) contain detailed guidance as to the tax treatment of benefits and expenses. The latter also analyses the NICs treatment of a wide range of payments and benefits.

More specific advice can always be obtained from the tax office, the local office of the CA or a professional tax advisor.

It should be borne in mind that the advice given by the tax or CA office may not necessarily be that which is most tax or NICs efficient to the employer – the tax office in particular has a tendency to recommend that the employer should 'play safe' by taxing payments in the first instance. A professional advisor, on the other hand, may be able to suggest valid reasons why a payment should *not* be taxed, or recommend changes in procedures to support not taxing it.

The following are key points.

(i) Most benefits will involve a reporting obligation for the employer and a subsequent tax implication for the employees. Currently, NICs are not due on non-cash benefits, other than 'company' cars, fuel provided for private motoring and certain readily convertible assets referred to in 9.4 below. We have used the word 'currently' above since benefits in kind are specifically excluded from any NICs liability *unless* legislation exists which specifically includes them.

The creation of the Class 1A NICs charge (payable only by employers) might be seen by some to be the thin end of the wedge and, following the change of Government for the first time in 18 years, the principle of applying NICs to benefits in kind generally might be attractive to a Chancellor of the Exchequer keen to raise revenue without being seen to raise taxes.

Details of benefits in kind must be submitted to the Inspector of Taxes each year on Forms P9D or P11D as appropriate, with copies of the information being provided to each employee. We discuss the nature of these returns later in this section.

(ii) Holiday arrangements are very varied with little statutory regulation. Special tax and NICs implications exist for some workers, for example, those in the construction industry.

(iii) Schemes which exist for the provision of cars can vary widely and special tax regimes apply to these.

(iv) Payroll administrators may encounter company share schemes which can have payroll implications. These include Inland Revenue approved profit sharing schemes as well as unapproved share option and incentive schemes.

(v) Profit-related pay schemes can currently obtain special tax advantages. However, as we have commented earlier, the need for such schemes (as 'pump-priming' measures designed to boost the economy), has largely disappeared. As a consequence, the attraction of such schemes will decline as the tax advantages are phased out.

(vi) Many miscellaneous employee benefits can be provided, for example, free (or discounted) medical insurance, incentive prizes given to sales-men, the provision of Christmas parties and so on. As we subsequently discuss, certain such benefits (for example, a Christmas party) may not carry any tax implications by virtue of Inland Revenue Extra-Statutory Concessions.

In the case of other benefits, the employer may not consider that it is in his best interests to require that his employees should be taxed on them – incentive prizes are a prime example – because of the perceived 'demotivating' effect to the employee who receives such a reward and subsequently receives a demand to pay tax on it. In such cases, employers will often arrange to provide the benefit gross and to meet the employ-ees' tax liability under a 'PAYE Settlement Agreement' (PSA) or Taxed Award Scheme (TAS).

(vii) As we have commented earlier, the rates and conditions under which expenses allowances are paid need to be strictly controlled by the employer so as to avoid any suggestion by the Inland Revenue that they may be 'unjustified' or 'excessive'. A prudent employer will take steps to ensure that his internal control procedures are such that employees themselves are aware of how much they can claim and under what circumstances.

Equally, he will ensure that employees responsible for authorising or countersigning expenses claims know when to allow or (more importantly) disallow an employee's claim.

If 'round sum' expenses allowances are paid, the employer should ensure that these reflect an accurate estimation of the likely level of expenditure incurred by employees, and that the approval of the Inspector of Taxes to such round sums has been obtained.

(viii) The right of an employee to receive a payment on his being made redundant is enshrined in the *Employment Rights Act 1996* (*ERA 1996*). However, this only prescribes the minimum amounts which may be payable and employers are permitted to devise their own schemes either for use throughout the organisation as a whole or in relation to specific parts of the organisation.

In addition to the statutory requirements of *ERA 1996* therefore, employers need to be aware of what they can (and more particularly, what they cannot) do as far as granting redundancy terms to employees is concerned. A number of Statements of Practice (SPs) have been published by the Inland Revenue in this connection and employers should ensure that they are familiar with the terms of each of these.

(x) Whilst the legislation governing the tax treatment of termination payments has not changed in recent years, it is clear that the Inland Revenue's attitude towards such payments has hardened. A number of tax cases have taken place and it appears that the Inland Revenue will challenge any termination payment or payment in lieu of notice, the terms of which appear to overstep the legislation.

Income tax on benefits and expenses

9.3   Emoluments which are taxable under Schedule E include more than simply monetary payments to employees. 'Emoluments' also includes many 'benefits' such as the provision of a company car, medical insurance and accommodation.

Whilst 'benefits' such as those referred to above will undoubtedly be of some value to the employee to whom they are provided, it is important to note that, for income tax purposes, a 'benefit' need not be something which necessarily enriches or improves the quality of life of an individual. Thus, for example, if an employee incurs costs whilst travelling in the performance of the duties of his employment and is subsequently reimbursed those costs by his employer, the amount of the reimbursement will be regarded as a 'benefit' albeit not one upon which tax will necessarily be charged.

The basis upon which tax is charged on a benefit (if indeed any tax is payable) depends upon into which of the following two groups the employee falls:

(a)   company directors (irrespective of the level of earnings) and employees earning at a rate of £8,500 per annum or more; or

(b)   employees earning at a rate of less than £8,500 per annum.

Excluded from (a) above are certain full-time working directors and directors of charities or non-profit making concerns provided that the individual:

(i)   does not own or control a 'material interest' (broadly more than five per cent of the ordinary share capital) in the company; and

(ii)   is not remunerated at a rate of £8,500 per annum or more; and

(iii)   does not fall within (a) above in respect of any other employment with the same, or/and associated, employer.

Company directors and employees earning at a rate of £8,500 pa or more

The Inland Revenue used to describe persons falling into this category as 'higher paid' employees. However, the £8,500 annual threshold has not been revised for many years (and it seems unlikely that it will be changed) and the designation 'higher paid' is no longer appropriate.

Such person are now, more commonly, referred to as 'P11D employees' and this name derives from the tax form used by employers to report the expenses paid to them and benefits in kind with which they have been provided.

In determining whether or not an employee earns at a rate of £8,500 per annum or more, the employer must take account, not only of the total gross salary which the employee receives (including any overtime, commissions or bonuses), but also of the value of all taxable benefits in kind which he receives and all expenses which have been paid to him, except where covered by a dispensation.

Furthermore, employers should note the use of the words 'at a rate of' £8,500 per annum or more. An individual who is employed by an employer for, say three months, and who earns a total of £3,000 during that time, will be P11D liable, even though he has earned less than £8,500, since his earnings of £1,000 per month are paid at a rate of more than £8,500 per annum.

A P11D employee is taxed on the 'cash equivalent' of any benefit which he receives. The cash equivalent is either the cost to the employer of providing the benefit (less any payments made for the private use of the benefit by the employee) or such other amount as may be laid down by legislation, where specific legislation exists.

In this latter connection, legislation specifies the cash equivalents of benefits such as fuel provided for private use, mobile telephones, the private use of company vans etc.

We discuss the different tax treatments later in this section.

Employees earning at a rate of less than £8,500 per annum

Employees who earn at a rate of less than £8,500 per annum are known as 'P9D employees' and again, the name derives from the form used by employers to report the benefits with which they have been provided. The Form P9D is a far simpler form than the Form P11D and calls for a smaller range of benefits to be reported.

For instance, it is not necessary to report the provision of a company car to a P9D employee (as long as the value of the car does not bring the employee's annual rate of earnings to more than £8,500) and the employee will not therefore pay tax on such a benefit.

Where a P9D employee is taxed on a benefit, the basis of taxation differs from that which applies to a P11D employee. Instead of being taxed on the cost of providing the benefit (as is the case with P11D employees) the P9D employee is taxed on the 'money's worth' of the benefit, that is to say, the amount for which he could sell the benefit or the second hand value.

Thus for example, if a P11D employee were given a suit of clothes which cost his employer £100, he would be taxed on the full £100. The P9D employee, on the other hand, would be taxed on a far lower figure and he would normally agree this with his tax district. The amount on which tax is paid could be as little as £20 or possibly even less.

Some benefits in kind are taxable on all employees, others are taxable only on P11D employees and, as we have stated previously, the basis of taxation in connection with the same benefit will depend upon whether the employee is P9D or P11D liable. In Figure 9A below, we have shown the differences between some of the main types of benefit.

It will be seen that the tax treatment of P9D employees is far more favourable than that which applies to higher earners.

Certain benefits which might otherwise be considered to be taxable, for example, the provision of free meals to all employees in a canteen and the provision of luncheon vouchers, do not in fact give rise to a reporting requirement or an income tax liability by virtue of Extra-Statutory Concessions granted by the Inland Revenue. We discuss certain of these issues later in this section.

The 'cash equivalent' of a benefit includes any element of VAT which relates to it, whether or not the VAT is recoverable by the employer. In the case of 'in-house' benefits, that is to say, those which are supplied to the public in the course of the employer's business and which are enjoyed by employees at a lesser cost or at no cost at all, the cash equivalent is any additional or 'marginal' cost incurred by the employer in providing the benefit for the employees.

The cash equivalent of an in-house benefit is *not* determined by reference to an appropriate proportion of the total cost to the employer. This principle was determined following the case of *Pepper v Hart [1992] STC 898 HL*. In brief, the case, which was ultimately decided by the House of Lords, concerned the valuation of the benefit in kind of free education provided to the children of schoolteachers at the fee-paying school at which they taught.

The Inland Revenue had initially been successful in the lower courts in arguing that the quantum of the benefit was the average cost to the school of providing each place rather than the marginal or additional cost to the school of educating the teachers' children. That is to say, only the extra direct costs without taking into account any of the normal running costs of the school such as salaries, property expenses etc.

The House of Lords overturned the earlier decisions of both the High Court and the Court of Appeal and ruled that in-house benefits shared with others, such as goods or services provided at less than cost price, should be taxed on the direct extra (or marginal) cost which the employer incurred in providing the benefit for his employees, rather than on the average cost, less any payments made by the employees in question.

The decision does not affect company cars, beneficial loans, living accommodation or most types of benefits which are purchased by employers but it does affect benefits such as free in-house legal and financial advice, reduced price travel tickets for airline and rail staff, subsidised sports facilities and cut-price goods in staff shops.

The Inland Revenue's view is that the *Pepper v Hart* decision also affects the calculation of the cash equivalent of some assets which are both used in the business and placed at the disposal of employees. Certain fixed costs will no longer need to be taken into account in determining the total value of the asset where the private use is incidental to the business use. Any additional costs incurred as a result of private use must, however, continue to be included. Assets which are provided solely for private purposes are unaffected by the *Pepper v Hart* principle.

As we have stated, the employer must declare most benefits on Forms P9D or P11D (as appropriate) for each employee, at the year end. Those returns to be made in respect of the 1996/97 and subsequent tax years differ however in certain respects. In past years, it has been sufficient simply to notify the

Inspector of Taxes that a benefit has been provided, without, in all cases, quantifying the cash equivalent of the benefit. Furthermore, whilst many employers did so, there was no statutory requirement to provide that same information to the employees.

However, with the introduction of self assessment, the employer is now under a statutory obligation, not only to calculate the cash equivalent of *every* taxable benefit which he provides for each employee, but also to provide mirroring information to employees to enable them to complete any self assessment tax return which they may receive. The information must, by law, be provided to both the Inland Revenue and the employees no later than 6 July, following the end of the relevant tax year and employers who fail to do so will render themselves liable to penalties.

Certain information need not be reported, either to the Inland Revenue or to employees. We have already discussed items such as those in respect of which an Extra-Statutory Concession relates, however, there are other circumstances which can render unnecessary the requirement to make a return.

The employer might, for example, have opted to meet certain employee tax liabilities himself under what is known as a PAYE Settlement Agreement (discussed separately later), or he may have negotiated a 'dispensation' from certain P11D reporting requirements.

A dispensation is a written agreement from the Inspector of Taxes that a specific expense or benefit need not be reported on Form P11D. A dispensation will normally be granted, for example, in connection with expenses which have been paid to an employee which do no more than reimburse him for costs which he has been required to incur in the performance of his duties. In other words, he has not profited from receiving the payment. The employer may have provided a free eye test to those of his employees who are required to use visual display equipment in the course of their work and may, in addition, have contributed towards the costs of any special spectacles which the employees need in order to use such equipment.

Benefits and expenses such as these will commonly be made the subject of a dispensation although employers should note that Inspectors of Taxes will occasionally refuse to allow the contribution towards the cost of the spectacles to be made free of tax. Such a refusal might occur where, for example, the contribution is in respect of particular frames, tinting of the lenses or, if it is determined that the employee needs to wear spectacles for purposes other than operating a VDU.

Taxpayers (employees) who pay tax under Schedule E face a somewhat stricter tax regime (as far as expenses are concerned) than those who are taxed under Schedule D (the self-employed). Expenses refunded to (or paid on behalf of) an employee by an employer must be included in his total emoluments and will not always be allowed as a deduction for tax purposes.

The test for the allowability of expenses for Schedule E taxpayers is by reference to the *Income and Corporation Taxes Act 1988, s 198* which, in relation to periods to 5 April 1998, stated that travelling expenses would only be allowed if they were 'necessarily' incurred in the performance of the duties. Any other types of expenses must be incurred 'wholly, exclusively and necessarily' in the performance of the duties. (The position has changed with effect from 6 April 1998 as we discuss at 9.7 below.)

A self employed person, on the other hand, does not have to meet the 'necessarily incurred' test in respect of all types of expenses.

Figure 9A

Benefit	Tax Treatment	
	P11D employees	*Other employees*
Car for private use	Car Benefit Charge*	Nil
Private fuel	Scale Benefit Charge*	Nil
Van for private use	Scale Benefit Charge*	
Assets for private use (other than cars and vans)	'Annual Value' (20% of market value)	Nil
Living accommodation	Higher of Gross Rateable Value or rent paid by employer	As aside
Vouchers for cash, goods or services	Cost to employer	As aside
Purchases using employer's credit card	Cost to employer	As aside
Beneficial Loans	Difference between interest paid and 'official' interest rate	Nil
Medical Insurance	Cost to employer	Nil
Travel tickets (Non-business)	Cost to employer	As aside
Free meals on employer's premises available to all employees	Nil	Nil
Luncheon vouchers up to 15p per day	Nil	Nil

* *See Appendix D*

NICs on benefits and expenses

9.4   *Regulation 19(1)(d)* of the *Social Security (Contributions) Regulations 1979 (SI 1979 No 591),* specifically excludes from the computation of earnings for NICs purposes:

> 'any payment in kind . . . the provision of board or lodging or of services or other facilities.'

On this basis, it would appear that none of the benefits in kind which have been discussed earlier in this section should attract a liability to NICs. This is, however, not the case.

With the removal of the upper earnings limit for secondary (employers) NICs in 1985, it became apparent that the cost to employers of employing highly paid employees could increase considerably. This was particularly the case in respect of those employees who were accustomed to receiving large annual cash bonuses, the whole of which would thus become liable to secondary NICs.

As a consequence, and with a view to avoiding the additional NICs liability, practices were devised whereby such employees received their bonuses in forms other than in cash. Some of the favourite earlier methods involved the use of payments in gilt edged securities, units in unit trusts and gold bullion.

Bonuses paid by such methods had three considerable advantages. The first was that, since they constituted 'payments in kind', they avoided the imposition of secondary Class 1 NICs. The second was that as payments in kind, they did not attract a charge to PAYE – instead, they fell to be reported on Forms P11D. As a consequence, the point at which tax became payable could be deferred, often by twelve months or more, after the submission of the Forms P11D.

The third major advantage was that such payments in kind were easily convertible into cash.

These initial NICs avoidance schemes flourished for a number of years until special provisions were introduced to outlaw them. However, they were replaced by a succession of other schemes, many of which too have now been outlawed. Details of some of the most popular (and bizarre) schemes are detailed below:

(*a*)   gilts;

(*b*)   shares;

(*c*)   debentures;

(*d*)   units in unit trusts;

(*e*)   futures;

(*f*)   options;

(g)   Premium Bonds;

(h)   National Savings Certificates;

(j)   gold bullion;

(k)   other precious (and semi precious metals)

(l)   Persian carpets;

(m)   vintage and other rare cars;

(n)   fine wines;

(o)   works of arts and antiques; and

(p)   platinum sponge.

As NICs avoidance schemes flourished, so successive Chancellors moved more and more quickly to introduce amendments to the *Social Security Regulations* to counter them and there are now few schemes which will go unchallenged. In addition to introducing amendments of this type, Regulations were introduced, with effect from 1991/92, which imposed a new Class of NICs on two of the most common benefits in kind, company cars and fuel provided for private use in such cars. The new charge, known as Class 1A, is payable at the secondary rate of contribution, by the employer only, and the amount of NICs payable is calculated using the same figures as are used to calculate the tax liability.

The *Social Security Act 1998* has taken matters further, introducing, with effect from 6 April 1999, a NICs liability on payments made using vouchers – a point which we discuss at 9.13 below.

Whilst (apart from the exceptions referred to above) NICs are not payable on benefits in kind provided by employers, it should be noted that, if the employee purchases the benefit himself, and is reimbursed the cost by the employer or the employer pays the supplier on behalf of the employee, NICs *will* be payable on the amount reimbursed or paid.

NICs are not due on genuine business expenses by virtue of *Social Security (Contributions) Regulations (SI 1979 No 591), reg 19(4)(b)* which states that, in calculating NICs, employers may disregard:

'any specific and distinct payment of, or contribution towards, expenses actually incurred by an employed earner in carrying out his employment'.

It will be noted that the Regulation is somewhat less restrictive than the 'wholly, exclusively and necessarily' requirements contained in *ICTA 1988, s 198*. Nevertheless, the CA have, until relatively recently, interpreted the 'specific and distinct' test almost as rigorously.

As a consequence, CA inspectors could be expected to insist that NICs were payable on genuine business expenses unless the employer could demonstrate conclusively, by producing receipts or vouchers, that the expense had been incurred. The CA has now relaxed this rigid approach and will now accept other forms of evidence of expenditure, including the 'probability' or 'likelihood' that an employee incurred the expense in question.

Problems initially arose in connection with the application of dispensations (discussed earlier) for NICs purposes. The legislation which permits the Inland Revenue to grant a dispensation is not mirrored in the Social Security regulations and whilst, for many years, it had been assumed that a dispensation for tax purposes would apply equally for the purposes of NICs, the CA ruled that this was not the case.

As a consequence, CA inspectors could be expected to charge NICs on expenses which, in their view, did not meet the *Regulation 19(4)(b)* test despite the fact that it was the subject of a dispensation for tax purposes. Fortunately, this state of affairs was rectified with effect from 6 April 1995 when the CA announced that a dispensation would have equal applicability for the purposes of both tax and NICs.

Holiday schemes

9.5   An employee's entitlement to holiday will usually be addressed in his contract of employment. There are, however, certain official regulations concerning holidays and these are addressed in section 5.20 above. In practice, most regular employments will involve formal holiday schemes and, under a typical such scheme, an employee might, for example, be entitled to receive pay on public holidays, plus 21 days holiday per year plus one extra day for each year of service, up to a maximum of four days.

In practice, there can be a whole host of complications within a holiday scheme, including:

(*a*)   non-uniform accrual of holiday within a year;

(*b*)   a prohibition or restriction on carrying over any surplus holiday entitlement from one year to the next;

(*c*)   the taking of unpaid leave;

(*d*)   a stipulation that holidays must be taken at a specified time, for example, during an annual works 'shut-down'; and

(*e*)   variations in the holiday entitlements of employees according to grade and length of service.

The administration of holiday schemes might be shared between the personnel and payroll departments and the employee's own employing department or may be the primary responsibility of any one of the three. The payroll department is, of course, always responsible for the calculation and payment of holiday pay.

Needless to say, it is essential that the rules and employee entitlements relating to holidays should be clearly documented. Assuming that the entitlement used is recorded and monitored separately, the pay office is concerned with:

  (i)   checking the authorisation;

  (ii) converting the entitlement into pay; and

  (iii) the payment date.

In the case of weekly paid employees, it is usual to pay the requisite number of full weeks' holiday pay in advance, usually on the last pay day before the commencement of the holiday. Income tax and NICs are deducted as if the employee had worked during the holiday weeks. Multiple deductions in respect of items such as SAYE and any attachment of earnings orders are also taken by reference to the holiday period. Certain deductions or earnings elements may not be appropriate during holiday periods.

On occasions, employers may pay additional sums to employees, based on the average earnings over a preceding pay period in order to avoid or reduce any significant drop in earnings when an employee takes a holiday.

Monthly salaries are normally paid at the usual pay interval irrespective of holiday periods and similar procedures may adopted where appropriate for fortnightly and four-weekly paid employees.

In order to ensure that payments are made at the correct time, sound administrative procedures must be established. Provided that this is done, the need for emergency payments can be minimised, if not eradicated totally. One such method by which this can be achieved is to require employees to complete a holiday request form within certain specified time constraints, stating when the holiday is to be taken and when the payment of the wage or salary should be made.

Provided that the request is made and signed by a supervisor or manager, it will serve both as a holiday record for personnel department and a pay request for the payroll department. Holiday stamp and credit schemes are often used in cases where employees change jobs on a regular basis within specific industries. For this reason, they are particularly common in the construction industry. Employers who use the scheme purchase stamps from the administrators of the scheme and these are placed weekly on each employee's holiday card.

Some holiday pay tax and NICs complications are described below and these mainly affect weekly-paid employees.

(a) ***Advances*** — A computer will normally be programmed to calculate tax and NICs in advance for holidays taken by weekly-paid employees. For example, if an employee goes on holiday for two weeks and is paid weekly, his tax weeks should be advanced by an extra two weeks. The NICs are calculated either by treating the payment for each week as if it had been made at the regular time (DSS Method A) or by treating the whole payment as one calculation for the whole holiday period (DSS Method B).

Under Method B, both the lower and upper earnings limits ('LEL and UEL') are effectively increased according to the length of the holiday, for example, to twice the weekly level for two weeks pay. Methods A and B can be chosen freely and can give different results. Method B can be used for employees who are paid in multiples of a week, for example fortnightly, but not for those paid monthly.

(b) ***Stamp schemes*** — As stated earlier, the provision of holiday pay through the purchase of stamps is a practice that is relatively common in areas of the construction industry. However, the treatment for tax purposes will vary depending upon whether or not the scheme has been approved by the Inland Revenue. Where the scheme is unapproved, PAYE must be accounted for at the time the credits are allocated to the employee (that is to say, when the stamps are attached to the card).

In the case of approved schemes, the employer is not required to operate PAYE. Where the holiday pay is paid from an approved holiday pay fund, the fund itself is required to deduct tax at basic rate and will issue a certificate of tax deducted to the employee.

No NICs are payable on either the amount spent on the stamps or credits used in holiday pay schemes or on the holiday pay paid to the employee, whether this is paid by the employer or directly by the fund.

(c) ***Credits*** — Money is set aside from pay until such time as the employee requests that the accrued credits are repaid to him. PAYE and NICs are deducted from his pay at the time of taking the credit. The accrued amounts of credit may therefore be paid to the employee without any further PAYE or NICs liability arising.

However, if the employee can only have the money at his holiday time, rather than on demand, it is subject to NICs at the time the credit is paid to the employee and not at the time it was set aside for the purpose by the employer. PAYE is still payable at the time the money was first aside.

(For further clarification of the above points, see CWG2 'Employer's Further Guide to PAYE and NICs', paragraphs 32–37.)

Entertainment, meals and gifts

9.6   The income tax treatment of expenses or benefits in respect of entertainment, meals or gifts is affected by a number of issues and is also subject to the possible application of several Extra-Statutory Concessions.

(*a*)   ***Meals*** — A common employee benefit is that of free or subsidised meals provided by the employer on his premises or elsewhere, or the provision of a ticket or token to obtain such a meal. (The use of meal vouchers is subject to separate taxation provisions.)

Tax is not charged if the meals are provided on a reasonable scale and either all of the employees may obtain free or subsidised meals on such a scale or the employer provides free or subsidised meal vouchers for those to whom meals are not provided. The concession regarding the tax free treatment of meals does not apply in the case of hotel, catering or similar businesses which provide meals for employees in a restaurant or dining room, at a time when meals are being served to the public, unless part of the premises is designated for the use of the employees only (ESC A74).

The provision of food to employees at other times may be a taxable benefit. For instance, it is not uncommon for food to be provided when employees work through the lunch break, work late after normal hours or carry out extra duties at the weekends. In these circumstances, it may be possible to escape liability by, *inter alia,* the *de minimis* principle if the amount divided amongst the employees is small, for example, £1 or less per head.

(*b*)   ***Entertainment*** — The tax treatment of entertaining expenses reimbursed to employees has frequently created problems for employers. As a consequence of *ICTA 1988, s 577*, an employee may not always be entitled to claim tax relief for entertaining expenses met by the employer. These rules apply to all employees and not just those to who the P11D rules apply.

In general, as long as the costs of providing the entertainment are disallowed in arriving at the employer's liability to tax, the employee is allowed to claim relief in respect of those amounts against his Schedule E tax liability.

The normal expense rules of Schedule E apply in order to determine whether or not the expenses allowance for the employee will be allowed. Where, for example, an employee's own meal is part of an entertainment function, it will not be disallowed for Schedule E purposes. However, where the only persons being entertained are other employees of the employer, the expenses will not normally be allowable.

Where an employee meets entertaining expenditure from either an inclusive salary or a round sum expense allowance, the expenditure is disallowed to the employee as it cannot be disallowed to the employer.

The rules for allowing entertaining expenditure for employees of non-trading organisations, for example, local authorities or the civil service, differ from those referred to above. Provided the expenditure is incurred 'wholly, exclusively and necessarily' in the performance of the duties, it will be allowable without the need for any disallowance to the employer.

Employees are not taxed on the value of a Christmas party or other function provided that the VAT-inclusive cost of the event does not exceed £75 per attendee and the event is open to the staff generally. This amount may be apportioned between more than one annual event, for example, a Christmas dinner and a summer party, provided that the total cost per head for both is no more than £75 (including VAT) (ESC A70). If the cost of an event exceeds £75 (including VAT) per head, tax will be payable on the full amount.

(c)   ***Gifts*** — Gifts of goods made to employees by their employer normally give rise to a taxable benefit. The measure of the benefit for a P9D employee is the second-hand value, but for a P11D employee, it is the greater of the second-hand value and the cost to the employer.

A gift received from a third party will not give rise to a taxable benefit on the employee provided that it has not been given *because* the recipient happens to be an employee of the employer. Such a gift is not exempt if it is received specifically in return for carrying out the duties of an employee.

The exemption can only apply if the cost of the gifts to any recipient is £150 or less from the same third party per tax year and the employer did not arrange for the third party to make the gift. This exemption is also provided for by ESC A70. If the cost of the gifts from the same third party exceeds £150 in the tax year, the whole cost of the gift is taxable rather than just the excess over £150.

Travelling and subsistence expenses

9.7   The position concerning the allowability, for tax purposes, of travelling and subsistence expenses has changed dramatically with effect from 6 April 1998. It will be recalled that, in the previous edition of this publication, attention was drawn to a consultative document that had been issued by the Inland Revenue proposing major changes to the tax treatment of such expenses. Many of these changes have now been introduced into the legislation.

In view of the fact that both the Inland Revenue and the CA can seek recovery of arrears of PAYE and NICs for a retrospective period of six years, it is important that employers are aware of the legislative requirements prior to 6 April 1998 (described below under the heading, 'The old legislation') and those which apply with effect from 6 April 1998 ('The new legislation').

The old legislation

The old legislation is contained at *ICTA 1988, s 198* and imposed a number of tests which had to be met before expenses could be allowed for tax purposes. In order to qualify for tax relief, the expenses of travelling had to have been incurred 'necessarily' whilst those connected with any other aspect, for example, subsistence expenses, had to have been incurred 'wholly, exclusively and necessarily' – in each instance, 'in the performance of the duties of the employment'.

The effect of these tests was to limit both the circumstances under which tax relief was available and the range of employees to whom it was available. For example, the costs of travelling between an employee's home and his normal place of work would not qualify for tax relief since the employee was not considered to be travelling 'in the performance of his duties', rather he was travelling in order to 'put himself in a position to perform the duties'.

As a consequence, tax relief would not be available, even if the employee was required to make a subsequent journey to the normal workplace, say, in the event that he was called out to deal with an emergency situation.

The costs of business journeys to places other than the normal workplace were, however, allowable on the grounds that the employee was considered to be travelling in the performance of the duties of the employment.

If the business journey commenced from a place other than the normal place of employment (say, the employee's home), the Inland Revenue required employers to ensure that the amounts of expenses reimbursed free of tax were limited to the lesser of the costs of the journey from the employee's home and the normal workplace. For obvious reasons, this was known as the 'lesser of or triangular travel' rule.

Although relatively simple in concept, the triangular travel rule was widely misunderstood by both employers and employees alike and was disliked because it was regarded as cumbersome and time consuming to administer.

The old rules were also regarded as discriminating against certain types of employee. For example, if an employee had no normal place of employment but was, instead, required to work at a number of sites, for periods of time varying between several days and several weeks, the Inland Revenue took the view that he was site based.

In this case, each site at which he worked was regarded as the normal place of work with the result that, in travelling to each site, the employee was not travelling in the performance of his duties, rather he was putting himself in a position to perform those duties.

The old rules had been tested before the courts on numerous occasions but in all but a very few instances, the Inland Revenue's view was upheld.

The proposed changes

The original consultative document proposed that the legislation should be amended with a view to making it easier to understand and fairer in its application. It was proposed that the new legislation should take effect from 6 April 1998. The major advantages were that the necessity that the costs of travel should be incurred in the performance of the duties of the employment would be replaced with a broader test, that is to say, that the travel should be necessary *either* in the performance of the duties *or* that attendance at the place visited was necessary to the performance of those duties.

This would, clearly, operate to the benefit of those employees who had hitherto been disadvantaged by being unable to claim tax relief in respect of any of the journeys which they made, for example, site based workers.

For the first time, a link would be established between travelling expenses and 'expenses connected with travel' – in other words, subsistence expenses.

However, the most controversial proposal was that account should be taken of the savings which the employee made when making a business journey by not making his ordinary commuting journey. Thus, for example, if an employee incurred travelling expenses of £20 when making a business trip to a place other than his normal workplace, and would have expended £5 in travelling from his home to the normal workplace, the amount of tax free reimbursement which he could receive would be limited to £15 (£20 — £5).

The triangular travel or lesser of rules would therefore cease to be appropriate.

Logical and reasonable though this sounded in theory, the proposal was, in practice, flawed. It was pointed out to the Inland Revenue that in order to operate the scheme properly, employers would need to know the normal commuting costs of every employee, not just those who made regular business journeys. Those costs would be subject to change, not just if an employee changed his home address, but on every occasion that the bus or rail company increased its fares.

In addition, employees' commuting methods might change – they might walk or cycle in fine weather or use their cars or public transport in times of rain or snow. In short, the proposed new procedures were more likely to *increase*, rather than *decrease* the administrative burden on employers.

As a consequence, the Inland Revenue announced a surprising about turn in September 1997 when it issued a Press Release stating that the requirement to take account of normal commuting costs would no longer apply although all other aspects of the proposed changes would remain in place.

The new legislation

The new legislation took effect from 6 April 1998 and the main points are set out below.

Tax relief is available in respect of the full costs of a journey which an employee makes when attending a temporary workplace. A 'temporary workplace' is one that an employee attends to perform a task of limited duration or for a temporary purpose. Thus, for example, a brief visit to a supplier's premises to discuss production delays would be regarded as a visit to a temporary workplace.

Since the full costs of the journey can be claimed, there is no longer a need to take account of the 'lesser of' rules or to deduct any home to work mileage. As a consequence, if an employee begins his business journey from home and drives 50 miles to the place to be visited, he is entitled to tax relief in respect of the whole of the journey. This notwithstanding that he might have only driven 30 miles had he commenced the business journey from his normal place of work – referred to in the new legislation as the 'permanent workplace'.

This will still be the case, even if the employee drives past the front door of his permanent workplace *en route* to his business appointment – regardless of whether or not he stops there. However, the Inland Revenue has stated that the reason for any such stop must not be to perform 'substantive duties'. Thus, if the employee stopped to collect a file or to make a quick telephone call, the journey would qualify for relief in its entirety.

On the other hand, if he spent an hour or so completing a report before continuing to the business appointment, only that part of the journey from the permanent workplace to the business appointment would qualify for relief.

There is no statutory requirement that the employer should reimburse employees with the *full* cost of their travelling expenses (or indeed with *any* of those costs). Thus, for example, if the employee commenced the business journey from home, the employer could, if he wished, apply the 'lesser of' rule and reimburse travelling expenses as if the employee had commenced the business journey from the permanent workplace.

Using the figures in the example given earlier, the employee would, therefore, receive travelling expenses from his employer for business mileage of 30 miles and would be entitled to claim tax relief from the Inland Revenue in respect of the 20 allowable business miles for which he had not been reimbursed.

Alternatively, the employer could require employees to deduct the costs of normal commuting from the expenses that they incur and reimburse the net amounts to the employees. As in the previous example, the employees would then be entitled to claim tax relief in respect of the amounts that the employer had not reimbursed them.

The tax relief can be claimed in one of three ways. The employee may either:

(*a*)   complete a self assessment tax return;

(*b*)   complete Form P87; or

(*c*)   simply request that relief be granted by writing to the tax district.

Site-based workers who, prior to 6 April 1998, were unable to obtain tax relief in respect of journeys that they made between their homes and the sites at which they performed their duties can now obtain that tax relief.

The Inland Revenue has estimated conservatively that the cost to the Excheq-uer of giving the additional tax relief will be in the region of £100 million per annum.

Despite the assertion that the new rules would be simpler than those that they replaced, in practice, many of them remain confusing and require a degree of objectivity on the part of the employer. The Inland Revenue has attempted to give its view as to how they should be interpreted in a new Booklet 490 'Employee Travel – A Tax and NICs Guide for Employers' and also in a new leaflet for employees – IR161.

A full resumé of the technical points contained in Booklet 490 is beyond the scope of this book and it is therefore recommended that employers should make themselves fully familiar with it if potential exposure is to be avoided. In cases where the reimbursement of expenses remains in doubt, professional advice should be sought.

It goes without saying that both the Inland Revenue PAYE auditors and CA inspectors will pay particularly close attention to the manner in which employers operate the new rules and they can also be expected to review expenses claims for periods prior to 6 April 1998 with a view to ensuring that the 'lesser of' rules have been applied correctly.

Claims for travelling expenses where the employee uses his own car on his employer's business are, again, not usually considered to be a taxable benefit. Claims in these circumstances are usually expressed as a rate, say 30p, per mile, to cover wear and tear, fuel etc. Where the rate used contains an element of 'profit' for the employee, the excess amount of the allowance will be liable to both PAYE and NICs.

However, the task of quantifying the profit element is not simple. In strictness, the employer should report the full amount of such allowances paid to each employee and they, in turn, should submit claims for tax relief based on the actual expenses incurred. In order to simplify the exercise, employers can agree with their tax offices that they operate the voluntary Fixed Profit Car Scheme (FPCS), whereby any profit element is determined by reference to the engine size of the employee's car and the related Inland Revenue Authorised Mileage Rates (IRAMRs). These were previously known as the FPCS rates.

The IRAMRs are determined annually by the Inland Revenue and take into account each of the factors in respect of which an employee would be able to claim tax relief if he were to undertake the arduous task of calculating, on a precise basis, the amount of relief to which he was entitled, for example, depreciation, running costs, standing charges etc.

If the employer chooses to use the IRAMRs (those for 1998/99 are shown below), he may pay these to his employees free of tax and NICs. If the rates which he pays to his employees are less than the IRAMRs, employees may compare the rates which they receive with the IRAMRs and claim tax relief on the difference.

The Inland Revenue authorised mileage rates for 1998/99 remain at 1997/98 levels and are as follows.

Size of car in cc	First 4,000 miles	Each mile over 4,000 miles
Up to 1,000 cc	28p	17p
1,001 cc to 1,500 cc	35p	20p
1,501 cc to 2,000 cc	45p	25p
Over 2,000 cc	63p	36p

Employers may choose to use one rate, irrespective of the engine capacity of each car and, if they choose to do so, they may take the average of the two middle bands above. For 1998/99, this will allow rates of 40p and 22.5p respectively.

The revised legislation contained at *ICTA 1988, s 198*, with effect from 6 April 1998, now regards travelling expenses as covering associated subsistence expenditure, for example, meals and accommodation, where they form a part of the costs of making a business journey. Thus, subsistence costs will normally qualify for a deduction on similar terms as for travelling expenses.

With effect from 6 April 1995, changes to the income tax legislation have permitted employers to reimburse employees free of tax with the costs of certain personal expenses which they may incur whilst staying away from home overnight on business, which would not qualify for tax relief. For example, an employee who is required to stay away from home overnight in an hotel might make a telephone call to his home, buy a drink, or amuse himself by visiting the cinema. Whilst the costs of doing so would, in all likelihood, not have been incurred had the employee not been away from home, they would nevertheless fail the 'wholly, exclusively and necessarily' test for the allowability of expenses imposed by *ICTA 1988, s 198*. In other words, the employee did not have to incur those costs in order to carry out his duties.

ICTA 1988, s 200A, however, exempts from tax the reimbursement of such personal incidental expenses (PIEs) up to a maximum of £5 per night (or £10 per night if the overnight stay is overseas). To qualify for exemption, the PIEs must be incidental to the employee's being away from his usual place of abode during a 'qualifying absence from home'.

A qualifying absence from home is any continuous period throughout which the employee is obliged to stay away from his usual place of abode and during which he has at least one overnight stay away from that place but does not on any occasion stay overnight at a place, the expenses of travelling to which would not be allowable for tax purposes.

Whilst PIEs are not intended to represent round sum allowances, there is no requirement on employees to provide evidence of having incurred any, or all of the amount claimed. Employers may however insist that employees provide such evidence before they will pay the PIE.

If the employee is away, for say, three nights, the maximum amount which may be paid tax free is £15 (or £30 if he is overseas). However, if the amount paid to him exceeds the equivalent of £5 (or £10) per night, the whole amount, and not just the excess, is taxable.

If the employer chooses not to reimburse such costs to the employee, the employee cannot claim tax relief in lieu.

(See 9.18 below for further guidance on expenses.)

Medical insurance

9.8   There is a wide range of medical and health insurance schemes, BUPA and Private Patients Plan (PPP) being two of the best known. The membership terms imply that insurance is used to pay doctors' fees and hospital charges for private treatment obtained outside the NHS. Medical insurance is often provided as a perk but it can be an effective way of maintaining and restoring the health of essential employees. It may also be a necessity for employees on foreign service. The employer can pay the insurer's premiums and provide cover free of charge but, where the employee works in the UK, this will be treated as a taxable benefit. Relief will normally be granted where the facility is provided for employees travelling overseas.

In many cases, the employee pays, either partly or wholly, the cost of the medical insurance whilst the employer provides the administration. Where the employer simply arranges the insurance so that employees can take advantage of a group discount, without actually making any contribution himself, no taxable benefit arises. Families of employees can also take advantage of such schemes.

Where the employee subscribes towards the cost of the scheme, the premiums are usually deducted via the payroll. The value of any benefit to be reported on Forms P9D or P11D should reflect both the cost to the employer of providing the benefit and any contribution made by the employee. It is common practice to allow employees to 'opt out' of medical insurance so as to avoid a charge to tax on a benefit which they do not enjoy.

More basic contributory schemes are commonly found. These may be provided to assist with other 'medical' expenses, such as dental treatment, spectacles or the cost of family visits to people in hospital. Permanent health insurance, discussed at 8.18 above, is a misnomer and is basically a method of providing a disability pension.

Basic rate tax relief was previously available to any individual paying medical insurance premiums in respect of a person aged 60 or over (or for a married couple where one spouse was aged 60 or over). Such tax relief was given at source. However, in the July 1997 Budget, the Chancellor of the Exchequer announced the withdrawal of the relief. Contracts in existence at that time would continue to attract tax relief until they expired. New contracts, however, would not receive tax relief. It is likely that most premiums would cease to qualify for tax relief after July 1998.

The provision of routine health checks or medical screening for employees does not confer a taxable benefit. However, the Inspector of Taxes may seek confirmation that the medical report is submitted to the employer in the first instance. Similarly, a pre-employment medical intended to assess a potential employee's fitness to work, does not constitute a taxable benefit.

Relocation and removal expenses

9.9   Until the *Finance Act 1993*, the taxation treatment of removal expenses was covered by Inland Revenue Extra-Statutory Concessions A5 and A67. Under this concessionary treatment, there was virtually no limit as to the amount which an employer could pay to an employee free of tax. Since 6 April 1993, relocation and removal expenses and benefits have been governed by a statutory exemption contained at ICTA 1988, 11A Sch.

The legislation places a cap of £8,000 on the amount in respect of which exemption from tax will be allowed. This amount includes the eligible removal expenses incurred by the employee as well as any eligible benefits in kind which the employer may provide, in connection with a job-related change in the employee's sole or main residence.

The eligible removal expenses fall into seven categories:

(*a*)   disposal charges such as estate agents' and solicitors' fees and disconnection charges;

(*b*)   acquisition charges, such as survey fees, Stamp Duty and solicitors' fees;

(*c*)   abortive acquisition expenses, where for example, the purchase falls through for reasons beyond the control of the employee;

(*d*)   transportation expenses, including insurance and temporary storage;

(*e*)   travelling between the two places involved and associated subsistence expenses;

(*f*)   duplicate expenses, for example, where replacement items have to be bought for the new home because the old ones are unsuitable;

(*g*)   bridging loan expenses.

There are categories of eligible removal benefits corresponding to headings (*a*) to (*f*) above.

In order to qualify for the exemption, the employee does not have to dispose of the previous home but he must be able to demonstrate that the main place of abode has changed because of the employment relocation.

If a beneficial bridging loan is provided by the employer, a special calculation is needed if the qualifying removal expenses and benefits fall below the £8,000 limit. Where an employer grants or facilitates an interest free or 'cheap' bridging loan to a relocated employee, the legislation requires that the normal beneficial loan rules at *ICTA 1988, s 160* (see 9.16 below) are postponed for a certain number of days. This is found by equating the interest payable on the loan at the 'official rate' for that number of days with the amount by which the qualifying removal expenses and benefits falls short of £8,000.

Example

Qualifying removal benefits and expenses provided	£7,000
Amount of unused exemption	£1,000
Interest free bridging loan provided	£50,000

Official interest rate 10% pa $\times$ £50,000 =   £5,000

Operation of *ICTA 1988, s 160* delayed for:

$$\frac{1,000}{5,000} \times 365 \text{ days} = 73 \text{ days}$$

PAYE is not applied to payments of qualifying removal expenses made under a relocation package, even if the qualifying limit of £8,000 is exceeded. Instead, any taxable payments are reported on Form P11D or Form P9D. Payments of non-qualifying removal expenses, for example additional housing cost allowances, must, however, be treated as pay for PAYE purposes.

One other condition should be noted which may impact upon the qualifying status of any relocation expenses whether or not they exceed the £8,000 cap. The legislation states that in order to qualify, the expenses must be incurred or the benefits provided on or before the 'relevant day'. In this context, the relevant day is defined as the last day of the tax year, following the tax year in which the employee began to perform his duties at the new location.

ICTA 1988, 11 Sch 6(2), states however:

'If it appears reasonable to the Board to do so, having regard to all the circumstances of a particular change of residence, they may direct that in relation to that change the relevant day is a day which:

(a) falls after the day mentioned in sub-paragraph (1) above; and

(b) is a day on which a year of assessment ends'.

Accordingly, therefore, the time limit referred to earlier can be extended by the Inland Revenue where any delay in changing residence is due to circumstances which are outside the control of the employee.

The fact that relocation expenses can be paid over a period of time can, in itself, create problems for the employer. Take, for example, the employee who is notified in March 1997 of the fact that he is due to be relocated. The employee may take early steps to find a new house and be successful in finding one by the end of March and having a survey carried out. The survey costs will fall within the 1996/97 tax year.

The bulk of his remaining expenses are, therefore, likely to be incurred within the following (1997/98) tax year. The employer must ensure that his procedures are such that he can 'capture' relocation costs paid over both tax years for the purposes of reporting the taxable expenses on the Forms P11D or P9D for both 1996/97 and 1997/98.

The conversion of the previous Extra-Statutory Concessions into statutory relief has resulted in a far less generous tax-free régime for the relocation of employees. As a consequence, employers will often be faced with demands for recompense from relocated employees for the tax element which they will have to suffer on relocation costs not covered by the statutory exemption.

House purchase schemes are sometimes used by employers to help their employees who are making a job-related move to dispose of their existing homes. These typically involve the employer, or a relocation company, purchasing the property at the current market value as established by independent professional valuations.

The tax treatment depends on the precise contractual obligations entered into by the parties. The Inland Revenue normally accepts that costs met by the employer relating to the employee's old residence *after* the beneficial interest in the property has been transferred from the employee, including any loss on eventual resale, will not be chargeable to tax on the employee.

Where, instead of acquiring the employee's old home, the employer makes good any loss on the sale incurred by the employee in disposing of the property to a third party, the payment is taxable in full and does not qualify for any exemption.

Employees may be able to mitigate their tax liability through the availability of an Extra-Statutory Concession (ESC D37) and the revised treatment of removal expenses introduced by the *Finance Act 1993* (see above) may allow relief from capital gains tax where the employee has a right to additional proceeds from the onward sale of his property by the employer or a relocation company, where he satisfies the conditions for the private residence exemption in respect of the property. Where there is no provision for the employee to receive any additional proceeds as a right, but an amount is nevertheless paid over to him, the Inland Revenue takes the view that the amount would give rise to a charge under Schedule E, as an emolument from the employment.

Car schemes

9.10   Despite increasing tax charges, cars provided for an employee's private use continue to be a popular benefit in the private sector. Public sector employers tend to restrict themselves to either the provision of loans for car purchase or to an allowance paid to employees who must provide vehicles for use in the course of their duties. The use of a hire car or an employer's pool car is not a taxable benefit subject to certain conditions being met.

(Reference (5) in 9.21 below contains a full survey of current practices as far as car schemes are concerned.)

Car schemes range from providing a car, complete with chauffeur, to the payment of a mileage allowance for the use of the employee's own car on the employer's business. In many cases, but by no means all, a company car is necessary for the employee's work, a sales representative is a typical example. The type of vehicle provided will usually be related to the employee's status within the organisation or to the level of his salary. Where a car is provided, road tax, insurance and maintenance will usually be included. Company policies on the replacement of cars varies widely. Some employers insist that the car is replaced every year whilst others will impose a minimum period of say three to four years or a mileage figure, after which the car must be changed.

Common arrangements include:

(*a*)   the provision of a car plus fuel for private and business use;

(*b*)   the provision of a car with no fuel provided for private use but business mileage expenses being reimbursed at an appropriate mileage rate (say, between 6p and 10p per mile);

(*c*)   the ability to obtain a car of better quality than the 'benchmark' model, to which the employee would normally be entitled, subject to the employee making a private contribution;

(*d*)   the payment of a regular allowance to help to purchase and maintain a car to be used for business purposes; and

(*e*)   the provision of a loan at a reduced rate of interest with which to purchase a car.

Employers may also provide, or pay for, a car parking space at or near to the employee's place of work – such a benefit does not fall to be regarded as taxable (*ICTA 1988, s 197A*) or NICable.

A car which is provided for an employee's private use (including use by members of his family or household) is subject to a special tax charge – the car benefit charge.

The mere fact that an employee is offered an alternative, for example, a higher salary, to a car, does not make the car subject to the general Schedule E tax rules. The car benefit charge specified by *ICTA 1988, s 157* still applies.

This rule was introduced with effect from 6 April 1995, in order to counter a, then popular, tax and NICs avoidance scheme based on such 'salary sacrifice' arrangements.

The car benefit charge is only applicable to directors and employees in respect of whom a Form P11D is appropriate (see 9.3 earlier).

The car benefit charge does not apply to motorcycles, invalid carriages or certain other vehicles 'of a type not commonly used as a private vehicle and unsuitable to be so used'. This latter category includes cars such as those commonly provided to firefighters and police officers which, although they may not be in a distinctive livery or carry any other visible identifying features, may nevertheless be equipped with permanent flashing blue lights – often concealed behind the radiator grille or disguised as driving lights or headlights.

The principle, that such cars could not be taxed as 'company cars' under *ICTA 1988, s 157*, was established in the tax case, *Gurney v Richards [1989] STC 682*. This fact is likely to be of interest to only a limited number of employers – primarily, police forces, fire brigades, and possibly ambulance services. Nevertheless, it is worth making some observations here. The outcome of the case established that cars such as have been described, do not fall to be taxed under the car benefit charge – but they do not fall out of a tax charge altogether. The cars will still attract a liability to tax under that section of the Schedule E charging provisions at *ICTA 1988, s 154* which deals with 'use of employer's assets'. However, the tax treatment is still more beneficial, relying as it does on a cash equivalent calculated by reference to 20 per cent of the market value of the car, (that is to say, the price paid for it) rather than 35 per cent of the manufacturer's list price (applicable regardless of any discounts which the employer may have been able to negotiate). Furthermore, the cash equivalent can be apportioned between the business and private use of the car – the same does not apply to cars taxed under the car benefit charge.

It follows that a car which is not taxed under *section 157* cannot attract the fuel scale charge imposed by *ICTA 1988, s 158*. Similarly, a charge to Class 1A NICs on either the car or the fuel cannot arise since the Class 1A NICs liability is contingent upon the car being taxed under *section 157* in the first instance. Thus there are savings to be made for both the employer and the employee.

Finally, it is of interest to note that certain police officers and firefighters continue to believe that no income tax liability arises whatsoever in connection with such cars and that Mr Richards won his case on the basis that, as a firefighter, he was on duty (or at least, on call) at all times. This is not the case – the deciding factor in this case was simply the fact that the blue lights (whether operating or not) rendered it illegal for such a vehicle to be driven on the public roads by someone who was not employed by the emergency services. The vehicle was thus 'unsuitable to be used as a private vehicle'.

The car benefit charge is based on the manufacturer's list price (MLP) of the car and its accessories. The legislation covers in detail what is to be taken as the MLP of the car and the accessories but it is important to note that any discounts which the employer may have been able to obtain when purchasing the vehicle (for example, because of bulk buying, payment in cash, or absence of a 'trade in' vehicle), are disregarded for the purposes of establishing the MLP.

The cash equivalent is calculated by reference to 35 per cent per annum of the MLP and accessories (but with a cap at a total MLP of £80,000). However, the cash equivalent can be reduced by reference to certain circumstances as follows:

(i) *business mileage at least 2,500 p.a. but less than 18,000 p.a.* — the 35 per cent benefit is reduced by one-third;

(ii) *business mileage at least 18,000 p.a.* — the 35 per cent benefit is reduced by two-thirds;

(iii) *car only available for part of the tax year* — the benefit (after adjustment for business mileage) is further reduced according to the number of days of unavailability within the year;

(iv) *car not available for 30 or more consecutive days* — the benefit (reduced by reference to any business mileage) is further reduced according to the number of days of unavailability;

(v) *more than one car made available concurrently* — only the car used most for business travel can attract the two-thirds reduction. All other cars can attract the one-third reduction if applicable;

(vi) *older cars* — where the car is four or more years old at the end of the year, a further reduction of one-third of the calculated benefit is allowed;

(vii) *contribution by employee* — the calculated benefit is to be reduced by an amount paid by the employee which **he is required to pay as a condition of the car being made available for his private use;**

(It is important to note that the emboldened phrase must appear in the car scheme documentation if the employee is to obtain tax relief in respect of any such contribution.)

The MLP of the car and accessories is to be reduced by any capital contribution made by the employee towards the cost of the car. However, where the capital contribution exceeds £5,000, the reduction of the MLP is limited to £5,000;

(viii) *classic cars* — the market value of the car on the last day of the tax year concerned will be substituted for the original list price of the car. The definition of a 'classic car' is set out in detail in the legislation but, briefly stated, is as follows:

- the definition of list price under the new legislation would result in a figure less than the market value for the tax year;

- the car is more than 15 years old at the end of the relevant tax year; and

- the market value of the car at the end of the relevant tax year is £15,000 or more;

(ix) *pool cars* — no tax charge arises in connection with a genuine pool car, that is to say:

- one which is used by more than one employee and not used by one employee to the exclusion of others; and

- any private use of the car is incidental to the business use of it; and

- the car is not normally kept overnight at, or near to, any employee's home.

In view of the impact on car benefits by virtue of income tax, NICs and VAT, the necessity to maintain accurate and detailed records of the usage of cars by employees is of paramount importance. The extent of the liability under these heads depends on the business mileage driven by each employee and, because of this, record keeping cannot be avoided. Whereas, in the past, employers were allowed to enter 'don't know' in response to the question on the Form P11D which asked for details of the annual business mileage, such a response is no longer permitted.

Where the car benefit charge applies, a further charge to tax arises if any fuel is provided for private use. The fuel scale charge is an 'all or nothing' charge and applies if as much as one pounds worth of fuel is provided for private motoring. The charge can only be avoided if the employee repays the whole cost of any private fuel which he has received and there is no reduction for any partial contribution which an employee may make in respect of any such fuel. No special rules apply in relation to the extent of an employee's annual business mileage or in respect of older or second cars.

The fuel scale charges applicable for 1998/99 are shown below:

	£
Petrol cylinder capacity	
0–1,400	1,010
1,401–2,000	1,280
2,001 and over	1,890
Diesel	
0–2,000 cc	1,280
2,001 and over	1,890
Cars without a cylinder capacity	1,890

Vans

9.11   A van which is made available to an employee for his private use has, since 1993/94, been subject to a scale charge. The basic scale charge is £500 reduced to £350 if the van is more than four years old at the end of the relevant tax year. Further reductions are allowed where the employee makes a contribution towards the private use of the van or where the van is not available for the whole of the tax year. It should be noted that the contribution made by the employee must be made as a condition of the van being made available for his private use.

In addition, a charge arises on any employee who uses a 'shared van'. If a variety of vans is made available for the private use of employees during a year, the appropriate scale benefit (£500 or £350) of each must be aggregated and apportioned amongst each of the employees to whom they are available for private use. If the calculation results in a cash equivalent of more than £500, the excess is ignored. Again, any contribution made by employees for the private use is deducted from the cash equivalent and the cash equivalent is also reduced *pro rata* where the van or vans are unavailable for part of the tax year.

An alternative method of calculating the cash equivalent on shared vans is provided for within the legislation. This allows for the imposition of a daily taxable benefit of £5 where the employee makes a claim for this method to be used.

Telephones

9.12   The Inland Revenue will generally allow a deduction for tax purposes in respect of the cost of business telephone calls made from an employee's home telephone. However, a deduction in respect of any part of the telephone rental will *normally* not be permitted.

The Inland Revenue's justification for this is that the rental cost serves to make the telephone available for both business and private use and, accordingly, the rental element of the telephone bill fails the 'wholly, exclusively and necessarily' test imposed by *ICTA 1988, s 198*. This view was confirmed in the case of *Lucas v Cattell ChD [1972] 48 TC 353*.

The italicised use of the word 'normally' should be noted. Whilst the *section 198* test is absolute (in other words, if any private use is made of the telephone, no statutory entitlement to relief in respect of the telephone rental can exist), Inspectors of Taxes can occasionally be persuaded to agree some measure of concessional relief where, for example, an employee has a contractual requirement to be called out to deal with emergency situations.

The Inland Revenue will be prepared to grant some relief to employees in the electricity and gas industries who are likely to be called out to deal with life and death emergencies. By the same token, it follows that they should be prepared to allow similar claims in respect of workers in the nuclear industry, certain police and firefighter officers and, possibly, certain health service employees. The extent to which such relief will be granted depends upon the Inspector of Taxes in question.

Inspectors of Taxes can normally be expected to require some form of evidence to support any claim for relief in respect of business calls. In the past, they would usually require that a detailed log of such calls be maintained and produced as evidence, although since itemised bills are now far more common-place than hitherto, such a bill, with the business calls clearly identified, will usually suffice. The costs of any private calls which are met by the employer will be treated as a taxable benefit and NICs will be due thereon.

If the employer is the subscriber, no liability to NICs will arise. However, the question of the extent of the benefit in kind regarding the line rental is an interesting one. Following the decision in *Pepper v Hart*, it would seem reasonable that the line rental should be disregarded for tax purposes since this cost would have had to be paid in any event by the employer in order to make the telephone available for business purposes. This being the case, the only taxable benefit would fall to be the cost of any private calls and a proportion of any capital costs. Whether the Inland Revenue in fact takes this point is not known.

Mobile telephones

The tax treatment of mobile telephones is more clear cut. Where the employer provides a mobile telephone that is available for private purposes, it is subject to a scale charge of £200. This scale charge applies in respect of both hand portable and car telephones.

The scale charge is reduced to 'nil' if the employee either makes no private use of the mobile telephone or is required to (and in fact does) reimburse the employer in full for any private use. The Inland Revenue defines the full cost of the private use as being the cost of all private calls (including VAT) plus a proportionate share of the higher of:

(*a*)   the equipment rental; and

(*b*)   20 per cent of the market value of the equipment (the annual value) when it was first provided.

It should be noted that, if the telephone was provided specifically for business use, the line rental can be ignored on *Pepper v Hart* grounds. If, on the other hand, it was not so provided, the line rental must be taken into account.

Few if any employers now actually rent mobile telephones – the cost of buying these has decreased quite dramatically in recent years. It follows therefore that (*a*) will rarely be a consideration in calculating the amount to be repaid by employees. Furthermore, since the costs of acquiring such equipment can be extremely low (many service providers will actually give the handset away free, secure in the knowledge that they will make a good profit on the air time) the annual value of the telephone will, itself, be very low. Take as an example, a telephone which has been purchased for £50 and which is used privately for 10 per cent of the time.

The 'annual value' is 20 per cent of the purchase price (£10) and a proportionate share is 10 per cent of £10 (£1). In order to avoid the scale charge, the employee must repay his private call costs (plus VAT) plus £1 per year. Many Inspectors of Taxes will take a pragmatic approach and agree to disregard the 'annual value' element provided that the call costs are repaid. Again, however, this is a subjective issue and not all Inspectors of Taxes will agree the point.

Vouchers

9.13   One area of benefits which has attracted a great deal of attention in recent years is that of the provision of vouchers. One of the reasons why they have attracted such interest is their value as a NICs avoidance measure – vouchers are generally excluded from a NICs liability unless they are exchangeable for cash. Another reason is the fact that payment by way of vouchers offers the potential for deferring the point at which the tax becomes payable – provided, of course, that the voucher is only exchangeable for goods or services, and cannot be exchanged for cash. Where a voucher is exchangeable for cash, it is subject to PAYE and NICs at the time it is provided, as if it were cash. The NICs advantages of vouchers that cannot be exchanged for cash will disappear with effect from April 1999. Legislation introduced in the *Social Security Act 1998* imposes a liability to Class 1 NICs on almost all vouchers with the exception, for example, of those supplied for the provision of childcare.

Provided that the voucher can only be used to obtain goods or services, the cash equivalent for Form P9D/P11D reporting purposes is taken to be the cost to the employer of providing the voucher. This will usually be the face value of the voucher, although it may be the case that the employer has been able to obtain the vouchers at a discounted price, in which case the lower value will be substituted.

A voucher which is capable of being exchanged for a readily convertible asset (for example, gold bullion) or which is itself a readily convertible asset, is treated as if it were cash and the employer is required to calculate PAYE on the notional cash value. Similarly, such a voucher attracts a NICs liability with effect from 6 April 1995.

Luncheon vouchers do not give rise to either a PAYE or NICs liability provided that certain conditions are met:

(*a*)   the vouchers must be non-transferable and used for meals only;

(*b*)   where any restriction is placed on their issue to employees, the vouchers must be available to lower paid staff; and

(c)   the daily value of the vouchers must not exceed 15p per working day.

Where any of these conditions is not met, the value of the voucher or part of the value is taxable.

Employee share schemes

9.14   The basic intention of employee share schemes is to provide employees with a stake in their employer's business and thus give them an incentive to maximise profits. The method by which this is normally done is to provide the employees with ordinary shares in their company (or rights to acquire such shares) on special terms.

'Approved' share schemes carry certain tax incentives. There are several types of schemes currently available and the details of each vary to some extent. The three types of approved scheme are briefly described below.

(a)   *Profit-sharing schemes* — In profit sharing schemes, shares are held in trust for the employee for a minimum of two years and an income tax charge will arise if the shares are disposed of within three years. The limit on the value of shares which may be allocated to the employee is ten per cent of the employee's salary (excluding benefits), subject to a maximum of £8,000 and a minimum of £3,000. [*ICTA 1988, s 186*].

(b)   *Savings-related schemes* — In savings-related option schemes, the employees set aside a certain amount each pay period (currently up to £250 per month) under Save As You Earn (SAYE) via the payroll. (See 15.5(*h*) and 15.5(*k*) below.) The employees have the option of purchasing the shares at a fixed price using these savings. [*ICTA 1988, s 185*].

(c)   *Company share option plans* — In company share option plans (formerly known as 'executive' schemes), share options can be given to an employee as long as they do not exceed £30,000 worth. The options can be exercised tax-free at any time between three and ten years after they are granted, although not more frequently than once every three years. [*ICTA 1988, s 185*].

Reference (12) in 9.21 below gives an in-depth examination of share option schemes.

Profit-related pay

9.15   Performance (or Profit) Related Pay (PRP) schemes were introduced in the mid-1980s with the objective of giving employees an incentive to increase the productivity of the company for which they worked by sharing in the success of the company. In brief, it was felt that employees would be more inclined to help the employer to do well if they felt that part of their remuneration was dependent upon the company trading profitably or achieving a previously set benchmark.

Such schemes, offering as they did, the potential for employees to receive a substantial tax free (but not NICs free) payment became extremely popular. However, in the 1996 Budget, the Chancellor of the Exchequer announced that, in view of the fact that the national economy had improved dramatically, 'pump-priming' methods of this type were no longer necessary and, accordingly, PRP schemes would be phased out over a period of years. The method by which this would happen would be by a gradual withdrawal of the tax concessions which gave them their popularity, such that no tax relief will be due for profit periods commencing after 31 December 1999.

PRP schemes, subject to their gaining Inland Revenue approval, currently qualify for certain tax concessions. [*ICTA 1988, Pt V, Chapter III*]. The basic idea behind PRP is to grant tax relief to private sector employees in schemes which link part of their pay to the profits of their employer's business. Employers could design their own schemes subject to certain restrictions. The features of an approved profit-related pay scheme include, *inter alia*, the following:

(*a*)   tax relief is calculated for profit periods (which may differ from the tax year) on the whole of an employee's pay under such a scheme up to the lower of £4,000 and 20 per cent of total pay for the period. The first limit is reduced to £2,000 for profit periods commencing after 31 December 1997 and to £1,000 for profit periods commencing after 31 December 1998 and before 1 January 2000;

(*b*)   PRP and tax relief can be given through the operation of PAYE, although NICs are still payable on the whole of PRP in the normal way;

(*c*)   a PRP scheme must cover 80 per cent of the employees in an employment unit excluding people who have not been employed for a minimum period specified in the scheme;

(*d*)   PRP may be distributed each pay period on the basis of interim payments;

(*e*)   an annual return (Form PRP20) must be completed and sent to the Inland Revenue PRP office. The figures in the form must be independently audited.

'Special schemes' can be implemented for smaller groups of employees (once there is a 'general scheme' which meets the statutory requirements), giving considerable scope for designing schemes to enable most employees to benefit from the tax relief available and to arrange that, if desired, different groups can obtain different levels of PRP and thereby, different amounts of tax savings.

The *Finance Act 1994, ss 98* and *99* introduced provisions to prevent perceived abuse of PRP 'special schemes'. Some 'special schemes' were designed as devices to reward and benefit, for example, senior managers, while their associated 'general schemes' were designed only to produce limited sums, for instance, £50 per head, for other employees. *ICTA 1988, 8 Sch* (as amended by *FA 1994, ss 98* and *99*) made provision that for 'special schemes' registered on or after 1 December 1993, the fixed percentage or distributable pool may not exceed a limit calculated by reference to the ratio of total pay to PRP in the 'general scheme'.

If it is established that, whether by mistake, or otherwise, an Inland Revenue approved scheme does not, in fact, meet the statutory requirements, any tax relief which an employer has given under a defective scheme is recoverable from the employer. The employer, for his part, has no statutory right to recover the excess relief from his employees. The careful and proper drafting of the scheme rules and careful operation of the scheme itself by the payroll department are, therefore, essential if the employer is to avoid incurring an irrecoverable cost.

ICTA 1988, s 177B(8)(g) allows an employer to correct a defective set of rules in order to bring a scheme back within the statutory framework, although this will only apply in very limited circumstances.

In order to be successful, the design and drafting of schemes is a complex matter and employers who, despite the loss of the tax advantages, nevertheless wish to introduce a PRP scheme would be as well to refer to their tax advisors.

See References (7) and (13) in 9.21 below.

Employer loans

9.16   Employers will frequently make loans available to staff for a variety of purposes. Typically, these will be in respect of:

(a)   house purchase;

(b)   car purchase;

(c)   season tickets;

(d)   study loans; and

(e)   personal loans.

Most loans by employers to employees are offered at either a nil rate of interest or at preferential low interest rates. Depending upon the purpose of the loan, the employer may take little regard of the status of the employee or the requirements of the job. However, local authorities will often only grant car loans to those employees who are designated as essential car users. The employer will usually impose a minimum period of employment, say one year, before the employee can be considered for a loan.

House purchase loans are most commonly encountered amongst financial institutions, for example, banks, building societies and insurance companies. A simple scheme might offer, say, up to four times the employee's annual salary as a loan covering up to 95 per cent of the value of the house. The interest rate might be five per cent per annum with repayments being made monthly by deduction from salary. More complex schemes may increase the interest rate in accordance with the size of the loan.

Loans for season tickets are common, particularly in and around the London area. The purpose of such loans is to enable employees to take advantage of the significant discounts which are available when purchasing annual season tickets and London based employers will frequently offer the facility of such a loan as an incentive to attract and retain staff. Repayment of a season ticket loan will typically be over a period of between ten and twelve months.

Loans may also be offered to employees to assist them during a period of financial hardship or to provide them with bridging finance when being relocated to a new geographical location.

Loans made to directors or P11D employees (see 9.3 above) which are at either a nil or low rate of interest are known as 'beneficial loans' and will frequently attract a tax liability. The cash equivalent of such a benefit is the difference between the interest paid to the employer by the employee in the year and the amount of interest calculated as being payable had the official interest rate (OIR) been used. The OIR is set by the Inland Revenue and is reviewed on a regular basis. The rate usually reflects changes in market lending rates.

Different OIRs apply to certain foreign currency loans.

From 6 April 1994 (the 1994/95 tax year), no cash equivalent is deemed to arise if the amount of the beneficial loan outstanding at any time in the year does not exceed £5,000. [*ICTA 1988, s 161*]. Where an employee has more than one beneficial loan outstanding at any time, the outstanding balances must be aggregated for the purposes of this £5,000 limit.

Any loan which is written off or released by the employer is treated as giving rise to a taxable benefit, except where this occurs on or after the employee's death.

Special mention should be made concerning the method of calculating and charging interest by local authorities in connection with low interest loans to employees – typically those made under 'Assisted Car Purchase Schemes'. Guidance on the method of calculating and charging interest is given to local authorities in the 'National Joint Council Conditions of Service Manual – the Green Book' (previously known as the Purple Book).

Employers are advised that two alternative methods of calculating and charging interest may be used and the decision as to which one is used is left to the authority.

The first method allows for the calculation of interest using a 'flat rate' of interest – say 4.55 per cent. Thus, for example, if an employee borrows £7,500 over three years, the interest will be calculated as follows:

£7,500 × 4.55% × 3 = £1,023.75

The interest is added to the amount of the loan to give a total to be repaid of £8,523.75. The amount of the monthly repayment is £8,523.75 divided by 36 (months) or £236.77.

The second method involves using an annual percentage rate (APR) of interest – say 9.1 per cent calculated at six monthly intervals on the reducing balance of the loan.

The amount of interest payable by the employee will be almost identical regardless of which method is used. However, the Inland Revenue will often argue that the flat rate method (using as it does, a lower rate of interest) gives rise to a greater tax liability than might otherwise be the case, particularly where the supporting documentation makes no reference to the apportion-ment between the amount of capital and interest which is repayable each month or, more importantly, where it does address the position, but does so in a manner which appears to show that the ratio between capital and interest repaid remains constant.

Employers will frequently take the view that if this method is used, the ratio of capital to interest will remain constant. Thus, in the instance referred to above, the monthly repayment of £236.77 may be described in the supporting loan schedules as representing the repayment of capital of £208.33 and interest of £28.44 in each and every month.

If, on the other hand, the interest was to be recalculated on the six monthly basis, the amount of interest repayable would vary according to the amount of the outstanding capital – the amount of the repayment would remain constant but the percentage of it which represented the interest would decrease as the amount originally borrowed reduced.

Local authority employers should, therefore, ensure that any loan schedules which are prepared are capable of demonstrating that interest is recalculated on the basis of six monthly 'rests' if a challenge from the Inland Revenue is to be avoided.

(See Figure 9A above and IR Booklet 480, Chapter 17 for the tax details).

Redundancy and termination payments

9.17   When an employee's contract of service comes to an end, the employer may be obliged, or will choose, to make a payment (or payments) to him which have, as their source, either contractual or statutory provisions. Such termination payments may be liable to income tax and/or NICs depending upon various factors such as their source, nature or size. (The term 'termination payments' is used here to describe any payments made on the termination of the contract of service and includes redundancy pay, payments in lieu of notice, compensation for loss of office, payments in respect of restrictive covenants etc.)

If an employee ceases to be employed by virtue of redundancy, he will often be entitled to a statutory minimum payment. 'Redundancy' is defined in the *Employment Rights Act 1996* which lays down a strict procedure to be followed by employers, including consultation with employee representatives and notification to the Department of Education and Employment.

ERA 1996, s 139(1) defines 'redundancy' as dismissal wholly or mainly attributable to either the employer ceasing (or intending to cease) to carry on the business for which the employee was employed (or ceasing the business in the place where the employee was employed), or to a cessation or diminution of the requirements of the business for the employee to carry out work of a particular kind.

The statutory minimum for redundancy payments, as now laid down in *ERA 1996, s 162*, varies with the employee being entitled to one and a half weeks' pay or one weeks' pay or half a weeks' pay for each year of service according to his age and length of service. This payment is subject to a maximum of 20 years' service; a maximum of £220 as a week's pay; and an overall maximum of £6,300. (The maxima for a week's pay and overall payment are reviewed annually by the Department for Education and Employment.) Appendix G contains a redundancy pay ready reckoner.

Over time, many employers have developed redundancy schemes which exceed the statutory minimum level of redundancy benefits. For example, there may be a flat-rate addition for each year of service; a minimum payment irrespective of length of service; enhancements to the statutory minima; and early retirement terms, such as no actuarial reduction in the early retirement pension.

The tax and NICs position of termination payments is not straightforward and a full description of the position would undoubtedly be beyond the scope of this handbook. However, it is clear that the Inland Revenue has, for a number of years, taken an increasingly harder line on payments made, free of tax, at the termination of an employment.

A great deal depends upon the nature of the employment contract which exists between the employer and the (former) employee. However, if the contract provides for the making of a particular payment, the probability is that the payment will be liable to both PAYE and NICs. The tax and NICs treatment of the various types of payment is explained below.

(a)   ***Income tax*** — The principal tax position can be found at *ICTA 1988, s 148* which applies to all termination payments which are 'not otherwise chargeable to tax'.

It is necessary in the first instance, to examine any termination payment with a view to establishing whether or not it falls to be taxed under any other section of the income tax legislation. For example, if the payment is deemed to be an emolument, it will be taxed under Schedule E by virtue of the standard provisions contained at *ICTA 1988, s 19*. All payments which, after this, fall to be taxed under *ICTA 1988, s 148* will be exempt from tax to the extent that the total of such payments does not exceed £30,000. Where the £30,000 threshold is exceeded, only the excess amount is taxable. In addition, there are certain types of payment which are specifically not taxed.

(i)   ***Fully taxable payments*** — The following types of payment are considered to be taxable in full:

(A)   ***Payments for services rendered*** — Where an employee is paid a sum which represents deferred remuneration, for example, a terminal bonus, that sum is taxable under *ICTA 1988, s 19(1)*. Similarly, a payment which is made to a prospective employee as an inducement to render service in a new employment is taxable in full.

The Inland Revenue can be expected to argue that a payment which an employee expects to receive, because it is the practice of the employer regularly to make such payments, should be taxed under *section 19(1) ibid*. (See *Corbett v Duff [1941] 23 TC 763*.)

(B)   ***All-employee payments*** — Redundancy payments are occasionally made to all employees even though some of them will be keeping their jobs. Those payments made to employees who are not leaving are not regarded as compensation for loss of the employment and so are regarded as fully taxable.

(C)   ***Gardening leave*** — (So called because it is assumed that the employee in question will spend his time at home tidying the garden.) An employee may be sent on 'gardening leave' on the proviso that he will remain at home during the notice period and will not be called upon by the employer to render any other service and furthermore, will not seek, or undertake, any other work in the interim. Any lump sum paid in respect of such leave is deemed to arise as a consequence of the employer/employee relationship and is therefore treated as taxable remuneration.

(D)   ***Contractual payments*** — Any payment which an employee receives from his employer, to which he has a contractual right, is treated by the Inland Revenue as fully taxable. This is the case, even where the payment is described as being of a compensatory nature. Thus, for example, the employee's contract may state that, in the event of his being made redundant, he will receive payment of one, three or six months' salary. Such a payment is taxable and NICable since the employee has a contractual right to receive it at the end of his period of employment.

On the other hand, the contract might state that the employee is entitled to one, three or six months' notice. In the event that the employee is not given such notice but is instructed to leave immediately, he will be entitled to receive the payment free of tax (subject to the over-riding £30,000 limit) since the payment will then effectively fall to be regarded as compensation for the employer's breach of contract in not allowing the employee to work the notice period. (The payment would be taxable under *ICTA 1988, s 148* rather than under *section 19 ibid.*)

A court would normally award the employee compensation in an amount equivalent to the wages which he has been denied the opportunity of earning, if the matter were to be taken that far. Payments made by way of compensation for redundancy are free of NICs without any maximum limit being imposed.

Contracts will occasionally give the employer a choice as to whether the employment may be ended by giving a period of notice or by paying a sum of money in lieu of notice. It has been argued in the past that a payment of this type should not be taxable on the grounds that it is made, not in return for being or acting as an employee, but because the employment is being brought to an end. The Inland Revenue would, invariably, challenge such a claim and, in the recent past, it would appear that the Revenue's argument has been strengthened following its success in *EMI Group Electronics Ltd v Coldicott (Inspector of Taxes)*.

The employer and the employee can agree to set aside the contract on terms such that the payment is made under that agreement and not under the contract. This being the case, it is arguable that the payment should be taxed under *ICTA*

1988, s 148 rather than *section 19 ibid* although the Inland Revenue is likely to dispute such a contention strongly.

(E) ***Payments on retirement*** — Lump sum payments are occasionally made when an employee retires. For this purpose, an employee retires when he leaves an employment at an age, or in circumstances, when he is unlikely to seek further employment. The Inland Revenue takes the view that such a lump sum *ex gratia* payment constitutes a payment under a retirement benefits scheme and, if such a scheme is 'unapproved', the payment will normally be regarded as taxable under *ICTA 1988, s 596A(1)*.

Statement of Practice 13/91 (SP13/91) gives details of the Inland Revenue's view of such payments and states that there may be certain exceptional circumstances when the payment can be regarded as not taxable. These are, however, likely to be few and far between.

(F) ***Restrictive covenants*** — Employers will occasionally make payments to employees in return for a 'restrictive covenant'. A restrictive covenant is an undertaking given by the employee to the employer that he will not, for example, trade in competition with the employer or attempt to solicit clients of the former employer for a specific period of time. Such a payment is fully taxable under *ICTA 1988, s 313*.

(ii) ***Partially exempt payments*** — The following types of payment all fall within the ambit of *ICTA 1988, s 148* and thus qualify for the overall exemption subject to the overriding £30,000 limit.

(A) ***Redundancy*** — Payments made under either a statutory or non-statutory redundancy scheme fall within this category provided that they represent genuine compensation for the loss of the employment.

Statutory redundancy payments are exempt from the basic charge to income tax under Schedule E by virtue of *ICTA 1988, s 579* but fall within the scope of *section 148*.

Payments under non-statutory redundancy schemes may also qualify for the £30,000 exemption provided that they meet certain conditions and these are prescribed in Inland Revenue Statement of Practice 1/94. Employers are invited to submit details of their proposed schemes to the Inland Revenue for advance clearance. Such applications should be made in writing and be accompanied by the scheme documentation.

A payment under a non-statutory scheme can be conditional upon the employee agreeing to work beyond the redundancy date and this too can be made free of tax provided that the amount paid is not calculated by reference to the period of additional time worked. If the payment is calculated in this way, it will be regarded as a terminal bonus and taxed accordingly in the normal way. Payments which are made for meeting production targets prior to the redundancy taking effect will be similarly taxed under *ICTA 1988, s 19*.

The Inland Revenue might attempt to argue that a redundancy payment made to an employee who is at, or near to, retirement age should not be accorded the exemption provided for by *ICTA 1988, s 188* and that it should, instead, be treated as an *ex gratia* payment from an unapproved retirement benefit scheme.

Such an argument can be resisted on the grounds that it would be unreasonable to discriminate against an older employee who has genuinely been made redundant, when younger redundant employees would not be so taxed.

(B)   ***Termination remuneration*** — If a payment made on termination contains any element which is stated to be 'in settlement of past claims' of the employee, it will be taxable under *ICTA 1988, s 19(1)* in accordance with *Carter v Wadman [1946] 28 TC 41*. In this case, the claim related to unpaid bonuses.

In practice, a termination agreement should not be drawn up too far in advance of the termination date or the Inland Revenue may argue that the agreement supplements or alters the terms upon which the service was rendered. The payment may thus be deemed to have arisen from the supplemented or revised contract of service.

(C)   ***Payments for restricted rights*** — Inland Revenue Statement of Practice 3/96 (SP3/96) clarifies the position regarding payments made to employees which are stated to be in 'full and final settlement' of all outstanding claims against the employer. It was initially thought that such sums would be fully taxable under *ICTA 1988, s 313*. However, SP3/96 confirms that these payments will not be caught if they are made in respect of claims which the employee could have pursued in law. They will, however, be caught under *ICTA 1988, s 148*. A termination payment which goes beyond such an undertaking could, however, still be caught by *section 313*.

(D)   ***Damages for unfair dismissal*** — *ICTA 1988, s 148* applies to damages paid for wrongful or unfair dismissal which have been awarded by an industrial tribunal or court. Where an employer agrees to make such a payment in order to settle out of court, the payment should be similarly treated.

(E)   ***Ex gratia payments*** — A true *ex gratia* payment is one which is not provided for in the employee's contract, is not made in accordance with an established policy and is not made in pursuance of some other legal obligation. Provided that the payment is not made on the retirement of the employee, it will probably fall to be taxed under *ICTA 1988, s 148* and relieved accordingly.

(iii)   ***Fully exempt payments*** — The following termination payments are considered to be fully exempt from income tax.

(A)   ***Payments on retirement*** — Lump sum payments made on retirement can be paid free of tax provided that they are made as a commutation of pension rights under an approved retirement benefits scheme, retirement annuity contract or personal pension scheme. Lump sum payments from funded unapproved pension schemes are taxable in accordance with *ICTA 1988, s 596A.*

(B)   ***Payments on death*** — Many payments made on the death of an employee are not liable to income tax, for example, payments from an approved retirement benefits scheme. The death need not have occurred during working hours.

(C)   ***Disability*** — Provided that a termination payment is made on account of a disability arising from an accident or injury at work, the payment will not be liable to tax. Inland Revenue Statement of Practice 10/81 (SP10/81) explains what is meant by 'disability' in this context.

As a consequence of a decision given by the Special Commissioners in January 1981, a 'disability' is regarded not only as a condition resulting from a sudden affliction, but also a continuing incapacity to perform the duties of an office or employment arising out of the culmination of a process of deterioration of physical or mental health caused by chronic illness.

(D)   ***Legal Fees*** — The payment of legal fees incurred in connection with the termination of an employment is not taxed under *ICTA 1988, s 148* in accordance with Inland Revenue Extra-Statutory Concession A81 (ESC A81).

(E)   ***Other retirement payments*** — Under Inland Revenue Statement of Practice 13/91 (SP13/91), certain *ex gratia* payments on retirement are exempt from tax. The payment must be below limits specified by the Inland Revenue and the employee must not be a member of his employer's pension scheme.

(Reference 14 in 9.21 below offers a view on the income tax treatment of termination payments.)

(b)   **The NICs position** — The NICs legislation is less prescriptive than the comparable income tax legislation. The general principles are as follows.

(i)   **Voluntary payments** — Any payment made voluntarily by an employer to compensate an employee for the loss of his employment is not regarded as earnings for NICs purposes – see the case of *Henley v Murray [1950] 1 AER 908*. However, a payment made under the express or implied terms of the employee's contract will be treated as earnings and must be subject to NICs in the normal way – see *Henry v Foster [1931] 16 TC 605*.

(ii)   **Payments in lieu of notice** — Such payments are subject to NICs if they are contractual, but otherwise they are excluded from earnings. The Contributions Agency differentiates between a contract ending on an agreed date with an agreed payment (which would be NICable) and one where the contract is terminated immediately with the employee having the right to damages for breach of contract (when the payment made would not be NICable).

Employers will occasionally protect themselves by inserting a clause in the contract which reserves the right to make a payment in lieu of notice. In such a situation, the employee would be deemed to have a contractual right to receive the payment and, as such, it would be liable to NICs.

(iii)   **Ex gratia payments** — Genuine *ex gratia* payments are not classed as earnings for NICs purposes, provided that they are not made in recognition of past services. However, if it is the employer's practice to make such payments and the practice is well-known to the employees, the payments will be treated as earnings. It may be possible to avoid a charge to tax and/or NICs if the employer can demonstrate that there have been instances where such a payment has been denied to an employee in the past.

(iv)   **Employment protection payments** — Certain payments made under the provisions of employment law, for example, the *Employment Protection Act 1996* are treated as earnings and subject to NICs. These include guarantee payments, medical suspension payments, maternity pay payments and payments arising from a protective award.

(v) **Redundancy pay** — Any redundancy payment is excluded from earnings even if it is not a statutory payment, since such a payment is merely compensation for the loss of rights attached to the person's job.

(vi) **Restrictive covenant payments** — Such payments are made by an employer to an employee in consideration of the employee agreeing not to compete against the employer for a specified period of time, and are treated as earnings for NICs purposes. [*SSCBA 1992, s 4(4)*].

Expenses

9.18   As has been stated previously, expenses may only be considered to be tax-free to the extent that they represent sums which have been incurred by the employee 'wholly, exclusively and necessarily' in the performance of the duties of the employment [*ICTA 1988, s 198*]. The costs of travelling in the course of business (excluding home to work travel costs) and subsistence costs are subject to the criteria laid down in *ICTA 1998, s 198*.

The legal position in connection with the tax and NICs treatment of expenses is explained in more detail in 9.3 and 9.7 above and in 12.14 below.

The application of aspects of the legislation is occasionally challenged and resolved through the courts. For example, the case of *Smith v Abbott [1994] STC 237* considered the payment of an allowance paid by employers to employees to purchase publications produced by competitors. The employees (who were journalists) were required to view such publications prior to commencing their own work. The House of Lords decided that the expenditure by the journalists on these publications was in preparation for, and not in the performance of, their duties. Accordingly, they were disallowed as a business expense. This decision has wider implications, for example, training courses which are not necessary for the performance of the employee's duties may be disallowable.

The strictness of the law with regard to the allowability of expenses paid to employees contrasts sharply with the treatment of self-employed persons in the case of whom the 'necessarily' test is absent. It is partly for this reason that Inland Revenue Inspectors can be expected to take a keen interest in those who seek self-employed status.

The payroll administrator is often responsible for the payment of expenses either directly through the payroll along with salaries and wages or as supplementary payments in cash or by cheque. The fact that details of many expenses must be reported on Forms P9D or P11D is another reason why detailed expenses records must be maintained. (See 20.15 below.) The position is complicated by the fact that certain expenses contain an element of profit which may be liable to tax or NICs or both.

The expenses payable to employees are usually authorised according to a set of rules with a fixed scale of all standard expenses, for example second class rail travel for all ordinary employees and first class travel for senior managers. Claims must be authorised by an appropriate person, usually the employee's line manager and should normally be supported by evidence of expenditure, such as receipts or vouchers in order to satisfy the employer, the Inland Revenue and the Contributions Agency.

In some circumstances, the employer may make an advance against expenses in the form of a loan or float. The employee will then use this to meet expenses as they arise and the float will be 'topped up' by the employer when the employee submits an expenses claim. Provided that the amount of such a float is modest, the employee submits expenses claims on a regular basis and he repays it on leaving the employment, such a float will not carry any tax or NICs implications.

Problems can occasionally arise if the employee is given a round sum allowance intended to cover his expenses regardless of the actual amount of expenses incurred. In strictness, an employee receiving an allowance of this type should suffer PAYE and NICs on the whole of the round sum and then submit a claim for tax relief under *ICTA 1988, s 198*, supporting his claim with receipts and vouchers.

In practice, it will often not be necessary to take matters to this extreme since Inspectors of Taxes can usually be persuaded to issue a special authorisation (a dispensation) to the effect that the round sum does no more than reimburse the employee for expenses which he has actually incurred. However, such authorisation should not be assumed and must be sought before any such payments are made. The Inspector of Taxes may be reluctant to issue a retrospective authorisation but he can do so if he wishes.

(For further details on the tax position, see Booklet CWG2, paragraphs 131–134 and 140, and Booklet 480, Chapters 2,3,7,8 and 9.)

PAYE Settlement Agreements

9.19   For some years, individual tax offices have been prepared to enter into informal arrangements with employers whereby the employer may pay tax liabilities on behalf of their employees in respect of a range of minor benefits or taxable expenses payments. Such arrangements were known as 'annual voluntary settlements' or AVS.

The tax due is calculated on a 'grossed up' basis, that is to say, the tax borne is itself treated as a benefit upon which further tax is payable. If the employee is a higher rate(40 per cent) taxpayer, the employer effectively pays tax at a rate of 66 per cent. However, neither the employer nor the employee have to report such expenses or benefits on Form P11D or Form P9D.

This informal procedure has now been formalised with the introduction of self-assessment and, with effect from 1996/97, placed on a statutory footing. The procedure is known as a PAYE Settlement Agreement (PSA).

PSAs are intended to apply where it would be difficult or impractical for the employer to identify the cash equivalent of a particular benefit in relation to each individual employee, for example, the cost of working lunches provided to certain staff. The cost to the employer is still expensive since the tax payable under a PSA still needs to be grossed up. However, against this cost must be weighed the potential savings in administrative time.

Although NICs are not due on the tax paid under a PSA for years to 1998/99 inclusive, a new Class 1B charge to NICs, initially at a rate of 12.2 per cent will be imposed from 6 April 1999.

Administration

9.20   The general administration of benefits has already been discussed in 6.11 above. A key point to bear in mind in connection with expenses and benefits is the need to ensure that detailed records are maintained so that these can not only be produced to an Inland Revenue Inspector or auditor but also to a Contributions Agency inspector should the need arise.

Computer payroll systems often contain facilities for administering the financial aspects of benefits, for example, SAYE deductions for an employee share scheme and holiday credits information. Often entirely separate systems are used for administering different benefits and expenses such as the use of individual systems for share schemes and company cars. This can lead to a proliferation of manual and computerised systems.

The number of systems is likely to increase following the introduction of self-assessment since employers must now not only provide information on Forms P11D to the Inland Revenue, but must also provide mirroring information to each employee. Accordingly, a variety of new software packages have been developed which will calculate cash equivalents and produce both of the types of return which are needed.

References

9.21

(1)   Booklet CWG2 (1998), 'Employer's Further Guide to PAYE and NICs', Contributions Agency/Inland Revenue.

(2)   Booklet 480, 'Expenses and Benefits — A Tax Guide', Inland Revenue, 1997.

(3)   Booklet 490, 'Employee Travel — A Tax and NICs Guide for Employers'.

(4)   Moores Rowland, 'Completing the Form P11D', PMR, April 1996, Supplement.

(5)   'Tolley Swan National Survey of Company Car Schemes 1997–98', Tolley Publishing Co Ltd, 1997.

(6)   'Employer's Payroll Health Check', a looseleaf, Tolley Publishing Co Ltd, 1998.

(7)   PRP2, 'Tax Relief for Profit-Related Pay: Notes for Guidance' (as amended), Inland Revenue.

(8)   IR 1, 'Extra-Statutory Concessions', Inland Revenue.

(9)   Slade E, 'Tolley's Employment Handbook', Tolley Publishing Co Ltd, Twelfth Edition, 1998.

(10) Saunders G and Smailes D, 'Income Tax 1998–99', Tolley Publishing Co Ltd, 1998.

(11) Golding J, 'Not Quite a Free Lunch', PMR, June 1996.

(12) Woodhouse S, 'Employee Share Incentives', PMR, April and May 1996.

(13) Biggs M, 'Operating Profit-Related Pay', PMR, February 1996.

(14) Ferrar L, 'Termination Payments', PMR, July 1996.

10   Pension Schemes

Scope of this chapter

10.1   This chapter contains a brief outline of the various types of pension scheme and their administration. It concentrates on the payroll aspects. Chapters 14 (Pension Contributions) and 21 (Pension Payroll Procedures) develop these two main areas of payroll involvement further. Both private and public sector pensions are discussed but with an emphasis on the former.

Private pension provision in the UK can be made through two types of tax approved schemes: the occupational pension scheme, which is provided by employers or groups of employers, and the personal pension scheme which is sold by a number of different financial institutions, notably the life offices of insurance companies. Together, occupational and personal pension schemes cover the majority of the UK working population. However, many others are not covered by private pension schemes, although they do contribute to State social security pensions. Also, some people on low earnings may not qualify for any pension provision, not even from the State.

Some brief statistics can indicate the importance and scale of pensions. There are about 10.5 million employees in membership of UK occupational pension schemes and over six million members of personal pension plans. In 1998 approximately 10.5 million people are in receipt of the contributory State retirement pension. About seven million people are currently receiving pensions from occupational schemes. There are over 50 UK pension schemes each with over £1 billion in assets. The total assets of all UK pension funds exceeds £650 billion.

A primary purpose of a pension scheme is to provide an income in retirement. Taking 65 as the ostensible retirement age, a man can expect to live a further 13 years, and a woman, a further 17 years. The situation is, however, understated, as retirement at 65 has never been common for women. Also there has been a marked increase in early retirement. The net result is that perhaps over half of current retirements take place before the age of 60, with many before the age of 55. As a result a retirement pension may have to provide an income for over a quarter of a century.

Pensions form a large and somewhat arcane subject. For a good introduction to private pensions see the bibliography given at 10.26 below.

Readers should note two important legislative developments in pensions which particularly affect this chapter and Chapter 14 (Pension Contributions).

(a)   The *Pension Schemes Act 1993 (PSA 1993)* —This came into force in 1994. It consolidated, but did not change, previous social security legislation concerning pensions. Recent editions of the *Payroll Management Handbook* have changed the legal references to those in the new Act. However, references to the old Acts, e.g. the *Social Security Act 1986* which introduced personal pensions, are likely to be found elsewhere for some time.

(b)   The *Pensions Act 1995 (PA 1995)* —This has changed and extended pensions law quite radically. Most of its provisions came into force on 6 April 1997. Section 10.25 below outlines the main provisions of this important Act.

Key points of pension schemes

10.2   The main aspects are listed below.

(a)   Pensions are an expensive and socially vital employee benefit.

(b)   Pensions are usually controlled, separately from the employer, by a legally-distinct entity, for example a trust. The practical administration may also be undertaken by a separate organisation, such as an insurance company.

(c)   The collection of pension contributions is an important payroll function.

(d)   One payroll operation can be responsible for pension payments from several schemes. In some cases pensions and employee payrolls are run side by side.

(e)   Pensions administration is usually handled by a department or organisation separate from the employee payroll department. However pensions, payroll, and personnel procedures must be carefully linked together.

(f)   While most public sector pension schemes are governed by Statute and regulations, most private sectors are primarily governed by the trust law provisions set out in their trust deed and rules although they are also subject to the provisions of the two main Pension Acts and the regulations made under them.

(g)   Occupational and personal pension schemes are subject to strict contribution and benefit levels which are policed by an executive agency of the Inland Revenue known as the Pensions Schemes Office (PSO).

(*h*)   There are many different possible pension arrangements all within a complex legal framework.

(*j*)   An individual may claim several different pensions on retirement, for example a basic State pension, a graduated pension, an earnings-related pension from the State Earnings-Related Pension Scheme (SERPS), an occupational pension and a personal pension.

(*k*)   Different pensions may come into payment at different points in an employee's life; for example the occupational pension may begin from age 50 if an employee is taking early retirement and be used to supplement earnings from casual work while, in the case of a man, the State retirement pension is not payable until age 65. The transition from work to retirement is often a phased process.

(*l*)   Pension schemes can have a significant effect on the calculation of NICs as a result of employees contracting-out of the State Earnings-Related Pension Scheme (SERPS).

(*m*)   History demonstrates that pension matters have been subject to continual change with knock-on consequences for payroll administration. Examples are the introduction of contracted-out pension schemes in 1978 leading to a new NIC structure and *PA 1995* which includes, amongst other things, changes to the contracting-out arrangements of pension schemes.

There is every reason to expect continual change to persist into the immediate and middle future. Indeed there have been several recent proposals for the radical reform of State and private provision of pensions and related matters. At the time of writing, a Green Paper on pension provision is expected from the Government which may make some radical proposals for change, including moves towards extending compulsory pension provision.

Pensions background

10.3   It is worth noting that there is no practical difference between a 'superannuation' or 'pension' scheme. Other terms may also be used for a pension, for instance a retirement annuity. In financial terminology the term 'annuity' means a series of regular payments and hence includes not only pensions but also other types of regular payments, such as rent from property. However, the word annuity, when unqualified, tends to imply a pension of some kind bought from an insurance company. Insurance company annuities themselves, of course, represent a special kind of pensions payroll operation.

The fundamental objective of any pension scheme is the continuance of income after retirement. In the UK private occupational pension scheme sector this means collecting contributions from the employer and usually from the employee and investing these monies in a fund. This is in contrast to the main government pension arrangements, for example the basic State pension, which are unfunded. These pensions are paid mainly out of current NICs on a 'pay as you go' basis. The money invested through an occupational scheme is ultimately paid out, usually in part as a tax-free lump sum and as a pension for life. Strictly controlled tax privileges are granted to pension schemes. Certain other benefits such as life assurance cover and ill-health pensions may also be provided as part of the occupational pension scheme.

Although the basic idea of a pension scheme appears simple, in practice pensions work is a complicated combination of law, finance and business practice. This arises because of the need to prevent tax evasion and to ensure that the large assets of most pension schemes are correctly and fairly administered. Further complications arise when occupational pensions are linked to NI benefits and where, under recent legislation, the employee can opt out of any occupational provision in favour of a personal pension.

There are many different pension schemes and a payroll administrator may have to deal with several. So in a large local authority this would include the Local Government Pension Scheme and the Teachers' Pension Scheme. In the private sector the employer may administer its own schemes. Alternatively, it may participate with other employers in national, local or industry schemes or choose an insurance company or other third-party administrator to administer its scheme. An individual may receive several pensions on retirement, for instance one pension from each of the schemes of his or her previous employers.

For the payroll administrator the main administrative links with pensions are as follows.

(*a*)   Both employer and employee pension contributions are usually collected via the employee payroll.

(*b*)   Regular pension payments, for example to retired employees, require payroll procedures; pension payroll systems are similar to those used for employee payrolls, but they are usually simpler.

(*c*)   Changes in employment status have major pension implications, such as when joining or retiring from an employer and one common consequence is the requirement to make occasional payments from the pension scheme, for example refunds of contributions on leaving, or lump sums when a pension scheme member dies.

Other connections between pensions, payroll and personnel work are as follows.

(i)   Pensions are expensive and long-term employee benefits which are tax-efficient. This means that they play an important role in employee benefits planning. (See Chapter 6 (Background to Pay and Benefits).)

(ii)   State social security rights are often taken into account when planning employee benefits. In the pensions field this can have an important impact on NICs. (See Chapter 12 (National Insurance Contributions).)

(iii)   Pensions have become of more interest to employees and trade unions over the last few years. One consequence is an increase in employee queries on pension matters, employer-sponsored consultative committees on pensions, personal financial planning courses for employees, and pre-retirement courses for employees. Pensions have also become more important in trade union bargaining.

(iv)   Developing the comments in the previous paragraph, on a more personal level, employees have their attention drawn to pensions by press articles on financial scandals, the salesperson from an insurance company, and so on. The result is that payroll and personnel administrators are often consulted concerning pension matters. Therefore, they should be familiar with the rules of their own pension scheme and pension matters generally.

Like most other areas of payroll and employee benefits, pension administration is vulnerable to constant change. Changes in political views give rise to new legislation which then influences current fashions in business thinking. Invariably there is a 'knock-on' effect as the pension changes require further changes in the personnel and payroll areas. One obvious example is an employee's legal right to refuse to join an employer's pension scheme.

The above discussion tends to imply a standard occupational pension scheme, usually a pension plan operated by the employer. However, personal pension schemes have become very popular since 1988 because of legislative changes and government incentives. Personal pensions are usually offered through banks, building societies, and insurance companies. Personal pensions compete with employer schemes, although in recent years it has become clear that many smaller employers have forsaken occupational pension scheme provision and moved over to facilitate the sale of personal pensions to their employees via the setting up of group personal pension arrangements. Here the employer will run a payroll check-off for employee contributions to personal pensions and may also directly contribute to the personal pension of individual employees. In addition, FSAVC schemes are effectively personal pension plans designed to supplement employer schemes. (FSAVC stands for Free Standing Additional Voluntary Contributions.)

The net effect of all this and other more general changes in employment is to weaken the appeal of employer schemes and complicate both payroll and pensions administration. For example, employees can choose from: no pension provision other than the State retirement pension, the employer's scheme, or a personal pension. The employee may also change between these options. The effect is, of course, to complicate the employee's own personal financial planning.

The business environment for pensions is currently rather confused and changing rapidly. Recent key developments are listed below.

(A)   ***New types of pensions*** — Entirely new types of pension scheme have been introduced over the last decade, e.g. COMPS (Contracted-Out Money Purchase Schemes) in 1988 and COMBS (Contracted-Out Mixed Benefit Schemes) in 1997.

(B)   ***Sex discrimination*** — The *Barber* case concerned sex discrimination against a man in a pension scheme, and was decided by the European Court of Justice on 17 May 1990. The detailed consequences of this and related cases such as *Coloroll* are now reasonably established. Broadly, sex discrimination is now prohibited in occupational schemes. One consequence has been to equalise normal scheme retirement ages for men and women. Employers have often responded by 'levelling down', that is to say reducing for future service the advantages enjoyed by the favoured sex to the level of those of the disadvantaged sex. For example, this has been done by raising the traditional retirement age of women from 60 to that of the traditional male retirement age of 65.

(C)   ***The Maxwell scandal*** — Before his rather dramatic death at sea in 1991, Robert Maxwell misappropriated the pension scheme assets under his control. The funds were used to support his ailing business 'empire' in printing, publishing and communications. The net loss ran into hundreds of millions of pounds, but a substantial amount was recovered. The pensions of Maxwell employees and pensioners could have been severely jeopardised. This has led many people to doubt the security of their own pension arrangements and question the current regulatory arrangements imposed by the authorities.

(D)   ***The Goode Committee*** — This was set up after the Maxwell affair and investigated the law and regulation of pension schemes. It reported in late 1993 with an extensive report containing many recommendations. The main proposals of the Goode Report have been broadly incorporated into the *PA 1995*.

(E)   ***Social security*** — Social security payments are the largest part of government expenditure. This is now about £100 billion per year. The Government is continually reviewing social security and related areas. Examples of recent social security changes are the replacement of invalidity benefit for the long-term sick by the incapacity benefit, and the upward revision of female State retirement ages in the *PA 1995*. Such changes have consequences for personal financial planning and the design of employee benefit schemes.

Purpose of establishing a pension scheme

10.4   The reasons for establishing a pension scheme can vary (see 6.6 above). However, as already mentioned, the primary purpose is, by exploiting the tax advantages, to provide the following main benefits:

(*a*)   old-age retirement pensions;

(*b*)   death benefits, e.g. life assurance and widow's/widower's pension;

(*c*)   ill-health and disability pensions.

There are other ancillary benefits. Typical examples include contribution refunds subject to a standard tax rate, transfers of pension rights to other schemes, retirement lump sums, early retirement pensions and lump sum payments to beneficiaries free of inheritance tax in the event of a member's death.

Pension scheme trust deed and rules

10.5   All pension schemes are governed by extensive legally binding rules. In the public sector these can be regulations made under statute. In the private sector occupational pension scheme rules are usually established under deeds and operate under trust law. The documents which then control their operation are the scheme's trust deed and rules. Another example of pension scheme rules are the details of a personal pension policy from an insurer. Whatever their origin, whether in the public or private sector, the governing documents define such matters as:

● membership;

● retirement ages;

● contribution levels;

● benefits payable;

● investment powers;

● discretionary powers;

● administrative powers.

The employee booklet of an occupational pension scheme contains only a simplified summary of the rules. It should, therefore, be used with caution in payroll and personnel work.

The trust deed and rules provide for the retirement age which might range from age 50 to 75 although commonly the normal retirement age is between 60 and 65. With regard to pension scheme membership there are variable rules covering such matters as the type of employee who qualifies as a member and the minimum age for entry to the scheme.

Benefit structure

10.6   The principles of pension benefit calculations are illustrated below in round numbers. In this example we are dealing with a typical 'final salary' scheme i.e. a scheme offering defined benefits which are related to the employee's salary at the date of retirement, leaving the scheme or death.

Example

Betty is a sales administrator who retires aged 62, the normal male and female retirement age in her pension scheme. Her gross earnings are £17,000 in her final year (£16,500 basic pay plus £500 overtime). She has 20 years' pensionable service. Her scheme gives a pension of 1/60th of final pensionable pay for each year of service. Using the rules of her scheme her retirement pension benefit is:

$$(£16,500 - £3,328) \times 1/60 \times 20 = £4,391 \text{ p.a.}$$

Some comments on the calculation are given below.

(*a*)　Both pensionable pay and pensionable service are defined in the scheme rules. Usually both are different from definitions of pay or service used for other purposes. For instance pensionable service is not the same as employment service as Betty may have entered the pension scheme several months or even years after joining her employer's business.

(*b*)　In Betty's case pensionable pay is defined to exclude her overtime. This is common but by no means universal.

(*c*)　£3,328, which is the annual value of the National Insurance Lower Earnings Limit in 1998/99, is deducted from Betty's pensionable earnings because her scheme is 'integrated' to take account of the basic State pension. Not all schemes use such integration factors.

(*d*)　Usually a scheme like this is contracted-out of SERPS (the State Earnings-Related Pension Scheme). In benefit terms, this kind of contracted-out scheme has usually provided a pension that equals or exceeds the Guaranteed Minimum Pension (GMP) earned in pensionable service from 6 April 1978 to 5 April 1997. The GMP is broadly equivalent to the SERPS benefit forgone by contracting- out. In Betty's case, as in most others, the scheme pension is comfortably in excess of the GMP. See 10.21 below for further details. For pensionable service after 6 April 1997 the scheme pension must satisfy an overall quality test if it is to be permitted to contract employees out of SERPS on a defined benefit basis.

(*e*)　There are many other benefits that might be claimed throughout Betty's life each with their own calculation rules. Some examples of these benefits are a refund of contributions, an ill-health pension, a transfer of her pension rights to another scheme, and a widower's pension following death in retirement. Some benefits may be optional, for example a retirement lump sum could be chosen in exchange for giving up some of the retirement pension (see 21.9 below, for an example).

(*f*) Betty's retirement pension depends on her final pay and service and, as explained above, is known as a 'defined benefit' arrangement. However, there is one radically different concept which is also commonly met, i.e. defined contribution or money purchase schemes as discussed in 10.16 below.

Some benefits can be optional, e.g. a lump sum on retirement could be chosen by sacrificing some of the retirement pension. Within legal and financial limits a benefit structure is designed to meet employee needs which leads to the numerous variations which are met in practice. A further complication is the frequent retention of old benefit structures alongside the new as schemes are changed or replaced. Often the old benefit structures can only be phased out slowly.

As already indicated an outline of the rules for calculating various pension benefits, for example an orphan's pension, are usually found in the employee pensions booklet. However, for the professional administrator this is only useful for obtaining a broad view of how a particular scheme works. Officially the benefit structure (and other) rules are found in the scheme's trust deed and rules. These documents may, however, be silent about some of the finer points in calculations such as rounding rules. They may also explicitly or implicitly refer to other sources for information. For example, the details of calculating pension transfer values from a defined benefit are often obtained from an actuary. (A transfer value is the amount pension rights are worth and it is calculated when these rights are transferred to another scheme.) Pension calculations can be complicated. So in practice, when occasionally done manually, the common pension calculations are laid out as a series of steps on pre-printed worksheets. In practice, of course, pension software has significantly improved the quality, reliability and speed with which calculations are completed.

Financing of a pension scheme

10.7 Most pension benefits are financed from a fund created by the joint contributions made by the employer and the employees. The fund is further increased by investment returns, made all the more valuable due to the tax-exempt status of the fund. As already stated, however, some public sector schemes, for example, the Principal Civil Service Pension Scheme, are financed out of current contributions on the 'pay as you go' system. However, the vast majority of schemes are pre-funded. In a defined benefit scheme contribution rates are recommended by the pension scheme actuary who is a professional financial mathematician specialising in pensions, life assurance and related matters. The actuary 'values' the liabilities (benefit promises) and the fund assets. The recommended contribution rates are designed to maintain a fund adequate to meet present and future benefit rights. The emphasis is on a long-term view. Actuarial valuations take place at three yearly intervals or more frequently when a major change in the benefit structure is contemplated.

Pension benefits are expensive to provide and typically employer and employee contributions might currently be ten per cent and five per cent respectively of pensionable earnings.

Inflation and pension increases

10.8   Inflation affects pension rights as follows.

(a)   ***Up to retirement*** — Pension rights earned early in life may not compare sensibly with price levels and expectations on retirement. Final salary schemes try to avoid this by relating the pension to earnings at or near retirement.

(b)   ***Deferred pensions*** — People often receive a deferred pension on leaving their employer. This is payable on their eventual retirement. These pensions are usually based on pay at the date of leaving and in the private sector prior to 1985 were rarely increased to cope with inflation. Under *PSA 1993, ss 83–86*, employees in a final pay scheme who now leave service must have their deferred pension revalued. The revaluation over the period of deferment is the cumulative rise in the retail prices index or five per cent per annum compound if this is less. Prior to 1991 only benefits accruing for service after 1985 had to be revalued in this way. Special rules apply to the revaluation of GMPs.

(c)   ***Pensions in payment*** — Current pensions in payment continue to lose their value unless revalued in line with inflation. Many public sector schemes do this. In private sector schemes it has become increasingly common to offer regular but limited pension increases on either a discretionary or guaranteed basis or, as is most common, a minimum guaranteed increase with the scope for discretionary increases on top. However, until 6 April 1997, some schemes offered no increases whatsoever. The pension increase typically applies to that part of the pension above the GMP. Private sector schemes are usually unwilling to guarantee matching inflation completely.

(d)   ***GMPs*** — As already mentioned, GMPs are a statutory component of many occupational pensions although no further right to GMPs have accrued since 6 April 1997. The GMP part of a pension is subject to separate statutory increases both as a deferred pension and when in payment. When in payment any GMP accrued between 6 April 1988 and 5 April 1997 must be increased by the scheme each year in line with price inflation up to a ceiling of three per cent in any one year. The State is responsible for inflation-linked increases to GMPs accrued before 6 April 1988 and for any supplementary increases on GMPs accrued between 6 April 1988 and 5 April 1997 needed to match price inflation. All this explains why the GMP is usually excluded from the pension increases discussed above.

(e) **The *Pensions Act 1995*** — The *Pensions Act 1995, ss 51–55*, has introduced the requirement for Limited Price Indexation (LPI) for pensions in payment which derive from pensionable employment after 5 April 1997. LPI involves mandatory minimum increases of up to five per cent or RPI whichever is the lesser. *PA 1995* has also abolished future accrual of GMPs though GMPs previously accrued are still payable. The result is that pension benefits accrued prior to 1997 and after 1997 will be increased in a different way unless the schemes go beyond the minimum requirement of the *PA 1995* by providing LPI on all pension rights and not just those accruing since 6 April 1997.

(See 21.18 below for further details on pension increases.)

Preservation of pension rights

10.9   On leaving an employer prior to retirement, an employee could be faced with one or more pension possibilities:

(a) a refund of his or her own contributions with the loss of occupational pension rights;

(b) a deferred pension payable at normal retirement age; or

(c) a transfer of deferred pension rights to another pension scheme or an insurance company plan.

In all cases the employee's rights are defined by a combination of circumstances, legislation, and scheme rules. Refunds are only legally possible if the employee's scheme service is less than two years. [*PSA 1993, s 71*]. Early leavers with at least two years' service have the legal right to transfer the value of the deferred pension to another scheme under *PSA 1993, ss 93–101*). In addition to the above options the employee's right to the State pension benefits is always preserved in one form or another.

Private sector, public sector and personal pensions

10.10   There is no sharp distinction between the private and public sector pensions. Any difference, as far as everyday pension administration is concerned, is not particularly dramatic anyway, especially for the payroll. The main practical difference lies in the source of the rules.

Public sector pension scheme rules are defined by regulations made under Acts of Parliament, for example the Local Government Pension Scheme, which is governed by the *Local Government Pension Scheme Regulations 1997 (SI 1997 No 1612)* made under the *Superannuation Act 1972, ss 7* and *12*. Public sector schemes usually provide pensions that are index-linked under the *Pensions Increase Act 1971, s 2*.

Private sector schemes are usually established by a trust deed. Investments are held in trust for the members of the scheme by trustees who manage the fund. The trustees must comply with the terms of the legally binding trust deed and rules. The trustees are legally separate and distinct from the employers. However, the employers usually have the major say in appointing them. Sometimes a trustee company is used instead of individual trustees. The *PA 1995* introduces the requirement for at least one-third of the trustees of an occupational scheme to be nominated by the general membership unless the employer proposes an alternative arrangement through a statutory consultation procedure. An employer's alternative proposal will be adopted unless more than ten per cent of those consulted register an objection (or 10,000 members if this is less than ten per cent).

The other type of private sector arrangement is the personal pension plan. The self-employed can contribute to a personal pension plan which is usually administered by an insurance company. Employees who are not members of an employer's scheme can also take out these plans. Personal pension plans have an entirely different system of tax relief compared to company occupational schemes.

Responsibility for the operation of a pension scheme

10.11   The ultimate legal responsibility for managing a pension scheme does not fall on the employer as such. In the private sector either a trustee company or a group of individual trustees is responsible. In the public sector specific divisions of government are authorised to administer pensions, for example County Councils run the Local Government Pension Scheme for the local authorities in their area.

Legal regulation for pension schemes

10.12   Pension arrangements are subject to extensive legal controls. The main relevant areas of law relate to trusts, social security and taxation. There is a certain amount of discretion allowed within the law and this has been fully exercised by employers. The Pensions Schemes Office (PSO) of the Inland Revenue, the Contributions Agency (CA) of the DSS and the Occupational Pensions Regulatory Authority (OPRA) supervise the operation of pension schemes. The main concerns of government are in the following areas:

- tax evasion;

- contracting-out of SERPS;

- protecting beneficiaries' rights;

- adequate funding.

Recent changes in pensions regulation are summarised below.

(*a*)   The Pensions Ombudsman was established in 1991 to receive and deal with complaints about occupational and personal pension schemes. There are a number of other organisations whose responsibilities border on that of the Pensions Ombudsman, for example the various Ombudsmen operating in the financial services industry.

(*b*)   The introduction of the Pension Schemes Registry in 1991 enables employees who have lost contact with their former pension schemes to trace their benefits. The register contains details of most pension schemes and is kept up to date by means of regular returns. Some pension arrangements consisting of pension schemes for single members are excluded, for instance '*section 32* buy-outs', old *section 226* policies, etc.

Other regulators exist for pensions. The most obvious ones are the pension scheme's own auditors and the regulators of financial services, for example for personal pensions there is the Financial Services Authority (FSA), formerly known as the Securities and Investments Board (SIB) and the Personal Investment Authority (PIA). Finally there is OPAS (the Pension Advisory Service) which offers a free advisory service to a scheme member in difficulties and tries to resolve problems with the member's scheme trustees or pension administrators. There is, in fact, a four-stage process for resolving problems with occupational pension schemes:

(i)   an internal disputes procedure must be established by each occupational pension scheme whereby a specified person (usually the pensions manager) must deal with complaints in accordance with the requirements of the *PA 1995* and the *Occupational Pension Schemes (Internal Dispute Resolution Procedures) Regulations 1996 (SI 1996 No 1216)*;

(ii)   an appeal system, built into the internal dispute resolution procedure allows a complainant, who is still dissatisfied, to take the complaint directly to the scheme trustees for a decision;

(iii) if still dissatisfied, the complainant is advised to contact OPAS;

(iv)   if OPAS is unable to resolve the problem to the complainant's satisfaction, the complainant may then go to the Pensions Ombudsman (see (*a*) above). *OPAS itself is able to refer cases directly to the Pensions Ombudsman if it feels the scheme is at fault but is unable to persuade the trustees to rectify the problem.*

In the event of the appointment of receivers, and/or liquidators, an independent trustee must be appointed to protect the interests of the members. But most importantly, the *PA 1995* has introduced OPRA (the Occupational Pensions Regulatory Authority) in place of the former OPB (Occupational Pensions Board) with the overall task of policing occupational pension schemes and ensuring that the statutory requirements of the *PA 1995* are observed. OPRA has the power to prohibit individuals and companies from acting as scheme trustees and can impose fines. OPRA is also empowered to bring criminal prosecutions. In addition, the Pensions Compensation Board (PCB) administers the new compensation scheme that can come to the aid of scheme members when assets have been dishonestly removed from the pension fund and the employer has become insolvent.

Broad categories of pension schemes

10.13   There are several different types of pension arrangement that a payroll administrator may encounter. Pension schemes can conveniently be classified under two broad headings.

(*a*)   ***Benefit structure*** — There are two main types of pension scheme structure:

   (i)   defined benefit schemes;

   (ii) defined contribution schemes.

These terms are explained in 10.15 and 10.16 below. Hybrid schemes combining defined benefit and defined contribution features are also common.

(*b*)   ***Type of pension source*** — Pensions may be received from several sources such as the State, occupational schemes and personal pension schemes. Each of these pension sources has its own purpose and arrangements.

In practical payroll work it is the source of a pension that matters most. The benefit structure determines the actual amount to be paid and is the responsibility of the pensions department. However, a general knowledge of pension matters is often essential for handling the payroll aspects and employee queries.

Combination of pensions

10.14   Different types of pension are often met in pensions and payroll administration. It is possible for an individual to claim many types of pension in virtually any combination, depending on his or her career history and the deferred pension entitlements earned in previous employments. A payroll system often has to consolidate two or more different pensions all of which are payable to one pensioner. This is illustrated in the example given below. All the terms used are explained later in this chapter.

Example of combined pensions — Mike is single and has a job as a production manager in a small factory. His basic salary is the equivalent of £440 per week. He retires aged 65 after 13 years' service in his current job. He is entitled to various pensions. These are paid at different intervals, but they are listed below in weekly terms.

Mike, as a pensioner, must deal with several organisations regarding the payment of benefits. These organisations include the employer's scheme administrators, the Benefits Agency for State pensions, and an insurance company for the self-employed pension.

		£ per week
(1)	Basic State Pension	64
(2)	His SERPS entitlement is £75. The State only pays £10 to cover the short period when he was not contracted-out of SERPS. The remaining £65 is included in his contracted-out occupational pension	10
(3)	State graduated pension. (Based on earnings prior to 1975.)	6
(4)	Basic occupational pension. (This includes the GMP which replaces his SERPS for the same period.)	76
(5)	*Ex gratia* pension.	20
(6)	Deferred pension from previous employment.	9
(7)	AVC pension. (AVCs have been used to purchase a further pension.)	30
(8)	Insurance company pension from a period of self-employment.	25
(9)	Total pension.	£240

It should be noted that Mike's total pension receipts are about 55 per cent of his earnings. Of course, he might have been in his employer's scheme for 40 years instead of changing jobs and working as a self-employed person. In this case his pension including State benefits could have been a much higher percentage of his final salary at retirement. Mike has anticipated this potential loss of pension rights and tried to compensate for it with a self-employed plan, AVCs, etc. This sort of scenario is not uncommon in an era where people are tempted or forced to change jobs several times during their working life.

In return for tax concessions the Inland Revenue has quite complicated rules for restricting the level of pension benefits and scheme contributions. For instance, the maximum pension payable by the scheme is usually two-thirds of pensionable pay. For scheme entrants from 1989 the maximum amount of pensionable pay is currently £87,600 p.a. There are also restrictions on the lump sum payable on retirement in certain cases.

Defined benefit schemes

10.15 Many of the major occupational schemes fall into this category. These schemes operate by defining the benefits to be paid. The contribution rates estimated by the actuary are aimed at meeting the overall cost of pensions and other benefits defined in the scheme rules. In practice, the employer's contributions fluctuate over the years according to the actuary's estimates. The rules, of course, usually allow the employer to curtail or terminate its commitment. The *PA 1995* has codified the legal responsibility for an employer to maintain adequate funding.

The calculation of Betty's retirement pension in 10.6 above is an example of how the rules of a typical final salary scheme define the pension payable. Other examples of defined benefit provision are the death benefits which in Betty's scheme are set out below.

(*a*)   A lump sum of 4 × gross annual pay; and

(*b*)   a spouse's pension of $\dfrac{1/2 \times \text{pensionable pay} \times \text{notional service}}{60}$

Notional service in this case is generously defined as service at the date of death plus the remaining service had the member lived to normal retirement. The various types of 'pay' would be defined in the rules. Pensionable pay, for instance, is in many cases defined as basic pay less an allowance for the basic State pension. Fluctuating 'emoluments' such as a salesman's bonus or commission, averaged over a few years, may or may not be included in pensionable pay.

Defined benefit plans are often termed 'final pay' or 'final salary' schemes. These schemes, like the previous examples, include definitions of pay at or near retirement or death, often with some kind of averaging over the last few years. Other defined benefit schemes are, however, occasionally met. An example of these alternative schemes is where pension rights are based on earnings during each year of a person's career. To take into account modern conditions these 'career average' schemes would have to include an allowance for inflation. SERPS is a form of career average scheme with inflation-proofing. In recent years another form of defined benefit scheme, known as the 'cash balance' scheme has begun to appear in the UK. In such schemes an employee's entitlement is defined in terms of a 'cash balance' or 'capital sum' which accumulates as a defined proportion of a employee's pensionable earnings.

Defined contribution schemes

10.16   In defined contribution or 'money purchase' schemes the pension is not related to earnings at or near retirement or death. In these schemes an employee builds up a share of the fund based on his or her own contributions together with those made by the employer. Over the years the fund is augmented by the investment growth. On retirement the employee's share of the fund is used to purchase a pension annuity. Only rough-and-ready calculations are used in the text to illustrate the principles of purchasing pensions. However, there are several complications in practice such as the type of annuity purchased, for instance does it include a spouse's pension? A key problem is also that the price of an annuity fluctuates in line with business conditions, particularly the yield on 15 year gilts. This can be illustrated from the price of an annuity published in 'Pensions World'. So each £1,000 would have purchased the following annual annuities, payable monthly in advance and guaranteed for five years for a male aged 65.

(*a*) January 1991 — £142.14.

(*b*) January 1996 — £106.15.

(The rates are those of the Norwich Union with similar rates available from other insurers.)

The contribution rates are fixed to produce estimated target benefits. The predictable cost of defined contribution plans can make them attractive to some employers. The final benefits are not, however, predictable for the employee. The pension depends, not only on the accumulated employee and employer contributions, but also on the unknown investment growth as well as on the age and sex of the pension recipient and on the scale of any management charges made by external administrators or investment managers.

Actuaries work on the basis that women live longer than men and therefore they calculate for women a smaller pension for the same age and purchase sum.

For example, Dave and Joan both retire at the age of 65. Each has accumulated £100,000 in the scheme fund which is used to purchase a pension annuity from an insurance company. So whilst Dave might receive a pension of £10,553 p.a. Joan could receive £9,457 p.a.

The use of sex as a factor to determine benefits has a clear scientific and economic justification in this case. However, it is a principle which has been criticised both in the UK and abroad. In some countries the use of unisex annuity rates is mandatory and in the UK unisex annuity rates are mandatory when any 'protected rights' derived from contracted-out elements of a pension are used to purchase an annuity.

Additional voluntary contributions (AVCs) are often used as a supplementary money purchase arrangement to increase the benefits from the main pension scheme. Free-standing AVCs (FSAVCs) are AVCs administered by an independent organisation, usually an insurance company, chosen by the employee. However, the FSAVC scheme contribution levels and benefits are linked to the employer's scheme. (See 14.10 and 14.13 below for further details.) With the exception of self-employed and AVC schemes, money purchase arrangements were out of favour for many years. However, *SSA 1986* (now part of *PSA 1993*) deliberately and successfully encouraged the growth of money purchase schemes both in the form of personal pensions and occupational pension schemes for groups of employees.

Different types of pension

10.17   There are many types of pension which are encountered in one way or another in payroll work and which can be classified as follows.

(a)   ***State pensions*** — There are several social security pensions and pension-related benefits which offer employees a standard but usually low level of pension provision. The table in Appendix D contains the current rates. The most important State 'pensions' are as follows:

   (i)   the basic State pension;

   (ii)   the additional pension provided by SERPS which 'tops up' the basic State pension;

   (iii)   the graduated pension payable on relevant earnings between 1961 and 1975 and which is also additional to the basic State pension;

   (iv)   incapacity benefit for long-term ill health;

   (v)   industrial disablement benefit for long-term disablement following injury at work;

   (vi)   the various widow's benefits; and

   (vii)   income support, and the other means-tested benefits, which are becoming increasingly important as a top-up element to the poorest pensioners.

There are many qualifying conditions to be satisfied if one is to successfully claim these benefits, e.g. a widow must be over 45 years old to receive a widow's pension. [*SSCBA 1992, s 38*]. An extensive NIC history, or entitlement to NIC credits, is particularly important to claim full State retirement benefits. Unlike occupational pensions, State retirement pensions can only currently be received on or after the State pensionable age of 60 years for women and 65 years for men. It is, therefore, not possible to obtain pension on early retirement from the State.

It should also be noted that even full social security pensions are quite modest. In 1998/99 the basic State pension is £64.70 per week for a single person. The State 'top-up' pension (SERPS) has eased this situation. The total State benefit (basic pension and SERPS) received by a person could currently reach 40 per cent of typical earnings (taken as approximately £350 per week in 1998 for a male adult manual worker). However, these are current figures and the SERPS benefit is to be progressively cut as a percentage of career revalued earnings in the long-term. Also with State benefits much depends on the individual's employment and contributions history. Furthermore, as there is a maximum that can be received, State benefits fall as percentage of earnings for the better paid. The relatively low level and inflexibility of State benefits is one of the main justifications for the existence of occupational pension schemes, particularly for the higher paid employees.

(b)   ***Employer pensions*** — Private sector employers are generally at liberty to devise their own pension schemes within legal limitations to supplement or replace the State pension provisions. Large occupational schemes are usually 'contracted-out' of SERPS. As mentioned before this means that in return for reduced NICs the pension scheme must provide a substitute for the additional pension provided by SERPS. Contracting-out is explained further in 10.21 below. Sometimes an employer grants an extra or '*ex gratia*' pension which is paid by the employer without any legal obligation. Some senior or 'key' executives could receive an additional pension either from an individual scheme or from an 'executive scheme'. These were termed 'top hat' schemes at one time. See also 10.17(*k*) below for a discussion of unapproved pensions.

(c)   ***Pensions for specific occupations*** — Within the public sector employers are often obliged to administer schemes for particular occupations, for example local authorities must admit all their teachers to the relevant national scheme.

(d)   ***Industry-wide pension schemes*** — Where there is a widespread common 'trade' with multiple employers it often makes sense to offer their employees a common pension scheme. An employee moving between employers can then remain in the scheme provided all those employers are affiliated to the scheme. Examples of industry-wide schemes are those for the plumbing trade, merchant navy and the academic staff of traditional universities.

(e)   ***Supplementary pensions*** — Several kinds of supplementary or 'top-up' pensions exist. They are useful where the employee has insufficient time to build up a full pension in the main scheme. The most common method is the use of AVCs where the employee receives extra pension rights in return for additional contributions deducted through the payroll. Some senior executives may also receive additional pensions (see (*b*) above).

(f)   ***Previous schemes*** — When an old pension scheme is closed to new members the benefits are often 'preserved' until payable. For instance, under an old scheme an employee may be entitled to £1,000 p.a. plus statutory revaluation on retirement together with the new scheme pension. This is often called a 'paid-up' pension. Alternatively, the earlier pension rights may be waived in return for past service rights in the new scheme. Alternatively, the old scheme may be wound up and its obligation to pay pension benefits transferred to a new scheme.

Schemes are wound up for a variety of reasons, such as takeovers, mergers, liquidations or replacement generally by superior schemes.

(g)   ***Insurance company pension plans and services*** — Life insurance companies have traditionally offered differing pension plans on an individual or group basis. However, other financial institutions, such as building societies and banks, are active in this field. They all provide a means of pension provision where self-administered schemes are not convenient or possible, for instance for the employees of small companies or the self-employed. More controversially, the financial institutions during the late 1980s and early 1990s offered pension provisions in competition with the schemes provided by employers. Occupational pension schemes can be administered by an insurance company for an ordinary employer. These schemes are popular with smaller organisations which cannot afford to employ pension specialists or run a self-administered scheme with its own fund. Insured schemes are, therefore, a pooled investment vehicle.

However, in recent years the insurance companies have begun to emphasise group personal pensions rather than occupational pension schemes (see (*h*) below).

A purchased life annuity is a regular income for life which is bought from an insurance company with a lump sum. It is, in theory, available at any age, but is usually bought by the elderly. It is treated partly as a return of capital and partly as a taxable payment of interest. [*ICTA 1988, Pt XIV, Ch V*]. By way of contrast, a pension or retirement annuity is purchased from an insurance company with money from a tax-approved pension fund and is taxed, usually at source, as earned income on the entire pension amount. [*ICTA 1988, ss 597, 619(1)(b), 643(3)*]. One tax mitigation arrangement involves taking the lump sum retirement benefit from a pension scheme and using it to buy a purchased life annuity. This only involves partial taxation (on the interest element), so the tax paid is less than leaving the purchase money in the scheme to generate a pension which is fully taxable.

An important practical point for payroll practice is the payment of insured pensions. Sometimes they are paid directly to the individual by the insurance company. Alternatively, they are remitted to the pension scheme to be sent to the pensioner. In both cases, of course, the pension has to be paid through PAYE.

Insurance companies also offer individuals and employers a wide range of pension-related services which include:

(i)   life assurance arrangements for pension schemes;

(ii)   accepting transfers of pension rights for ex-employees. These transfers are often called '*section 32* buy-outs' (see (*h*) below);

(iii)   permanent health insurance;

(iv)   pension scheme investment; and

(v)   operating AVC plans on behalf of employers and FSAVC plans for employees in competition to the occupational pension scheme's AVC arrangements.

(*h*)   ***Personal pensions*** — These pensions were introduced in 1988 and cover both the employed and self-employed. They are an extended version of the old self-employed money purchase pension plans which were available for many years. These were called '*section 226*' policies which is a reference to a superseded section of *ICTA 1970*. Although these plans have not been available since 1988, old *section 226* plans taken out prior to that date still remain in force.

Concentrating on employees rather than the self-employed, the basic idea of the new personal pension plans is that employees pay contributions into their own independent 'earmarked' account. This contains the employee's own personal tax exempt fund. The account is administered by a financial institution, typically an insurance company, which also manages the investment of the fund. All personal pensions are based on the 'money-purchase' principle.

On retirement the proceeds of the fund are normally used to purchase a pension annuity although high net worth individuals may find it more profitable to defer the purchase of an annuity and to draw down income from a fund which is still actively managed and invested. Employees can select the personal pension plan and financial institution of their own choice. Personal pension plans can also be contracted-out if the employee so wishes – they are then termed 'appropriate personal pensions'. Contracted-out plans are not applicable to the self-employed.

With minor exceptions an employee can only have a personal pension plan when he or she is not a member of the employer's scheme. Employees who are members of an employer's scheme have to opt out of them if they wish to take up a personal pension. Employees who, either by choice or circumstance, are covered by neither an occupational pension scheme nor a personal pension plan are usually in SERPS.

Under the tax legislation, an employee is able to contribute directly to a personal pension taken out by an employee. If so, the amount of the employer's contribution does *not* give rise to income tax charge as a 'benefit in kind'. No NIC charge arises on employer's contributions directly paid to an employee's personal pension.

As mentioned above, there is also the concept of GPPs (Group Personal Pensions). A GPP arrangement is not strictly a pension scheme as such, but a set of personal plans grouped together for marketing and administrative convenience. The employer may or may not contribute directly to the individual personal pension contracts in a GPP.

As regards payroll operations employees in personal pension plans are always treated as not contracted-out even where their personal plans are 'appropriate' (contracted-out). The Contributions Agency is then responsible for paying any contracted-out rebates over to the appropriate personal plan administrators. The employee is responsible for paying any extra contributions to the personal plan. The employer can, if he wishes, assist either financially or with the administration but is under no statutory obligation to do so.

The tax provisions for personal pensions are contained in *ICTA 1988, Pt XIV, Ch IV* as amended. The contributions and fund investment growth enjoy tax relief on a different basis from company schemes. For example, an employee, if aged 35 or less, who is not in a company pension scheme may contribute up to 17½ per cent of earnings with full tax relief. The higher percentages for those who are older than 35 years range from 20 per cent to 40 per cent. The employee may also receive death benefit cover as part of the personal pension plan. The capital sum accumulated in the fund, say £27,000, might buy a pension of around £2,000 p.a. on retirement at age 65. Personal pension contributions (after the deduction of income tax) may be collected through the payroll as a service to employees who are not in a pension scheme (see Reference (1) in 11.18 below for a full description of the tax position of personal pension plans).

(*j*)   ***Foreign pensions*** — In the area of 'foreign' pensions the main complications are tax, social security and foreign currency. The Inland Revenue has special arrangements for tax relief with overseas pensions arrangements. Foreign pensions are an increasing feature in an age of multinational companies and internationally mobile executives or technicians. They require specialist advice and are not considered further in this book. Paying a UK pension to a person living abroad is considered in 22.11(*c*), 22.11(*d*) and 22.12(*b*) below.

(*k*)   ***Unapproved pensions*** — Under the *Finance Act 1989* employers are allowed to 'top up' ordinary occupational pension rights with further benefits. Such arrangements are 'unapproved' by the Inland Revenue and hence do not enjoy the normal tax reliefs given to approved pension schemes. The impetus for the adoption of an unapproved scheme has been the introduction of pensionable earnings cap which limits the amount of a high-earning employee's pension from an approved scheme. When unapproved pension arrangements are pre-funded by the employer they are known as Funded Unapproved Retirement Benefit Schemes (FURBS). Employers' contributions to a FURBS give rise to income tax charge on the employee, and since April 1998, to a NICs liability on the employees (employees in membership of a FURBS are usually earning over the Upper Earnings Limit so the NICs liability does not normally result in a higher cost for the employee).

(*l*)   ***Related benefits*** — These benefits which are related to pensions are usually provided by insurance. Premiums may be paid by an employer. A common example is PHI (Permanent Health Insurance) which provides an income for long periods of disability. Another example is long-term care policies which insure a person for nursing home care.

Outline of pensions administration

10.18   The main areas of pensions administration are as follows:

(*a*)   keeping membership records;

(*b*)   collecting contributions;

(*c*)   calculating benefits;

(*d*)   paying benefits including pension payroll;

(*e*)   managing investments;

(*f*)   maintaining accounts;

(*g*)   engaging in employee communications and counselling;

(*h*)   undertaking pensioner welfare;

(*j*)   liaising with advisors, e.g. the actuary, solicitor, etc.;

(*k*)   reporting to the supervising authority, e.g. pension scheme trustees in the private sector;

(*l*)   liaising with the Inland Revenue and Contributions Agency.

The complexity of the pensions field demands computer assistance. The result is that, like payroll work, pension administration is usually computerised. Payroll and pension systems often communicate electronically, for example by an intranet or modem. This provides a convenient method of transferring, for instance, employee earnings and contributions data from a payroll to a pensions system.

Relationship between pensions, payroll and personnel departments

10.19   Many large organisations have in-house pensions departments which liaise with the personnel/HR department and the payroll department. There are many ways of sensibly dividing pensions responsibilities between these three departments. The two extreme methods are as follows.

(*a*)   *Maximum centralisation* — Here the pensions department handles as much as possible itself. This includes the department running its own pension payroll and handling all pension queries. The employee payroll department merely deducts contributions and accounts for them to the pensions department.

(*b*)   *Maximum decentralisation* — In this case the pensions department delegates as much as possible to the payroll and personnel departments. For instance, the payroll department runs the pension payroll for the pensions department. Wherever possible pension queries are handled locally by the payroll or personnel departments depending on the nature of the query.

Either method, or a combination, can be effective depending on the particular circumstances of each case. Another option is to unite pensions, payroll, and personnel work in one combined human resources department. There is also the possibility, as elsewhere in business, of contracting-out pensions administration to an outside service provider. Many organisations do not maintain an in-house pensions administration department but rather use a third-party administrator to run their pension scheme. Where an employer provides an insured scheme, the insurance company will normally act as the pension administrator. In cases where a third-party administrator is used, the pensions–personnel–payroll interface will straddle a client-based commercial relationship between the scheme trustees and the third-party administrator. The choice depends partly on circumstances and partly on the business policy of a company. What matters is the close integration of pensions, payroll, and personnel practices. Good office procedures, and well-designed documentation and electronic communications, are essential. (See Chapter 16 (Payroll Organisation) for more details.)

Status changes of employees

10.20   Pension scheme administrators are normally dependent on local representatives to inform them of changes in employment status. This usually means that the personnel and payroll departments must despatch forms containing the relevant details. The main employment status changes which affect pension rights are as follows:

(*a*)   joining the employer opens the possibility of voluntarily joining the pension scheme, although there may be age limits or a waiting period or even special eligibility criteria depending on status;

(*b*)   wage increases usually increase the pension benefits and contributions;

(*c*)   promotions may involve not only an increase in salary but a change of pension scheme, for example a change from the staff to the executive scheme;

(*d*)   withdrawal, i.e. leaving, dying or retiring, involves the pension department in benefit calculations;

(*e*)   transfers of staff to different locations or associated organisations such as subsidiaries which should be notified to the pension department.

Note: There is of course a direct effect on the payroll when each of the above occurs.

Contracting-out of SERPS

10.21   A majority of large occupational pension schemes 'contract-out' of SERPS. Occupational pension schemes in the past could do this on a defined benefit basis by providing as a bare minimum a guaranteed minimum pension

(GMP) from the scheme. GMPs are no longer built up in schemes but any GMP accrued before 6 April 1997 remains a scheme liability which can only be discharged in prescribed ways. The DSS makes good any deficiency between the GMP entitlement and the entitlement from SERPS which would otherwise have been paid on retirement had the employee not been contracted-out. Normally the scheme pension benefits are superior to the GMP. In return for providing the GMP both the employee and employer paid reduced NICs. The amount of the reduction is called the contracted-out rebate. From 6 April 1993 to 5 April 1997 the NIC rebate was 1.8 per cent for employees and 3 per cent for employers. (The percentages refer to the employee's 'banded earnings' – i.e. those earnings lying between the Lower and Uper Earnings Limits.)

From 6 April 1997, the GMP test has been abolished for future pensionable service and has been replaced by an overall scheme quality test as the basis for contracting out on a defined benefit or Contracted-Out Salary Related (COSR) scheme basis. Furthermore, from that date, links between all forms of contracting out and SERPS have been broken: either an employee is in membership of SERPS or in membership of the contracted-out provision. The DSS will no longer 'top up' an employee's contracted-out provision as it does for GMPs. The NIC rebate for COSR schemes from 6 April 1997 is fixed at 4.6 per cent of an employee's 'banded earnings', split 1.6 per cent for employees and 3 per cent for employers.

Contracted-out money purchase schemes (COMPs) for groups of employees were introduced on 6 April 1988. In this case the contracted-out rebate was assumed by the DSS to pay for a GMP in place of the entitlement from SERPS. Whether it does or does not depends, of course, on fund investment returns and the money purchase terms, i.e. in this case there are guaranteed minimum contributions, called protected rights, and not a guaranteed minimum pension. From 6 April 1993 to 5 April 1997 employees could be contracted out by means of a COMP scheme if the employer undertook to pay by the 14th day after the end of each tax month 'minimum payments' equal to 4.8 per cent of each employee's 'banded earnings' (i.e. equal to their NIC rebate) although the employer could recoup the employee's share (1.8 per cent) from the employee's earnings. From 6 April 1997, the total flat-rate percentage payable each month by the employer fell to 3.1 per cent, split 1.5 per cent to the employer and 1.6 per cent to the employee. This is equal to the NIC rebate that applies to COMP schemes. From 6 April 1999 the total flat-rate percentage payable falls from 3.1 per cent to 2.2 per cent, split 0.6 per cent to the employee. The employer may still recoup the employee's share (1.6 per cent) from the employee's earnings. In addition, following the end of the tax year, the Contributions Agency pays an age-related percentage for each employee.

From 6 April 1997, a new form of scheme, the Contracted-Out Mixed Benefit (COMB) scheme has come into existence. In essence, this is a scheme with two separate sections – one which can retain liability for past GMPs and benefits from the new COSR schemes; and the second which holds protected rights as in a COMP scheme.

As already noted occupational pension schemes are often contracted-out of SERPS, i.e. the occupational scheme effectively replaces SERPS in exchange for the NIC reduction. Some schemes are 'not contracted-out', i.e. their members can receive both the benefits of SERPS, and the benefits of the occupational scheme. This also means paying twice, via contributions, to belong to both schemes. In this case the occupational benefits are sometimes reduced to allow for the SERPS benefits, and thus reduce the total pension and NIC costs. Only the employer sponsoring a scheme can decide to contract-out. If they do not their scheme members by default are members of SERPS, and they do not expressly need to 'contract-in'. However in informal speech and writing the term 'not contracted-out' is considered too clumsy, and the term 'contracted-in' is used, even though this is strictly incorrect. Also, of course, ordinary employees, who for one reason or another are not members of an occupational pension scheme, are usually automatically members of SERPS, i.e. contracted-in.

Employees who are members of a contracted-in occupational pension scheme may choose to contract out on an individual basis. To do this they become members of an Appropriate Personal Pension (APP) to which the DSS will pay an age-related sum after the end of each tax year. Neither the employee or employers can contribute directly to a personal pension when it is used simply to contract out an employee who is also a member of an occupational pension scheme. The employee and employer pay NICs at the higher, not contracted-out rate.

Much of the State administration of contracting-out is handled by COEG (the Contracted-Out Employment Group) which is part of the Contributions Agency. Contracting-out involves extensive procedures. For example, there are COEG forms which must be completed, usually by pensions staff, each time an employee leaves a contracted-out pension scheme. The payroll implications of contracting in or out by means of an occupational pension scheme are significant in that contracted-out employment results in reduced NICs. This is reflected in the use of NIC table letters, which system has recently been extended to allow for *PA 1995* changes.

Implications of pension scheme membership

10.22   Membership of an occupational scheme is a vital consideration for the payroll staff. Membership could result in:

(*a*)   ordinary pension scheme contributions being made by the employer and often the employee;

(b)   supplementary pension contributions such as AVCs being deducted from salaries;

(c)   reduced NICs (if contracted-out) being due to the Contributions Agency.

Note: Personal pension contributions may also be administered by the payroll department as a service. This occurs only where the employer wishes to do so, usually where the employer sponsors a Group Personal Pension arrangement. NICs at the not-contracted-out rate are payable and employee contributions are made after the deduction of income tax.

Members can obviously be concerned about an important and expensive benefit such as their pension plan. After all pensions are now almost universally accepted as a form of 'deferred pay'. As already mentioned there is a heightened interest by individuals in their pension rights and a wider concern resulting from events like the Maxwell case in 1991. Personnel, payroll and pensions departments can all be involved in dealing with members' requests for information.

The need for both personal and general information has been met in many voluntary and statutory ways. These can involve improved communications, e.g. benefit statements as discussed below, presentations by the pension department, or courses on personal financial planning. Access to general information such as the trustees' annual report and the actuarial valuation report are also a right.

Returns to the pension department

10.23   The pension department depends on being correctly notified by the payroll and personnel departments of the following:

(a)   employment status changes (see 10.20 above);

(b)   contributions and pay details (see Chapter 14 (Pension Contributions)).

Normally this is done on forms or transmitted electronically by a large employer. Usually the returns are made whenever an event like joining or retirement occurs. Contribution and pay details for current employees are often reported annually to the pension department. The actual employer and employee contributions themselves are usually paid over to the pension fund monthly. From 6 April 1997, employee and employer contributions to occupational pension schemes should be paid strictly in line with a schedule listing amounts and the due date for payment. The pension scheme trustees must report any failure to observe the schedule to the Occupational Pensions Regulatory Authority (OPRA).

Benefit statements

10.24   Benefit statements provide an estimate of an employee's pension benefits. Typically they are based on current earnings, issued annually, and include estimates of the following:

(*a*)   retirement benefits;

(*b*)   death in service benefits;

(*c*)   leaving benefits.

All the relevant personal data is also shown. Benefit statements have been used for many years to:

 (i)   allow employees to conduct their own financial planning, e.g. when buying life assurance;

(ii)   bring the employee's attention to the range of (expensive) benefits provided mainly by the employer;

(iii)   foster an interest in the pension scheme.

Benefit statements are usually computer-produced and sometimes refer to other employee benefits, for example medical insurance and company cars. These statements can be a useful part of the general employee benefits strategy. (See 6.8 above.)

Regulations originally made under the *Social Security Act 1985* make benefit statements effectively mandatory. [*Occupational Pension Schemes (Disclosure of Information) Regulations 1996 (SI 1996 No 1655)*]. Figure 10A below illustrates the layout of a typical benefit statement.

The Pensions Act 1995

10.25   This legislation is derived from the Goode Committee proposals and the 1994 Pensions White Paper 'Security, Equality, Choice: The Future for Pensions'.

The *PA 1995* is complicated, but the main provisions which may be of interest in payroll administration are outlined below. The equal treatment provisions came into force on 1 January 1996. Most of the other measures came into force on 6 April 1997.

(*a*)   ***Occupational Pensions Regulatory Authority*** — The Act establishes this new authority (OPRA) to regulate pension scheme trustees.

(*b*)   ***Member-nominated trustees*** — The members are allowed to nominate at least one-third of the trustees of a pension scheme unless the employer

Figure 10A

The XYZ limited pension scheme

Personal benefit as at 31 December 1998

Personal details

Name:	BILLY BLOGGS	Date of birth:	17 04 42
Sex:	MALE	Normal pension date:	01 05 07

Pensionable service	Years	Months
Completed to date (includes transfer credits)	27	8
Future to normal pension date	8	4
Total (prospective)	36	0

Current pensionable pay _____ £15,300 p.a.

Retirement pension

1/60 x pensionable service (years) x final pensionable pay (£)

Pension calculated on current pensionable pay and

completed service _____ £ 7,055 p.a.

prospective service _____ £ 9,180 p.a.

On your death after retirement the pension continuing to a widowed spouse would be one half of your own pension

Benefits bought by your voluntary contributions will be paid in addition

Benefits on death in service

Lump sum (3 x current pensionable pay) _____ £45,900

Pension for widowed spouse
(½ x retirement pension on prospective service) _____ £ 4,590 p.a.

Your own contributions to date	**normal**	**voluntary**
Paid in the year just ended	£ 765.00	£ 459.00
Paid before the year just ended	£7,120.50	£ 414.00
Total paid to date	£7,885.50	£ 873.00

Illustration of the layout of a typical benefit statement

(By courtesy of Payroll Manager's Review)

successfully proposes an alternative arrangement. Employees must be allowed reasonable time off work with pay to attend to their duties as trustees.

(*c*)   ***Pension increases*** — These must be provided annually at the specified amount (RPI or five per cent whichever is the lesser) on pensions earned in employment after 5 April 1997. GMP increases payable by schemes will only apply to GMPs accrued between 1988 and 1997 and are limited to the increase in the RPI or three per cent, whichever is the lesser.

(*d*)   ***Minimum funding requirement*** — Specifies rules for measuring and maintaining a minimally funded defined benefits pension fund.

(*e*)   ***Equal treatment*** — All occupational pension schemes are now regarded as containing a rule on equal treatment. Some exceptions are allowed, for example different actuarial factors for men and women in benefit calculations (which reflect different longevity).

(*f*)   ***Compensation*** — The Pension Compensation Board will provide up to 90 per cent compensation to an under-funded trust scheme. The employer must also be insolvent and the shortfall due to illegal acts.

(*g*)   ***Equal State retirement ages*** —The Act brings the State pension retirement age of women up to that of men, i.e. 65 years. The increased female retirement age will be introduced in steps between 2010 and 2020.

(*h*)   ***Abolition of GMPs*** — The new contracting-out provisions in the Act abolish the need for GMPs in a defined benefits scheme after 1997. However, such a scheme must provide benefits that meet the benefits provided by a 'reference scheme' for at least 90 per cent of the employees.

(*j*)   ***Age-related NIC rebates*** — These are now provided for COMPs and contracted-out ('appropriate') personal pension plans.

It should be noted that much of the *PA 1995* retrospectively amends the *PSA 1993* and that many of the details have been provided in regulations.

References

10.26   References (1) to (3) below contain general information on pensions. The remaining references are further reading on specific topics.

(1)   Mathewman J and others, 'Social Security and State Benefits 1998–99', Tolley Publishing Co Ltd, 1998.

(2)   Fenton J, Sabel J, and Ham R, 'Pensions Handbook', Second Edition, Tolley Publishing Co Ltd, 1995.

(3) Nabarro Nathanson's Pensions Group, 'A Guide to UK Pension Law', Tolley Publishing Co Ltd, 1997.

(4) Self R, 'The Pension Fund Trustee Handbook', Fourth Edition, Tolley Publishing Company, 1998.

(5) Freshfields' Employment, Pensions, and Benefits Group, 'Guide to the Pensions Act 1995', Tolley Publishing Co Ltd, 1995.

(6) 'Pensions Administration', Tolley Publishing Co Ltd, 1998. (A comprehensive looseleaf book which is regularly updated.)

(7) 'Reviewing Pensions', PMR, September 1997. (A background to the Government's pension review.)

(8) 'Credit Where Credit's Due', PMR, September 1997. (The abolition of advanced corporation tax credits for pension schemes.)

(9) 'FURBS' and NICs', PMR, October 1997. (The National Insurance treatment of funded unapproved retirement schemes.)

(10) 'Reviewing Higher Rate Relief', PMR, November 1997. (Tax relief on pensions contributions.)

(11) 'Excess Contributions', PMR, December 1997. (Part-time workers' pension rights.)

(12) 'Stake in the Future', PMR, January 1998. (Stakeholder pensions.)

(13) 'Reviewing Rebates', PMR, February 1998. (National Insurance rebates.)

(14) 'Low Earner Challenges Exclusion', PMR, March 1998. (Low earners and occupational pension schemes.)

(15) 'Passing the Buck', PMR, April 1998. (Employers' compliance with the *Pensions Act 1995*.)

(16) 'Rebating Zero NICs', PMR, May 1998. (National Insurance refunds and pensions.)

(17) 'Calculating Pension Entitlement', PMR, June 1998.

(18) 'The State of Pensions', PMR, July 1998. (The future of pensions provisions.)

(19) 'Making Life Simpler', PMR, August 1998. (NICs and tax alignment – the effect on pensions.)

(20) 'Solving Pensions Problems', PMR, September 1998. (Complaints – OPRA, OPAS, the Ombudsman etc.)

11 Income Tax

Scope of this chapter

11.1   The income tax legislation places a statutory obligation on employers to deduct income tax from the earnings paid to employees through the Pay As You Earn (PAYE) system. Income tax is deducted by way of the same system from any occupational and personal pension payments which an employee might receive.

Social security pensions paid by the State are not subject to a direct deduction of tax and any tax which is payable in connection with such pensions is recovered by other means. For example, if the employee also receives an occupational pension, his code number may be reduced and the tax collected from that source. Alternatively, the employee may be required to pay the tax under the Direct Collection procedure.

An employee may also be required to pay tax other than under Schedule E, if, for example, he also has a source of income from self-employment or investment income.

This chapter outlines the legal background to UK income tax on earnings from employment and pensions. Most of the administrative and calculation details relating to income tax are contained in Chapters 20 (PAYE procedures) and 25 (Manual Calculation Methods). Chapter 4 (Payee status) describes, *inter alia*, the effect of a payee's legal status as far as the income tax and NICs positions are concerned.

Other chapters describe the tax position of specific types of pay or benefits, for example, Chapter 9 (Benefits, Expenses and Termination Payments) outlines the tax background to approved profit-related pay schemes.

Key points of income tax

11.2   The salient features of taxation as they apply to the payroll operation can be summarised as follows.

(*a*)   Employees' remuneration (including taxable benefits) and pensions are taxed under Schedule E.

(*b*)   Pay As You Earn (PAYE) is just a method of collecting tax under Schedule E.

(c) With effect from 6 April 1996, the Inspector of Taxes does not normally assess employees to tax under Schedule E – with the introduction of self assessment, those employees who receive an income tax return are required to assess themselves. They have the option of calculating their tax liability if they wish or can let the Inspector of Taxes do so instead.

(d) The Board of Inland Revenue supervises direct taxes such as income tax whilst indirect taxes such as Value Added Tax (VAT) are the responsibility of the Commissioners of Customs and Excise.

(e) The main officials of the Inland Revenue are Inspectors of Taxes who calculate employees' tax liabilities and the Collectors of Taxes who are responsible for collecting, enforcing and accounting for taxes. The Commissioners, who hear appeals relating to tax issues are not employed by the Inland Revenue, rather they are an independent body of persons experienced in income tax and legal issues.

(f) For the purposes of Schedule E, 'emoluments' includes not only earnings which are paid in cash, but also most benefits in kind.

(g) For Schedule E purposes, expenses paid to an employee are subject to a very strict test for allowability under the *Income and Corporation Taxes Act 1988, s 198 (ICTA 1988)*. However, with effect from 6 April 1998, a major change occurred to the way in which expenses may be claimed in relation to business travelling and subsistence costs.

Up until that date, in order to qualify for tax relief, expenses relating to business travelling had to have been incurred 'necessarily' and 'in the performance of the duties of the employment'. Other expenses, for example subsistence, had to have been incurred 'wholly, exclusively and necessarily' and 'in the performance of the duties of the employment'.

With effect from 6 April 1998, the legislation was amended such that travelling expenses *and* expenses connected with travel (such as subsistence) became liable to a new test for allowability. Such expenses will now be regarded as allowable if they are incurred *either* in the performance of the duties *or* if attendance at the place visited was necessary to the performance of those duties.

(h) Expenses details, together with details of benefits in kind, must be reported to the Inspector of Taxes each year on Form P11D where the employee is either a director or where his earnings (including the value of all benefits in kind) are paid at the rate of £8,500 per annum. In the case of employees who earn at a rate of less than £8,500 per annum, it may still be necessary to report the provision of certain types of expenses and/or benefits in kind but in their case, the return is made on form P9D. Employees are entitled to make claims for relief in respect of eligible expenses under *ICTA 1988, s 198* described above.

(j) Appendix D contains details of current income tax rates.

General taxation background

11.3   This topic can be dealt with under the following heads:

(*a*) ***Main personal taxes*** — Individuals who are resident in the United Kingdom (UK) are taxable on their income arising in the UK whether it is 'earned' income or 'unearned' income (for example, income from bank or building society interest, stocks, dividends etc.). They are also liable to tax on income arising abroad in certain circumstances. Residents in the UK who have a foreign domicile are not liable to UK income tax on foreign income unless the income is remitted to the UK.

Individuals who are not resident in the UK are taxable on their income arising in the UK subject to any double taxation relief (DTR), either unilaterally or under an agreement between their home territory and the UK.

Individuals resident or ordinarily resident in the UK are also taxable on their capital profits made anywhere in the world under the Capital Gains Tax (CGT) rules. CGT is not levied on any gains made when the individual is neither resident nor ordinarily resident in the UK.

Individuals who are domiciled in the UK are also subject to inheritance tax on death or on certain lifetime transfers of capital. Non-domiciled persons are liable only on any UK property.

The basic rate of income tax is currently (1998/99) 23 per cent and is charged on a band of taxable income between £4,300 and £27,100. Tax at the lower rate of 20 per cent is charged on the first £4,300 of taxable income and any taxable income in excess of £27,100 is charged to tax at the higher rate of 40 per cent. CGT is charged as if the gain forms the top slice of the individual's income.

(*b*) ***Income tax schedules*** — An individual's income is taxable if it falls within one or other of the relevant 'Schedules' contained at *ICTA 1988, ss 15 to 20*. All of the Schedules and types of income to which they relate are described briefly below for the sake of completeness. Schedule E is of primary importance to payroll administrators whilst Schedule D is primarily of relevance in relation to self-employment.

With the introduction of self assessment, self-employed persons are responsible for preparing accounts for submission to the Inspector of Taxes and for calculating their own tax liabilities ('assessing'). However, persons who choose not to do so may continue simply to submit their accounts to the Inspector who will calculate the extent of their tax liability and issue a demand for payment.

Self-employed persons are responsible for making payment direct to the Inland Revenue, unlike employees, whose tax is deducted at source by the employer under the PAYE system.

(i) Schedule A covers all income from UK property, including rents from furnished and unfurnished lettings and lease premiums.

(ii) Schedule B formerly covered the assessable value of woodlands which were managed on a commercial basis, with a view to the realisation of profit. This Schedule was abolished in 1988.

(iii) Schedule C formerly covered interest, public annuities, dividends or shares of annuities out of public revenue of any government and the revenue of any public authority or institution outside the UK which were payable in the UK and which were paid through paying agents (bankers and others). This Schedule was abolished in 1996.

(iv) Schedule D is divided into the following separate 'cases':

Case I	— profits or gains of traders;
Case II	— profits or gains of professions or vocations;
Case III	— interest received, annuities and other annual payments;
Cases IV and V	— overseas income from certain investments, possessions, property and businesses;
Case VI	— miscellaneous profits not falling within any of the other cases of Schedule D.

(v) Schedule E covers wages and salaries from offices and employments (including directorships). This Schedule is also divided into cases as follows:

Case I	— normally applicable where the employee is resident and ordinarily resident in the UK irrespective of where the duties are actually performed;
Case II	— applies to employees who are non-resident, or if resident, then not ordinarily resident, in the UK, in respect of duties performed in the UK;
Case III	— applies to employees resident in the UK, whether ordinarily resident or not, so far as their main emoluments do not fall within Case I or II and which are remitted to the UK during the course of overseas employment.

(vi) Schedule F covers dividends and other distributions of UK companies.

(c) *Allowances* — Every individual is entitled to receive certain allowances which are set against his or her income before income tax is charged.

271

Every person receives a basic allowance (£4,195 in 1998/99) and a married man is entitled to an additional married couple's allowance (MCA) which is £1,900 in 1998/99 although tax relief in respect of the MCA is given at a rate of only 15 per cent. The wife can claim 50 per cent of the allowance if she so chooses. The allowances are increased for individuals aged 65 or over and further increased for those aged 75 and over, subject to their income not exceeding specified figures.

(*d*)   ***Self-assessment*** — As has already been mentioned, the whole basis of income tax assessment changed radically on 6 April 1996 (the beginning of the 1996/97 tax year) with the introduction of self-assessment. Prior to the introduction of self-assessment, the Inland Revenue issued assessments to taxpayers, one for each Schedule of income as appropriate. It was then left to the taxpayer to appeal against the assessment if he considered it to be incorrect (for example, if it was estimated or excessive) and to request any necessary postponement of the payment of the tax. Once the relevant tax return had been submitted, the Inland Revenue would amend the assessment as required and seek payment of the revised amount from the taxpayer.

This has now all changed. Under the self-assessment procedure, the taxpayer may be required to complete a tax return and, at the same time, make a calculation of his or her own total tax liability for the year. Self-employed persons will have to pay their tax in two installments each equal to 50 per cent of the expected liability.

For the majority of employees who pay tax under Schedule E, the self-assessing procedure is a formality since they will have paid the tax which they are due to pay on their earned income under the PAYE system. It is unlikely, therefore, that they will receive a self-assessment return unless they specifically request one from the Inspector of Taxes. However, certain employees will automatically receive a return – for example, those whose tax affairs are not straightforward because, say, they have additional income from interest or dividends, because they make payments under maintenance orders, or those who pay tax at 40 per cent and directors. Such persons will still be required to complete the return and pay over any additional tax which may be due.

The operation of self-assessment also has implications for employers in that the information which they have been accustomed to providing to the Inspector each year on Form P11D or P9D must now, under threat of penalty, be provided to each employee.

(See 20.19 below for a discussion of the impact on employers and employees).

(*e*)   ***The PAYE system*** — The PAYE system under which an employer is obliged to deduct tax from the salaries and wages which he pays to his employees applies to all income from offices and employment, except those earned by certain divers and diving supervisors and a few isolated types of employee in respect of whom employers are given special instructions.

PAYE is simply a method of collecting tax under Schedule E from the vast majority of employees. The system also applies to occupational and personal pensions payments. The PAYE system has been extended to cover the collection of National Insurance contributions (NICs).

The statutory authority for the deduction and repayment of tax from wages and salaries etc. under Schedule E is contained in the *Income and Corporation Taxes Acts 1988, ss 203* to *204* and in the *Income Tax (Employments) Regulations 1993 (SI 1993 No 744)*. In practice, however, payroll managers and administrators are likely to refer to Inland Revenue publications such as Booklet CWG2 (Employer's Further Guide to PAYE and NICs) rather than to the legislation, although it should be noted that these simply provide an interpretation of the legislation and, in themselves, have no statutory force.

The operation of PAYE is outlined in 11.14 and 11.15 below and at Chapter 20 (PAYE Procedures). The territorial scope of PAYE was considered in *Clark (H M Inspector of Taxes) v Oceanic Contractors Incorporated [1983] 56 TC 183*. In this case, it was held that payments made by a non-resident company to individuals working in the North Sea which constituted emoluments within the scope of *ICTA 1988, s 830(5)* were taxable under Schedule E and subject to PAYE because of the trading presence of the company in the UK.

(*f*) **The history and source of UK taxation** — The modern system of UK taxation can be traced back to the introduction of income tax by William Pitt (the younger) in 1799 when it was introduced as a temporary measure to fund the Napoleonic Wars – the 'temporary' measure has remained with us for some 200 years! However, the temporary nature of taxation is still demonstrated by the fact that it is still necessary to have a Budget each year when the *Finance Acts* are renewed.

The 'Schedule' system of income tax was introduced in 1803 by Lord Addington, Pitt's successor. The system of assessment and collection, together with the right of appeal, evolved throughout the nineteenth and twentieth centuries and has resulted, apart from the introduction of self-assessment, into the detailed and complex structure of taxation which we currently have today.

It was precisely the complex nature of the UK's taxation system which led to the introduction of self-assessment – described as 'the biggest change to tax in the UK for 50 years'. The previous major change was the introduction of the PAYE system itself.

Tax law is largely a creature of statute – its primary source. However, this is supplemented by case law, which represents the judicial interpretation of the fiscal legislation, and the guidelines published by the Inland Revenue – representing its interpretation of the legislation. The annual *Finance Act* is also a regular source of tax law. From time to time, the various Finance Acts are consolidated, most notably on the income tax side by the *Income Tax Act 1918*, the *Income Tax Act 1952*, the *Income and Corporation Taxes Act 1970* and the current consolidating act, the *Income and Corporation Taxes Act 1988*. Capital gains tax is currently consolidated in the *Taxation of Chargeable Gains Act 1992* and inheritance tax, in the *Inheritance Tax Act 1984*. The main procedural and operational provisions are currently contained in the *Taxes Management Act 1970*.

Administration of taxation in the UK

11.4   Direct taxes such as income and corporation tax are supervised by the Commissioners of Inland Revenue ('the Board'). Indirect taxes such as Value Added Tax (VAT) are supervised by the Commissioners of Customs and Excise. These bodies have a duty to collect the relevant taxes or duties.

Income tax, capital gains tax and corporation tax are dealt with in Inland Revenue tax districts, each of which is responsible for administering its own area. The tax districts are supervised by the Board's head office and each is in the charge of a District Inspector, whose main responsibility is to supervise the assessment and agreement of tax liabilities.

The job of collecting taxes is the responsibility of the Collector of Taxes.

Under the Inland Revenue's New Office Structure (NOS) arrangements, many of the Inspectors' and Collectors' offices have been combined into new large Taxpayer District Offices (TDOs) and Taxpayer Service Offices (TSOs). The new structure should be fully implemented by the middle of 1998.

Outline of income tax calculations

11.5   The principle for calculating the annual amount of tax payable and an illustration of this calculation is given below:

(a)   calculate the annual total income;

(b)   deduct the unrestricted tax-free allowances;

(c)   the resulting figure is the taxable income;

(d)   calculate the tax payable, applying the various income tax rates consecutively on the taxable income;

(e)   deduct any restricted allowances, for example, the married couple's allowance, on which tax relief is given at only 15 per cent.

Example — Tom is a senior business executive. He receives an annual income from employment of £66,000 after deducting allowable expenses. He also receives £3,000 per annum in rents from a small cottage. His annual pension contributions are £3,000. He is married and claims the married couple's allowance. The calculation (or 'computation') of tax for 1998/99 is as follows:

	£
Salary etc.	66,000
Less: Pension contributions	3,000
Taxable earnings	63,000
Income from property	3,000
Total income	66,000
Less: Personal allowance	4,195
Taxable income	61,805

Tax payable:

	£
On first £4,300 at 20% (reduced rate)	860
On next £22,800 at 23% (basic rate)	5,244
On balance of £34,705 at 40%	13,882
Total	19,986
Less: Married couple's allowance £1,900 at 15%	285
Net tax liability	19,701

The PAYE system spreads the collection of the tax due on Tom's salary over the whole of the tax year. Tom is assigned a tax code by the Inspector of Taxes which governs the amount of tax to be deducted under PAYE in each pay period according to his personal allowances and other relevant factors. PAYE calculations and other details are explained in Chapter 25 (Manual Calculation Methods).

In the example given above, Tom's whole tax liability for the year would have been recovered under PAYE. As a consequence, if he were to receive a self assessment return, he would be able to calculate his liability as £19,701, less tax paid in an equivalent amount, with a 'nil' balance payable.

If, on the other hand, Tom had income from bank or building society interest, tax would be deducted at source at the 20 per cent reduced rate. On completing his self-assessment return, he would need to calculate the additional tax payable on the interest based on the difference between the reduced rate deduction and his marginal (higher) rate of tax – that is to say, at 20 per cent.

Self-assessment

11.6 As mentioned above, the introduction of self-assessment places significant burdens on employers to enable their employees properly to comply with their obligations under the new rules. The first self-assessment returns were issued in April 1997 covering income received in the 1996/97 tax year.

Employers have until 31 May to provide employees with Form P60 giving details of the pay received and tax paid in the preceding tax year. Failure to provide a copy to the employee can give rise to a penalty of £300 per form plus an additional daily penalty of £60 per form for each day that the failure continues.

Employers are also now required to give a copy of the information reported on Forms P11D and P9D to each employee by 6 July following the end of the tax year. A failure to do so will also incur penalties similar to those outlined above.

Distinction between the self-employed and employees

11.7 A question of great importance for payroll administrators is that of being able to distinguish between employees (those to whom Schedule E is applicable) and the self-employed (those who pay tax under Schedule D).

The tax advantages of self-employment are clearly attractive. Quite apart from the fact that tax is not deducted at source and the self-employed person therefore has the use of the money until such time as it is due to be paid, the expenses rules relating to self-employed persons are more generous than those applying to employees.

However, both the Inland Revenue and the CA can be expected to take a close look at the position of those claiming to be self-employed. A simple declaration by the employer or the self-employed person to the effect that the person is self-employed is unlikely to be accepted without corroborating evidence. If no such evidence is forthcoming, and the employer has treated a worker as self-employed, when in fact he should have been treated as an employee, the employer could be held liable to pay the tax which he should have deducted from the worker under PAYE and may, in addition, face penalties for non-operation of PAYE. This issue is discussed in some depth at Chapter 4 (Payee status).

General points relating to Schedule E

11.8 Schedule E brings into a charge to tax the earnings from employment as opposed to earnings from self-employment. The latter, as we have discovered earlier, are taxed under Schedule D. Under the self-assessment procedure, there is no longer a separate Schedule E assessment but it is still necessary to be able to identify what is, or is not, Schedule E income.

Tax is charged under Schedule E on 'all salaries, fees, wages, perquisites and profits whatsoever' *(ICTA 1988, s 131(1))* derived from an office or employment. Examples of 'office holders' are company directors and Members of Parliament. (See Chapter 4 (Payee status) for a discussion of the legal definition of office and employment.)

An example of the strict interpretation of taxable earnings is found in *Hamblett v Godfrey [1987] 1 AER 916* (the 'GCHQ' case). Here a £1,000 payment made by the Crown to an employee in recognition for losing the right to be a member of a trade union was held to be taxable under Schedule E.

From 6 April 1989, and subject to transitional arrangements, the earnings of all directors and employees are taxed according to the tax year in which they are received and not according to the tax year in which they were earned. [*ICTA 1988, ss 36–45*].

Schedule E Cases

11.9   As we discussed earlier, assessment under Schedule E is split into three Cases, as follows:

(a)   **Case I** — This Case applies where the employee is both resident and ordinarily resident in the UK. It does not cover earnings from an employment performed wholly abroad for a non-resident employer by an employee not domiciled in the UK, which may, however, be chargeable under Case III.

A 100 per cent foreign earnings deduction may be available in charging tax under Case I as discussed in 11.11 below.

(b)   **Case II** — This case applies where the employee is either not resident in the UK or resident but not ordinarily resident in the UK and the earnings are from duties performed within the UK.

(c)   **Case III** — This Case applies to the earnings of a UK resident which do not fall within Case I or Case II. The assessment is based on the actual amounts remitted to this country in the relevant tax year. This Case now only applies to those persons who are not domiciled in the UK and who work wholly abroad for a non-resident employer and to persons not ordinarily resident in the UK in respect of earnings for work carried out outside the UK.

Domicile and residence

11.10   The Schedule E Case to be applied depends upon an employee's domicile and residence. These two concepts are important in all areas of tax law and not just to Schedule E.

(a)   **Domicile** — All individuals acquire at birth what is called a 'domicile of origin'. This is the country in which their father is domiciled at the time of their birth. An individual can only lose that domicile of origin by acquiring a 'domicile of choice', meaning that the individual has formed a clear intention of remaining in another country for the rest of their life with no intention of returning to make their home in the previous country of domicile.

If, for any reason, an individual loses their domicile of choice, unless another domicile of choice is established, they re-acquire their domicile of origin.

(b)   **Residence** — For tax purposes, residence is something which is determined by reference to a person's circumstances from year to year and the determination of residence can become very complicated. A person can be treated as being resident in more than one country at the same time and the question of where one is resident will depend upon the facts of the given case. Residence depends upon the length of time a person lives in a country, his purpose in living there and his future intentions regarding his stay.

There is little statutory guidance on the subject of residence but there are three specific provisions as follows:

(i)   an individual who is in the UK for a temporary purpose will be deemed to be UK resident if he is physically present in the UK for at least 183 days in a tax year, ignoring days of arrival and departure;

(ii)   a Commonwealth or Irish citizen whose 'ordinary residence' (see below) has been in the UK and who has left the UK for 'occasional' residence abroad will continue to be UK resident throughout;

(iii)   the availability of accommodation in the UK for an individual working full-time outside the UK will not have a bearing on his residence status.

Apart from the above, the Inland Revenue's approach to residence has evolved over a number of years and their current practice is set out in Inland Revenue Booklet IR20. The booklet has no statutory force but is merely the Inland Revenue's interpretation of what few provisions there are. The following are the main points.

A person leaving the UK to work abroad full-time will be treated as non-resident provided that both the absence from the UK and the employment cover a complete tax year, and that return visits to the UK do not amount to more than 182 days in any tax year or more than an average of 90 days per year (averaged over four years).

A person coming to the UK will be regarded as resident immediately if he comes here permanently or with an intention to stay for three years or more. (The purchase of accommodation in the UK will be taken to indicate an intention to stay for three years or more.) Otherwise, the individual will be treated as resident from the fifth tax year where, in the preceding four tax years, visits to the UK averaged 91 days or more per year.

Any decision by the individual which shows an intention to stay on a more permanent basis will result in UK residence beginning in the tax year in which the decision is made.

In strictness, one's residence status is determined by reference to complete tax years but, by concession, an individual coming to the UK to take up permanent residence or to stay for at least three years will be treated as UK resident only from the date of arrival. Similarly, a person leaving the UK to take up permanent residence abroad will be treated as UK resident only up to the date of departure (ESC A11).

In a similar vein, an individual coming to the UK to take up employment which is expected to last at least two years will be treated as UK resident only from the date of arrival in the UK and an individual leaving to take up full time employment will be treated as resident only up to the date of departure (ESC A11).

Another important concept is that of 'ordinary residence', a term which denotes a greater degree of permanence than mere residence. A person can be resident under the 183 day rule without becoming ordinarily resident. On the other hand, a person can be ordinarily resident without being resident for a particular year, for example, if he is absent from the UK for one complete tax year whilst on holiday.

A person will be treated as being ordinarily resident if he visits the UK regularly and either has accommodation available in the UK or the visits average 91 days or more per tax year.

The 100 per cent foreign earnings deduction

11.11   For periods up to 16 March 1998, a deduction from earnings, chargeable to tax under Case I of Schedule E is due where, in a given tax year, the duties of the employment are performed wholly or partly outside the UK in the course of a 'qualifying period' which falls wholly or partly in that year and consists of at least 365 days (*ICTA 1988, s 193(1)* and *12 Sch*).

The deduction is 100 per cent of the earnings attributable to the qualifying period. A qualifying period is a period of consecutive days which consists either:

(*a*) entirely of days of absence from the UK; or

(*b*) partly of such days and partly of intervening days of presence in the UK within certain limits.

The intervening days of presence in the UK which may be included in a qualifying period must not exceed one-sixth of the overall period nor amount to more than 62 consecutive days. In the case of seafarers, the limits are one-half of the overall period and 183 consecutive days respectively. For these purposes, an individual is not regarded as absent from the UK on any day unless so absent at the end of it.

The 100 per cent foreign earnings deduction has been withdrawn for the generality of employees in relation to:

(i) earnings attributable to qualifying periods beginning on or after 17 March 1998; and

(ii) earnings attributable to qualifying periods beginning before 17 March 1998 which are received on or after that date.

The foreign earnings deduction for seafarers remains, although in relation to earnings falling within (i) and (ii) above, employment as a seafarer is redefined to make it clear that this only covers the performance of duties on a ship (*ICTA 1988, s 192A*). Under previous legislation, certain individuals working on particular types of oil rigs had qualified to be treated as seafarers.

Further aspects of Schedule E

11.12 Schedule E includes payments and benefits from employment other than direct monetary earnings and these will usually be subject to some form of special treatment. Common cases are listed below and more details are given in Chapters 9 (Benefits, Expenses and Termination Payments), 10 (Pensions), 14 (Pension Contributions) and 20 (PAYE Procedures).

(*a*) Pensions and retirement annuities are taxed when received but contributions to pension schemes are almost invariably free of tax. Further details are given in Chapters 10 (Pensions) and 14 (Pension Contributions).

(*b*) Benefits in kind such as company cars are also chargeable to tax under Schedule E. Such benefits may be taxed more leniently than an equivalent cash benefit. Chapter 9 (Benefits, Expenses and Termination Payments) gives further details of common benefits.

(*c*) Redundancy payments receive preferential tax treatment. This is discussed in Chapter 9 (Benefits, Expenses and Termination Payments).

(*d*) Expenses incurred by an employee in the course of his duties are, in principle, not subject to tax. Unless the expenses are covered by a dispensation, the employee must enter these items in his tax return and claim tax relief on the amount of the expenditure by means of a *section 198* claim.

(*e*) Details of benefits and expenses are often reported to the Inland Revenue on Forms P11D or P9D. See Chapter 20 (PAYE Procedures) for further details.

Special cases

11.13 Certain employments are governed by special rules arising from case law or statute. Thus, for example, in the case of *Cooper v Blakiston [1909] 5 TC 347*, offerings received by a vicar at Easter were held to be emoluments. North Sea divers' income is excluded from a charge to Schedule E and is taxed under Schedule D. [*ICTA 1988, s 314*].

Where a business carrying out construction work (the contractor) pays a sub-contractor, the contractor must withhold from the sub-contractor's earnings, an amount equivalent to income tax at the basic rate (unless the sub-contractor has been granted an 'exemption certificate' by the Inland Revenue).

The contractor is then required to pay the amount of the withholding to the Inland Revenue who then retains the money as a payment on account of the sub-contractor's eventual tax liability. Despite the requirement for this withholding, the sub-contractor is still taxed under Schedule D. (It has to be said that the Construction Industry Tax Deduction Scheme is to be radically revised from 1 August 1999 and the status of many sub-contractors may change as a result.)

Chapter 4 (Payee Status) contains further details.

Background to the PAYE system

11.14 As has been explained previously, PAYE is simply one method of collecting income tax under Schedule E. The system not only caters for income tax but is also used as a medium for the collection of certain classes of National Insurance contributions (NICs).

The basic intention of PAYE is to ease the difficulties of paying and collecting tax infrequently in large lump sums and this is achieved by spreading the deductions over the tax year. PAYE is complicated because it must cover many eventualities. As an illustration, there are numerous different forms which must be used by the payroll administrator who operates the scheme on behalf of an employer or pension scheme. A list of the main PAYE forms together with a selection of facsimiles are given in Appendix C. Details of the PAYE system are contained in Inland Revenue Booklet CWG2 'Employer's Further Guide to PAYE and NICs' and CWG1, 'Employer's Quick Guide to PAYE and NICs'.

Operating PAYE

11.15 The operation of PAYE requires the maintenance of pay and tax records for virtually all employees. The records must be retained for three complete tax years (*Income Tax (Employment) Regulations 1993 (SI 1993 No 744), reg 55(12)*). The calculation of income tax and NICs is explained in Chapter 25 (Manual Calculation Methods). The details of gross pay and the statutory deductions for tax and NICs must be recorded on deduction working sheets – Forms P11 – (see Figure 25A) or substitutes including computer systems. A full list of standard forms and their purpose is contained in Appendix C. The operation of PAYE, including the use of the various forms, is described in Chapter 20 (PAYE Procedures).

PAYE penalties

11.16 The penalties for late submission of PAYE end of year returns (Forms P35 and P14 (OCR)) can be severe, as can the penalties for incorrect returns.

With effect from May 1995, automatic penalties are levied on employers who do not submit end of year returns by the fixed filing date of 19 May, following the end of the tax year. However, by concession (ESC B46), the Inland Revenue has confirmed that it will not charge a penalty if the returns are submitted by the last working day within seven days following the usual deadline. ESC B46 states that:

> 'This concession should not be regarded as an extension of the statutory time limits. It will be kept under review'.

The maximum penalty allowed by statute is dependent upon the number of employees shown on the annual return. The penalty bands are based on multiples of 50 with an additional band for the additional part number above a multiple of 50.

The penalty is £100 for each month, or part of month, (up to twelve), during which the failure continues, for each 50 employees (or part, where the total is not a multiple of 50). If the failure continues beyond twelve months, an additional penalty arises, not exceeding the amount payable for the year of assessment which remained unpaid at 19 April following that year.

Examples of how statutory penalties are arrived at are as follows:

Assume X Ltd had 565 employees to return on the 1996/97 P35. (The actual number of current employees could be significantly lower than this figure but the test to be applied is the number of names required to be returned on the Form P35. It therefore includes employees who left or joined part way through the tax year.)

Example 1: P35 submitted 1 July 1997

565/50 = 12 (rounded up)

Penalty = £100 × 12 × 2 months = £2,400

Example 2: P35 not submitted until 1 June 1998

Initial penalty = £100 × 12 × 12 months (max)

= £14,400

Assuming total due per P35 = £2,250,000 and amount paid by 19 April 1997 = £2,000,000.

Unpaid by 19 April 1997 = £250,000

Total maximum penalty = £14,400 + £250,000 = £264,400.

Penalties are also charged for late filing of Forms P11D and P9D. There is an initial penalty in respect of each form of up to £300, with a daily continuing penalty of up to £60 per form for each day that the failure continues.

Where an end of year return understates the amount due through fraud or negligence, the maximum penalty permitted by statute is the difference between the amount declared on the return and the correct amount which should have been shown. An employer who fraudulently or negligently provides incorrect information in a Form P11D or P9D is liable to a penalty of up to £3,000 for each form.

It will be seen from this that employers face potentially serious financial consequences if they are dilatory or careless in making end of year returns. Care, and the institution of procedures to ensure that information can be collated promptly, are of the essence if correct returns are to be submitted timeously and penalties avoided.

Collection of taxes

11.17   Under the PAYE system, employers pay income tax and NICs to the collector of taxes together with an official payslip (P30BC). In the event of non-payment, the collector can take enforcement proceedings through the courts or by distraint (known as 'poinding' in Scotland). In other words, the Inland Revenue can seize the employer's goods or assets and sell them at auction to meet the tax liabilities.

The Inland Revenue is only a preferential creditor regarding statutory deductions etc. [*Insolvency Act 1986, Sch 6*]. Tax paid under PAYE is due from the employer within 14 days of the end of each income tax month or each quarter in the case of a small employer. Where tax is lost through the taxpayer's negligence or fraud, he may incur a penalty up to the amount of tax not paid as a result of the incorrect return. [*TMA 1970, ss 95–99*]. The taxpayer may also be prosecuted under the *ThA 1968, PjA 1911* and *FCA 1981*.

The Inland Revenue will charge interest automatically on an employer's remittances of PAYE and NICs which are received after 19 April. The interest charge on the amount of unpaid tax and NICs will automatically be applied, subject to *de minimis* limits set by the Inland Revenue. The interest rate is regularly updated to reflect ongoing base lending rates.

References

11.18   Because tax legislation changes rapidly the reference works below are revised regularly. They should be supplemented by the Inland Revenue booklets which are similarly updated as required.

(1)   Saunders G and Smailes D, 'Tolley's Income Tax 1998–99', Tolley Publishing Co Ltd, 1998.

(2)   Dolton A and Saunders G, 'Tolley's Tax Cases 1998', Tolley Publishing Co Ltd, 1998.

(3)   Homer A and Burrows R, 'Tolley's Tax Guide 1998–99', Tolley Publishing Co Ltd, 1998. (A useful practical guide covering taxation generally.)

(4)   Maas R, 'Tolley's Taxation of Employments', Fifth Edition, Tolley Publishing Co Ltd, 1997.

(5)   Gravestock P, 'Tolley's Guide to Self-Assessment 1998–99', Tolley Publishing Co Ltd, 1997.

(6)   'Festive Pastime or New Year Tax Headache', PMR, December 1997. (Self-assessment.)

(7)   'Building Regulations', PMR, May 1998. (The construction industry.)

Note: A full list of the Inland Revenue booklets can be found in Reference (1) above.

12   National Insurance Contributions

Scope of this chapter

12.1   National Insurance contributions (NICs) are paid to finance State social security benefits such as jobseekers allowance, incapacity benefits and widow's and retirement pensions. These contributory benefits form part of the much wider UK social security system which includes many non-contributory benefits such as family credit and child benefit. This chapter briefly describes the main payroll rules for NICs. It concentrates on employees and employers but gives some consideration to the position of the self-employed. The main benefits available are also outlined. NICs are not levied on pension payments which are, of course, subject to income tax. However, the employers of people over State pensionable age — 60 for women and 65 for men, still pay NICs although the employees themselves do not. Readers are recommended to refer to References (1) in 12.21 below and (4) in 6.13 above which provide the details of both NICs and social security benefits on an annual updated basis.

Key points of National Insurance contributions

12.2   A summary of the key points is stated below.

(a)   NICs paid by employees provide rights to contributory social security benefits.

(b)   The National Insurance number (NINO) is essential for recording and identifying a person's NIC history and subsequent benefit rights.

(c)   The Contributions Agency administer NICs.

(d)   NICs are usually collected through the PAYE system and paid to the Inland Revenue acting on behalf of the Contributions Agency.

(e)   NIC calculations are divided into classes and categories depending on a person's employment status and the type of pension arrangement into which they have entered. Married women and widows can, in some cases, pay reduced rates.

(f)   NIC calculations involve a multiplicity of rates and earnings bands. Calculations can be performed either by using the official NIC tables or

by using 'exact percentage' rates. There may be slight differences in the contributions payable depending on the actual salary.

(*g*)   NIC regulations also cover special circumstances, for example company directorships, multiple employments, holiday pay and overseas employment.

(*h*)   There is an extension of NIC to be applied to certain benefits- in-kind, e.g. shares and share options which are not part of an Inland Revenue approved arrangement, private use of company cars and private petrol provision and items which can be traded on a recognised exchange or where other trading arrangements exist. A further extension of the rules will levy an employer only NIC charge on payments of tax under a PAYE settlement agreement.

Background of National Insurance contributions

12.3   NICs are collected from employees and employers. Chapter 25 (Manual Calculation Methods) describes manual payroll calculations and shows how the National Insurance procedures are integrated into the PAYE system. With computer systems many of the calculation details are concealed from the payroll user. However, a general understanding of NICs and benefits is useful, if not essential, in many areas of payroll, pensions and personnel administration. For example, a married woman or widow had the right to elect to pay reduced rates of NICs in return for reduced NI benefits. This right was lost in May 1977 for women married after that date. However, a married woman or widow already paying reduced NICs at that time was allowed to continue doing so subject to her continuing to satisfy certain conditions. In this case the employer must restore standard NIC deductions if there is a change in her marital status, for example on divorce or a widow remarrying. It is, therefore, essential for employers to be aware of such changes and to have procedures in place whereby speedy action can be taken when changes occur.

The National Insurance system is administered by the Contributions Agency, which is now part of the Department of Social Security, although, as already explained, most NIC details and payments are collected by the Inland Revenue through PAYE procedures on behalf of the Contributions Agency. The Agency will merge with the Inland Revenue in 1999. The employee's NIC history stored by the Contributions Agency is a major factor in determining his right to contributory benefits. In the case of State pensions the relevant contribution history can cover up to 50 years. Any errors in the NIC calculations or records could, therefore, prejudice an employee's future benefit rights.

NICs are a major financial burden which can cost employer and employee together 20 per cent of pay and this will increase significantly from April 1999 when the standard employer rate increases to 12.2 per cent. The yield from NICs is a major source of revenue to the Government. Virtually all of this sum is paid by employers and their employees. The social security system is operated on a 'pay as you go' basis and, at any one time, the National Insurance fund normally has only sufficient money (including State scheme premiums and income from fund investments) to cover a few months' benefit expenditure. In recent years expenditure from the NI Fund has greatly exceeded the income and has only remained solvent by virtue of sizeable grants being made from general taxation. The deficit to be made up from general taxation in the 1997/98 tax year was around £1.4 billion but it is expected that the Fund will break even in the 1999/2000 tax year or perhaps even end in surplus.

Legal basis for NICs

12.4   The law governing NICs is mainly contained in the *Social Security Contributions and Benefits Act 1992*, the *Social Security Administration Act 1992* and the *Social Security (Contributions) Regulations 1979 (SI 1979 No 591)*. A number of other SIs also contain provisions relating to NICs. General commentary and guidance on NIC matters is given in leaflets available from offices of the Contributions Agency and reference is made to them and to the relevant law where appropriate. The most important of these leaflets is CWG 2 'Employer's Further Guide to PAYE and NICs') and the latest edition is for use from April 1998.

Contribution classes for NICs

12.5   Contributions are payable under one or more of five classes which are as follows.

(a)   *Class 1* — Earnings-related NICs payable by employed earners (the 'primary contributions') and their employers (the 'secondary contributions').

(b)   *Class 1A* — Employers' NICs on taxable benefits for cars and fuel.

(c)   *Class 2* — Flat rate NICs payable by self-employed individuals.

(d)   *Class 3* — Flat rate NICs payable on a voluntary basis to protect or enhance benefit entitlements.

(e)   *Class 4* — Profit- or gains-related NICs payable by self-employed individuals in respect of certain amounts which are also charged to income tax.

A further class of contribution, Class 1B, will be introduced from April 1999. This will be an employer only contribution payable on income tax due under a PAYE settlement agreement.

Only Class 1 and Class 1A are usually of direct relevance to payroll administrators. Class 2 NICs can sometimes be of interest, for example, when part of the workforce operate on a self-employed basis. The appropriate rates of NICs are available in DSS leaflet NI 196 and the current NIC rates are listed in Appendix D.

The definition of an employed earner includes normal employees who perform under a contract of service or apprenticeship, but also includes persons in an elected office such as company directors, MPs and Church of England clergy. The distinction between the employed and the self-employed is vital as it determines the NIC Class and the amount of the contributions as well as other matters. This issue and the related matter of determining which NIC class applies to employees is discussed in Chapter 4 (Payee Status) but because of the increasing interest shown by Inspectors, the question of employment status is not one to be taken lightly.

Summary of National Insurance benefits

12.6   The main social security benefits provided by the various NIC Classes are outlined below. The contribution and other qualifying conditions vary according to the benefit.

(*a*)   *Jobseekers allowance* — Only recently paid standard rate Class 1 contributions and certain credits count for this benefit, therefore, it is not available to those individuals who have not worked for some time, to the self-employed or those paying reduced rate Class 1 contributions, i.e. some employed married women or widows.

(*b*)   *Statutory sick pay (SSP) and statutory maternity pay (SMP)* — Individuals must be working for an employer and have earnings which reach a certain average in a specified eight week or two-month period. Although there is no requirement to pay contributions to receive these benefits, because of where the average figure is set, it is safe to say that if contributions have not been paid then neither SSP nor SMP will be paid. Both benefits are paid by the employer and are both taxable and liable for NICs.

(*c*)   *State incapacity benefit and maternity allowance* — Class 1 or Class 2 contributions must be paid for a claimant to receive these benefits. SSP and SMP will remain the benefits most likely to be paid to employees. Where, however, an employee is not entitled to SSP either because he does not satisfy the basic conditions or because he is sick for more than 28 weeks then incapacity benefit may be payable. Maternity allowance is a National Insurance benefit which may be payable to women who do not qualify for SMP, for example the self-employed or employees who have not been long enough with their employer.

(*d*)   *Basic State pension, widow's pension and widowed mother's allowance* — Class 1, Class 2 or Class 3 contributions are required to be paid to qualify for these benefits. A widow's benefits may depend on her husband's contribution record.

(e)   ***State Earnings-Related Pension Scheme (SERPS)*** — Only standard
rate Class 1 contributions paid on earnings which fall between the lower
and upper earnings limits count towards this additional pension, which is
available to both contributors and their widows. Widowers are included
under *Social Security Contributions and Benefits Act 1992, s 41*. Chapters 10
(Pension Schemes) and 14 (Pension Contributions) explain the SERPS in
greater detail.

(f)   ***Widow's payment*** — The husband's Class 1, Class 2 or Class 3
contributions count towards this benefit. It was replaced by a £1,000
lump sum payment under *SSA 1986, s 36* (now *SSCBA 1992, s 36*).

(g)   ***Accidents at work and industrial diseases*** —These are covered by the
non-contributory industrial injuries disablement scheme.

(Appendix D contains the current rates of the main social security benefits.)

Department of Social Security

12.7   The DSS is the government department responsible for implementing
legislation on matters relating to social security. The DSS, in the form of a
number of agencies (see below), administers the various contributory and
non-contributory State benefit schemes including SSP and SMP throughout the
UK. The agencies, however, remain within the overall control of the Department of Social Security. The agencies will have their own business plan
approved by the appropriate ministers and together will cover the DSS's major
executive functions. The main agencies are as follows:

(a)   ***The Information Technology Services Agency (ITSA)*** — This agency
began on 2 April 1990 and services the computing and telecommunications required by the DSS. It employs around 4,700 staff, many of them
highly specialised in information technology. The locations of this agency
are at Livingston, Norcross, Washington and Swindon. National implementation of a pensions strategy project, local office project and a central
index has already been undertaken. The strategy systems are available to
assist the enforcement and collection activities of the Contributions
Agency (see below) by identifying potential under-payments and non-
payments.

(b)   ***The Social Security Benefit Agency (SSBA)*** — This agency began in
April 1991 and is located at Leeds. It is responsible for the administration
of all social security benefit entitlements worth approximately £80
billion to about 20m individual claimants. It has a staff of around 70,000,
most of whom work in the local office network.

(c)   ***The Contributions Agency*** —The Contributions Agency is an executive
agency of the DSS and exists, on behalf of the Secretary of State for

Social Security, to ensure compliance with the law relating to National Insurance contributions (NICs) and to operate the National Insurance (NI) scheme.

The Agency can be divided into three main areas:

(i)   Field operations, based mainly in local offices situated throughout the UK, but with a central support group based at Longbenton, Newcastle upon Tyne. These deal mainly with NI matters that require a local presence (e.g. visiting local firms to ensure compliance with the law relating to National Insurance).

(ii)   Central operations, which occupy various sites in the Tyneside area, are responsible for maintaining and correcting NI records for employed, self-employed and non-employed persons. Basically they deal with all matters not requiring a local presence.

(iii)   Corporate services, based at Longbenton, are responsible for future planning, finance and personnel matters.

This agency replaced the National Insurance Contributions Unit on 5 April 1991 and is located at Newcastle upon Tyne. It is responsible for:

(A)   collecting NICs and enforcing compliance on employers for payment and notification;

(B)   maintaining about 60 million individual contribution records;

(C)   providing NI-related information to enable benefits to be paid promptly and accurately.

This agency employs around 10,000 staff but this is expected to drop rapidly as the full effect of a recent move to greater automation works through the system.

As mentioned at 12.3 above, the Contributions Agency and Inland Revenue will merge in 1999.

(*d*)   There are three other agencies: the Resettlement Agency, which came into existence on 24 May 1989, the Child Support Agency, which started in early 1992, and the War Pensions Agency, which began in April 1994.

The headquarters address of the DSS is Richmond House, 79 Whitehall, London SW1A 2NS (see Appendix F) and it operates through numerous divisions. The main divisions are as follows:

(i)   Central Office, Newcastle upon Tyne NE98 1YX, at which office are held all contribution records regarding computer and specialist matters, deferment regarding multiple employments, refunds, contracting-out matters, determination of questions to the Secretary of State and the liability of mariners are dealt with.

(ii)   The Adelphi, 1–11, John Adam Street, London WC2N 6HT where the international relations division is situated. This office will deal with all questions of policy regarding international matters. Also at this address are a number of contributions policy branches which deal with various questions related to the assessment and collection of contributions and the categorisation of earnings.

Field operations — All contributions and compliance work which requires a local presence is within the jurisdiction of the Contributions Agency operating through almost 5,000 staff and 30 or so field operational divisional managers, and approximately 220 field operational area managers, each of whom is responsible for between one and six local offices.

Local offices — These offices, some under regional control, are about 500 in number of which some 325 have a contributions section, and these offices are the means of communication with the public, even though decisions come from elsewhere. The number of offices is expected to drop dramatically in the next couple of years.

The powers of an inspector — DSS inspectors are permanent civil servants appointed by the Secretary of State, and they number in the region of 2,200 – this is an increase over recent figures but can be explained by the spend and save initiative announced in the last Conservative Budget. A DSS inspector's powers are contained in *Social Security Administration Act 1992, s 110* and are extensive. It is an offence to obstruct an inspector in the exercise of his powers. (Further information, including details of maximum penalties chargeable in various situations, is contained in leaflet CA 28.)

He is entitled to:

(A)   enter at all reasonable times any premises used for trade or business if there is reason to believe that anyone is employed there;

(B)   interview anyone on the premises;

(C)   see, take or copy any documents which would help him to check whether the conditions of the Social Security and National Insurance Acts are being or have been followed, and to enforce the Acts if necessary, and look into the circumstances of any industrial accident or disease for which a benefit claim is being or has been made.

An inspector has similar powers in relation to SSP, SMP, income support, family credit and personal pension arrangements.

Appeals with regard to NIC decisions — In order to appeal against NIC matters it is necessary to pose a question to the Secretary of State on Form CF90 or CF93 which is available from the Office for the Determination of Contribution Questions (ODCQ) based at Newcastle, although local offices will generally become involved. There is no effective time limit for posing a question and employers may go through this procedure in relation to a contested liability to Class 1 NICs. An independent inquiry is normally held and it is possible for a further appeal on a point of law to be made to the High Court against the resulting decision. Appeals against assessments to Class 4 NICs are, however, handled by the Inland Revenue and the General or Special Commissioners under *TMA 1970, s 31*. When the Contributions Agency and Inland Revenue merge it is expected that appeals will be dealt with under the Inland Revenue procedures.

Information — The information division of the DSS is situated in the head office in Whitehall (Tel: 0171 712 2171). Explanatory leaflets can be obtained from GPA Interface, Rosepark House, Upper Newtownards Road, Belfast, BT4 3NR. Fax No: 01232 526121. There is also a free social security advice line for employers and the self-employed, which is 0345 143 143.

Collection of NICs

12.8   The Inland Revenue handle the collection of NICs under Class 1 and Class 4. Class 1A contributions may be payable to either the Inland Revenue or the Contributions Agency, depending on the choice made by an employer. NICs under Classes 2 and 3 are normally paid directly to the Contributions Agency either by direct debit or via a bill issued in arrears by the Agency. As already explained, the collection of Class 1 NICs normally takes place through the PAYE system which every employer is required to operate. The employer is responsible for paying to the collector of taxes both primary and secondary Class 1 NICs less, where appropriate, any SSP, SMP and SMP compensation which he is entitled to recover. He is entitled to deduct the primary NICs from the employee's earnings. Payment of these contributions in most cases should reach the collector within 14 days of the end of the tax month. A tax month starts on the sixth day of the calendar month.

Class 1A contributions which were payable from 1991/92 onwards will be a once a year collection, carried out in July 1998 for the year 1997/98. The current rate is at ten per cent and will be levied on the taxable car benefit appropriate to the type of vehicle and business mileage, and where relevant, to the fuel scale charge applicable to each individual. The contribution is levied on the employer and there is no liability on the employee. (See 20.15 below for details of methods of paying Class 1A NICs.) Although the Inland Revenue are now assessing tax liabilities based on the original cost of the vehicle this has no real implications for NICs. This is because the Class 1A is due on whatever is taxable.

National Insurance numbers

12.9   The National Insurance number (NINO) identifies an employee's personal national insurance account. It is also used as an identifier by the Inland

Revenue and is quoted on many PAYE forms; it is sometimes used by employers as the individual's internal payroll or pension number. The number is usually assigned through the Child Benefit system in the year before a person reaches 16 years of age. It is now issued to the person concerned on a plastic card but such cards are available to all employees on request. Card 6 of CWG 1 'Employer's Quick Guide to PAYE and NICs' gives details of the procedures for dealing with missing NINOs. Employers are encouraged to notify the Contributions Agency of any employee who fails to produce a NINO within eight weeks of starting work. The format of a NINO is XX 99 99 99 X where XX can be any two letters, 99 99 99 any six digit number and X a letter (e.g. AB 12 34 56 A). The final letter is always A, B, C or D. Employers can now obtain NI numbers by completing the new page on Form P46 or by completing Form CA 6855.

Two methods of calculation for Class 1 NICs

12.10   Class 1 NICs can be calculated either on an 'exact percentage' basis or by reference to tables supplied in booklets by the Contributions Agency. The exact percentage basis is used in this chapter and involves applying the NIC percentage rates to exact earnings to determine the liability. NIC tables are, in fact, only an officially approved ready reckoner containing pre-calculated NICs for all earnings. These tables are not precise as the earnings are listed in £1 steps for weekly pay and £4 steps for monthly pay, although the contributions are calculated on the mid point between the steps. Where tables are used, pay is rounded down to the nearest earnings entry in the tables. The exact percentage method is often used by computer systems. When comparing the two methods of NIC calculations, small differences can occur because one calculation is based on mid point amounts and the other on exact amounts. The maximum difference will be 40 pence a month split evenly between the employee and his employer. The NIC rates on which the tables are based and which are used for exact percentage calculations are found in Appendix D.

NIC table letters

12.11   A brief explanation of the broad differences between the calculation of NICs and income tax is given in 25.5 below. The NIC calculations are broken down into categories which are represented by the letter of the corresponding NIC table. This NIC table letter is sometimes confusingly called the NI 'code' or 'category'. The main NIC table letters are listed below and a different set of calculations applies to each.

A — for not contracted-out employees.

B — for married women or widows who are not contracted-out on reduced rate NICs.

C — for the employees who do not pay NICs because they are entitled to deferment by virtue of another employment or because they are over State pensionable age. The secondary (employer's) NICs remain payable. There are two separate tables with Category C calculations: one for not contracted-out employments and the other for contracted-out. Employees over State pensionable age must always be treated as not contracted-out.

D — for contracted-out employees.

E — for married women or widows who are contracted-out on reduced rate NICs.

X — where NICs are not payable. Often, however, this letter is not used and a blank is left on any form or computer screen, although it is subsequently allocated by the Contributions Agency. It should be used for pension payments, earnings which never reach the lower earnings limit in the year or where an employee is exempt from the NIC system either via a treaty provision or because he has not been in the UK for the required length of time. The DSS check regularly to ensure that the use of category X is not abused.

From 6 April 1997 employers have needed to use three new category letters for employees who are members of a contracted-out money purchase (COMP) pension arrangement. These categories are:

F — where full standard rate contributions are payable.

G — where married women or widows are paying reduced rate contributions.

S — when the employee has been granted deferment.

There are further NIC tables and letters for certain special categories of employee. For example, a contracted-out ocean-going mariner may be allotted the table letter 'N'.

Appendix D contains the calculation rate structure corresponding to the above conditions. These are the rates to be used for the exact percentage method. The method of applying the rate structure is explained below.

The table letters are not only important for determining the appropriate NIC table or exact percentage calculation to be used but must also be shown on PAYE records or their computer equivalents. It is the responsibility of the employer to determine an employee's correct NIC table letter. In most cases this is straightforward but mistakes can occur. For instance, the Contributions Agency are likely to take a strict view of employers who have not transferred a woman from reduced to full NIC liability after being told of her divorce or widowhood, i.e. changed her table letter from E to D or B to A, as the case may be.

NIC rate limits

12.12   Although the details differ between table letters the essence of the NIC calculation is to apply different rates between earnings bands or 'brackets' formed by limits. These limits are currently as follows:

(*a*)   the lower earnings limit (LEL) of £64 per week;

(*b*)   the lower graded contribution limit of £110 per week;

(*c*)   the middle graded contribution limit of £155 per week;

(*d*)   the upper graded contribution limit of £210 per week;

(*e*)   the upper earnings limit (UEL) of £485 per week.

The graded contribution limits only apply to employers' contributions. The LEL represents roughly the level of the basic State pension and the UEL is around seven times the LEL. The State Earnings-Related Pension Scheme (SERPS) is accrued on earnings between the LEL and UEL.

No NICs are levied on earnings which do not reach the LEL. For earnings at or above the LEL there are two earnings bands and rates for employee NICs.

 (i)   A lower percentage rate on that part of pay up to the LEL, i.e. on 'lower band' earnings currently up to £64 per week.

(ii)   A higher rate on any pay between the LEL and UEL, i.e. on 'middle band' earnings currently from £64 up to £485 per week.

There are no NICs on 'upper band' earnings over the UEL of £485 per week levied on the employee.

The actual percentage rates used depend on the NIC table letter. However, with table letter A (for a typical not contracted-out employee) the rate is 2 per cent on lower band earnings and 10 per cent on the middle band. With table letter D (for a typical contracted-out employee) the lower band rate is 2 per cent and the middle band rate is 8.4 per cent.

NIC exact percentage calculations

12.13   The rates in Appendix D have to be selected with care. NICs are calculated separately for each earnings band and totalled. The calculation for each band is rounded prior to totalling (0.5p and below is rounded down). Figure 12A is an illustration of the graded structure for contracted-out secondary contributions. Examples of NIC calculations using the exact percentage method can be found in 12.14 and 25.10 below.

NIC calculation examples for the 1998/99 tax year

12.14   The following are examples of NIC calculations with notes relating to the calculations, earnings periods and earnings on which NICs are paid. Where different rates apply to different earnings bands this is shown as two or three figures, for example 2/10 for 2 per cent on the lower band and 10 per cent on the middle band.

Example – Employee not contracted-out (table letter A)

Not Contracted-out

Weekly Wage	Employees (%)	Employer (%)	Note
£40	Nil	Nil	(a)
£70	£1.88 (2/10)	£2.10 (3)	(b)
£115	£6.38 (2/10)	£5.50 (3)	(c)
£160	£10.88 (2/10)	£11.20 (7)	(d)
£220	£16.88 (2/10)	£22.00 (10)	(e)
£490	£43.38 (2/10/0)	£49.00 (10)	(f)

Notes:

(a)   Earnings are below the weekly lower earnings limit of £64.00, therefore NICs are not due.

(b)   Earnings are in the bracket £64.00 to £109.99 and therefore the employee pays 2 per cent up to £64.00 and 10 per cent on the remainder of his earnings. The employer pays 3 per cent on all earnings.

(c)   Earnings are in the bracket £110.00 to £154.99, and therefore the employee pays 2 per cent up to £64.00 and 10 per cent on the remainder of his earnings. The employer pays 5 per cent on all earnings.

(d)   Earnings are in the bracket £155.00 to £209.99 and therefore the employee pays 2 per cent up to £64.00 and 10 per cent on the remainder of his earnings. The employer now pays 7 per cent on all earnings.

(e)   Earnings are in the bracket £210.00 to £465.00, and therefore the employee pays 2 per cent up to £64.00 and 10 per cent on the remainder of his earnings. The employer now pays 10 per cent on all earnings.

(f)   Earnings are in the bracket above £485.00, and therefore the employee pays as previously 2 per cent up to £64.00. However, he only pays 10 per cent on earnings up to a ceiling of £485.00. He pays nothing on earnings above the ceiling whilst the employer pays 10 per cent on all earnings.

An example of a contracted-out calculation is given in 25.13 below.

Figure 12A   1998/99 graded structure of NICs for employers

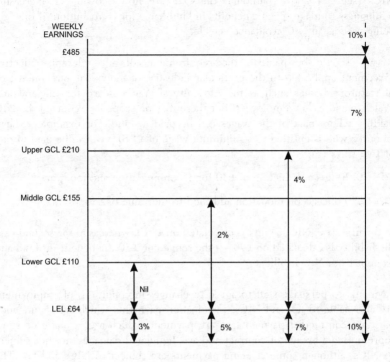

Illustration of the 1998/99 graded structure of contracted-out secondary contributions for an ordinary employee (Table letter D): there is a similar structure for other types of Class 1 NICs. These secondary contributions are paid by the employer

Earnings periods — All NIC tables and limits are published in a weekly or monthly form. For periods which are multiples of a week or month the pay is split into an equivalent weekly or monthly amount. The NIC is calculated on this figure in the normal way. The result is multiplied by the number of weeks or months concerned to give the total liability. For example, an employee is paid £400 per fortnight. The NICs are calculated on the equivalent weekly amount of £200 and multiplied by two. (For complications such as company directors and irregular payments see leaflets CA 44, and CWG 2, as well as 12.16–12.18 below.)

Earnings on which NICs are paid — Virtually all normal earnings of employees are subject to NICs. Pension payments are not subject to NICs. From a payroll viewpoint some payments included in the gross pay of an employee may not be subject to NICs. The most obvious example is actually incurred business expenses: Chapter 25 (Manual Calculation Methods) shows how the pay subject to NICs can differ from that subject to income tax. Chapter 5 of Booklet CWG 2 lists common payments which should or should not be included as 'NICable' pay. Benefits in kind are usually exempt from NICs (see 9.4 above) although the DSS are now showing an increasing willingness to make specific benefits in kind liable for contributions if they are being used as an NIC avoidance vehicle.

Regard should be paid to the requirements of any relevant collective agreement applicable to the particular industry, of individual agreements, or of statutory bodies such as the Agricultural Wages Board for England and Wales, when paying employees, but there may be scope for reducing the NIC liability where part of the wages can be paid in kind. For example, a farm labourer who is entitled to a minimum wage of £120 p.w. can be paid in one of two ways:

  (i)   £120 less a deduction of £30 for accommodation and food, or

  (ii) £90 plus accommodation and food to the value of £30.

In the first case, NIC liability is calculated on £120, whereas in the second case the liability is calculated on £90 — the remaining £30 is a benefit-in- kind and exempt from NIC liability.

Payments to persuade staff to agree to changes in conditions of employment are also liable to tax and NICs. Termination payments which are redundancy pay, non-contractual payments or are payments which are *ex gratia* or sums representing a breach of contract and are 'liquidated damages' are not subject to NICs, although some *ex gratia* payments are subject to NICs and tax. The NIC legislation is nowhere as detailed as that for tax. There is no NIC-free equivalent of £30,000 and all termination payments must be carefully considered. In short, payments linked to previous service will be liable for NICs whilst compensatory payments for something which is lost will be NIC-free. A recent change, however, means that contractual payments in lieu of notice are liable for NICs. A NIC inspector will carefully scrutinise *ex gratia* payments and look at all the background circumstances of the payment in order to arrive at a decision.

Provision of company car and petrol for private use — Where there is an element of private use the income tax provisions will apply depending on the business mileage. The change in Inland Revenue practice, whereby tax liabilities will be assessed on the initial cost of the car, has no NIC implications because the taxable amount is what is subject to Class 1A liabilities. The taxable figure is subject to NIC at the rate of ten per cent for the payments due in July 1998. The DSS has clarified the situation for periods prior to 6 April 1991 that there are no NICs payable on the private use of a car, and that the old regime regarding the fuel provided for private purposes will apply, i.e. where the employer contracted with the supplier and payment was made by company credit card with prior consent of the supplier, this is sufficient to avoid liability. In fact, the Contributions Agency have gone even further and stated that where employers have not paid NICs on fuel used privately by employees no action will be taken to pursue NIC arrears for the 1989/90 and 1990/91 years. This is now largely irrelevant because of the six year statute of limitations.

It is necessary to keep accurate mileage logs, as the tax charge depends on the mileage. It appears that some employers who could not present logs have been able to strike a deal based on the fuel scale charge for previous years, but where in some cases this was not agreed, full liability was claimed. The DSS were insisting that back payments are collected from 1989 for company cars and for six years back where employees purchase petrol for their own car and are then reimbursed by their employer. There was, however, some confusion with the DSS saying that contributions were due back to 1989 on company cars but they have now agreed they will not pursue such liabilities but employers should bear in mind that the situation regarding private cars is still subject to scrutiny. The DSS have conceded, however, that any Inland Revenue dispensation agreed for earlier years will now apply to NIC. Where such a dispensation has not been granted the DSS will now accept any reasonable split between business and private use. Refunds are therefore available for earlier years.

Telephone allowance — Detailed logs of business telephone calls are no longer required. From 6 April 1993 as part of a joint Inland Revenue/DSS study it was agreed that where the Inland Revenue accept a part of a reimbursed telephone bill as being tax free then no NICs will be due on that same portion. The DSS have now agreed that any dispensation given by the Inland Revenue will now apply to NICs. Refunds are available for earlier years when the DSS insisted on the availability of detailed logs or itemised telephone bills.

Round sum allowance — If round sums are paid whether or not an expense is incurred, the whole amount should be included in gross pay. However, if any specific or distinct business is incurred, only the profit element should be included. This recovery is not always possible due to the time lag and therefore care should be taken when paying round sum allowances. When no profit is intended and it can be shown that the amounts paid are the result of a reliable survey no NIC liability will generally arise. The Agency is, however, beginning to argue that cost of living allowances will always be liable for NICs irrespective of whether there is a profit or not. As part of the Inland Revenue/DSS study mentioned above, working rule agreements accepted by the Inland Revenue as tax free will now be NIC free.

This list of expense items is not exhaustive and readers are advised to clear all problem expense items with the Contributions Agency after checking with the written guidance in Booklet CWG 2.

Comments on the effect of the NIC structure

12.15 Prior to 5 October 1989 the NIC structure presented a kind of poverty trap for lower paid employees. A small rise in earnings could result in a very high increase in the NICs due from both the employee and employer. The revised NIC structure from April 1995 has improved but not eliminated this situation. The use of higher paid staff is also penalised as the employer, but not the employee, pays full rate NICs on all earnings over the UEL. Furthermore these extra NICs earn no additional social security rights. Needless to say the uneven and relatively heavy burden of NICs is further compounded by the effect of income tax. Some of this imbalance will be addressed by the contribution changes due to be introduced from April 1999, but that is outside the scope of this chapter.

The overall effect of the NIC system at most levels of pay is to encourage benefits in kind most of which do not attract NICs and which may also result in lower tax being paid if the earnings on which contributions are paid fall below the minimum qualifying level for the year in question. (See 9.3 above.) However, avoiding NICs may prejudice entitlement to social security benefits.

Company directors and NICs

12.16   Company directors are in a special position. All company directors who are in post at the beginning of a tax year are on an annual earnings period for NICs purposes. This is the case whether or not earnings are paid at shorter intervals, for instance monthly. (Contributions Agency Booklet CA 44 explains the NIC position of company directors in some detail.) A particular problem with company directors is the fact that some computer PAYE programs do not have the facility to use the annual earnings rules for company directors. In these cases, the NIC calculations have to be done manually.

The annual earnings bands and rates for directors' NICs in 1998/99 are shown below to illustrate the system. The table and example below are for not contracted-out directors.

Earnings Brackets	Employee (%)	Employer (%)
£0 – £3,227.99	Nil	Nil
£3,228 – £5,719.99	2/10	3
£5,720 – £8,059.99	2/10	5
£8,060 – £10,919.99	2/10	7
£10,920 – £25,220.00	2/10	10
More than £25,220.00	2/10/0	10

Example — A director receives a salary of £2,500 per month in 1998/99; his NIC position is as follows. (The exact percentage method is used.)

Cumulative Pay		Employee (%)	Employer (%)	Cumulative Total NICs	NIC payments	Notes
April	£2,500	Nil	Nil	Nil	Nil	(a)
May	£5,000	2/10	3	£383.76	£383.76	(b)
June	£7,500	2/10	5	£858.76	£475.00	(c)
July	£10,000	2/10	7	£1,433.76	£575.00	(d)
August	£12,500	2/10	10	£2,233.76	£800.00	(e)

Notes:

(a) Earnings amount to £2,500, which is below the limit of £3,228.00, therefore NICs are not due.

(b) Earnings now total £5,000 and total NICs of £383.76 (for both employer and employee) are due.

(c) Earnings now total £7,500 and total NICs of £858.76 are due. However, £383.76 has already been paid so that the remittance for June is £475.00.

(d) Earnings now total £10,000 and total NICs are £1,433.76. However, £858.76 has already been paid so that the remittance for July is £575.00.

(e) Earnings now total £12,500 and total NICs are £2,233.76. However, £1,433.76 has already been paid so that the remittance for August is £800.00.

If the director had been earning more than, say £3,000 per month, then after nine months his earnings would exceed the UEL of £25,220 and no further employee contributions would then be due. The employer's contributions, of course, would continue to be paid on earnings beyond the UEL.

Variations and complications of the above annual earnings period method, such as the use of NIC tables, are explained in Reference (1) in 12.21 below.

The Contributions Agency did issue a consultation document on whether the cumulative system of assessment for company directors should continue. Their intention was to treat directors paid at regular intervals in the same way as employees paid at that interval. Those who responded to the document wanted the Agency to go even further. This proved too much for the Agency and, in the short term, no changes will be made to the existing system.

Multiple employments

12.17 Where an individual has several employments with the same employer the earnings from each employment are usually aggregated to calculate the NIC due. Where an individual holds a number of employments with different employers, but the employers carry on business in association with each other, the earnings are also usually aggregated to calculate the NIC due. According to the Contributions Agency, employers are in association with each other if they share profits, losses or, to a sufficient extent, resources. The effect of aggregation is normally to reduce or cancel out any NIC savings where earnings in one or more of the relevant employments would otherwise attract NICs at the lower rates. An individual can pay excess Class 1 NICs if he has earnings from more than one employment. The general rule is that refunds can be claimed if the employee NICs amount is more than the annual maximum calculated assuming that earnings are paid for 53 weeks at the weekly upper-earnings limit for the year. For 1997/98 the maximum NICs are (53 × £64 × 2%) plus (53 × £421 × 10%) = £2,298.14. (See Reference (4) in 12.21 below for a brief discussion of maximum NICs and single employments.)

NICs on holiday pay

12.18   There are sometimes NIC complications with holidays. These mainly affect weekly-paid employees. (See 9.5 above.)

NICs on overseas employment

12.19   The NIC position of employees sent abroad to work for an employer resident in Great Britain is complex and is described in the DSS leaflets NI 38, NI 132 and the SA series of leaflets. There are basically three sets of rules which depend on whether the overseas country is:

(*a*)   in the European Economic Area, which for social security purposes includes Austria, Finland, Iceland, Norway, Sweden and Liechtenstein;

(*b*)   a country with which the UK has a reciprocal agreement (see the DSS leaflets in the SA series, e.g. SA22 Turkey); or

(*c*)   a country with which there is no reciprocal agreement.

The purpose of European Community Council regulations and reciprocal agreements is to ensure equal treatment when an employee moves from one country to another and to protect entitlement to State benefits. In general the position outside the EEA countries and those countries which have reciprocal agreements with the UK, is that full Class 1 NICs are due on all earnings paid by an employer based in the UK during the first 52 weeks of employment abroad provided that the employee is ordinarily resident in the UK (i.e. he intends to return to the UK within five years) and he was resident in the UK immediately before starting his employment abroad. Where an employee is being sent to an EEA country, for a period which is not expected to exceed twelve months, and he is not replacing someone whose tour of duty has ended, his earnings are liable to UK NICs. Liability to UK NICs is, in these circumstances, certified on a Form E101 which can be obtained from the DSS international services branch. It is possible to extend this treatment by a timely completion of the Form E102 if, after the term of duty has started, the period of duty is unexpectedly thought likely to exceed a period of twelve months, but not twenty-four. In other cases the employee will be governed by the contributions rules of the EC country of employment from the outset although in certain cases it is possible for an employee to remain in the UK contribution system for up to five years. This is usually possible where the employee has a skill which is not available locally or where he is carrying out a specific task for his UK employer. Where the employee is gainfully employed outside the UK he may voluntarily pay NICs under Class 2 or 3. Further information is available in Contributions Agency leaflet CA 08. (See also, Reference (4) in 12.21 below.)

Self-employed workers and NICs

12.20   The self-employed worker pays far less NICs than his employed counterpart. The following examples show the differences in NIC liability in various circumstances for 1998/99 for a not contracted-out situation:

	Employee £	Employer £	Total £	Class 2 £	Class 4 £	Total £	Notes
Example 1 Where one employee receives £15,000 p.a.	1,233.76	1,500.00	2,733.76	330.20	461.40	791.60	(a)
Example 2 Where one employee receives £50,000 p.a.	2,255.76	5,000.00	7,255.76	330.20	1,074.60	1,404.80	(b)

Notes:

(a)   The total of employed NICs due is £1,942.16 more than the NICs due on a self-employed individual.

(b)   The total of employed NICs due is £5,850.96 more than the NICs due on a self-employed individual.

Clearly, the self-employed individual not only pays less NICs in his own right but the notional 'employer' avoids paying a great deal of NICs: £1,500.00 in Example 1, and £5,000.00 in Example 2. It follows that a self-employed workforce is attractive to an organisation because it is cheaper. However, as already discussed, if an individual is incorrectly classified as being self-employed the Inland Revenue will look to the employer for arrears of PAYE income tax and Class 1 NICs.

References

12.21 References (1) and (3) below provide a comprehensive description of National Insurance and social security. For the payroll practitioner the most important DSS publications are CWG 1 'Employer's Quick Guide to PAYE and NICs' (a series of advice cards) and CWG 2 'Employer's Further Guide to PAYE and NICs'. There is an April 1998 edition of both publications. There are, however, approximately 100 Contributions Agency booklets, many of which may be relevant to the payroll administrator. Some are designed for the employer and some for the employee. Reference (1) below contains a list of the more common NIC leaflets.

(1) 'Tolley's National Insurance Contributions 1998–99', Fourteenth Edition, Tolley Publishing Co Ltd, 1998.

(2) Some other useful DSS booklets

Leaflet Number	Subject
CA 44	National Insurance for company directors
CA 08	National Insurance voluntary contributions
CA 07	National Insurance: Unpaid and late paid contributions
NI 196	Social security benefit rates and NI contribution rates
CA 38	National Insurance tables: not contracted-out
CA 39	National Insurance tables: contracted-out

(3) Matthewman J, 'Tolley's Social Security and State Benefits 1998–99', Tolley Publishing Co Ltd, 1998.

(4) 'Maximum NICs', PMR, May 1996. (A response to a query from a Payroll Alliance member.)

(5) 'The Social Security Maze', PMR, June 1995. An article discussing the social security issues which vex employers when employees are sent to or obtain work in foreign countries.

(6) 'International Rescue', PMR, November 1997. (NICs for workers abroad.)

(7) 'Looking into the Future', PMR, May 1998. (New NICs regime.)

(8) 'Question Time', PMR, August 1998. (Latest NICs changes.)

The references in 4.9 above include a list of DSS booklets covering special cases, such as people employed through agencies.

13 Attachment of Earnings Orders

Scope of this chapter

13.1   This chapter concerns itself with the range of AEOs (attachment of earnings orders) which may be encountered by payroll administrators in their work. There are several different types of AEO available in the UK, under English and Welsh law, under Scottish law, and under the law of Northern Ireland. Although the methods of operation of each type are similar, there are significant differences to which the payroll administrator must be alert.

The use of attachment of earnings orders (AEO) has become a favoured method of government for recovering money in respect of debts, fines and liabilities from workers' pay. Accordingly, what was a relatively straightforward area in payroll administration has been subjected in the last few years to a surge in legislation to deal with a range of issues. These comprise non-payment of Community Charge and Council Tax, enforcement of payments of child support by absent parents and recovery of income support. The employer is, therefore, required to operate another set of statutory deductions, alongside PAYE and NICs. Failure by an employer to comply with an AEO carries fines.

The surge in the range of AEOs and complexity of their operation has prompted some suppliers of payroll computer software to decline to maintain or develop programmes to meet in full the requirements of payroll administrators. However, other suppliers have endeavoured to develop and maintain accurately functioning programmes. Those payroll administrators who have to intervene in their computerised payroll system calculations are likely to suffer the greatest compliance costs as compared to those who either have accurate programs or perform the payroll function completely manually.

In view of the range of AEOs and the attendant legislation there are few regulatory references in the text of this chapter. Reading of the relevant legislation given at the end of the chapter is, therefore, recommended.

Key points of AEOs

13.2   The following are important points in regard to AEOs.

(*a*)   The location of a centralised payroll processing point may be irrelevant as to the legal duty on the employer to operate any type of order. For instance, an employer with a centralised payroll department in England may have an employee working at a branch in Scotland for whom an order issued under the *Debtors (Scotland) Act 1987* (*DSA 1987*) is to be applied. A further complication, as yet unresolved, is where an employer has received two or more orders of different types which have originated under the jurisdictions of England/Wales and Scotland. For example, an employee originally employed at a branch in Scotland has a Scottish Earnings Arrestment (SEA) made against him. He is transferred to England and has a 1971 Act AEO made against him for another debt. Does the SEA remain valid, and in which sequence should the orders be applied? Questions on jurisdiction have been receiving the attention of the LCD but a decision is unlikely soon, if at all.

(*b*)   Although there are exceptions, virtually all earnings are subject to AEOs, after the deduction of income tax, NICs and pension contributions. There is a view that the value of certain benefits in kind should be included when calculating a deduction under an AEO. (See Reference (13) in 13.18 below.) Exceptions are found in the text.

(*c*)   A deduction for an AEO is based usually on the level of net or attachable earnings in each pay period. This level of net or attachable earnings is reduced by the value of any deduction by other AEOs previously operated in the same pay period. Accordingly subsequent orders are applied to the residue of net or attachable earnings.

(*d*)   Where the level of net or attachable earnings or the residue of net or attachable earnings falls below a prescribed amount, sometimes referred to as protected earnings, which is specified either in the relevant legislation or the order, then no deduction can be made. For some types of AEOs, such as the 1971 Act Priority Order, arrears of both protected earnings and deductions may be required to be maintained and carried forward to the next available pay period.

(*e*)   There may be legal problems in applying AEOs to pensioners.

(*f*)   The employer is required to notify the employee of deductions made under an AEO.

(*g*)   The employer is required within a prescribed time to notify the originating source of the AEO when the employee leaves, or where the employee specified in a new AEO is not in employment. The employer may also be required to give a notice concerning the order to the employee when he leaves.

(*h*)   The employer is permitted to deduct an additional amount each time a deduction is made under certain AEOs, in respect of administration costs.

(*j*)   Where more than one AEO is held for an employee then the AEOs have to be applied in a priority sequence.

(*k*)   Each type of AEO has its own calculation rules. In some cases the deduction is based on net or attachable earnings as shown in tables, but in other cases it is based on the amount of pay left after deduction of protected earnings. In the case of a Scottish Current Maintenance Arrestment the deduction is based, uniquely, on the number of days in the pay period.

(*l*)   Employers are required to make remittances of the amounts deducted under an AEO to the originating source or to the creditor.

(*m*)   Where an employee has more than one order of the same type then in some cases the orders can be merged into one AEO.

Types and usage of AEOs

13.3   The following AEOs can be raised for the purposes shown by the originating sources shown.

(*a*)   *1971 Act Priority Order (1971 Act AEO)* — used for the collection of family maintenance and fines. Raised by the High Court, magistrates' courts and the county court in England and Wales. [*AEA 1971*].

(*b*)   *1971 Act Non-Priority Order (1971 Act AEO)* — used for the collection of civil debts. Raised by magistrates' courts and the county court in England and Wales. [*AEA 1971*].

(*c*)   *Judgments Enforcement (Northern Ireland) Order* — used for the collection of civil debts. Raised by Enforcement of Judgments Office (Northern Ireland) or the High Court (Northern Ireland). [*JENI 1981*].

(*d*)   *Magistrates Courts (Northern Ireland) Order 1981* — used for the collection of family maintenance. Raised by magistrates' courts in Northern Ireland. [*MCNI 1981*].

(*e*)   *Scottish Earnings Arrestment (SEA)* — used for the collection of civil debts or fines. Raised by Sheriff courts in Scotland. From 1 July 1997, Commissioners of Customs and Excise have been able to raise SEAs in respect of any duty of Customs and Excise (except vehicle excise duty, value added tax, insurance premium tax, landfill tax or any agricultural levy of the European Community. [*DSA 1987*].

(*f*)   *Scottish Current Maintenance Arrestment (SCMA)* — used for the collection of family maintenance. Raised by Sheriff courts in Scotland. [*DSA 1987*].

(g) *Scottish Conjoined Arrestment Order (SCAO)* — used for the collection of multiple civil debts, fines and maintenance. Raised by Sheriff courts in Scotland. [*DSA 1987*].

(h) *Community Charge AEO (CCAEO)* — used for the collection of unpaid Community charges. Raised by Local charging Authorities in England and Wales, subsequent to obtaining a Liability Order at a magistrates' court. [*LGFA 1988*].

(j) *Council Tax AEO (CTAEO)* — used for the collection of unpaid Council Tax. Raised by Local Authorities in England and Wales, subsequent to obtaining a liability order at a magistrates' court. [*LGFA 1992*].

(k) *Child Support DEO (deduction from earnings order) (CSDEO)* — used for the collection of payments of child support from absent parents' earnings. Raised by the Child Support Agency of the DSS, throughout the UK. [*CSA 1991*; *CSNI 1991*].

(l) *Income Support Deduction Notice (ISDN)* — used for the recovery of income support paid to an employee for up to 15 days after his return to work following a trade dispute. Raised by the Benefits Agency of the DSS. [*SSCBA 1992*].

Priority of and sequencing of AEOs

13.4   The recent introduction of new types of AEOs has caused some difficulties for the payroll administrator particularly when operating more than one AEO for an employee.

In Scotland the DEO takes precedence over both the SEA and the SCMA. The SEA takes precedence over the SCMA. Where a Conjoined Arrestment Order is received an existing SEA and SCMA are to cease to be applied.

In England and Wales the 1971 Act Priority Order, the CCAEO, the CTAEO, and the DEO all have equal precedence, the priority being decided by date of issue, i.e. the AEOs are operated chronologically. The 1971 Act Non-Priority Order is operated regardless of date after other orders, although it may in certain circumstances affect the operation of a CCAEO.

In Northern Ireland AEOs raised under *MCNI 1981* and *JENI 1981* are to be applied in a priority sequence such that orders for maintenance take precedence over orders for civil debts. A DEO takes precedence over civil debt AEOs. Orders under *MCNI 1981* and *CSNI 1991* are to be dealt with in date of issue sequence.

An ISDN raised under *SSCBA 1992* is deducted after all amounts lawfully deductible by the employer.

The sequencing of orders, subject to the above, is chronological, using the date of issue of the AEOs. In the case of CCAEOs and CTAEOs a Local Authority can apply to and obtain from a court a Liability Order in respect of the debt, but not actually issue the AEO until much later.

There is a complication to the sequencing of AEOs. Where a 1971 Act AEO (Priority or Non-Priority) is in payment and has a date of issue earlier than 1 April 1993 then no CCAEO dated later can be operated. In effect all later dated CCAEOs are blocked from being operated until the extant 1971 Act AEO is cleared. Further, where a CCAEO is in payment and has a date of issue earlier than 1 April 1993, then all other CCAEOs for that employee which are dated later cannot be operated until the former has been cleared. In effect, a CCAEO in payment and dated before 1 April 1993 blocks the operation of any later CCAEO. Where all the AEOs for an employee are dated on or after 1 April 1993, then the blocking effect given above does not apply.

Earnings from which deductions are made

13.5   Virtually all 'earnings' are attachable for the purpose of applying attachment of earnings orders, but there are exceptions and minute differences between the range of attachment of earnings orders in what constitutes earnings. In addition there are questions as yet unresolved as to whether or not certain other emoluments and payments on termination of employment count as attachable earnings. There is a view that emoluments, such as a contribution made by the employer to the employee towards the cost of a season ticket, should be included as attachable earnings for a Council Tax AEO. (See Reference (13) in 13.18 below for a discussion of this particular issue.) Further, the treatment of some payments on termination of employment is uncertain. For instance, should redundancy pay be included or excluded as attachable earnings? Does such a payment arise out of or on the cessation of the employment? Under the *DSA 1987* redundancy pay due under *EPCA 1978, s 81(1)* is specifically excluded from being attachable earnings for arrestment orders. Where there is any doubt as to the treatment of a particular payment or emolument the employer can apply to the originating source of the AEO and seek guidance.

In principle, earnings are any sums payable by way of:

(a)   wages or salary, including any fees, bonus, commission, or overtime pay, or other emoluments payable in addition to wages or salary or payable under a contract of service;

(b)   pension, including an annuity in respect of past services, whether or not rendered to the person paying the annuity, and including periodical payments by way of compensation for the loss, abolition, relinquishment, or diminution in the emoluments, of any office or employment;

(c)   statutory sick pay.

Payments under (*b*) are not attachable to ISDNs, nor to CCAEOs and CTAEOs, nor to orders raised under *DSA 1987* where the payment is made under an occupational pension which precludes any assignation of such payments.

The following payments are not to be included in attachable earnings.

 (i) Income payable by any public department of the Government of Northern Ireland or of a territory outside the UK. This exclusion does not apply to orders raised under *DSA 1987*.

 (ii) Pay or allowances payable to the debtor as a member of Her Majesty's Forces.

(iii) Allowances or benefits payable under any Social Security enactment (except statutory sick pay). In particular statutory maternity pay is not subject to AEOs.

 (iv) Pensions or allowances payable in respect of disablement or disability.

 (v) Except in relation to a maintenance order, wages payable to a person as a seaman, other than wages payable to him as a seaman of a fishing boat. This exclusion does not apply to DEOs raised under *CSA 1991*.

 (vi) A guaranteed minimum pension within the meaning of the *Social Security Pensions Act 1975*. This exclusion does not apply to CCAEOs raised under *LGFA 1988* on or after 1 April 1992, or to CTAEOs raised under *LGFA 1992*.

Some of the above inclusions and exclusions may not be applicable to ISDNs.

The attaching of payments made under a pension scheme is fraught with difficulties. Pensions payable to a member of Her Majesty's Forces may be excluded by specific legislation, for example, the *Army Act 1955, s 203*. Pension scheme rules usually prohibit the assignment of or charge on a pension benefit so as to ensure the beneficiary alone receives the benefit and it is not used for any other purpose. In some instances the pension benefit is often void or is forfeited to be applied as the trustees of the scheme think fit. The question of a distinction between voluntary and involuntary assignments may need to be resolved. As an AEO is an involuntary assignment legal advice may need to be sought to resolve the situation, although the AEO may prevail. (*Edmonds v Edmonds [1965] 1 AER 379* and *Cotgrave v Cotgrave [1992] Fam 33.*)

Operation of the 1971 Act Priority Order

13.6   There are several elements to the operation of this order. The normal deduction rate is the amount specified in the order, which the court thinks reasonable to take from the employee's attachable pay. The protected earnings rate is also specified in the order, and is the amount of pay that the court allows the debtor to retain. No deductions are to be made which reduce the pay below the protected earnings level. Arrears of the normal deduction rate and of the protected earnings rate have to be maintained by the employer and used in subsequent pay period calculations. Arrears can arise where there are insufficient attachable earnings in a pay period to fully meet either or both the protected earnings level and the deduction rate. The deduction rate and the protected earnings level can be specified as either a weekly or monthly amount. In some situations, such as pay periods of a length which is neither weekly nor multiples of a week, nor monthly, then recourse may have to be made to daily rates for calculating the order. Where an employee receives holiday pay in advance then the deduction rate and the protected earnings rate are, in effect, multiplied by the appropriate number of weeks. Usually there is no balance or outstanding amount specified in the order.

To operate a 1971 Act Priority Order, the employer should follow the procedure stated below on each pay day.

(*a*)   Deduct the sum of normal protected earnings and arrears of protected earnings from the attachable earnings.

(*b*)   Carry forward any arrears of protected earnings.

(*c*)   Deduct the sum of normal deduction rate and arrears of deduction from the residue of pay left after operation of (*a*) above.

(*d*)   Carry forward any arrears of deduction where there was insufficient pay available in (*c*) above to meet the full deduction.

The following example illustrates the operation of a 1971 Act Priority Order.

Example — John's attachable earnings fluctuate weekly. A court has instructed his employer to operate weekly a normal deduction of £60.00 and a protected earnings level of £70.00. In week 5 John receives one week's holiday pay in advance.

Week number	Attachable earnings £	Deduction under the order £	Take home pay £	Comments
1	140	60	80	Normal deduction is taken.
2	110	40	70	Arrears of deduction of £20 are carried forward as there is insufficient pay available for a full deduction to be made.

311

3	65	Nil	65	Arrears of deduction of £80 (£20 brought forward, and £60 current period) are carried forward as there is insufficient pay available. Also, arrears of protected earnings of £5 are carried forward as there is insufficient attachable earnings to meet in full a week's protected earnings.
4	170	95	75	The £5 protected earnings arrears are cleared, plus the normal protected earnings. The residue of pay is sufficient to meet a deduction of £95, representing £80 arrears brought forward and £15 in the current period. Arrears of £45 deduction are carried forward.
5	310	165	145	The protected earnings is £140 representing two weeks. Thus, there is £170 available to meet a deduction of £165, representing arrears of £45 brought forward and £120 being two weeks' deduction.

Operation of a 1971 Act Non-Priority Order

13.7   Although the 1971 Act Non-Priority AEO has similarities to the Priority Order, it has distinctive features. The normal deduction rate and the protected earnings level are specified in the order. These are operated in the same way as for a Priority Order, except that arrears are not operated. The originating court also specifies in the order the amount which represents the balance to be paid in total over time by the employee. The deductions made each pay period reduce this balance. When the balance has been cleared the order ceases to apply. Where more than one 1971 Act Non-Priority Order is held for an employee then the employer can apply to the court to merge the orders into one consolidated AEO.

To operate a 1971 Act Non-Priority Order, the employer should follow the procedure stated below on each pay day.

(*a*)   Deduct the normal protected earnings from the attachable pay.

(*b*)   Deduct as much as possible up to the normal deduction amount, from the residue of attachable earnings left after (*a*).

(*c*)   Record the total amount of deductions.

The following example illustrates the operation of a 1971 Act Non-Priority Order.

Example — Joanna's attachable earnings fluctuate weekly. A court has instructed her employer to take a weekly normal deduction of £30.00 with protected earnings of £80.00. The balance outstanding on the order is £73.66.

Week number	Attachable earnings £	Deduction under the order £	Take home pay £	Balance on the order £	Comments
1	115.00	30.00	85.00	43.66	Normal deduction.
2	74.00	Nil	74.00	43.66	Insufficient protected earnings, so no deduction taken.
3	111.00	30.00	81.00	13.66	Normal deduction.
4	94.66	13.66	81.00	Nil	Normal deduction, but restricted to the outstanding balance.

Operation of the Northern Ireland AEO

13.8   An AEO raised under *MCNI 1981* or *JENI 1981* operates in the same way as for orders raised under *AEA 1971*. (See 13.6 and 13.7 above.)

Operation of the Community Charge AEO

13.9   The Community Charge AEO has little similarity to a 1971 Act AEO. There are no protected earnings, nor a normal deduction rate, but there is a debt specified in the order. Once the balance is cleared the order ceases. A deduction made under the order in a pay period is calculated by reference to a table, which is defined in the legislation and shows the amount or percentage of net attachable earnings to be deducted according to bands of earnings. (See Appendix H.) There is a minimum level of net or attachable earnings from which no deduction can be made. There is a given maximum band of earnings above which the excess is subject to a standard percentage charge. Prior to 1 April 1992 the deduction was taken as a set amount within a net or attachable earnings band. On and from 1 April 1992 the deduction is taken as a percentage within a net or attachable earnings band. The date of issue of the CCAEO is fundamental to deciding which calculation method is to apply.

Orders raised prior to 1 April 1992 also use a different definition of net or attachable earnings as compared to those CCAEOs raised on or after 1 April

1992. For orders issued prior to 1 April 1992 the employee's pension contributions do not reduce the level of attachable earnings. For orders raised on or after 1 April 1992 the level of attachable earnings is reduced by pension contributions. When holiday pay is paid in advance, then, for CCAEOs issued before 1 April 1992, the pay received on the one pay day is treated as a single payment, but for CCAEOs issued on or after that date the number of weeks involved is to be considered. For orders issued on or after 1 April 1992 the net or attachable earnings are reduced by the value of any loan repayment, whereas this does not apply to orders issued prior to 1 April 1992 or to those issued on or after 1 April 1995.

To operate a Community Charge Order, the employer should follow the procedure stated below on each pay day.

(*a*)   Deduct the amount calculated by reference to the table.

(*b*)   Reduce the balance outstanding on the order.

CCAEOs cannot be issued more than six years after a community charge debt arose. It follows that no new CCAEOs can be issued after 31 March 1999.

The following example illustrates the operation of a CCAEO issued prior to 1 April 1992. For an illustration of a CCAEO issued on or after 1 April 1992 see the illustration given under operation of a Council Tax Order (see 13.10 below).

Example — Jake's net or attachable earnings fluctuate weekly. A Local Authority has instructed his employer to operate a CCAEO for him until a balance of £200.00 has been cleared. In Week 2 Jake receives two weeks' holiday pay.

Week Number	Net or Attachable Earnings £	Deduction under the order £	Balance on the order £	Comments
1	120	11	189	Normal deduction.
2	360	98	91	Although representing three weeks' pay, the net or attachable earnings are still treated as if a single payment. (Compare with Council Tax deduction.)

Operation of the Council Tax AEO

13.10   A Council Tax AEO is identical in operation to a CCAEO issued on or after 1 April 1992. However, the earnings values in the deduction tables for CTAEOs were increased on 1 October 1998. These new tables apply only to

CTAEOs issued on or after 1 October 1998. (See Appendix G for the tables to calculate the deduction.) The same rules are used to determine net or attachable pay, for example, pensions contributions are deductible in full. Where holiday pay is paid in advance then the calculations are based on the number of weeks involved.

From 1 October 1998 not more than two CCAEOs can operate as an individual from anyone charging authority. Employers must operate more orders when, say, they have three orders from two different authorities.

To operate a Council Tax Order, the employer should follow the procedure stated below on each pay period:

(*a*)   deduct the amount calculated by reference to the table;

(*b*)   reduce the balance outstanding on the order.

The following example is an illustration of both a Council Tax Order, and a Community Charge Order which was issued on or after 1 April 1992 but before 1 October 1998.

Example — June has weekly earnings which rarely fluctuate. A Local Authority has issued an order showing a balance of £300 to her employer. In week 2 June receives two weeks' holiday pay.

Week number	Net or attachable earnings £	Deduction under the order £	Balance on the order £	Comments
1	120	14.40	285.60	Normal deduction.
2	360	43.20	242.40	The payment represents three weeks' pay. Each of the three weeks is assessed for a deduction.

Operation of the Child Support DEO

13.11   The Child Support DEO is basically identical in operation to the 1971 Act Priority Order. A normal deduction and protected earnings rates are specified in the order issued by the Child Support Agency, and arrears of both may have to be applied by the employer. Although basically the same as the 1971 Act Priority AEO, there are distinguishing features.

(*a*)   The first significant difference is that a DEO may specify two or more normal deduction rates with dates when each is to be applied. There are no limits to the number of rates which can be specified nor how far ahead the dates can be set. The employer is required to implement the new rate at the appropriate date.

(*b*)   The second difference concerned the treatment of holiday pay made in advance. The legislation governing the operation of DEOs was amended from 19 January 1998 so that it is now similar to 1971 Act AEO. This was really a technical amendment as it now puts the law in line with the practice adopted by most employers and the guidance provided by the Lord Chancellor's Department (see reference (1) in 13.18 below).

For an example and illustration of operation of a DEO see 13.6 above for a 1971 Act Priority Order.

Operation of the Scottish Earnings Arrestment Order

13.12   The SEA has similarities to those orders used in England and Wales. 'Attachable' earnings are those left after deductions of income tax, NICs, and pension contributions, but are not reduced by loan repayments. The calculation of a deduction under an SEA is made by reference to a weekly, monthly or daily table, but there is no normal deduction rate nor protected earnings. The tables show ranges of earnings bands with set deduction amounts. New tables (see Appendix J) were issued in 1995. There is a minimum earnings amount below which no deduction can be made, but also a maximum amount above which a percentage of the excess is deducted. A significant difference in the operation of a SEA is when a payment of holiday pay in advance is made. The holiday pay is aggregated with other payments made at the same time and the whole amount treated as if it was a single payment in the pay period. In this respect, the SEA is similar to a CCAEO issued prior to 1 April 1992. A balance is specified in the order. An employer can operate only one SEA at any one time. A second SEA cannot be applied but must be returned to the originating Sheriff's court.

To operate an SEA the employer should follow the procedure stated below each pay period:

(*a*)   deduct an amount under the SEA by reference to the appropriate table;

(*b*)   reduce the balance outstanding on the order.

The following example illustrates the operation of an SEA.

Example — Julie's weekly attachable earnings are almost static. A Sheriff has instructed her employer to apply an SEA. In week 3 Julie receives three weeks' holiday pay in advance. A balance of £201.00 is specified.

Week number	Attachable earnings £	Deduction under the order £	Balance on the order £	Comments
1	135.00	14.00	177.00	Normal deduction.
2	135.01	16.00	161.00	Normal deduction, but note that the extra 1p attachable earnings meant the next higher earnings band was used.
3	560.00	159.00	12.00	A deduction of £149.00 on the first £540 attachable earnings, and 50% of the remainder, produces a deduction of £159.00.
6	135.00	12.00	Nil	A deduction of £12.00 is made, clearing the outstanding balance, although the table showed a deduction of £14.00 as due.

Operation of the Scottish Current Maintenance Arrestment Order

13.13   Although the SCMA has a definition of attachable earnings similar to that for the SEA, it has a unique method of deduction calculation. There is a standard daily rate of protected earnings, currently set at £9 (with effect from 30 November 1995). The deduction rate specified by the Sheriff has to be applied also on a daily basis. The daily basis is inclusive of weekends and non-working days. The levels of protected earnings and deduction are to be equated to the actual number of days in the pay period. Thus, for a monthly payroll the calculations would have to refer to the number of days (31, 30, 28 or 29) in the month being processed. A second SCMA cannot be applied but must be returned to the originating Sheriff's court.

The following procedure should be followed by the employer in each pay period:

(*a*)   multiply the standard daily protected earnings rate by the number of days in the current pay period;

(*b*)   calculate the deduction amount by reference to the number of days in the current pay period;

(*c*)   apply the amount in (*b*) to the residue of attachable earnings after deduction of the amount in (*a*).

The following example illustrates the operation of an SMA.

Example — Jeremy is paid monthly. A sheriff has instructed his employer to operate a monthly deduction of £240.

Month	Number of days	Attachable earnings £	Protected earnings £	Deduction under the order £	Comments
February	28	800.00	252.00	220.92	The protected earnings are calculated as follows : £9 × 28. The deduction is calculated as follows : £240 × 12 / 365 × 28.
March	31	800.00	279.00	244.59	The protected earnings are calculated as follows : £9 × 31. The deduction is calculated as follows: £240 × 12 / 365 × 31.

Operation of the Scottish Conjoined Arrestment Order

13.14   While a Conjoined Arrestment Order (CAO) is in force no SEA, SCMA or another CAO is to be operated for the employee. Any SEA or SCMA already in force at time of receipt of a CAO is recalled (cancelled).

Where all the debts in the CAO are fines or civil debts, the calculation method to be used is that for an SEA. Where all the debts in the CAO are in respect of maintenance, the calculation method is that for an SCMA. Where the debts are a mixture of fines/civil debts and maintenance, then the calculation method is a combination of those methods used for SEAs and SCMAs. Where the CAO comprises maintenance orders and civil debts/fines, the CAO continues in operation until the Sheriff's court cancels the order.

Operation of the Income Support Deduction Notice (ISDN)

13.15   The income support attachment of earnings order has features similar to the 1971 Act Non-Priority Order. There are attachable earnings (referred to as available earnings), protected earnings, and an amount specified in the Deduction Notice which is to be recovered over time. There are, however, a number of characteristics which are unique to the ISDN. The protected earnings rate specified in the Notice is to be multiplied by a factor of 1, 2, 4 or 5 depending on whether the employee is paid weekly, fortnightly, four weekly (lunar monthly), or monthly, respectively. The amount to be deducted from the employee's pay in the pay period is based on the difference between the available earnings and the protected earnings in the pay period. Where the difference exceeds £1 (or £2 for fortnightly, or £4 for four weekly, or £5 for monthly, paid employee) the amount to be deducted is 50 per cent of the difference. Fractions of 1p are rounded down. The Deduction Notice has a limited life, and ceases to be valid after 26 weeks from the date of its issue.

To operate an ISDN the employer should follow the procedure given below for each pay period;

(*a*)   calculate the protected earnings according to the employee's pay frequency, and deduct this amount from the available earnings;

(*b*)   multiply the amount calculated in (*a*) by 50 per cent if it exceeds £1 for a weekly paid employee (or multiples thereof for other pay frequencies). Deduct this amount from the employee's pay;

(*c*)   reduce the balance on the Deduction Notice.

The following example illustrates the operation of an ISDN.

Example — Jane is paid monthly on the 20th day of the month. The DSS has instructed her employer to operate a Deduction Notice. The Notice is dated 14 March 1997, and shows protected earnings of £120 and a recoverable amount of £143. In months 3, 4 and 5 Jane's earnings are affected by a period of absence.

Month number	Available earnings £	Protected earnings £	Deduction under the notice £	Balance on the notice £	Comments
1	700	600	50	93	The deduction is 50% of the excess (£100) of available earnings (£120 × 5).
2	700	600	50	43	As for Month 1.
3	650	600	25	18	The deduction is 50% of excess (£50) of available earnings over protected earnings.
4	460	600	—	18	No deduction is taken as available earnings are below the protected earnings.

5	604	600	—	18	No deduction as the difference (£4) between the available earnings and the protected earnings is less than the monthly minimum (£5).
6	700			18	No deduction as 26 weeks have elapsed since the date shown on the Deduction Notice issued by the DSS.

Administration of orders

13.16   When an order is received it is usual for it to be applied to the next available pay period. Orders raised under *AEA 1971*, *MCNI 1981* and *JENI 1981* are to be actioned within seven days of receipt. Orders raised under *DSA 1987* are to be actioned immediately except that for conjoined orders seven days are allowed.

If an AEO is received (or held) which is considered to be defective, e.g. no protected earnings specified for a 1971 Act AEO, the employer should contact the originating source. (See References (14) and (15) in 13.18 below concerning the validity of and treatment of defective AEOs.)

Orders are administered until the amount outstanding on the order is cleared by operation of the order, or the originating source discharges the order by notifying the employer or the employee leaves. It may be necessary to have a record of the balance outstanding and/or the amounts paid under the order.

When an employer makes a deduction from an employee's pay under an AEO then he is entitled to deduct a further sum in respect of the administration costs. A deduction of £1 can be made in respect of AEOs made under *AEA 1971*, *CSA 1991*, *CSNI 1991*, *JENI 1981*, *MCNI 1981*, *LGFA 1988* and *LGFA 1992*, but a deduction of £0.50 made in respect of AEOs made under *DSA 1987*. No deduction can be made under *SSCBA 1992*. This deduction is in addition to the deduction made under the order and may, depending on the circumstances, reduce the employee's pay below protected earnings. Although it is necessary to calculate the deduction under an AEO each pay period, employers may make a deduction for their administration costs only on occasions when a deduction is paid to the court or debtor.

The employee must be informed in writing of each deduction made under an order and in the case of CCAEOs and CTAEOs either the amount paid to date under the order or the oustanding balance. A similar requirement applies to the deductions made in respect of administration costs. This right is in addition to the right to an itemised pay statement as provided for by *ERA 1996*. (See 5.13 above.) The employee's payslip can of course meet these requirements.

When either an order is received for a person who is not employed or an employee for whom any type of AEO is operated leaves then the employer is to notify the originating source within a prescribed time. In the case of orders made under *AEA 1971*, *JENI 1981*, *MCNI 1981*, *CSA 1991* and *CSNI 1991* the time allowed is ten days. For orders made under *LGFA 1988* and *LGFA 1992* the time allowed is 14 days. For orders made under *DSA 1987* the notification should be made as soon as possible. For an order made under *SSCBA 1992* the notification is to be made within ten days.

When an employee for whom an AEO under *AEA 1971* is operated leaves employment, the employer should notify him of his obligation to inform the originating court within seven days that he has left his employment and to provide details of new employment.

Remitting the deductions

13.17   The order will carry details of the payee and the address to which the money that has been deducted is to be paid. The details to be included with the remittance vary according to the nature of the order, but the following is the minimum necessary:

(*a*)   the employer's name and address;

(*b*)   the employee's name and initials;

(*c*)   the reference number provided by the originating source, in the order;

(*d*)   the amount of the deduction;

(*e*)   the payee's name and address.

In the case of the Child Support DEOs an employer can make the remittances by electronic funds transfer (EFT). The reference number to be quoted for EFT is of a different length to that used when the remittance is by cheque. Where the employer chooses to change the method of remittance he should contact the Agency to apply for a new reference number. Separate remittances are required in respect of the Northern Ireland Child Support Agency.

In the case of 1971 Act Orders, remittances are made to the originating court.

In the case of orders raised under Northern Ireland legislation, the remittances are made to the Enforcement of Judgments Office, the creditor, or to the magistrates' court.

In the case of SEAs or SCMAs the remittances are made to the creditor or to the originating Sheriff.

In the case of Community Charge and Council Tax orders the remittances are made to the originating Local Authority.

In the case of income support deduction notices the remittance is to the local DSS office.

Where the remittance is by cheque for a number of different deductions then in some instances a computer listing bearing the appropriate details may be sufficient documentation to accompany the cheque. Where the remittance is by EFT then no listing or documentation may need to be sent as the individual transactions will be for each employee involved.

The frequency of remittances to the originating sources may vary. It is common practice for remittances to be made monthly in respect of the previous month. In the case of CCAEOs, CTAEOs, ISDNs and DEOs the regulations require remittances by the 19th of the month following the month of deduction.

Since 2 December 1996, the Centralised Attachment of Earnings Payment System (CAPS) was introduced nationally. This applies to AEOs for judgment debts and maintenance, initially only single case orders. The principle behind CAPS is to provide an automated (and more efficient) system to issue notices to employers, receive payments from employers and to pass on these payments to creditors. Employers will benefit by having a single point of contact and issuing a single payment to cover a number of AEOs. CAPS provides a helpline for employers concerning single county court or maintenance orders on telephone no. 01604 601555.

References

13.18   Reference (1) below gives a practical description of the administration of attachments of earnings orders. It has been updated once since its issue, but unfortunately still contains some out of date information.

(1)   'Attachment Orders — A Handbook for Employers', issued by the Lord Chancellor's Department.

(2)   'Income Support Deduction Notice', PMR, February 1995.

(3)   Attachment of Earnings Act 1971.

(4)   Administration of Justice Act 1982.

(5)   Child Support (Collection and Enforcement) Regulations 1992 (as amended).

(6)   Community Charges (Administration and Enforcement) Regulations 1989 (as amended).

(7) Council Tax (Administration and Enforcement) Regulations 1992 (as amended).

(8) Debtors (Scotland) Act 1987.

(9) Judgments Enforcement (Northern Ireland) Order 1981.

(10) Magistrates' Courts (Northern Ireland) Order 1981.

(11) Social Security (Payments on Account, Overpayments and Recovery) Regulations 1988.

(12) Finance Act 1997.

(13) Thompson M, 'Are Benefits Attachable Earnings', PMR, December 1995.

(14) 'AEOs and Redundancy Pay', PMR, March 1996. (A discursive response to a question raised by a subscriber.)

(15) 'Council Tax AEO', PMR, April 1996. (A response to a subscriber's question about a defective order.)

(16) 'DEOs', PMR, May 1996. (Report of two cases concerning the powers of magistrates' courts to quash defective DEOs and order the CSA to repay the deducted amounts.)

(17) 'Employers gain national CAPS', PMR, December 1996 (Payroll News section).

(18) 'Payroll News', PMR, February 1998 (details of new CTAEO rates).

14   Pension Contributions

Scope of this chapter

14.1   Chapter 10 (Pension Schemes) contains an outline of pensions as a whole. Prior understanding of Chapter 10 is desirable before reading this chapter. It describes the collection and payment of pension contributions and related matters which are important parts of payroll administration. There are several different types of pension contributions commonly payable by both employers and employees. These include the following:

(*a*)   National Insurance contributions (NICs);

(*b*)   ordinary employer contributions;

(*c*)   special employer contributions;

(*d*)   employee contributions;

(*e*)   additional voluntary contributions (AVCs);

(*f*)   free-standing AVCs (FSAVCs);

(*g*)   personal pension contributions.

In addition, some contributions are payable directly by the DSS Contributions Agency into occupational pension schemes as well as personal pensions.

The calculation and collection of contributions often require close liaison between payroll and pension departments. As well as details of contributions, many pension schemes require earnings data as well. These are usually collected at the same time. The calculations and procedures are more complicated in practice than might be expected. For instance, some computer payroll systems initially had difficulty coping with all the NIC and pension contribution requirements. (See References (2) and (3) in 14.24 below for a general discussion of the employee payroll procedures concerned with pension matters, including the collection of contributions. Reference (4) in 14.24 provides encyclopaedic coverage of pension matters and covers contributions administration in some detail.)

The coming into force on 6 April 1997 of the *Pensions Act 1995 (PA 1995)* had a considerable impact on the making of pension contributions. The main points in summary are:

  (i) all employee contributions deducted from pay must be passed by the employer to the trustees within a strict deadline, with criminal sanctions for failure to comply;

  (ii) a schedule of contributions must be put in place and enforced by the trustees where a defined benefit scheme is subject to the minimum funding requirement (MFR);

  (iii) a payment schedule must similarly be put in place and enforced by the trustees in the case of defined contribution (money purchase) schemes;

  (iv) there are now two contracted-out rates of NICs in addition to the not contracted-out rate.

Readers should note that this chapter tends to focus on common pension arrangements for ordinary employees and how they impinge on payroll administration. Other aspects, for example tax relief on self-employed pension contributions, may only be mentioned briefly, or not considered at all.

Key points of pension contributions

14.2   Pension contribution procedures need to allow for the following:

(*a*)   Many pension schemes are linked to SERPS. Therefore, details relevant to NICs are often collected and recorded by the pensions department.

(*b*)   Most schemes are 'contributory', i.e. the employee makes a contribution. In some schemes the employee can choose which tier of benefits and associated employee contributions he or she wishes to join. Also the level of the employee contribution can be related to the employee's age or length of service.

(*c*)   The employer must usually pay contributions to an occupational pension scheme which it sponsors although in the case of defined benefit schemes temporary 'contribution holidays' are commonly adopted as a method of reducing overfunding. In defined contribution schemes the employer's contributions can be directly related to the employee's age or length of service.

(*d*)   In a defined contribution or money purchase scheme, all contributions including those from the employer must be correctly attributed to individual employees. In a defined benefit scheme, employer contributions are normally calculated on an overall basis, for example as a percentage of total pensionable pay.

(e)   It is always important to keep a proper record of employee contributions.

(f)   Employee contributions may be based on gross pay but usually the definition of 'pensionable earnings' will differ leading to a separate calculation to identify the earnings on which the employee's contribution will be calculated.

(g)   AVCs are supplementary contributions paid by employees to enhance their benefits. Under *PSA 1993, s 111* it is a legal obligation for all occupational pension schemes to offer this facility, including non-contributory schemes.

(h)   Free-standing AVCs (FSAVCs) are paid by the employee to outside financial bodies and there is normally no effect on the payroll system.

(j)   Personal pension contributions if used to contract out are collected via the NIC system. The employee pays any additional contributions directly to the personal pension provider in the same way as FSAVCs. There is normally little effect on the payroll system except that the employer and employee must pay national insurance contributions at the higher not contracted-out rate. However, if the employer facilitates a GPP (Group Personal Pension) arrangement, the payroll department is likely to offer a facility to deduct these contributions from employees' pay after the deduction of income tax and pass them to directly to the personal pension provider.

(k)   Usually total employee contributions must not exceed 15 per cent of pensionable pay. Where the pension scheme has received Inland Revenue approval, under the 'net pay' arrangement occupational pension contributions are deducted from pay prior to income tax calculations but they are not deductible for NIC purposes.

(l)   The pensions department usually collects contributions and earnings data annually or, increasingly, more frequently on paper schedules or electronically. Data must also be collected when employees join and leave. Reconciliation of contributions data is vital for revealing discrepancies between the payroll and pension records.

(m)   Refunds of contributions are usually the responsibility of the pensions department. Under the *PSA 1993, s 71* the maximum period of pensionable service up to which a refund of contributions can be granted is two years. The scheme rules may specify a shorter period.

(n)   The *PA 1995* has introduced some radical changes for occupational pensions administration as explained below.

National Insurance contributions

14.3   National Insurance contributions are effectively a combination of tax and insurance premiums. The insurance element of NICs determine a person's right to many 'contributory' social security benefits, for example a basic State pension. For this reason alone care needs to be taken in the payroll department when NIC details are calculated and sent to the DSS Contributions Agency on PAYE returns. The details of social security benefits and their contribution conditions are explained in Reference (5) in 14.24 below. A description of the National Insurance system is given in Chapter 12 (National Insurance Contributions). This chapter briefly describes the aspects relevant to pensions.

SERPS and contracting-out

14.4   The State Earnings-Related Pension Scheme (SERPS) was introduced to provide an earnings-related pension for all employees in addition to the flat-rate basic State pension. Employers with occupational pension schemes are allowed to contract out of SERPS, paying lower rates of NICs if their occupational pension scheme has obtained a contracting-out certificate from the Contributions Agency. (See also 10.21 above for a further discussion of contracting-out.)

The technically incorrect but convenient term 'contracted-in' is often used in place of the cumbersome but accurate phrase 'not contracted-out'. Some relevant pensions terminology is explained below with further details in Chapter 10 (Pension Schemes).

(a)   *Additional pension* — This is the official name for the benefit provided by the State Earnings Related Pension Scheme (SERPS), so-called because it is additional to the basic State pension. It is calculated from the 'earnings factors' for each year of an individual's working life. Each year's earnings are revalued in line with national average earnings inflation up to the date of retirement. The earnings factor for each tax year is obtained from NIC data sent by the employer to the DSS on the end of year return, Form P14.

(b)   *Guaranteed minimum pension (GMP)* — This is the minimum amount of pension which a scheme that has been contracted-out on a defined benefit basis during the period 6 April 1978 to 5 April 1997 guarantees to pay to a member in respect to contracted-out employment. It is calculated from earnings factors in a similar but not identical way to the employee's SERPS entitlement.

The GMP is included in the scheme pension but is normally exceeded by the amount derived in accordance with the pension formula. Occasionally the GMP could be higher than the scheme pension. This is because the GMP is based on all NIC middle band earnings (i.e. earnings between the lower and upper earnings limits). However, a scheme pension, for example, might be calculated on basic pay alone, hence excluding significant overtime and bonus payments which would be included in a GMP scheme entitlement.

(c) **Reference scheme test** — From 6 April 1997 employers sponsoring an occupational pensions scheme which is to be contracted-out on a defined benefit basis must do so by ensuring that the scheme satisfies an overall quality test. In brief, the scheme actuary must be able to certify that at least 90 per cent of the employees will receive a pension equal to, or better than, 1/80th of 90 per cent of their averaged final middle band earnings for each year of pensionable service. Occupational pension schemes contracted-out by the reference scheme test are known as COSR schemes.

(d) **Protected rights** — These are the employee's rights to money purchase benefits under a scheme which is contracted-out on a money purchase basis (known as a COMP) or an 'appropriate' (contracted-out) personal pension scheme (known as an APP). Protected rights are usually, but need not be, restricted to the benefits derived from the NIC rebate and appropriate age-related payments. The amount of the protected rights pension entitlement may be lower or higher than the amount the employee would otherwise have received from SERPS had the employee not been contracted-out. The amount of pension payable depends on the capital sum accumulated by the employee at the time the pension needs to be secured.

(e) **COMBS** — Contracted Out Mixed Benefit Schemes were introduced on 6 April 1997 as a consequence of *PA 1995*. These schemes have two parts: one is contracted-out by the defined benefit 'reference scheme' test, the other is contracted-out by the defined contribution protected rights test. For many purposes the two parts are seen as distinct sections but the whole COMB is contracted-out by a single contracting-out certificate.

(f) **COMPS** — Schemes which were contracted-out by the GMP test immediately prior to 6 April 1997 may switch to becoming a COMP scheme which contracts out using the protected rights test for employment from that date. Although a COMP scheme, the scheme may retain its existing liabilities to pay GMPs when they fall due. Such schemes are known as '*Regulation 76A*' schemes or simply as 'COMPS preserving GMP rights'.

Calculation of National Insurance contributions and payments

14.5   Contracted-out NICs are currently paid on all earnings between the NIC lower earnings limit (LEL), which is approximately equal to the basic State pension for a single person, and the upper earnings limit (UEL), which is about seven and a half times the lower limit provided the employment is contracted-out by virtue of the employer holding a current contracting-out certificate.

Pay between the LEL and UEL has various names such as contracted-out earnings, second tier earnings, and middle band earnings. Members of contracted-out schemes and their employers pay lower contributions on this earnings range but, prior to 6 April 1999, pay the full rate on earnings below the LEL. (From 6 April 1999 employees will not be required to pay any contributions on the slice of earnings below the LEL whatever their total earnings. From that same date employers will not be required to pay contributions on the slice of earnings below the prevailing weekly PAYE threshold, again irrespective of the employee's total earnings.) Relating to earnings above the UEL, the employers continue to pay contributions on all earnings but the UEL effectively serves as an earnings cap as regards employee contributions.

The reduction in NIC liability is often called the contracted-out rebate. Since 6 April 1997 there are, in fact, two different contracting-out rebates depending on which method the occupational pension schemes uses to contract out. In the case of an employee who is contracted-out by the reference scheme test, the amount of the rebate is set from 6 April 1997 at 4.6 per cent of middle band earnings, split 3 per cent to the employer and 1.6 per cent to the employee. In the case of an employee who is contracted-out by the protected rights test, the amount of the rebate from 6 April 1997 to 5 April 1999 is set at 3.1 per cent of middle band earnings, split 1.5 per cent to the employer and 1.6 per cent to the employee. From 6 April 1999 the amount of the rebate will be 2.2 per cent of middle band earnings, split 0.6 per cent to the employer and 1.6 per cent to the employee.

The reduction in NIC liability on middle band earnings is obviously attractive. If the scheme is contracted-out by the reference scheme test from 6 April 1997, the scheme must demonstrate that it will provide benefits to at least 90 per cent of its active members that satisfy the statutory standard set by the reference scheme.

If the scheme is contracted-out by the protected rights test from 6 April 1997, the employer must undertake to pay the whole 3.1 per cent rebate (2.2 per cent from 6 April 1999) over to the trustees of the scheme by the 14th day after the end of the tax month to which these minimum payments relate (i.e. by the 19th day of the following calendar month). The employer is entitled to recover the employee's share of these minimum payments from the employee's earnings. It should be noted that this 1.6 per cent of middle band earnings counts as an employee contribution to a tax approved retirement benefits scheme and so is paid before the deduction of income tax. There is an interaction between the measures announced by the Chancellor of the Exchequer in his 1998 Budget and the requirement on employers to pay minimum payments over to the scheme trustees:

- the Chancellor's Budget announced that employers would not pay National Insurance contributions (NICs) on the slice of an employee's earnings below the PAYE threshold; but

- the employer is required to pay the employer's share of the minimum payments to a COMP where the minimum payments are calculated on earnings over the Lower Earnings Limit and recovery is made through the COMP rebate.

A problem arises because if employers are paying zero NICs on an employee's earnings between the LEL and PAYE thresholds, they cannot have those contributions rebated by the 0.6 per cent of banded earnings in the case of any employee who earns in excess of the LEL but earns less than the PAYE threshold or only a few pence more than the PAYE threshold.

The solution to this problem has been announced by the DSS minister. He explained that the Government would ensure that employers still receive a rebate on earnings above the LEL even though they will not necessarily pay National Insurance contributions on them. Amendments to the *Pension Schemes Act 1993* were tabled to the *Social Security Act 1998*. These will enable a rebate to be paid on earnings between the LEL and the PAYE threshold and also allow employers to deduct the rebate from their overall National Insurance contributions liability.

The *PA 1995* has introduced two separate systems of age-related payments from the National Insurance Fund directly to pension schemes of employees who are contracted-out by the protected rights test.

(*a*)   The first case relates to employees who are members of an occupational pension scheme which is contracted-out by the protected rights test. These are known as COMP schemes. (However, contracted-out money purchase schemes can in fact be schemes which provide salary-related benefits like the final salary scheme but use the protected rights test, which is a money purchase test, as the method of contracting-out.)

At the end of the tax year, the Contributions Agency will make an age-related payment to the trustees of the pension scheme in respect of each contracted-out employee. The amount of the payment will be the difference between the 3.1 per cent (2.2 per cent from 6 April 1999) minimum payments and the figure given in Table 1 in Appendix D below.

(*b*)   The second case relates to employees who have contracted-out on an individual basis using an Appropriate Personal Pension (APP), although this may be within an arrangement known as a Group Personal Pension (GPP) whereby the employer's payroll operates a 'cheque and disk' service to collect any employee contributions for the personal pension provider involved. In all cases, however, both the employee and employer continue to pay NICs at the higher not contracted-out rate and employee contributions are not deducted using the net pay method that applies to occupational pension schemes – instead employee contributions must be deducted from their earnings after the deduction of tax.

The Contributions Agency will make an age-related contribution to the personal pension provider in respect of each APP policyholder. The amount will be the figure given in Table 2 in Appendix D below. In addition, tax relief at the basic rate is paid on the employee's share of the flat rate rebate (i.e. tax relief at the basic rate of 23 per cent (1998/99) on the 1.6 per cent of middle band earnings).

Employer contributions

14.6 An occupational pension scheme established by an employer, ranging from an individual arrangement to a scheme for over 100,000 members, can only obtain tax relief if the employer contributes to it. In a defined benefit scheme the contribution rate is usually expressed as a percentage of pensionable pay.

The assets and liabilities of a scheme, including estimated future income and benefits, are subject to a three yearly actuarial valuation. As part of this process the actuary arrives at the contribution rate to be applied until the next valuation. A typical current rate might be ten per cent for employers if employees contributed five per cent to the scheme, or 15 per cent for employers if the scheme is 'non-contributory' i.e. where the employees do not contribute. The total contribution rate does, of course, depend on a whole series of factors such as the level of the benefits and the age of the contributors, salary increases, inflation, and investment returns.

By their very nature, defined benefit schemes tend to produce a fund which is either in deficit or surplus. This is because the underlying assumptions on which the scheme is costed can only be approximate. For example, the investment returns may have been better than expected or changes in actuarial factors such as the age and sex distribution of the membership may make a scheme more expensive. The main purpose of regular actuarial valuations is to identify whether a scheme has moved into a deficit or surplus and make adjustments accordingly.

If a defined benefit fund is in deficit, i.e. where the actuary predicts that in the long term its assets and income are not enough to meet the accruing liabilities, the contribution rate must be increased to meet the promised level of benefits. This may be achieved by raising the existing employer rate, say from nine per cent to ten per cent, and leaving it at the higher rate indefinitely or by not altering the existing rate but paying special contributions at a higher rate for a short period, e.g. an additional five per cent for the next five years.

An employer could make special payments or special contributions occasionally in addition to the ordinary contributions. Technically, a special contribution is defined as an employer contribution which is neither a fixed amount paid annually, whether in instalments or otherwise, nor an annual amount that is payable over a period of three years or more and is calculated on a consistent basis in accordance with actuarial principles by reference to the earnings, contributions or number of members of the scheme.

For example, a company is taken over and its employees are brought into the acquiring company's defined benefit pension scheme which has superior benefits. If the original fund had insufficient money at the time of the takeover for providing the new structure of benefits, the acquiring company may consider paying additional contributions for a few years to provide for the taken-over employees' past service benefits in the new scheme. Depending on the amount of the special contribution the Inland Revenue will treat special contributions as spread over several years when granting tax relief, even if the actual payment is made in one year.

Figure 14A   Spreading of tax relief for special contributions

£500,000 or over but less than £1,000,000:	2 years
£1,000,000 or over but less than £2,000,000:	3 years
£2,000,000 or over:	4 years

If there is a surplus in a defined benefit pension fund, i.e. more assets than would be needed to meet the predicted liabilities, the employer may decide to reduce the excess by stopping contributions for one or more years (contribution holidays). Indeed, the Inland Revenue requires surpluses, calculated using a prescribed method and set of assumptions, to be reduced once they exceed a set threshold. The employer could then restart paying contributions at the previous rate or at a new rate recommended by the actuary. Contribution holidays became common in the 1980s and in some cases are still continuing. An alternative to a complete stoppage would be to lower the contribution rate, for example from ten per cent to eight per cent, thereby allowing the surplus to be eroded over time. Another way of dealing with surpluses is for them to be used to pay for increased benefits. More controversially a payment out of surplus may be made over to the employer where this is allowed by law and the scheme rules. The usual argument in these cases is typically that the benefits promised are secure and that the employer's contributions have effectively over-funded the scheme in the past. There is also the 'swings-and-roundabouts' argument that many employers have voluntarily increased contributions to pension schemes in the past when schemes were in deficit, so they are entitled to such a payment when there is a surplus. Needless to say these arguments have not always convinced scheme members who may regard the employer's contributions as deferred pay.

Employer contributions to a pension scheme are tax-deductible as a business expense, provided they are reasonable. Tax relief is restricted if a defined benefit fund is considered to have a 'surplus' of more than five per cent of the liability, as calculated using the Inland Revenue's prescribed method and set of assumptions. To retain full tax relief the surplus must be eliminated within five years. Payment of surplus to the employer is taxed at a standard rate of 40 per cent and this fact may tip the balance in favour of a 'contribution holiday' or a long-term reduction in the contribution rate or an increase in pension benefits rather than a payment out of surplus to the employer. [*ICTA 1988, ss 601–603, 22 Sch*].

As explained above, one perceived problem with defined benefit schemes is that the inevitable changes in costing assumptions lead to fluctuations in the overall contribution rate. The employer usually absorbs these fluctuations rather than the employee, but see 14.11(*e*) below for an explanation of the shared-cost approach. By way of contrast, a defined contribution scheme, as the name implies, attempts to avoid these problems by fixing stable contribution rates and letting changes in investment returns affect the benefits. Furthermore the cost of actuarial factors like sex and age are not averaged across the whole fund. As explained in 10.16 above, in defined contribution schemes the individual's sex and age at retirement, as well as investment conditions, determine the amount of pension that can be bought. On average, of course, a defined benefit and defined contribution scheme might, in theory, produce the same final benefits for the same total contributions. However, the average conceals large fluctuations and a defined contribution scheme transfers the risks or benefits of these fluctuations to the member. The greater stability of contribution rates with defined contribution schemes is particularly welcome to smaller employers. It should be noted that if an employee wishes to contract out of SERPS on the defined contribution (or protected rights) basis, the employer must ensure that the minimum payments (3.1 per cent (1998/99) and 2.2 per cent (1999/00) of 'banded earnings') are paid over each month. The employer may recover the employee's share (1.6 per cent) from the employee's salary.

PA 1995 has introduced further restrictions on the funding arrangements of defined benefits schemes. These include a minimum funding requirement (see 14.14 below) and controls on payments of surpluses to employers.

Calculation of employer contributions

14.7   Actuaries have many ways of calculating the total contributions required each year to keep the fund solvent. How the total contributions are split between the employer and various types of employee can be contentious. The actuarial cost of providing pensions for an employee depends on factors such as the level of benefit, the individual's sex, as women live longer than men, and the age on joining the scheme which determines the period for which contributions are made. If different classes of member accrue different levels of benefit, this is also reflected in the costs. The rules of the scheme determine to what extent, if any, the variation in cost between individual scheme members is taken into account.

The principal methods of funding for pension schemes are dealt with below. Unless stated to the contrary the comments apply to defined benefit schemes.

(a) **Overall contribution rate** — This is the simplest method. All the cost variations are averaged out and a single contribution rate, i.e. the funding rate, is determined as a percentage of the total pensionable pay. The amount due can be calculated easily by applying the funding rate to the total pensionable salary. The sum so derived can be paid to the trustees monthly or at the beginning or end of a scheme year.

(b) **Company rates** — If the age and sex distribution of employees among the various participating employers differs considerably, it may be more appropriate to apply a different rate to each employer. This again would be relatively easy to calculate. If each company operates its own payroll the method is no different from the previous case.

(c) **Individual calculations** — A very complicated situation arises where an individual calculation is performed for each scheme member and one of a series of rates is applied according to some formula based on sex, age, service, and benefit class. These individual amounts are then totalled and each contributing company charged accordingly. This process is often an once-a-year task because of the complications involved. The contributions, calculated from employee's pay at a particular date, may be for the year just completed or the year following.

(d) **Estimated rates** — In very many cases the employers' contributions are calculated as a percentage of wage and salary payments already made. In some cases, however, they are based on estimates of pay for the following year. If such advance calculations have been performed, adjustments are inevitably needed at the end of the year for changes in membership and pay which occur during it.

(e) **Money purchase schemes** — In a defined contribution scheme, employer contributions must be calculated exactly for each member. For COMPs the minimum payments are equal to the COMP NIC rebate of 3.1 per cent of banded earnings (2.2 per cent from April 1999). The DSS pays an additional age-related sum after the end of each tax year. As mentioned above, the employer may recover the employee's share of the NIC rebate (i.e. 1.6 per cent of banded earnings) from the employee. Any additional contributions are calculated as a percentage of either gross or band earnings or pensionable earnings or sometimes as a flat amount per pay period. Different rates of contribution may be paid for different categories of employee.

(f) **Unapproved schemes** — As mentioned in Chapter 10 (Pension Schemes) separate employer contributions may now be made to an unapproved scheme. The employee is taxed on the amount of the employer's contributions. The employer can claim tax relief on such expenses which were incurred by him to provide these benefits as a normal business expense. The employer can only claim if the pension provision is taxed in the employee's hands. Since April 1998 the employer's contribution to an unapproved scheme also gives rise to a National Insurance liability.

(*g*)   **Shared costs** — See 14.11(*e*) below.

Accounting for pension contributions

14.8   Details of contributions must be shown in two separate sets of accounts, firstly in those of the pension scheme and secondly in those of the employer where its own contributions are of primary relevance. There are some extra requirements specifically for pensions accounting. These additional accounting rules are contained in the SORP (Statement of Recommended Practice) for schemes and SSAP24 (Statement of Standard Accounting Practice 24) for employers. The *PA 1995* has introduced the necessity for a separate pension scheme bank account and further requirements for pension scheme financial records. Also, the auditor (and actuary) to a scheme have a duty to 'whistle-blow'. This means giving a written report to the new Occupational Pensions Regulatory Authority (OPRA) where there is reasonable cause to believe that there are any material infringements of any legal duties.

Employee contributions

14.9   Contributions from employees are required in the majority of occupational schemes. The money for these contributions can be considered to come ultimately from the employer but it forms part of the employee's nominal earnings and therefore increases his or her awareness of, and involvement with, the scheme.

Tax relief

14.10   Any retirement benefit scheme may be approved if it satisfies Inland Revenue requirements, and approval, by virtue of *ICTA 1988, s 596*, exempts the member from liability to income tax on the employer's contributions under *ICTA 1988, s 595*. Employer's contributions to approved schemes are also not liable to National Insurance contributions. It is, however, only an exempt approved scheme that will qualify for the special tax reliefs on contributions, investment income, etc. under *ICTA 1988, s 592* or for premiums paid to an insurance company to qualify for tax relief on 'pension business'.

Broadly, tax relief is given on basic employee scheme contributions and on AVCs up to a maximum of 15 per cent of the relevant remuneration (see 14.13 below). The restriction to 15 per cent can, exceptionally, be increased by the Inland Revenue in special circumstances by virtue of *ICTA 1988, s 592(8)* but, if so, the tax relief will be restricted to the first 15 per cent. In payroll terms pension contributions are the first deduction from gross earnings, and tax is then calculated on the remaining net figure. This is known as the 'net pay arrangement'. NICs are calculated on gross pay before deduction of the pension contributions. Furthermore, NICs themselves are not eligible for tax relief.

FSAVCs (Free-standing AVCs) are effectively a special kind of personal pension plan which supplements an occupational scheme pension. Typically an employee takes out an FSAVC plan with an insurance company. The combined benefits and contributions from the occupational scheme and FSAVCs must be within Inland Revenue limits. For tax relief the total pension contributions (ordinary, AVC, and FSAVC) must not exceed the normal 15 per cent limit. The FSAVC plan contributions must of necessity lie outside the net pay arrangement. Hence they are unlikely to concern the employer's payroll staff. Checks against Inland Revenue limits are done by the provider based on details given by the employee. With an FSAVC plan the tax relief is claimed by the plan provider at the basic rate, and by the employee for any higher-rate relief.

Scheme contribution rates paid by members

14.11   Many pension schemes levy a single rate of contribution. Typical rates range between four per cent and six per cent of pensionable pay. There are, however, several possible reasons for having multiple contribution rates. These types of contribution rates are listed below.

(*a*)   ***Benefit-related contributions*** — By definition, benefits are related to contributions in money purchase schemes. However, in some defined benefit schemes members may pay one of two or more different rates to obtain corresponding levels of benefit. For example, some members may pay five per cent and receive benefits based on one-sixtieth of pensionable pay per year of service while others may pay only three per cent but receive benefits based on one-eightieth of pay. The level paid may be determined by the job category or grade but is sometimes an option to be exercised by the member. In some cases different levels exist because of options given in the past but new employees have to pay the higher rate.

(*b*)   ***Cost-related contributions*** — In a few cases contributions from employees are related to the cost of providing benefits (see 10.16 above), by charging a higher rate to members with less potential service. For example, the rate could be five per cent for those joining the scheme before the age of 40 and six per cent for those joining later. The rate, once set, would not normally be affected by changing to a different contributing company within the scheme.

(*c*)   ***Pay band-related contributions*** — Contributions may be based at one rate on earnings within certain limits and at a higher rate on any earnings above the upper limit. For example, in a contracted-in scheme topping up SERPS, the members could pay two per cent on earnings between the lower and upper SERPS limits (LEL and UEL) and five per cent on any earnings above the upper limit. The benefit levels would correspond, i.e. a lower level for the band of earnings partially covered by the State additional component and a higher rate for the earnings not so covered.

(d) ***Fixed amount contributions*** — These are deducted as a fixed amount per pay period, regardless of variations in actual earnings. This method is almost obsolete for defined benefit schemes, but might occasionally still be found in old, established defined contribution schemes.

(e) ***Shared costs*** — Most occupational schemes share the costs between the employer and employee, but the employee costs, i.e. their contributions, are usually carefully defined. However, in the narrow-sense a shared-cost scheme assumes that any increase in the total contributions for a defined-benefit scheme does not become an open-ended liability for the employer. In some way the increase (or decrease) in the total cost must be shared with the employees. The most obvious way to do this is to share the total costs of a defined-benefit scheme in a fixed ratio, for example the employer pays £2 for every £1 paid by the employee. In this situation the employee contribution rate would rise or fall in line with total costs.

Section 49(8) of the *PA 1995* concerns the deduction of employee contributions. If the employer's payroll department deducts pension scheme contributions from employees' pay but fails to pass them on to the scheme's trustees or managers within the prescribed time in circumstances where 'there is no reasonable excuse for the failure to do so', the employer is guilty of an offence and liable, on summary conviction, to a fine not exceeding the statutory maximum and, on conviction on indictment, to imprisonment, or a fine, or both.

The *Occupational Pension Schemes (Scheme Administration) Regulations 1996 (SI 1996 No 1715)* stipulate that the prescribed time for ensuring that employee contributions are passed from payroll to the scheme trustees or manager is 19 days beginning from the end of the calendar month in which the contributions were deducted from employees' salary. (In the case of minimum payments payable in contracted-out money purchase schemes, the same deadline is set but expressed as 14 days from the end of the tax month in which the contributions were deducted.)

Pensionable pay

14.12 The earnings figure on which contributions are calculated is always defined by the scheme rules. It may be based on a basic weekly/monthly salary or on gross PAYE earnings. In the past, the latter was the most common method for 'works' pension schemes while the former was used for 'staff' schemes. The pay figure used for calculating the benefits is usually the same as that on which contributions are paid. The difference between basic salary and gross PAYE earnings consists usually of such pay elements as bonus, overtime, commission, etc. in addition to the basic salary. These amounts are often recorded separately for pension purposes so that they can be averaged for benefit calculations. For example, a typical 'final pensionable pay' may be the final year's basic pay plus the average of the fluctuating emoluments for the last three years. In the example of John, the salesman, shown below, commission, which is a 'fluctuating emolument', is pensionable but overtime payments are not. Contributions may be payable only on earnings in excess of a fixed 'off-set' figure. This is very often the State basic pension or the NIC lower earnings limit or a figure derived from one of these. Such deductions are known as 'integration' factors because they attempt to integrate the occupational pension with the State retirement pension. Usually the same deduction is made from the earnings used for benefit calculations. The rationale is that the State basic pension covers the relevant band of earnings. In recent years, integration factors have gradually been removed from many schemes. They are seen to affect most adversely the pension entitlement of lower paid individuals.

Under *FA 1989, 6 Sch* pensionable pay was restricted to a maximum of £60,000 p.a. This has been progressively increased, and it is £87,600 p.a. from 6 April 1998.

If contributions are based on actual earnings or the pay rate in each pay period then any increases are applied automatically. If contributions are based on a 'snapshot' rate of pay, for instance where the pay rate applicable at the start of the scheme year determines the contributions to be paid for the entire current year, pay increases do not affect contributions until the start of the following year. In this case the payroll must hold separately a 'contributions salary' figure or the actual contribution amount to be deducted in each pay period. Scheme contributions are normally deducted at the standard rate from any accumulated back-dated salary payment. If part of the increase relates to a previous tax or pension scheme year, however, there may be problems in recording it correctly.

Example — John is a salesman in a staff scheme. The rules stipulate that pensionable salary is basic salary plus commission less an off-set of £3,328, the current lower earnings limit. Employee contributions are five per cent of pensionable pay. John earns £12,000 basic, £16,000 commission, and £1,000 in overtime when working at trade exhibitions. Overtime is not, however, pensionable.

His annual contributions are arrived at as set out below.

$$\frac{5}{100} \times ((12{,}000 + £16{,}000) - £3{,}328) = £1{,}233.60$$

From a payroll viewpoint certain pay elements are classed as non-pensionable. In this case overtime payments are not eligible either for pension contributions or pension benefits.

An employee may be temporarily absent, for example because of sickness, maternity absence or seconded to another employer. Subject to certain rules regarding international secondments the Inland Revenue permits him to remain in full membership of an approved pension scheme, even where no remuneration is paid. Broadly, the conditions are that there is an expectation of the employee returning to work, except where he is incapacitated, and that the employee is not a member of another scheme during the absence. The scheme rules may impose further conditions. Special rules apply in cases of maternity leave.

Where an employee's reduction in remuneration is compensated by a corresponding payment by the employer to the pension scheme for the benefit of that employee, the 'salary sacrifice' should be notified to, and permission obtained from, the appropriate Schedule E inspector of taxes. If this permission is not forthcoming then the 'salary sacrifice' will be treated as a member's contribution and will be subject to the 15 per cent maximum rule. Any excess should be repaid to the member at the earliest opportunity and the Schedule E inspector of taxes will advise on the tax treatment of this amount.

Additional voluntary contributions

14.13   Additional voluntary contributions (AVCs) are often paid by a substantial number of employees, most of them in the older age groups when they have started to consider their pension situation seriously. The proportion of members paying AVCs in a scheme may vary from one per cent up to 40 per cent or more, depending on average age and how well the AVC arrangement has been publicised. *PSA, s 111* requires all occupational schemes to offer an AVC facility.

Contributions are normally calculated as a percentage of the same pensionable earnings figure used for scheme contributions. The percentage paid is at the option of the member and may change from time to time. It is possible to pay two or more types of AVC although these can usually be consolidated into a single payment rate for payroll purposes. Some AVCs are paid as a fixed amount per pay period rather than as a percentage of earnings. Fixed amount AVCs are less common in final salary schemes, but they are used with money purchase schemes. In principle AVCs can be stopped, re-started or varied as the member chooses. [*ICTA 1988, ss 592(7)(8), 594*].

The maximum contribution rate which can be paid by an employee, adding scheme contributions and AVCs together, is usually 15 per cent of remuneration (*ICTA 1988, ss 592(7)(8), 594* and the Pension Schemes Office Practice Notes IR 12). For all practical purposes remuneration is equated with emoluments and consequently AVCs could equal a maximum of 15 per cent of the employee's income assessed under Schedule E which is inclusive of benefits in kind, such as car benefits, BUPA, etc. As already mentioned, *FA 1989* introduced some changes which mean that for scheme entrants from June 1989 the maximum remuneration for contribution purposes is now £87,600 p.a.

AVCs may be retained within the normal pension fund, either buying additional service benefits or accumulating on a money purchase basis (see 10.16 above for details on money purchase arrangements). Alternatively and, perhaps, more frequently, they are paid into a money purchase scheme run by an insurance company or building society. The member in effect has an individual investment or savings account with this body, and the pension scheme is acting as an agent for administration and tax relief purposes.

As mentioned in 14.10 above, any member of an occupational pension scheme can pay FSAVCs to any pension provider of his or her choice, but most of the providers are insurance companies. [*ICTA 1988, s 591(2)(h)*]. The combined contributions and benefits with the FSAVC and occupational schemes are subject to the usual Inland Revenue limits.

Commutation of the AVC to a lump sum payment is not permitted for AVCs under arrangements entered into after 7 April 1987. The same is true for all FSAVCs. However, where the maximum lump sum depends on the total pension payable, the pension provided by AVCs and FSAVC can be included with the main scheme pension. For example, if the main scheme pension is £8,304 p.a. and the annuity provided by AVCs is a further £1,204, then under the Inland Revenue rules for a member joining after May 1989, the maximum tax free lump sum is 2.25 × (£8,304 + £1,204) or £21,393. The commutation factor would be applied to reduce the main scheme pension, not the annuity bought by AVCs.

Schedules of contributions

14.14 A very important new requirement affecting all defined benefit schemes that are subject to the minimum funding requirement (MFR) introduced by *section 56* of the *PA 1995* is the requirement to have in place a schedule of contributions. The schedule of contributions must be applied within twelve weeks of the signing of each MFR valuation.

At the three-yearly actuarial valuation, the scheme actuary must check to see whether the scheme meets the MFR requirement. If the MFR valuation shows that the scheme is seriously underfunded (i.e. less than 90 per cent funded), the employer must take urgent action within a year to secure that the 90 per cent target is reached. In effect the employer will usually have to pay a one-off contribution or ring-fence unencumbered assets for the use of the fund. However, if the scheme is more than 90 per cent funded, the scheme actuary must recommend a minimum contribution rate that will ensure that after a five year period (with an extension during the introductory transitional period for the MFR) the scheme is at least 100 per cent funded. If the scheme is found to be already at least 100 per cent funded at the valuation, the scheme actuary must recommend a minimum contribution rate that will continue to ensure that the scheme is 100 per cent throughout the next five-year period.

The scheme trustees and the employer must then discuss the actual schedule of contributions to be put in place. In most cases this will be in excess of the rate needed to secure the MFR requirement but the trustees cannot agree to any schedule of contributions that is less than that recommended by the actuary in order to meet the MFR.

At the next three yearly actuarial valuation the schedule of contributions may need to be revised. During the inter-valuation years the actuary must certify that the schedule of contributions continue to be sufficient to meet the MFR.

Under the *PA 1995, s 58* and the *Occupational Pension Scheme (Minimum Funding Requirement and Actuarial Valuations) Regulations 1996 (SI 1996 No 1461)*, the schedule of contributions must show separately:

(*a*)   the rates and due dates of all contributions (other than AVCs) payable by the scheme's active members;

(*b*)   the rates and due dates of all the contributions payable by the employer or employers;

(*c*)   any separate contributions, and their due dates, to cover expenses payable by the trustees and which are likely to fall due during the five year period covered by the schedule.

Any contributions that are not paid on or before the due date automatically become a debt due from the employer to the trustees.

The trustees must report to OPRA (Occupational Pensions Regulatory Authority) any failure by the employer to pay the required contributions by the due date set out in the schedule of contributions. The trustees must report the failure within 30 days of the missed due date. Moreover, if the employer has still not made the contribution required by the schedule of contributions within a period of 60 days of the missed due date, the trustees must disclose this failure to contributing employees and the other scheme members. This disclosure to the members must be made within a period of 90 days of the missed due date.

Trustees who fail to take all reasonable steps to enforce the schedule of contributions or who fail to report missed contributions to OPRA or the trustees, can be removed by OPRA and can face fines of up to £5,000 in the case of an individual trustee or up to £50,000 in the case of a corporate trustee.

Payment schedules

14.15 A similar requirement is made for most kinds of defined contribution or money purchase scheme by virtue of the *PA 1995, s 87* whereby the trustees must ensure that there is prepared, maintained and from time to time revised a 'payment schedule' which shows separately:

(a) the rates of contributions payable to the scheme by the employer and the due dates for payment;

(b) the rates of contributions payable to the scheme by the active members of the scheme and the due dates for payment (but excluding additional voluntary contributions);

(c) any amounts payable to the scheme by the employer to meet scheme expenses likely to be incurred in that scheme year (an example is the levy payable to the Registrar).

In cases where an insurance premium is payable, the payment schedule need not contain separate entries for identifying the contributions payable by the employer and the employees.

Any amounts which remain unpaid after their due date (whether payable by the employer or not) are automatically treated as a debt from the employer to the trustees.

Normally all the payments and the due dates shown in the payment schedule are specified in the scheme rules or have been agreed between the employer and the trustees.

The trustees must monitor events to ensure that the employer complies with the payment schedule. As with the schedule of contributions underpinning a defined benefit scheme, if the employer fails to make a payment by the due date on the payment schedule, the trustees must report the failure to the OPRA. The notice must be given to OPRA within 30 days of the failure. If the employer has not made the payment within 60 days of the due date, the trustees must in addition send a written notice reporting the failure to each scheme member. This notice to members must be sent within 90 days of the missed due date.

If the employer fails to make the payment by the due date, OPRA has the power to levy a fine of up to £50,000 in the case of a company, and up to £5,000 in the case of an individual employer. Trustees who fail to take all reasonable steps to enforce the payment schedule or who fail to report missed payments to OPRA or the trustees can be removed by OPRA and can face fines of up to £5,000 in the case of an individual trustee or up to £50,000 in the case of a corporate trustee.

Introduction to personal pensions

14.16   Personal pensions were introduced in 1988 following the implementation of *SSA 1986, s 1* and *ICTA 1988, Pt XIV, Ch IV*. Most of the details have been issued in Inland Revenue and DSS regulations which have little direct effect on payroll administrators. Personal pensions are discussed in 10.17(*h*) above.

Minimum contributions to a personal pension plan

14.17   As explained at 14.5 above 'minimum contributions' consist of the age-related payments made by the DSS Contributions Agency, including also basic rate tax relief on the equivalent of 1.6 per cent of the employee's 'banded earnings', after the end of each tax year during which the employee was contracted-out of SERPS by membership of an 'appropriate' personal pension. The employee, who is a member of an appropriate personal pension, and that employee's employer pays National Insurance contributions at the higher not contracted-out rate.

Additional contributions in the case of personal pensions

14.18   In addition to an appropriate personal pension, or if the employee prefers not to be contracted-out of SERPS, a simple personal pension can be used to provide a pension fund for an individual employee. If the employee makes contributions to a personal pension this will not necessarily involve the employer unless the employee has agreed, as part of a group personal pension arrangement, to provide a check-off facility for employee contributions. Few employers running company pension schemes offer additional contributions to members opting out in favour of personal pensions. Employers who do not have company schemes are more likely to be willing to make direct contributions to the personal pension contract of their employees. They are allowable as an expense for corporation tax purposes in the same way as employer contributions to a company scheme. The 'net pay' arrangement does not apply to personal pension contributions deducted from an employee's pay, i.e. there is no immediate tax relief as there is with occupational pension contributions. However, any employer contributions to a personal plan do not incur the employee any extra tax. NICs are not levied on the amount of the employer's direct contributions to a personal pension. An employer's contributions count towards the total allowed for tax-free contributions.

The total employee and employer contributions payable into a personal pension are limited by a percentage limit which depends on the employee's age. The percentage limit is applied to the employee's net relevant earnings which are capped at the permitted maximum (currently, in 1998/99, £87,600). Figure 14B below gives the limits by age.

Figure 14B   Maximum percentage for contributions into a personal pension

Age on 6 April	Maximum percentage
35 or under	17.5
36 to 45	20
46 to 50	25
51 to 55	30
56 to 60	35
61 or above	40

14.19   The employee (but not the employer) can carry forward unused tax relief from any of the previous six years. Similarly, the employee (but not the employer) can carry back a contribution made by 5 July to the previous tax year.

There is no necessity for employers to become involved in the payment of contributions to personal pensions by employees. The normal procedure is for the employee to send contributions, net of tax, to the personal pension provider; the latter reclaims basic rate tax from the Inland Revenue. The employee can claim any higher-rate tax relief personally. This system is similar to that used for tax relief on house mortgage payments. Given the multiplicity of personal pension providers to whom contributions might have to be paid, employers are unlikely in most cases to complicate their payrolls with personal pension contributions. Group personal pension plans, however, are now becoming very common, especially among small employers. In this case the employer collects contributions from its employees for one personal pension provider. The employer may also make direct contributions to some or all of the personal pensions held by its employees in the group personal pension arrangement.

With regard to any aspect of personal pensions an employer must be careful to respect the *Financial Services Act 1986* and not provide unauthorised investment advice. In April 1994 the DSS issued a leaflet, 'A Guide to the Financial Services Act for Employers'. (See Reference (1) in 14.24 below.)

Where the personal pension provider has not received an employee or employer contribution by the date on or before which it was expected to be made, the personal pension provider must inform the employee within three months of the non-payment, unless the contributions are received within that period.

Collection and payment of contributions

14.20   Some procedures concerning contributions to occupational pension schemes are performed in each pay period. Other procedures are required at the year end. There may be two sets of year-end procedures if the pension scheme year does not coincide with the tax year.

Pay period procedures

14.21   Contributions to occupational pension schemes from employees must be deducted from earnings in each pay period, and accumulated towards year-end totals at the same time. There are also usually joiners and leavers during each pay period. All deductions from pay must be itemised on the employee's payslip. NICs, occupational scheme contributions and AVCs should be shown separately. Personal pension contributions, if any, should be shown as a separate deduction. (An example of an itemised payslip is contained in Figure 22A below.) If employees are members of two schemes (see 10.17 above) and both are contributory, the contributions to each scheme must be calculated and recorded separately.

The legal requirement for payment of employee contributions to occupational pension schemes, as explained at 14.11 above, is particularly strict. Employers must pay employee contributions to the scheme trustees by the 19th day of the calender month following the month in which the employee contributions were deducted. Minimum payments due to an occupational pension scheme contracted-out by the protected rights test must be paid over by the same day. Schedules of contributions (MFR schemes) and payments must also be observed. As explained, there are penalties for non-compliance. This implies rigorous procedures for the payroll department as well as the pension scheme administration.

Payroll procedures will need to be put in place for entrants to, and leavers from, the pension scheme. New employees may join the pension scheme immediately on starting work. Alternatively, they may join the scheme after a fixed period (for instance six months, a year or at the start of the next scheme year). There may also be an overriding minimum age, for example they cannot join until their twenty-first birthday. The payroll procedures must identify the start date for contributions, the appropriate rate, and the effect on NI contributions.

Details of leavers must be sent from payroll to pension departments frequently. These details such as NICs, pension contributions, salary, etc. are necessary for several purposes, such as making a refund where scheme service is less than two years, or calculating deferred pension rights. Section 10.21 above explained how the DSS Contracted-Out Employment Group (COEG) must be sent details of a contracted-out leaver. COEG provides special forms for this known as 'termination notices' or more informally as 'CA' forms (the form codes are prefixed by 'CA'). The CA forms allow the DSS to conduct its part of contracted-out pensions administration, and the forms contain NI details. These forms are usually completed by pension administrators, though much of the information comes from payroll returns. Pensions computer systems print the common CA forms. Contribution refunds and associated matters are usually handled by the pensions administrator and subject to scheme and statutory rules. There may be two deductions from the refund. Firstly if the scheme is contracted-out by the defined benefit method there is the certified amount (CA). This is the employee's share of the contributions equivalent premium (CEP) paid to the DSS. The CEP effectively transfers the employee's GMP back into SERPS. Secondly, income tax is deducted at a current rate of 20 per cent.

Year end and other procedures

14.22 To ease the administration many pension schemes have their scheme year ending on the same date as the tax year or very close to it, for example 31 March. If the two are separate, scheme and NICs are then passed to the pension scheme on separate lists at their respective year ends.

For defined benefit schemes the following procedures should be considered at the year end although in some cases they may be done more frequently.

(a) *Recording annual contributions* — The pensions administrator normally requires at the year end a list of all contributions paid by each member and containing details such as his pensionable pay. This list may be produced manually or as a computer print-out. Alternatively, if the pension scheme records are on a computerised system, a schedule of members may be produced so that the appropriate figures can be inserted by payroll staff. If both the payroll and pensions system are run on computers, it is usually more efficient to transfer information between them electronically, for example by a personal computer magnetic disk or via a common server, saving time and effort, and eliminating transcription errors.

(b) *Reconciliation of payroll and pensions records* — The transmission of contribution records from one system to the other necessitates the reconciliation of the payroll and pensions records and discrepancies often come to light at this stage. These can be kept to a minimum by internal procedures which ensure that joiners and leavers during the year are processed by both systems.

(c) *Payment procedures* — Contributions of all types are usually paid over to the pension scheme monthly. The same method is normally used for both employer and employee contributions although it may differ. Computer payroll systems print the requisite totals for controlling and paying contributions.

Multiple schemes

14.23 AVC plans may be regarded as separate 'schemes'. In some companies a supplementary 'executive' scheme is operated for senior employees, who are also in the main company scheme. These supplementary or 'top up' schemes are often non-contributory even if the main scheme is contributory but they may include an AVC facility. As already mentioned unapproved top up schemes may also exist. From an administrative point of view if contributions are being paid by one member to two schemes, they must be kept entirely separate. This may necessitate multiple deductions for the payroll system which must be separately itemised.

References

14.24   The general references given in 10.26 above also apply to this chapter.

(1)   'A Guide to the Financial Services Act for Employers', leaflet PP4, DSS. (This leaflet clarifies the position of employers giving general pension advice to employees.)

(2)   Homer A and Burrows R, 'Tolleys Tax Guide 1998–99', Tolley Publishing Co Ltd, 1998. (This covers the tax aspects of the various types of pension contribution as well as the tax treatment of employee benefits generally.)

(3)   Self R, 'The Payroll/Pensions interface', PMR, February 1995.

(4)   'Pensions Administration', Tolley Publishing Co Ltd, 1998. (A comprehensive looseleaf book which is regularly updated.)

(5)   Mathewman J and others, 'Social Security and State Benefits 1998–99', Tolley Publishing Co Ltd 1998.

15 Voluntary Deductions

Scope of this chapter

15.1   This chapter outlines non-statutory deductions from pay, their administration, their position regarding income tax and NICs (National Insurance contributions) and their itemisation on the payslip.

Income tax, NICs and attachment of earnings orders are statutory deductions which the employer has the right, and indeed duty, to make without authority from the employee. These statutory deductions are each described in their own separate chapters — see Chapter 11 (Income Tax), Chapter 12 (National Insurance Contributions) and Chapter 13 (Attachment of Earnings Orders). All other deductions are a matter of agreement and are generally called 'voluntary' deductions even though, in some cases, the employee may have no choice in the matter where they are covered by a provision in the contract of employment. Voluntary deductions include trade union dues, medical insurance premiums and regular charitable donations. Pension contributions have several peculiarities and form a separate class of voluntary deductions. (See Chapter 14 (Pension Contributions).)

Employee payrolls almost invariably involve voluntary deductions and these deductions can also occur in pension payrolls, for example contributions to medical insurance.

Key points relating to voluntary deductions

15.2   Key points on voluntary deductions are summarised below:

(a)   all voluntary deductions must be authorised either by the contract of employment or by a separate written agreement signed by the employee;

(b)   each type of voluntary deduction has a separate arrangement, which often involves a third party, and places a duty on the employer;

(c)   the agreement of the employer is required before a voluntary deduction can be operated through the payroll;

(d)   the employer's right to make deductions, fine employees and recover retail cash and stock losses is controlled by *ERA 1996, ss 13–22*;

(*e*)   pension scheme membership and hence contributions are on a voluntary basis;

(*f*)   payroll giving schemes allow employees to make tax-free charitable donations directly from their pay by means of a deduction through the payroll;

(*g*)   all deductions should be shown on the payslip;

(*h*)   the employer's right to make deductions in respect of trade union dues is controlled by *TULRCA 1992, s 68*. The rules were eased during 1998 by the *Deregulation (Deduction from Pay of Union Subscriptions) Order 1998 (SI 1998 No 1529)*.

Administration of voluntary deductions

15.3   The administration of voluntary deductions can be dealt with under the following headings.

(*a*)   ***Deduction arrangements*** — Voluntary deductions must be collected and disbursed according to an agreement. There are many arrangements found in practice and only the common or important deductions are discussed here. Up-to-date details of deduction arrangements should be held in the payroll department library. (See 18.4 below.)

Some deductions may apply to all employees in a particular group, and may be fixed or variable. For instance, some employees who are members of a trade union may pay a fixed subscription each month; other employees, members of a different union, may pay a variable amount according to a pay-related scale. (The rules governing the deduction of trade union subscriptions from pay are covered in full at 15.5(*a*) below.)

The level of other deductions are often dependent on the wishes and decisions of the individual employee. For instance, members of a medical insurance scheme, such as the Hospital Savings Association (HSA), pay an amount which accords with the level of benefits required.

Facilities usually exist to terminate an arrangement at the wish of the employee or the employer, or when the employee leaves. The cancellation by an employer of a deduction arrangement is unlikely to be a quick process as it may involve consultation with employees, their representatives and third parties. Cancellation without the agreement of the employee may be a breach of the contract of employment and damage employer/employee relations. In the case of trade union dues, however, a worker's authorisation of a deduction arrangement does not oblige the employer to make or continue to make deductions. (See 15.5 below.) Often the employees and third parties may have to make new arrangements, such as bank standing orders or direct debits to effect continuing payments.

Deduction arrangements may be classed as:

(i)   external, e.g. medical insurance premiums;

(ii)   internal, e.g. season ticket loans made by the employer; and

(iii)   pension contributions.

In an external arrangement money, and often payer details, must be transferred to a third party, for example a charitable giving deduction. An internal arrangement, however, merely requires an accounting transfer of the relevant payer details from the payroll to the employer's accounts. Deduction arrangements covering pension contributions can be either external or internal. They are often paid to an organisation which is at least notionally independent of the employer, such as a pension trust. In practice this may just be a different department within the employing organisation, but it could require payment to an external body such as a life assurance company. (See 10.17 above for a list of different types of pension arrangement.)

Employers may sometimes charge external organisations an administrative fee for making payroll deductions. For example, the fee could amount to 2.5 per cent of total dues collected on a trade union's behalf.

Many deduction arrangements involve a third party, for instance a trade union, and require three agreements, all of which should be compatible. The agreements are between:

(A)   the employer and third party;

(B)   the employee and third party; and

(C)   the employee and employer.

In practice, the three agreements are often made as follows. The employer agrees to an arrangement with a third party to provide the facility to make deductions from employees' pay and to forward money and payer details to the third party (A). The arrangements will define the duties of both the employer and the third party and should provide for a number of situations which can occur, such as frequency of deduction, underdeductions, administration of arrears of deduction, handling of inaccurate documentation and annual review and increase of deduction amounts. The employee and the third party agree to a level of benefit and deduction (B). Documentation, often in a prescribed form, is forwarded by the employee either directly, or indirectly via the third party, to the employer as the authorisation to make deductions from his pay and to forward the amounts to the third party (C).

If the deduction arrangement is internal, the employer and employee will have agreed to the benefit, if any, and the deductions to be made. The agreement should provide for a number of situations which may occur, such as the employee leaving.

(b)   **Signed authorisation** — The pay office must hold a signed authorisation from the employee consenting to all voluntary deductions unless they are provided for in the contract of employment. *[ERA 1996, s 13].* Special rules govern the deduction of trade union subscriptions from pay. (See 15.5 below.) An example of a deduction commonly provided for in the contract of employment is the recovery of the net pay rounding amount for employees paid in cash. (See 22.7 below.)

The signed authorisations may need to be retained over a number of years, and at least until superseded by a later authorisation. It is common for auditors (both internal and external) to require sight of such documents during an audit.

It is not usually necessary to obtain a new agreement each time the amount of a deduction changes, providing the authorisation wording allows variations. It is, however, a common practice for employers to invite employees to renew their authorisation to make certain deductions, such as participation in medical insurance cover, annually. (See Reference (2) in 15.6 below.)

Wherever practicable the information received should be in a format suitable for input to computer systems with a minimum of clerical work, and be submitted in a prescribed form. The authorisation should show any reference number which identifies the agreement between the employee, the third party and the employer.

(c)   **Changes in deductions** — If the deductions are based on a formula or a scale for all employees rather than unique to each individual, and a computer system is in use, automatic changes in the amounts deducted may be effected. This avoids making a data entry for each person on the payroll subject to the deduction. A good example of this sort of change in deduction is a sports and social club contribution which is increased due to inflation. The right to make changes should, of course, be contained in an authorisation. In the past, special rules have applied to increases to trade union subscription deductions, and they may still apply to such arrangements authorised by employees before 23 June 1998. (See 15.5 below.)

(d)   **Frequency of deduction** — The frequency of deduction will be covered by the deduction arrangements (see (a) above). Care should be taken to ensure the correct deductions are made if monthly or annual amounts have to be deducted based on equivalent weekly amounts (or *vice versa*), or the employee's pay frequency changes, from weekly to monthly, for example. It is not always possible to calculate a weekly equivalent of a monthly or annual amount. For instance, savings-related share option schemes require fixed monthly deductions. It may prove impractical to arrive at a weekly equivalent for employees paid weekly. Some months will be of four weeks' duration but others will be of five weeks, and for a four-weekly payroll there are thirteen pay periods in a year as compared to twelve for a monthly payroll. In the case of weekly deductions, a deduction 'holiday' may be the practical solution. It is less common to find a single deduction made annually but an example may be a subscription to a sports club.

Where unusual arrangements exist an administrative burden will fall on the payroll department. If a computer payroll system is in use it can be instructed to deal with any type of deduction frequency. For instance, it can be programmed to make or not to make deductions in certain pay periods thereby relieving the payroll administrator of the responsibility of monitoring the deductions.

(e)　**Payment documentation** — Suitable output documentation will be needed to support the payment of deductions to the relevant body. The documentation may be as prescribed by the agreement with the third party.

The minimum information needed is likely to be the employee's name, payroll number, the amount of deduction for the period and perhaps a reference number, such as the employee's building society roll number. The recording and use of reference numbers will usually be important for both the third party and for internal purposes. However, not all deductions require reference numbers, and their usage should be controlled to limit the amounts of information and data which have to be maintained.

A magnetic tape or disk is sometimes used to transfer the payment details. Ideally, listings of deduction details should be reconciled to the payroll deduction totals prior to paying the recipient. (See 19.9 below.) EFT (electronic funds transfer) can also be used for paying third parties.

The frequency of payment will form part of the agreement, but it is common practice for monthly or four-weekly remittances to be made. Deductions made in one month will be paid over in the following month. Thus, some remittances will cover four weeks and others five weeks.

Income tax and NICs

15.4　Most voluntary deductions are taken from pay after statutory deductions, but there are exceptions, for example most pensions contributions and some payments to charities. Unless otherwise stated the individual deduction discussed below is paid from income after the deduction of income tax and NICs.

Some deductions imply a taxable benefit. For instance, the sum deducted may not fully pay for the benefit received, i.e. the employer provides a subsidy. A common example is the provision of medical insurance where the employee's contribution does not extinguish the value of the benefit. In such cases reporting of the benefit and the employee's contribution is required on end of

Voluntary Deductions **15.5**

year returns, e.g. Form P11D. (Reference (1) in 15.6 below discusses aspects of tax and NICs in relation to deductions from pay.)

Typical deductions

15.5   The number of deductions operated by a pay office is only limited by the attitude of the employer. Each deduction operated carries an administrative cost which may be mitigated by the making of a charge, deductible from the remittance to the third party or by an internal recharge of costs. Computer systems may also have a limit to the number of different voluntary deductions that can be set up. The calculation of the deduction is usually straightforward, although some, especially contributions to occupational pension schemes, may be complex. The administration and maintenance of under-deductions, arrears and recovery of balances can be effectively performed by computer systems. Typical deductions can be classified as follows.

(*a*)   ***Trade union deductions*** — The rules governing the deduction of trade union subscriptions from pay ('check off' arrangements) were eased during 1998. The *Deregulation (Deduction from Pay of Union Subscriptions) Order 1998 (SI 1998 No 1529)* amends *TULRCA 1998, ss 68, 68(A)* with the effect that:

- employers no longer have to get individual employees' approval every three years in order to deduct trade union subscriptions under a check off arrangement; and

- employers no longer have to notify employees at least one month in advance of any increase in the amount to be deducted.

Other aspects of the rules remain unchanged, notably that:

(i)   employers must ensure that they have employees' written authorisation before they make check off deductions;

(ii)   employers must give every employee an itemised pay slip listing the amount of any deductions, as required by the *Employment Rights Act 1996, s 8*;

(iii)   employees are free to withdraw from a check off arrangement at any time. Employees withdraw their authorisation by writing to their employer in time for it to be 'reasonably practicable' for the employer to ensure that the deduction is not made; and

(iv)   employers are not obliged to make, or continue to make, check off deductions, even if employees have authorised them to do so.

The Deregulation Order came into effect on 23 June 1998, and the new rules apply to any authorisations given by employees from noon on that date. Transitional arrangements apply to existing authorisations signed by employees before 23 June 1998.

353

The transitional arrangements permit employers or unions to issue a notice to individual employees whose deductions are covered by existing authorisations, allowing the employee to choose whether he wishes the authorisation to be treated under the old or new rules. The notice must use the form of words shown at Figure *15A* below.

The notice tells the employee that his existing authorisation will be treated as indefinite, unless he lets his employer know, in writing within 14 days, that he wants it to expire at the end of its three-year period. If the employee chooses to have his authorisation treated under the old rules, it will expire at the end of its three-year life in the usual way. Any new authorisation he subsequently makes will be covered by the new rules.

Figure 15A

DEDUCTION OF TRADE UNION SUBSCRIPTIONS FROM PAY

Following the coming into force of the Deregulation (Deduction from Pay of Union Subscriptions) Order 1998 you no longer need to re-authorise payments of trade union subscription by 'check off' (deduction from pay by your employer) every three years and your employer need not give you advance written notice of any increase in the .rate of deductions. The law continues to require your written authorisation before check off can start, and you continue to have the right to stop paying by check off at any time, by giving notice in writing to your employer.

This notice affects you if you pay your union subscription by check off and you gave your current authorisation before the date on which the Order came into force.

If you are content for the new arrangements to apply for you, <u>you need do nothing</u>.

If, however, you wish the previous arrangements to continue to apply to you, you must give notice to that effect in writing to your employer at [*name and address of employer*] <u>within 14 days of receiving this notice</u>.

If you do so, your current authorisation will expire three years after you gave it, but any subsequent authorisation will be subject to the new arrangements.

Illustration of a form of notice that may be given by employers or trade unions to employees under the Deregulation (Deduction from Pay of Union Subscriptions) Order 1998, Article 3(2)

The notice can be issued at any time before the existing authorisation expires, and need not be issued until its three-year life is due to end. Employees must, however, be given at least 14 days to respond before their old authorisation expires. Note that until the notice is issued and the employee has been given the chance to respond, employers must still give advance warning of any increase in deductions.

If an employer does not issue a notice, existing authorisations will expire in the usual way, and any new authorisations made after 23 June 1998 will be governed by the new rules.

Deductions through the payroll provide the trade unions with a steady source of revenue that is comparatively inexpensive to collect, and accurate financial documentation relating to their dues. Some trade unions' branches endeavour to have separate remittances and documentation forwarded for their members. In such situations, where the employer has agreed to such a practice, then the use of the reference number may be necessary to identify membership of particular branches. Normally the dues are paid over on a monthly basis with supporting documents itemising details even though some employees are paid weekly.

(b) **Loans** — Loans may be made for a variety of reasons, e.g. the purchase of a car, and are discussed as a benefit in 9.16 above. The interest, if any, the nature of the loan and amounts outstanding on the loan during the year, should be readily identifiable for each tax year in order to assist completion of end of tax year returns (i.e. beneficial loan details on Form P11D) where a taxable benefit arises.

It is good practice to arrive at a figure for the total repayment, including interest where a fixed rate of interest is used, and to show this amount as a decreasing balance on the payslip for each pay period. The employee should be given a statement as part of the agreement, showing the calculation of interest over the period of the loan. It should be noted that where interest for the full term of the loan has been included in the original balance an adjustment may be necessary when the employee leaves or the loan is cleared before the end of the term.

It is important that the loan agreement signed by the employee provides for and authorises a normal level of deduction from wages for each pay period and for the balance of the loan to be payable immediately in full by the employee if he leaves the employment. The agreement should also make provision for the loan to be recovered in part or in full from final payments of earnings. The agreement may also provide for interest to be chargeable and payable by the employee if the loan is not repaid immediately on termination of employment.

An example of the need to structure loan agreements with employees carefully is the case of *Potter v Hunt Contracts Ltd [1992] IRLR 108*. Mr Potter received a loan from his employer to pay for an HGV driving course. It was recovered in part (£278.50) from his final wages when he left employ leaving a balance outstanding (£244.50). He was successful in his claim before the EAT that as the loan agreement did not authorise repayments from his wages such deduction was unlawful under the *Wages Act, s 1* (now *ERA 1996, s 13*). In such circumstances an employer would be obliged to repay the unlawful deduction and would have no way of getting that money back [*ERA 1996, s 25*] although it might be able to pursue recovery of any outstanding balance by county court proceedings. (See 5.12 above.)

Some employers make provision in the contract of employment to treat as a loan payments of occupational sick pay to employees who have suffered an accident for which either a third party or the employer may subsequently prove liable to pay compensation for loss of earnings. When the employee receives such compensation only the net pay element of the loan is repayable to the employer. (See 8.19 above for details of a court case on this point.)

It is the practice of some employers to give an advance of net pay (after notional deductions of tax, NICs etc.) when an underpayment has occurred, and to pay the gross amount with recovery of the advanced sum in the next pay period. In these circumstances employers may consider it prudent to obtain the signature of the underpaid employee to a carefully worded agreement which authorises both the delayed payment and recovery of the advance from wages. (See 5.12 above.)

Computer systems can be utilised successfully to improve administration of loans. For example, as the end of a loan period draws near, or when the employee is about to leave, a computer can be programmed to give a warning message. The computer can be instructed to recover automatically in full or part the outstanding balance from the final payment of earnings when an employee leaves. Further, the computer can be instructed to recover only the balance oustanding on a loan if this is lower than the normal deduction rate.

(c)   ***Medical insurance and health benefits*** — If an employer pays for medical insurance the benefit is often taxable. (See 9.8 above.) If the employee contributes and deductions are taken from pay the administration, documentation and procedures required may be similar to the administration of arrangements with other third parties, e.g. trade unions. Alternatively, the employee's contributions may be transferred from one account to another internally.

(d)   ***Rent, council tax and mortgage payment for local authority employees*** — Employees working for a local authority usually have the facility for their council house rent, council tax or mortgage payments to be deducted from pay. The transaction is an internal financial transfer from one account to another and may be effected either by listings or more efficiently by automatic computer transfers. In both cases a reference number identifies the employee's details and should, ideally, be passed into the organisation's accounting system each time a transfer occurs.

(e)   ***Fines*** — The contract of employment or other written agreement may give the employer the right to make deductions for bad or negligent work, or other failings which are the responsibility of the employee. Examples of deductions in respect of a failing of the employee and authorised by the contract of employment are car parking fines incurred by the employee but served on and paid by the employer, and related standard administration charges.

Deductions to recover the total amount due are restricted in the case of retail workers and must sometimes be spread over several pay days. Workers must receive written notification of the total liability and a demand for payment. The case of *Tobacco & Confectionery Ltd v Williamson (1993) ICR 371 EAT* has demonstrated that authorisation to make deductions in respect of, for instance, stock deficiencies from the pay of a retail worker, must predate the event which led to the deduction. [*ERA 1996, ss 13–22*].

The authorisation of such fines is dealt with mainly by the personnel department but the pay office needs to ensure that it receives properly authorised documents as this area of activity is likely to lead to poor industrial relations unless care is taken. (See 7.7 (*l*)(vi) above for further details.)

(f)   ***Jury service*** — There is no requirement for an employer to pay an employee for the time taken in performing jury service. The employee's contract of employment should state what payment, if any, will be made for attending jury service, and will usually require the employee to pass to the employer details of any money received from the court. An employee may claim expenses and a financial loss allowance from the court; these allowances are not subject to tax or National Insurance. The financial loss allowance is based on loss of earnings certified by the employer and is capped at a daily maximum.

It is not uncommon for employers to deduct an employee's financial loss allowance from his usual pay or to withhold wages altogether, the contract of employment permitting. Unless specified in the contract of employment, any deduction made may be from net or gross pay; no particular method is required by law.

(g)   ***Occupational pension schemes*** — Employers cannot insist on the membership of pension schemes as a condition of employment. Membership of such schemes is therefore voluntary. (See Chapters 10 (Pension Schemes) and 12 (Pension Contributions) for further details.) It should be noted that scheme membership does not of itself provide authorisation for the deduction of pension contributions from an employee's pay.

(*h*) **Building society savings** — Save as you earn (SAYE) schemes can be used for ordinary savings or for savings-related share options schemes (see (*k*) below). An ordinary SAYE contract involves a commitment to save a fixed amount each month for five years. At the end of the period the saver receives a bonus, and if the money is left in the account for another two years there is a further bonus.

Restrictions on the amount saved and on withdrawals and the removal of tax exemption on the interest and bonus by *Finance Act 1995, 12 Sch* have led to a decline in popularity of ordinary SAYE schemes.

(*j*) **Account transfers** — Payroll deductions can be transferred to almost any savings account with limited withdrawal facilities or to ordinary building society accounts, some of which allow the use of cash cards. Some computer payroll systems allow for transfer of savings deductions as well as the facility to split an employee's net wages between two or more different bank or building society accounts. (See 22.12(*c*) below).

(*k*) **Savings-related share option schemes** — The objective under a share save scheme is to allow employees the option to purchase their company's shares at a pre-determined price. They use the proceeds of an approved savings-related share option scheme, of either three or five years duration, to exercise their option to buy shares. Contributions to the scheme must be in the range from £5 to £250 a month and are usually deducted through the payroll. (See 9.14 above for share schemes generally.)

(*l*) **Charities** — Employers can allow employees the facility of having deductions made from pay as a contribution to registered charities under 'payroll giving' schemes. [*ICTA 1988, s 202*]. These payments are free of tax provided they do not exceed £1,200 a year. [*FA 1996, s 110*]. In some cases the old practice of paying charitable deductions out of taxed pay may continue.

Employers can make the deductions and forward them to an approved agency for onward transmission to the relevant charities. The contributions need to be reported in a listing showing the employee's name, amount and reference number. An employee must complete forms authorising the deductions and showing how they are to be distributed by the agency to the charities he supports. Alternatively, the agency can send vouchers to the employee who sends them to the charity. The vouchers can then be redeemed for cash from the agency. Although no charitable giving details are shown on Form P45 or Form P60 the employer must give an employee who leaves a statement of the amount deducted under the scheme in the current tax year. The employee and not the employer is responsible for ensuring that only £1,200 is deducted during the tax year. [*Charitable Deductions (Approved Schemes) Regulations 1986 (SI 1986 No 1046)*].

(m) **Overpayments** — Strictly, the recovery of overpayments has little in common with voluntary deductions except that the written authorisation of the employee may be essential in certain circumstances. The legal position regarding overpayment and related matters is examined in detail in 5.14–5.19 above. Further examination of recovery of overpayments is given at 18.22(g) below.

(n) **Miscellaneous** — Examples of other commonly found deductions include contributions towards the personal use of the employer's assets such as a house or car. Details of deductions made from an employee's pay in respect of personal use of an asset or provision of car fuel may reduce the taxable amount of the value of the benefit and may need to be shown on the end-of-year Forms P9D or P11D.

The common practice of allowing for State benefits when providing an occupational benefit is also sometimes considered a deduction. For example, State incapacity benefit received during illness is usually deducted from OSP (occupational sick pay) to ensure that the total payment from both sources does not exceed the basic rate of pay. (However, this is often expressed the other way round, i.e. the State benefit is made up to the employee's basic rate of pay by OSP.) Such 'deductions' are made before tax, NIC and AEO calculations but may have implications for pension contributions and other deductions.

Under *ERA 1996*, an itemised payslip is mandatory for all employees. The payroll administrator also regards a well-designed payslip showing all deductions clearly as both his 'shop window' and invaluable where subsequent reference to a copy held by the payroll office is necessary, perhaps months or years later. Where either a pay statement is in use which has limited space for itemising all deductions, or an employee has a large number of deductions, it is common practice for two or more deductions to be shown as, for example, 'Others'. Keeping the provisions of *ERA 1996, ss 8–9* in mind, the payroll administrator may need to provide an additional statement where this occurs. (See 5.13 above.)

References

15.6 The legal and tax positions with regard to the various deductions are covered by the References in 5.42 above. Most deductions agreements are covered by documents with a restricted circulation, for example trade union handbooks or literature issued by medical insurers.

(1) Whiscombe D, 'Elementary Deductions', PMR, December 1995.

(2) 'Help Desk: Deduction Authorisations', PMR, February 1996.

(3)   Prime V, 'Pay Deductions: Case Round-Up', PMR, October 1996.

(4)   'Help Desk: Charitable Giving', PMR, May 1997.

(5)   'Case Law: Actual Deduction Necessary', PMR, September 1997.

(6)   'Help Desk: Deducting Jury Service Payments', PMR, August 1998.

16　Payroll Organisation

Scope of this chapter

16.1　In any business the payroll function must be organised in such a way as to allow the employer to meet statutory and contractual obligations in the most effective and efficient manner. The prime aim is, of course, the prompt and accurate payment of wages, salaries and other sums due, but, there are also a multitude of other tasks to consider as well.

Today's payroll office administers staff loans and other employee benefits and compiles statistical returns as well as providing advice and guidance on pay, tax and National Insurance matters, especially since the introduction of Self-Assessment.

Payroll and employee benefits work combines aspects of personnel, finance and general administration and this often raises the question concerning to which part of the organisation payroll belongs. This is quite apart from the general discussions about business organisation that will affect all other departments such as job structures, staffing and technology.

In many organisations payroll is expected to operate like an outside business selling its service to the other departments and charging as near a commercial rate as possible for so doing. This necessitates payroll managers, like many other service functions, knowing precisely all relevant costs and being able to closely control these and thus minimise charges to users.

This has led to increased pressure on payroll managers to justify the costs and wherever possible reduce them and even examine ways of raising income, for example charging for voluntary deductions or advertising on payslips. (See Reference (1) in 16.15 below for a discussion on payroll advertising.)

Even further, there has been moves to 'externalise' the payroll function, either voluntarily as in the private sector or often forced as evidenced in the 'Compulsory Competitive Tendering' (CCT) exercises found in Local Government, where in-house payroll teams are forced to compete against private sector providers for the cheapest rates.

Whilst CCT is the brainchild of the Conservatives, the change of Government has so far made little difference to Local Government payroll offices. 'Best Value' is the new Governments replacement for CCT but until its details are tested, finalised and implemented CCT remains a major threat for public sector payroll.

Throughout this chapter, suggestions concerning payroll organisation must be tempered with personal experience because arrangements which work well in one organisation may not always be transferable to another, even in the same sector. The placing, structuring and scope of the payroll function will be influenced by many factors though increasingly this will be determined by the demands of the 'users' and the employing body but the drive will be for the efficient and most effective use of resources possible.

Payroll offices have to respond positively to these demands and adapt their procedures, structures, even their attitudes and culture, accordingly.

Key points of payroll organisation

16.2   The main features of payroll organisations can be summarised as follows.

(*a*)   Payroll organisation is determined by many factors, such as the pay structure, the number of employees and the history of the employer.

(*b*)   The method of determining pay, benefits and conditions of employment is useful background knowledge for payroll staff. The details differ considerably between organisations and industries.

(*c*)   Effective payroll work depends on good working relationships with almost all the other departments of an organisation.

(*d*)   The payroll department can be validly placed within any one of the finance, personnel or general administration functions of a business.

(*e*)   Payroll departments can be organised in several ways, for instance by dividing it into wages and salaries sections or sections handling input, processing and output or queries. Some allied functions may be fully or partially included within the payroll ambit. Common examples are pensions, bonus calculations and benefits in kind.

(*f*)   The number of payroll staff required depends on many factors. It is, therefore, difficult to provide a typical figure as rarely are any two payroll functions identical in every respect. Pay periods and transaction levels can have a dramatic effect on the employee to pay clerk ratio as can the level of computerisation.

(*g*) Some organisations adopt the total human resources approach by combining payroll, personnel and pensions into one department.

(*h*) Like all managers, the payroll manager has to reconcile many requirements which sometimes conflict, for example a payroll manager will need to balance out the drive for excessive automation, efficiency and security against the desire to keep the job varied and interesting.

(*j*) Payroll work demands constant research and training to keep up to date with continual changes, e.g. in pay structures, law and new technology.

(*k*) All of the above factors plus others, personal preference for example, determines the actual job title for payroll staff. The term 'payroll clerk' or 'payroll assistant' has become somewhat outmoded, often replaced with 'payroll technician' or 'payroll officer' which may tend to reflect better the skills and expertise now required.

Main factors determining payroll organisation

16.3   Figure 18A below illustrates the basic work of a payroll department. The total amount of payroll work is often, but not always, directly proportional to the number of payees. Pay structures tend to be more complex in large organisations. The larger the number of payees, or diversity of payee types, e.g. expatriates and/or impatriates, the more staff required and that can give more scope to employ specialists within the department.

Specialists could, for instance, cover pensions, occupational sick pay, SSP, SMP, Form P11D preparation and completion or specific groups of payee with particularly complex employment conditions. This provides an in-depth knowledge of certain areas of payroll procedure but may reduce the options available for staff movements to cover sudden emergencies due to absences. This again requires a delicate balancing act by the payroll manager.

Pay and employee benefits structures are dependent on the different contracts of employment of the workforce. The contract of employment to a large extent dictates how a payroll is organised. The contract will stipulate that employees are paid monthly, weekly or at some other interval. It also covers the complexity of the pay and benefits structure which has a major bearing on the number of employees handled by each payroll technician.

Where there is a longer interval of payment there will usually be fewer payroll technicians. Employers operating from one location tend to need fewer payroll technicians than ones spread over several, geographically dispersed sites.

The amount of work completed on raw data at stages prior to receipt in the pay office affects the staffing numbers in the pay office. For instance, clock cards or time sheets submitted to the pay office without any preliminary work require more payroll staff work than data that has been processed already by the employees' supervisor. Another example is the situation where a data collection system has eliminated the need for 'paper' submissions and has performed certain calculations to arrive, for instance, at payable hours. Payroll managers need to be aware of the cost of such 'prior' work even if it is not part of the central payroll function.

It may be administratively convenient to combine certain duties or functions but sensible financial control dictates that to minimise the risk of fraud, certain duties should be kept distinct from each other wherever possible. This is referred to, by auditors, as Internal Control. Whatever procedures are operated it is essential that adequate controls are applied. Examples of such segregation of staff duties are as follows:

(*a*)   payroll staff who are involved in systems work, i.e. parameter definition, should not be responsible for payroll transactional input;

(*b*)   staff responsible for authorising wages or allied payments should be different from those responsible for the input of data or pay calculations;

(*c*)   staff involved on input or calculations should be different from those involved in the cash handling or distribution function;

(*d*)   where pay packets or cheques have to be returned they should be handled by the cashier's or payment's section rather than the pay office. However, the latter is required to be notified so that it can take appropriate action.

Every organisation has its own culture, history and traditions which need to be accommodated or changed only gradually after careful thought. Whereas the view 'we have always done it this way' is not a good reason for continuing a practice, there may be sound reasons for the continuance of an established method. Payroll managers must always be aware of a 'ripple effect' and ensure that change is of benefit to the organisation as a whole. It is not unknown for departmental improvements to inconvenience the rest of the organisation.

The stamp of the individual payroll manager is important and has a major effect on all aspects of payroll organisation, especially motivation. Consequently, the payroll manager must be aware of his unconscious, as well as conscious, acts of communication. The payroll manager is the hub around which the payroll wheel revolves. A well-motivated group of pay technicians achieves far more than a demotivated group. Consequently, the staffing ratios may be lower with a high level of motivation. Much of this has to do with the payroll manager but there are other contributory factors, such as training, career progression and personalities within the pay office.

The payroll office does not exist in isolation and payroll is not an end in itself but it is an important part of the personnel and financial procedures. As such, the degree of support demanded and given by other departments is crucial to the way a pay office operates. The speed, accuracy and courtesy of the payroll service determines how it is viewed by others. There is mutual dependence between cashiers, payroll, personnel, accountancy and computer staff. The fostering of good working relationships is essential.

This is an area of staff relations which payroll managers should monitor carefully to ensure that they receive and give the appropriate level of service and support. (Chapter 17 (Management Skills) discusses the payroll manager's role in more depth and see also Reference (2) in 16.15 below for a profile of a payroll office which has been awarded a high accolade by other departments within its company. Changes in working practices, including a report to the Board concerning late receipt of termination advices, significantly improved the operation of the payroll function.)

Many different business structures

16.4   Organising a business into a rational set of separate departments and sections can be a major contribution to effectiveness and efficiency. This is, however, quite difficult with payroll and allied business functions. Organisational structures vary significantly even between apparently similar businesses, for example large local authorities differ from each other as do health authorities, social security departments etc. Normally these public sector bodies, where a high degree of public accountability is required, have well-formulated structures with little staff movement between the major administrative functions.

The same comments apply to large private sector companies although there are occasions where the use of combined payroll, personnel (and even pensions) functions provide for better staff movement. (See Reference (3) in 16.15 below for a profile of payroll and pension functions combinations.) There is often, however, a more flexible approach to the transfer and use of staff between different business functions, for instance private sector payroll staff could be transferred from or to other departments such as sales or accounting.

The range of skills and disciplines required by a member of the payroll office supports the view that it is often easier to temporarily move someone out of payroll and into another function rather than vice versa. Further, payroll is a highly sensitive area and is the custodian of confidential and personal information so that the temporary transfer of staff from other functions into payroll should occur only after careful consideration.

Smaller related functions such as pensions and employee benefits can be difficult to place in the organisational structure even in large businesses. They require specialist knowledge and skills but the volume of work may not justify the creation of a whole department. A small company frequently has the personnel, payroll and even accounting functions merged, perhaps under the company secretary. (See also 16.8 below on the human resources concept.)

Data processing (sometimes called 'computing' or 'information services') may also be difficult to place in the organisation structure. This is further complicated by the tendency for some business departments to control their own computer equipment. The increased availability of good payroll software systems which will run on mini or personal computers has led to some payroll departments containing or 'owning' their own computer equipment.

In these situations the payroll department may be responsible for all aspects of the hardware and software, for example contracts for maintenance, taking and reloading of back-up copies of masterfiles data and the development and loading of new software. Some large payroll departments may have their own systems development team. Alternatively, a central information, management services or computer department may have overall responsibility. Careful investigation and planning will be required before major changes are introduced.

The place of the payroll department in an organisation

16.5   As referred to above, the culture and history of an organisation will have shaped its current procedures and structure. It is rare to find any two organisations exactly the same and although many broadly conform to general structures there is no definitive organisational structure for the location or shape of the payroll function. In Figure 16A below an example of the functions and reporting structure of one large public body is shown. In Figures 16B and 16C below examples of private sector companies are shown. A recent trend has been for the payroll function to be placed with the personnel function in small UK organisations. There are, however, arguments for establishing payroll as a separate function away from the personnel, accounts or administration functions, with a direct reporting line to a director. For instance, the need for confidentiality and separation of duties may be considered as essential.

Organising a payroll department

16.6   Management Services personnel can be of considerable help in determining the structure of a department. They can help to systematically examine the workload, methods of working and office automation. Together with the general and payroll management they can devise and recommend new staff structures, computers, data collection systems and working methods. Of course, techniques such as job evaluation apply in payroll administration as much as anywhere else. There are a variety of ways to organise a payroll department, some of which are described below.

(*a*)   ***Separate wages and salaries sections*** — Figure 16D below shows a traditional payroll department split into wages and salaries sections. It is not unusual in the private sector for there to be a separate payroll, perhaps administered by the company secretary, for the organisation's executives and senior managers. Broadly the distinction is between a wages section paying traditional hourly paid employees and a salaries section paying the office based staff monthly. Such an arrangement produces staff with expert detailed knowledge of the conditions of service of individual areas but suffers the disadvantages of specialisation, friction between sections and inadequate cover during illness and holidays.

(b)   ***Multi-disciplinary teams*** — There is an increasing trend to opt for multi-disciplinary teams, each team dealing with a complete section of the wages and salaries payroll involving all the functions, e.g. PAYE, NIC, SSP, SMP etc. This is illustrated in Figure 16E below.

With such an arrangement it is important that one team leader alone has an overall co-ordination role for each payroll. This person liaises with other parts of the organisation on most matters.

This type of approach has the disadvantage that a good deal of co-ordination is necessary between the teams but the complication is outweighed by the advantages of:

   (i)   broader work experience for staff;

   (ii)   better cover during sickness and holidays;

   (iii) less friction between sections;

   (iv)   increased motivation and job satisfaction;

   (v)   better opportunities for promotion.

It is important to retain work identification, i.e. staff like to see a process through from beginning to end. Consequently, it is preferable to divide the team's workload into identifiable units.

(c)   ***Functional teams*** — This approach defines teams according to specific functions. For instance, the input or calculation functions can be divided from the checking and distribution of the outputs. Separate teams to handle pay queries (including enquiries from external bodies, e.g. the DSS) or to prepare and complete Forms P11D could be set up. This approach has the disadvantage of being less flexible than other systems as staff may be unoccupied awaiting work unless their role is combined with other duties. It does, however, provide a built-in segregation of duties reducing the possibilities for fraud and error. This approach is illustrated in Figures 16F and 16G below.

(d)   ***A payroll administration service*** — This type of service virtually eliminates the payroll department. All payroll work is subcontracted to an external organisation for an agreed fee. It is basically an extension of the familiar computer payroll bureau service to cover all aspects of payroll.

16.6 *Payroll Organisation*

Figure 16A

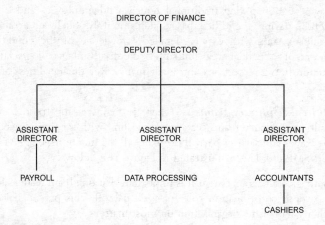

Illustration of the payroll and other departmental structures of a large public body

Figure 16B

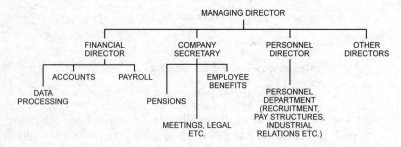

Illustration of the payroll and other departmental structures in a large private sector company

Figure 16C

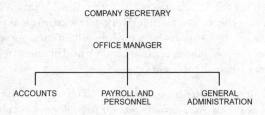

Illustration of the structure of the administrative functions of a small private company

Figure 16D

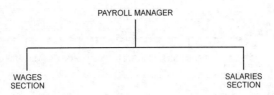

Illustration of separate sections of a payroll department (see 16.6(a))

Figure 16E

Illustration of a division of a payroll department's staff into three teams, each team handling a section of the work from start to finish (see 16.6(b))

Figure 16F

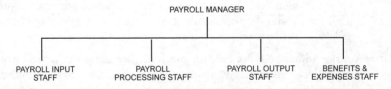

Illustration of the division of a payroll department's staff into functional teams (see 16.6 (c))

Figure 16G

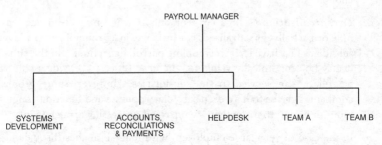

Illustration of a payroll department in a large company with its own systems development section, and separate teams to handle queries from the branches, process the payroll and deal with payroll accounts (see 16.6(c))

Figure 16H

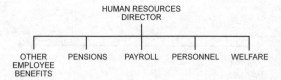

Illustration of the activities of a human resources department (see 16.8 below)

Outsourcing, or externalising as it is sometimes known, some or all of the administrative functions of a business is increasingly viewed as a viable option by UK companies. It allows businesses to concentrate on their 'core' activities. Payroll is clearly one non-core activity which can be easily out-sourced. There is also continuing pressure, especially in the form of compulsory competitive tendering, generated initially by government on public bodies, and particularly on local authorities, to out-source a number of functions. It is not unusual to find both the payroll department staff and the responsibility for the payroll are transferred to an outside agency. It can be an economical and reliable approach for a smaller business or a pension scheme to use a payroll administration service.

Most organisations will find, however, that some payroll work is usually still required as the administration service needs a member of staff in the user organisation for contract management and liaison purposes, someone to collate and despatch all the basic data such as joiner and leaver details and distribute output such as management reports.

A major advantage is not only the much smaller amount of payroll work but a reduced requirement for payroll expertise. The users of such an administration service must, of course, rely on the suppliers for advice on new payroll developments. Careful ongoing monitoring of the level and quality of the service provided by the external agency is recommended. The need for a tight, well defined, contract managed by someone strong and with sufficient understanding cannot be emphasised enough.

(e)   ***Decentralisation*** — In a large organisation the payroll service may be fully or partially decentralised. For instance, in a group of companies each subsidiary may have its own complete payroll department. In this situation it may be economically viable for the head office to provide a computer payroll bureau service to the subsidiaries. However, some groups of companies prefer to have each subsidiary operate and function as autonomous units and to make their own payroll processing arrangement.

In the case of very large employers with many branches throughout the UK, a combination of a centralised payroll function and devolvement of some aspects, for example responding to enquiries, to these branches may prove the most satisfactory.

With such a large employer having say, 100,000 employees scattered across the UK, preparatory work may be performed at local administrative centres prior to forwarding data to the central payroll office.

Another example found both in local authorities and manufacturing concerns is attendance recording and incentive scheme administration, such as bonus calculations. These tasks are often performed by staff outside the payroll department, for example, timekeepers and bonus clerks who are part of the employee's own department or another department such as management services. In some businesses with several geographically remote employment units cash wages are made up locally according to the central pay office instructions. (See 22.6 below.)

Payroll department staffing

16.7   The number of staff required to operate a particular payroll function can be a controversial issue. Simple statistics need careful qualification, for instance, it could be stated that there should be one member of payroll staff for every 250 employees. However, the payroll staff may or may not do other payroll related or non-payroll work.

Similarly, some payroll work, e.g. SSP, can be done in the user or personnel department. The content of the workload needs to be carefully scrutinised before deciding on staffing levels. The following questions need to be discussed in arriving at a final decision.

(*a*)   How much preparatory work is done before data arrives in the pay office?

(*b*)   How complicated is the work? For example, a time sheet containing only plain hours requiring totalling needs much less effort than one requiring complex calculations for shift work, night work and weekend working.

(*c*)   How much of the work is automated?

(*d*)   How much peripheral payroll work is attached to the job, e.g. correspondence and pensions work?

(*e*)   What proportion of the workforce is paid weekly or monthly?

(*f*)   Are payments made in cash, or by cheques, credit transfers, or BACS?

(*g*)   How many non-UK employees are there on the payroll, e.g. UK expatriates working overseas, and impatriates (i.e. foreign nationals) seconded from an overseas associate company working in the UK?

(*h*)   How many individual payrolls are there? Many small ones may be more time consuming collectively than a single payroll with the same or higher number of employees.

(*j*)   Are there any payrolls being processed in respect of subsidiaries or companies outside the UK, e.g. Republic of Ireland, which demand an understanding and application of different legislation?

(*k*)   What level of detail in management information is to be produced by the payroll function? Does this impose, for example, special data entry routines?

(*l*)   How many pensioners are there on the payroll? A pensions payroll requires fewer payroll technicians than an employee payroll with the same number of records.

(*m*)   Is the payroll office responsible for compiling details of benefits in kind and expenses and issuing Forms P9D and P11D?

(*n*)   Do payroll staff advise employees and directors on income tax issues arising out of the introduction of self-assessment?

Bearing in mind these and other factors, staffing ratios are likely to vary widely between, say, 1:100 for a small manual payroll to 1:3,000 for a very large computerised payroll with, for example, over 100,000 employees. The ratios may be much lower where payments are processed for expatriates, impatriates or foreign payrolls, or much higher where there is a pensioners' payroll or where highly-developed payroll procedures and software are in use.

In summary, there is no set calculation that can be used to determine the number of payroll staff needed to complete the work. Payroll Managers must be prepared to experiment with various structures and data processing methods before arriving at a staffing level that is both cost effective and able to produce quality work.

The human resources concept

16.8   A recent development is for companies to combine in one department the staff engaged in all aspects of employee management (Figure 16H above). This results in the integration of payroll, personnel, pensions and possibly part of management services (organisation and methods and work study). Such an amalgamation may tend to exist in theory rather than in practice because although there is one head for such a department the disciplines tend to operate independently though, hopefully, in a co-ordinated manner.

One variant of this approach is to merge only the paper work aspects of personnel and related activities, together with payroll, under an administration manager. There are beneficial aspects to this structure. Career opportunities are facilitated by easier transfers between the various sections. The computer systems can be more easily integrated by having these groupings under one head (see Chapter 28 (Selecting a Computer System) for further details).

Overall planning for human resources is made more meaningful and fosters the feeling in staff that they are of sufficient importance to the organisation to warrant a major department.

The counter argument to the human resources approach is that payroll is a complicated high-volume 'number-crunching' operation. It involves large amounts of money and is a major proportion of the costs of running an organisation. Therefore, like, for example, sales invoicing, it properly belongs to the accounting and finance functions. This counter argument can be summarised by stating that the financial aspects of payroll outweigh any personnel considerations.

Relationships with other departments and organisations

16.9   No matter how well organised the office, its effectiveness is reduced if the individual payroll members do not have sound and effective working relationships at an individual level with all other sections and departments. Good communications between sections must be clear and two way. Arrangements based on agreement tend to be more effective than those imposed by the pay office or by anyone else. It is necessary to encourage an atmosphere of mutual co-operation which is sometimes difficult in a pay office environment where rigid deadlines can lead to friction and tension.

The prime area for friction, dissent and misunderstanding tends to be the scheduling and meeting of the dates by which information must reach the pay office for inclusion in the payroll calculations. (Reference (2) in 16.15 below reveals how one payroll office put in place changes, such as regular reports to the Board of directors of late notifications of leavers, which led to improved relationships with other departments.) It is advisable to inform all concerned at frequent intervals of deadlines even though there may be no change during the year. This reinforces the message, especially where new employees are providing the information.

The data gathering stage is the most crucial stage in payroll production because inaccurate, late or missing information results in inaccurate or omitted payments and returns, such as Form P11D. The provision of, for example, the information for SSP is often irksome. Accuracy and moderate discipline must therefore to some extent be imposed.

Irrespective of where the responsibility for the error lies the failure and responsibility to effect corrections are often laid at the door of the payroll department. Consequently, it is important to ensure that payroll staff cultivate good relationships with the providers of information to ensure that data arrives on time and, equally important, in the prescribed format. Wherever possible it is desirable that data is in a format suitable for passing directly to the computer stage with a minimum of extra work.

Figure 18A below summarises the work and relationships of the payroll department with other business functions and outside organisations.

It is important to remember that payroll work is not an end in itself. It is a contribution to the overall functioning of the organisation. Consequently, the output of reports to the accounts, personnel, audit, pensions and management services departments is important. There is often, however, a tendency to devote less effort to these types of output than to the 'pure' payroll outputs, for example payslips and pay control documents.

It is very much in the interest of everyone that impractical pay and benefit structures are not agreed with employees or their trade union representatives. The payroll and computer departments should provide advice on the administrative and technical feasibility of any proposals which affect them. Delays to the implementation of revised pay and benefits schemes are likely to occur when resources are not available to give effect either to changes in procedure or to amending the computer programs.

As PAYE is enforced by law, it is prudent to cultivate a good relationship with the local tax office. This encourages sympathetic treatment in such matters as, for instance, P11D queries, correcting errors and applying for dispensations.

A good relationship with the local office of the Contributions Agency of the DSS should be cultivated also as this can prove helpful when dealing with enquiries or errors related to SSP, SMP, NIC or national insurance numbers. Good relations may provide a more favourable and speedier response to pay office queries.

Enquiries from shop stewards or trade union representatives should be dealt with honestly. Courteous co-operation should be displayed by the payroll staff and not resistance which is occasionally encountered. Normally, by helping the trade union official to do his job, the best interests of everyone are served. Trade unions also have a major impact on payroll and other employee benefit administrators when they negotiate new remuneration packages for their members (see 16.10 below).

Of course, payroll staff should be alert not to reveal information of a confidential nature which may be either personal in respect of an employee, or be about the employer's plans or intentions which have not been divulged yet outside the payroll department. There may also be aspects of the *Data Protection Act 1984*, and any subsequent amendments (the *European Data Protection Directive* was brought into UK law and comes into force in Spring 1999), which would be infringed by disclosure of personal details; see 23.16 below.

Negotiating pay and conditions

16.10   The payroll administrator is obviously interested in the various methods of negotiating employee pay and conditions. These range from national agreements between employers and trade unions to individual agreements between one employer and one employee. Important examples are the Whitley Councils found in the public sector which are joint negotiating councils where employer representatives and trade unions settle pay and conditions. Often there are multi-tier agreements, for instance in engineering. In the latter case the national agreement between employers and unions forms a minimum which can be supplemented by further negotiations at company and plant level.

The National Minimum Wage is something that not only has to be implemented (the *National Minimum Wage Act 1998* comes into force April 1999), but managed as well and agreement is needed between the employer and employee representatives concerning any effect on local pay bargaining, age changes etc.

The documentation of collective bargaining agreements is often very extensive but essential for payroll work. (See 18.4 below for further comments on documentation.) For instance, the National Joint Council for Local Authorities' Services publishes the results of its negotiations as handbooks covering many different types of employee, for example car park attendants, school cleaners, general labourers, gardeners etc. Although the new single status conditions of service covers most local council employees the documentation is actually a lot more straightforward and simple than its predecessors.

Until recently statutory wages councils were important for setting minimum levels of pay and conditions in certain industries, e.g. clothing manufacture. Though the last remaining wages councils were abolished with effect from 30 August 1993 by *TURERA 1993*, the Agricultural Wages Board for England and Wales continues to operate. Pay review bodies (see 4.5 above) advise the Government on the remuneration of certain occupations, such as armed forces personnel or doctors.

An important general trend is the move away from national or central bargaining to local negotiations. This is true of both the public and private sectors and has been encouraged by central government policies. The general argument in favour of local bargaining is flexibility. It allows managers to negotiate pay and benefit schemes which match the needs of each separate business unit and its employees. National bargaining tends to impose a general compromise.

This trend to local bargaining increases the differences between payroll operations even within the same group of companies. The move to local bargaining is, however, opposed by some trade unions and not all employers support it. As already mentioned national and local bargaining can be combined to form multi-tier arrangements.

All employers will need to reconsider their pay policies, though, when the National Minimum Wage (NMW) is introduced by regulation. Local bargaining will no doubt continue but the new regulations introduce a start point of £3.60 per hour for adult employees.

Requirements which can conflict with job satisfaction

16.11   Very often in the time-constrained area of payroll the manager satisfies one set of criteria only to discover that this has worked against other operational needs. There are no rules guaranteed to avoid these pitfalls but the payroll manager needs to be aware of these problems. Some aspects are dealt with below.

(*a*)   *Performance* — Job satisfaction and performance can be closely linked. A payroll technician obtaining job satisfaction is likely to be a high performer. However, arrangements made to achieve high performance sometimes militate against job satisfaction. For example, a technician given a large number of similar time sheets to complete each week should be capable of achieving expertise and quick performance. However, lack of variety may lower job satisfaction and performance could drop.

(*b*)   *Segregation of duties* — Similarly, segregation of duties, whilst assisting financial checks and forming part of the internal controls, often reduces efficiency as staff movement may be prevented in certain areas. From a motivational point of view it is important that the payroll manager fully explains to his staff why they are prevented from performing certain duties. Alternatively, the rotation of staff through the range of duties over a period, for instance twelve months, will improve efficiency, motivation and promotion opportunities.

(*c*)   *Confidentiality, security and control* — Payroll confidentiality is often a contentious issue. Employees tend to protest aggressively about perceived breaches of confidentiality on personal pay details whereas they are likely to be quite open about other aspects of their lives. As a consequence the general attitude within the payroll field quite rightly tends to be one of continual vigilance.

This can present problems when carried too far within the pay office. It is often not necessary to insist on a high degree of segregation and the withholding of information from colleagues within the pay office. It is a matter of striking the correct balance and not de-motivating individual technicians by unnecessarily preventing access to some areas of work. Commonsense has to be the payroll manager's guide in this field.

Payroll security is a vital activity concerned with minimising the risks of fraud and disaster. Control is concerned with the monitoring of the payroll service and taking corrective action when problems and errors occur. (Chapter 23 (Security and Administrative Controls) deals with these issues in detail.)

(*d*)   ***Flexibility*** — As far as possible flexibility has to be an important aspect of the payroll function. Whereas change for the sake of change is futile and costly, the payroll manager must foster flexible attitudes in his staff to meet constantly changing priorities and unpredictable events. There can be no room within the pay office for the 'it is not my job' attitude.

Recruitment

16.12   The recruitment of payroll staff requires the same care as selecting any other employees. All the standard rules of good recruitment practice should be followed. (See 17.5 below and Reference (4) in 16.15 below for an outline of interview procedures and alternatives.) There are, however, some special considerations. It is advisable for payroll managers to have a significant role in the appointment of staff to ensure that:

(*a*)   the appointee fits suitably in with the rest of the office. An efficient but disruptive person is of little benefit to the organisation;

(*b*)   the appointee has either adequate potential for training or already has suitable skills. It is advisable to test these skills at the interview stage. (See Reference (6) in 16.15 below.) A competent payroll technician should be able to do a fairly complicated gross to net calculation in 20 minutes when provided with the relevant documents and a quiet room. The introduction of certificates and diplomas in payroll by payroll organisations, such as the IPPM and Payroll Alliance, provide a measurement by which employers can set standards for new employees;

(*c*)   the appointee has appropriate literary skills as pay technicians should be involved in writing letters and memoranda. The further test of writing a simple business letter may assist a decision on appointment where matters are fairly equal at the interview stage.

Recruitment agencies specialising in finding, selecting and placing payroll staff of all levels, for instance pay technicians, payroll manager, have become established in the last few years. In addition, recognised payroll standards and qualifications are being increasingly requested by both employers and, consequently, recruitment agencies.

Staff training

16.13   Having obtained staff it is desirable to provide training both to enhance performance and to assist motivation. This demonstrates to the staff that they are worth the time and money spent on them. Formal payroll and related training courses are available commercially and many are of high quality. The charges of, perhaps, £250 per delegate per day, or £1,700 for a two-year distance learning course, may appear expensive.

Whatever the charges, any form of training needs to be viewed as an investment for the future for payroll becomes more complex and demanding with each passing year. Care must be taken to ensure that the training is linked to real training needs and managers should not forget their own ability to deliver in-house training where and when it is needed. (see Reference (6) in 16.15 below.)

New entrants to payroll need to be taught how to manually calculate income tax, NICs, SSP and SMP. They must be able to interpret conditions of employment correctly. Progress should be monitored and payroll technicians encouraged to learn quickly. To this end it is practical to nominate one individual, perhaps a section leader, to tutor an individual in the rudiments of payroll.

Care should be taken to ensure this tutor is competent and does not pass on bad working habits or inaccurate practices. Some tests should also be used to assess progress. Access to a procedures manual, covering all aspects of the operation of the payroll office, will be of great help to new employees. (See 18.4 below.) As circumstances change frequently the necessity arises for group tuition. For example, major SSP, SMP, income tax (such as the introduction of self-assessment) or NIC changes need to be conveyed to staff.

Often this is difficult or too large a task on an individual basis. A seminar involving the entire pay office is best for such training. This may involve closing all or part of the pay office for a morning to undertake the training. Whilst this may present difficulties it is usually possible to arrange for such a seminar provided adequate notice of the closure is given to other departments.

A large part of the payroll manager's training role must be to keep himself and his staff abreast of current legislation and modern trends in management and technology. The payroll professional associations can help considerably in this area as well as reading the payroll and related journals. Seminars, courses and training materials on topical issues are offered by several professional and employer's associations as well as commercial organisations. The Contributions Agency of the DSS has also committed resources to providing free seminars and educational visits to employers. These cover SSP, SMP and NICs.

Training in the use of computer systems should also be available. Most suppliers of payroll software offer training courses in the usage of the software which will serve to help achieve maximum benefit of the system. Many of these companies supplement their systems training programme with other payroll related subjects giving a further source of education and development.

One essential aid for staff development, day-to-day administration and proferring advice to other departments is the maintenance of a library covering such matters as payroll legislation and related subjects, for example, social security. (See 18.4 below.)

Additional roles for the payroll administrator

16.14   Pay and benefits represent a major cost and opportunity for most businesses. There is as a result considerable scope for the payroll administrator to use his skills and knowledge to support overall corporate objectives in a pro-active rather than reactive manner. The IPPM has a clearly defined code of conduct and guides to good payroll management practice which may serve to help the payroll practitioner.

Some typical areas where constructive contributions are made:

(*a*)   supporting human resources and other corporate strategies;

(*b*)   the automation of pay and benefits administration (see Chapters 26 to 29 for further details);

(*c*)   providing better management information (see Chapter 19);

(*d*)   use of external services, e.g. security companies and banks;

(*e*)   providing consultancy advice on the design of pay and benefit schemes, particularly on the administrative aspects;

(*f*)   the payment of non-employees such as sub-contractors.

Payroll professional associations can help the payroll administrator fulfil this expanded role. (See Appendix F for their addresses.)

References

16.15   The work of the modern payroll office combines a wide range of various aspects of business and human resource administration. The payroll administrator will be required to assimilate and apply technical, administrative and personnel management skills and knowledge. The area of remuneration continues to receive attention from government, employers, and professional and commercial bodies. Further, 'payroll management' is relatively new. It is still evolving and trying to find its place and role in today's business environment. Accordingly, as there is a growing body of information available, it would be inappropriate to offer here a list of publications. However, it is suggested that any guidance, comprising of books, articles, journals and training courses, etc, which covers administration and the human resource would be worthwhile reading. The following articles, which have appeared in Payroll Manager's Review, contain material relevant to payroll organisation and management.

(1)   Browne D, 'Payslip Advertising', PMR, January 1996.

(2)   'HMV on the Record', PMR, February 1996.

(3)   'Administering a Pensions Payroll', PMR, January 1996.

(4)   Courtis J, 'Interviews and Alternatives', PMR, February 1996.

(5)   'Making Payroll Processes Efficient', PMR, October 1997.

(6)   'Certain in Payroll', Tolley Publishing Co Ltd. Software to assess a candidate's payroll skills and can be used for staff appraisal and training.

17   Management Skills

Scope of this chapter

17.1   Effectiveness as a payroll manager depends on a series of overlapping skills. In this chapter these skills are described and the key issues in each are highlighted.

The ability to lead and influence people are the initial areas of focus. These in turn are underpinned by interpersonal skills. Firstly face-to-face interview situations are examined. This is followed by a discussion on the application of those skills to the most common interview situations; recruitment, appraisal, discipline and grievance interviews.

A section on presentation skills follows next. These include, making oral presentations, writing reports and handling meetings. This leads to a section on the skills of negotiation. The final set of skills relate to the payroll manager's ability to organise and maximise the time that is available. The chapter concludes with a series of key points which underlie good management practice.

Leadership

17.2   An effective leader is someone who:

- defines the direction and general aims of the payroll department;

- decides on the goals by which those general aims will be achieved;

- gains the commitment of staff to achieve those goals;

- pursues those goals with the help and co-operation of staff.

This is a dynamic view of management based on the notion that the key to being an effective payroll manager is in the ability to initiate and implement change.

Influencing people

17.3   A payroll manager will often be in situations where the authority to give instructions or directions is either absent or inappropriate. The ability to influence or persuade others will be critical here. Persuasion is about having well prepared arguments and being able to negotiate. However, it also depends on strong interpersonal skills. Those who are best at influencing others tend to display the following characteristics:

(*a*)   **Trust** — Trusting others is the first step towards being trusted. Like many of the skills described here, there is a strong mutual element. The payroll manager should initiate this. People are most influenced by those who trust them and whom they trust.

(*b*)   **Respect** — Respect is shown in many ways – at its most basic, asking the person their opinion and valuing that opinion are clear demonstrations of respect. The mutual aspect is present strongly here also.

(*c*)   **Knowledge** — Perhaps this could also be described as, 'credibility'. Stated simply, to have influence, others must believe that the person in authority knows what he or she is talking about.

(*d*)   **Good relationship** — Time spent developing good interpersonal relationships within the payroll department can be very valuable. However, this does not mean that the payroll manager has to be liked by everyone. Most managers will have to take unpopular decisions. A good working relationship is based on features such as consistency, looking after staff's interests and fairness.

(*e*)   **Clear instructions** — There are very few people who are satisfied with doing a bad job or who wish to be associated with failure. Those managers who are able to state clearly what they want their staff to do and their expectations of how the job should be done are less likely to have to rely on fear to get a job done properly.

(*f*)   **Constructive feedback** — Real improvement in performance only comes when people are given feedback on whether they have done well or even badly and, most importantly, how they could do better next time. That focus on how to improve and how the manager will help the person improve is a key skill of influencing.

(*g*)   **Timing** — The same message can have a positive or negative reaction depending on whether or nor it is timed properly. Knowing when staff are most receptive to correction or development is a skill all managers should have.

Face-to-face interview skills

17.4   Listed below are the key aspects of face-to-face interview skills.

(*a*)   **Ask open questions** — Open questions usually begin with, 'Who?' 'What?' 'Why?' 'When?' 'Where?' 'Which?' 'How?'. Closed questions usually begin with 'Did you?' 'Could you?' 'Have you?' 'Are you?' 'Will you?'. Open questions will help find out information whereas closed questions tend only to be of value in confirming prior expectations.

(b) **Be particularly careful of asking leading questions** — For example, 'Do you not think . . .?' or 'Have you considered . . .?' or 'Why didn't you . . .?'. Leading questions will result in the answer the manager wants to hear.

(c) **In all interview situations aim to get the truth or the person's genuine opinions** — The interviewer is not there to 'catch the interviewee out'. The purpose is to get the truth. So while questions may be probing or challenging, they should not be aimed at provoking the interviewee.

(d) **Keep questions short** — If the content of the question is long, outline the main details and ask the question at the end. Otherwise the point of the question will be lost by both the interviewee and interviewer.

(e) **Situational questions can be a useful way to test knowledge and are of value, particularly, in selection interviews** — Situational questions are those which ask how the interviewee would handle a particular set of circumstances (or situation). Care should be taken to ensure that the question will help the interviewee to genuinely demonstrate understanding or skill. A simple test of memory or the ability to recite a procedure will not disclose much about what the person would actually do if the situation arose. The best situational questions probe the interviewee on how he or she would handle a clash of priorities.

(f) **Avoid 'double-barrelled' questions** — Doing this will make it more difficult for the interviewee who is genuinely trying to answer the question and easier for the interviewee who is trying to avoid answering.

(g) **Use follow-up questions** — The real skill in asking questions is in the interviewer's response to the answer. The interviewer should listen for vague statements or answers which do not give detail and ask follow-up questions to find out more information. For example, 'You said that you would . . .What experience have you actually had of doing this?' or 'You mentioned good communication as being important. What do you mean by "good communication"?'

(h) **Watch the interviewee as well as listening** — Body language does not tell what the other person is thinking. However, a change in facial expression or posture at a critical moment, or an overreaction to a question, or an air of defensiveness when discussing certain issues, can all indicate an area where an interviewer should ask more questions.

(j) **Demonstrate interest in the interviewee's answers** — An interviewer is likely to get more information if the interviewee believes that he or she wants to hear more.

(k) **Change the tone and atmosphere of an interview as needed** — An interviewer should recognise when an interview is so relaxed that it is not giving what the interviewer needs or when it has become so challenging that the interviewee feels defensive. Being able to respond to that and changing the tone is a key skill.

Selection interviews

17.5   The essence of good selection is:

- having a clear idea of what it is that the person will do;

- having thought through the blend of experience, qualifications and qualities which the successful applicant should have;

- advertising in such a manner as to attract enough suitable candidates to make the selection;

- selecting on the basis of suitability;

- the selection process should be rigorous enough to allow the best candidate to demonstrate his or her suitability. It must also be fair to all candidates and should not be the means by which those selecting humiliate or mistreat the candidates.

Preparation for selection interviewing

17.6   Good interviewing depends on good preparation. A clear definition of the job is critical. Interviewers should be clear on the precise purposes of the job. Why does the organisation need someone to do this work? Arising from that, what are the specific duties and tasks that the post holder will carry out? These can be flexible but should contain enough detail that those carrying out the selection have a good understanding of what the job will entail. This information will then enable them to define the personnel specification.

The personnel specification is the set of essential and desirable skills, qualifications, personal qualities and attitudes which the ideal candidate would have. Enough flexibility should be written into this document to allow for a reasonable judgement to be made about the suitability of the less than ideal candidate.

Interview questions should then be devised. These will help the interviewers focus on the suitability of various candidates, how well they match the personnel specification and, therefore, how good they will be at carrying out the duties.

Preparation should also include a check on the organisation's procedures and approaches to filling vacancies. Where organisations are criticised by external bodies for failing to be fair or give equality of treatment to all candidates, it is often a failure in this respect. However, selecting the right people for the right jobs should be the main motivation.

Keep notes of all interviews – these will help interviewers clarify their thinking and decision making. Be careful of making notes about irrelevant issues. It will be assumed that if interviewers have recorded something in writing that it was part of the decision-making process. In the event of a complaint after a selection decision, notes will be an important record of the thinking of the selection panel. It should be noted that the *Data Protection Act 1998* also includes regulations governing manual records.

Appraisal interviews

17.7   The main purposes of appraisal interviews are as follows:

(*a*)   to let the person know how well their performance is meeting expectations;

(*b*)   to clarify what those expectations are;

(*c*)   to discuss what are the next set of actions needed and how the manager will support the person in carrying them out.

The suggested approach to appraisal is as follows:

(i)   Wherever possible, the feedback should be kept factual. Information on what the employee actually did, said or achieved are of more value than opinions or assumptions about motives.

(ii)   Ask the person for his or her opinion on the factual feedback, particularly if it is negative. A person declaring that his or her own performance is unacceptable is worth any number of pronouncements from the payroll manager.

(iii)   Turn the discussion towards how performance could be made acceptable. Again, staff saying what they could or should do to make things better is more effective than the manager telling them what should be done.

(iv)   Take ownership of the problem. As a rule of thumb, '*You* did well but *we* have a problem'. The same applies to failure. If something did not work as expected, the approach should be, 'What could *we* have done differently?' or 'What will *we* do differently next time?'.

(v)   Ask the person to set targets for improvement. Perfect performance is the aim but improvement is usually a slower, step-by-step process. With many employees the payroll manager's task will be to get them to lower their sights from perfection to something that is more achievable.

(vi)   Most people will be willing to review their behaviour or performance critically when they do not feel under threat or the need to defend themselves.

(vii)   If there are a lot of problems in the person's performance then it is probably better to focus on one or two aspects.

Discussion in an appraisal interview should focus on:

(A)   **Key performance areas** — These will be the tasks or responsibilities from the person's job description which are critical to the job being done well.

(B)   **Team work and communication** — These two areas are important in any organisation in terms of the effectiveness of the whole operation. Unless the individual is working and communicating closely with others, their efforts elsewhere will be less productive.

(C)   **The future** — What changes and/or developments is the payroll department and the whole organisation likely to experience over the foreseeable future? What are the implications of this for the employee?

(D)   **Targets** — Simple, achievable, challenging, measurable, time-bound performance targets focused on key areas of the employee's performance will give the person a clear idea of the payroll manager's expectations and increase motivation.

(E)   **Development** — Few jobs remain the same and few people will be genuinely motivated if they are not being developed or trained.

Disciplinary interviews

17.8   The purpose of a disciplinary interview is not to punish, even though that might be the outcome. The interviewer should be aiming to ascertain the facts of what occurred and to give the person, thought to have committed the 'offence', the opportunity to tell his or her side of the story.

While the full requirements of proof, as needed by a court of law, are not necessary, certain basic requirements of fairness are important. These could be summarised as follows:

(*a*)   Everyone has the right to privacy in having their 'offence' examined. The interview should not be conducted publicly.

(*b*)   Everyone has the right to be accompanied. This is often the trade union representative but may be another person, usually another employee. On the other hand, it is not advisable for a manager to conduct such an interview without also being accompanied. This would normally be another manager, more senior than the interviewee, or a member of the personnel/HR department.

(*c*)   Decisions should not be made in advance of the interview. However damning the evidence, managers must genuinely conduct the interview with an open mind. Apart from fairness, which is the most important issue, any indication that those conducting the interview have made up their minds in advance will not be helpful should the case go to an employment tribunal (previously known as an industrial tribunal).

(*d*)   If possible the interview should be conducted by at least one person who has not been involved in the initial incident.

(*e*)   If the organisation has disciplinary policies and procedures they should be followed. Such procedures are laid down away from the heat of the immediate incident and usually will indicate what those who drew them up believe to be fair. At a more practical level, if there are procedures and they are not followed, it is difficult to demonstrate to an outside body that the organisation has acted fairly.

If the organisation does not have a disciplinary procedure that issue should be addressed.

(*f*)   Staff should not be disciplined for breaching rules which they did not know existed. If that is the case then normally only an informal warning should be issued. In general, the formal disciplinary interview should come at the end of more informal steps to stop the problem from occurring. There are, of course, exceptions to this where the 'offence' is so serious that an informal warning is not adequate.

The same requirement for advance knowledge should apply to the procedure itself. All employees should know in advance what the disciplinary procedures are. An aspect of this is consistency. While each case is individual, it is reasonable to expect that individuals who commit the same 'offence' will be treated in the same way.

(*g*)   The theory of good disciplinary interviewing rests on the assumption that there is a gap between what the manager can reasonably expect and the behaviour and/or working performance of the interviewee. The process of interviewing should be aimed at doing this, as should any action taken as a result of the interview.

In very serious cases, where the misconduct has been 'proved' the above will not apply, there the outcome is dismissal.

(*h*)   It is common to have the option of being able to suspend the employee between the misconduct and the interview, and between the interview and the decision. If this is done, the person should be suspended on full pay. If the person is not paid then it could be argued that the issue has been pre-judged. Be careful also, when suspending, of the implications surrounding that decision. For example, expecting someone to drive home who appears to be intoxicated could be seen as being either negligent or providing proof that the person was not intoxicated.

The structure of a disciplinary interview is quite similar to other types of interview and is summarised in the following paragraphs.

Preparation

17.9   Details of the problem or incident should be investigated prior to the interview. Managers should be clear on the aspects which need to be investigated or discussed during the interview. Preparation of the questions to be asked and the points needed to be answered, is very important if the interview is to be conducted properly.

In addition, managers should be aware of the organisation's policies and procedures, as they relate to this type of situation and of the outcome of any other recent similar cases. This will not determine the decision but may influence it. Managers should also be very aware of the rights of the interviewee and ensure that they are met in full.

Preparation also refers to organising the interview so the interviewee knows when and where the interview will be held and of his or her rights to be accompanied. The two or more managers present also need to decide between them how the interview will be conducted, what each of their roles are, what questions will be asked and what areas need to be covered.

Opening

17.10 The interviewee should be told the nature of the interview. The reasons why the interview is taking place and/or the offence which the interviewee is thought to have committed should be described. The stage which the disciplinary procedure has reached should also be outlined. Normally, the purpose of an initial interview will be investigatory, this should be stated.

Main body

17.11 As in other interviews, this section is taken up mainly with questions and answers. The interviewee should be asked open questions and asked to comment on whether he or she actually did do what he or she is accused of and/or offer any explanation or extenuating circumstances. Answers should be listened to and further follow-up questions asked, as needed, to clarify issues.

In some interviews there is clear evidence that the interviewee has breached the disciplinary code. It is important to remain calm here and ensure that the issue is fully investigated despite the apparent certainty of the outcome.

Decision and action

17.12 In many cases the decision is not reached at the time of the interview. If managers are in any doubt about the circumstances or need to check an aspect, an adjournment should be called. Managers may simply wish to discuss the interview with each other. However, it is necessary, for fairness, that the interviewee is told the decision as quickly as possible.

In some cases the interview will end in an agreement about future actions and behaviour on the part of the interviewee and/or the manager. If this is the case such agreements should be recorded and a copy given to the interviewee as soon as possible. The manager must carry out any agreed actions to retain credibility for the future.

Administrative follow up

17.13   The interviewee must be informed in writing of:

(*a*)   the outcome and any requirements on (or reviews of) his or her future behaviour and/or working performance;

(*b*)   the employee's rights to appeal, the time limits for this and who the appeal should be made to.

For their own purposes, managers should record details of the decisions made and their reasons for making them. This may be separate from, or part of, what is sent to the interviewee.

Sanctions

17.14   The sanctions normally used in misconduct cases include the following.

(*a*)   *Verbal warnings* — These are misnamed since they are recorded, in writing, and the person is given written notice of the warning, the reason for it and how long it will remain on their record (normally eighteen months, after which it will be removed if there has been no recurrence). Verbal warnings are given for minor misconduct. If the same misconduct is repeated within the prescribed period, then the matter moves on to the next stage — which is a written warning.

(*b*)   *Written warnings* — For a repeated minor misconduct, a first written warning is issued. This also records the offence, reasons and the duration of the warning on the person's records (normally, two years). If the offence is repeated again, or if the matter is one of serious misconduct, then a final written warning is issued. The written warning should give details of the offence, duration (usually two years) and make clear that a repeat of the offence will result in dismissal.

(*c*)   *Dismissal* — This is given where there is gross misconduct that has been established in the manner described above in 17.8 (interviews etc.). It can also be given for a less serious offence that has been repeated and where the proper procedure of written warnings has been followed correctly. As with all procedural steps, the employee should be informed, in writing, of the decision, the reasons for it and his or her rights of appeal, how that can be done and who it should be made to.

Where there are mitigating circumstances managers may choose to apply one of the less serious sanctions but the reasons for so doing should be recorded.

The organisation should also clearly define who has the right to apply each level of sanctions. Very often the decision to dismiss can only be taken at the most senior levels and the involvement of someone with personnel knowledge is a requirement at all stages.

Other sanctions and/or punishments are possible, for example demotion is used in some organisations.

In all written communication of decisions to the employee, his or her right to appeal and how this can be done, should be outlined.

Appeals also should be made within a limited time period (usually within five days of the decision being received) and the person should be informed of this period. However, employers seldom adhere rigidly to this particular time limit.

Different types of misconduct are treated separately. In unusual circumstances, the organisation may take a number of offences of different kinds into account (usually minor misconducts) and issue a final written warning.

Being fair to the employee also means that managers and others do not provoke the person. For example, if a person is publicly accused of theft, their subsequent behaviour might be unacceptable normally, but would be excused in the circumstances.

Grievance handling

17.15   Many of the same principles apply to both discipline and grievance handling. These include:

(*a*)   the right to a fair hearing;

(*b*)   privacy and the right to be accompanied, if desired;

(*c*)   speed in responding to the notification of the grievance;

(*d*)   the desirability, where possible, of sorting matters out without recourse to formal procedures;

(*e*)   the existence of formal procedures, when the informal approach has not worked;

(*f*)   the right of appeal to higher management;

(*g*)   confidence in the process and trust that the individual will not be victimised if the grievance is found not to be justified;

(*h*)   the existence of a procedure for dealing with problems that would develop into more serious issues if not addressed.

Oral presentation skills

17.16   The basic requirements for good presentations are the same whatever the format. These are discussed below.

(*a*)   *Clear objectives* — There is a need to be very sure exactly why a presentation is being made, i.e. what does that the payroll manager hope to achieve? Some of the more common objectives are to inform, persuade or get agreement for an action.

(*b*)   *Simplicity* — A clear simple message will have more impact than a complex one, however well it is presented. If the message is of necessity complicated then thought must be given as to how this can be presented in a way that will build the understanding of those receiving it.

(*c*)   *Involvement* — Where possible a presenter should try to involve the 'audience'. Participation can be encouraged by asking questions or leading a discussion.

(*d*)   *Key points and repetition* — A message will seldom be effective if only given once. Thought should be given as to how the message can be repeated or restated in a number of different ways.

(*e*)   *Illustration* — The presenter should try to illustrate all points in some way. People generally absorb information better when there is a visual element. A photograph, a diagram or a prepared slide for an overhead projector, with the key points outlined, are the most used methods.

(*f*)   *Think of the 'audience'* — Although many presentations will have more than one audience, all formal types of communication should be directed at a specific individual or group. Without this focus the presentation will become bland and general.

Information is usually not neutral and it is seldom possible to tell the audience everything. A presenter must be selective in a way that suits the audience and the objectives of the presentation.

(*g*)   *Preparation* — A good presentation is one where the person delivering it has put in the preparation necessary to communicate effectively. Preparation will also help ensure that the presentation is focused on the audience and enhances the possibility of the objectives being met.

Report writing

17.17   Effective reports must be well focused and easily accessible to the 'audience'. Reports have many different formats and purposes and it is difficult to give advice that is specific to each. The points relating to oral presentation skills in 17.16 above also have relevance here.

The length of the report will determine the structure. In general, it is better that the report is short rather than long. For a proposal for action, it is usually difficult to effectively get the message across if the report is longer than two (typed) sides of an A4 page. If the report needs to be longer than this then the summary should be that length or shorter if possible. There should be very compelling reasons why it needs to be longer if it is a proposal for action. However, sometimes a longer report is needed to demonstrate how comprehensive the investigation and analysis has been.

All reports tend to reflect the most basic structure of introduction, main body and conclusion. The content of each of these is discussed below.

Introduction

17.18   The introduction could also be called the summary. It gives a broad overview of what the report contains but does not go into detail. It tells the audience what the subject matter is going to be and acts to engage them. Each sentence in the introduction should be the basis for a paragraph or a section in the main body of the report.

Main body

17.19   The main body is not a single section but a series of sections and/or paragraphs. It is where the main message is passed in detail to the reader and the main arguments are made.

Usually, it will open with a review of the current situation. This could be headed 'Background' or 'Current Situation'. Use could be made of one of the analytic techniques. For example, A SWOT analysis (i.e. an outline of the strengths, weaknesses, opportunities and threats of the current situation). Another popular analytic technique which could be used is the PEST or STEP analysis which is an outline of the general factors effecting a situation under the headings of, 'Political', 'Economic', 'Social' and 'Technological'.

There are other methods and approaches but these tend to be specific to particular topics or areas of work. This analysis starts the argument as to why the action that is going to be recommended later is necessary. Therefore, the decisions that are made here about what to include will be critical to how well the argument is made.

The focus on the current situation can lead to consideration of the future. What is new and/or likely to develop along with possible problems and challenges.

The above often leads on to a section where the problems are specified. In some reports, it is the opportunities that are defined at this stage. Again, the way that this is presented or worded will be significant for the strength with which the recommendations are made later on.

If any research or surveys have been carried out, these usually follow next. Key findings are detailed. If there are additional interesting findings which would be distracting to the main thrust of the report, it is probably better to give these in the Appendix. Enough detail should be given in the main body of the report to make the case. Anything else to be included should be put at the end of the report for those that are interested to read.

If findings have been formally analysed in any way, it may also be of value to give the raw data in the Appendix. If the report is based on a piece of research, then this section together with interpretation and discussion of those results will probably form most of the main body.

Reports on research should comment on the following, the 'experimental design' or 'method' (i.e. what was done and how), 'results' (i.e. the actual findings), 'interpretation' (i.e. the significance or otherwise of particular findings), 'discussion' (i.e. the author's opinions on the significance of the findings), 'further research needed' or 'recommendations'.

Alternatively the report may be focused on someone else's research. Again, the main determining factor as to how this is presented is the relevance to the case that is being made.

Even if the report is a factual one, for example into operations, it would be unusual not to present options for improvement or change. It is in this part of the main body, that the case for options is made. The headings of this section should again reflect the type of report that it is.

Where the report is intended as a description of a change which has already been implemented, the next section often outlines problems encountered and steps taken to overcome them. There is a need to be selective in what is chosen for inclusion. Generally speaking, if the steps taken are unexpected or unusual, then it is in this section that the justification is offered.

Arising out of the evidence or information presented, the next step is to suggest what to do as a result. In a report on action already taken, this section will be on the outcome of that action. However, in most reports the next step is to present proposals or recommendations. These are usually better if they are written in a fairly brief style. With longer recommendations there could be a brief statement, as a heading, followed by an in-depth description of what is being proposed.

If the recommendations have cost or savings implications, these can be laid out as part of this section or separately in a 'financial implications' or 'financial analysis' section. The most difficult aspect of this is when there are a number of possible paths to be taken and the cost will depend on decisions that the person writing the report cannot make.

The options could then be outlined along with the cost and pay-back period of each. Alternatively, the additional costs that will be incurred, or savings made if various options are followed, could be given. Costs may not only be about the financial costs of the recommendations – they can equally be about the time, effort, amount of co-operation and commitment needed to make the proposals happen.

Conclusion

17.20   The conclusion sometimes is used to outline the action that will be taken. However, in most reports this has already been done in the main body. The conclusion, therefore, becomes the means by which the author reinforces the main message or learning points or key recommendations of the report. Like the introduction, it is a summary and no new information or arguments should be made. Whereas the introduction outlines the main issues to be discussed, the conclusion gives an overview of the main conclusions in the opinion of the author.

Report lay out

17.21   Presentation tends to be extremely important in terms of the credibility that the report is given. With a long report, particular consideration of the needs of the reader is required, with the use of page numbers, tables of contents or other means to enable quick location of content. In addition, the following should be adopted.

(*a*)   ***Good spacing and wide margins*** — Plenty of white space makes the text easier to read. Too much white space makes it look as though it lacks content.

(*b*)   ***Bold headings and use of indentation and bullet points*** — These will make the report more accessible for the reader and will help to visually emphasise the main points.

(*c*)   ***Short paragraphs and sentences*** — These also make reading and understanding the report easier.

The writing style will vary with the type of report. For example, a conversational style may not be appropriate in a scientific report. However, it is generally true that the writer should try to 'speak' to the audience in language they can relate to.

The first draft should be corrected for poor expression, ambiguous comments, factual inaccuracies, grammar and spelling. Often this drafting process is about taking out repetition, simplifying and reducing the total amount written.

In addition, the author should ask, does the report achieve the objectives set for it? If not, it may not require a lot of change to make it right – it is often a simple matter of an extra sentence at the end of a section, a point restated to enhance an issue or the removal of an irrelevant or distracting point.

Handling meetings

17.22 The reasons for having meetings could be summarised in so far as they:

- enable information to be passed quickly and problems to be sorted out with all those effected present;

- develop teamwork and co-operation;

- enable co-ordination of effort between individuals, groups and departments;

- maintain a regular forum for views to be expressed and problems aired in order to avoid individuals, groups and departments becoming caught up in their own problems and losing sight of the 'bigger picture';

- help involve staff in developments which effect them.

However, many meetings fail to live up to the above for the following reasons:

- the meeting has no focus or direction, with people wandering off the point and nothing being decided;

- even when decisions are made they are not acted on;

- the meeting starts late and then has to be rushed at the end to cover the content within the time;

- some people hold the meeting back by raising irrelevancies or spending too long discussing minor matters;

- people do not do what they agree to – this brings the whole process into disrepute and those who *do* complete their assigned tasks become de-motivated;

- the same problems arise again and again with the same solutions offered but no progress is ever made.

Understanding the processes of meetings

17.23 Meetings are structured gatherings of people for the purpose of communicating. Certain rules must be followed if they are to be effective. The formal parts of a meeting are in the roles and, arising from those, the procedures. There are three main roles: Chair, Secretary and Member.

The Chair (also called, Chairperson, Chairman, Speaker etc.) is the person who chairs the meeting and has responsibility for:

(*a*)   fixing the date, time and location of the meeting;

(*b*)   deciding the agenda and circulating it to the others attending a reasonable period before the meeting;

(*c*)   setting the timings for the different agenda items and sticking to those;

(*d*)   giving all participants the opportunity to speak, drawing out the quieter members and stopping those who have had their say from dominating the meeting. This is a disciplinary role which requires diplomacy and strength and it can be particularly difficult if the Chair is not the line manager of those at the meeting;

(*e*)   ensuring the meeting starts and finishes on time and that the agenda is followed. However, all participating members have a responsibility to make sure the meeting is successful. The Chair can only create the conditions where this might be possible;

(*f*)   ensuring that all participants receive the minutes of the meeting as soon as is practical after the meeting;

(*g*)   ensuring that decisions are made, tasks are clearly allocated and agreeing what to do with those items where a decision is not possible;

(*h*)   reviewing decisions made at the last meeting and progress made by the members towards doing what they were charged to do. For those in a line management position, this may also take the form of calling those individuals to account, who have not done what they had agreed to do. This may be done at the meeting or, if appropriate, in private afterwards;

(*j*)   the Chair, usually, is also a full participating member of the meeting but this should not be used unfairly to his or her own advantage. In many meetings the Chair is also the line manager of those present and, therefore, it could be expected that he or she would have strong opinions on many issues – that can make it more difficult to be fair in the handling of those who disagree.

The Secretary (sometimes called the 'minute taker') may overlap with that of the role of Chair in smaller meetings. It is preferable that this does not happen as both roles are quite distinct and demanding.

The main role of the Secretary is to record the Minutes of the meeting. The Minutes comprise of a record of all present, the agenda and decisions taken. Some Secretaries try to record the discussion also. However, this is not usually possible so it becomes a very selective record. Unless there are compelling reasons for doing otherwise, it is better to restrict the record to actual decisions made.

At the meeting the Secretary has the role of ensuring that it runs according to plan by alerting the Chair to problems or potential problems.

Outside the meeting the Secretary supports the Chair in organising the meeting. For example, the secretary may be involved in drafting and distributing the agenda, arranging the location and timing of the meeting and refreshments etc. Generally speaking, the Chair has responsibility for seeing decisions about organising the meeting are made and the secretary has responsibility for actually doing or seeing that those decisions are implemented.

The Secretary is also, usually, a full participating member of the meeting. This can be at odds with having to take minutes. The real influence of many Secretaries comes in the writing up of minutes. It is possible to put some 'slant' or 'spin' on to the wording of a decision. Integrity is a very important quality in a Secretary.

The third role is taken by Members. Their main responsibilities are:

(*a*)   arriving on time;

(*b*)   attending to the business of the meeting;

(*c*)   ensuring the meeting is well run (this is the Chair's role, primarily, but every member has some responsibility for it);

(*d*)   reading the Agenda and being prepared to comment on and discuss the items;

(*e*)   not wasting the time of the other members by irrelevant comments or questions. Not wasting the time of other members by taking up the meeting's time on matters which could be sorted out individually;

(*f*)   taking seriously the decisions of the meeting. Ensuring that any tasks allocated are performed, as agreed or informing the Chair of any problems in that regard, as early as possible before the next meeting;

(*g*)   being willing to state a point of view in a constructive manner. A meeting should not degenerate into a competition or a point scoring exercise. Another aspect of this is allowing and encouraging others to have their say even those with whom the person does not agree. The theory of good team work and good meetings is that by bringing problems out into the open better solutions are found;

(*h*)   contributing to the setting of the Agenda for the meeting.

If meetings fail, all the participants lose, so it should be in everyone's interests to make them work. This may seem like an idealised version of reality, but it is only if everyone genuinely tries to work towards this that the meeting is likely to be successful.

Negotiation skills

17.24   There are few managers who do not have to negotiate from time to time. These negotiations may be very formal and involve a number of other people or they may be something that happens very informally, involve only one other person and happen without much warning or opportunity for preparation. The basic principles and approaches are similar whatever the circumstances.

Principles of negotiation

17.25   Modern theories of negotiation emphasise the need to maintain the relationship and for both sides to perceive that they have won. At the very least, there should be a change away from a competitive to a co-operative style of negotiation.

There are many problems in changing from a competitive to a co-operative approach. The principal one being that, in an environment where competitive negotiation has been the accepted approach, any attempt to change towards co-operation appears weak.

In the long term, it is usually possible to change but it takes time to build trust and to get away from the attitude of winning and 'split-the-difference' style bartering. Co-operative negotiation involves trying to get beyond the demands that either side and/or the individual makes in order to address the *needs* or *wants* or *interests* that lie beneath those demands. As long as the focus is on demands, both sides will be pushing apart from each other with the potential for winners and losers.

Trust is the second element in this type of negotiation. This is not easily achieved, particularly if it has not been a feature in the past. However, people do recognise someone who is honest, who does keep their word (or explains why, when they cannot) and someone who does not try to make them look foolish. Unfortunately, if the manager trusts, it will almost certainly result in disappointment in the early stages. Trust takes time to build and will not be given quickly or easily by either side – it is usually a matter of small steps. It must, therefore, be part of the payroll manager's aims and objectives.

From trust comes openness. Openness in setting out, not only the demands, but also the interests that underlie those. This is the most difficult part of this approach. For negotiators to reveal the real interests and needs to the other side leaves them open to what they have revealed being used as bargaining counters.

Knowing the other side's needs can make bargaining positions very powerful. However, without openness there is unlikely to be a reasonable settlement. It would be naive, therefore, to try to move from a competitive negotiating style to an open and trusting one in a single move. But it is only when this transformation has been achieved that negotiation, where both sides can win, will happen.

As a start, management negotiators should not tell any lies or deliberately mislead. Real trust will only exist when both can tell the other side everything and know that they will not use it against them. That may never be realistically possible in some situations – but a move in that direction would be beneficial.

Even where trust is built and co-operation becomes a feature of negotiations, there will still be aspects and issues where there is no meeting point. It is here that the real commitment to co-operative negotiation is demonstrated. A fair or objective means for deciding between competing claims is what is required in these circumstances. This can take a number of forms but should be by reference to a set of principles or a model of resolution which is acceptable to both sides.

The publicity with which a negotiation is conducted will have a bearing on the likelihood of success. Negotiation is about movement and compromise from both sides. If every move is examined and investigated in detail, it becomes very difficult to make any changes. It is usually better if the audience sees the final outcome rather than the process by which that outcome came about.

Where the outside audience has a genuine interest in the outcome, it can be difficult to get a reasonable balance. No communication looks like there are secret deals being done. Balance between these two extremes is needed.

Successful negotiation relies heavily on preparation, this should include:

(a) What is the case or position of the side represented by you and what are the interests which underlie this?

(b) What is the case the 'other side' have or are likely to bring?

(c) What are the strengths and weaknesses of your own case?

(d) What historic factors are at play, there will normally be at least precedent and a perception arising out of past events?

(e) What are your three outcomes?

- What is the ideal outcome for your side?

- What is the least you can settle for?

- What you can realistically expect?

(f) Looked at, as objectively as possible, what are the rights and wrongs of the situation? Try to view the situation from the point of view of the other side.

(g) What are the long term consequences of the various possible outcomes likely to be? Will the short term gains of 'winning' now be worth it in the future?

(*h*)   What are the tactics of the other side likely to be? If they are likely to use unfair or aggressive tactics, what approach can be taken to minimise the effects of that?

(*j*)   What room for manoeuvre is available to you? In addition, what authority to settle do you have? It is difficult to negotiate if the negotiater does not have the authority to settle.

Effective use of time

17.26   Good personal organisation will ensure effective use of the time available to you. The following are some of the critical issues to be considered:

(*a*)   Managers should make realistic goals or targets each day. It is useful for a payroll manager to spend a little time each day writing down a list of things that are hoped to be achieved. This should be in order of importance. Most managers who do this find that they do manage to achieve most of the things on the list.

(*b*)   Payroll managers should have one place where they can record ideas, thoughts or important information.

(*c*)   Targets and deadlines should be set for routine tasks. Performance against these will need to be reviewed regularly. That, in turn, will help to give those tasks the priority that they deserve.

(*d*)   Time management should be checked regularly. Every three to six months a payroll manager should review performance with regards to this.

(*e*)   Effective delegation should be integral to management practice. Delegation is about giving people power while the manager continues to take responsibility for what is done. The approach to delegation needs to be handled with care. Good training coupled with a step-by-step hand over of decision-making power is essential. A proper review procedure needs to be in place from the start.

(*f*)   The payroll manager's job and department should be reviewed regularly in terms of the purposes and tasks. In addition, payroll managers should look at how performance is measured and at how well targets are being achieved within the department.

(*g*)   Perhaps the most important advice about time management relates to how a payroll manager manages those who work in the department. Staff should be looked after, helped to develop in their jobs and care taken that management actions add to their motivation. It will be easier for payroll managers to manage their own time well if those who work for them are productively employed and motivated in what they do.

Key points

17.27   The following are a set of approaches and principles which are the key to good management practice:

(*a*)   measure key areas of performance regularly and accurately and review the results;

(*b*)   recognise, reward and praise those aspects of staff's behaviour that the payroll manager wishes to become the normal;

(*c*)   develop people by giving them training and opportunities to use what they have learned;

(*d*)   plan the first few steps in any change very carefully, the ease or difficulty of these will have an inordinate effect on the likelihood of success;

(*e*)   look behind what people say to how they say it and their non-verbal behaviour. This will be a more accurate gauge of what they are thinking;

(*f*)   being serious about change means being willing to take some action immediately;

(*g*)   motivation for change is related to these four factors:

- fear, of the change and of its consequences;

- current habit and behaviour patterns;

- wanting the change to happen or being convinced that it is necessary;

- feeling in control of the change;

(*h*)   people will support change in those situations where they have a feeling of ownership or involvement;

(*j*)   people work better with deadlines and structure;

(*k*)   a clear, achievable and understood target will increase the chances of success.

References

17.28   A recommended reading list including articles from 'PMR' is listed below.

(1)   Blanchard K, Zigarmi P, Zigarmi D, 'Leadership and the One Minute Manager', Fontana/Collins, 1985

(2)   Dell T, 'How to Motivate People', Kogan Page, 1995

(3)   Boutall T, 'The Good Manager's Guide', Management Charter Initiative, 1997

(4)   Munroe-Faure L, Munroe-Faure M, 'Implementing Total Quality Management', Pitman Publishing, 1992

(5)   Fisher R, Ury W, 'Getting to Yes', Business Books Limited, 1991

(6)   Covey S, 'The Seven Habits of Highly Effective People', Simon and Schuster, 1990

(7)   McCallion P, 'The Competent Manager', PMG Publications, Belfast, 1995.

(8)   'Taking Control of Your Career', PMR, September, 1997

(9)   'Effective Time Management', PMR, October, 1997

(10) 'The Winning Team', PMR, November, 1997

(11) 'Selling Ideas', PMR, April, 1998

(12) 'How to be a Model Manager', PMR, May, 1998

(13) 'Speech Therapy', PMR, July, 1998

(14) 'Successful Staffing', PMR, September, 1998

18 Employee Payroll Procedures

Scope of this chapter

18.1 Employee payroll procedures depend to some extent on the business organisation concerned and, as mentioned elsewhere in this handbook, the payroll function may form part of another function such as personnel or financial administration or employee benefits. However, the actual division of work between various departments should not make too much difference to the overall payroll processes. After all, PAYE, SSP, SMP, normal business practices etc. impose standard requirements, forms and procedures.

Probably the type of business and type of employee has a more significant effect on pay and benefits administration than the details of departmental organisation. Compare for instance the payroll and related administration of an insurance company, with predominantly monthly-paid salaried staff, to a construction or manufacturing company, with many employees paid weekly and possibly still paid in cash. (Chapter 16 (Payroll Organisation) discusses this in more depth.)

A great deal of this handbook concentrates on the theory and practice of payroll administration involving application of law and computers. Although these subjects are of practical value because they influence or govern the process of paying employees, pensioners and other types of payees such as government trainees, this chapter, however, focuses on ordinary employees and outlines the features of the payroll processes that are common to most businesses. It shows how the various specialist topics fit together. It is the combination of the various statutory requirements, like SMP, with an employer's own rules and regulations that makes payroll and related administration so complex.

Chapter 20 (PAYE Procedures) concentrates on the administrative aspects of collecting income tax and NICs and contains extensive coverage of the changes to PAYE imposed by the self-assessment system. Chapter 21 (Pension Payroll Procedures) covers the special requirements of pension scheme beneficiaries. Other chapters, such as Chapter 19 (Payroll Accounting) and Chapter 15 (Voluntary Deductions), in this book contain details which are relevant to employee payroll procedures.

Key points of employee payroll procedures

18.2   The salient features of payroll procedures can be summarised as follows.

(*a*)   Payroll procedures are partially determined by the nature of each business. However, legal requirements and good business practice tend to impose a similar general framework on all businesses.

(*b*)   Strict compliance with all internal and external regulations is essential. This demands a library of up-to-date documentation.

(*c*)   There are two main payroll work cycles, i.e. one every pay period and the other every year.

(*d*)   The status of each new payee must be carefully determined for income tax, NICs and other purposes. Common special cases include government trainees, casual employees, expatriates and students.

(*e*)   Each payee's personal details such as basic pay, tax code, national insurance table letter etc. must be carefully established and recorded.

(*f*)   Pay elements must be classed as subject or not subject to tax, NICs, attachments of earnings orders or pension contributions.

(*g*)   Expenses need particularly careful administration if they are to meet Inland Revenue and DSS requirements.

(*h*)   All pay elements such as SSP, SMP, bonus, profit-related pay, tax, etc. must be carefully calculated according to the relevant rules.

(*j*)   All permanent changes or temporary variations in pay such as overtime must be properly authorised.

(*k*)   PAYE and NICs forms and procedures apply to all employees.

(*l*)   Voluntary deductions and benefits require correct authorisation by the employee.

(*m*)   The regular and timely notification of pay data to the payroll office is essential but often causes problems in practice. The payroll department must make every effort to process late pay data.

(*n*)   The payroll office sometimes shares administration with other departments, such as holiday schemes jointly administered with the personnel department.

(*p*)   There is a vast amount of data which will need to be accumulated by payroll either separately or in conjunction with other departments in respect of benefits in kind, for instance, company cars, for reporting after the end of the tax year.

(*q*)   The payment of wages and salaries and distribution of payslips are major tasks.

(r)   The system of self-assessment for income tax has altered PAYE procedures.

(s)   Today all but the smallest payrolls are computerised. Using information technology requires some modifications to administrative practice.

(t)   Strict security, control and confidentiality procedures are essential with both manual and computer payrolls.

(u)   The primary objective of the payroll function can be summarised as delivery of accurate and punctual net pay.

(v)   The accurate recording and reporting of all dispersals of money on behalf of the organisation is vital, so that the organisation's assets, liabilities and expenditure are properly recorded in the accounts.

Determinant issues of payroll procedures

18.3   Although a general similarity can be found between payroll procedures in all organisations, the details vary enormously. The similarity results from common statutory requirements and common business principles. Some of the main determinant causes of the differences are:

(a)   the pay and benefit rules applicable to the employees;

(b)   the method and frequency of payment, e.g. weekly cash;

(c)   the size, occupational structure and geographical distribution of the workforce;

(d)   the division of responsibility between payroll and other functions such as the cashier's department;

(e)   the level of human resources automation.

These issues are discussed in more depth in Chapter 16 (Payroll Organisation).

Documentation

18.4   An up to date payroll library should exist in each payroll office. Its purpose is to be both an educational and a guidance resource. Effective payroll administration demands as a minimum an up-to-date library of employer and government regulations and guidance. The library should include the following.

(a)   *Guidance* — All relevant government publications, for example, Booklet CWG 2, 'Employer's Guide to PAYE and NICs', are essential in every payroll library. Text books on employment law, taxation etc. can be very useful, too. Further payroll publications are listed in Reference (1) in 18.23 below.

(b) **Legislation** — Copies of the relevant legislation and regulations, for example, '*Income Tax (Employment) Regulations 1993 (SI 1993 No 744)* is also helpful.

(c) **Employer procedures** — Details of the employer's standard terms and conditions of service, together with usually numerous supplements covering such matters as the procedure for claiming expenses, calculating incentive pay, provision of luncheon vouchers and availability and operation of pension schemes, must be held including copies of all appropriate employee handbooks.

(d) **Computer system manuals** — These manuals explain the operation of the specific equipment and payroll software system used. The manuals issued by the software or hardware suppliers should be added to, where necessary, to reflect an organisation's usage or customisation.

(e) **Office procedures** — These procedures cover all the administrative functions such as filing procedures. Details, such as lists of authorised signatures for documenting overtime claims, are held here together with key addresses and telephone numbers, for example, those of BACS Ltd and the local tax office. The procedures should also encompass disaster recovery procedures and relate to computer system processes if appropriate.

Payroll cycles

18.5 There are two main cycles to payroll work which are repeated:

(a) each pay period, for example weekly, when the objective is to pay employees and produce all the associated data reports and documentation including payslips and employment (accounting) costs analyses;

(b) each year, when the purpose is to produce tax year-end forms for the Inland Revenue, the DSS and employees, and perform end of year processing for the employer.

The pay period cycle, which is the same with manual or computer systems, is illustrated in Figure 18A below. A typical weekly payroll cycle is illustrated in more detail in Figure 18B below. In practice, of course, a payroll department may have to manage several of these recurring payroll cycles simultaneously, for example, a weekly manual workers' payroll, a monthly staff payroll, and a monthly pension payroll; and cope with various other tasks, such as paying and/or employee expenses.

In addition to the work involved in the regular payroll cycles there is '*ad hoc*' work such as producing special reports and analyses on demand. This could include, for example, producing a time and attendance record for an individual employee.

Figure 18A

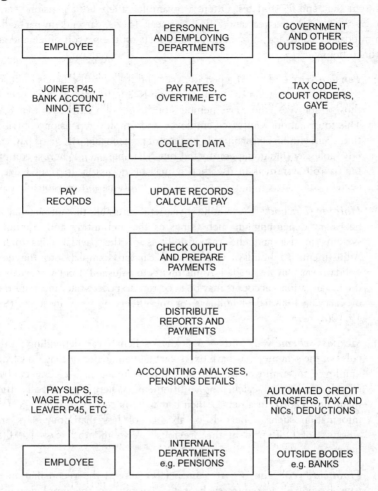

Illustration in outline of the pay period cycle usually repeated every week or month

Figure 18B

MONDAY	Payroll data collected and entered.
TUESDAY	Payroll data collected and entered, payroll processed.
WEDNESDAY	Payroll reports produced and reconciled. Net pay transmitted to BACS Ltd.
THURSDAY	Benefits and expenses data updated.
FRIDAY	Pay day: payslips distributed.

Illustration of a weekly pay cycle

Superimposed on the main payroll cycles are other yearly cycles often with different start and finish dates. Often, as examples, there are a pension year, a holiday year, a sickness year and a financial year. These year ends in particular can impose demands for information and reports on the payroll office and are outlined below.

(i) **Pension year end** — At a pension year end the payroll office is required to supply information to the pension funds' administrators in respect of those employees who were members of the pension scheme in that year. This information comprises employee and employer pension contributions, and employee earnings in respect of pensionable pay, gross pay, and NIC-able pay (including contracted-out NIC-able pay). Where a computer payroll system is in use then it may be necessary to reset to zero certain cumulative values of pension contributions and pensionable pay.

(ii) **Holiday year end** — At a holiday year end a number of routines may be necessary depending on such things as the accounting and computer systems in use and the responsibilities of the payroll department. Adjustments to holidays untaken and carried forward into the next holiday year may be needed. Adjustments to values of holiday accruals in the organisation's accounts may be necessary to reflect the cancellation of or carrying forward of holidays, or the effects of a pay increase. (See 19.10(*a*) below.)

(iii) **Sickness scheme year end** — A sickness scheme year, depending on the rules of the scheme, may have fixed start and end dates or may vary from employee to employee being based, for example, on a rolling twelve-month period for calculating entitlement. Where the payroll office maintains records of absences then it may be necessary to delete certain information such as periods of absence of less than four days and amounts of OSP paid in the previous twelve months. (See 19.10(*b*) below.)

(iv) **Financial year end** — At a financial year end the reconciliation of payroll control accounts, such as the balance on the employee loan accounts, is usual. (See 19.9 below.) Other information to be prepared may include details of directors' earnings and benefits, average numbers of employees, and an accrual for the estimated value of Class 1A NICs, for inclusion in the organisation's statutory accounts. (See 19.10(*c*) and 24.19 below.)

Pay period procedures

18.6 The most fundamental payroll procedures are those associated with each pay period cycle which are outlined in Figures 18A and 18B above. These basic procedures are described in a little more detail below and must be carried out to strict deadlines to meet the payment date.

(*a*)   Collect all the basic data on payees, such as: hours worked, overtime, bonus, holidays; details of starters, leavers and sickness; and 'across-the-board' increases to pay rates or voluntary deductions.

(*b*)   Ascertain the legal and internal status of each payee, for example, a temporary student employed as a warehouse operative ineligible for pension scheme membership. The status of an employee can occasionally change, for instance, a married woman may be widowed or divorced and lose the right to pay reduced rate NICs. Steps should be taken to ensure that the payroll office is notified of all such details.

(*c*)   Obtain authorisation and update the official pay records. Not all of these are computer records, for example, voluntary deduction authorisation forms could be stored in ordinary filing cabinets.

(*d*)   Calculate the various pay elements such as commission on sales (this may be done by another department). Calculate the gross pay of each individual from the various pay elements, such as: basic pay, sick pay, overtime.

(*e*)   Calculate the statutory and voluntary deductions to arrive at the net pay.

(*f*)   Prepare all the various control reports, such as the payroll summary and cash analysis.

(*g*)   Prepare the payslips and management reports.

(*h*)   Prepare payment media, for example, inserting cash in a paypacket.

(*j*)   Deliver net pay, for example, electronic funds transfer via BACS Ltd, and distribute the payslips and the cash wages.

(*k*)   Send remittances covering income tax and NICs to the Inland Revenue within two weeks of the tax month end (or quarter end for small employers).

(*l*)   Distribute management reports and payments to outside organisations, such as union deductions.

(*m*) Follow all security and control procedures at all stages of the payroll cycle.

There are innumerable variations on the above basic themes. Chapter 28 (Selecting a Computer System) details the requirements for computerising the pay period cycle. Chapter 25 (Manual Calculation Methods) explains the PAYE and NICs calculations in some depth. Some important aspects of the pay period cycle are considered in 18.7–18.21 below.

Legal status of the payee

18.7   The status of each payee must be established every pay period because, as explained in Chapter 4 (Payee Status), this can have a significant effect on the payroll process. For example, employees such as mariners and the police are governed by special legislation; 'ordinary' employees in the same group of job titles or grades may belong to different trade unions and enjoy different conditions of employment; company directors have their NICs calculated cumulatively; and those employees over State pensionable age pay no NICs. As well as accurately determining status, all changes in employee status must also be handled correctly, for example, an employee taking late retirement and continuing to work beyond State pensionable age might continue contributing to the pension scheme but ceases to pay NICs.

It is particularly important to establish each pay period the actual status of such people as government trainees and the self-employed, such as those in the construction industry. (See 4.7 above for commentary on various types of non-employee.) Further, employment of an illegal immigrant can lead to the employer being fined on summary conviction.

Collection of basic details

18.8   Basic details of a personal nature, such as address, date of birth, National Insurance number (NINO) and bank account details, must be obtained from the application form or from the employee on commencement of employment.

The information obtained is then used in determining status issues (see 18.7 above). For instance, receipt of Form P45 will indicate which tax code is to be operated for a new employee.

With some computerised systems the payroll department records can be linked with the personnel records allowing both departments access to common employee data so that either duplication of records is avoided or the updating of common data is performed in one system and transferred into the other system. In the case of manual systems this information is often duplicated as both departments need to refer to common details.

Some computerised systems insist on a temporary number where the NINO is missing, for example, TN010168F for a female born on 1 January 1968. Many systems will automatically create a temporary NINO from the DOB and the sex indicator. The use of a temporary NINO is only required at the end of the tax year for entering on Form P14 which is sent to the Inland Revenue or DSS.

Pay rates and scales

18.9   The rate of pay for an employee is normally finalised by the personnel department. The payroll department is then advised of the employee's pay rate and the point on the pay scale if any. Where pay scales are used then it is often the payroll department's responsibility thereafter to ensure the correct rate of pay is paid in accordance with the employee's automatic progression through the scales. This is most common with the public sector. Where neither pay scales nor automatic progression are applicable then the payroll department will require individual notification of any pay rate change. The growing popularity with employers of merit pay awards, performance-related pay and the spread of personal contracts in place of collective bargaining has led to an increase in the need for each pay change to be separately authorised and notified.

In some organisations although there are fixed pay rates and scales, managers often have the discretion to vary an employee's rate of pay. This causes problems for the payroll department when applying pay reviews and in auditing the quality of payroll data.

Contract of employment

18.10 As explained in Chapter 5 (Payroll Law) employees are to be given a written statement of the main terms and conditions of employment (see 5.4 and 5.5 above). This statement is sometimes incorrectly and misleadingly termed a 'contract of employment' but it is in fact a summary of certain features of the contract as required by *ERA 1996, s 1*, and includes, *inter alia*, details of entitlement to pay, hours and holidays. Other terms and conditions, which form part of the contract of employment, may be held elsewhere or are implied.

With notable exceptions, such as guarantee payments in respect of lay-offs from work, periods of notice of termination of employment, or redundancy, etc, the contract of employment, either express or implied, is the source of the terms and conditions of employment which will apply to the employee. (Of course, the contract of employment may provide for better terms than those specified by legislation, for instance enhanced redundancy scheme.) In some instances the contract of employment will refer to the employee handbook for full details of the terms and conditions of employment. Accordingly, any payment, other than those provided for by statute, e.g. SSP, which is not provided for in the contract of employment is likely to require authorisation from someone in whom such authority has been vested. For example, if an employee claims a minimum payment of, say, five hours at flat rate for attending a break-in on a Sunday at the business premises but such payments are only given to a different group of employees, then the payroll administrator may need to refer the claim for authorisation. This does not detract from the normal authorisation required for payments such as overtime.

Pay frequency

18.11 Of all the terms and conditions of employment which affect payroll procedures, the most fundamental effect is that of the pay frequency (or frequencies) at which the employee is paid. This is because it determines the manner and timing of calculations of pay, statutory and voluntary deductions, thereby affecting payroll procedures and the processing schedule.

Provisions in the employee's contract of employment determine their pay frequency (or frequencies). Where the contract is of indefinite length, i.e. not a fixed-term contract, then it is usual for at least one regular pay frequency to be stipulated, whereas with definite length contracts, as for harvest workers, the pay frequency could be irregular or non-existent where the employee is paid once only for the entire job.

The most commonly encountered regular pay frequencies are:

(*a*)   weekly;

(*b*)   calendar monthly;

(*c*)   four-weekly ('lunar' monthly);

(*d*)   fortnightly.

However, an employee may have more than one pay frequency. This may occur, for example, where an annual bonus is to be paid separately to the normal monthly salary or the employee has more than one job with the same or an associated employer. This multiplicity of pay frequencies has implications for the calculation of various pay elements, including Statutory Maternity Pay, and deductions. For example, aggregation of earnings paid at different frequencies may be required for the purposes of calculating NICs.

The day when payment occurs is usually the same in each pay period, such as every Thursday for weekly pay. For calendar monthly, a pay day or date of the month may be specified, for example, the last Thursday in the month or the 28th of the month. (See Reference (2) in 18.23 below for discussion of NIC implications for a pay frequency of monthly but in number of weeks, i.e. 4, 4, 5.)

The longer the pay period the less demands made on the payroll office administration and major savings may be achieved by reducing the pay frequency. (See 16.7 above for a discussion of payroll department staffing levels.)

Three commonly encountered situations which affect payroll procedures are where employees are engaged, their employment is terminated, or their pay frequency alters. In each case, care must be taken to ensure the accuracy of the calculations and delivery of net pay. This often involves intervention by the payroll administrator; for example, where an employee commences employment mid-month but too late for inclusion in that month's payroll, and the first payment of earnings is made in the following month for both months, then some action will be required to ensure that the PAYE income tax and NICs are correctly calculated. (See References (3) and (4) in 18.23 below for discussion of aspects of the procedures for starters and leavers.)

Deferred weeks

18.12   The need to pay an employee weekly in arrear may arise due to time delays in calculating pay, for example, where there are production bonuses and piecework calculations to be performed. The employee may start on the Monday of the first week and will not receive any pay for that week until, for example, the Friday of the second week. This means that, as wages are paid one week in arrears, when an employee leaves, either the final week's pay must be forwarded to the employee or arrangements must be made for the pay to be collected. (See 22.5(*a*) below for a practice where a weekly paid employee leaves.)

A payment can sometimes be a combination of current pay, pay in arrears and pay in advance. A simple example of this is a salaried employee receiving in the middle of a month basic pay for the entire month (i.e. pay in arrears for the first half of the month, and pay in advance for the second half) with overtime pay from the previous month.

Deductions

18.13   Part of setting up the employee's payroll record involves establishing details for the statutory and voluntary deductions. The main requirements are:

(*a*)   the tax code;

(*b*)   pension scheme membership if applicable; and

(*c*)   NIC table letter.

The tax code usually comes from PAYE documents such as the Form P45 or the Form P6. Alternatively the employer uses the Inland Revenue procedures to determine the code to be used, for example where no Form P45 or Form P46 are provided by a new employee.

Pension scheme membership may depend on the employee's job or age. For example, there could be 'manual workers', 'staff' and 'executive' schemes each with their own contribution rules.

The NIC table letter is determined by the employer from the employee's status. For example, an employee who has joined the employer's contracted-out money purchase pension scheme has a table letter of 'F'.

Details of voluntary deductions such as trade union contributions, charitable donations and loan repayments are authorised on the appropriate documents by the employee. (Chapter 15 (Voluntary Deductions) gives an extensive commentary on non-statutory deduction arrangements and authorisation.)

The statutory deductions of income tax, NICs and various types of AEOs, although involving complicated calculations, are at least standardised. The calculations are often facilitated by computational aids such as the Form P11 and tables for tax, NICs and AEOs. PAYE and NICs are advantageously performed by a computer for even small numbers of employees. The details of PAYE and NIC calculations are described in Chapter 25 (Manual Calculation Methods). Attachment of earnings orders stipulate deductions to be made from an employee's pay. (See Chapter 13 (Attachment of Earnings).) Pension contributions including AVCs, unlike ordinary voluntary deductions, are usually deducted from gross pay before income tax is calculated. Chapter 14 (Pension Contributions) discusses the main administrative requirements.

The payroll administrator is often responsible for a large number of voluntary deductions such as savings for an employee share option scheme, repayment of loans, union deductions, medical insurance, etc. Some voluntary deductions are characterised as having balances, i.e. an opening balance, a reducing balance or an increasing balance. Other deductions may require arrears to be maintained and administered with arrears accumulated where the making of the deduction from the employee's pay in a particular pay period is not possible. The recovery of those arrears may then be made in subsequent pay periods in accordance with defined rules, such as by 'double-deduction'. The incidence of arrears and balance type deductions place additional duties on the payroll administrator.

The order in which deductions are processed can also be important when there is insufficient pay to collect the full amount. An employer may prefer deductions for, say, a loan to take preference over sports club deductions.

The duty of reconciling the payroll deduction control accounts in the organisation's ledgers often falls on the payroll administrator. This reconciliation may occur as part of the procedures to be followed prior to the payment of the deduction to outside organisations but also at the financial year-end. (See 19.9 below for commentary on reconciliation of control accounts.)

Build-up to gross

18.14   The process of determining the total pay from the various pay elements is often called 'build-up to gross'. This process is partly manual, i.e. by the payroll administrator, and partly automatic, for example performed by computerised payroll system.

There are various ways in which gross pay is calculated. For some employees there is no such thing as standard pay, for example those on piecework as their rate per piece may vary as they move between different tasks. Also many manual workers are still paid by the hour though the rate remains constant for long periods. Salaried staff are often paid overtime and sometimes expenses through the payroll. There are, of course, employees who are on a flat salary which does not change for months on end.

Where there are large numbers of workers paid on an hourly basis there may be a separate 'time-keeping' function to handle clockcards etc. The increased availability of data collection systems, which are also able to apply conditions of employment to calculate payable hours, has served to offer a highly efficient alternative method to the traditional manual method of 'time-keeping'. These systems are often known as time and attendance systems.

Similarly, extensive piecework or bonus schemes may require a separate department to deal with that part of the build-up to gross calculations. Although many of those may be calculated using alternative computerised systems excluding spreadsheets. Clearly in this environment, carefully co-ordinated administrative procedures are required to ensure that the gross pay is calculated correctly and fed through to the payroll system for the payments to be made on time.

To cope with these various pay methods, and to minimise data entry require-ments, some computer systems were designed as either 'positive' or 'negative' payroll systems. In a 'positive' system the computer must be given input each pay period to calculate the pay of an employee, usually a manual worker. In a 'negative' system the computer continues to pay the employee, for instance, someone who is paid monthly, until the instruction is countermanded.

The complications of modern pay structures and both statutory and opera-tional (e.g. job costing) requirements, however, have caused a modification of the concept of 'positive' and 'negative' systems. Nowadays computer systems classify each pay element as 'temporary' instead of positive and 'permanent' instead of negative. For example, a monthly-paid person would have any overtime pay classified as a temporary pay element only to be paid at time and a half when the overtime hours are input. The salary of such a person would be classified as a permanent pay element, albeit subject to variation by entry of a temporary adjustment because, for example, of unpaid absence, and would continue to be shown at the basic rate until changed.

In addition to being classified as temporary or permanent, each pay element could also be classed under:

(*a*)   taxable or not, e.g. part, none or all of a profit-related payment may be taxable;

(*b*)   NIC-able or not, e.g. a first-aid allowance is NIC-able;

(c)   pensionable or not, e.g. overtime pay is often non-pensionable for salaried workers, but pensionable for manual workers, especially if it is deemed to be contractual;

(d)   attachable or not, e.g. SMP is not attachable earnings for the purpose of calculating AEOs.

With a modern computer system each pay element is usually stored as a parameter containing the above and other details i.e. a formulae to perform specific calculations. The computer uses these parameters primarily for calculating both the gross and net pay. Needless to say these parameters are extensive for a large organisation and must be carefully set up, documented and changed as necessary.

Appendix E provides, at (b) of 'Payroll facilities', notes to requirements for a computerised payroll system.

PAYE and NICs

18.15   A major part of the pay period procedures involve the operation of PAYE income tax and the National Insurance contribution systems. For instance, a Form P11 (deductions working sheet) or computer equivalent is required for most employees.

The PAYE aspects are explained in Chapter 20 (PAYE Procedures) together with the use of the relevant forms and the impact of the self-assessment system. Chapter 12 (National Insurance Contributions) explains aspects of NICs. Chapter 25 (Manual Calculation Methods) explains the effect of PAYE and NICs on pay calculations.

Sickness and maternity

18.16   The administration of sickness and maternity benefits is complex. SSP and OSP often operate in tandem, but SMP is less frequently supplemented by OMP. The basic principle is to establish an employee's entitlement according to the rules of the State and employer's schemes. For instance, a monthly-paid employee would not be entitled to SSP if he had two days' sickness (see 8.5 above for a guide to SSP rules), but may, however, depending on the contract of employment, be entitled to OSP.

Good historical records are required in order to ascertain the entitlement as both State and employer schemes often have qualifying conditions. These usually determine the benefit according to such factors as length of service, previous periods of sickness, earnings history, etc. (see 8.15 for a typical example of OSP rules). Once the entitlement has been determined the State benefit represents a minimum to be paid by the employer through the payroll.

Where OSP and/or OMP is paid it is not unusual to express this entitlement as being at a particular rate of pay less any SSP or SMP or State benefits due or received (State incapacity benefit may be payable by the DSS where there is no SSP entitlement). So, for example, where an employee is entitled to basic pay of £225 per week, expressed as OSP of £45 per day, then SSP of £11.14, if appropriate, may be included in the OSP. Many employers show occupational sick pay, SSP and a SSP offset item on the payslip.

It is not unusual for SSP and SMP details to be calculated by and stored in either another computer system or in a separate module within the payroll system. Often the calculations for SSP occur as part of those performed for entitlement to OSP. The entitlement to SSP and SMP (and OSP and OMP) may sometimes be defined as a number of days and passed into the payroll system where the cash equivalents are calculated. Nor is it unusual for absence to be entered by HR and payroll to process SSP and any adjustments to pay due to reduced or nil OSP entitlement.

Other benefits and expenses

18.17   There are numerous benefits which either directly affect pay in some way, for instance holidays, or are administered by payroll staff, such as luncheon vouchers. Some vouchers, such as those exchangeable for cash, are to be included for National Insurance purposes in pay for the period. The value of tradeable commodities or assets, for example gold bullion, or vouchers exchangeable for such commodities, are to be included for both income tax and National Insurance calculations in the pay for the period. In recent years more and more of these commodities have been caught by legislation so that they are included in pay for tax and National Insurance calculations and, therefore, reduce the potential for tax and National Insurance avoidance by employees.

Benefits may be the responsibility of other departments, for example company cars may be administered by the vehicle fleet manager. Whilst these benefits do not affect pay directly, in most cases it is essential that information is properly collected as it is needed to process end of year PAYE returns and possibly linked to the payment of expenses which may be processed by the payroll department.

These end of year PAYE returns are the Form P9D for the 'lower-paid' and the Form P11D for those earning at a rate of, or more than, £8,500 p.a. where the value of the benefits is included in the £8,500 threshold figure. These forms show details of each employee's expenses and benefits and contributions. (See 20.16 and 20.19 below for further details.) A particular aspect of the provision of each benefit is the essential requirement to fully and accurately record the values in the organisation's accounts. (See Chapter 19 (Payroll Accounting) for a discussion of requirements of payroll accounting.)

Employees' and directors' expenses incurred in the performance of their duties may have to be paid, either by reimbursement to the employees or direct to a third party, for example to a hotel for accommodation. These expenses may be reimbursed or settled by one or more methods, for instance through the payroll, petty cash, or the creditors/purchases ledger, depending on various factors such as an organisation's internal procedures. However, whatever method is used by employers, there are PAYE income tax and NICs implications where:

(*a*)　the payment made by the employer is for more than the expense actually incurred by the employee; or

(*b*)　the expense, or part of it, was not a genuine business expense, e.g. an employee's personal debt; or

(*c*)　the employee has obtained a saving on the home to normal place of work commuting costs when working temporarily away at another place, such as a client's site – see below for further comment.

In some cases, it may be necessary to process parts of expenses through the payroll system in order to calculate the tax and NIC liabilities and report values on the end of year tax return, i.e. Forms P9D or P11D, as appropriate. Exceptions to this include where a valid dispensation is held, an Extra-Statutory Concession applies or a PAYE Settlement Agreement (PSA) operates.

From the start of the 1998/99 tax year, a significant change to the Schedule E rules on the income tax treatment and, to a lesser extent, for the National Insurance treatment, of travel and subsistence expenses came into effect. This change could have a major impact on payroll procedures, perhaps leading to the payroll department being responsible for the processing of all employees' business expenses claims to ensure that the correct treatment occurs for income tax and NICs. All employers are encouraged to review their expenses payments procedures and current dispensations in respect of this new legislation.

(Reference (5) in 18.23 below is a profile of a large employer which operates a highly-developed benefits and expenses control system.)

Besides pension scheme membership and contributions, local payroll and personnel functions may provide pensions advice and liaison on behalf of a central pensions department. Where advice is given care should be taken to ensure that the employer does not fall foul of the *Financial Services Act 1986*.

Chapter 9 (Benefits, Expenses and Termination Payments) outlines the administration of common benefits and expenses. Chapter 10 (Pension Schemes), Chapter 14 (Pension Contributions) and Chapter 21 (Pension Payroll Procedures) give details on how the payroll function links with pension administration.

Flexitime and flexible work practices

18.18   Changes in working practices in many industries are affecting payroll procedures. There has been an increase in part-time working and in flexitime systems such as annualised hours. Home-working is increasingly possible for some workers, as telecommunication systems improve and computers and other hardware become comparatively cheaper to purchase and operate. Flexible working arrangements enable employers to organise employees' hours to meet the peaks and troughs in production schedules.

Different conditions of employment might apply to these groups, for example part-timers may not be eligible for overtime premia until completion of the standard working week. Separate provisions may need to exist for determining sick pay entitlement (both statutory and occupational sick pay) for employees who are employed on annualised hours contracts.

Flexitime systems can operate effectively where fixed time-keeping is not essential, for instance where there are no production lines to be staffed. Employees can then have some discretion in their starting and finishing provided they average a standard number of hours in a working week and are present during a 'core time' which is the main part of the working day. An easy way to handle flexitime is to use an automated time and attendance system. This automatically calculates any surplus or deficit in working hours as 'credits' or 'debits'. Alternatively, employees may be asked to 'log' themselves in and out by signing a register.

There are a number of practical problems involved in the operation of flexitime. Who is responsible for working out the times of logging in and out? Who calculates the credits/debits and advises the employee? Who decides if an employee has to take time off in lieu of credits or is paid overtime and at what rate? If these responsibilities do not belong to the payroll department then it is essential that the payroll department is notified in good time to be able to make any appropriate amendments to the payroll in the correct pay cycle.

The flexitime system needs to be clearly documented before it is implemented so that both the employer and employee are familiar with and understand its rules. These rules need to specify factors such as:

(*a*)   the average hours per working period;

(*b*)   the core time when the employee must be present and the limits of flexibility, e.g. the standard number of hours per working week could be 35 hours and the core time 10.00–12.00 and 14.00–16.00;

(*c*)   starting before 08.00 and finishing after 18.00 without specific authorisation may be prohibited;

(*d*)   credit calculations can be made every week, month or at any other convenient interval;

(*e*)   negative or positive adjustments to pay, overtime payments or time in lieu may be granted according to the credit situation;

(*f*)   medical appointments, sickness and holiday leave can be credited at normal time depending on the rules of the scheme or the terms of the contract of employment.

Many employers use time and attendance systems in the management of flexitime, this information can often be fed into the payroll system to process appropriate payroll adjustments.

Payment

18.19   The delivery of actual payments to employees and the recipients of deductions, such as the Inland Revenue or trade unions, is an essential part of payroll work. In larger organisations, however, it may be the work of the finance department as this achieves the advantages of specialisation, security and segregation of duties. Chapter 22 (Payment Methods) and 23.12 below outline the main payment procedures for employees and the recipients of voluntary deductions. The payment of statutory deductions is covered in 13.17 above and 20.12 below.

Leavers

18.20   Employees may leave for several reasons, the main ones being:

(*a*)   resignation or dismissal;

(*b*)   maternity;

(*c*)   redundancy;

(*d*)   disability;

(*e*)   retirement; or

(*f*)   death.

A primary requirement is the application of PAYE procedures, particularly issuing a Form P45 correctly. (See Chapter 20 (PAYE Procedures) for further details.) Other typical requirements include:

(i)   pro rating final pay if the employee leaves part way through a pay period;

(ii)   forwarding cash payments to employees who leave before their last pay day;

(iii)   SSP procedures (see 8.5 above for details of the SSP1 Form);

(iv)   late payments, e.g. due to a retrospective pay award settled after the employee has left;

(v) recovering outstanding employer loans;

(vi) adjustments for holiday pay, either recovering any excess taken or paying any that is outstanding; and

(vii) AEOs, which may require employers to notify the employee and the originating source (see Chapter 13 (Attachments of Earnings));

(viii) adjusting pay and recovering overpayments where employees are paid in advance and leave before the end of the current pay period.

Further, good controls must be observed to ensure that leaver records are secure and not open to fraudulent access, for example keeping the record open to generate ongoing payments. Many payroll systems will give warning messages where payments to leavers are processed. Often these payments cannot be made without actively changing a flag/indicator on the payroll system.

Tax year end

18.21   The yearly pay cycle consists of:

(*a*) preparing the PAYE Forms, e.g. Forms P14/60 and P11D. (See 20.14 and 20.16 below for further details);

(*b*) preparing annual management and control reports, e.g. employee statistics for company accounts or central government returns by a local authority;

(*c*) preparing manual or computer systems for the new tax year, e.g. preparing new deduction working sheets for a manual payroll or setting up new NIC parameters in a computer; and

(*d*) clearing down any old year-to-date totals in readiness for the new year.

As already mentioned there may be several different year ends, for example the tax year end may not be the same as the employer's financial year end, (see 18.5 above) hence care needs to be taken that the year to date totals for the different year ends are not cleared down erroneously.

Miscellaneous

18.22   There are innumerable miscellaneous responsibilities in a payroll department. A few that are commonly required are listed below.

(*a*) *Clockcards* — Preparing and issuing clockcards, or their electronic equivalent for time and attendance systems, is an on-going task in many organisations. This may be the responsibility of a separate time-keeping section.

(*b*) *Queries, correspondence and liaison* — Payroll departments receive many queries about pay and benefit matters from employees, for example enquiries on when overtime and bonuses can be expected in gross pay and requests for guidance and explanations of implications of self-assessment. Sometimes it will be necessary to write to an employee, such as notifying details of an overpayment. Regular liaison or correspondence with the Inland Revenue and Contributions Agency is an essential part of their work. In addition, there may be requests for advice from general management on such matters as the employee tax refund position during a strike or taxation of expenses and benefits in kind.

Mortgage providers such as building societies may want earnings of employees to be confirmed. There are numerous statistical surveys conducted by government departments which require earnings details, etc. to be supplied by payroll departments. For example, there is an annual earnings survey requiring submission of details for employees who have been selected on the basis of a part of their National Insurance number.

(c)   ***The preparation of management reports*** — These reports can range from simple personnel statistics, for example the number of casual employees last year by department, to complex labour-costing reports. Chapter 19 (Payroll Accounting) gives an outline of aspects of the preparation of costs analyses.

(d)   ***Computer operations and office automation*** — Most payroll departments of any size have a computerised system and other forms of payroll automation such as a word processor. At one extreme the computer system can be a 'batch' system where data is entered on forms which are then batched together and despatched to a computer bureau or department for processing. At the other extreme, the payroll department controls a network of computers and terminals for payroll and allied work such as time and attendance recording.

This spectrum of computer facilities implies an increasing involvement and skill in the general operation of computers. Also, the administrative procedures have to be adjusted for an automated environment, for example when batch system printouts are replaced by VDU screens. Advances in technology can be applied successfully in the payroll department. For example, optical character recognition (OCR) can reduce substantially both manual data entry and levels of input errors. Document image processing (DIP), computer output to laser disc (COLD) and computer output to microfiche (COM) offer methods of both reducing the volumes of reports and documents to be retained on the computer and enhancing retrieval speeds. (See Chapter 26 (Payroll Technology) for further details of automation.)

(e)   ***Controlling and participating in payroll automation*** — The payroll administrator must control the development and maintenance of automated payroll systems. The payroll administrator/manager often participates with computer and management services staff in the design and implementation of such systems, and is the final authority on the quality assurance of these systems, certifying that they meet the specified requirements. Acceptance testing is a particularly important part of the quality assurance role. (See Chapters 26 to 29 for further details.)

(*f*)   *Security and control procedures* — These procedures are essential and have to be of high quality as the payroll service is inherently vulnerable to fraud and errors. (Chapters 23 (Security and Administrative Controls) and 24 (Payroll Audits) give details on this vital area.)

(*g*)   *Overpayment of wages* — Overpayments of wages inevitably occur and raise problems for the payroll administrator as to whether recovery is possible and, if so, the method to be used and the procedures to be followed. The legal position on overpayments and recovery is given in 5.14–5.19 above.

Almost every instance of overpayment of wages has its own set of circumstances which distinguishes it from any other. Where recovery of the overpayment from the employee is possible, then a number of aspects will or may need to be considered, such as the size of the overpayment, whether the recovery will cause hardship for the employee, and the date(s) when the overpayment occurred, for example, in the previous or the current tax year. There are also the effects on industrial relations which may need to be considered. Consultation with the employee, the line manager and usually the personnel officer will be necessary.

The actual recovery of the overpayment can be problematic. It may be acceptable to effect recovery of the gross amount, i.e. before any deductions such as tax and NICs, from the employee's wages. Alternatively, repayment of the net amount, i.e. after PAYE income tax and NICs deductions, whether through or outside the payroll, will involve adjustment of the year to date values of earnings, income tax, and NICs, etc. with attendant reflection in the appropriate remittance to the Collector of Taxes. Where the recovery as a net amount is sought or occurs in a later year the employer will need to seek repayment of the income tax and the NICs from the Inland Revenue and DSS as appropriate. It will then be necessary to provide corrected details of Form P14 and Form P35.

References

18.23   Most of the references in the other chapters are relevant to employee payroll procedures.

(1)   Payroll publications obtainable from Tolley Publishing Co Ltd: Payroll Fact File; Payroll Manager's Review; Payroll, Remuneration and Benefits; Employer's Payroll Health Check.

(2)   'Monthly Earnings Periods', PMR, May 1997.

(3)   'Education or Simplification?', PMR, March 1997.

(4)   'NICs for Starters and Leavers', PMR, January 1997.

(5)   'It's all Under Control', PMR, November 1996.

19 Payroll Accounting

Scope of this chapter

19.1 The modern payroll department plays an important role in the collation, processing and production of financial and management information. This is not surprising as employment costs often constitute the biggest slice of expenditure in organisations. It is usually the case that the organisation requires at least one highly detailed analysis of payroll costs in each pay period. Cost analysis is essential for the measurement of the success of the business, and it can also help as a way of identifying items or areas of costs which may then be the subject of investigation and, perhaps, cost-cutting exercises.

Accounting procedures are an integral element of the payroll function. Other than standard accounting techniques and principles there is, however, no established system for payroll accounting. Every organisation will have developed methods to meet its particular requirements.

This chapter outlines the basic features and principles of payroll accounting, and illustrates them with straightforward examples. Other chapters, such as Chapter 23 (Security and Administrative Controls), Chapter 24 (Payroll Audits) and Chapter 26 (Payroll Technology), are also relevant.

Key points of payroll accounting

19.2 The main aspects can be summarised as follows.

(a) Accurate details of employment costs are necessary for the organisation to meet its statutory obligations, e.g. under the *Companies Act 1985*.

(b) Employment costs are often an organisation's biggest single item of expenditure.

(c) Collation, processing and analysis of employment costs frequently form part of payroll procedures. Post-payroll calculation routines may require further input or processing of costing data.

(d) Recording of some elements of employment costs, e.g. expenses, may be necessary for reporting on end-of-year returns such as Form P11D.

(e)   Payroll costs analysis modules may be either part of the payroll system or a stand-alone system or both. Interfaces between systems may expedite transfer of details.

(f)   Technology, such as computers and data-capture systems, has affected payroll accounting procedures.

(g)   Each organisation has its own accounting requirements which are subject to frequent change. As these impact on the payroll function it is essential that the payroll administrator understands the accounting system and the operational requirements.

(h)   Regular liaison with managers of other departments, such as information technology and finance, is essential.

(j)   The month-ends and the various year-ends of the organisation, such as for the financial year or the holiday year, are periods when additional accounting routines have to be performed.

(k)   The pay frequency may affect payroll accounting procedures.

(l)   General or nominal ledger journals may have to be prepared manually by the payroll administrator where, for instance, there have been manual payments which supplement the payroll.

Impact of information technology

19.3   Computerisation has brought about substantial changes in payroll and accounting practices and procedures. Where previously manual preparation of payroll journals could take days, computerised modules have cut the time to minutes. Up-to-date and accurate management and financial information is generated by, and can be swiftly extracted from, the data held on computerised systems such as payroll and the general or nominal ledger. (For ease of purpose, the term 'general ledger' is used from this point in this chapter.) This means that organisations now have easier access to more and better information on which business decisions can be based. In the past obtaining information on employment costs by manual methods may have been a protracted process and one liable to produce data that was not wholly reliable. The information may have been incomplete and out of date by the time it was received and examined.

The input of payroll data, from timesheets for example, now frequently involves the entry of costing information. The computerised pay record for the employee may hold details of the cost centres and departments in which he normally works, often with the appropriate general ledger codes to which the costs are to be posted. Even voluntary deductions, such as loan repayments, may be given a reference code to facilitate recording in the ledger (see 15.5(b) above). Timesheets may show values of hours worked according to job, department and cost centre, details of which have to be input by the payroll administrator. Various pay elements may have to be held individually on the employees' pay records to enable separate costings for them to be analysed. Reimbursement of business expenses may be made through the payroll, thereby involving analysis according to purpose and to meet taxation require-ments.

General ledger journals can be created by extracting information held on computerised employee pay records. Either the payroll system itself has a costings module that performs the necessary routines or an interface exists to pass the data to another system which then generates the journals. The values and codings of additional manual payments or of cancelled payments can be included either automatically in the main payroll journal or separately.

Structure of general ledger codes

19.4   General ledger codes are often composites of cost centre, department and account codes. Sometimes a further division is achieved by the introduc-tion of sub-analysis or project codes. The length of ledger codes will vary according to business requirements. However, the longer the full code the greater the number of key depressions that may be required during data entry.

In view of the possible length of full ledger codes and the impact on payroll data entry, it is not unusual to find that ledger codes are abbreviated when used in payroll either on the computerised employee pay record or within tempo-rary pay data or both. Where such abbreviation occurs, the costings analysis programs may contain instructions which will generate the full ledger codes prior to transfer to the general ledger.

If there is more than one code on the employee's computerised pay record, for example some of his time is attributed to one department and the balance to another, then it is usual to enter percentage values to a total of 100 per cent against these codes. (See Example 4 in 19.8 below.) Percentage values are used in costings analysis programs to apportion employment costs to the codes.

Ledger codes will usually be designated either as expenditure or balance sheet codes. Occasionally they may be designated as a 'budget' code. Budget codes are used only for comparative purposes and do not accept postings of actual values.

Some payroll costs may be coded directly to balance sheet codes; examples include research and development costs for a new product or the employment costs of an employee in the maintenance department constructing a wall in a part of the premises (i.e. adding to the value of a fixed asset). Balance sheet codes are sometimes also used in job costing (see 19.6 below), for instance the creation of debtor accounts, but almost always for posting gross-to-net items such as income tax, NICs, loans, AEOs, net pay, etc.

Sub-analysis (or project codes) are sometimes appended to ledger codes for the purpose of identifying for whom or why the cost was incurred. Thus, a full ledger code may have any number of sub-analysis codes by which the year-to-date value of that code can be analysed. A particular usage of sub-analysis codes is for accumulating data for individual employees for the purpose of completion of Forms P9D and P11D after the end of the tax year.

Costs analysis methods

19.5   The purpose of a costs analysis system, whether manual, computerised or both, is the preparation and extraction of financial and management information. Financial information requirements are concerned with the accurate recording and reporting of transactions, such as purchases of assets and materials, sales and employment costs. Management information requirements are concerned with the analysis of data so as to project and measure the success of new or existing parts of the business. The provision of accurate employment costs is, therefore, an important element in supplying data which is used in the preparation of financial and management information.

Details of employment costs may be presented in any number of ways, and it is rare to find two organisations with the same information requirements. The following, however, are common to most:

- an analysis of the elements of gross pay ('up to gross'); and

- an analysis of gross-to-net pay.

The analysis of the make-up of gross pay is achieved in the main by four methods and it is not unusual to find all of these methods in use in some organisations, sometimes within a single payroll:

- by budgetary costings analysis;

- by job costings analysis;

- by individual analysis of certain pay elements; and

- by sub-analysis and project code analysis.

Often the work of coding payroll elements, cash amounts and hours falls on the payroll department. The work is either accommodated in data-entry routines before the payroll is processed or as a separate procedure after the pay calculations. The former has the advantage, perhaps, of reducing the overall amount of input but has the disadvantage of increasing the level of work (which is usually time critical) in the time available prior to the pay calculations.

Budgetary costings are those coded to the general ledger codes which may have been set up with estimates of employment costs as part of the annual budget preparation exercise performed by almost all organisations prior to the start of each financial year. Accordingly, the posting of payroll costs to these ledger codes provides a method for organisations to compare actual costs against the budgeted values. Examples 4, 4.1 and 4.2 at 19.8 below illustrate the principles of budgetary costing.

Job costings are used where values are to be coded to ledger codes which have been set up to monitor and account for the costs of specific jobs. Sometimes these job costs are then used as part of the charges raised on third parties, for example maintenance work on Council owned properties to be recharged and invoiced to the tenant. The use of job costing, either by payroll input or from an automated data collection system, such as from production lines in a manufacturing environment, allows organisations to monitor and account for time and costs incurred on individual contracts. Example 5 at 19.8 below is an illustration of the principles of job costing.

Some pay elements, such as group bonuses, may need to be coded to particular ledger codes regardless of where the employee's costs are normally coded. Indeed there may be specific ledger account codes set up in the employee's cost centre or department code. Examples of this are separate ledger codes to accumulate expenditure in respect of employer's NICs and pension contributions, and overtime costs.

Basic principles

19.6   Every action and transaction that carries a financial cost for the organisation will have to be properly recorded and the appropriate entries passed into the organisation's general ledger. Thus, the basic employment costs of, for example, salary, overtime and expenses payments, must be fully and correctly recorded and reported.

Some costs, which are referred to as 'on-costs', such as employer's National Insurance and pension contributions, will also need to be treated in the same way. Other costs, such as those incurred in the provision of meal vouchers or medical insurance, which usually do not form part of the payroll calculations, will have to be properly recorded and reported in the general ledger.

The general ledger code of accounts is usually carefully structured by the organisation so that it meets its financial and management information requirements. Much attention is given to the structuring of the general ledger codes which are used to identify items of expenditure and income, assets and liabilities. Expenditure and income determine the success of the business, e.g. the profit and loss account, whereas assets and liabilities comprise the organisation's balance sheet.

Payroll processing generates entries that will be used in measuring the levels of success and viability of the business. The vast majority of payroll-generated entries are to the expenditure accounts, a few may be to the income accounts, and there will always be entries to the balance sheet accounts. (See 19.4 above for a discussion of general ledger coding structures and the effect on payroll processing.)

Certain general ledger codes are designated as control accounts. These are often balance sheet account codes, and form part of the financial controls applied in the maintenance of the ledger. The accounts serve several purposes, such as identifying liabilities, e.g. unpaid wages, and discrepancies that have occurred in the posting of entries.

The posting of entries to the general ledger is made via journals, prepared manually or by computer program, and every entry in the journal should be given an identifying reference, e.g. 'April Tax Week 2'. This makes it easier to locate records and reconcile the postings to, and the balance on, the account codes.

Each journal contains debit and credit entries that must balance in total, and meet the double-entry principle on which all accounting systems operate. This basic and fundamental principle is demonstrated in the following example.

Example 1

Sydney receives £140 gross pay in the month, from which there are no deductions.

		Dr	Cr
Cost centre	(GL code A123)	£140	
Wages control	(GL code DD88)		£140

In this basic example, Sydney's gross pay of £140 has been debited to the cost centre which is identified in the general ledger (GL) as A123. The corresponding credit entry is to the wages control account DD88. When the payment of Sydney's net pay is effected, further entries to the general ledger need to be made as follows in Example 1.1 below.

Example 1.1

		Dr	Cr
Wages control	(GL Code DD88)	£140	
Bank	(GL Code DD99)		£140

There are variations to this example of basic payroll accounting. For instance, the entries to the wages control account could be omitted. The general ledger entries would then be as follows in Example 1.2 below.

Example 1.2

		Dr	Cr
Cost centre	(A123)	£140	
Bank	(DD99)		£140

This method may be suitable if, for instance, the organisation's accounting system is uncomplicated or if wages are paid out of petty cash. Another more commonly found variation is shown in Example 1.3 below. A separate control account exists for the purposes of recording net pay.

Example 1.3

		Dr	Cr
Cost centre	(A123)	£140	
Net pay	(DD91)		£140
Net pay	(DD91)	£140	
Bank	(DD99)		£140

The first set of entries debiting the cost centre and crediting the net pay control account may have been created from the payroll system records, e.g. by a costing analysis module, and passed into the general ledger. The second set of entries may have been created by the cashier. An advantage in creating a separate account for net pay is that the employer's net pay liability can be easily identified in the general ledger. A credit balance on the account may indicate that the employer has not fully paid his employees, whereas a debit balance may indicate a discrepancy.

The above simple example shows that payroll entries to the general ledger fall into two distinct areas: the postings of employment costs (debits, usually) and the balancing liabilities (credits, usually). These two areas are referred to here as 'up-to-gross' and 'gross-to-net'. It is possible, as shown in Example 1.3 above, either to combine in one journal the 'up-to-gross' and 'gross-to-net' postings or to have separate journals for each.

Gross-to-net

19.7   The term 'gross-to-net' implies that the journal entries are concerned only with the posting to the general ledger of the amounts of net pay, deductions from pay and other items. Almost invariably these entries will be credit entries, made either to individual accounts or to some suspense account. Usually, the corresponding debit entries will be to either the expenditure account codes or to a wages (or salaries) control account. (See the example in 19.6 above.)

Separate balance sheet accounts for net pay and deductions will assist in the maintenance of financial controls, particularly when reconciliation of these accounts is required, such as at the end of the financial year. (Reconciliation of payroll-related ledger accounts is discussed in 19.9 below.) If, however, a large number of voluntary deductions are operated through the payroll or there is a limit to the number of balance sheet account codes which can be used, then two or more payroll deductions will have to be posted to the same ledger code.

Ideally, separate codes for net pay, PAYE income tax, NICs and for contributions to pension funds should be created. Consideration can also be given to setting up an account code to hold the recoverable values of statutory maternity pay and statutory sick pay, although such amounts could be posted directly to the NI account.

Usually, only total values are posted to the ledger. For example, the sum of all employees' pension contributions rather than individual amounts for each employee is posted. It may be worthwhile, however, in some cases, for example loan repayments, for the individual amounts to be passed into the ledger to assist in reconciliation routines, but this should be carefully considered as too many entries in an account may be obstructive rather than helpful.

The following is an example of a gross-to-net journal. The employees' subscriptions to more than one trade union have been posted to the same general ledger account as total values for each trade union.

Example 2

Account name	GL code	Reference	Dr £	Cr £
Salary control	BS0001	December 98	154,950.03	
Net pay	BS0050	December 98		72,625.78
PAYE income tax	BS0051	December 98		29,629.63
NICs	BS0052	December 98		23,464.32
NICs	BS0052	December 98 SMP	212.34	
Pension fund 1	BS0054	December 98		6,138.76
Pension fund 1	BS0054	December 98		17,052.11
Pension fund 2	BS0054	December 98		803.95
Pension fund 2	BS0054	December 98		2,090.27
AVCs	BS0055	December 98		1,200.00
Trade unions	BS0060	December 98		385.70
Trade unions	BS0060	December 98		521.85
Medical insurance	BS0062	December 98		850.00
Loans	BS0063	December 98 700259		150.00
Loans	BS0063	December 98 03518		250.00
			155,162.37	155,162.37

In this example, the values posted to the NI account are total NICs, comprising employees' and employer's contributions, and an amount in respect of SMP which is recoverable (i.e. £230.80 × 92%). No separate control account is held here for SMP. (Examples 8, 8.1 and 8.2 below utilise a separate control account for SMP.)

The four entries for the two pension funds show employees' and employer's contributions. The entries to the loans account show the payroll numbers of the two employees making repayments.

In the case of medical insurance, only the total of the employees' payments is shown. A more sophisticated general ledger system could hold separate sub-accounts for each employee as a method of providing further analysis of the main account code. In this way, each employee's payment would be passed separately into the ledger although only one total entry appears in the main account.

Up-to-gross

19.8   The term 'up-to-gross' is used here to describe all components of earnings, including basic wages, overtime, occupational and statutory sick pay, statutory maternity pay, bonuses, shift premia – in fact anything which is processed through the payroll. It includes on-costs (see 19.6 above), such as employer's NICs. These entries will almost invariably be debit entries made to expenditure accounts. The corresponding credit entry or entries will be either to a wages (or salary) control account or to the net pay and deduction accounts. (See 19.7 above.)

The structure of the account codes in the organisation's general ledger (see 19.4 above) will determine the degree of analysis of gross pay that is required. Separate accounts may have been set up to hold, for example, basic pay, overtime pay, holiday pay, sick pay, and employer's NICs and pension contributions.

The following is an example of an up-to-gross journal.

Example 3

Account name	GL code	Reference	Dr £	Cr £
Salary/basic	EXAA1000	May 98	16,666.67	
Overtime	EXAA1001	May 98	330.85	
Employer's NICs	EXAA1003	May 98	1,538.28	
Employer's pension	EXAA1005	May 98	2,178.95	
Sick pay	EXAA1008	May 98	98.19	
Salary control account	BSAA5501	May 98		20,812.94
			20,812.94	20,812.94

Costing analyses can be much more complex than this simple example. For instance, if an employee works for several cost centres during the period his costs may need to be apportioned between them. This may be dealt with automatically through the costs analysis module by accessing details held on the employee's computerised pay record or on a timesheet record which was entered in the period. In the former case, the apportionment continues to apply until the employee's pay record is amended. In the latter case, the apportionment is temporary and applies only for the one period but is actioned by the analysis module before the pay record details.

In Example 4 below, the employee works for several departments. His computerised pay record holds details which apportion his pay accordingly.

Example 4

Steven's pay record shows that 40% of his costs are to be coded to cost centre EX01, 25% to cost centre EX18, and the balance of 35% to cost centre EX61. In May 1998, the total payroll costs for him are £2,200, comprising £2,000 basic pay and £200 employer's NICs. The journal debit entries to be generated are as follows.

Account name	GL code	Dr £
Basic pay	EX010001	800.00
Employer's NICs	EX010005	80.00
Basic pay	EX180001	500.00
Employer's NICs	EX180005	50.00
Basic pay	EX610001	700.00
Employer's NICs	EX610005	70.00
		2,200.00

If Steven had been paid £325.00 in that month for overtime performed for another department (cost centre EX23), thereby increasing the amount of employer's NICs to £232.50, the analysis of the employment costs might appear as follows.

Example 4.1

Account name	GL code	Dr £
Basic pay	EX010001	800.00
Employer's NICs	EX010005	80.00
Basic pay	EX180001	500.00
Employer's NICs	EX180005	50.00
Overtime	EX230002	325.00
Employer's NICs	EX230005	32.50
Basic pay	EX610001	700.00
Employer's NICs	EX610005	70.00
		2,557.50

This variation of the initial example shows that the additional employer's NICs incurred because of the overtime payment have been fully coded to cost centre EX23. The amount of employer's NICs to be charged were separately calculated and then the percentages held on Steven's pay record applied to the remainder.

To calculate the amount of NICs to be charged to EX23, the employer's NICs (£232.50) were divided by the total employment costs (£2,325) which were liable to NICs: £232.50 ÷ £2,325. This produces a value of 0.1, which is then multiplied with Steven's overtime: £325 × 0.1 = £32.50. This amount is then deducted from the value of the employer's NICs: £232.50 − £32.50 = £200.00, which is then used in the percentage-based apportionment. If this principle is not adopted, then the additional employer's NICs incurred on the overtime would have been charged proportionately to cost centres EX01, EX18 and EX61.

There may, of course, be situations where it is decided that on-cost elements such as employer's NICs, are to be charged to the employee's 'home' cost centre(s). An example may be payment of annual bonus, where only the bonus amounts and not the on-costs are to be charged to a specific cost centre.

If Steven had worked in another department for part of his normal time, then the principle outlined above would still hold good. For instance, £300 of Steven's salary in May 1998 is to be recharged to cost centre EX10. The journal entries would then appear as follows in Example 4.2 below.

Example 4.2

Account name	GL code	Dr £
Basic pay	EX010001	680.00
Employer's NICs	EX010005	68.00
Basic pay	EX100001	300.00
Employer's NICs	EX100005	30.00
Basic pay	EX180001	425.00
Employer's NICs	EX180005	42.50
Overtime	EX230002	325.00
Employer's NICs	EX230005	32.50
Basic pay	EX610001	595.00
Employer's NICs	EX610005	59.50
		2,557.50

The above examples have been based on budgetary costing, but different cost analysis principles apply where job costing is involved. (For a discussion of budgetary and job costing, see 19.5 above.)

Where an employee is engaged in work that requires analysis by jobs, for example as a property maintenance worker for a local authority, then it is usual for his employment costs in the pay period to be recharged to the general ledger codes which have been set up for that purpose. For instance, one or more codes may have been set up to record the costs of repainting the external woodwork of properties owned by a local authority. The time spent on each job is analysed and the employment costs apportioned accordingly. Example 5 below illustrates the entries and principles required for job costing.

Example 5

Sandra, a decorator, has gross pay in the week of £185.65. The total on-costs are £37.13, comprising £13.00 and £24.13 in employer's NICs and pension contributions. Sandra worked on six jobs in the week for a total of 37.50 hours.

Account name	GL code	Reference	Dr £	Cr £
Job no. 19,612	ZZ19B13	Wk 10	48.42	
Job no. 19,710	ZZ19C83	Wk 10	19.48	
Job no. 19,711	ZZ19C84	Wk 10	38.20	
Job no. 19,760	ZZ19D20	Wk 10	64.46	
Job no. 19,872	ZZ19G85	Wk 10	29.11	
Job no. 19,873	ZZ19G86	Wk 10	23.11	
Direct labour control	ZZ01A56	Wk 10		222.78
			222.78	222.78

The apportioning of employment costs has been achieved by the use of hours: 8.15, 3.28, 6.43, 10.85, 4.90 and 3.89, respectively. The total cost of £222.78 is divided by the total hours of 37.50 to arrive at a multiplicand of £5.9408 which is then multiplied against the hours for each job. The exception is the last job, where only the remainder of the uncharged costs is allocated in full. The credit to the direct labour control account would be a contra entry to the debit made to it by the main payroll journal. A more complex example might involve, for example, sick pay, holiday pay, incentive payments, unchargeable (lost) time and a predetermined multiplicand. Separate accounts may have been set up for sick pay and holiday pay, perhaps as part of the budgeting process. Unchargeable costs may have to be absorbed as unplanned expenditure by the organisation. Where a standard hourly rate is used for recharging a surplus (profit) may arise.

Reconciliation of payroll control accounts

19.9 The task of reconciling the balances on the payroll control accounts in the organisation's general ledger will often fall to the staff of the payroll department. An advantage of this is that, as the payroll is the source of most of the journal entries on these accounts, the payroll staff are better placed to check details, make corrections and explain the balance.

It is good practice for the payroll control accounts to be regularly reconciled. This may be every month when payments, for example settlement of PAYE income tax and NICs, have to be made or could be at longer intervals. Ideally, the interval should not be too long as recollection of events by the payroll and accounts office staff will fade and, moreover, there will be a greater volume of entries to examine.

At the very least, all the payroll control accounts should be reconciled annually. In some cases, this may be at the end of the financial year when certain items of liability have to be reported in the statutory accounts that have to be completed and filed by almost every organisation. In others it may be after the end of the PAYE tax year prior to the finalisation of details on the end-of-year returns, Forms P14 and P35.

It may be, of course, that such is the extent and scope of the operational processing controls in the payroll and the ledger, that devoting resources to reconciliation work is considered to be unnecessary. Each organisation and payroll administrator will have to decide policy.

In reconciling certain control accounts, the payroll administrator may find that, as a preliminary step, it is helpful to reconcile balances and values held on the employees' pay records. For example, normally the sum of loan balances on the employees' pay records should equal the balance on the control account at the end of the period in question. This is because deductions made from employees' wages will have reduced the outstanding amounts on their loans, and appropriate entries will have been made to the control account via the payroll journals. The same principle can be applied to all the statutory and voluntary deductions. In the case of those deductions which require a remittance to a third party, such as pension contributions, reconciliation of the balances and values held on the employees' master files can form part of the verification and preparation of the payment.

In performing a reconciliation of the balances on the employees' pay records, the payroll administrator will need to be alert to certain situations which may cause difficulties. For example, if there are both monthly and weekly payrolls, transfers of pay records between the two may occur, such as when a weekly paid employee is promoted and is placed on the monthly payroll. This could have the effect of reducing the balances and values on the original payroll but increasing them on the receiving payroll. Where, however, the pay record on the original payroll is retained until the end of the tax year because the two payrolls have separate PAYE references, the values of PAYE income tax and NICs, and probably other deductions, will be retained.

Example 6 below illustrates the principle of reconciliation of balances and values on employee pay records.

Example 6

National Insurance contributions			£
Balance as at end of September 1998 b/fwd			6,123,152.83
Less, transfer of S Stanley to monthly payroll			(1,601.35)
			6,121,551.48
Add, payroll for tax week	27	246,815.29	
	28	215,731.55	
	29	223,215.70	
	30	229,561.79	
Manual payments week	28	220.19	
	29	176.23	
Less, cancelled payment week	28	(325.88)	
			915,394.87
Total to date at end of October 1998			7,036,946.35
Total of NICs on employee pay records c/fwd (see computer listing)			7,038,662.39

The difference of £1,716.04 is explained as follows:

(1)   The adjustments to S Smith's (pay no. 65198) pay record in respect of cancelled payment and manual payment (see tax week 28 entries) have not been made. Changes to employee's master file record are being actioned in tax week 32. Difference = (£105.69).

(2)   S Stanley's (pay no. 09361) pay record has not been deleted from the weekly payroll. This was actioned in week 31. Difference = (£1,601.35).

(3)   Transposition of figures occurred when details of a manual payment for S Symon (pay no. 44316) in tax week 29 were input: £67.83 input as £76.83. Correction to employee pay record being actioned in tax week 32. Difference = (£9.00).

A reconciliation like the one shown above serves only to verify the values held on the employees' pay records. Further work is necessary to reconcile the balance on the NI control account and to establish the amount of NICs to be remitted to the Collector of Taxes. The following example illustrates the reconciliation of the control account using the details in Example 6.

Example 7

NIC control account 10AA95			Dr £	Cr £
Balance b/fwd				1,570,348.12
Weekly payroll	tw 27	Jnl 6801		246,815.29
Corrective entry (see Jnl 5318)		Jnl 6575		900.00
Weekly payroll	tw 28	Jnl 6802		215,731.55
Monthly manual payment:	August	Jnl 6723		148.79
Accrual for Class 1A NICs		Jnl S100		6,800.00
Cheque no. 491813		Jnl 6413	1,530,596.91	
Weekly payroll	tw 29	Jnl 6803		223,215.70
Monthly payroll	October	Jnl 7019		518,600.82
Weekly payroll	tw 30	Jnl 6804		229,561.79
Petty cash		Jnl 6972		23.68
Weekly payroll	tw 28	Jnl 7012		220.19
Cancelled payment	tw 28	Jnl 7013	325.88	
			1,530,922.79	3,012,365.93
Balance c/fwd				1,481,443.14

This balance is explained as follows:
Journals entries to come:
(1) Corrective journal in respect of Jnl 6972: 23.68
(2) Journal for manual payment in tax week 29, posted in October : (176.23)
(3) Accrued Class 1A NIC c/fwd: 47,600.00
(4) Cheque no. 493068: 1,433,995.69
Balance per ledger: £1,481,443.14

In the above example, although the NI control account shows a credit balance of £1,481,443.14, the actual remittance to the Collector of Taxes settles the employer's true liability, which is the sum of the NICs from the weekly and monthly payrolls for the preceding month. Class 1A NICs are not included in the remittance as settlement is required annually. The accrual and treatment of Class 1A NICs and recovery of SMP and SSP is discussed briefly in 19.10 below.

Miscellaneous issues

19.10   There are a number of other issues that may affect payroll accounting procedures, and will be encountered in most organisations. In some cases, it is a question of accruing for a future liability, such as holiday pay, in others it is a question of how the particular employment cost item should be recorded in the organisation's accounts. Some of the most commonly found issues are outlined below, with suggestions on how they may be treated.

(a)   *Annual holiday pay* — There are several aspects to the accounting treatment of annual holiday pay. These concern how actual payment of holiday pay is to be shown in the ledger, and how the organisation is going to identify and record the ongoing value of liability for untaken holidays. Some employers may simply ignore the issue, perhaps on the basis that the sums involved are comparatively insignificant, or treat it as an employment on-cost.

If the actual costs of holiday pay are to be recorded in the ledger, there may be an effect upon payroll processing. Data-entry routines may be affected, as the value of holiday pay may need to be entered as a separate pay item in each pay period. This value may be a cash amount or a number of hours or days which then generates the appropriate amount of pay. Alternatively, the values of holidays may be calculated by the costs analysis program as a percentage of gross payroll costs in the pay period or by using information obtained from another source, such as a time and attendance system, job costing timesheets or perhaps the absence monitoring system operated by the personnel department.

A further aspect of holiday pay is the requirement to make accruals in the general ledger for the value of untaken holiday pay. The contract of employment determines how and when an employee is entitled to holidays. It is common for a number of days to be 'earned' for every complete month of employment. When an employee leaves he may receive payment for the untaken holidays. Less often, employees are sometimes allowed to carry forward a number of untaken holidays from one year to the next. One situation encountered by almost every employer, is a pay rise awarded to employees which increases the value of their untaken holidays. Occasionally, employees are transferred internally between departments and carry forward untaken holidays which, it could be argued, when taken should be charged to the original department. A value of on-costs may have to be built into the holiday pay accounting entries. All these situations have liability implications for the employer and may have to be handled by a holiday pay accounting system.

Whether or not the entries, if any, in the general ledger in respect of holiday pay are made by the payroll department, almost invariably they will be based at least in part on data held by this department. Data may comprise, for example, details of individual or average rates of pay, numbers of employees by cost centre and department and values of holidays taken or untaken.

(b)   **Sick pay** — The accounting treatment of sick pay in the ledger has some similarities to that of holiday pay. Some organisations will choose to ignore it for accounting purposes, whereas others will wish to know precisely how much it is costing the business.

A few employers will be eligible to recover a portion of SSP paid in a month (see 8.7 above) and will have to decide how the sum involved will be coded in the ledger. It may be that the sum will have to be credited either proportionately to the cost centres of the employees who were paid SSP in the period or in full to a general income account (perhaps of the payroll department).

If the organisation requires the actual costs of sick pay to be coded separately in the ledger, then this may affect payroll procedures. For example, the amount of sick pay, inclusive of SSP, will need to be recorded. Alternatively, information about costs of sick pay may come from the same sources as those shown above for holiday pay, for example, an absence monitoring system.

Some employers also generate an on-cost for anticipated additional costs which could arise because of an employee's sickness absence. The on-cost may be, for example, in respect of overtime that will have to be worked to make up the lost time. The amount accrued may be calculated as a percentage of payroll costs or by some other method, such as historic levels of absence and costs.

(c) **Class 1A NICs** — Employers are required to pay Class 1A NICs on the cash equivalent of the taxable benefits of provision of company cars and fuel (see 20.15 below). Normally this amount is calculated and paid annually, but some employers may prefer to accrue for the estimated liability over the financial year rather than make the expenditure entries in the general ledger only in the month when payment is made.

If an accrual for Class 1A NICs is made, then estimated rather than precise calculations of the amount may be preferable. This estimate could be based on historic information, such as the total Class 1A NICs in the previous year, but modified perhaps to reflect changes, such as fewer employees with company cars.

Where an organisation accrues for Class 1A NICs then some consideration will have to be given as to where the credit entry of the journal will be posted. In Example 7 above, the NI liability was posted to the NI control account, but if an employer adopts this practice then care has to be taken when the monthly remittances to the Collector of Taxes is made. A separate control account for Class 1A NICs would avoid this particular difficulty.

(d) **Expenses** — The accurate accounting of employees' expenses is important both for financial reporting reasons and because the amounts involved may need to be reported on the end-of-year returns, Forms P9D and P11D.

Some employers have moved to reimbursing expenses through the payroll, but many organisations continue to operate arrangements whereby employees are reimbursed through petty cash or perhaps the purchases or creditors ledger. Others combine both methods, so that preparatory work on the expenses claims is performed before it is passed to the payroll department for payment.

Whichever method is adopted, VAT must be treated correctly and the purpose of the expenses must be recorded, as, for example, entertainment. Some items may have to be subjected to PAYE income tax and NICs but still recorded for reporting at the end of the tax year.

Ideally, the expense items should be posted to account codes which have been set up for each employee, or to their sub-analysis codes. This may serve to facilitate extraction and collation of details for the end-of-year returns. Alternatively, if reimbursement is through the payroll, expenses could be itemised and accumulated in employee pay records.

(e) **Statutory maternity pay** — SMP has similarities to SSP. However, as a portion of it can be recovered, the payroll accounting treatment differs slightly. The treatment may depend on whether or not the employer is a 'small employer' (see 8.11 above) and where the NI compensation, if any, is to be coded. As for SSP, this compensation may have to be coded to the employee's cost centre or, perhaps, to an income account of the payroll department. Example 8 below illustrates the principles.

Example 8

Sally is on maternity leave, and receives OMP (occupational maternity pay) of £800.00 in the month, which includes £230.80 SMP.

Account name	GL code	Reference	Dr £	Cr £
Basic pay	A915	Month 4	587.66	
Employer's NICs	A916	Month 4	56.00	
SMP control	B123	Month 4	212.34	
Salary control	B100	Month 4		856.00

In this example the recoverable portion of SMP (£230.80 × 92%) has been coded to the separate control account, and the OMP to the basic pay account. If this were a 'small employer' the entries might be as follows in Example 8.1 below.

Example 8.1

Account name	GL code	Reference	Dr £	Cr £
Basic pay	A915	Month 4	569.20	
Employer's NICs	A916	Month 4	56.00	
SMP control	B123	Month 4	246.96	
Income account	A918	Month 4		16.16
Salary control	B100	Month 4		872.16

In this example the full recoverable amount of SMP (£230.80 × 107%) has been coded to the separate control account. Often the compensation element is not coded until the remittance to the Collector of Taxes is made, when the recoverable amount of SMP is deducted from the amount of NI that is payable. Based on the above example, the following entries as illustrated in Example 8.2 below would then be made.

Example 8.2

Account name	GL code	Reference	Dr £	Cr £
NI control	B124	Month 4	1,669.06	
SMP control	B123	Month 4		230.80
Income account	A918	Cheque 556		16.16
Bank	B001	Cheque 556		1,422.10

References

19.11   Standard textbooks on accounting should be consulted for details of principles of accounting.

(1)   Glynis Morris, 'Manual of Accounting', Tolley Publishing Co Ltd, 1998.

20 PAYE Procedures

Scope of this chapter

20.1   This chapter contains an outline of the Pay As You Earn (PAYE) system and related National Insurance contribution (NIC) procedures. It is a vital part of payroll work and is much the same for all employers and pension administrators.

The chapter concentrates on the administrative features of PAYE, such as the requirements under self-assessment and the use of standard forms. Chapter 25 (Manual Calculation Methods) describes the tax and NIC calculations. Chapters 11 (Income Tax) and 12 (National Insurance Contributions) give details of the legal and regulatory framework. The incorporation of PAYE into other aspects of payroll practice is covered by Chapters 18 (Employee Payroll Procedures) and 21 (Pension Payroll Procedures). The tax treatment of benefits, expenses and termination payments are dealt with in Chapter 9 (Benefits, Expenses and Termination Payments). Deductions from pay often have PAYE implications and aspects of these are discussed in Chapter 15 (Voluntary Deductions), which deals with, *inter alia*, employee donations to charities.

Key points of PAYE procedures

20.2   The essential features of PAYE administration are summarised below.

(a)   PAYE is a system whereby the employer continuously collects income tax chargeable under Schedule E and Class 1 NICs from his employees on behalf of the Government. PAYE is obligatory for the employer.

(b)   PAYE is inevitably complex because it must cater for all circumstances. It involves about 30 different Inland Revenue Forms, but only about ten are in common use. (See Appendix C below.)

(c)   Income tax and Class 1 NIC calculations are a major part of PAYE. They involve a full set of tax tables and an official deductions working sheet for recording manual calculations. Computer and proprietary manual systems are permitted as substitutes.

(d)   Virtually all employees and pensioners are covered by PAYE. NICs are not collected from most pensioners and some employees.

(*e*) Benefits in kind and expenses are within Schedule E and may need to be included in the PAYE system.

Background to PAYE

20.3   The PAYE tax system was introduced into the UK at the end of the Second World War and has been continuously developed ever since. In 1975 the system of collecting NICs using stamps on cards was abolished for Class 1 NICs and the NIC collection was merged with the PAYE system. The use of stamps for Class 2 contributions for the self-employed was abolished after 5 April 1993. Employers' computerised payrolls have handled PAYE since the early 1950s. The Inland Revenue applied computers on a national scale in the 1980s with COP (computerisation of PAYE).

The Inland Revenue and DSS distinguish between PAYE (as an income tax deduction system) and the collection of NICs. However, as income tax and NICs have been collected together as part of the same system since 1975 many people consider NICs as part of PAYE. Indeed, the phrase 'pay as you earn' is sometimes applied to any kind of regular deduction from employee pay. SSP and SMP, although separate systems, are also linked in to PAYE. (See Chapter 8 (Disability and Maternity Benefits).)

Essential reference documents commonly used by all payroll practitioners are the joint Inland Revenue/Contributions Agency Booklet CWG2 (1998), 'Employer's Further Guide to PAYE and NICs'; CWG1, April 1998, 'Employer's Quick Guide to Pay As You Earn and National Insurance Contributions'; CA29 'Employer's Manual (SMP)'; CA30, 'Employer's Manual (SSP)'; CA 33 'Cars and fuel – A manual for employers'; CA44 'National Insurance for company directors'.

Principle of PAYE

20.4   The principle of PAYE is straightforward even though the details are complicated. The basic idea is for the employer to collect income tax in each pay period from the employee. The amount of tax is calculated by the employer according to a tax code, and involves a set procedure using standard tax tables. The tax code is set by the Inland Revenue so that the correct total amount of tax should be recovered from the employee over the tax year despite fluctuations in earnings. Refunds or changes to the tax code can be made by the Inland Revenue if there is any over- or under-deduction of tax. Sometimes the tax codes are applied on a non-cumulative basis, commonly called a Week 1/Month 1 basis. In this situation the tax in each pay period is calculated without regard to that deducted in previous periods, as is broadly the case with NICs. The principles of PAYE calculations are explained in Chapter 25 (Manual Calculation Methods). NICs must also be calculated using a separate set of tables. The various PAYE forms are used to allow the employee, employer and the Inland Revenue to keep track of the calculation details and basic data such as the tax code changes. So, for instance, a Form P45 transfers earnings and tax data from an old employer to a new employer. The PAYE system becomes complicated because it must allow for events such as the death of an employee and matters like benefits in kind. In the first case the tax position of the employee's estate must be settled and in the second case the employer and the Inland Revenue have to monitor and value the benefits for tax purposes.

The National Insurance number (NINO) is used as a payee identifier for PAYE and social security purposes by both the Inland Revenue and the DSS.

Computerised payroll systems automate many of the requirements of PAYE, particularly the tax and NIC calculations. The Inland Revenue issue special notes for computer users. (See Booklet CWG2, and Reference (3) in 25.16 below.) These systems usually only print PAYE forms where it is worthwhile. For instance, in many computer systems it may not be worthwhile printing a Form P45 for a leaver. In these cases the work is done by hand and the data copied from a screen or print-out onto the Form P45. The point at which it is preferable to move to computerised production of Forms P45 is determined usually by such factors as the volume of leavers and costs.

The employer's duties under PAYE can be summarised as follows:

- correct deduction of income tax and NICs;

- keeping good records of pay, benefits and expenses;

- paying the total amount due to the collector of taxes each month (or quarterly in some instances); and

- producing a correct set of annual returns for each employee.

PAYE Forms

20.5 A list of the main PAYE Forms is given in Appendix C together with facsimiles of a selection of these. There are other forms not listed in Appendix C that the payroll administrator may occasionally use in special circumstances such as registering an entirely new business with the Inland Revenue. The forms most frequently used by an employer are listed below.

(*a*)   P6 — Notice of an employee's tax code. (See Appendix C below.)

(*b*)   P9 — Notice of an employee's changed tax code for the coming tax year. (This is basically the same as a Form P6, but can be in list form or provided in magnetic media.)

(*c*)   P9D — Annual return of expenses payments and income from which tax cannot be deducted for a 'lower-paid' employee. (See Appendix C below.)

(*d*)   P11D — Annual return of expenses and benefits for 'certain' employees or directors. (See Appendix C below.)

(*e*)   P14(OCR) — Annual return of pay, NICs etc. for each employee. (See Appendix C below.)

(*f*)   P30B — Payslips to accompany the employer's payment of income tax and NICs to the collector of taxes.

(*g*)   P35 — Employer's annual statement showing a summary of each employee's PAYE details. (See Appendix C below.)

(*h*)   P45 — Starter's/leaver's tax details. (See Appendix C below.)

(*j*)   P46 — Form for new employees who do not possess a Form P45. (See Appendix C below.)

(*k*)   P46 (Car) — Form to report changes to company cars provided to employees. (See Appendix C below.)

(*l*)   P60 — Employee's copy of the Form P14(OCR). (See Appendix C below.)

(Minor variations of the above form numbers occur in practice. More commonly forms issued by a computer have a 'T' suffix after the standard form number.)

See Figure 25A below for an example of Form P11.

Starting a new payroll

20.6   The PAYE aspect of starting a new payroll is outlined below.

(*a*)   The employer notifies the relevant tax office (which depends on the place of the company's registered office or the taxpayer's place of business or the place from which the wages will be physically paid) of his intention to start a new payroll. They determine the tax district which is to supervise the new payroll.

(*b*)   A P4 'starter pack' is despatched by the tax office to the employer. The pack contains all the basic forms, tables, and Booklets such as CWG2, 'Employer's Further Guide to PAYE and NICs'. The pack contains enough material to establish a manual payroll, some of which is only occasionally required with a computer payroll, such as the P11 deductions working sheet.

(*c*)   The employer is assigned a tax district and payroll reference which should always be quoted in any correspondence.

(*d*)   The tax office notifies the Collector of Taxes who forwards the P30BC payment book containing the payslips which are to accompany and detail the monthly or quarterly payments of income tax and NICs less any SSP and SMP.

(*e*)   The tax office is contacted to obtain extra forms and queries relating to the operation of PAYE are raised with it. Any queries on NICs are addressed to the Contributions Agency of the local DSS office.

New employees with a Form P45

20.7   As Chapter 4 (Payee Status) explains, establishing the legal status of each payee is essential for PAYE and other purposes. (See also 18.7 and 18.13 above.) Assuming the payee is an ordinary employee then he must be correctly classified for NIC purposes, i.e. the employer must determine the appropriate NIC table letter for the employee. Normally a new employee (and often a new pensioner) produce a Form P45 containing all the tax details from the previous employment. These can then be used for the new employment. (See Appendix C for an example of a Form P45.) The employee surrenders parts 2 and 3 of the form to his new payroll department, part 1 having been sent to the Inland Revenue by the previous employer. The employee is to retain part 1a to enable him to meet requirements under the self-assessment system. The tax details on the form should be checked by the new employer, for example, that the tax deducted agrees with the tax code and pay according to the current tables. If any discrepancy is noted then appropriate steps, such as informing the tax office, must be taken. (See CWG1, Card 7.) Employers are required to record on part 3 of Form P45 the tax code used where this differs from the code shown on the Form. Part 3 is then sent to the current employer's tax office.

The procedure with pensioners is similar except that the tax code shown on the Form P45 is applied initially on a non-cumulative basis and the copy returned to the tax office is marked 'Pensioner — Week 1/Month 1 basis applied'. (See Booklet CWG2, paragraph 21.)

New employees without a Form P45

20.8   A typical case of a new employee without a Form P45 would be someone recruited straight from school or college. Another is a taxpayer starting a second (or third, etc.) job. In this situation the new employee should be given a Form P46 to complete. This is sent to the local tax office when the employee's earnings reach the current tax threshold. (See 20.9(*b*) below.) This allows the employee's tax code to be calculated. Until the employer is notified of the new employee's tax code he uses the current emergency code on either the cumulative or non-cumulative basis for calculating the tax to be deducted. (See CWG1, April 1998, Card 8.)

Broadly speaking, new pensioners without a Form P45 are treated in the same fashion as employees, for example the Form P46 is issued without the pensioner being asked to consider the certificates A or B thereon and the emergency code is used until further notice with regard to the pension payments. (See Booklet CWG2, paragraph 21.)

Exceptions with new employees

20.9   Several exceptional cases may occur with new employees (and pensioners). The main ones are summarised below.

(*a*)   *An out-of-date Form P45* — In general terms the details are accepted. Where the Form P45 originated in a previous tax year then the pay and tax details are ignored, and either the emergency code applied or, in certain circumstances within the first seven weeks of a new tax year, the code on the Form P45 is used. (See CWG1, Card 7.)

(*b*)   *Low pay* — Where the rate of pay is below the PAYE tax threshold limit (£81.00 per week in 1998/99) then no tax is deducted but pay records must be kept. NICs are deducted unless the pay is less than the LEL (£64.00 per week in 1998/99). The Form P46 is not required to be sent to the tax office until the tax threshold is exceeded. When the tax threshold or LEL is eventually exceeded tax and/or NICs, as appropriate, must then be deducted. (See CWG1, Cards 7 and 8.)

(*c*)   *Form P46 not signed* — Where the employee does not sign the form it is still sent to the tax office and tax is deducted at the basic rate. (See CWG1, Cards 7 and 8.)

(*d*)   *Casual employees* — Where the employee works for a week or less the procedure is similar to that of an ordinary employee except that a Form P46 need not be issued, i.e. tax is deducted using the emergency code or at the basic rate where it is known that the employee has another job. No tax and NICs are deducted if his pay is below the appropriate limits. Again, records must be kept. (See Booklet CWG2, Chapter 4 and CWG1, Card 7.)

(*e*)   *Tax refunds* — Because of the cumulative nature of income tax an employee may be entitled to a refund of tax on joining his new employer, for example where he had not been earning between employments. In the 1995/96 (and previous) year(s), where the refund exceeded £200 on the employee's first pay day the employer had to seek permission to give the refund by despatching a Form P47 to the tax office. Permission was given on a Form P48. From 6 April 1996, the limit on tax refunds on a new employee's first payday was abolished and Forms P47 and P48 cease to be used. Details of special procedures which apply in respect of tax refunds during and after the end of trade disputes are given in Booklet CWG2, paragraph 41. (See also 20.18 below.)

Pay calculations and records

20.10   Pay calculations including the statutory deductions of income tax and NICs are described in Chapter 25 (Manual Calculation Methods). Statutory calculations are described in the official literature as being performed on a PAYE P11 deductions working sheet but the use of the Form P11 is not mandatory and substitutes can be used. The prime requirement when using any manual or computer system is that full details are recorded for each payee and each pay period. This is not only necessary for the Inland Revenue and DSS officers to audit the PAYE operations, but also for the employer's internal and external auditors as well. Though this is an obvious and essential requirement it is not always easy to maintain good records. Similar comments apply to benefits and expenses which are discussed in 20.16 below. The other key point is deciding what part of the 'pay' and benefits is subject to income tax and NICs. This is discussed in several chapters and particularly in Chapter 9 (Benefits, Expenses and Termination Payments) above. Briefly, a complicated situation can be summarised as follows. Money payments excluding genuine expenses are subject to NICs. Income tax is levied on all such money payments with the exception again of genuine expenses and also of pension contributions, some charitable payments and approved profit-related pay within certain limits. Most benefits in kind do not suffer NICs and they sometimes receive tax concessions. In practical terms, this means it is essential to distinguish between pay elements which are taxable or not, and NICable or not. (See 18.14 above for further details.) Benefits are, of course, usually handled separately. However, the *Income Tax (Employments) (Notional Payments) Regulations 1994 (SI 1994 No 1212)* apply to any 'notional payments' made on or after that date. The regulations give effect to provisions in *ICTA 1988*. They have the effect of imposing PAYE liability on items to be known as 'tradeable commodities'. Their impact is to treat as earnings subject to PAYE items which previously were regarded as benefits in kind, such as the transfer to an employee of certain assets. (See 20.17 below for further details.) (For details on the tax and NIC treatment of pay and benefits see Chapter 5 of Booklet CWG2 and Booklet 480.)

SSP and SMP

20.11   SSP and SMP are linked into the PAYE and NIC system as described below. They are examined in detail in Chapter 8 (Disability and Maternity Benefits).

(*a*)   Both SSP and SMP are social security benefits paid by the employer. To a limited extent they depend on the employee's level of earnings.

(*b*)   Both SSP and SMP are subject to income tax and NICs.

(*c*)   The employer may be able to recover in part or in full the cost of these benefits from the NICs collected.

(*d*)   The annual totals paid for SMP are to be shown on the year-end returns, Forms P14(OCR) and P35. (See the example in Appendix C below where the fields for these figures are shown on a Form P14(OCR).)

(*e*)   It is unnecessary to show the annual totals of SSP on Forms P14(OCR) or P35. However, where there is recovery of SSP under the percentage threshold scheme the values for the months for which recovery occurred must be shown. (See 8.11 above.)

Payment of PAYE deductions

20.12   PAYE income tax and NICs deductions for each tax month (or quarter) are paid to the Inland Revenue accounts office by the nineteenth day of the following month. There is a payslip booklet (P30BC) and a payslip from this booklet must accompany each payment except where the remittance is by electronic funds transfer. The employer can use either or both Form P30BC or Form 32 to record details of payments. The payment details should be recorded and calculated as outlined below.

(*a*)   The deductions from gross NICs for SSP and SMP are the total of the following:

   (i)   the amount of SSP paid in the tax month which is in excess of 13 per cent of the total employer's and employees' Class 1 NIC liability for that tax month;

   (ii)   100 per cent or 92 per cent of SMP, depending on whether the employer is a 'small employer';

   (iii)   nil or 6.5 per cent of NIC compensation on SMP, according to circumstances indicated in (ii) above.

(*b*)   The total amount due to the Inland Revenue is the sum of:

   (i)   income tax;

   (ii)   gross NICs less the total deduction for SSP and SMP in (*a*) above. Where the total deduction exceeds the gross NICs the balance can be deducted from the income tax due.

Example — Deductions and Inland Revenue payments

Deductions	£
(A) SSP (£272.00 – (£1,800 × 13%))	38
(B) SMP	1,000
(C) SMP compensation	65
(D) Total deductions	£1,103

Inland Revenue payment details	£	£
(1) Income tax		1,000
(2) Gross NICs	1,800	
(3) Total deductions as above	(1,103)	
(4) Net NICs ((B) less (C))		697
(5) Total amount due to the Inland Revenue		£1,697

Special provisions apply where exceptionally the amount 'due' to the Collector of Taxes is negative, i.e. the employer is due a refund. (See CWG1, Card 18.)

Leavers

20.13   With ordinary leavers the four-part Form P45 is completed giving details of pay and tax in the year and in the employment. (See Appendix C below.) The top part is sent to the Inland Revenue and the remaining three parts are generally given to the employee. Parts 2 and 3 are to be handed over by him to his new employer and the third part, 1a, retained by him for self-assessment purposes. (See CWG1, Card 21.)

Some common complications are given below.

(a)   *Maternity* — In principle a woman on maternity leave is treated as an ordinary employee for PAYE purposes. The procedures regarding issue of Form P45 and subsequent taxation of pay are detailed in Booklet CWG2, paragraph 23, and outlined at 8.12 above.

(b)   *Retirement* — Where the ex-employee is not paid a pension directly by the employer, a Form P45 is issued marked 'Pensioner'. A common example would be where the employer's trust fund, which is a legally separate entity, pays the pension. Where the employer pays the pension directly, a Form P160 is sent to the tax office. Form P160 is a two part set from the start of the 1996/97 tax year. The second part is given to the employee for self-assessment purposes. (See Booklet CWG2, paragraph 20.)

(c)   *Death* — A 'D' is entered in the appropriate box on the Form P45 together with details of the deceased employee's personal representative if known. All four parts are sent to the tax office. (See Booklet CWG2, page 16.)

(d)   *Payments after issue of Form P45* — After the issue of Form P45 to a leaver, any further payments are subject to income tax at the basic rate in force at the time. For self-assessment purposes the former employee is to be provided with a letter giving details of the payment(s), the gross amount of each and the amount of tax deducted from each. (See Booklet CWG2, page 15.)

Year end

20.14   The main PAYE annual returns must be completed soon after the end of the tax year. (The submission dates are given at the end of this section.) These returns, which give tax and other details for employees, are listed below:

(*a*)   Form P14(OCR) for each employee;

(*b*)   Form P35 which is a schedule of employee details;

(*c*)   supplementary returns for employees not entered on the Form P35;

(*d*)   Form P60 for each employee; and

(*e*)   Forms P9D and P11D which are returns of expenses, payments and benefits. (See 19.16 below for an examination of these forms.)

Forms P14(OCR) and P60 are a three-part set produced for each employee summarising the tax and NICs paid as well as any SSP and SMP. The top copy of the set is sent to the DSS, the middle copy to the Inland Revenue, and the bottom copy is the Form P60 which is handed to those employees working at 5 April each year, i.e. not leavers before this date.

Form P35 is an annual statement, declaration and certificate by the employer that the summarised information shown on it is correct. This information is a schedule showing the Form P14(OCR) data for each employee and is shown in Appendix C below. A P35(CS) continuation schedule (or substitute) is used where there are many employees. The requirements for pensioners are similar except there are, usually, no NIC, SSP, or SMP details. The figures on the Form P35 have to be reconciled with those on the P30B monthly payslips. Late or inaccurate submissions of Forms P14(OCR) and P35 can lead to penalties being automatically incurred. (See Reference (5) in 11.18 above, and 11.16 above.)

The details on the Forms P14(OCR), P60 and P35 are often printed on a computer using substitute stationery in accordance with Inland Revenue specifications. Although an employee must always receive the Form P60 the details to be shown in the Forms P14(OCR) and P35 may be sent to the DSS on magnetic tape or diskette. This arrangement can reduce the work involved for all parties. These details are then passed onto the Inland Revenue by the DSS. The employer is sent a microfiche or print-out of the magnetic media details. (Further details are given in Booklet CWG2, Introduction and in CWG1, Card 6.)

Supplementary returns must be completed for those people not entered on the Form P35, for example those on low earnings below the tax and NIC thresholds for whom a Form P38A must be prepared. Forms P38(S) are to be sent to the Collector of Taxes. (See Booklet CWG2, Chapter 4 (for casuals, students and foreign workers).) Supplementary returns must also be completed for those employees for whom tax refunds are still withheld because of involvement in a trade dispute at the end of the tax year. (See Booklet CWG2, paragraph 41.)

The annual PAYE returns for 1996/97 and subsequent tax years must be with the Inland Revenue by the following dates:

- *19 May* — Forms P14(OCR), P35, P38A and P38(S); and

- *6 July* — Forms P9D and P11D.

An Extra-Statutory Concession provides that automatic penalties will not be charged where employers' end of year returns, for example Form P35, are with the Inland Revenue on or before the last business day within seven days following the statutory filing date.

The annual returns which are issued to employees must be given by the following dates:

- *31 May* — Form P60; and

- *6 July* — copy of information contained in Forms P9D or P11D.

New tax year procedures

20.15   At the beginning of the new tax year all cumulative cash totals in respect of pay, tax, NIC, SSP, SMP pension etc. should be cleared and recommenced from zero. Tax codes remain unaltered and should be carried forward to the new tax year unless new tax code notices (Forms P9) are received from the Inland Revenue. Any person who was on a non-cumulative (i.e. Week 1/Month 1) coding in the previous year reverts to a cumulative tax coding. (Note that a prefix D tax code is always operated on the non-cumulative basis. (See 25.6(iv) below).) Where a tax coding advice (Form P6) was received too late for operation in the previous tax year then it is still to be carried forward to the new year. Tax codes brought forward are to be amended in accordance with instructions in Form P9X for the year in question. (See 25.7(*a*) below.) All tax coding advices are to be applied in strict date of issue sequence. Where a student, for whom a Form P38(S) is held, works over the end of one tax year into the next, then another Form P38(S) must be completed for the next tax year.

New rates for NICs, SSP etc. should be checked and all payroll staff should ensure that they have the correct tables for the current year.

All leavers in the previous tax year should be cleared so that at the beginning of the year the payroll commences with only the current employees. There is one complication to this procedure which has been created by the introduction of the Class 1A employer's NI contributions on car and car fuel taxable benefits.

Under present arrangements the Class 1A contribution has to be remitted via the PAYE system with the July payment. It is an annual payment comprising of the contributions due for the previous income tax year, for example, the payment due on 19 July 1998 had to include the Class 1A contribution for 1997/98. In order to facilitate the correct contribution payment an amount has to be recorded on the P11 working sheet for each employee who had a company car and/or received car fuel at any time during the previous income tax year. It can be seen then that a P11 working sheet will have to be prepared at the start of a new income tax year for any employee who left in the previous year and is, therefore, not on the payroll at the start of the current year but who had a company car/car fuel at any time in the previous tax year. However, two procedures have been introduced by the DSS which can help employers.

(*a*)   Employers can choose to pay the Class 1A NICs via the Alternative Payment Method (APM), which eliminates the requirement to show the NICs on the Form P14(OCR). To be able to operate the APM the Contributions Agency insist that the employer's application (Form CA 34) is submitted before the end of the fiscal year to which it applies, i.e. to adopt the method for 1997/98 (payment due by 19 July 1998) the application had to be received by the Contributions Agency no later than 20 May 1998. Once the method is adopted it is not necessary to reapply for permission to use it for subsequent tax years.

(*b*)   Where the APM is not in use an employer can choose to pay and report Class 1A NICs for leavers in the year of leaving thereby avoiding the need to open employment records in the subsequent tax year.

Details of these arrangements are given in Leaflet CA 33, 'Cars and fuel — A manual for employers', at paragraphs 124–132.

Benefits in kind and expenses

20.16   Chapter 9 (Benefits, Expenses and Termination Payments) explains the tax position of benefits in kind. Most benefits and often expenses must be reported at the year-end to the Tax Inspector by 6 July on the following PAYE forms. (Note that different dates applied to previous tax years.)

(*a*)   *Form P9D* — For those earning less than £8,500 inclusive of the value of benefits in kind and expenses.

(*b*)   *Form P11D* — For those earning at a rate of £8,500 p.a. or more inclusive of the value of benefits in kind and expenses and all directors.

In general terms the exceptions that do not need to be reported include some expenses where the Inland Revenue has specially granted a dispensation, incidental overnight expenses which meet certain criteria and benefits such as tax-free contributions to an approved pension scheme. A dispensation only covers certain groups of employees and certain types of expense. These expenses need not then be reported. It is only granted to the employer where the expenses concerned are strictly controlled. (See Booklet CWG2, paragraph 136, and Reference (5) in 20.20 below for a discussion of scope of, and applications for, dispensations.)

The reporting of benefits and expenses to the Inland Revenue is sometimes done by staff other than the payroll administrator, for example those working for the company secretary. This is often a question of convenience and ready access to the necessary data and may ensure greater confidentiality for senior executives. (See Chapter 16 (Payroll Organisation) for a discussion of the effects of 'peripheral' payroll work.) The reporting can be made in schedule form (e.g. computer listings) or, rarely, magnetic media (e.g. disk) where the agreement of the tax office has been received.

The Inland Revenue can apply penalties for late submission of or errors in Forms P9D and P11D. Where returns are not submitted by 6 July, under *TMA 1970, s 98(1)* an initial penalty of up to £300 per document may be levied, with a further £60 per day for each day that the failure continues. In addition, under *TMA 1970, s 98(2)*, if a form is incorrectly completed (either fraudently or negligently), a penalty of up to £3,000 per document may be levied. These penalties have been extended to cover a failure of the employer to furnish the employee with a copy of the information contained in Form P9D or P11D. (See 20.19 below and Reference (5) in 11.18 above.)

The maintenance of accurate records of benefits and expenses is essential (by employees also, under self-assessment). For example, Class 1A NICs are charged on the taxable benefit of company cars, which is based on business mileage, etc. (See Reference (6) in 20.20 below for an article on calculating car benefits.) Under the requirements of the self-assessment system, employers are to calculate the cash equivalent of benefits and expenses provided to their employees. These values are to be reported in the Form P11D (or P9D). Apportionment of benefits may be possible where the employee has had use of the benefit for only part of the year, for example the use of a company van shared by several employees.

The *Income Tax (Employments) Regulations 1993 (SI 1993 No 744)* require employers to submit details of changes to company cars, including accessories and fuel, on a quarterly basis. The Form P46 (Car) is used for this purpose, although substitutes, such as computerised lists, may be acceptable to the Inland Revenue. These returns are required within 28 days of the end of the quarter to 5 July, 5 October, 5 January and 5 April and are to detail changes in the preceding three months. Submission of the details allows the Inland Revenue to change an employee's tax code in-year to reflect movements in the amounts of taxable benefits. (See Appendix C below for an example of the form.)

PAYE counter-avoidance measures, etc.

20.17   The *Finance Act 1994* introduced a number of measures to counteract schemes used by employers to avoid accounting for income tax under PAYE and also liability to Class 1 NICs. The *Finance Act 1998* has introduced further anti-avoidance measures to enforce the operation of PAYE on non-cash remuneration.

The main features are covered below:

(*a*)   ***Intermediary Employers (ICTA 1988, s 203B)*** — The simple aim of the new section is to treat the employer as being the payer of earnings where an intermediary of the employer makes a payment of assessable income on his behalf. The exception to this is where the intermediary has deducted and accounted for PAYE from the payment.

A payment is deemed to fall within these provisions where either the payment is made:

(i)   by someone acting on behalf of the employer and at the expense of the employer or of a person connected with the employer; or

(ii)   by trustees who hold property for any person or class of persons which includes the employee.

(*b*)   ***Tradeable readily convertible assets (ICTA 1988, s 203F)*** — The 1994 legislation was intended to stop the avoidance of PAYE on non-cash remuneration in the form of assets or commodities, then defined as 'tradeable assets'. A number of schemes have successfully circumvented the 1994 legislation and the new measures are designed to finally close the door. The definition of tradeable assets has been widened and a new term, 'readily convertible assets' has been introduced into the legislation.

Employers must now account for PAYE in respect of the cash value of the following readily convertible assets:

(i)   any asset capable of being sold or otherwise realised on a recognised investment exchange, or the London Bullion Market; and

(ii)   any asset capable of being sold or otherwise realised on any market specified in the PAYE Regulations; and

(iii)   an asset consisting in the right of an assignee, or any other rights, in respect of a money debt that is or may become due to the employer or any other person; and

(iv)   an asset consisting in, or in any right in respect of, any property that is subject to a fiscal warehousing regime; and

(v)   an asset consisting in anything that is likely (without anything being done by the employee) to give rise to, or to become, a right enabling a person to obtain an amount or total amount of money which is likely to be similar to the expense incurred in providing the asset; and

(vi)   an asset for which trading arrangements are in existence; or

(vii) an asset for which trading arrangements are likely to come into existence in accordance with any arrangements of another description existing when the asset is provided or with any understanding existing at that time.

The employer is required to operate PAYE on the amount of each notional payment and deduct the tax from the employee's cash remuneration for that month. A further taxable benefit will arise if the employee does not make good any shortfall within 30 days (*ICTA 1988, s 144A*).

Further measures that apply from 6 April 1998 require employers to operate PAYE on readily convertible assets, including:

(A)   any gains from share options, etc. relating to shares that are readily convertible assets;

(B)   non-cash vouchers and credit cards (tokens) used to acquire readily convertible assets;

(C)   anything which enhances the value of an asset in which the employee (or a member of his family or household) already has an interest and which is a readily convertible asset. This will include payments by the employer to enhance the value of a life policy owned by the employee.

(c)   ***Non-cash vouchers (ICTA 1988, s 203G)*** — A non-cash voucher is subject to 'trading arrangements' if, when it is provided to an employee, it is capable of being exchanged for assets which at the time the voucher was provided were capable of being sold or otherwise realised under (b)(i) or (ii) above or 'trading arrangements' exist as outlined in (b)(vi) above; or the voucher itself is capable of being sold or realised in a market specified in (b)(i) or (ii) above or itself is subject to 'trading arrangements'.

(d)   ***Credit tokens (ICTA 1988, s 203H)*** — Where by reason of employment an employee is provided with a credit token and that token is used to obtain goods or money capable of being sold on a market within the definitions at (b)(i) and (ii) above, or capable of being subject to 'trading arrangements' referred to at (b)(vi) above, then the employer is regarded as being liable to PAYE. The amount of the payment is an amount equal to the expense incurred by the employer. [*ICTA 1988, s 142(1) (a)*].

(e)   ***Cash vouchers (ICTA 1988, s 203I)*** — An employer providing an employee with a cash voucher [*ICTA 1988, s 143(1)*] is liable to PAYE in respect of the sum of money for which the cash voucher is capable of being exchanged.

(*f*) **Deducting and accounting for PAYE tax (ICTA 1988, ss 144A, 203J)**
— The new *section 203J* introduces the concept of 'notional payment' and provides that PAYE regulations are to be made or altered to achieve what is required in terms of PAYE tax deductions. 'Notional payment' is defined as a payment treated as made by virtue of any of *ICTA 1988, ss 203B, 203C* and *203F–203I*, with certain exemptions. The *Income Tax (Employments) (Notional Payments) Regulations 1994 (SI 1994 No 1212)*, came into force on 25 May 1994. The Regulations set out, *inter alia*, what are to be excluded from the definition of 'notional payment'. Shares acquired under employee share option schemes and the use of a credit token or cash voucher to obtain money to defray expenses are excluded from the definition.

The Regulations also set out when an employer will be required to operate PAYE on a 'notional payment', and the accounting arrangements associated therewith. Basically, the employer is required to deduct PAYE income tax on the 'notional payment' from any other earnings subject to PAYE which are paid in the same PAYE period (e.g. 6 April – 5 May, etc.) and to account for it to the Collector with the remainder of the PAYE/NIC remittance for that period no later than the 19th day of the following month.

Where the PAYE income tax due on the 'notional payment' cannot be deducted from other earnings in the same tax period, any underdeduction of PAYE income tax has to be met by the employer who must remit the total tax due on all of the employee's earnings inclusive of the 'notional payment'. A period of 30 days is allowed from the date of the 'notional payment' in which the employee can make good the underdeduction of PAYE income tax. Tax paid by the employer is treated as paid by the employee. The amount of this tax is to be reported on end of year return, Form P11D, and will be assessable on the employee under Schedule E. [*ICTA 1988, s 144A*].

(*g*) **Employees not resident or not ordinarily resident in the UK: work done in the UK and abroad** — Provisions (*ICTA 1988, s 203D*) facilitate an employer to approach the Inland Revenue to obtain a direction that only a proportion of an employee's earnings should attract PAYE. The employees affected are those who are either resident but not ordinarily resident in the UK, or not resident in the UK. It is recognised that the direction by the Inland Revenue will be a best-estimate of what proportion of earnings will be liable to UK taxation where some duties are performed in the UK and the balance elsewhere.

(*h*) **Employees working for someone other than their employer** — Two new sections have been added to *ICTA 1988*. The first of these deals with the situation where a person is working for someone in the UK but whose employer (or the person who pays the employee) is based overseas and to whom the application of the PAYE Regulations do not apply. The provisions of *ICTA 1988, s 203B* require the person for whom the employee is working in the UK to account for PAYE income tax which would have been deducted from the payments to the employee had the PAYE Regulations applied to the person making the payments.

The second of the two sections applies where both the employer/payer and the person for whom the employee is working are in the UK. Usually the employer/payer would be expected to operate the PAYE Regulations on earnings. *ICTA 1988, s 203E* provides that where it appears that it is likely that PAYE income tax will not be deducted by that person, the Inland Revenue are able to make a direction that PAYE should be deducted from payments to the employee.

Special situations

20.18   Booklet CWG2, 'Employer's Further Guide to PAYE and NICs', gives a fairly exhaustive list of special situations. Some of the more important ones are summarised below.

(*a*)   *Week 53, etc.* — Because a calendar year contains 52 weeks plus one (or two) days it is possible to have 53 weekly, or 27 fortnightly or 14 four-weekly pay days in a year. Generally, the tax for this extra pay day is worked out as if the person were being paid for the first pay day of the tax year. Where, however, the tax free pay, obtained by reference to the employee's tax code, is equal to or greater than his taxable pay in the year, inclusive of the week 53 etc. pay, then the tax calculations are performed cumulatively. (See CWG2, paragraph 6.)

(*b*)   *Trade disputes* — When an employee is involved in a strike tax refunds can arise under PAYE because of the period of nil earnings. In this situation the employer must retain the refund until the employee returns to work. (See CWG2, paragraph 41 and also 20.9 and 20.14 above.)

(*c*)   *Free-of-tax payments* — Employers sometimes agree to make payments to their employees which are free of tax and NICs. In this situation the employer must make these statutory payments himself on behalf of the employee based on 'grossed-up' figures. Special tax tables and deductions working sheets are available to help with the calculations. (See Booklet CWG2, paragraphs 24 to 28.)

Self-assessment

20.19   The implementation of the income tax self-assessment regime from the start of the 1996/97 tax year has brought many changes to PAYE procedures. These changes radically affect employees (and directors and pensioners) and employers. (See 11.3(*d*) above for further information regarding self-assessment.)

(*a*)   *Impact on employees* — Although self-assessment is applicable to all taxpayers, the vast majority of employees who are taxed only under

Schedule E are not affected. This is because the PAYE system collects
Schedule E income tax on a current year basis through coding adjustments. For instance, the tax due on benefits in kind (e.g. company cars)
and expense payments (such as mileage allowances where there is a
profit element if the rates exceed the Inland Revenue's Authorised
Mileage Rates (formerly known as the Fixed Profit Car Scheme)) are
collected in-year wherever possible, sometimes by use of prefix 'K'
codes. In addition, the new system provides for underpayments of
income tax to be collected by coding adjustments where:

(i)   the employee has filed his tax return with the Inland Revenue by
      the 30 September following the tax year in question, i.e. 30
      September 1998 for the 1997/98 tax year; and

(ii) the tax to be collected is less than £1,000; and

(iii) there are sufficient personal allowances available; and

(iv) the employee agrees.

(See Reference (7) in 20.20 below for an article on tax allowances and
codings and the effect of self-assessment.)

Where the tax cannot be collected by coding adjustment (such as where
the employee does not file the tax return by the due date) the taxpayer
will not know for sure whether the Inland Revenue have taken into
account information about expenses and benefits received for the first
time.

To create certainty for those affected by the six-month limit the Inland
Revenue issued a Statement of Practice, 'SP 1/96 Notification of Charge-
ability to Income Tax and Capital Gains Tax for Tax Years 1995–96
Onwards'. This Statement of Practice makes clear that employees who
receive a copy of Form P11D information from their employers can
assume that the Inland Revenue know about any items on the form and
that they will be taken into account for PAYE, provided that:

(A)   the employees are satisfied that the information is correct and
      complete; and

(B)   they have no reason to believe that the information has not been
      passed to the Inland Revenue.

In completing his tax return the employee has to collate all information
and details of earnings etc. from all sources. Against income from
employments it is no longer acceptable for the taxpayer to enter
comments such as 'See Form P11D' or 'Per PAYE'.

(b) *The impact on employers* — Though the original concept of the new
     system was limited to simplifying the tax assessment process for the
     self-employed, the extension to include employees means that all
     employers are now affected. The main impact of the new system is in the

provision of information to employees, but the requirement to calculate and state the cash equivalent of benefits in kind and expenses in the annual returns Forms P9D and P11D has imposed a significant new duty on employers.

All employers are required to provide, by certain dates, detailed information about earnings and benefits in kind from the employment. This information is to be returned to the tax office and also provided to the employees. Without this information the employee will not be able to complete his tax return and comply with the new system. Penalties can be imposed by the Inland Revenue for failures to meet the requirements; see later in this section.

(i)   ***Form P45*** — From 6 April 1996 a new four-part Form P45 was introduced containing an additional part 1a. It requires more information about earnings and tax in the current year. When an employee leaves, part 1 is to be sent to the tax office and parts 1a, 2 and 3 given to the employee. Part 1a is to be retained by the former employee to enable him to complete his tax return.

Where the Form P45 has been issued and another payment is subsequently made to the employee, the employer is required to give the employee a letter showing the payment and the tax deducted, and to forward the details to the tax office. (See Booklet CWG2, page 15.)

(ii) ***Form P60*** — The employer is required to give each employee who was in employment at 5 April a Form P60 (or approved substitute) by 31 May following the end of the tax year, i.e. 31 May 1999 for the 1998/99 tax year. The form may be sent by post or delivered by hand (e.g. with a payslip) etc. If the employer fails to provide the Form P60 by the due date an initial penalty of up to £300 per form can arise.

(iii) ***Forms P9D and P11D*** — The employer is required to complete for each employee who received benefits in kind or expenses during the tax year, either a Form P9D or a Form P11D. (See 20.16 above for a guide to determining which form is appropriate for each employee.) These forms are to be with the Inland Revenue by 6 July following the end of the tax year. (See 20.14 above.)

The employer is required to calculate the cash equivalent of expenses payments and benefits in kind provided to employees. This is a significant extension of the burden of completing these forms. (See Reference (4) in 9.21 above for an annual guide to completion of Form P11D.)

The general rule for calculating the cash equivalent is to take the cost (including Value Added Tax) to the employer or other provider and report any amounts made good by the employee, or from which tax is deducted. For instance, contributions made by the employee towards private use of a company car are deductible in full. Some benefits, such as cars, vans and mobile telephones, have special rules for determining the taxable benefit. (See Chapter 9 (Benefits, Expenses and Termination Payments) for a discussion of the income tax treatment of various benefits and expenses.)

The calculation of the cash equivalent of certain benefits, such as beneficial loans, accommodation and cars, is complex. The Inland Revenue provides P11D working sheets which employers can use when calculating these particular items. (See Appendix C below.)

To ease the onerous compliance burden imposed by the requirement to return details of benefits and expenses, employers should consider applying to the tax office for a dispensation to cover certain items, for example travelling and subsistence expenses, which are received by groups of employees, such as sales staff. Any existing dispensation should be located, checked and renewed or extended where appropriate to ensure it remains valid and valuable. The Inland Revenue leaflet IR69 includes an application form, Form P11DX, which employers can use to apply for a dispensation. The employees should be informed of a dispensation which the employer holds so that they do not have to include in their tax return the particular items nor make a claim for any allowable deductions, for example for business travel expenses necessarily incurred. (See Reference (5) in 20.20 below for a discussion of dispensations.)

Another way of reducing the burden is to enter into a PSA (PAYE Settlement Agreement) with the tax office. This formalised arrangement will mean that employers can agree to meet their employees' tax liabilities on certain benefits in kind and expenses, and will not have to report the details on Forms P9D and P11D. (See 9.19 above for further details about PSAs.)

Another important feature of the new rules for self-assessment is that a copy of the information in the Forms P9D and P11D must be given to employees. The legislation requires that those employees in employment on 5 April are given a copy of the information by the following 6 July. For employees who have left between 5 April and the date of providing the information, the employer can satisfy the requirement by posting the copy to the employee's last known address.

There is no requirement on the employer to automatically send a copy of the Form P11D or P9D information to a former employee who left before 5 April. However, these employees will require the information to complete their tax return if they receive one. Accordingly it is provided that such ex-employees can request a copy of the information from their former employer(s). The request must be made within three years of the end of the tax year in question. On receipt of the request the employer must provide the information to the ex-employee within thirty days or, if later, 6 July following the end of the tax year in question. Once the request has been made and met the employer does not have to deal with further requests for the same information from the employee.

The legislation does not specify in what form the information is to be provided to the employee (or ex-employee). For many employers a photocopy of the Form P11D or P9D will prove the most convenient medium.

(iv)   *Form P160* — This form is now a two-part set. The additional second part is to be given to the employee, who is to retain it for self-assessment purposes. (See 19.13 (*b*) above. Note that, similar to the comments in (i) above where a further payment is made after the Form P160 has been issued, a statement of pay and tax deducted is required to be given to the ex-employee.)

(c) .   ***Benefits and expenses provided by a third party*** — Under the self-assessment system new rules have been introduced for the reporting of benefits provided by third parties. These new rules affect both employers who have 'arranged' the benefit and third parties which have provided them outside of such an arrangement. (Payroll administrators should note that their employer may fall to be considered as both a third party provider of benefits and also as having arranged benefits from third parties.)

'Arranged' means guaranteeing or facilitating the provision of expenses payments or benefits in kind by third parties. In determining whether the employer has arranged the benefit the Inland Revenue say that the test to be applied is whether the employer has played an active part in the expenses and benefits being provided.

If the employer has 'arranged' the benefit then he is required to return details in Forms P11D or P9D. If, however, the employer can demonstrate that he played no active part in the provision of the benefit, there will be no requirement for him to report the details.

Where the employer has not arranged the benefit, then the third party is required to inform the recipient (the employee) of the cash equivalent. The third party does not have to report the details to the tax office, unless required to by the Inland Revenue under provisions of *TMA 1970, s 15*. The information, which must be supplied to the recipient by 6 July following the end of the tax year, can be given in any format. Accordingly, for example, it is possible to provide the recipient with the details each time the benefit (or payment) is made or by a yearly return.

(*d*) **Retaining records** — A fundamental change introduced by the self-assessment system is that the taxpayer is required to keep all such records as may be requisite for the purposes of making a correct and complete tax return. These records will have to be kept for at least one year following the 31 January following the year of assessment. For example, records for the 1997/98 year will need to be kept at least until 31 January 2000 Exceptions are where the tax return is filed later than the 31 January and where the taxpayer has income from self-employment or from letting of property. [*TMA 1970, s 12B.*]

The new system does not impose any new requirements on employers to keep records of payments, benefits, etc. This is because *regulation 55* of the *Income Tax (Employments) Regulations 1993 (SI 1993 No 744)* requires an employer to keep full records relating to emoluments and PAYE. This includes all records for wage earners, salaried employees, directors and executives; time sheets, clockcards and tachographs records; cash books and cheque stubs which show payments to employees; petty cash vouchers and records, and ledger records. Records must be kept for at least three years after the end of the tax year to which they relate.

(*e*) **Penalties** — The following is a summary of the penalties which can be imposed on employers. In some cases these penalties are automatic but in others they require referral to the General or Special Commissioners.

  (i) **Forms P14(OCR) and P35** — There is an automatic penalty of £100 for every 50 employees (or part of 50) for each month or part of month the return is late.

  (ii) **Form P60** — If the employer fails to provide this form, or the amount of tax involved is significant, a penalty of up to £300 per form can be imposed. A further penalty of up to £60 per form per day can be imposed where the failure continues.

  (iii) **Forms P9D and P11D** — Failure to file by the due date can give rise to a penalty of up to £300 per form with a further penalty of up to £60 per form per day that the failure continues. A maximum penalty of £3,000 per form can be imposed where the form is incorrect or incomplete.

  (iv) **Third parties** — A penalty of £300 per form with £60 per day for continued failure can be imposed on a third party which does not meet its obligations. An incorrect or fraudulent return can lead to a penalty of up to £3,000.

(See 11.16 above for further information and examples of the calculations of penalties.)

References

20.20   The Inland Revenue and DSS guides are essential references for points of detail. Other chapters have references which may have a bearing on PAYE, e.g. Chapter 9 (Benefits, Expenses and Termination Payments).

(1)   CWG2 (1998), 'Employer's Further Guide to PAYE and NICs', Inland Revenue/CA.

(2)   CWG1, April 1998, 'Employer's Quick Guide to PAYE and NICs', Inland Revenue/CA.

(3)   CA 33, 'Cars and Fuel – A manual for employers', DSS, 1996.

(4)   Booklet 480, 'Expenses and Benefits – A Tax Guide', Inland Revenue, 1998.

(5)   Evans M, 'Self Help on Dispensations', PMR, March 1996.

(6)   Perkins H, 'The Taxation of Company Cars', PMR, October 1995.

(7)   Gravestock P, 'Tolley's Guide to Self-Assessment 1998/99', Tolley Publishing Co Ltd, 1998.

(8)   SABK4, 'Self-Assessment — A General Guide to Keeping Records', Inland Revenue, 1997.

(9)   'Facing up to Year End', PMR, March 1998.

(10)   'Gearing up for Form P46 (car)', PMR, September 1998.

The Inland Revenue and DSS publish many useful leaflets which explain aspects of PAYE and related matters. They are aimed at employers, employees, and others such as students. References (1) in 11.18 and 12.21 above both contain a full list of these leaflets and some are mentioned elsewhere in this book. For instance, an Inland Revenue leaflet such as IR 33, 'Income Tax and School Leavers', can be useful in helping employees with their payroll queries.

21   Pension Payroll Procedures

Scope of this chapter

21.1   This chapter describes the main aspects of pension payroll procedures. Annuities paid by an insurance company are also briefly discussed. Broadly speaking, pension payroll procedures are a variation of those used on employee payrolls, but there are significant differences. The following paragraphs concentrate attention on these differences and ignore the many common features. Pension payrolls are not, of course, just concerned with paying pensioners but also include paying other beneficiaries, such as widows and orphans. Chapter 10 (Pension Schemes) covers the pensions background, Chapters 18 (Employee Payroll Procedures) and 20 (PAYE Procedures) cover many of the general features of payroll administration.

Key points of pension payroll procedure

21.2   The main features of pension payroll procedure are as follows.

(*a*)   Pension beneficiaries have different legal rights from employees.

(*b*)   Pension beneficiaries are subject to PAYE tax but not NICs (unless the pensioner has also been re-engaged as an employee and is under State pension age, and if over State pension age and also an employee, NICs are still due from the employer but not the employee).

(*c*)   Broadly speaking, employee payroll practice applies to pension payrolls although certain features, such as SSP, do not apply to them (unless the individual employed retired on pension and then was re-employed on a new contract while still under age 65).

(*d*)   Pension payrolls involve some special procedures, for example monitoring the right of child beneficiaries to receive a pension after age 16 which usually depends on their continuing in full-time education.

Comparison with employee payrolls

21.3   Despite being similar in many ways, pension payrolls differ from employee payrolls in the following respects.

(a) **Legal status** — Legally a pension is paid according to the terms of a trust deed or in the public sector under the applicable statutory regulations. Pension payments are not governed by employment legislation.

(b) **Multiple sources of pension** — It is common for one pension department to pay pensions from several different funds. Some payroll systems may consolidate these pensions where possible into a combined pension for some individuals, although this may not always be desirable. A common example is where an administrator pays pensions out of the current scheme fund and also pays pensions from a separate pension scheme fund established by a subsidiary company acquired many years ago. Certain beneficiaries may qualify for pensions from both sources.

(c) **Simpler pay structure** — Pension payments can remain constant for long periods because variations such as overtime pay do not occur. Payments such as OSP, contractual maternity pay, SSP, SMP and holiday pay also do not figure in a pensioner payroll. (Unless, exceptionally, the pensioner has been re-employed on a new contract by the employer and the common payroll deals with both pensioners and employees.) It is a common practice, however, for welfare visitors (see 20.5 below) to be reimbursed their expenses through the pensions payroll. There are usually none of the on-costs associated with an employee, for example employer's NICs and pension contributions. Pensions are specifically excluded from NICs. [*Social Security (Contribution) Regulations 1979 (SI 1979 No 591), reg 19(1)(g)*]. Pension beneficiaries may, of course, have to pay NICs on any money earned by working whilst also receiving a pension provided they are aged under 60 years (women) or 65 years (men). If working pensioners are over State pension age, their employers will remain liable to pay their NIC liabilities.

(d) **Geographical locations of payees** — Pension payees are often scattered across the country and some are resident in foreign countries. Access to banks, building societies or post offices may not always be possible. Contact with both the pension administrators and the ex-employer is usually very limited. This leads to both communication and payment problems that are not experienced in employee payrolls.

(e) **Incapacity of payees** — Some pension payees are very old or in poor health, whilst others are dependent children. In these cases it may be necessary to pay the pension to a legal representative. Even if this is not the case some pensioner payees are not as capable in handling their financial affairs as the ordinary employee. This can lead to special administrative problems.

Besides statutory obligations everything that is mentioned in the following paragraphs is subject to the detailed regulations or trust deed and rules governing any particular scheme. The fine details of the rules and regulations differ considerably between different pension schemes. However, discretion is often allowed in matters of administration such as the method of pension payment.

Links with other systems

21.4   In outline the main links that a pensions payroll has with other manual or computer systems are as follows.

(a) ***Employee payroll*** — Often tax details are transferred from the employee payroll to the pension payroll on Form P45 at retirement. Where the PAYE tax reference is the same for both the employee and pensions payrolls, Form P160 rather than Form P45 is issued. (See 20.7 *et seq* above.)

(b) ***Pensions administration*** — The pensions administration system contains detailed records of all beneficiaries. Not only are these records used to calculate the initial pension but often any increases that become due. Other details such as the current address are also often held by the pensions administration system.

(c) ***Pension accounts*** — The pension payroll may be paying beneficiaries on behalf of several different pension funds. Each of these funds maintains its own accounts. Therefore, total payments to beneficiaries, properly analysed into various categories, should be posted to the relevant accounts.

(d) ***External organisations*** — Pension payrolls must, of course, be linked with the Inland Revenue tax system via PAYE procedures. There will be contact with the DSS where submission of the end of year return (Form P14) is made by magnetic media or details of pre-6 April 1997 GMPs are forwarded from the Contracted-Out Employment Group. There must also be links with banks and the recipients of any voluntary deductions. In this area there is very little difference between the pension and employee payrolls.

Welfare and service issues

21.5   Some employers take great pride in the welfare services that they provide for their pensioners. These services can range from special additional payments/benefits and organising parties for pensioners to providing welfare visitors. Sometimes a separate welfare department is established, although more commonly welfare is administered by the pensions department. The extra benefit payments may be discretionary or paid by the employer from a separate trust fund. Because some pension beneficiaries are very old or ill the welfare visitor can play an important role in resolving pension payment queries and problems. The pension payroll department has to be more sympathetic than usual when responding to queries or giving advice when requested. A large volume of correspondence occurs with beneficiaries, and a familiar approach in letter writing is adopted by the pension and payroll administrators. The payment of pensions is the *raison d'être* of the pension scheme. Any failure in the service not only damages the credibility of its administration but also the image of the sponsoring employers.

Tax implications of pensions

21.6   The tax implications of pensions can be dealt with under the following headings.

(*a*) **PAYE** — The pension scheme administrator is responsible for ensuring that PAYE is applied to the pension payments. Income tax deducted from each pension must be paid over to the Collector of Taxes in the usual way. When a pension trust fund is established formal undertakings are given to the Inland Revenue which require the administrators to operate PAYE. This is part of the conditions for granting tax privileges to a pension scheme. [*ICTA 1988, s 597*].

(*b*) **Compulsory purchase annuities** — Compulsory purchase annuities can be purchased from life assurance companies. The purchase money is provided from an approved pension scheme and the pension is then taxed under PAYE. The pension can be paid directly and taxed by the insurance company. Alternatively it can be paid gross to the scheme administrators and tax is deducted by them prior to payment. There are no special tax implications in this arrangement, which is only implemented for financial and administrative convenience. [*ICTA 1988, ss 597, 619(1)(b), 643(3)*].

(*c*) **Personal pensions** — Since 6 April 1995 personal pension scheme annuities have been taxable on the same basis as pensions paid by occupational pension schemes. [*ICTA 1988, s 648A*]. This means PAYE references are to be used for these personal pension payments, as they fall within Schedule E.

(*d*) **Pensioner tax codes** — Pensioners, once they reach age 65 and then again when they reach age 75, receive a special age allowance which reduces their tax liability. The tax due on any state social security pension is often recovered by imposing the applicable tax on the occupational pension. As usual these circumstances are reflected in the PAYE tax code. The P and V tax suffices are unique to pensioners. Normal employee tax suffices and prefixes also occur (see 25.7 below for the meaning of various tax codes).

(*e*) **Purchased life annuities** — A regular income for life can be purchased from a life assurance company by means of purchased life annuities. For tax purposes they are treated differently from ordinary pensions. [*ICTA 1988, Pt XIV, Ch V*]. Tax is deducted at the basic rate from the income element of the annuity and the net amount is paid to the individual by the insurance company. They are strictly not within the pensions area as they do not necessarily concern retirement. However, some pensioners invest their retirement lump sums in purchased life annuities because of tax advantages, i.e. tax is levied only on the income proportion of the annuity.

Auditing

21.7   Pension scheme accounts are regularly audited in the normal way and this includes the pension payroll. The Inland Revenue can also audit a pension payroll although in practice this is infrequent. (Chapter 24 (Payroll Audits) has further details.)

Types of beneficiary

21.8   There are several classes of beneficiaries who receive pensions. It is not unusual to find a pensioner in receipt of two pensions, one in his own right, and another as a beneficiary, for example a widower, from the same pension fund. The validation and calculation of pension claims are the responsibility of the pension department. The processing of these claims is governed by the pension scheme rules. The main classes of beneficiaries are as follows.

(a)   ***Ill-health or disability retirements*** — People in this class can be of any age. They suffer long-term illness or disablement which prevents them from working normally. The pension will normally cease on recovery before retirement age.

(b)   ***Early retirements*** — These are people who have been granted early retirement, i.e. before reaching the scheme's normal retirement age. The Inland Revenue accepts that scheme rules may allow members to retire on pension at any age between 50 and 75. Early retirement is frequently offered as part of a redundancy package or as a result of a partial decline in ability. Sometimes an extra 'bridging' pension is paid as well until the State pension also becomes payable.

(c)   ***Normal retirements*** — The pension scheme's normal pension age must be sex equal at least in relation to all pension benefits built up from 17 May 1990, the date of the *Barber* judgment. Most schemes have equalised at age 65 but many will allow members to retire on an unreduced pension from age 60.

(d)   ***Late retirements*** — It is now comparatively rare for any employees to be asked or be allowed to work beyond normal retirement age. Common exceptions are male employers (especially manual workers) whose pension scheme stipulates a normal retirement use of 60 because the State pension is not payable for a further five years — although bridging pensions may be available from the pension scheme. One complication is that it may be possible for employees to defer receipt of their pensions or for them to receive their pension and pay at the same time. Thus a person may be on both the employee and pension payrolls. However, this is often not attractive because of the consequent abatement of the pension under the scheme rules in certain public service schemes and the payment of tax at the higher rate on the joint incomes. Deferring pension payment until actual retirement will mean that the eventual pension is increased.

(*e*)   ***Deferred pension*** — These pensions are due to those employees who ceased to be scheme members before normal pension age and chose to preserve their pension rights in the occupational scheme. In some cases it may be difficult to trace the recipient. The Letter Forwarding Service, provided by the DSS, Contributions Agency, Newcastle-upon-Tyne, offers a route for pension fund providers to trace recipients.

(*f*)   ***Spouses*** — Pensions are usually payable on death to the spouse of a member, deferred pensioner or pensioner. There are, however, complications such as divorce, common law partners and occasionally a rule requiring such pensions to cease on re-marriage. A spouse's or dependant's pension may be reduced if the survivor was considerably younger than the member at the date of the member's death. These situations are resolved according to the rules of the pension scheme or where permitted at the discretion of the trustees.

(*g*)   ***Dependants*** — A dependant's pension may be paid in place of, or as well as, a spouse's pension, for example to a member's common-law partner or dependent sister. There must be financial dependency or inter-dependency in order for a dependant's pension to be payable.

(*h*)   ***Children*** — Not all schemes provide pensions for dependent children on the member's death. Where they are provided, such a pension is often paid to the legal guardian who is often the member's spouse. This may lead, however, to a tax deduction at source, whereas payment to the child may be immediately tax-free as the child can claim his or her own tax allowances. The local tax inspector will often award the single person's allowance against a pension paid to a guardian who has given a written undertaking to use the money for the benefit of the child.

Obtaining pension details

21.9   Whether or not the pension department actually pays pensions it is invariably responsible for calculating them. Obviously the pension department must first be notified that the pension is payable. Typical circumstances for the payment of pensions to employees or dependants include:

(*a*)   ill health or disability;

(*b*)   redundancy and early retirement;

(*c*)   normal or late retirement;

(*d*)   death.

The pension department can use its own manual or computer system to signal who is due for normal retirement, although the employee may have the option of continuing in work beyond the normal retirement date. Usually with employees the authoritative notification comes from the personnel department. In the case of deferred pensions due for payment the pension department may be required to trace the ex-employee if contact has been lost. The DSS, for a small fee, can help a pension scheme trace missing beneficiaries via the Letter Forwarding Service (see DSS leaflet CA 14, paragraph 93, and 21.8(e) above). Where a beneficiary cannot be traced the benefit is usually forfeited after a specified period, generally six years. In the case of deferred pensioners, a considerable lead-time is desirable in order for the pensions administrator to establish the individual's preferences regarding options, and the necessary bank details etc. Deferred pensioners, keen to trace who now has responsibility for paying a preserved pension, perhaps following a series of scheme mergers, can make use of the tracing service offered by the Pension Schemes Registry run by the Occupational Pensions Regulatory Authority. This tracing service is offered free of charge.

Once in payment, proper procedures should be put in place to verify periodically that the recipient is still alive and that the pension is not being misappropriated. Where a pensioner dies the pension department should be notified by the relatives or by the pensioner's bank. Verification, however, is desirable. The pension must be stopped and the spouse's, dependant's or children's pensions can then be calculated and payments made accordingly. One important function of the pension department is checking the documentary basis of a pension claim. Birth, marriage and death certificates are needed to carry out this check. Medical evidence would be required in the case of retirement due to ill health. Where death benefits like a lump sum or dependant's pension are paid at the discretion of the trustees, a member's wishes can be taken into account. These can be documented on an 'expression of wish' or 'nomination' form completed in advance by the member – this is preferable to relying on directions given in the member's will.

The pension is calculated in accordance with the scheme rules (10.6 and 10.14 above contain some simple examples). There are often options within the rules which can be exercised by a retiring employee. The most obvious example is the surrendering of part of the prospective pension for a lump sum or an increased prospective spouse's pension. For example, Ted has a prospective pension of £9,000 p.a. He opts within the rules to take a lump sum of £13,500. According to the rules of the scheme, given Ted's age and sex, the annual pension sacrificed is one-ninth of the lump sum. Therefore, Ted's payable pension is reduced to £7,500 i.e.

$$£9,000 - \frac{£13,500}{9} = £7,500$$

A transfer from the employee payroll to the pension payroll is required in the event of a retirement. The normal procedure is to treat the employee as a leaver and to issue a Form P45 in the normal way. Part 1 of the Form P45 should be marked 'pensioner' at the top. The P45 procedure applies to the normal situation where the pension administration is legally distinct from the employer. As usual, the Form P45 transfers the tax details from one payroll to another and from one PAYE reference to another. Form P160 is forwarded to the tax office in the more uncommon situation where the employer pays the pension rather than a legally separate organisation. Where either Form P45 or Form P160 has been issued, the employer should then normally use the employee's tax code to deduct tax on a Week 1/Month 1 basis until a new tax code is received or until 5 April whichever is the sooner. Where the pensioner payroll has been given a P45 for a new pensioner, part 3 of the P45 should be marked 'pensioner — Week 1 (Month 1) basis applied' before sending it to the tax office. If the tax office has not contracted the pensioner payroll by 5 April, the existing code should be carried forward to the new tax year, but used on a cumulative basis. (See Booklet CWG 2, 'The Employer's Further Guide to PAYE and NICs', pages 19–20, for details.)

Pension components

21.10   As already explained, one pension payroll system may be responsible for paying several different types of pension. One pensioner may be entitled to two or more of these pensions. Holding these components separately will facilitate both the reconciliation of the payments each pay period and the preparation of statistical returns. These pensions are part of gross pension payable and, ideally, should be shown separately on the payslip along with any deductions. The total payment for each type of pension must be allocated to the various pension funds, for example executive, staff and old scheme funds. Computer payrolls should handle this situation satisfactorily.

Changes to a pension payroll

21.11   Compared to employee payrolls, pension payrolls have relatively few changes for a beneficiary in a year. However, the sheer size of some pensions payrolls, such as 530,000 pensioners on the Civil Service Pension Fund, brings problems of volume and communication quite distinct from those sometimes experienced on employee payrolls. The main data fields subject to change include:

(*a*)   each pension component in the total payment which may be subject to separate rules regarding annual increases;

(*b*)   tax codes;

(*c*)   voluntary deductions;

(*d*)   address(es);

(*e*)   payment details, e.g. bank or building society account.

To ease the volume of data entry required for input of bulk quantities of Forms P9 or P6, the Inland Revenue may agree to supply tax code changes at certain times of the year in magnetic tape form. This feature can be very effective but will require accuracy in the National Insurance numbers held for the beneficiaries on the pension payroll. Some care will be required where a beneficiary is held on the payroll as two records.

Methods of payment of pensions

21.12   Chapter 22 (Payment Methods) describes the various methods of handling payroll payments. There are, however, some variations between employee and pensioner payrolls. This is mainly due to the different circumstances of pensioners and employees. The rules of a private sector pension scheme often leave the choice of the method of payment to the trustees. The methods of payment employed can be classified as follows.

(*a*)   ***Cash*** — This method is not often practical because pensioners are almost certainly geographically scattered. However rare now, it has been the case that some pension payroll procedures allow beneficiaries to collect their pensions in cash from the employee payroll office. Naturally it is not a practice to be recommended either from the point of view of convenience for the payroll department or the physical security of the pensioner.

(*b*)   ***Cheques*** — A considerable number of pensioners prefer payment by cheque which can be paid into a bank, building society or post office account. Cheques may also be used in a few special cases, for example the initial pension payment. There is a greater risk of misappropriation and in practice cheques are frequently now only used where the pensioner is resident abroad. (See (*d*) below.)

(*c*)   ***Credit transfer*** — The method used, whether paper or electronic funds transfer (via BACS Ltd), makes no difference to the beneficiary. The net result is a credit in his or her bank account. In the past, and still on occasion today, pensioners may have difficulties dealing with a bank or building society, for instance opening an account or finding a suitable branch location. For these reasons credit transfer to a Girobank account may be more desirable. The Girobank offers free most of the services of a bank, making them available through post offices. The rationalisation of banks' and building societies' branches may cause pensioners difficulties in being paid by credit transfer.

(*d*)   ***International payment*** — Many pension schemes have pensioners who have retired abroad. As explained in 22.12 below payment may be made through either a bank or the post office. (See, also, Reference (5) in 21.22 below.) The cost per payment can be high, depending on the method of transfer used and the destination country. The administrative burden can be placed on the pensioner by paying the pension into a UK bank account. Pensioners have then to make the necessary arrangements with their bank to transfer money abroad at their own expense. It may be that the cost of the arrangements significantly diminishes or extinguishes the benefit of the pension payment. Commutation of small pensions may then need to be considered. Under a double taxation relief agreement and subject to Inland Revenue approval, a pension may be paid gross and then taxed in the pensioner's country of residence.

Advice slips for pension payments

21.13   Generally, if and when issued, a pension advice slip (payslip) can be simpler than an employee payslip. Usually there are fewer pay components and deductions. However, the layout is often similar. Because a pension beneficiary is not an employee there is no employment law obligation to provide an itemised payslip, and, in practice, it is rare for pensioners to be advised of their pension payment each month. Under the social security legislation (*Occupational Pension Schemes (Disclosure of Information) Regulations (SI 1996 No 1655)*) a pensioner must be informed of any variation in the amount of pension to be paid (e.g. each annual increase). The variation must be provided to the pensioner automatically before or within one month of the effective date of the change. However, technically, if when the pension originally became payable, the pensioner was provided with full information as to how increases would be made, there is no need to supply further notices. In practice, many pension payrolls provide a single pension advice note at the end of the tax year and, if not at that date, when pension incomes are put into effect.

Where the pensioner payroll practice is to send out payslips only on a change of designated items, such as tax code, annual amount of pension, or voluntary deductions it may be appropriate to include an estimate of the next period's payment. Clearly any such arrangements have to be within the pension scheme rules and approved by the scheme authorities. Further, the issue of the payslip may form an important part of regular communication with the pensioner. Payslips are almost invariably mailed, rather than handed, to pension beneficiaries. This means that a list of addresses must be maintained. The different types of payslip and mailing methods are described in 22.6 below.

Payment of pensions

21.14   Pensions are paid at various frequencies which include:

(*a*)   weekly;

(*b*)   fortnightly;

(*c*)   four-weekly;

(*d*)   monthly;

(*e*)   quarterly;

(*f*)   half-yearly;

(*g*)   annually.

Monthly payments are by far the most common, although pensioners may sometimes be encouraged to accept less frequent payment periods to reduce administrative costs. Very small pensions not exceeding £260 p.a. may be commuted in their entirety for a lump sum. Usually all payments are made on a fixed day within each pay period, for example the fifteenth day of each month in the case of monthly pensions. Occasionally, however, payment is made by reference to the date of commencement of the pension. Therefore, if a particular monthly pension is payable from 3 March then it is always payable on the third of each month. This is obviously administratively inconvenient in most cases.

One common complication with pension payments is the 'guarantee period'. Pensions are often guaranteed for up to five years. If a pensioner dies during the guarantee period the full pension entitlement continues to be paid to the estate or to the spouse until the period has expired. In most cases, as an alternative, a lump sum is paid to discharge the liability. The spouse's reduced pension can be paid from the date of death according to the scheme rules. However, where the guarantee is discharged by paying the full pension entitlement for the balance of the guarantee period, procedures must be in place to ensure that any spouse's or dependant's pension becomes payable, at the correct rate, upon the expiry of the guarantee period.

Apportioning payments

21.15   When a four-weekly pension commences there may be only two weeks before all pensioners are paid. Many pension schemes would apportion the payment so that only two-fourths of the pension would be paid on the first payment date. Other schemes would pay the full four-weekly amount on the first payment date irrespective of the fact that the pension entitlement started part way through a pay period. Similar considerations may apply when a pension is terminated. Again, as in all pension matters, everything depends on the scheme rules and the decision of the scheme authorities where discretion can be exercised.

Overpayments and suspension of pensions

21.16   The legal situation with regard to overpayments is almost identical to the corresponding employee payroll situation. Whether recovery of an over-payment is sought will often depend on the decision of the scheme authorities in administering discretionary powers, and the circumstances of each case. Generally, mistakes of fact or fraud allow money to be recovered whereas a mistake of law may result in the overpayment being retained by the beneficiary (see 5.14–5.19 above for further details). From a practical viewpoint the easiest way is to write to the beneficiary informing him or her that the overpayment is to be recovered from the following pension payments allowing time to handle any protests with sensitivity and diplomacy.

Another common situation is where an overpayment arises due to late notification of death. The usual method of effecting a recovery in this case is to apply to the executor or solicitor controlling the estate of the deceased. Where, due to the pensioner's death, an overpayment has occurred, the amount may be offset against any guaranteed lump sum payment or the first instalment of any dependant's pension. Sometimes, however, the return of a pension payment from the deceased's bank account is the first indication that a pensioner has died, although this may be insufficient evidence of a death. Occasionally the returned payments relate to a previous tax year and are identified only after the end of year tax returns have been sent to the Inland Revenue and DSS. In such circumstances the pension payroll administrator will have to write to the Inland Revenue to correct the figures reported.

In view of the difficulties of communication with beneficiaries and pensioners, some pension payrolls are able to suspend payments of pensions from specified dates. Such suspension would not be made without good cause. These causes may arise from, for example, a return of a payment (such as returned credit transfer or cheque), a change of payee's address (deduced from correspondence returned from last known address), non-return of a certificate of existence (see 21.19 below), and a child beneficiary reaching age 16 or leaving full-time education (see 21.21 below). Suspension may avoid overpayments in some cases but cause underpayments in others where payment has to be reinstated. Where reinstatement occurs, payment of the unpaid pension payments to the date of suspension will have to be made.

Incapacity of pensioners

21.17   Incapacity of a pensioner can lead to administrative problems. Pensioners who are hospitalised or senile need a representative to control their affairs. The pension scheme welfare officer can be of help in these situations. Clearly, however, strict precautions must be taken when paying the pension to a beneficiary's representative. This requires documentary proof of the power of attorney or a declaration signed by the beneficiary that a named representative, for example a spouse, is entitled to collect the pension on the beneficiary's behalf. The representative needs to produce proof of identity before payment can be made. Often in the short-term the problem of incapacity is dealt with by the bank where the pensioner holds the account into which the pension is paid. Also, the scheme rules frequently contain special provisions for the trustees to make pension payments to others for the benefit of an incapacitated beneficiary. A more straightforward situation is a child's pension which is paid to a surviving parent or guardian. The use of joint bank accounts, in the name of the beneficiary and the nominated payee, may serve to obviate some difficulties.

Private and public sector pension increases

21.18   Many public sector pension schemes increase both deferred pensions and pensions in payment according to the provisions of the *Pensions Increases Act 1971*. Generally this grants increases of pensions in line with price inflation.

A few private sector pension schemes prior to 6 April 1997 did not contain provisions for increases to pensions in payment or, if they did, offered relatively modest guaranteed increases for example three per cent p.a. or the rate of inflation, whichever was less. Since 6 April 1997, all occupational pension rights built up after that same date must increase once in payment at least in line with the Limited Price Indexation requirement – i.e the annual rise in inflation capped at five per cent.

In practice many private schemes have operated under a mixture of guaranteed increases and discretionary top-ups. For example, a common formula used by many large pension schemes is that the rules stipulate an annual guaranteed increase in line with the year-on-year rise in prices but subject to a cap at five per cent, i.e. the Limited Price Indexation explained above, but applied to all pension rights, not just those built up since 6 April 1997. In addition, the trustees, with the agreement of the employer, may use their discretionary powers to grant further increases, perhaps to all pensioners because inflation is higher than five per cent, or perhaps special targeted increases directed to those whose pensions have been in payment longest.

From the viewpoint of the pensions and payroll administrator the essential point is the formulae for granting a pension increase. Sometimes, as with employee payrolls, backdating an increase causes additional administrative complications. Nowadays even in the smallest schemes, the calculation of the increase and revised pension is computerised. Where there are several different sources of pension payments each pension may be increased in a different way. The calculations are often based on pension records rather than the payroll records since the former are likely to be more extensive.

In practice, pension increases can become administratively more complex because the pension is made up of different components which receive different increases and it may be subject to different increases depending on how long it has been in payment.

(a)   ***Different components*** — Schemes which have been contracted out of SERPS during the period 6 April 1978 to 5 April 1997 may have either a guaranteed minimum pension (GMP) component or a protected rights component. In addition there will be the components in excess of these contracted-out elements.

(i) GMPs accrued in employment before 6 April 1988 are increased each April by the State in line with the year-on-year rise in the retail prices index (RPI) for the previous September.

(ii) GMPs accrued in employment during the period from 6 April 1988 to 5 April 1997 inclusive are also increased each April in line with the year-on-year rise in the RPI for the previous September but the occupational scheme is responsible for the increase up to a ceiling of three per cent in any one year, with the State paying increases above the three per cent limit in years when the RPI increase is higher.

(iii) Protected rights pensions accrued in contracted-out employment from 6 April 1998 to 5 April 1997 inclusive must, whether or not secured by an annuity, have a minimum increase in payment in line with the rise in the RPI up to a ceiling of three per cent in any one year.

(iv) The excess pension rights over the GMP or protected rights pension and which have been accrued before 6 April 1997 are not required by legislation to increase at all unless the sponsoring employer has received a payment from surplus. In this case pensions must increase with the LPI formula — see (vii) below.

(v) Where GMPs are in payment and increases are granted under the scheme rules and/or by the exercise of trustee discretionary powers on the excess pension over the GMP, those increases may occasionally also be granted on the GMP element, although this is relatively uncommon since it can be seen as a 'double increase'.

(vi) Any pension rights, in excess of any GMP or protected rights, built up before 6 April 1997 may be secured when they come into payment by a compulsory purchase annuity (see 21.6 (*b*) above). This is very likely to be the case in a money purchase scheme. If so, the arrangements for annual increases will be defined at the time of the annuity purchase. The more generous the provision for subsequent increases to the pension, the lower the initial amount of pension that can be purchased by the capital sum in the member's account.

(vii) GMPs have been abolished for employment after 5 April 1997. Any pension rights built up in an occupational pension scheme from that date must give rise to a pension which increases each year in payment at least in line with the rise in the RPI up to a ceiling of five per cent in any one year. This requirement for Limited Price Indexation (LPI) also therefore applies to protected rights pensions accrued after 5 April 1997. Naturally, scheme rules or trustee discretion with employer's consent may ensure more generous increases if inflation is higher than five per cent.

(*b*) ***Increases dependent on when the pension came into payment*** — It is common to find that the rules of an occupational pension scheme lay down that the full increase designated each year is only applied to pensions which have been in payment for at least twelve months at the date the increase is applied. Commonly, in cases where the pension has been in payment for less than one complete year, 1/12th of the increase is granted for each complete month that the pension has been in payment.

As explained above, the rules of many occupational pensions give the trustees the power to grant discretionary pension increases, usually with the need for the consent of the sponsoring employer. Such increases may on occasion not be given in the form of an across-the-board general increase but may be special increases targeted at pensioners whose pensions have been in payment longest. Such pensions will have been the most eroded by the effect of inflation if previous increases have not always matched the annual RPI movement.

There can be complications in defined benefit schemes where the actual final pensionable pay figure on which the initial pension is to be based will not be known until much later that year. An example might be a bonus payment which cannot be determined in advance. In such cases, the pensioner may receive a special increase the following year to take account of this payment.

(See 10.8 and 10.16 above for further comment about pension increases.)

Certificates of existence

21.19   As indicated in 21.9 above, one of the problems with regard to pension payrolls is to ensure that the pension payments cease on death. There is, of course, no guarantee that the pension or payroll office will be told that a pensioner has died. Death may be notified either by a relative, a friend or by the beneficiary's bank where credit transfers are used. Pension payments may continue to be made or may be fraudulently misappropriated by a relative. To ensure that the pensioner is still alive some schemes issue 'certificates of existence' regularly, for instance once a year. These certificates are intended to be signed by a responsible person who certifies the continuing existence of the beneficiary. They are then returned to the pension office. Suitable signatories include doctors, ministers of religion or bank managers. Where certificates are not returned a visit can then be made by a welfare officer or enquiries made. With some schemes the pension is suspended if the certificate is not returned (see 21.16 above). However, certificates of existence can be an irritation and they probably have little effect in cases of fraud. Where they are not issued on a regular basis, i.e. every one or two years the auditors may check the existence of a sample of pensioners.

Payments into single rather than joint accounts can provide a method of detecting the death of a pensioner. The return of a payment may indicate the death of the beneficiary.

Remarriage of pensioners

21.20   Some pension schemes stipulate that a spouse's pension ceases or is reduced on remarriage. Most are in the public sector. The scheme administrators might be notified when the spouse remarries. However, the remarriage may also be detected from a change of bank account details or by the issue of a certificate of existence which requires the relevant information to be given.

Children's pensions

21.21   Children's pensions usually cease at the age of 16, but often continue in the case of full-time education, sometimes up to the age of 26. In this case a declaration is often required annually from the education authority or college to confirm the situation. The Inland Revenue has confirmed that it has no objection if young people, with a confirmed place at university or college, continue to receive a benefit from the pension scheme during a year off between school and university/college.

References

21.22   The References in 10.26 above contain some information on pension payments. In addition the references in 11.18 above are useful for tax matters.

(1)   Fenton J, Ham R and Sabel J, 'Pensions Handbook', Tolley Publishing Co Ltd, 1995.

(2)   CA 14, 'Termination of Contracted-out Employment, Salary Related Pension Schemes' and CA 14A 'Termination of Contracted-out Employment, Money Purchase Schemes'.

(3)   IR 78, 'Personal Pensions, A guide for tax', Inland Revenue, 1991.

(4)   IR 121, 'Income Tax and Pensioners', Inland Revenue, 1995.

(5)   NI 106, 'Pensioners or widows going abroad', Benefits Agency, 1997.

(6)   'Pensions Administration', Tolley Publishing Co Ltd, 1998. Section 3.15 of Part 3 of this looseleaf work provides information on the operation of a pensions payroll.

(7)   Self R, 'Administering a Pensions Payroll', PMR, January 1996. This is a profile of Tate & Lyle's pension payroll department.

(8)   'Gearing up for Form P46 (car)', PMR, September 1998.

(9)   'Facing up to Year End', PMR, March 1998.

22 Payment Methods

Scope of this chapter

22.1   The main objective of payroll offices is the delivery of punctual and accurate payments of wages, salaries and pensions. The same objective applies to payments made to the self-employed, subcontractors and government trainees. Besides the main payee, who is usually the employee or pensioner, there are others who are entitled to receive payments, for example the Inland Revenue and charities.

A variety of payment delivery methods exist. The main methods are cash, cheques and credit transfer (including, and predominantly, the increasing use of EFT (electronic funds transfer)).

Of the 25 million people currently employed in the UK, a total of 4.5 million weekly wages and 12 million monthly salaries are paid by automated credit transfer using EFT. Although 95 per cent of the UK's working population have a bank or building society account, this means that in excess of a third of employees receive their salaries and wages by cash or cheque. This is not a situation exclusive to small companies or particular industries, where, for instance, part-time work is common; some major employers continue to pay part of their workforce in cash. The term 'automated credit transfer' is used here to describe generically the various electronic funds transfer methods. These EFT methods are discussed below.

As well as actually paying people there is the requirement to notify employees and, usually, other payees through the use of paystatements with accompanying documentation. Although today there are several proprietary stationery systems available which can assist in the preparation and distribution of the paystatements (see 22.11 below), many organisations use stationery including cheques and payslips which they have designed themselves. Use of sophisticated equipment, such as laser printers, has also offered choices in the way organisations prepare their payment statements.

This chapter looks at the various means by which the payment objective may be discharged, recognising that it is not met until an accurate payment is given in an acceptable form to the payee at an agreed place and time. Payment methods are also mentioned in other chapters, particularly Chapters 18 (Employee Payroll Procedures), 21 (Pension Payroll Procedures) and 23 (Security and Administrative Controls).

Key points of payment methods

22.2   The following are important aspects of payment methods.

(*a*)   The selection of payment methods includes considerations of convenience, notification, distribution, payment medium, frequency, advance or arrears of payment and legal obligations.

(*b*)   There is a wide range of common payment media including cash, cheques paper and automated credit transfers.

(*c*)   Other methods are available for special situations including proprietary credit transfer services, postal orders and international money transfers.

(*d*)   Payslips (pay statements) can be prepared by using a wide range of special stationery systems which simplify handling and preparation.

(*e*)   There is a continuing general move towards cashless and monthly pay. Changing payment terms in this direction requires careful planning, consultation and, preferably, the consent of the employees.

(*f*)   Careful structuring of pay location codes, such as department numbers, which are then used in a computer payroll system can substantially improve and simplify handling of payslips, various listings (such as cash analysis) and cheques.

Selection of payment methods

22.3   The disbursement of pay, pensions and expenses requires as much care as their calculation and attention must be given to various issues. Selection of payment methods involves the following major administrative considerations.

(*a*)   **Payee convenience** — Some payees may not have easy access to a bank or building society, which means credit transfers may not be acceptable to them.

(*b*)   **Payer convenience** — All methods involve costs to the employer or the pension fund. Moves towards automated credit transfers and longer payment intervals are attempts to reduce these costs. (See 16.7 above for a discussion of the effects of payment intervals on payroll department staffing.)

An independent survey conducted by BDO Consulting in 1994 (Source: Reference (6) in 22.18 below) quantified the cost of paying in cash or cheque as being over six times more expensive than direct credit. This was based solely on a company's internal costs and showed that a company paying 100 employees in cash every week could make savings in excess of £6,000 annually.

(c)   ***Security and control*** — The control of cash and cheque payments is more onerous than automated credit transfers and is more susceptible to fraud. Cash pay, in particular, presents grave security risks as the employer runs the risk of danger to his staff from armed robbery and there is the possibility that employees can be mugged for their wage packets outside the workplace.

However, sophisticated technologies, such as high quality colour photo-copiers and solvents to remove computer-printed text and figures on cheques have led to an increase in cheque fraud. Consequently, employers using cheques should ensure these meet certain standards and are supplied from an approved printer. (See 22.8 below.)

(Chapter 23 (Security and Administrative Controls) deals with this topic in more depth: see, for example, 23.12 below.)

(d)   ***Payment media*** — Generally, cash payments are to be avoided where possible and automated credit transfers encouraged. (See 22.10 below.)

Also to be taken into consideration are the requirements of the recipients of the statutory and non-statutory deductions, such as the Inland Revenue, courts, pension funds, trade unions, charities and savings institutions. These organisations are usually, but not always, paid by cheque but there is a growing usage of EFT facilities, for example the Inland Revenue and the Child Support Agency accept payment by this method as does the Court Service.

(e)   ***Pay period frequency*** — The less frequently payment is made generally the lower the overall administrative costs.

(f)   ***Payment in advance or in arrears*** — Payment in arrears has cash flow advantages for the payer at the expense of the payee. Some element of payment in arrears may be inevitable given the time taken to process overtime and incentive scheme returns. However, basic pay can be paid in advance. Some payment systems include pay partly in arrears and partly in advance, for example, payment for the whole of the month paid on the 20th of each month. Where there is a payment in advance there is a potential problem in recovering the excess, for instance when an employee leaves or dies.

(g)   ***Documentation and stationery systems*** — Supporting documentation to accompany payments must be considered. (See 15.3(e) above.) These could be computer produced listings, but in some cases the method of payment, for example EFT, may obviate the need for supporting listings as each employee's payment may be individually transferred. Well-designed stationery systems, whether proprietary or internally designed, reduce handling costs and queries.

(*h*) **Distribution** — The secure distribution of cash wages presents considerable problems, particularly in a large organisation. Distributing payslips alone is a more straightforward operation.

(*j*) **Legal compliance** — Payment methods must comply with the relevant terms and conditions in the contract, for example the contract of employment, whether express or implied. There may also be collective and individual agreements to be honoured whether legally binding or not.

(*k*) **Payment of expenses** — Employee expenses are often paid separately to net pay, although sometimes payment is made with wages and salaries. Where they are paid separately a different payment method may be used, for example salaries may be paid by automated credit transfer and expenses by cheque. The separate payment of expenses can create problems for the payroll administrator as part or all of the payments should be subject to PAYE procedures, i.e. tax and NICs.

Range of payment methods

22.4   The following payment methods are commonly used:

- cash;
- cash cheques (uncrossed or open cheques);
- crossed cheques;
- paper credit transfers (or GIRO tranfers);
- automated credit transfers.

The use of the BACSTEL service involving transmissions over telephone lines to BACS Ltd to effect electronic funds transfer of wages has become an increasingly popular method and this is discussed in 22.10 below.

Other methods of paying people include:

- proprietary methods, e.g. Barclays Bank's 'Payflow' (see 22.11 below) where credit transfer details are sent verbally over a telephone;
- postal orders;
- international money transfers for foreign payments;
- a combination of any of the above.

Legal considerations in paying wages

22.5   Payment methods for manual workers were previously covered by *TAs 1831–1940*. These Acts gave manual workers the right to insist on payment in cash but the *Wages Act 1986* abolished this requirement. This means that the method of paying wages and salaries for all employees is now governed by the contract of employment alone. Other types of payee, for example contractors, have their own method of payment covered by express or implied terms in the contract or in the governing rules of the trust deed in the case of pensioners. However, pension payment methods are often at the discretion of the administering authority. Any reasonable payment method can be imposed on new employees by incorporating specific clauses in their contract on appointment but for existing employees any change in the way they are paid is a variation of the payment terms. The contract may specify the procedure for varying its terms, for instance as a result of trade union negotiation. Where the change is negotiated there should be no legal difficulties. An imposed change, however, could expose the employer to possible legal action by the employees. Such an imposed change is clearly undesirable on industrial relations grounds alone.

Even when payment changes are acceptable to the majority of employees and their representatives it is advisable to seek legal advice. No matter how beneficial the arrangement, there could still be a few litigious, truculent or aggrieved individuals who are prepared to contest the change.

(See 5.7 above for further details of variation of the contract of employment.)

The following are two examples of pay practices which are sometimes found.

(*a*)   Where an employee who is paid weekly in arrear leaves, the employer pays the last week's wage on the day of leaving rather than on the normal pay day which would usually be in the subsequent week. This may be an unnecessary practice but its withdrawal may need to be the subject of consultation.

(*b*)   Where a payment is delayed, perhaps as a result of the wrong processing date in the transmission to BACS Ltd, the employer may be obliged to compensate employees, e.g. for any bank charges incurred as a direct result of the delay in the pay being credited.

A payslip (pay statement) must be provided to all employees. (See 5.13 above.) This, of course, does not cover other types of payee such as pensioners, but the provision of payslips is generally good practice.

Distribution of cash pay packets and payslips

22.6   In the distant past, wages were paid directly by selecting the money out of bulk cash at the time of payment. This was superseded by the method of placing cash in numbered containers, each container referring specifically to an employee. Similar methods are still occasionally met, although today, cash or cheque payments are almost invariably placed together with the payslip in a pay packet.

Basically, there are two solutions for paying out cash wages. The first method is for the employee to collect his pay packet from a secure central point. The second method is less secure and involves handing over the pay packet in the employee's own department. This, however, reduces the working time lost in travelling to and queueing at the pay point. Handing out pay packets with cash presents considerable control and security problems which are discussed in 23.12 below.

Employers with a geographically dispersed workforce have a distribution problem with cash wages. The problem can be solved by:

(*a*)   using a central pay office to prepare all the pay documentation and using local staff to make up and pay the wages with cash drawn from a local bank or from cash sales, e.g. a retail store;

(*b*)   using a security company to perform part or all of this work;

(*c*)   establishing separate local payroll offices.

Pay packets containing cash must permit the cash to be checked without the seal being broken. Any discrepancies between the net pay shown in the payslip and the cash can be rectified provided the seal is not broken. There are several ways of achieving this. All systems allow sealed cash to be checked easily against net pay. Normally coins, if used, are clearly visible through a transparent pay packet window. Notes project out of the sealed envelope to facilitate checking. Sometimes a staple is placed through the notes and the envelope as a further security measure: if the staple has been removed, then any claim for cash shortage may be refused.

A system for proving the receipt of the wage packet is necessary. This can be achieved, for instance, by collecting the recipients' signatures on a computer printed list of payee names. An old method is for the payee to return his signed clockcard as a receipt. The card also contains pay details and is issued in advance for checking. This procedure may be necessary where the payslip shows only gross pay and does not list the components.

With credit transfers, the payslips are distributed on their own. Here, confidentiality demands that the payslips should be placed in envelopes although it is not unknown for them to be issued loose. Envelopes containing a cheque and a payslip are also fastened by a staple to provide an additional seal.

The distribution of payslips alone in sealed envelopes is rarely a problem. They can be easily handed out by a manager or foreman, however, secretaries and clerks are often designated to carry out this duty. (Reference (7) in 22.18 outlines the position regarding retention of pay statements where these are not issued to employees.)

Figure 22A

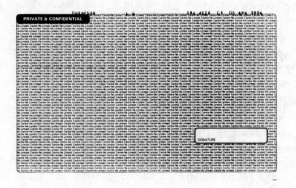

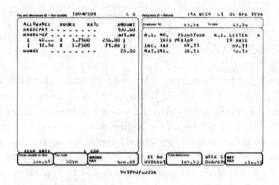

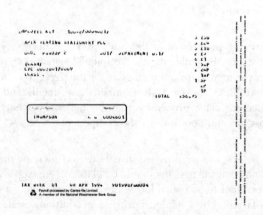

Illustration of a typical payslip (pay statement), confidential envelope and cash envelope for an employee paid in cash. The cash envelope displays the employee's net pay and the numbers and denominations of notes and coinage required. These details are concealed upon the folding and affixing of the flap which carries an adhesive strip

(By courtesy of Centrefile Limited)

Figure 22B

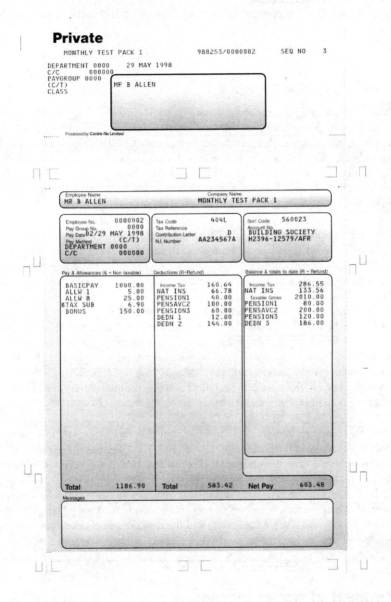

Illustration of a payslip (pay statement) for an employee paid by credit transfer. The payslip folds at two lines and is heat sealed, to form a confidential envelope
(By courtesy of Centrefile Limited)

In the case of absences through sickness, holidays etc, or perhaps a cash payment due to a former employee, it may be necessary for the employer to use registered post to ensure that the pay packet with cash is received at the correct time. Besides the expense, this method is exposed to the vagaries of the post.

Making up cash wages

22.7   Cash wages are often handled by security firms. Working with payslips, pay packets and computer prepared information provided by the employer they draw cash from the employer's bank and make up the wages at their depots, etc. This not only protects the wages in transit but also protects the money whilst it is being issued to employees. Where the employer makes up the wages himself, he uses cash drawn from the bank and sometimes from business takings, for example from till money in retailing.

Wages are usually made up by the 'exhaust method' whereby a fixed amount of cash, usually identified from computer analyses (see below), is issued to make up the wages of each group of employees. Any errors in packeting the wages are then easy to locate.

To ease the make-up process wages are often rounded up to the nearest £1 or £5. This reduces or eliminates coin handling. The rounding amount is recorded as a 'carry forward' amount and deducted from the payment in the following period as a 'brought forward' amount and, of course, this practice should be provided for in the contract of employment (see 15.3(*b*) above). When the employee leaves, the previous period's rounding amount is recovered but no rounding is made for the final payment.

All good computer systems include a pay rounding facility as well as a coinage analysis (more strictly termed a cash analysis). The coinage analysis shows the total number of each denomination of coins and banknotes required to make up the total wages and the wages of each group of employees. A coinage analysis at group level is very useful for making up wages by the exhaust method. Many computer payroll systems now include features which allow the user to specify the levels of rounding and the minima and maxima of coins and denominations of notes to be used when making up cash wages packets.

Payment of wages by cheque

22.8   Cheque payments can be divided into the following two categories.

(*a*)   Cash cheques – sometimes called 'open' or 'uncrossed' cheques – are payable in cash on presentation and are usually restricted to one bank branch or a small geographical area.

(*b*)   Crossed cheques can only be paid into the payee's bank or equivalent account and are much more secure than 'open' cheques. They normally take three working days to be cleared which may be a handicap for some payees. The *Cheques Act 1992* imposes duties on banks, etc., when handling cheques bearing 'a/c payee', for example, crediting can only be made to the payee's account.

Cheques can be prepared manually, by special machines, or by computer. Subject to certain restrictions they may be personalised and contain the payer's designs, such as the employer's logo. Where they are prepared by computer, it is usual for a listing containing details of each cheque to be produced at the same time.

Producing large numbers of cheques creates a considerable amount of bank reconciliation work. This can be eased by using a separate bank account purely for employee payments. Alternatively, or in addition, the cheque details may be passed automatically into a computerised bank reconciliation system. The employer's bank regularly supplies a tape to update the employer's bank reconciliation system with details of the presented cheques. The effort required for signing cheques may be reduced by the use of cheque signing machines.

By agreement with the employer's bank, the payslip may be combined with a cheque for ease of printing and handling. This is done by having, for instance, the payslip on the left of the combined stationery and the cheque on the right. They are separated by a perforated line which makes them easy to be taken apart when required. Any name and address details on the payslip can be designed for use with window envelopes.

The use of cheques to pay employees attracts the attention of auditors who will be obliged to audit the controls in their issue, authorisation and settlement. One procedure in the auditing of controls has become more difficult due to a deregulatory measure which was introduced under provisions of the *Deregulation and Contracting Out Act 1994*. The *Bills of Exchange Act 1882* has been amended so that cheques can be retained at an earlier point in the clearance cycle, so that they do not have to be returned and presented at the payer's bank. (See Reference (3) in 22.18 below.)

Paper credit transfers

22.9   These transfers are merely documents instructing the bank to debit the employer's account and credit the respective employee's account but because of bank restrictions their use in computer payroll systems is declining. The banks insist on special high quality printing of the transaction details along the bottom of the document to meet the requirements of their optical character reader machines. The transfer instructions can be prepared manually or printed by computer. (See Figure 22C below.)

Figure 22C

FROM		🌀 bank giro credit

BRANCH   DATE

Destination Branch Sort Code

£

Bank & Branch   Credit Account

By order of

Please do not write or mark below this line.

Illustration of a bank giro credit

Automated credit transfers

22.10   The term 'automated credit transfer' is used here to describe generically the various electronic funds transfer methods. These EFT methods are discussed below.

BACS — Automated credit transfers are processed through BACS Ltd (formerly the Bankers Automated Clearing Services Ltd). The 'BACS' service, which has existed since 1968, is also used for transferring funds other than payroll payments, for example business purchase payments and direct debits. Payments may be made into accounts held at the branches of most UK banks and building societies.

The service is designed for the use and benefit of business account holders of the UK banks. A business organisation must be sponsored by its bank before it can use the service.

All the computer data containing credits and debits must be sent to the BACS Ltd premises in Edgware, Middlesex. The magnetic media options include 3480 cartridge, ½ inch tape and 3½ inch or 5¼ inch diskette but these are being phased out (see below). The data may also be sent by telecommunication links (using BACSTEL) which has become the preferred method of most employers (see below).

On receipt of the data BACS Ltd operates a number of validity checks and procedures designed to minimise fraud and error. Its computers check all incoming data and the individual transactions are streamed and sent to the destination banks for posting to the appropriate accounts. Figure 22D below is

Figure 22D

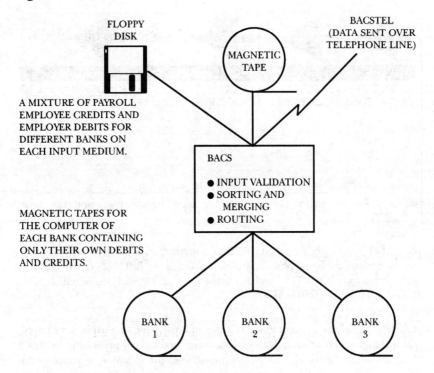

Illustration of a simplified view of how the BACS computer system routes payroll credits and debits to the appropriate bank

a diagram of a simplified view of how the BACS Ltd computer system routes payroll credits and debits to the appropriate bank.

The BACS service time cycle, i.e. the whole process culminating in the debiting of the payer's account and the crediting of the payees' accounts, takes 36½ hours. All items submitted before 9.00 p.m. on day one (input day) result in the payer's and payees' accounts being debited and credited by the opening of business at their branches at 9.30 a.m. on day three (entry day). Figure 22E below illustrates the direct payment process. Because both debiting and crediting take place on the specified payment day there is no loss of interest on the user's part, unlike in the case of paper credit transfers where the payer's account is debited at least two days before the payees' accounts are credited. However, in the case of automated credit transfers to building society accounts these may require an extra day to reach the destination account if they have to pass through a Head Office Collection Account.

There are a number of advantages to using BACSTEL rather than tapes and diskettes. Costs may be lower, thousands of transactions can be transmitted in a short space of time, and the employer is able to immediately register the

Figure 22E

Illustration of the three-day processing cycle where BACS is used

success or failure of the transmission. Tapes and diskettes have to be sent by a delivery service either provided by the bank or the user, and this takes considerably longer.

BACSTEL is now the favoured submission method of BACS Ltd, and magnetic media options are being phased out. New users of the BACS service must make submissions via BACSTEL, and from the start of 1999 all users will have to adopt this method.

CHAPS — Where an immediate transfer of a payment to a payee is required, for instance when an employee's salary is rejected during processing by BACS Ltd, and other methods are clearly unsuitable, for example, a paper credit transfer will usually take three days, then the use of CHAPS (Clearing House Automated Payments System) may be appropriate as it enables same-day transfer of funds between UK banks. There is no minimum payment criterion for CHAPS: the £1,000 test was abolished in January 1993.

Use of CHAPS is open to all organisations whether by written or telephonic instructions, or a bank proprietary EFT system or a dedicated CHAPS terminal. The latter option may only be viable for high volumes as the costs can be considerable.

Accounts overseas — The use of automated credit transfer to effect payments of wages, salaries and pensions to beneficiary accounts worldwide is somewhat restricted. Some countries do not have automated clearing houses (ACH). Accordingly, making international payments can be difficult and, comparatively, more expensive.

However, the 'high street' banks have introduced products and facilities to expedite large volumes of payments (as compared to single transactions of high value) as cheaply as possible to a growing number of foreign countries which have an ACH. The payments can be converted into local currency automatically. These products and facilities may achieve automated international transfers to beneficiaries' accounts within four to six days of submission of the transaction.

Some banks have also introduced interfaces between CHAPS and the SWIFT (Society for Worldwide Interbank Financial Telecommunications) network which enables them to transmit instructions enabling rapid processing of international payments.

Proprietary services for paying wages and pensions

22.11   The major banks and payroll bureaux provide special payment services. Examples of these are outlined below. The first two examples are more suitable for small numbers of payees whereas the last two examples concern facilities for making international payments.

(*a*)   'Payflow' is a service offered by Barclays Bank. A full list of payees and their bank details is stored in the bureau computer. The payee details are printed out on a sheet which is returned to the payroll administrator. When payment is required he enters the amounts on the sheet and telephones the details to the Payflow bureau and specifies the payment day. Security procedures such as passwords and batch totals are, of course, used. The bureau transmits the details directly to BACS Ltd and a print-out of payment details is despatched for reconciliation with the payroll records.

(*b*)   'Autopay' is an automatic credit transfer service offered by the National Westminster Bank to customers of all banks. It is designed to replace paper credit transfers used in small numbers. Bank account details for each payee are stored in the Autopay 'library' which is held on the bank computer. Each payee has an Autopay 'library' reference number. Payment is made by submitting to the bank a schedule of 'library' reference numbers and amounts together with the payment date. The schedule can either be a standard bank form or an approved computer print-out in the same format. The payer's account is debited on the payment date and the payees' accounts credited by electronic funds transfer two banking days later.

(*c*)   'Tempo' is an automated credit transfer service offered by Midland Bank which enables organisations to effect international payments of wages and pensions through use of BACS Ltd. The sort code quoted in the transactions submitted by the user is specific to Tempo. In addition to reaching many countries in Europe, including Scandinavia, automated transfers can be made to the USA, South Africa, Canada, Australia, Hong Kong, Singapore and New Zealand. On receiving the details sent via BACS Ltd, Tempo automatically converts the sterling amount into the local currency, which had been previously notified by the user, reformats the transaction for purposes of compatibility and forwards an output file to the appropriate overseas automated clearing house. The beneficiary account to be credited will be included in the transaction record and must have been obtained by the user using standard stationery supplied by Midland Bank.

(*d*)   'TAPS' (Transcontinental Automated Payment Service) is a service operated by Bank of Scotland to effect payments to beneficiaries resident overseas. Payment can be made to any of the countries on the TAPS network. Either the remitter or the Bank can hold the payees' details. Payment can be made via BACS Ltd to TAPS which then converts the amount into local currency and forwards value to the ACH in the destination country. Payment to the beneficiary's account is made within prescribed timescales.

(*e*)   'Payments Accounting' is a service operated by Centrefile to provide a BACS service for the processing of bank credit and debit transactions. Using Centrefile's software 'AutoCredit' and 'AutoDebit', details of the payments are entered and transmitted via modem for processing. Centrefile transmits details directly to BACS Ltd and provides various management reports.

Other payment methods

22.12   Less popular payment methods are noted below.

(*a*)   Postal orders are limited to £20 each and as such they are only used occasionally, perhaps as a temporary measure.

(*b*)   International money transfers, which may be arranged through a high street bank, the post office or the Girobank, can be used for payments to employees and pensioners in foreign countries in sterling or in the local currency. Payment may be made through a foreign bank account or by the recipient presenting documentation at a specified bank in the foreign country. The bank collects the payee details in the form of an International Banker's Draft, and then makes all the arrangements.

The charges (costing several pounds per transaction) can be high compared to the value of the payroll payment. This sometimes obliges the payer to increase the payment by the estimated charges.

(*c*)   Mixed payment methods are sometimes offered, for example, an employee is paid partly in cash and partly by automated credit transfer. It is not unusual to find that the employee can specify two or more bank or building society accounts to be credited with parts of his net pay. Sometimes, where the employee is paid normally in cash but a large one-off payment has occurred, such as an annual bonus, paying part of the net pay by cheque or credit transfer avoids the risks associated with large sums of cash. Employers also sometimes use this feature, for instance, when paying a bonus for which they wish to present a separate cheque to the employee.

Payment advice slips

22.13   Although pay advice slips (pay statements) are a legal requirement for employees, they are also used as a matter of good practice in the case of payments to pensioners. See 5.13 and 21.13 above for the legal position of pay advice slips for employees and pensioners.

There are likely to be increased costs in supplying a pay advice slip for each pensioner in each pay period. For instance, as the payslip will usually have to be sent by post there could be high postal, stationery and handling charges incurred. As an example, 'Paymaster' (HM Paymaster General) pays monthly 1.5 million pensioners of various public sector pension funds, such as the Civil Service Pension Fund, the Armed Forces Pension Fund, and the Teachers' Pension Fund. The annual postal charges alone could exceed £3.5 million if payslips were issued to each pensioner each month.

Pay advice distribution costs can be reduced in a number of ways. Special postal rates could be agreed with the Post Office where the quantity exceeds a particular level and, for instance, the items are pre-sorted and bundled into sets of 50 by postal code. A further method of reducing costs is to issue a payslip to a pensioner only when a change occurs to a designated item, for example, changes in the annual pension amount, tax code or amount of voluntary deductions.

The general principle in the printing of payslips is that all necessary information is given showing the build-up to gross and the gross to net calculation. Usually the pay and deductions are itemised and supporting information, such as the tax code, is included. It may even be possible to have printed only on the employer's copy of the payslip other details such as dates of birth, entering service and entering the pension fund.

A very useful feature is the ability to include general or individual messages on the payslip. For instance, a general message may state that a pay increase for the whole workforce was effective from a particular date and that back pay has been shown separately, or that tax codes have been amended in line with Budget announcements.

Some organisations have explored the use of the payslip as an advertising medium and reached agreement with external companies to promote their products in return for a fee which is then treated as revenue of the payroll department. (See Reference (4) in 22.18 below for a discussion of payslip advertising.)

Some employers have also utilised the final payslip of the tax year to act as the employee's Form P60. This serves to eliminate both the need to purchase extra stationery, especially where the end of year returns to the Inland Revenue and DSS are made by magnetic media, and handling costs, i.e. sorting and distribution. Inland Revenue approval is required prior to using the final payslip in the tax year in this way, particularly as now OCR (optical character recognition) is being used to process Forms P14.

Figures 22A and 22B above show designs for confidential payslips, where cash and non-cash methods of payments are in use.

Copies of payment advice slips

22.14 It is common practice to retain copies of payment advice slips as the official record of a particular pay calculation and the payment details. However, although there is no statutory duty on employers to retain a facsimile of the employees' payslips it is essential to be able to demonstrate the make up of gross pay, deductions, and net pay. This is necessary to respond to queries, to provide earnings details (e.g. DSS and mortgage enquiries) and a trail for internal and external auditors, including Inland Revenue and Contributions Agency Inspectors.

Payslip copies of the original are sometimes made as part of the payslip stationery using carbon or NCR (no carbon required) paper, or may be produced in tabulation form on standard computer stationery. Their retention places demands on storage space, they can be cumbersome to use and may be difficult to access immediately, for example if archived off site.

Other methods of retaining copies of payslips include, for example, holding details on microfiche, on laser disc and electronically within the computer system (i.e. payslip history). These methods provide simplified access and, in some cases, can allow for enhanced automated search facilities thereby improving retrieval speeds with, perhaps, subsequent usage in management information analyses, such as costs analysis comparisons over a number of years.

Special payment stationery

22.15 There are many kinds of proprietary stationery used in payroll for both manual systems and especially for computer systems. Some manual systems combine the pay calculations with the payslip production. (See 25.15 below.) Computer stationery payslips come in several formats, and suppliers seem to vie to develop and market the latest state-of-the-art product. Most computer payslip stationery uses NCR (no carbon required) paper either exclusively or with limited carbonised areas. The formats include:

- a payslip already in an envelope which serves to conceal certain details;

- separate payslips;

- combined payslip and cheque;

- payslips which can be folded and heat-sealed to form an envelope; and

- payslips with pockets for cash.

Consequently there is a wide range of proprietary pay advice stationery which can be purchased 'off-the-shelf'. Further, employers can design their own stationery and have this produced by a supplier. The advent of advanced laser printers and automated equipment which cuts, glues, folds and heat-seals has provided a further option.

Background to changing payment methods

22.16   For many of the reasons identified above there is a continuing movement away from weekly cash pay. Often this is part of a general change in pay and conditions of employment, particularly in the case of manual workers. In this context there are several concepts that are often associated and confused with each other. These concepts are set out below.

(*a*)   Cashless pay merely means using cheques or credit transfer systems rather than cash.

(*b*)   Monthly pay means monthly or four-weekly pay periods (or a pay period of four or five weeks) although sometimes it implies 'staff status'.

(*c*)   Harmonisation involves rationalising terms and conditions of employment, particularly between groups with similar status. Unjustifiable anomalies are removed, for example, different bonus or overtime rates between employee groups.

(*d*)   Staff status granted to manual workers could imply the rights to benefits such as a pension scheme and sick pay.

(*e*)   Single status usually means granting consistent terms of employment to all employees. It is an extreme form of harmonisation which could mean that all employees could use the same workplace canteen or restaurant, or could be eligible to join the occupational pension scheme or to receive medical cover.

Moves to cashless pay and longer pay periods have figured in agreements between employers and employees to reduce the working week in the engineering industry. (See Reference (5) in 22.18 below for details of a survey.)

Although not strictly part of the wages and salaries system, employers often offer facilities, sometimes as part of moves to cashless pay (see 22.17(*a*) below), for employees to obtain cash. This can involve cashing employees' cheques, usually with notice for time to clear the cheque. Alternatively cash dispensers (ATMs) may be installed, or in the case of a very large organisation bank sub-branches may be set up on the site.

Introducing changes of payment methods

22.17   Changing payment methods can be part of a general change in pay and benefit structures but it does not have to be so. The reasons for changing from cash to cashless methods of payment include a reduction in administrative costs, greater security and a general trend towards single status. There is thus an ongoing move towards cashless and monthly pay for all employees. The *Wages Act 1986* removed all the statutory restrictions which previously made cash pay virtually mandatory in the case of manual workers. (The provisions of this Act are now contained in *ERA 1996*.) However, introducing new methods of payment as opposed to an improved pay and benefit structure requires the following considerations to be taken into account.

(*a*)   **Methods of payment** — Replacing cash requires careful research into the alternatives which may be used in combination, e.g. EFT with an ATM on site (see 22.16 above).

(*b*)   **Overcoming employee problems** — The use of bank accounts and more infrequent pay cycles can cause real problems for some employees. These problems need sympathetic handling and positive action to reduce the genuine difficulties.

(*c*)   **Legal considerations** — The contract of employment is usually changed when switching payment methods and extending the payment frequency. Such alterations may require professional advice.

(*d*)   **Packaging** — The new payment terms can be combined with pay and benefit improvements to provide an overall incentive to the employees to improve performance. (See Reference (5) in 22.18 below.)

(*e*)   **Inducements** — Various incentives, for example one-off payments, have been used to persuade employees to accept changes. Note that if a pay supplement is given to the employees for agreeing to a change in pay method, for instance cash to EFT, unilateral withdrawal of the supplement will amount to an unlawful deduction from wages, contrary to *ERA 1996, s 13* (*McCree v London Borough of Tower Hamlets* [1992] *IRLR 56*).

(*f*)   **Consultation** — Consultation involves not only the trade union representatives but also educating employees on the new payment methods and advising them, for instance on the use of bank accounts etc. BACS Ltd have produced material which employers can utilise to encourage employees to move to automated credit transfers. The material includes posters, a video, leaflets, etc. (See Reference (6) in 22.18 below.)

(*g*)   **Special factors** — There are always several special factors in each change-over situation, for example, employees may be on sites remote from banking services.

(*h*)   **Documentation** — A reasonable amount of documentation must be produced when changing payment methods. The main documents include new contracts of employment, informative literature for employees and new administrative and computer procedures.

References

22.18   The information on payment methods can be obtained from high street banks and specialist stationery suppliers as well as from the sources stated below.

(1)   Banking Information Service (see Appendix F below for the address).

(2)   BACS (see Appendix F below for the address).

(3)   'Cheques', PMR, March 1996.

(4)   Browne D, 'Payslip Advertising', PMR, January 1996.

(5)   'Counting the Cost: the Impact of Reducing the Working Week', IRS Employment Review, November 1995 Number 596. This is an analysis of the introduction of a shorter working week at 21 engineering companies.

(6)   'The Business Guide to Cashless Pay', BACS Ltd. A free pack offering guidance and assistance on implementing cashless pay. The pack includes a computer disk which enables an employer to evaluate the financial benefits of moving to EFT.

(7)   'Retaining pay statements', PMR, December 1996. (A response to a query concerning retention of pay statements.)

---

23 Security and Administrative Controls

Scope of this chapter

23.1   Security and administrative controls are essential in all financial and computer work. The changing technology available and continued use of more sophisticated software means greater emphasis on IT security controls. They assume even greater prominence in payroll systems. This is because of the volume of money involved and because they are inherently more vulnerable than other business systems. Security is concerned with minimising the risks and losses due to events such as robbery and fraud. Essentially the administrative controls ensure that errors are quickly identified and corrected. Auditors use the term 'internal control' to describe many of the procedures and precautions which are necessary to avoid costly mistakes and fraud. Their application requires the advice and assistance of computer staff, security officers and auditors. Chapter 24 (Payroll Audits) describes how an auditor would check the adequacy of the control procedures.

A more modern view would not just concentrate on the negative aspects of administrative management such as minimising simple mistakes. It would also consider controlling the wider aspects of quality management like 'customer' satisfaction. A 'customer' in this context is anybody who relies on the payroll service, for example an employee, a manager receiving pay statistics, or the Contributions Agency.

Layers of control

23.2   Senior management has a general responsibility to ensure, usually via delegation and supervision, that the internal controls and security procedures of an organisation are adequate. These should ensure that the assets of a business are correctly used and proper accounting systems are operated. Payroll administration and its supporting IT are of course only a part of this responsibility. Figure 23A below shows how the control of a business can be represented as three layers. The higher controls can only work provided that the lower controls are operating satisfactorily. This chapter is primarily concerned with layers 2 and 3.

Figure 23A

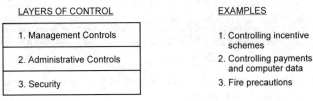

LAYERS OF CONTROL	EXAMPLES
1. Management Controls	1. Controlling incentive schemes
2. Administrative Controls	2. Controlling payments and computer data
3. Security	3. Fire precautions

Illustration showing layers of control

Figure 23B

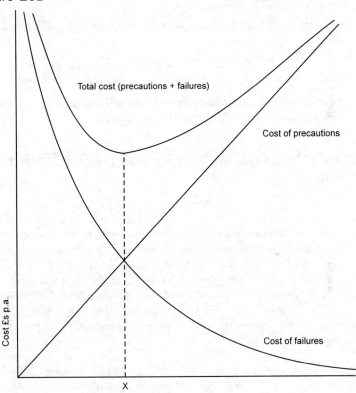

Illustration showing the balancing of the reduction in risk against the cost of security and controls

Notes:

(1) *All costs are expressed on an annual basis*
(2) *Increased expenditure on precautions reduces the cost of security failures*
(3) *Point X is the optimum level of expenditure on precautions where the total cost is minimised*

Key points of security and administrative controls

23.3   These features can be summarised as follows.

(*a*)   Payroll risk management is a systematic programme of identifying, measuring and controlling risks.

(*b*)   Payroll security should be seen as part of an overall organisation-wide risk management programme.

(*c*)   The *DPA 1984* usually applies to computer payroll and related systems.

(*d*)   Rigorous administrative control procedures are essential to detect errors and ensure good service.

(*e*)   A computer should be used to assist with control calculations and facilitate error detection.

(*f*)   In payroll, as in other areas of business, the management of the risks associated with computer systems is particularly important today.

(*g*)   Security and administrative control procedures require the careful co-ordination of all the departments concerned.

Cost-effectiveness of security and administrative controls

23.4   Clearly administrative controls and security have a cost. This cost must be balanced against the benefits. Figure 23B above is a diagram showing the balancing of the control and security costs against the benefits of reduced risks. In practice it is difficult to gauge the optimum point precisely. Also the idea of averaging the cost of control and security failures has its limitations. Thus catastrophes such as major fires cause relatively little damage to UK business as a whole. They are, however, devastating to the few businesses affected. This implies that some risks, the potential catastrophes, are so unacceptable that it is worth spending disproportionately more on precautions, and taking out insurance.

A common-sense approach to both security issues and administrative errors is that 'prevention is better than cure'. Take the possibility of a software virus attacking a computerised payroll system. Then it may be more sensible to reduce the probability of a successful attack rather than improve the means of detecting the virus and rectifying any damage.

General description of risk management

23.5   Risk management is the process of identifying, measuring and controlling business risks. The term is sometimes restricted to mean managing the numerous insurance arrangements required by the modern business. Here, however, risk management is interpreted in its original and wider sense which involves all methods of minimising business hazards and their consequences. Risk management in this context is only concerned with 'pure' risks and does not consider 'speculative' risks. The distinction is that pure risks involve the possibility of losses only, such as a result of fraud, whereas speculative risks can result in either losses or profits, for example when selling a new payroll bureau service. It should be noted that the term 'risk management' is also confusingly applied to managing speculative risks, for example with foreign exchange.

Risk management when applied to pure risks in payroll operations includes such matters as fraud and theft prevention, control procedures, alarm systems and the use of security guards to protect and move cash. What must be stressed is the systematic integrated approach to minimising the risks of the business organisation. This leads to the view that payroll risk management is only part of the overall management of the risks to which the business is exposed. For instance, in a large factory the payroll department benefits from security officers who guard the whole site and control the entry and exit. The payroll data may also share many of the security facilities provided for all the business systems run by a central computer department. Aside from the normal operations of the payroll department, risk management also involves the computer, security and internal audit departments. It should go without saying that it is essential that payroll risk management is proactive rather than reactive.

Risk management process

23.6   Risk management has three main elements.

(a)   **Risk identification** — Hazards must be systematically identified, for instance issuing a pay packet to the wrong person. This is the most crucial stage as failure to identify a risk means that it is never measured or controlled.

(b)   **Risk measurement** — The frequency and consequences of each hazard must be evaluated. For example, according to historical records overpayments in a company may occur ten times a year. The money involved may not be recovered in one case out of twenty while the other cases merely lead to embarrassment and inconvenience.

(c)   **Risk control** — The adverse effects of a hazard can often be minimised on a cost-effective basis. For instance, payroll robbery can be minimised by the use of a security company to deliver cash.

For computerised systems there is a government-supported approach to risk management called CRAMM (CCTA Risk Analysis and Management Method; the CCTA is the Central Computer and Telecommunications Agency). Risk management work can be supported by computer software.

Main payroll risk areas

23.7   Payroll precautions are detailed later in this chapter. The main risk areas are as follows.

(*a*)   **Shared risks** — These are the risks common to many business departments such as fire, flood and sabotage. The main risk of violence in payroll administration, as mentioned below, is armed robbery for wages cash. Other violent risks are fortunately uncommon and shared with other business functions. These risks include terrorist outrages, bombs, and kidnapping.

(*b*)   **Cash and cheque risks** — In some organisations only the payroll department and the cashier handle cheques and cash. The traditional demands of manual workers to be paid in cash leads to large concentrations of cash. Associated with this are the risks of armed robbery, theft and mistakes.

(*c*)   **Fraud** — Payroll systems are vulnerable to fraud simply because all employees are involved to some extent in the payroll operation. Opportunities for fraudulent time-keeping and bonus claims are frequent. Many of the other types of fraud can only be committed by specialist staff, e.g. supplier invoicing frauds often require the collusion of the purchasing staff. Of course, payroll and computer staff also have specialist opportunities for perpetrating frauds such as collecting the pay of fictitious employees.

(*d*)   **Mistakes** — Payroll systems combine complexity, large volumes of data, extensive communication with other departments and time pressure. Mistakes are easily made in these circumstances. There is a 'word' in computing to summarise the effect of errors in this situation — GIGO (Garbage In Garbage Out). Traditionally there are three types of mistake:

  (i)   errors of omission, e.g. forgetting to process a sickness notification;

  (ii)   errors of commission, e.g. entering the wrong rate of pay into a computer; and

  (iii)   errors of principle, e.g. not applying PAYE procedures to casual employees.

It should, of course, be noted that payroll errors are not confined to the administrative or computer staff of employers. Errors may, for instance, occur in payroll packages bought from software houses. Further examples come from the Inland Revenue. There were mistakes in calculating the 1994 tax codes which affected a large number of employees. Also printing errors affected a few entries in the 1993/94 tax tables.

(*e*)   **Records and computers** — The holding of essential records and the use of computers exposes the payroll department to special risks, for example faults in computer software.

(*f*) **Confidentiality** — Payroll information is highly confidential in the private sector. Even in the public sector where an individual's grade and salary band is widely known personal details are confidential.

Access to payroll information, including remote access third party data, by modem links means security controls must become increasingly more stringent and sophisticated in order to safeguard confidentiality.

Risk measurement

23.8   It is important to evaluate the probability and consequences of each risk identified. In some cases the consequences are qualitative, for example loss of employee goodwill may be one consequence of a pay calculation error. Risk frequencies can be gauged from historical records or national statistics. Measuring risks is probably the most difficult part of risk management. However, unless estimates are made it is impossible to judge reliably whether the risk control activities are cost-effective. (Figure 23B above illustrates the use of estimates to arrive at the most cost-effective level of control.)

Risk control

23.9   Besides good practice generally, risk control strategies relevant to payroll include the following.

(*a*) **Risk avoidance** — For example, some fire risks in the payroll office can be eliminated by prohibiting smoking.

(*b*) **Risk reduction** — The risk of faulty payroll computer programs can, for instance, be reduced by buying a reputable computer package and by testing when changes are made.

(*c*) **Risk transfer** — The use of a computer bureau transfers the problem of equipment failure to another organisation. Insuring against fire or theft transfers the financial consequences of these hazards to the insurance company. As described in 16.6(*d*) above the ultimate form of payroll risk transfer is to sub-contract the whole payroll function, including making payments, to another organisation. This is often done within groups of companies where, say, the head office may operate a full or partial payroll service on behalf of subsidiary companies. The provision of a complete payroll service is sometimes offered where there is no common association on a totally commercial basis. For example, employee benefit consultancies may operate a pension payroll for their clients. Where a full or partial payroll service is offered the risk transfer can never be total. Employers or pension trustees need to ensure that the service provider is reputable and reliable, as well as being bound by a strict contract including having some form of service level agreement.

(d)   **Risk retention** — This involves a conscious retention of both the financial and non-financial consequences of a hazard. Often some kind of contingency fund is established to cover larger risks.

(e)   **Damage limitation** — Clearly adverse incidents occur despite reasonable precautions being taken and any damage must be restricted if possible. For instance, if the net pay is incorrect on the weekly payroll due to a software error then not only must it be corrected immediately but the monthly computer payroll should also be checked for the same fault before it is also run.

(f)   **Recovery** — Damage must not only be limited but the normal service re-established as quickly as possible. This may be initially on a temporary basis. As an example computer departments keep copies of all payroll data stored on magnetic disks. If the original data is garbled when the computer is subject to a power cut then a copy is used to continue the payroll work when the power is restored. A system back up should be a part of the standard procedures.

(g)   **Contingency plans** — A major part of controlling risk is preparing plans to cover all possible and significant adverse events. These contingency plans limit damage and allow for the rapid recovery of the normal payroll service. A simple example is a list of reliable temporary staff who are willing to cover sickness or holidays. A more complicated case is a detailed plan covering the temporary transfer of payroll work to another computer following a protracted failure of normal data processing services. The ultimate contingency plan covers a major disruption of the payroll service itself due to a severe fire or industrial action. Regularly produced copies, in the chosen media (i.e. paper, microfiche, document imaging) of all data should be securely stored off site. As a temporary measure the net pay prior to the disruption can then be paid for one or two pay periods if necessary. Adjustments can be made when the normal payroll service is restored to allow for any under or overpayment. An agreement, with a similar sized local organisation for use of facilities is an option to consider. Alternative sites with a co-ordinated and established recovery procedure are increasingly common.

(h)   **Auditing** — Regular inspections of payroll and allied processes are essential to reduce risks and detect fraud. (See Chapter 24 (Payroll Audits) for further details.)

General points relating to payroll security

23.10   These matters can be summarised as follows.

(a)   **Advice and context** — The main payroll security measures are outlined below. The advice of security officers, computer staff, internal auditors, insurance brokers and the police is essential when implementing, reviewing or extending security measures. As previously mentioned there are considerable advantages in adopting a risk management strategy for the whole organisation of which payroll security is an integral part. Some aspects of security are also mentioned in Chapters 5 (Payroll Law), 24 (Payroll Audits) and 28 (Selecting a Computer System).

(b)   ***Staff*** — Both inside and outside the payroll department, staff are probably the most vital factor in security. The aspects which are important in this connection are:

    (i)   careful selection of new staff;

    (ii)   maintaining a high morale;

    (iii)   exercising good supervision;

    (iv)   consistent management interest in staff;

    (v)   a co-operative approach to security by all the departments of an organisation;

    (vi)   training in all aspects of payroll work including quality and security; this of course not only refers to training new staff, but also to refreshing and updating the skills and knowledge of existing staff;

    (vii)   continuous vigilance by staff;

    (viii)   maintaining a quality programme with a standard performance measuring routine.

(c)   ***Health and safety*** — Under the *HSWA 1974, s 2* it is the duty of an employer to provide safe equipment, a safe system of working, and safe premises. The main risk specific to the payroll and cashier's department is injury during armed robbery. This not only affects the staff concerned but employees could also be injured if the robbery takes place when paying cash wages. Organisations have been active in addressing this problem with a concerted move to automated payments and with it, inherent safety factors. However, this requires good office practice with regard to equipment, for example no trailing cables. An EC directive on using VDUs led to more strict health and safety regulations which were effective after 1992. As an example of one of the risks, a typist was recently disabled by RSI (Repetitive Strain Injury) and awarded £79,000 compensation.

See Reference (5) in 23.22 below which contains further details on office health and safety.

(d)   ***Insurance*** — Many insurance risks, for example water damage from burst pipes, are shared with other departments. Fidelity guarantee insurance can be used to reimburse an employer for losses caused by the fraud of his employees. Cash and cheques can also be insured against loss or theft etc.

(e)   **Security technology** — This has improved far beyond the traditional use of alarms and safes. There are numerous relatively cheap modern precautions. Familiar examples include identification cards, entry phones, special marking of equipment to hamper theft, smoke detectors, electronic access systems, remote signalling devices linked to police stations, and closed circuit television (CCTV). Some references to security technology are considered separately under other sections, for instance computer security in 23.15 below.

Shared risks

23.11   These risks are common to many departments and require a common approach. The risks that are particularly important to payroll are fire and intruders. Good fire precautions are essential as the extensive amounts of paper used in payroll work are not only a fire hazard but also contain vital information which requires protection. Access to the payroll and cashier's office should be denied to unauthorised personnel. All enquiries should be handled through small pay-out windows. Payroll offices, cashier's offices and pay stations should be placed, where possible, to take advantage of shared security and access control facilities. A central position within an employment site is usually best as this maximises the security barriers which robbers and vandals must overcome to be successful. Small remote pay stations can present some problems in this respect. Sometimes the payroll and cashier functions are associated or combined – one advantage of this being shared security.

Cash and cheque risks

23.12   The risk of successful robbery, theft or mistakes in the payroll or cashier's office can be minimised by introducing the following procedures:

(a)   reducing or eliminating cash payments, e.g. paying employees via BACS;

(b)   restricting access for ordinary staff to small armoured pay-out windows with 'scoops' cut in the base;

(c)   installing 'audible' alarms or 'silent' alarms connected to permanently manned security offices or to a police station;

(d)   strengthening all windows, doors and walls to prevent forcible entry;

(e)   keeping cash in a locked safe wherever possible. Cashless payment methods should be encouraged to reduce the amount of cash used;

(f)   ensuring that the activities of payroll staff are not visible from outside;

(g)   using a security company to collect cash from a bank and to perform all the pay packet preparations on its premises;

(*h*)   rounding pay up to the nearest five pounds eliminates coin handling problems. Computer systems can keep track of the employee's rounding credit for adjustments to be made in subsequent pay periods;

(*j*)   ensuring that strict controls are applied to petty cash and expense payments as well as payroll pay-outs;

(*k*)   strict controls to prevent useful information reaching robbers and thieves.

The risks with regard to cash transport and reception can be minimised by:

(i)   elimination of cash payments;

(ii)   using a security company rather than the payroll or cashier's staff;

(iii) using specially 'alarmed' cash bags which emit siren noises, coloured smoke etc;

(iv)   varying routes and times for collecting and paying wages;

(v)   using able-bodied staff in pairs;

(vi)   carefully checking the premises for intruders and suspicious circumstances immediately prior to the delivery of the cash;

(vii) using cash received through other business operations such as retail trading or collecting local authority rent and rates payments.

Cash pay packet distribution risks should be minimised using approaches similar to those required for cash transport and reception and are as follows:

(A)   elimination of cash payments;

(B)   paying out where possible from the payroll office itself thereby minimising the use of other less secure pay points;

(C)   using security companies for the pay-out rather than the company's payroll staff;

(D)   using special 'alarmed' cash bags;

(E)   varying routes, although pay-out times are difficult to vary;

(F)   using able-bodied staff in pairs;

(G)   careful checking for intruders in the area of the pay points;

(H)   using secure pay points;

(J)   insisting on independent identification of the payee, e.g. by the foreman or by using an identification card with a photograph;

(K)   ensuring that all employees sign for the receipt of pay packets. A computer-printed list of payroll numbers and names can be used for this purpose;

(L)   secure retention of any uncollected pay packets. These pay packets should only be collected by the payee or his authorised representative from the payroll office. Special arrangements must be made for any pay packets which remain uncollected for any length of time, e.g. the cash can be replaced by a cheque which can then be posted to the employee;

(M)   any errors in packeting the cash should only be accepted if the pay packet is returned unopened. This pay packet design must, of course, facilitate the checking of the cash without its being opened (22.15 above explains this further);

(N)   the signed receipts, uncollected pay packets and errors must be reconciled against the original total number of pay packets and the total cash amount for the pay period.

Similar precautions to the above should be taken with open cheques which can be cashed directly. Where payment is by EFT (BACS) or paper credit transfer the main concern is the distribution of payslips inside pay packets in a manner which respects confidentiality. This is primarily a question of secure handling of the pay packets and accurate identification of the payee. Here again undistributed pay packets can be a problem but as no cash is involved they can be retained by a responsible member of staff until collected. Cheques are preferably only used in occasional payroll circumstances when they can be issued by the cashier against a payroll cheque requisition. Such cheques then enjoy the same degree of security as all the other cheque payments made by the organisation. Cheques can be delayed or lost in the post creating further problems. Bank reconciliation can also be tedious because of the large number of cheques used although the process can be computerised.

There are unfortunately situations which may require large-scale use of cheques, for instance pension payroll. Where cheques are raised for the payroll department then typical precautions include:

(1)   strict control by serial number and total value;

(2)   taking care with the design of computer-printed cheques to minimise the possibility of fraudulent alterations;

(3)   the computer department must account for all cheques printed by the computer. All damaged cheques must be returned along with completed cheques and a regular reconciliation made;

(4)   cheques should be crossed 'account payee only' where acceptable to the payee. Banks impose strict restrictions on the use of cash cheques;

(5)   cheques should be kept in the safe;

(6)   all cheques should be raised and signed according to strict procedures and comply with the information on the requisition forms;

(7)   use of two signatories must be obligatory;

(8)   strict control of cheque-signing machines;

(9)   special care to be taken with pre-signed cheques;

(10)   security features such as the use of special types of ink and paper.

Fraud

23.13   Payroll systems are particularly vulnerable to a multiplicity of minor frauds which are capable of being committed by any employee.

Typical examples include inflated claims for expenses, time-keeping, bonuses, etc. One form of fraud, which was perhaps more common in the past, is employee 'truancy'. This is where an employee is 'clocked-on' for a whole shift at work. The employee then leaves work early, or may never have been present, the recording of his time being done by an accomplice. Another problem is 'phantoms'. These are non-existent employees, sometimes called 'dummies', 'ghosts' or 'deadmen', whose pay is collected by the person committing the fraud.

Standard precautions include:

(*a*)   installation of good controls and identification procedures;

(*b*)   rigorous insistence on the production of correctly checked and authorised documents from other departments, e.g. medical evidence with sickness claims, or a director's authorisation for a special bonus;

(*c*)   regular internal audits carried out of payroll procedures in all departments. Chapter 24 (Payroll Audits) contains further details on this. Remote pay sites should not be forgotten;

(*d*)   occasional spot checks on documents, individual payees, and departments. These checks can also be very useful for detecting errors;

(*e*)   segregation of staff duties both inside and outside the payroll department. One form of segregation of duties is to delegate the cash wage make-up and the pay-out to a separate cashier's department. This may not be feasible in small organisations and runs counter to job enrichment strategies. It also makes the payroll services vulnerable to staff absence;

(*f*)   regular job rotation. This helps uncover fraud and mistakes. It can also be part of job enrichment programmes;

(*g*)   strict disciplinary action taken when an offence is detected;

(*h*)   regular checks not only for phantom payees, but also for leavers who remain on the payroll with their wages being collected by a fraudster. A standard check for this type of fraud is to compare the personnel and payroll records.

Mistakes

23.14   The main precautions against mistakes occurring are:

(*a*)   thorough computer data validation checks;

(*b*)   rigorous controls and procedures;

(*c*)   reliable payroll computer software;

(*d*)   adequate time and resources devoted to the pay operations;

(*e*)   checking for staff errors and paying particular attention to recurring mistakes, i.e. looking for errors of principle;

(*f*)   thorough staff training;

(*g*)   rotation of staff duties and shared checking responsibilities;

(*h*)   a reduction in time pressure where possible by appropriate re-allocation of resources;

(*j*)   concern for staff welfare (health, holidays etc.) as part of company personnel policy;

(*k*)   a willingness to seek and provide assistance by the management;

(*l*)   the management being genuinely interested in payroll matters;

(*m*)   regular and vigorous audits, together with procedular reviews;

(*n*)   strict testing and monitoring of new payroll computer software and payroll office procedures when new requirements arise, e.g. the introduction of SSP in 1983 and SMP in 1987;

(*o*)   considering the use of certification schemes for assuring the quality of financial software, e.g. those of the IDPM (Institute of Data Processing Management);

(*p*)   the adoption of formal quality management procedures for all aspects of payroll and related work, e.g. British Standard BS5750 (now BS EN ISO 9000).

A common and worrying mistake with payroll and pension systems is wrong payments. Payroll underpayments are often corrected by paying the outstanding amount in the following pay period. Overpayments can of course be corrected in a similar manner by deductions from the succeeding wage or salary payments. However, recovering overpayments is usually more sensitive. It can lead to all sorts of practical and legal problems some of which are discussed in 5.14 to 5.17 and 18.22(*g*) above and in Reference (16) in 5.42 above. A further common mistake is failure to comply with legal requirements such as PAYE. Some of the consequences of a failure to comply with legal requirements, e.g. fines, are discussed in References (6) and (7) in 23.22 below.

Records and computers

23.15   Records must normally be held for six years. This is the period up to which a normal contract can be enforced at law. [*LA 1980, s 5*]. The Inland Revenue and Contributions Agency, however, insist on retaining payroll data for at least three complete tax years. Good practice should dictate that data is accessed and retained for an appropriate time period in relation to content and nature. Clearly the minimum retention period is determined by the nature of the potential problems for which the documentation is required. Long minimum periods may be appropriate in some circumstances, for example up to 50 years for health and safety matters, and maybe longer for pensions administration.

Good office practice requires secure but convenient filing methods. Microfilm and computer produced microfiche can be of great assistance in improving security. They are easy to lock away and security copies can be kept off site. Microfilm and microfiche are also extremely convenient to use. Optical storage and retrieval devices are seen as being important in the future for storing business records. The idea is to store the images of virtually any type of document. These are scanned into the IT system and retrieved by displaying them onto a computer screen. This type of document image retention also has built-in security features, not least being its inclusion in a general systems back-up and off-site storage. See 26.17 above for further details. The legal aspects of data storage should also be considered. For instance under *DPA 1984*, as discussed below, personal computer data should not be kept any longer than necessary, and this data must be secure. Microfilm and computer records can be acceptable as legal evidence. However, this is a complex and uncertain area.

With regard to computers the most important requirements are the keeping of security copies of computer payroll files, adequate testing of computer programs and contingency plans for failures in the computer service. Safeguards must prevent fraudulent or malicious interference with computer systems and guarantee the secure use of BACS, computer-printed cheques etc.

The continued expansion of the use of PCs lends itself to great system security measures, and automatic safe retention and storage of data. What should be borne in mind is that use of E-mail, intranet and even internet access, means security and confidentiality needs to be vigilantly controlled, at local, middle and the highest management levels.

In a little more detail the main security aspects of computer systems are listed below with some risk control measures.

(*a*)   ***Physical security*** — For example, special extinguishers designed for electrical fires should be installed. Precautions such as UPSs (Uninterruptable Power Supplies) as well as use of 'clean' electricity supplies (i.e. electricity not coming straight from the grid) are frequently used in

517

commercial computing. Theft of small computers and computer components has become a problem in recent years. This can be overcome, for instance, by special physical locking devices for office computers.

(b)   ***Access control*** — 'Hacking' can be a problem. This is unauthorised attempts to access and interfere with computer systems often via remote terminals or personal computers. Simple restrictions like limiting physical access to equipment and the careful use of passwords can be reasonably effective precautions. Security features are often built into the standard computer operating system as well as the payroll software itself. For example with mainframes and minicomputers there is a general 'log-on' procedure for whichever application system it is intended to use, and this procedure requires a password. The payroll software can then demand further passwords for different payroll functions like updating employee data. The limiting and restriction of access rights, i.e. read only access, are highly useful in the security process. Proprietary general-purpose security software is also available which can supplement or replace the security facilities of other software. This general-purpose software can prevent unauthorised access to any system or data on the computer. It not only hampers unauthorised administrative staff, but also unauthorised computer staff. Computer people could use their skills to try to by-pass the access controls in ordinary software, but they find security software a more difficult proposition. This general-purpose security software is particularly useful with PCs where the operating system provides notoriously weak security features. Security can be further increased by the use of hardware devices, for example electronic keys on computer workstations.

(c)   ***Data*** — It is essential to make regular security copies of payroll data. Normally at any one time there should be at least three recent copies of the main payroll computer files. Data can also be encrypted (specially encoded) to make it more secure. This means that it can only be read with special software routines built into the payroll system. Limited and restricted access rights can aid with security processes.

(d)   ***Software*** — There should be security copies of software. One risk is that staff may accidentally, fraudulently or maliciously change existing payroll software, for example to increase their own pay. Also in the last few years software viruses have been a growing and serious threat. Viruses are pieces of software which can infect any computer system and replicate themselves. They are often maliciously destructive, for instance making data unreadable. Sometimes they are merely mischievous. Viruses can, for instance, be inadvertently introduced to a system on a magnetic disk containing genuine data or software. There are several precautions which can be taken to deal with this problem. These include using special software which checks and removes known viruses. Also disks and tapes containing data and software should only come from approved reliable sources; otherwise they may be infected. Stringent and controlled use of virus checking and disinfecting routines and software on all media prior to the introduction to PCs or networks is vital to standard security.

(*e*) **Automated credit payments** — BACS (Bankers Automated Clearing Services) is used for most salary payments today, as well as many wage payments to manual workers. Automated payments to employees via BACS are discussed in 22.10 above and this is an inherently more secure method of payment than cash or cheque payments. The BACS service itself is secure, but at the employer's end there is still the possibility of accidents, fraudulent interference and sabotage. BACS provides the employer with security procedures, e.g. nominated individuals for contact purposes, the use of numbered labels for magnetic tapes, and passwords for BACSTEL when sending payments over telecommunication lines. Furthermore optional checks can be used to give warnings when a transaction value exceeds an agreed limit. BACS also provides controls to prevent a set of payments being processed twice. However, the employer preparing BACS payments with a computer system must take security precautions. For example, arrangements must be made so that it is virtually impossible to interfere with the computer payments data before it is sent to the BACS Ltd centre. A structured verification and authorisation procedure involving inter-departmental cross referencing is highly recommended within a quality business approach. Semi-automated credit transfer systems such as Autopay discussed in 22.11 above also require the employer to adopt common-sense security features. Basically this again means ensuring that the payment details sent to the bank are correct.

The *CMA 1990* has increased the legal protection against attempts to interfere with computer systems. This Act creates three categories of criminal offence:

(i) intentionally obtaining unauthorised access to a computer system;

(ii) obtaining such access to commit or facilitate further criminal offences;

(iii) intentionally causing unauthorised modification to the contents of a computer.

It is obviously sensible and clarifies matters if authorised access is explicitly defined for each computer function. As well as including the details in departmental circulars and office manuals authorised users can be shown on the start-up VDU screen of a system.

There is now a British Standard, BS7799, on information management security.

Most software and hardware is subject to restrictions as a result of IPR (Intellectual Property Rights). IPR problems concerned with patents are improbable in payroll, but copyright can be an issue. Reputable businesses are unlikely to be using 'pirated' payroll software, i.e. software used without the authority of its owner, usually because no payment has been made. However, with the proliferation of personal computers more copies of software products may be in use than are included in licence agreements. This is easy to do inadvertently with a popular software product like a word processor. Indeed most staff will be unaware of the details of the software contracts. It is the departmental manager's job, often with the assistance of IT staff, to monitor and control the use of software, and to ensure that everything in use is legitimate.

A strict monitoring of licence control and retention is essential as we move towards an age of expanding software availability and expansive usage.

Confidentiality and data protection

23.16   Virtually all payroll data can be regarded as confidential. This must be achieved by:

(a)   strict instructions to payroll and other staff not to reveal confidential information. These instructions should be documented in letters of appointment, office procedures etc;

(b)   strict access control for both manual and computer records;

(c)   shredding all surplus paper records. Computer magnetic tapes and disks must be 'scratched', i.e. the payroll data eliminated before general re-use.

Where individuals query pay details over the telephone, a legitimate proof of identity should also be requested. When outsiders seek pay information the payee's consent must be obtained. A typical case is a building society checking mortgage application details. Government officers and auditors, of course, have statutory rights to inspect payroll data. Access by others may be permissible but their authority and purpose should always be established. As a warning of the dangers, in one case bogus telephone calls were received. The callers pretended to represent the Contributions Agency. Their purpose was to collect employee addresses for debt collection purposes. The use of a return phone call, if in doubt, may be employed.

The *DPA 1984* has introduced various requirements for computer users who process personal data i.e. data concerning people rather than corporations, property, stock etc. In theory payroll, pensions and accounting systems are specifically exempt under the Act. [*DPA 1984, s 32*]. However, the exemptions are narrowly defined. Also in practice most computer payroll systems provide the general management and the personnel department with information which is not exempt. It should be noted that the Act only applies to computer data and not to the manual records. Word processing is usually exempt and so are some electronic communication systems, e.g. fax. Briefly the Act provides that all relevant computer systems which process personal data must be registered with the Data Protection Registry. [*DPA 1984, ss 4–6*]. Such computer systems must comply with the eight data protection principles which are listed below. Penalties can be imposed for non-compliance with the Act. Offending computer systems could be legally prohibited from operating. [*DPA 1984, s 11*]. Individuals may also be able to claim compensation where their data is misused. Generally the advice would be to register computer payrolls. However, there is little in the data protection legislation to worry most payroll departments as the principles mainly enshrine good practice. It is possible that data protection could result in some minor inconvenience, for instance principle (vii) below grants individuals access to their own computer data on demand. In the wider area of personnel computer systems there may be some concern about the consequences of the Act. This could be an important consideration if payroll and personnel systems are combined.

(*DPA 1984* uses the terms 'data user' and 'data subject'. In the payroll context a 'data user' is normally the employer or pension scheme trustee while a 'data subject' is the payee.)

The eight data protection principles [*DPA 1984, 1 Sch*] are reproduced below.

(i) *Fairly and lawfully obtained* — The information relating to personal data shall be obtained and the personal data shall be processed, fairly and lawfully. In considering whether information is obtained fairly the registrar considers whether any person has been deceived or misled as to the purpose for which it is to be held, used or disclosed.

(ii) *Held for specified purposes* — Personal data shall be held only for one or more specified and lawful purposes. Specified purposes are those described in the register.

(iii) *Restricted use and disclosure* — Personal data held for any purpose or purposes shall not be used or disclosed in any manner incompatible with that purpose or those purposes. Incompatible use or disclosure means otherwise than as described on the register.

(iv) *Adequate and not excessive* — Personal data held for any purpose or purposes shall be adequate, relevant and not excessive in relation to that purpose or those purposes.

(v) *Accurate and up to date* — Personal data shall be accurate and, where necessary, kept up to date. 'Accurate' means correct and must not be misleading as to any matter of fact. The data user may be unable to ensure the accuracy of data received from the data subject or a third party. There are provisions in the Act whereby by marking and processing such data appropriately the data user will not be considered to be in breach of this principle. Such marking or processing will also absolve him from any liability to pay compensation for damage caused by the inaccuracy of the data. Data should be kept up to date except where the purpose for which it is held does not require it to be updated.

(vi) **Limited retention** — Personal data held for any purpose or purposes shall not be kept for longer than is necessary for that purpose or those purposes.

(vii) **Individual access** — An individual shall be entitled:

    (i)   at reasonable intervals and without undue delay or expense:

- to be informed by any data user whether he holds personal data of which that individual is the subject;

- to grant access to any such data held by a data user; and

    (ii)   where appropriate, to have such data corrected or erased.

This principle introduces the right of subject access which is fully described in *DPA 1984, s 21*. 'Reasonable intervals' will vary with the nature of the data, the nature and frequency of processing etc. and is not defined. The Act stipulates that subject access requests shall be met within 40 days after receipt or determination of additional necessary information. The Secretary of State can make an order fixing the maximum fee which may be charged for subject access, thus ensuring that no 'undue expense' is incurred by data subjects. The current maximum fee that a data subject can be charged by the data user is £10.

(viii) **Security** — Appropriate security measures shall be taken against unauthorised access to, alteration, disclosure or destruction of personal data and against accidental loss or destruction of personal data. In considering whether security measures are appropriate regard should be had to the nature of the personal data and the potential harm which could result from unauthorised access etc. It will be necessary also to consider the place where the data is stored, security measures programmed into the equipment and measures taken for ensuring the reliability of staff having access to the data. This eighth principle applies to computer bureaux as well as data users.

It should be noted that the eighth principle ((viii) above) uses the term bureau in a wider sense than usual. Therefore, a central headquarter running a computer payroll for subsidiaries would be construed as a bureau. Similarly a company volunteering its computer as emergency back-up to other businesses would be a bureau.

Although external organisations are in a position to recommend and enforce the *Data Protection Act 1984*, it is the payroll department's responsibility to ensure the correctness and security of all data retained.

Courts may order data users to pay compensation for damage and any associated distress suffered by data subjects as a result of:

- loss of data;

- destruction of data without the authority of the data user;

- disclosure of, or access to, data without the authority of the data user;

- inaccurate data, i.e. data which is incorrect or misleading as to any matter of fact.

[*DPA 1984, ss 22, 23*].

(References (2) and (3) in 23.22 below contain further details on data protection.)

As a result of the European *Data Protection Directive*, UK data protection law has become more strict, for example, when the *DPA 1998* comes into force in Spring 1999, manual data will also be included. See References (8) to (11) in 23.22 below for a discussion of this.

Purposes of administrative controls

23.17   The primary purpose of administrative control procedures is the detection of errors. A secondary purpose is to provide simple statistics. Control procedures tend to concentrate on overall collections of data rather than individual items. Administrative controls are used with both manual and computer payrolls and the principles are the same in both cases. However, computer systems ease the work enormously and allow more detailed controls to be installed.

Types of control totals

23.18   Administrative controls have three basic formats:

(*a*)   *actual figure = expected figure*

(*b*)   *new figure = old figure ± adjustments*

(*c*)   *new cumulative figure (carried forward) = old cumulative (brought forward) ± increase (or decrease)*

Example — Using the first format a batch of forms has a header form stating ten forms are expected in the batch. The computer totals the number of forms entered and prints or displays the actual number entered, hopefully, ten forms. Any discrepancy is highlighted.

Example — As an illustration of the second format 5,000 employees are on a computer payroll file. Ten employees leave and twenty join. Clearly then the new number of active employees should be 5,010 (5,000 − 10 + 20).

Example — Gross pay can be used to show the use of the third format. If the total gross pay to date in week three is £300,000 and the total gross pay in week four is £90,000, then the week four total gross pay to date should be: £390,000 = £300,000 + £90,000. The computer calculates independently the current week's gross pay, the total brought forward and total carried forward gross pay. Manual calculations to arrive at these totals can provide a further check.

Administrative control procedures

23.19 These control procedures can be dealt with as follows.

(*a*) *Discrepancies* — Control procedures cover the formal recording of control checks and the corrective action to be taken in the event of an error being detected. Control checks are normally recorded either on a special control book or directly on computer print-outs. In either case the working must be clearly shown. If control totals do not balance then corrective action must be taken. For instance in the example at 23.18 above, a figure of 5,010 employees was expected. If the computer only recorded 5,005 on its file then the missing five must be explained. If five sets of joiner details had inadvertently been overlooked then they must be identified and promptly entered onto the computer payroll file.

(*b*) *Reconciliation* — Some control totals can be allowed to differ provided there is a good explanation for the difference. The most familiar example is the bank reconciliation where the cash book bank balance does not agree with the bank statement balance, example as a result of delays in presenting cheques to the bank. The term is often used where two systems are related or data is passed between them. A common case would be reconciling the total number of employees on a pension system with those on the payroll. The difference could be validly explained by the pension scheme membership rules, for instance if part-timers are on the payroll but are not members of the pension scheme. However, employees omitted from the pension scheme by mistake would also be revealed by this check. (See 19.9 below for reconciliation of payroll control accounts.)

(*c*) *Data errors* — The automatic checking of data for errors or warning conditions is a major benefit of computers. A common example is checking to ensure the sex data field only contains 'M' or 'F' or a blank (for unknown). A more sophisticated example is cross-checking the sex, date of birth and NIC table letter fields. This could reveal employees over state pensionable age who had not been assigned NIC table letter 'C'. Data which is rejected because of errors must of course be corrected and re-submitted in a controlled fashion. Examples of warnings are where the computer highlights very high or very low net pay figures for a particular employee. More sophisticated systems will provide a wider range of validation criteria. For example, generation of a report identifying percentage differences in basic or net pay compared to the last period.

(*d*) **Audit trails** — Audit trails provide a clear recorded detailed path of all the various stages of payroll processing. Normally this consists of input documents and copies of all computer outputs. Detailed controls can then be obtained by checking that each individual transaction has been correctly processed through all the payroll stages, manual and computer. For instance, an overtime return can be followed through to net pay on a payslip. In practice such detailed checking is often reserved for special queries, spot checks or work carried out by the auditors. The computer reports must be sufficiently detailed to follow a particular transaction through all the various stages of computer processing. Many standard systems produce audit reports that show old and new values of permanent data, thereby helping to highlight data that has been incorrectly changed, i.e. without having authorised input, such as a transposed employee number.

(*e*) **Verification** — This involves the checking of individual payee records and calculations in detail. It is expensive and only used occasionally, for example spot checks on records. One version of verification used with computer systems is to enter data from the forms twice and for the computer to request correction of any discrepancies before processing continues.

(*f*) **Independent control checks** — Examples of how control total errors are resolved are dealt with in 23.18 above. The important feature of control total procedures is ensuring that all figures in the equation are independently calculated. Independent calculations with computer systems implies either different pieces of software each calculating various parts of the equation separately, or some parts calculated by the software and the others calculated manually. In addition, of course, different sources of data are used for the calculations for example data on input forms and data on the computer file. This can be illustrated by once again using the example in 23.18 above. The computer can total the brought-forward figure of 5,000 whilst scanning the payroll file at the end of a week. It can total the carried-forward figure in a similar way at the end of the following week. The reconciling figures of leavers and joiners can hopefully be prepared from a manual count of the input forms.

(*g*) **Hash totals** — Sometimes control totals, i.e. 'hash totals' are produced for non-cash data. For instance the date of birth of employees could be treated as a number and totalled. Any of the three formats in 23.18 above can be used to check that all the data has been accurately entered into the computer. However, the use of such 'hash' totals is only used occasionally in payroll and associated systems.

Types of payroll controls

23.20 The following sections briefly outline typical controls used on computer payroll systems. It is not economic to control in detail all the data used in payroll systems. The main data which is controlled includes:

(a)   documents input and output, e.g. input forms, payslips and cheques;

(b)   number of payees;

(c)   gross pay elements, e.g. basic pay, hours, bonuses and allowances;

(d)   non-statutory deductions, e.g. recovering previous overpayments and pension contributions;

(e)   net pay, e.g. analysed by payment method such as cash, cheque and BACS.

Statutory deductions like income tax are totalled for accounting to the Inland Revenue. However, only a very rough control can be exercised over the amount because of the complexities and variations in each payee's calculation. So if tax last week was 15 per cent of the total payroll gross pay it should be approximately 15 per cent this week as well.

Cash needs special control procedures. The total net pay cash required is ordered from the bank according to the coinage analysis (now more correctly called the cash analysis). This is a computer print-out showing the required number of notes and coins of each denomination. The coinage analysis shows not only the total amounts required but also the amounts for each department. Pay packets can then be made up department by department. With this method any shortage or surplus only involves searching a relatively small number of packets to locate the error.

A more proactive view of payroll controls is based on modern quality management. This seeks more than technical assurance that the payroll service is good, and tries to maintain and develop 'customer' satisfaction. Obviously this view is of particular relevance to organisations offering commercial payroll services such as computer bureaux. In the context of a normal payroll department a 'customer' is any user of the service such as an employee, a pensions department, the Inland Revenue, or managers who receive pay and related reports. Feedback can still be obtained from these 'customers' to assess service provided.

At the simplest level quality management involves collecting broad statistics, and keeping records, on the various types of error. The statistics can be used by payroll administrators, perhaps in the form of graphs, to control the quality of the service. Hopefully they can demonstrate that preventive measures are resulting in a small and declining error rate. Another more qualitative approach is regular contact with users of the payroll service to seek their views. This can be done more formally with questionnaires.

Analyses and management reports

23.21   Detailed analyses and summaries are often produced from the payroll system for management. These analyses and reports are usually part of the management controls of a business. For instance the administrative controls may ensure that a management overtime report is correct and not based on fraudulent claims. It is then for the management to decide whether the overtime figures are excessive or not and to take the appropriate action. One of the most significant management control techniques is budgetary control. This involves, *inter alia*, a comparison of actual departmental total pay against the budgeted amount. Such close financial control usually requires computer payroll systems passing over detailed pay data to the accounts systems. Payroll reporting or accounts interfaces, if correctly used, provide vital cross referencing for cost centre and budgetary analysis. (Reference (4) in 23.22 below contains an explanation of the management accounting and control approach.) Chapter 19 (Payroll Accounting) discusses the accounting requirements placed on payroll.

References

23.22   The books below give a fairly complete coverage of the general and computer aspects of security and related topics. Many of the other control aspects can be found scattered across text books on accounting, business administration, management and business computing. However, none cover the payroll issues in depth.

(1)   'Tolley's Business Administration', Tolley Publishing Co Ltd. (This is a looseleaf publication which is continually updated. It contains major sections on document retention, health and safety, insurance, and security in general.)

(2)   The Data Protection Registrar, 'The Data Protection Act 1984 Guidelines'. There are eight guidelines published in the same series.

(3)   'Code on Employee Data', IPD, 1998.

(4)   Sizer J, 'An Insight into Management Accounting', Penguin, 1998.

(5)   'Tolley's Health and Safety at Work Handbook', Tolley Publishing Co Ltd, Eleventh Edition 1998.

(6)   Dugdale H, 'The Tax and NICs Men Cometh', PMR, April 1996. (Handling PAYE and DSS inspections.)

(7)   Dugdale H, 'The Tax and NICs Men Come and Go', PMR, June 1996. (Handling PAYE and DSS inspections.)

(8)   'Data Protection Consultation', CSR, 12 June, 1996. (Possible changes to data protection legislation as a result of the recent EU directive.)

(9)   'Safeguarding Rights in the Information Age', PMR, December 1997.

(10) Singleton S, 'Keeping it Personal', CSR, 18 March, 1998. (Considers provisions of the European Data Protection Directive.)

(11) Marke R, 'Internal Affairs', CSR, 14 October, 1998. (Practical issues arising from the implementation of the *DPA 1998*.)

24 Payroll Audits

Scope of this chapter

24.1   An audit is an independent examination of business activities and records. The scope of an audit and the persons performing the work depend on the audit objectives. The word 'audit' is sometimes loosely used to describe any special investigation into business activities, for example efficiency audits which check that a department or system is operating efficiently and is cost-effective.

Auditors can be classified as external or internal. External auditors are independent of the management of an organisation. Internal auditors are employees who report to the management.

Generally, external auditors concentrate on assessing that the published accounts of an organisation give a 'true and fair' view of its financial affairs. The payroll procedures and records must therefore be assessed along with all other systems that affect these matters. Internal auditors may extend their work to cover such matters as the efficiency and security of the payroll. In addition the Inland Revenue and DSS have auditors to inspect payroll systems for the correct operation of PAYE, NICs, SSP, SMP etc. This chapter describes the different types of payroll audit, the methods that are employed and the legal framework within which the auditor operates. It concentrates on the external private sector audit. Chapter 23 (Security and Administrative Controls) also describes many of the features that auditors would expect to find as part of the system of internal controls.

Key points of payroll audits

24.2   These matters are summarised below:

(a)   audit techniques include analytical reviews, compliance tests, re-performance, reviewing the work of other auditors and proof in total;

(b)   methods of control include physical security measures, segregation of duties, authorisation, re-performance of duties and reconciliation or balance checks;

(c)   external financial audits are usually necessary to comply with statutory requirements and must be carried out by appropriately qualified accountants. Internal audits complement and extend the work of the external auditor;

(d)   inland Revenue and DSS inspectors check regularly for employer compliance with PAYE, NIC and related regulations;

(e)   certain specified payroll data must be disclosed by statute in company accounts.

Types of payroll audit

24.3   Payroll audits can be classified under the following headings.

(a)   ***Statutory audits*** — There is a legal requirement for limited companies and public bodies such as local authorities to have their financial records audited. The auditor must be external to the organisation and is usually a firm of accountants or the District Audit Officer in the case of local authorities. In the case of audits of limited companies the auditor must be a 'registered' auditor. [*CA 1989, Part II*]. The *Companies Act 1985 (Audit Exemption) (Amendment) Regulations, 1997 (SI 1997 No 936)* exempts some smaller companies from the annual statutory audit (basically, those companies with an annual turnover less than £350,000).

(b)   ***Internal audit*** — Many large organisations employ their own internal audit staff. A degree of independence is obtained by reporting direct to senior executives. As well as performing authorisation and verification work the internal auditor may be used to investigate the efficiency of the procedures and systems in the payroll department.

(c)   ***Inland Revenue and DSS inspections*** — Payroll departments have a duty to collect income tax and NICs and pay SSP and SMP on behalf of the Government. The total value of such transactions can be high, and both the Inland Revenue and DSS have the power to inspect payroll records and procedures to ensure that everything is correctly administered. (See also 12.7 above.)

Auditing standards

24.4   The accountancy profession in the UK and Ireland has issued several Statements of Auditing Standards (SASs). These provide guidance on the objectives and principles governing external statutory audits. They also contain essential procedures with which auditors must comply.

Audit planning

24.5   Auditors should plan the audit work so as to perform the audit in an effective manner. To do this they should have a knowledge of the business of the entity being audited in order to assess the potential for error or misstatement.

The auditor may use a combination of techniques in order to obtain reasonable assurance that payroll details in the accounts give a true and fair view. The professional bodies' recommendations on audit evidence state that the auditor should perform tests for completeness, existence, ownership, valuation and disclosure. The most efficient approach is determined at the planning stage of the audit. The techniques used comprise one or more of the following:

(*a*)   analytical review;

(*b*)   compliance testing of systems of accounting and internal control;

(*c*)   verification of transactions by re-performance, commonly known as substantive testing;

(*d*)   reviewing the work of other auditors, either external or internal;

(*e*)   proof in total.

(These terms are explained in 24.8 to 24.12 below.)

The auditor must take into account the characteristics of the system being audited. He can then plan the use of the appropriate audit techniques to give the required level of assurance of the material fact at issue.

Example 1 — ABC Ltd has a well established and sound payroll system. Staff turnover is low and all employees are salaried. An outline audit plan may comprise:

● compliance tests of the key payroll controls;

● an analytical review of payroll costs; and

● the minimum of re-performance testing.

Example 2 — XYZ Ltd employs students for seasonal work. Wages are calculated by branch staff and paid from cash trading receipts. In this case an outline audit plan may comprise:

● a review of the regional office checks on cash disbursements;

● a substantial number of re-performance tests.

Generally it is not worthwhile seeking assurance from compliance tests if there is inadequate segregation of duties. However, a good system of internal control can substantially reduce the need for time-consuming re-performance tests.

Audit evidence

24.6   When performing their work, auditors should obtain sufficient appropriate evidence to be able to draw reasonable conclusions on which to base the audit opinion. The auditor will consider audit risk, materiality (see 24.7 below), previous experience and other audit findings when determining the quantity of audit evidence. The appropriateness of audit evidence depends upon its relevance to the objective of the audit test being performed (see 24.10(*a*)–(*e*) below) and its reliability.

Materiality

24.7   Auditors have recognised that it is not practicable to obtain 100 per cent assurance that the subject of their audit does not contain any errors or misstatements. Therefore, they have developed the concept of materiality.

Materiality is an expression of the relative significance or importance of a particular matter in the context of the financial statements as a whole. A matter is material if its omission or misstatement would reasonably mislead the reader of the accounts. Materiality has both quantitative and qualitative aspects and, therefore, is not capable of mathematical definition.

Analytical review

24.8   Numbers or values on their own are rarely of use to the reader of financial statements. The value has to be placed in context by comparison with another value. Examples are listed below.

(*a*)   Total payroll costs for current year   v   Total payroll costs for previous year

(*b*)   Sales per employee for company A   v   Sales per employee for company B

(*c*)   Actual departmental head count   v   Budgeted departmental head count

Comparisons can be made over time for a single operation or across operations within a single time period. Analytical review procedures involve studying and comparing interrelationships between the values subject to audit and other relevant data. The basic premise underlying these procedures is that, in the absence of any facts to the contrary, known operating relationships among data may reasonably be expected to continue into the future or to apply currently to other similar operations. Therefore analytical review procedures should be designed to identify for investigation unexpected fluctuations or variations in a relationship and the absence of such features where they are expected.

Most analytical review are performed by using one or more of the following procedures.

(i) **Ratio analysis** — This is used to express two or more values as a single unit, for example gross payroll costs per production hour could be compared at different times or between different factories.

(ii) **Tabulation or graphs** — Tabulating or plotting data on a graph or a bar chart often reveals trends or fluctuations. By using the statistical technique called 'regression analysis' to measure changes in relationships it is possible to identify those matters in the current period which should be investigated. The mathematics of regression analysis becomes cumbersome as the amount of data increases. Therefore, this technique is best exploited by using a computer.

Compliance tests

24.9   In most organisations the directors or senior executives are responsible for safeguarding its assets. This is because they have a duty of stewardship to the shareholders. It is often impossible or impractical for such persons to safeguard assets by personal supervision and, therefore, an adequate system of internal controls is installed. The 'Report of the Committee on the Financial Aspects of Corporate Governance' (The Cadbury Committee) recommends that the directors report annually on the effectiveness of their systems of internal control. Such a report must now be included in the Directors' Report of companies listed on the Stock Exchange.

For accounting periods beginning on or after 1 January 1995, the directors should include a statement on internal controls in the annual report. It is recommended that as a minimum the statement should include:

(*a*)   an acknowledgement by the directors that they are responsible for the company's system of internal financial control;

(*b*)   an explanation that such a system can provide only reasonable and not absolute assurance against material misstatement or loss;

(*c*)   a description of the key procedures that the directors have established, and which are designed to provide effective internal financial control;

(*d*)   confirmation that the directors (or a board committee) have reviewed the effectiveness of the system of internal financial control.

Controls can be preventive or detective and can be effective against error, irregularity or both. The basic methods of control are listed below.

(i) **Physical** — To prevent irregularities, for example pay packets delivered by a security company and kept in a safe until distributed.

(ii) **Segregation of duties** — To prevent irregularities and to detect error, for instance clockcards are distributed to employees by persons independent of those who calculate wages to prevent the creation of 'ghost' workers.

(iii) **Authorisation** — To prevent error or irregularities, for example a printout of the payroll has to be signed by the finance director before the cash can be drawn to make up pay packets.

(iv) **Re-performance of duties** — To detect errors, for example all clockcards are entered into a payroll system twice by two different data preparation clerks. The payroll programs are not run until after the input data has been compared.

(v) **Reconciliation of independently prepared balances** — To detect errors or irregularities, for example the gross payroll costs as computed by the payroll department are reconciled to the costing summary which has been prepared independently by, for instance, the costing department.

(See 23.12 to 23.15 and 23.17 to 23.21 above for further details on internal controls.)

The auditor may wish to place reliance on the system of internal controls to prevent or detect errors or irregularities. In order to gain reliance it is necessary for the auditor to understand the system, identify the controls upon which reliance is to be placed and to test that such controls have operated effectively throughout the period under review. This normally requires the auditor to document the system and controls in a narrative or diagrammatic form. It is important to ensure that any computerised features of a system are recorded according to the required level of detail. It is not sufficient to treat the computer as a 'black box'. The auditor should not need specialist knowledge to record a computerised system but it may sometimes be necessary to call in a specialist to evaluate and test the system. (See 23.15 above.)

Once the auditor has identified the key controls on which reliance is to be placed they should be tested. Such testing is known as compliance testing as the objective is to determine whether the controls have been operated in compliance with authorised procedures. Examples of compliance tests are given below.

(A) **Walk-through tests** — A single transaction is followed through the system, for example a clockcard is traced from issue to payment of wages.

(B) **Observation** — The operation of a control is observed in action, for example by attending a payout of wages.

(C)   ***Block tests*** — A set of documents is checked for evidence of control, for example all clockcards for a preselected week are checked to ensure that they have been signed by the foreman.

After compliance testing the auditor is able to conclude in one of three ways stated below on the system of internal controls.

- It is weak and no reliance can be placed on it.

- It is strong and reliance can be placed on it.

- It is generally strong but contains a few weaknesses.

In the latter case the auditor may be able to devise and perform pinpoint tests to cover specific weaknesses. The auditor needs to decide whether it is more efficient to perform the pinpoint tests or to gain reliance by using other methods.

If a weakness in internal control results in material losses which have to be disclosed in the financial statements, then the directors should either describe what corrective action has been taken or state why no changes are necessary.

Verification of transactions by re-performance

24.10   By re-performing some or all of the procedures which gave rise to a transaction being recorded the auditor can gain assurance on five matters listed below.

(*a*)   ***Occurrence*** — The transaction occurred during a given period.

(*b*)   ***Completeness*** — All transactions that should be recorded are recorded.

(*c*)   ***Rights and obligations*** — The transaction recorded a valid right or obligation.

(*d*)   ***Valuation*** — The transaction is recorded with the correct amount.

(*e*)   ***Allocation*** — The transaction is properly described, classified and disclosed.

When a transaction is found to be incorrect this indicates a misstatement in the financial statements. This may have been due to an error or an irregularity in the amount recorded or in the accounting principle applied. Further, if the misstatement is due to an irregularity then the perpetrator may have attempted to conceal the evidence. The auditor needs to consider these factors in designing the nature and extent of re-performance tests.

Examples of various types of re-performance tests likely to be used in a payroll audit are as follows:

(i)   agreeing the hours paid from the payslip to the supporting clockcard;

535

(ii)   checking that the rate used to calculate gross pay is from an authorised current pay scale;

(iii) testing the cast and crosscast of the individual pay details and payroll summary totals;

(iv)   checking postings from the payroll summary totals to the nominal ledger accounts;

(v)   reconciling the balance on subsidiary records (e.g. unclaimed wages) to the nominal ledger accounts.

Reliance on the work of other auditors

24.11   All organisations wish to perform audits as efficiently as possible. Some areas may be subject to the attention of more than one group of auditors. Therefore there is scope for savings if one auditor can rely on the work of another. The most usual example of this will be the external auditor who places reliance on the work of the internal auditor.

This may occur in three ways which are specified below.

(*a*)   Treating the internal auditor's work as part of a system of internal control.

(*b*)   Delegating the audit work in a particular area to internal auditors and then reviewing their findings.

(*c*)   Incorporating internal auditors within the audit team who then work under the direct supervision of the external auditors.

In all cases it is necessary to assess the competence, objectivity and independence of the other auditors. This can be done by determining their experience, qualifications and by reviewing previous reports and supporting documentation. In the case of a statutory audit, however, it remains the sole duty of the external auditors to express an opinion on the financial statements. It is not acceptable for the audit opinion to contain an exclusion clause such as '. . . except for the areas audited by the company's internal auditors . . .'.

Proof in total

24.12   In some circumstances it is possible to arrive at a close approximation to an accounting total by using other independent sources of information. Providing that the following requirements are met, the auditor is able to conclude on a value without performing tests on the individual components of the total.

(*a*)   The estimate must be computed from independent data which has a direct relationship with the amount being audited.

(*b*)   The estimate does not differ from the recorded amount by more than a pre-determined amount.

(*c*)   Explanations for the difference are obtained and corroborated.

Example — All salaried employees of XYZ Ltd are required to contribute five per cent of their basic pay to the company's pension scheme. This is matched by an equal contribution from the company. These amounts can be audited by either:

(i)   selecting a sample of employees, recomputing their pension contribution and following such amounts through various payroll summaries to the profit and loss account. It may be necessary to recast the payroll summaries; or

(ii)   multiplying the total gross salary of each department, as shown on schedules independently maintained by the personnel department, by five per cent. The totals are adjusted by the average pay increase awarded part way through the year as recorded in the minutes of a meeting of the board of directors. The proof in total computation may require to be refined if there have been significant staff changes in the year. However, it is likely to prove less tedious, and provide a greater understanding of the factors which determined the final value, than a series of detailed tests using individual pay details.

Legal requirements for an audit

24.13   The directors of a company are required to report to the shareholders each year and present accounts. Smaller companies may not need to have their accounts audited. (See 24.3 above.) Other business entities are also required to provide audited financial statements, such as local authorities and building societies. There are usually no legal requirements for sole traders and partnerships to have a statutory audit. Additional audits which have no legal status can be authorised by the management of an organisation. The most common example is the internal audit carried out by auditors employed by the organisation itself.

The following paragraphs explain the statutory audit of a limited company. The statutory audit of other business entities is in many respects similar.

Auditor's qualifications

24.14   Eligibility for appointment as a company auditor is governed by *Part II* of *CA 1989*. Basically, a person is eligible for appointment as a company auditor only if he is a member of a recognised supervisory body, and is eligible for appointment under the rules of that body. The rules are complex, but an external auditor will usually be either a member of one of the bodies of accountants established in the UK and recognised by the Department of Trade and Industry or individually authorised by the Secretary of State. [*CA 1985, s 389(1)*]. The recognised accounting bodies are the three chartered institutes (England and Wales, Scotland and Ireland) and the Chartered Association of Certified Accountants. (An internal auditor need not necessarily be such a qualified accountant.)

In practice a company will appoint a firm of accountants to act as auditors rather than a named individual. Thus, Jones Smith & Company, Chartered Accountants, may be appointed auditors and Mr Brown, a partner in the firm at the date of appointment, may be responsible for the audit. In turn, Mr Brown may delegate certain parts of the audit to other persons who need not be qualified as auditors, for example the person who performs audit work in the payroll department may be a trainee accountant.

Officers and servants of the company being audited, employees and partners of such officers and servants and associated undertakings of the company are disqualified from acting as the auditor. [*CA 1989, s 27*].

External auditor's legal duties

24.15   The auditor must report to the members (shareholders) of a company on the accounts examined by him, and state whether, in his opinion, they show a true and fair view and have been prepared in accordance with *CA 1985*. In order to determine if a true and fair view has been shown the auditor has to consider several factors, some of which are listed below.

(*a*)   Have proper accounting records been kept and are the accounts in agreement with them?

(*b*)   Have proper returns been received from branches not visited by the auditor?

(*c*)   Has all the information and explanations necessary for the purposes of the audit been provided?

(*d*)   Is the information in the directors' report consistent with the accounts?

(*e*)   Have details of directors' emoluments and other benefits and transactions between the company and its officers been included in the accounts? [*CA 1985, 6 Sch*, as amended by *CA 1989, 4 Sch*].

The procedures to be followed by the auditor in reaching his opinion are not specified in *CA 1985*, but the professional accountancy bodies have published Auditing Standards (SASs) with which their members must comply. (See 24.4 above.)

Audits should be planned so they have a reasonable chance of detecting material misstatements caused by fraud and error. Auditors should assess the risks that the financial statements contain material misstatements due to fraud or a breach of law or regulation. They will then need to design specific tests to consider whether the company has complied with relevant laws and regulations, particularly those laws and regulations where non-compliance may have a fundamental effect on the company's operations.

If an auditor discovers an impropriety or irregularity, it should be reported to the senior management. Depending upon the circumstances, it may be necessary for the auditor to refer to the matter in the audit report, or make a special report to the relevant regulatory body.

External auditor's legal powers

24.16   The auditor has a right of access to the books, accounts and vouchers of the company. He is entitled to receive from the officers of the company such information and explanations as is necessary for the performance of the audit. [*CA 1985, s 237A (1)*].

It is an offence for any officer of a company knowingly or recklessly to make a statement to the auditor which is misleading, false or deceptive in any material particular. [*CA 1985, s 237A (2)*]. A prison sentence of up to two years can be given to any officer of a company who knowingly or recklessly misleads an auditor. [*CA 1985, s 389A*]. The auditor of a holding company can request information or explanations from officers or auditors of subsidiary companies. [*CA 1985, s 237A(3)(4)*].

Liability of an external auditor for negligence

24.17   The standard of care and skill an auditor must use in performing his task is that of the reasonably careful and skilful auditor (*Re London and General Bank [1895] 2 Ch 673*). Today this indicates a high level of competence as there have been major increases in the standards laid down by the professional bodies and the powers granted by statute since 1895. Therefore, the statement that an auditor is a 'watchdog but not a bloodhound' (*Re Kingston Cotton Mill (No 2) [1896] 2 Ch 279*) may be considered out of date. The current situation is probably best summed up by Lord Denning who said that an auditor must approach his task 'with an inquiring mind — not suspicious of dishonesty, I agree — but suspecting that someone may have made a mistake somewhere and that a check must be made to ensure there has been none'. (*Fomento (Sterling Area) Ltd v Selsdon Pen Co Ltd [1958] 1 WLR 45*).

The external auditor has to express an opinion on the financial statements as a whole. Each component of the financial statements is subject to a level of examination which is proportional to its materiality (importance) and risk of misstatement. Thus the time spent by the external auditor in the payroll area may vary from one year to the next and from one company to another. The auditor is employed by the company and although he reports to the shareholders it is usually the company who brings an action for negligence. Examples of other persons who may rely on the auditor's work are potential shareholders and other interested parties such as banks and creditors.

The audit of computerised payroll systems

24.18   The computerisation of some or all of the functions in a payroll system may introduce new weaknesses which need to be detected, assessed and corrected as a result of the audit. These weaknesses are caused by the 'invisible' way in which data is held and manipulated by the computer. The assistance of a computer audit specialist may be necessary where the use of computerised data processing gives rise to a loss of the audit trail, i.e. where the computer programs do not produce sufficient printouts to enable a user to identify an item of input within an output total, and conversely to allow a user to ensure that only valid inputs are included in the output total.

In a payroll system there may be a printout showing individual gross pay and oncosts such as employer's NICs and another showing the total amount charged to various cost centres. Although the user could check that total payroll costs equal the total charged to all cost centres, there may be no record to prove that a named individual's costs had been allocated to the correct cost centres. In such a case the auditor may need to employ special audit software to verify or reperform the allocation process.

Other areas that may be addressed by the computer audit specialist are the computer access controls and the segregation of duties within the computer department. Computer access controls are often password based and restrict a user of the computer to those functions which are necessary for his work. Thus, the person who enters hours worked from clockcards should not be able to use the programs which set up details of new employees. Segregation of duties within the computer department is important to ensure that all new programs and modifications have been thoroughly tested before being used. Unless the computer is for the sole use of the payroll department, the computer audit specialist may perform a general review of the controls which are common to all control systems before concentrating on specific matters relating to the payroll applications.

If the payroll is prepared by an external bureau then management should ensure that the bureau will co-operate with the auditors, for example by providing a computer file of data for the auditors to test or by processing test transactions supplied by the auditors.

PAYE audit

24.19   The Inland Revenue may formally notify an employer that they intend to conduct an enquiry. This may be due to the discovery of an irregularity, as a result of a voluntary disclosure or on the basis of 'information received'. Businesses employing a large number of casual or part-time workers and those who make significant payments to consultants run an increased risk of being selected for such an enquiry. A PAYE audit is usually conducted by staff from the PAYE National Audit groups but PAYE compliance visits and special investigations are also undertaken by other sections of the Inland Revenue, for instance Employer Compliance. If the examiner comes from an Inland Revenue office of this type then this usually indicates that a serious breach of the regulations is suspected. In such circumstances it is appropriate to seek professional advice. The Inland Revenue examiner is looking for PAYE errors and omissions and consequently staff benefits are checked to ensure that they have been reported on a P11D return. The following records, *inter alia*, are reviewed during the audit:

(*a*)   cash books, petty cash books and cheque books are scrutinised for unsupported or round sum expense payments to employees;

(*b*)   payroll and PAYE records and computations are tested and agreed with the Form P35 entries;

(*c*)   Forms P45 and P46 and the procedures for their use, especially with regard to casual staff, are examined.

The remuneration package of directors and higher-paid employees is reviewed to identify benefits which should be subject to tax. As well as company cars, subsidised mortgages etc. the auditor may identify benefits which have not been recognised as such by the employer. These may include, for example, social events for employees and spouses accompanying employees on business trips. Although the tax on benefits is due from the employee, the employer may pay it to maintain employee relations. This in turn may be treated as a benefit and the Inland Revenue could require the sum involved to be grossed-up and the gross sum subject to tax. If an employer considers that his organisation may be at risk if subject to a PAYE audit it is of benefit to him to perform an internal audit. The Inland Revenue have been lenient on employers who can show that they have instigated preventive action. In addition to Inland Revenue audits, the DSS inspect NIC, SSP and SMP records and procedures. Employee benefit transactions can also be reviewed by the Customs and Excise officers to ascertain that VAT has been properly accounted for, such as VAT on employees' fuel benefit.

(See References (5), (6) and (7) in 24.21 below for further details on PAYE audits and related Inland Revenue investigations.)

Payroll audit checklist

24.20   Most payroll audits can be considered to have six objectives. These are listed below together with suggestions of the work to be performed to meet each objective. It is important that formal working papers are prepared (and retained) to record the planning of the audit work, the work done and the conclusions reached.

(*a*) **Objective 1** — To ensure that the gross payroll cost represents the amounts to which the employees of the organisation are entitled it is necessary to consider the following procedure.

(i) Proof in total is only suitable for payrolls with small numbers of employees and low staff turnover.

(ii) An analytical review can be performed using independent data on the number of employees, dates and percentage pay increases, overtime and bonus levels, accounting calendar (e.g. number of weeks per period, and holiday weeks) etc.

(iii) A representative sample can be chosen from the final accounting record of gross payroll costs (usually the general or nominal ledger) for re-performance testing.

(iv) An employee can be verified as genuine by reference to independently maintained personnel records or by personal contact. The payroll should be scrutinised to ensure that genuine employees are not recorded more than once.

(v) The calculation of gross pay can be reperformed by reference to authorised pay scales, clockcards, piecework records etc.

(vi) A check should be made that the liability to distribute the total net pay has been discharged by examining receipts for cash wages or the paid cheques. If the volume of payments in cash is large then the procedures for ordering the cash, making up the pay packets and distributing them should be observed. If payment is by credit transfer then the net pay amount should be traced to the payment details sent to the bank and the total of such payments should be agreed with the payroll and the bank statement.

(vii) In addition to a random sample of employees for substantive testing, the sample should include those persons who are in a position to adjust their own pay, i.e. those who prepare the payroll, handle or approve status change documents and have access to payroll records.

(viii) If the sample includes redundancy payments then they should be checked to ensure that they are at least equal to the statutory minimum and comply with the internal redundancy rules. Such payments should be followed up to confirm that the employer has received any government rebates to which he is entitled.

(*b*) **Objective 2** — To ensure that payroll costs are accounted for in full.

(i) Significant reliance may be placed on the fact that most employees have a strong interest in ensuring that they are paid promptly and correctly. Therefore, testing to ensure that payroll costs are not understated is confined to the end of the year accrual, for example where employees work a week 'in hand'. In most cases this amount is calculated and paid before the audit opinion is required.

(ii) If the examination of the system of internal control leads the auditor to consider that there is a reasonable probability of payroll costs being understated by a material amount then additional tests need to be performed. The nature of such tests is determined by the possible cause of the understatement. If a sample of employees is to be used for testing then they should be drawn from an independently maintained record of all employees, for example personnel records and not from the payroll records.

(c) **Objective 3** — To ensure that the employer's additional payroll costs represent payments for which they are liable.

(i) These additional costs are likely to comprise national insurance and pension contributions. As these amounts are related to gross pay it may be possible to use a proof in total technique. However, if there are large numbers of employees earning amounts at which NICs are charged at lower or zero rates then this may prove impractical. Similarly, pension contributions are often based on special rules which make their calculations difficult.

(ii) It may be possible to gain assurance from an analytical review of the relationship between the employer's NICs, pension contributions and employee's contributions because the latter are audited as part of the work on deductions from gross pay.

(iii) A representative sample of additional payroll costs selected from the final accounting records can be tested by reference to NIC tables or pension scheme rules. The posting of the total additional costs should be checked to the liability account.

(iv) Similar procedures can be applied in respect of other additional costs such as health insurance, luncheon vouchers etc.

(d) **Objective 4** — To ensure that all deductions from the gross payroll are authorised, correctly calculated and properly accounted.

(i) The major deductions are probably for taxation, national insurance and pension contributions. Other deductions should be supported by a written authority from the employee.

(ii) It is not normally possible to use either proof in total or analytical review to test deductions from payrolls.

(iii) Verification is obtained by testing a representative sample of deductions. It may be efficient to perform such tests on the same sample items that were selected to test gross pay. The sample size checked could be reduced in line with the importance of the deduction. The value of taxation is unlikely to exceed 25 per cent of gross pay for most payrolls, therefore, it is only necessary to perform taxation deduction tests on about one in four gross pay sample items. Similarly, it may only be necessary to test one in ten NICs and one in twenty pension deductions. Such reductions are only possible if the sample size is large enough.

(e)   ***Objective 5*** — To ensure that payroll costs are properly classified, described and disclosed in the financial statements.

The reporting requirements of the business organisation depend on the Acts of Parliament to which it is subject and various non-statutory regulations. For example, the accounts of a limited company must comply with *CA 1985, ss 226, 227, 231, 232, 4 Sch, 4A Sch, 5 Sch, 6 Sch* and Financial Reporting Standards (FRSs including SSAPs). If the company's securities are dealt with on The Stock Exchange then further regulations are imposed.

In many organisations the remuneration of directors and senior staff is recorded by means of a separate and confidential system. Audit work on the classification and disclosure of such emoluments may be concentrated in this area. However, the ordinary payroll should still be scrutinised to identify exceptional payments, commissions or bonuses which may cause an employee's emoluments to exceed the statutory disclosure limit. The auditor will also need to consider whether employees have received other non-cash remuneration. This is often done in an effort to avoid incurring tax and NIC liabilities, for example part of an employee's salary may be paid in vouchers.

The major payroll reporting requirements of *CA 1985* are listed below.

(i)   The average number of employees (including directors and employees working wholly or mainly outside the UK) in the year should be disclosed both in total and by category of employee. [*CA 1985, 4 Sch 56(1)–(3)*].

(ii) The aggregate of each of the following amounts should be disclosed in respect of the employees included above:

- wages and salaries paid or payable;

- social security costs incurred;

- other pension costs incurred.

[*CA 1985, 4 Sch 56(4)*].

(iii) In respect of directors, companies are required to show, separately:

(A)   the aggregate amount of directors' emoluments (in respect of services as directors and in respect of other offices in the company or its subsidiaries);

(B)   the aggregate amount of gains made by directors from share options;

(C)   the aggregate amount of money or other assets (other than share options) paid to or received by directors under long term incentive schemes;

(D)   the aggregate value of company contributions to pension schemes where those contributions are in respect of money purchase benefits; and

(E)   the number of directors who are accruing benefits under, respectively, money purchase pension schemes and defined benefit pension schemes.

However, a company need not show any information, other than that relating to share option gains, if it is readily ascertainable from other information which is shown. Small companies' full accounts can show just the total of the four aggregate values in (A) to (D).

'Emoluments' includes:

salary, fees and bonuses, sums paid by way of expenses allowance (so far as they are chargeable to United Kingdom income tax), and estimated money value of any other benefits received by him otherwise than in cash;

but excludes:

the value of any share options granted or the gain made on exercise of such options, company contributions paid or treated as paid in respect of him under any pension scheme or any benefits to which he is entitled under such a scheme, and any money or other assets paid to or for the received or receivable by him under any long term incentive scheme.

In addition, the following information is to be shown if the aggregate of (A) to (D) above exceeds £200,000:

●   the aggregate of the director's salary and cash paid or receivable under the long-term incentive scheme;

●   the amount of company contributions paid to the director's money purchase scheme;

●   in respect of a defined benefit scheme, the amount at the end of the financial year of the director's accrued pension and lump sum.

If the company is an unlisted company, it is not necessary to disclose the value of any shares received under long-term incentive schemes, only that the director did receive such shares. Similarly for gains on the exercise of share options.

[*CA 1985, 6 Sch,* as amended by the *Company Accounts (Disclosure of Directors' Emoluments) Regulations 1997 (SI 1997 No 570)*].

The Cadbury Committee's 'Code of Best Practice' recommends full and clear disclosure of directors' total emoluments and those of the chairman and highest-paid director, including pension contributions and stock options. The Greenbury Committee followed this up with further recommendations, including the recommendation that larger companies should form remuneration committees. Most Greenbury recommendations have been included in the London Stock Exchange's Listing Rules, which apply to quoted companies, and most are reflected in the *Companies Act 1985*. One additional requirement of the Listing Rules is to disclose either the transfer value of each director's accrued pension benefit, or to provide sufficient information to enable a reasonable assessment to be made of the increase in accrued benefit.

Provisions on the disclosure of loans and other transactions (e.g. consultancy agreements) with directors and other officers of the company are contained in *CA 1985, 6 Sch.* Such loans and transactions may be administered by the payroll department. Therefore, additional procedures need to be introduced to identify and audit the amounts, and to ensure they are properly classified and disclosed.

(*f*)   ***Objective 6*** — To ensure that amounts reported to the financial statements are in agreement with the accounting records.

This involves reviewing or preparing working papers to show that all payroll balances in the general ledger have been posted to the trial balance and hence to the financial statements and conversely that all payroll amounts in the financial statements are traced to the general ledger to ensure that there are no late adjustments which have not been subject to audit.

References

24.21   The following References provide an introduction to auditing in general.

(1)   Glynis M, 'Manual of Accounting Volume', a looseleaf service which is updated regularly, Tolley Publishing Co Ltd.

(2)   Venables J S R and Impey K W, 'Internal Audit', Butterworths, 1998.

(3)   Code of Practice 2, 'Investigations', Inland Revenue.

(4)   Code of Practice 3, 'Inspections of Employers' and Contractors' Records', Inland Revenue.

(5)   Dunn J, 'Auditing Explained — a Practical Guide for Managers', Kogan Page, 1991.

(6)   'Not a Shining Example', PMR, August 1998.

(7)   'Employer's Payroll Health Check', Tolley Publishing Co Ltd 1998. A new looseleaf which contains practical advice and information to prepare for, and protect against, investigations.

25 Manual Calculation Methods

Scope of this chapter

25.1   Large payrolls have been at least partially automated for over 50 years but there is still a role for manual pay calculation methods. Although it may be economic to computerise quite small payrolls of 20 payees or less, manual calculation systems may still be used in small businesses, or in a large company to pay a few senior executives in order to achieve confidentiality. Even if a computer payroll system is in use it may still be necessary to perform manual calculations of employees' pay. Another use of manual calculation methods is to prepare test cases for computer payrolls. Additionally, it is sometimes necessary to demonstrate manually how an individual employee's net pay is derived.

This chapter illustrates the principles and procedures for manually calculating pay. In particular it gives a brief description of PAYE (Pay As You Earn) income tax and NIC (National Insurance contribution) calculations. The use of certain PAYE and NI forms and proprietary stationery systems is also outlined. SSP (Statutory Sick Pay) and SMP (Statutory Maternity Pay) calculations are covered in Chapter 8 (Disability and Maternity Benefits). The calculation of deductions under an attachment of earnings order is explained in Chapter 13 (Attachment of Earnings Orders). Chapter 14 (Pension Contributions) describes contributions to various types of pension scheme. Chapter 15 (Voluntary Deductions) describes the implications of other non-statutory deductions.

Key points of manual calculation methods

25.2   The salient features of manual calculation methods are as follows.

(*a*)   Manual calculation methods are often used as a supplement to computer systems, for example to achieve confidentiality or for checking and demonstration purposes.

(*b*)   Income tax is usually calculated on a cumulative basis and NICs normally on a non-cumulative basis. (See 24.8 and 24.13 below.)

(*c*)   Although the payee's tax code is often notified to the employer by the Inland Revenue, sometimes the employer is required to determine a new employee's tax code in accordance with Inland Revenue instructions, e.g. CWG1 Cards, 'Employer's Quick Guide to Pay As You Earn and National Insurance Contributions'. (See 25.7 below.)

(*d*)   The NI table letter must be determined by the employer in accordance with various criteria, e.g. membership of an occupational pension scheme. See 25.12 below.

(*e*)   The calculations consist of a step-by-step procedure. First, gross pay is determined, followed by PAYE calculations for income tax, NICs and other deductions to arrive at the net pay. (See 25.3 below.)

(*f*)   Precise income tax calculations require either tables or computer procedures. NICs can be calculated using rates or tables. (See 25.8 and 25.13 below.)

(*g*)   Proprietary stationery systems can be a convenient means of administering a manual payroll. (See 25.15 below.)

(*h*)   Both manual and computer payroll systems must use Inland Revenue PAYE stationery or approved substitutes.

Outline of calculation procedures

25.3   Calculating pay manually comprises of the following steps.

(*a*)   ***Data input*** — To calculate pay and deductions manually the administrator must go through the following steps before starting the calculations.

   (i)   All general information must be gathered together, for example income tax and NI tables, conditions of service regulations and pay rates. (See 18.4 above for a discussion of documentation required for a payroll office library.)

   (ii)   The relevant payroll records for each employee must be obtained. These records include details such as the tax code, tax paid to date and NI table letter.

   (iii)   All current pay details for each employee, such as overtime and holiday information, must be collated.

(*b*)   ***Calculation procedure*** — The main steps in calculating each employee's pay details are as follows.

   (i)   Calculate the gross pay (the 'build-up to gross'), for example 40 hours @ £3.60 an hour plus £20 bonus = £164.

   (ii)   Calculate the statutory deductions, e.g. income tax and NICs.

   (iii)   Obtain details of and calculate the non-statutory deductions, for instance pension contributions and a subscription to the employer's sports and social club.

(iv) Calculate the net pay, i.e. the gross pay less total deductions.

(v) Record details of pay, income tax, NICs, and retain.

(*c*) **Data output** — Subsequent to calculating pay, payslips and other records and reports must be produced.

Example of a 'gross to net' pay calculation

25.4 Marion earns £160 a week as a shop floor supervisor. She has worked ten hours' overtime this week at time-and-a-half in addition to her usual 35 hours. Her pay calculation is as follows.

Example — Build-up to gross

	£	£	£
Standard week		160.00	
Overtime (10 × 1.5 × £160.00/35)		68.57	
Total gross pay			228.57
Gross to net			
Income tax	30.41		
NICs	15.10		
Total statutory deductions		45.51	
Pension contributions			
(0.05 × (£160.00 − £64.70))	4.76		
Trade union subscriptions	1.15		
Total non-statutory deductions		5.91	
Total deductions			51.42
Net pay			£177.15

Marion's statutory deductions, income tax and NICs, depend on her particular circumstances and earnings. These circumstances are represented by a tax code and NI table letter. In the above calculation the details are for tax week 30 (the end of October) during the 1998/99 tax year. All these terms and Marion's statutory calculations are explained in 25.8 to 25.13 below. Her pension scheme is contracted-out and the contributions, according to the rules of her scheme, are five per cent of basic pay less an allowance for the basic state pension. This formula results in a deduction of £4.76. The trade union subscription is a fixed amount which she has authorised.

Build-up to gross and non-statutory deductions are unique to a particular employer. Marion's case is straightforward but employee benefit and pay scheme arrangements can be very extensive and require considerable administration. Sick pay, including SSP, can also be part of the build-up to gross process. The same applies to SMP and OMP (occupational maternity pay). Chapters 6 (Background to Pay and Benefits), 7 (Pay Schemes), 8 (Disability and Maternity Benefits) and 9 (Benefits, Expenses and Termination Payments) provide further details.

Income tax and National Insurance

25.5   Taxation is dealt with in Chapter 11 (Income Tax) and National Insurance in Chapter 12 (National Insurance Contributions). Differences between income tax and NICs are also dealt with in those chapters.

PAYE is a method of collecting a payee's Schedule E income tax (see 11.39(*b*)) above). For convenience NICs are collected under the same system. Chapter 20 (PAYE Procedures) discusses PAYE, and the references in 25.16 below describe PAYE and NICs in greater detail. The complications covered in these references include such matters as applying PAYE and NICs to holiday pay, irregular payments and payments to starters and leavers.

The PAYE system is based on a series of formulae. The computer term for such formulae is 'algorithm' which is a calculation done as a set of steps following particular rules. The Inland Revenue issues a rather complicated specification containing income tax formulae for computers. (See Reference (3) in 25.16 below.) The tax table figures can differ slightly from those arrived at by using the computer formulae. The Contributions Agency also allows formulae to be used in a prescribed manner and again small differences can validly arise when the results are compared with the NI tables.

Normally the algorithms involve applying a series of earnings bands and rates. Thus, currently all earned income in excess of an individual's allowances is taxed at 20 per cent on the first £4,300 of taxable earnings, 23 per cent on the band £4,300–£27,100 and 40 per cent on earnings above £27,100. NICs are based on a more complicated set of bands and rates.

These bands and rates are incorporated in the income tax and NI tables which are issued by the Inland Revenue and Contributions Agency respectively. The CWG1 Cards issued jointly by the Inland Revenue and the Contributions Agency explain how to use the income tax tables and the NI tables. (The income tax and NI bands and rates for the current and prior years are contained in Appendix D.)

The major distinctions between income tax and NICs are briefly summarised below.

(*a*)   ***Income tax*** — The main features are listed below.

   (i)   Income tax is a personal tax on income including earnings and pensions. The tax due is based on the entries in the annual tax return and Form P11D. These forms are sent to the Inland Revenue by the taxpayer and the employer, respectively.

(ii)   Based on the details given in the annual tax return, or other forms such as Form P11D or Form P46 (Car), each payee is allocated a tax code which is used to determine the tax to be deducted through the PAYE system. (See 25.6 below for the procedures and forms used determining tax codes.)

(iii)   PAYE aims to deduct the correct amount of income tax over the whole tax year from 6 April to the following 5 April.

(iv)   PAYE is usually cumulative but, exceptionally, can be non-cumulative (see 25.6 (iv) below). The cumulative basis means that the tax deducted in each period is adjusted to allow for over or under-deductions in previous tax periods and allows for refunds of excess tax deducted in previous periods. The total tax deducted depends on the total annual earnings and not the pattern of earnings throughout the year. For example, the total tax paid on £13,000 a year is the same whether the money is paid at a rate of £1,083.33 a month or £950 a month with one extra payment of £1,600 as a bonus. Any tax due at the end of the year can be recovered by Inland Revenue adjustments (subject to certain limits) to the tax code for the following year or through the tax calculated and payable from the employee's annual tax return.

(v)   The cumulative nature of PAYE demands that the PAYE tax tables are based on tax weeks or months from 6 April to the following 5 April. A regular pay day falling on the 30th of the month would then have 30 April as (tax) Month 1, 30 May as Month 2 and so on. Other pay periods may involve special calculations; e.g. fortnightly or four-weekly pay periods will require using figures from tax weeks 2, 4, 6 *et seq.*, or 4, 8, 12 *et seq.*, respectively. Using the tax period, tax code and taxable pay the cumulative tax due to date is easily determined.

(b)   ***National Insurance*** — The main features are listed below.

(i)   In principle this is an insurance system and an employee's social security NI-related benefits (see Appendix D below) still depend partially on his contributions.

(ii)   Class 1 and 1A NICs only apply to employers and employees. (See 12.5 above.)

(iii)   Unlike income tax, NICs are not governed by individual codes. Employees are classified by table letters. (See 12.11 above and 25.9 below.)

(iv)   NICs are not usually collected on a cumulative, whole year basis like income tax. Each pay period is treated entirely separately from the others. This means that two people with the same total annual earnings but with a different pattern of earnings may pay different amounts of NICs. Company directors, however, are an exception as their NICs are calculated using an annual (or *pro rata*) earnings period. (See 12.16 above.)

(v) Unlike income tax, both the employer and employee usually pay NICs on the employee's earnings.

(vi) As NICs are usually non-cumulative the NI tables can be used to calculate the NICs for any pay period of any length. The most common pay period lengths are weekly and monthly and these are catered for in the NI tables. The weekly tables are used as the base for calculating NICs for those pay periods which may be multiples of a week or are irregular, e.g. ten days in length.

Description and operation of tax codes

25.6   There are several types of tax code. When calculating the tax due, the type of tax code indicates either:

(*a*)   an adjustment value (plus or minus) to be made to the taxable pay figure; or

(*b*)   the particular rate of tax (if any) to be used.

The various types of tax codes are discussed below.

(i)   *Suffix letter codes* – The vast majority of tax codes are of this type, and comprise of a numeric value usually in the range 0 to 500 followed by one of five letters. (In some cases the numeric value can exceed 500.) The value indicates the amount of tax-free allowance to which the taxpayer is entitled in the tax year, and the suffix letter usually denotes which personal allowance he receives. (The personal allowances for the current and prior years are given in Appendix D below.)

An example of a suffix letter code is 419L. In this case, the:

(A)   Numeric value 419 indicates that the taxpayer is entitled to £4,195 in tax-free allowances. (As a general rule, placing a '9' at the end of the numeric value produces the annual amount of tax-free allowances according to the tax tables.)

(B)   Letter L shows that the taxpayer is in receipt of the personal allowance.

The five letters currently used in suffix codes are as follows:

● *L* – this indicates entitlement to a personal allowance.

● *H* – this indicates entitlement to a personal allowance and the MCA (married couple's allowance).

- *P* – this indicates entitlement to a personal age-related allowance.

- *V* – this indicates entitlement to a personal age-related allowance and the MCA.

- *T* – this does not indicate a specific personal allowance, and can be used where, for example, the taxpayer does not want the tax code to reveal his personal circumstances.

The suffix letter is not used in the calculation of income tax but is used to apply general increases (or decreases) to tax codes when directed by the Inland Revenue. These increases (or decreases) follow any changes to income tax personal allowances announced by the Chancellor in the Budget statement and subsequently contained in the annual *Finance Act*. Tax codes with suffix letters L, H, P or V can be subject to general increases or decreases but codes with the suffix letter T must be individually altered by the Inland Revenue

Suffix letter codes can be operated cumulatively or non-cumulatively, and tax is calculated by reference to one or more of the tax rates in force. Examples of the cumulative and non-cumulative basis of operation of tax codes are given below in 25.8 to 25.10.

(ii) **Prefix letter codes** – There are two prefix letter codes: D and K codings.

(A)   *D* – Code D0 is the only prefix D code currently in use. It indicates that all income is to be taxed at the higher rate. The prefix D code is always operated on the non-cumulative basis.

(B)   *K* – This type of code, which comprises of a numeric value of 1 or more preceded by the letter K, indicates that when the Inland Revenue calculated the coding, the taxpayer's personal allowances were exceeded by the value of, for example, taxable items. A common cause of K prefix codes is receipt of high value benefits in kind from the employment, e.g. a company car.

K codes notionally increase taxable pay by the pay adjustment value obtained from the tax tables. In operation, therefore, they are the direct opposite of suffix letter codes.

An example of a prefix K code is K55. In this case, the numeric value 55 indicates that over the year an additional taxable amount of £555 is to be added to the employee's taxable pay for the purpose of calculating the tax due. (As a general rule, placing a '9' at the end of the numeric value produces the annual amount of taxable pay adjustment according to the tax tables.)

Prefix K codes can be operated cumulatively or non-cumulatively, and require a special calculation when working out the deductible tax. A regulatory limit, of currently 50 per cent of taxable pay in the period, is applicable. (See the example in 25.10 below.)

(iii) **Other types of tax code** – Other types of tax codings are often encountered. These denote either the status of the taxpayer or the rate of tax to be applied.

   (A)   *BR* – This tax code means that tax is calculated at the basic rate in force in the year. BR tax codes can be operated cumulatively or non-cumulatively.

   (B)   *NT* – This tax code indicates that no tax is to be deducted. NT codings are sometimes applicable to students working during vacation periods, and to employees working temporarily overseas.

   Usually the NT tax coding is applied cumulatively, but if there is any doubt as to whether tax already paid in the year should be refunded then the local tax office should be contacted.

   (C)   *Emergency* – The emergency coding, a suffix L tax code, is often applied to new employees. It can be operated cumulatively or non-cumulatively, at the various rates of tax in force.

   (D)   *OT* – Strictly this is a suffix T tax code with a numeric value of zero, and therefore can be applied cumulatively or non-cumulatively. Although there are no pay adjustment values to be deducted, the various rates of income tax in force in the year are applied.

   (E)   *NI* – This is not a tax code, but the CWG1 Cards indicate that 'NI' should be recorded in the tax code area of pay records, e.g. Form P11, if:

   - the employee's pay does not exceed the PAYE threshold but does exceed the NI threshold; and

   - the employee has signed Form P46 but not completed Statements B or C.

(iv) **Basis of operation** – As mentioned in 25.5 above, PAYE income tax is usually calculated by reference to the cumulative values of pay, income tax and pay adjustment obtained from the tax tables. This has the following two effects.

   (A)   The annual amount of pay adjustment allocated by reference to the numeric value of the tax code (prefix K and suffix codes only) is apportioned over the tax year, and increases *pro rata* to the tax period.

   (B)   If several rates of income tax are in use, e.g. 20 per cent, 23 per cent and 40 per cent, applying to certain bands of taxable pay (see Appendix D), these annual bands are also apportioned *pro rata* over the tax year.

   However, the income tax calculations may have to be performed on a non-cumulative basis which means that the tax due is calculated as though the tax period is the first period of the tax year. (Often the non-cumulative basis is referred to as 'week 1' or 'month 1' basis.) In other words, the tax due in the period is assessed separately from any other pay period within that tax year.

Non-cumulative calculations may be required where:

- the tax code is to be operated on a non-cumulative basis; or

- a payment of taxable pay is made in week 53, 54 or 56 of the tax year.

Tax codes to be operated on the cumulative basis are indicated by either a '0' (zero) or a blank immediately after the code. For example, a tax code of 486H would be operated cumulatively.

If a tax code is to be operated non-cumulatively it is indicated by a '1' immediately after the code. (The exception is prefix D tax codes, which are always operated non-cumulatively.) For example, a tax code of K130 1 would be operated non-cumulatively. (Note that sometimes the '1' may be shown as 'W1' or 'M1' indicating week 1 or month 1 basis respectively.)

Authority and source of tax codes

25.7   Authority for the use of a tax code is found either in a notice or the guidance issued by the Inland Revenue. The various notices and guidance currently in use are outlined below. The legislative source of the determinant issues and the procedures applied in the allocation of a PAYE tax coding is the *Income Tax (Employment) Regulations 1993 (SI 1993 No 744)*.

(a)   ***Forms P6 and P9(T)*** – Form P6 is used for in-year coding notifications, whereas Form P9(T) is used to give notice of the employee's tax code for the next tax year. Accordingly, Form P9(T) is issued only in the few weeks before the start of a tax year. (An example of Form P6 is shown in Appendix C below. Form P9(T) is almost identical.)

A feature of Form P6 is that the Inland Revenue can use it to advise the employer of a taxpayer's pay and tax from a previous employment. In such a case, the employer is required to include these values in the cumulative PAYE income tax calculations for the employee.

As a substitute for Form P9, the Inland Revenue may agree to submit tax code notifications to the employer either in paper listings or electronically, for example on magnetic tape. This method is only used where large numbers of codings are required. In April 1999 the Inland Revenue plans to introduce the electronic transfer of Form P6 information by EDI (electronic data interchange).

(b) **Forms P7X and P9X** – These two forms are used by the Inland Revenue to authorise a general increase (or decrease) to suffix letter codes and to inform employers of the emergency tax code. Form P9X is used to advise of such changes from the start of a tax year, whereas Form P7X is used to advise of in-year changes which take effect from a specified date.

(c) **Form P38(S)** – This form may be completed by students who are working during vacation periods. If the employer receives a valid Form P38(S), then income tax is not deductible from the employee's pay. Tax code NT applies.

(d) **Form P45** – This form is very important for the operation of the PAYE system, and contains details of the new employee's:

- pay and tax from previous employment; and

- tax code used in the previous employment.

The date of the Form P45 is crucial in determining the actions the employer is to take. For example, if the Form P45 is for the current tax year, then the above details shown in the form are used, but if the form is for a prior tax year:

- the details of pay and tax are ignored; and

- the tax code shown is either:

 — amended; or

 — ignored and the emergency code operated on the non-cumulative basis.

See Appendix C below for a facsimile of Form P45.

(e) **Form P46** – This form is used when a new employee who will be working for more than one week does not bring a Form P45 with him. Depending on which statements (A, B or C) the employee completes in the form, the employer determines the tax code to be operated. This could be:

- the emergency tax code on either the cumulative or non-cumulative basis; or

- tax code BR on the cumulative basis.

See Appendix C below for a facsimile of Form P46.

(f) **CWG1 Cards** – These cards, which are issued jointly by the Inland Revenue and the Contributions Agency, provide guidance on determining the tax code. (See Reference (1) in 25.16 below.)

Income tax calculations

25.8   The method for the usual cumulative calculation with common suffix tax codes is as follows:

(*a*)   calculate the gross taxable pay to date;

(*b*)   use the tax code to find the pay adjustment ('free pay') value to date from tax table A (details on how to use the official PAYE tax tables (see Reference (6) in 25.16 below) are given in the CWG1 Cards);

(*c*)   subtract (*b*) from (*a*) above to give the taxable pay to date;

(*d*)   find the tax to date using tax tables LR and B to D, whichever appropriate;

(*e*)   calculate the tax deduction – this is the tax to date amount at this period less the tax to date amount as at the last period.

The term 'gross taxable pay' used here, and in the examples below, is the gross pay less any non-taxable items, such as pension contributions.

Example of tax calculation for suffix codes

Marion the supervisor dealt with in 25.4 above is used in this example. Her tax code is 419L and she is to be paid for tax week 30. Based on the procedure above and using the figures from 25.4 above the calculations are as follows:

Gross taxable pay to date

(i)	Week 30 gross taxable pay (£228.57 – £4.76)	£223.81
(ii)	Week 29 gross taxable pay to date	£5,261.00
(iii)	Week 30 gross taxable pay to date	
	((i) plus (ii) above)	£5,484.81

Pay adjustment to date

(iv)	Week 30 pay adjustment to date (from tax table A)	£2,422.50

Net taxable pay to date

(v)	Week 30 net taxable pay to date ((iii) less (iv) above)	£3,062.31

Tax due to date

(vi)	Week 30 tax to date (from tax table B. Tables C and D do not apply here)	£629.83

Tax deduction

(vii)	Week 29 tax to date	£599.42
(viii)	Week 30 tax ((vi) less (vii) above)	£30.41

Note: These calculations are based on the 1998/99 tax tables and feature the basic rate of tax of 23 per cent, the lower rate of tax of 20 per cent and the single person's allowance of £4,195.)

25.9   The step-by-step layout shown above may be convenient occasionally. For instance, it may be used to demonstrate the tax calculation clearly to another person, particularly someone unfamiliar with PAYE calculations. However, it is not a convenient layout for practical payroll work. Figure 25A below contains an illustration of the use and layout of a P11 deductions working sheet.

Officially, correct tax calculations must use either the approved PAYE tax table or the equivalent approved computer formulae. Occasionally, however, a tax deduction is estimated using the approach in the following example.

Example of an approximate method of calculating tax

Joan has just had a pay rise. She has asked for an estimate of her monthly tax deduction during 1998/99. Her pay has been increased to £9,050 a year after deducting her pension contributions. Her tax code is 419L.

		£
(a)	Annual taxable pay	9,050
(b)	Annual tax-free pay	4,199
(c)	Net taxable pay	4,851
(d)	Annual tax due £4,300 × 20% =	860.00
	£551 × 23% =	126.73
		986.73
(e)	Monthly tax deduction ((d) divided by 12)	82.22

25.10   The general method for calculating the income tax due where there is a prefix K code is as follows:

(a)   establish the gross taxable pay to date;

(b)   use the numerical part of the tax code to find the pay adjustment to date in tax tables A;

(c)   add (a) and (b) to give the taxable pay to date;

(d)   find the tax due to date using tax tables LR and B to D;

(e)   the tax due in the current period is (d) less the tax to date as at the previous period. However, the tax deductible in the current period is limited to 50 per cent of the current period's taxable pay.

The term 'gross taxable pay' has the same meaning here as is given in 25.8 above.

Figure 25A

Deductions Working Sheet P11 **Year to 5 April 1999**

Employer's name
NETHER WAPPING COUNCIL
Tax Office and reference
NETHER WAPPING 999/1235

National Insurance contributions

For guidance on National Insurance and the completion of columns 1a to 1h see CWG1 'Employer's Quick Guide to Pay As You Earn and National Insurance Contributions' - card 9
For guidance on Statutory Sick Pay figures see leaflet CA30
For guidance on Statutory Maternity Pay figures see leaflet CA29
or contact the Employers Help Line - telephone number is in the CWG1

At the top of each section in the NI Tables there is a letter, for example *A, B, C, D* or *E*. Copy that letter from the Table you use to the box bottom left overleaf - see ▼ overleaf. If the employee's circumstances change part way through a year the letter may change as well. Record all letters with separate totals for each table letter used. Remember to record under letter *Y* any Class 1A on the last line of the box at ▼.
See the CWG1 card 11 for further information and examples

Earnings recorded in Column 1a should not exceed the Upper Earnings Limit

For employer's use	Earnings on which employee's contributions payable *Whole pounds only* 1a £	Total of employee's and employer's contributions payable 1b £	Employee's contributions payable 1c £	Earnings on which employee's contributions at contracted-out rate payable included in col. 1a *Whole pounds only* 1d £	Employee's contributions at contracted-out rate included in column 1c 1e £	Statutory Sick Pay in the week or month included in column 2 1f £	Statutory Maternity Pay in the week or month included in column 2 1g £	Statutory Maternity Pay recovered 1h £	Month no	Week no
D	228.57	33 02	15 10	164.57	13 82					1
	228.57	33 02	15 10	164.57	13 82					2
	228.57	33 02	15 10	164.57	13 82					3
									1	4
										5
										6
										7
									2	8
										9
										10
										11
										12
									3	13
										14
										15
										16
									4	17
										18
										19
										20
									5	21
										22
										23
										24
										25
									6	26
										27
										28
										29
									7	30
	Total c/fwd	Total c/fwd	Total c/fwd	Total c/fwd	Total c/fwd	Total c/fwd	Total c/fwd	Total c/fwd		

P11(1997) BMSD8/96

Illustration of a Form P11 partially completed (left-hand side)

Figure 25A (Cont'd)

Employee's surname *in CAPITALS* SMITH				First two forenames MARION			
National Insurance no. AB 12 34 56 A		Date of birth *in figures* Day 7 Month 6 Year 67		Works no. etc 1234		Date of starting *in figures* Day Month Year	
Tax code † 419L	Amended code † Wk/Mth in which applied					Date of leaving *in figures* Day Month Year	

PAYE Income Tax

For guidance on completing this form see CWG1 'Employer's Quick Guide to Pay As You Earn and National Insurance Contributions'

- Card 10 for general completion
- Card 12 specifically for K codes
- Cards 11 and 12 for examples using suffix and K codes

Pay in the week or month including Statutory Sick Pay/Statutory Maternity Pay 2 £	Total pay to date 3 £	Total free pay to date (Table A) 4a £	K codes only Total 'additional' pay to date (Table A) 4b £	Total taxable pay to date i.e. column 3 minus column 4a or column 3 plus column 4b 5 £	Total tax due to date as shown by Taxable Pay Tables 6 £	K codes only Tax due at end of current period Mark refunds 'R' 6a £	Regulatory limit i.e. 50% of column 2 entry 6b £	Tax deducted or refunded in the week or month Mark refunds 'R' 7 £	K codes only Tax not deducted owing to the Regulatory limit 8 £	For employer's use
223 81	223 81	80 75		143 06	30 40			30 40		4.76
223 81	447 62	161 50		286 12	60 81			30 41		4.76
223 81	671 43	242 25		429 18	91 22			30 41		4.76

SPECIMEN

† If amended cross out previous code.

⌀ If any week/month the amount in column 4a is more than the amount in column 3, leave column 5 blank.

Illustration of a Form P11 partially completed (right-hand side)

Example of tax calculation for prefix K code

Albert is a senior production manager with an annual salary of £39,000 and a PAYE code of K55. At month 5 in the 1998/99 tax year his gross taxable pay to date is £16,250.00 and tax deducted to date is £4,619.46.

	£
Month 6 gross taxable pay	3,250.00
Add Gross taxable pay to date at Month 5	16,250.00
Gross taxable pay to date at Month 6	19,500.00
Add Pay Adjustment Table figure	279.54
	19,779.54
Tax due per Table C (on £13,550 earnings)	3,052.00
Table D (£19,779.54 – £13,550	
= £6,229.54)	2,491.60
	5,543.60
Less tax deducted to month 5	4,619.46
Tax to be deducted month 6	924.14

The above example is straightforward. However, another feature of 'K' codes, as mentioned in (*e*) above, is the application of an overriding regulatory limit when computing the tax deduction in a pay period. The amount of tax deducted must not normally exceed 50 per cent of the employee's taxable pay, i.e. after allowing for deduction of tax-free items, such as profit-related pay, charitable giving, and pension contributions, in that pay period. An example of the operation of the regulatory limit is given below.

Example of application of overriding limit for prefix K code

Greg receives £2,200 gross pay in month 11 of 1998/99 which includes £400 profit-related pay (PRP) of which £200 is tax exempt. He gives £50 to a charity, and pays £110 in superannuation contributions. His tax code is K2100 operated non-cumulatively.

Month 11	£	£
Month 11 gross pay		2,200.00
Less tax exempt PRP	200.00	
Less superannuation contributions	110.00	
Less charitable giving	50.00	360.00
Gross taxable pay this pay period		1,840.00
Add pay adjustment*		1,750.77
Total taxable pay		3,590.77

Tax due per Tables	1,041.33
Tax to be deducted (£1,840 × 50%)	920.00
Difference in tax to be recorded	
(£1,041.33 − £920.00)**	121.33

* The pay adjustment value is taken from month 1 of Tables A as Greg's tax code is non-cumulative.

** The figure of under-deducted tax is recorded on the deductions working sheet (Form P11).

It should be noted that in the example above the K code is operated on a non-cumulative basis, so that the tax calculations are performed in isolation without reference to the cumulative values of taxable pay or tax paid. Consequently, the underpayment of tax (£121.33) in month 11 could not be recovered in month 12 if the tax code remained on the non-cumulative basis. However, if a Form P6 coding advice, changing the basis to cumulative, were received from the tax office in month 12 the underpayment of tax could be recovered in part or in full subject to the application of the regulatory limit in that month.

Description and operation of National Insurance table letters

25.11   There are several National Insurance table letters currently in use. These fall predominantly into two groups, comprising:

(*a*)   not contracted-out employment; and

(*b*)   contracted-out employment.

An employee is in contracted-out employment if he is a member of an approved occupational pension scheme. (See Chapter 10 (Pension Schemes) for further details.)

In April 1997, a sub-division to (*b*) above occurred with the introduction of new additional table letters for employees in COMP (contracted-out money purchase) occupational pension schemes. Before the start of the 1997/98 tax year, the same contracted-out table letters were used whether the employee was in a COSR (contracted-out salary related) or a COMP scheme.

The various table letters, which are explained at 12.11 above, can be grouped as follows:

- Standard rate: A, D, F

- Reduced-rate: B, E, G

- Age exception: C

- Employer only: C, S

- Non-liability: X

- Not contracted-out: A, B, C

- Contracted-out:

    (i)   COSR scheme: C, D, E

    (ii) COMP scheme: F, G, S

Note that table letter C serves more than one purpose, indicating that employer-only NICs are due in one of the following situations.

(A)   The employee has reached SPA (State pension age) — currently 65 for men and 60 for women — and has given his employer a certificate of age exception (Form CA4140 or CF384) or a certificate of earner's non-liability (Form CF381). Employees over SPA do not have to pay employee's NICs. Employer's NICs are still due, and are payable at the not contracted-out rate even if the employee remains a member of a COMP or COSR scheme.

(B)   An employee with more than one job has chosen to defer payment of employee's NICs and his employer holds Form CA2700. (See 25.12 below.) Table letter C applies only if the employment is not contracted-out, or is contracted-out via a COSR scheme. If the employment is contracted-out via a COMP scheme, table letter S applies.

The National Insurance table letters identify the rates and earnings bands to be used when calculating NICs, and to record and, at the end of the year, report in Form P14 details of NICs and NIC-able earnings. (See 25.14 below for recording NIC details, and 12.12 above and Appendix D for the NIC rates and bands.)

As explained in 12.10 above, NICs can be calculated by either of two methods:

- the exact percentage method; or

- by reference to the NI tables which are issued in the form of ready reckoners by the Contributions Agency.

The examples in 25.13 below demonstrate the manner of calculation of NICs.

Authority for NI table letters

25.12   Unlike the operation of PAYE where the Inland Revenue notifies employers via notices, e.g. Form P6, of an employee's tax code (see 25.7 above), the decision as to which NI table letter to apply for an employee rests entirely with the employer. Each pay period the choice of table letter for the employee must be reviewed in light of current facts, such as attainment of SPA.

The *Social Security (Contributions) Regulations 1979 (SI 1979 No 591)* are the basis of the procedures and guidance for determining NI table letters.

There are a few forms which must be considered when determining an employee's NI table letter. These forms and the guidance currently in use are outlined below.

(a) **Certificate of age exception** – The Contributions Agency will issue a certificate of age exception, either Form CA4140 or Form CF384, on request to the employee. If the employee has more than one job, then the Contributions Agency will issue additional copies.

(b) **Certificate of non-liability** – The Contributions Agency may have issued a certificate of non-liability, Form CF381, in respect of a person over SPA.

(c) **Certificate of reduced rate liability** – Some married women or widows who elected not to participate in the NI scheme before 11 May 1977 have the right to pay reduced rate NICs if they hold a valid certificate of election, Forms CA4139, CF383 or CF380A, issued by the Contributions Agency.

The right to pay reduced rate NICs may end for one of the following reasons:

- non-validity of the certificate, e.g. the expiry date has passed;

- the woman has divorced or the marriage is annulled;

- the woman requests return of the certificate;

- the woman has not paid any NICs in any two consecutive years since 6 April 1978;

- the certificate is cancelled.

(d) **Certificate of deferment** – If a person has more than one employment and will pay maximum NICs in one or more of his jobs, he can apply to the Contributions Agency for exemption from paying NICs in one or more of them. The Contributions Agency will issue a certificate of deferred liability, Form CA2700, to the employer which is valid only for that employment and the specified tax year.

(e) **CWG1 Cards** – These cards, which are issued jointly by the Contributions Agency and the Inland Revenue, provide guidance on determining the NI table letter. (See Reference (1) in 25.16 below.)

NI calculations

25.13   The procedure for NI calculations is outlined below. Examples of NI calculations are given in 12.14 above and a further example is given below. The main stages in performing NI calculations are listed as follows:

- calculate the NICable pay in the pay period;
- determine the NI rates to be used;
- calculate the employee's NICs;
- calculate the employer's NICs.

The NICable pay is the gross pay less any non-NICable items, such as expenses. Note that pension contributions are not deducted to arrive at NICable pay, in contrast to determining gross taxable pay. The NI rates to be used are determined by both the NI table letter and the level of earnings. Appendix D contains current and previous years' NI rates, as does the NI ready reckoner (see Reference (7) in 25.16 below).

Example of NIC calculations

Marion, the supervisor dealt with in 25.4 above, is used again in this example. She is a member of a contracted-out salary related (COSR) pension scheme and therefore the applicable table letter is D. Using the procedure above for the 1998/99 tax year, NICs are calculated as follows. The exact percentage method is used in this example.

Calculate the NICable pay

(a) Week 30 NICable pay. (Note that all her pay is
subject to NICs.)   £228.57

Determine the NI rates to be used

Marion's NIC table letter is D, therefore the NIC rates are as follows:

(b) Employee   2% on first £64.00
8.4% on excess earnings above £64.00 but below
£485 per week.

(c) Employer   Weekly earnings above £210.00, but do not exceed
£485.00
10% on first £64.00
7% on excess earnings above £64.00
but below £485.00

Calculate the employee's NICs

(d) Up to the lower earnings limit £64.00 × 2%   £1.28

(e) Up to the amount of earnings
(£228.57 − £64.00) × 8.4%   £13.82

(f) Marion does not earn more than the upper
earnings limit of £485.00 a week. Even if
she did there would be no employee NICs
payable on earnings above this limit.   £0.00

(g) Total of week 30 NICs ((d) + (e) + (f)).   £15.10

	Calculate the employer's NICs	
(h)	Up to the lower earnings limit (£64.00 × 10%).	£6.40
(j)	Earnings in the band £210.00 to £485.00 a week (£228.57 – £64.00) × 7%	£11.52
(k)	Above the upper earnings limit – this is not applicable to Marion. Any earnings above this limit, however, would require employer contributions at the rate of 10% to be charged.	£0.00
(l)	Total of week 30 employer's NICs ((h) + (j) + (k)).	£17.92

As in the case of tax calculations, the above step-by-step approach may be useful occasionally to check the accuracy of computer payroll systems. However, it is usually too laborious for practical payroll work. For this reason NI tables are used as a convenient ready reckoner for manual calculations, but it should be noted that generally, once a particular method is used to calculate NICs for an employee the other calculation method should not be used in the same tax year for him. For example, if the exact percentage method is used by a computer then this method must continue to be used even when a manually calculated payment is being made. (See 12.10 above.)

Recording of pay, PAYE and NI details

25.14 Details of pay, PAYE income tax and NICs are to be recorded each time there is a payment which is subject to PAYE and NICs, either in full or in part. The extent of the data to be recorded varies according to the particular circumstances; e.g. the recording requirements in respect of a payment to a casual worker vary from those relevant to a permanent employee for whom a prefix K tax code is being operated and who is a member of an occupational COMP scheme.

The following is the basic data to be recorded:

(a)   employee's name;

(b)   employee's address;

(c)   date of and tax period in which payment occurred;

(d)   National Insurance number;

(e)   amounts of:

- gross pay and:

    (i)   SSP paid (although recording of SSP at box 1f of Form P11 is now optional); and

   (ii) SMP paid.

- taxable pay;

- tax code;

- tax due;

- NICable pay*;

- NI table letter;

- employee's NICs;

- NICable pay* (whole pounds only – see comment below) between the NI lower and upper earnings limits where the employee is either in a COSR or a COMP occupational pension scheme;

- employee's NICs paid on earnings between the NI lower and upper earnings limits where the employee is either in a COSR or a COMP occupational pension scheme; and

- the total of the employer's and employee's NICs;

(*f*) the SCON (Scheme Contracting Out Number) where the employee is a member of a COMP occupational pension scheme.

* If NICs are calculated by reference to the NI tables, then the values to be recorded are those shown in the tables. If, however, the exact percentage method is used, then it is the values of pounds including the pence which are to be recorded.

In addition to the above listed items, the employer will need to record:

- the employee's date of birth;

- the employee's dates of commencement and termination of employment in the tax year;

- the PAYE reference number;

- the ECON (Employers Contracting Out Number) where the employment is contracted-out;

- whether the person is a director and, if so, the dates of appointment and resignation;

- business expenses reimbursed to the employee or director, even if these are not subject to PAYE income tax and NICs;

- benefits in kind, e.g. medical insurance; and

● deductions made from the employee's or director's pay, e.g. contributions to a pension scheme or towards the cost of provision of a benefit in kind.

Much of the above details may be recorded in Form P11 (the deductions working sheet) issued by the Inland Revenue or any substitute, whether computerised or paper-based. (Figure 25A above is an example of a partially completed Form P11.) Paper-based alternatives to the official Form P11 are discussed in 25.15 below.

Pay records need to be kept for a minimum of three years beyond the end of the tax year to which they relate.

Using a proprietary manual method

25.15   Simple wages books, pre-printed payslip forms and wages packets can be bought from any stationer but suppliers such as Kalamazoo and Moore Paragon provide well-established and advanced stationery systems for business administration. Such systems are entirely manual and consist of sets of NCR (no carbon required) forms. When these are placed on top of each other, written information is transferred from the top form to those underneath. A special 'copy-writer' board is used to ensure that the forms are correctly aligned.

Figure 25B at the end of this chapter contains an illustration of an NCR Form with copywriter board. The payslip, payroll sheet and payee record sheet are prepared simultaneously in this proprietary manual system.

The payroll system illustrated in Figure 25B lays out information and calculations vertically on the three different forms which are set up on the copywriter. All forms have the same vertical layout as shown in Figure 25C at the end of this chapter. The forms are loaded onto the copywriter in the following sequence:

(i)   a set of ten tear-off strip pay advice slips (bottom);

(ii)   a payroll sheet showing the details of up to ten payees (middle);

(iii)   an individual record sheet for each payee (top).

The manual calculations are performed in the vertical blank column and the results are copied through from the individual record sheet onto the payroll sheet and pay advice slips.

Figure 25B

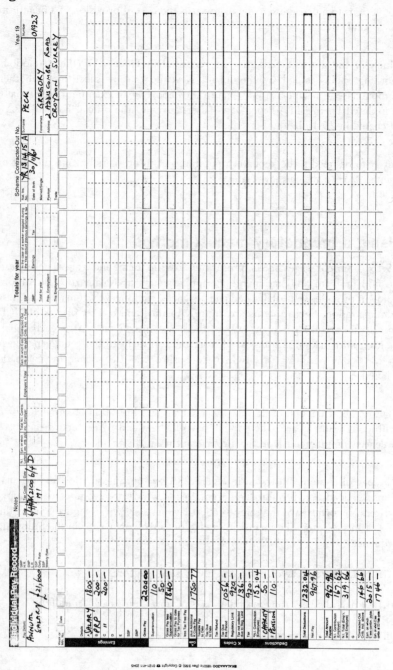

Illustration of an NCR form with a copywriter board

(By courtesy of Kalamazoo Plc)

Figure 25C

Place over first cone

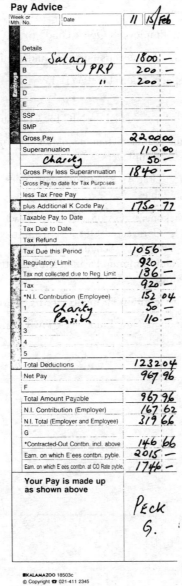

Pay Advice

Week or Mth. No.	Date	11 15/Feb
Details		
A	Salary	1800 —
B	PRP	200 —
C	"	200 —
D		
E		
SSP		
SMP		
Gross Pay		2200 00
Superannuation		110 00
	Charity	50 —
Gross Pay less Superannuation		1840 —
Gross Pay to date for Tax Purposes		
less Tax Free Pay		
plus Additional K Code Pay		1750 77
Taxable Pay to Date		
Tax Due to Date		
Tax Refund		
Tax Due this Period		1056 —
Regulatory Limit		920 —
Tax not collected due to Reg. Limit		136 —
Tax		920 —
*N.I. Contribution (Employee)		152 04
1	Charity	50 —
2	Pension	110 —
3		
4		
5		
Total Deductions		1232 04
Net Pay		967 96
F		
Total Amount Payable		967 96
N.I. Contribution (Employer)		167 62
N.I. Total (Employer and Employee)		319 66
G		
*Contracted-Out Contbn. incl. above		146 66
Earn. on which E'ees contbn. pyble.		2015 —
Earn. on which E'ees contbn. at CO Rate pyble.		1746 —

Your Pay is made up as shown above

PECK
G.

KALAMAZOO 18503c
© Copyright ☎ 021-411 2345

Illustration of the layout of NCR forms and payroll data in a vertical laid-out payslip
(By courtesy of Kalamazoo Plc)

References

25.16 In addition to the References in Chapter 11 (Income Tax) and Chapter 12 (National Insurance Contributions), more information relating to PAYE income tax and NIC calculations can be found in the following publications.

(1) CWG1 Cards, 'Employer's Quick Guide to PAYE and NICs'.

(2) Booklet CWG2, 'Employer's Further Guide to PAYE and NICs'.

(3) 'Computer Specification for PAYE Tax Table Routines', Inland Revenue.

(4) CA 44, 'Employer's Manual on NIC for Company Directors'.

(5) Inland Revenue leaflet, 'Thinking of Taking Someone On: PAYE Tax and NICs for Employers'.

(6) PAYE tax tables: Table A, 'Pay Adjustment Tables'; Tables LR + B to D, 'Taxable Pay Tables'.

(7) NIC ready reckoners: CA 38, 'Not Contracted-Out Contributions'; CA 39, 'Contracted-Out Contributions for Contracted-Out Salary Related Schemes'; CA 43, 'Contracted-Out Contributions and Minimum Payments for Contracted-Out Money Purchase Schemes'.

(8) Green N, 'Post-Cessation Payments', PMR, November 1996.

(9) Green N, 'Starting a New Employee', PMR, January 1997.

26   Payroll Technology

Scope of this chapter

26.1   Payroll departments have used office machinery for almost 100 years. Indeed payroll was one of the first business functions to be computerised in the 1950s. This chapter considers payroll technology in a large organisation in terms of business strategy, equipment, and the use of computer staff. It must be emphasised that the technology of business administration is wider than the use of computers. For example, it includes communication networks and specialised office equipment such as photocopiers and time recorders. Many terms are used rather loosely to describe the rapidly changing area of business systems and the supporting technology, each term having its own nuance. One defunct term is 'machine accounting'. Other terms still in current use are 'business automation', 'office automation', 'DP' (Data Processing), and IS (Information Systems). Perhaps the most general term is 'IT' (Information Technology). Computers, however, are such an important part of payroll automation that they are considered in greater depth in Chapters 27 (Computerising Your System), 28 (Selecting a Computer System) and 29 (Implementation of Your Computer System).

With the exception of the occasional machine specifically designed for payroll and related purposes most of the equipment and techniques used are common to all administrative automation. Usually it is a matter of applying standard equipment and techniques to payroll problems. With modern computing, the purchase or production of software is often seen as the major factor. It is usually more difficult to get the software to operate correctly than the equipment.

Payroll administrators continually need to update their systems for business reasons, for instance due to legislative change. They must also occasionally replace old IT systems. The continuing technical progress in computing and telecommunications means that everyone in business must constantly strive to stay up to date. Not only are improved versions of traditional systems continually emerging, but less frequently entirely new types of system. As discussed below there are many current and impending developments in information technology which affect payroll administration.

> When it comes to developing and amending payroll IT systems, managers, as in other areas of business, must decide between the apparently ponderous formal approaches of large organisations, and the informality common in small ones. Formality implies, for instance, careful and extensive documentation specifying IT systems, and detailed planning.

Key points of payroll technology

26.2   The main matters to be considered with regard to payroll technology are as follows.

(*a*)   Radical approaches to re-organising a business, in terms of its departmental structure and individual jobs, can exploit information technology. This approach could affect payroll and related functions; one example of this philosophy is called Business Re-engineering or Business Process Re-engineering (BPR).

(*b*)   Piecemeal approaches to payroll automation can be questioned, and fully integrated systems recommended. An example is the use of a human resources database for payroll, pensions, and personnel administration.

(*c*)   An opposing view to point (*b*) above is that developing systems piecemeal is sensible. Despite theoretical imperfection the flexibility of the piecemeal approach gives practical benefits in a world where the business and technical environment changes rapidly. According to this view large integrated systems are too expensive, take too long to develop, and are too inflexible.

(*d*)   A compromise viewpoint between points (*a*) and (*b*) is that systems can be evolved piecemeal within a general strategy. For example, different software suppliers can be used for both payroll and accounts work, provided that the different software packages run on a Unix computer and can be linked together.

(*e*)   Change is inevitable. Payroll computer systems must be adaptable, e.g. for new reward management arrangements such as performance-related pay schemes. They must also be maintained to cope with new statutory requirements, for example, the phased abolition of tax-relief on registered profit-related pay schemes from 1998. Business systems must also be continually changed to exploit the rapid progress of information technology.

(*f*)   Thorough cost-benefit analysis is essential prior to changing business systems.

(*g*)   Major considerations are standardisation, the use of compatible equipment and software, and integration with other applications.

(*h*)   In large organisations payroll system planning may have to comply with higher level business and technical plans.

(j)   Although computers are a major part of automated payroll systems traditional forms of office automation such as microfilm should not be ignored.

(k)   All administrative IT requires careful consideration of the human and industrial relations implications.

(l)   The systems analyst or an equivalent can be a key person in the development and maintenance of IT systems. However, with small systems, or simple extensions to large systems, the users of IT systems can do a lot of this work for themselves.

(m)   The normal way of developing larger computer systems is called the SDLC (Systems Development Life-Cycle). It normally implies a formal documented approach to producing computer systems.

(n)   Continuous and thorough quality control (QC) is imperative when developing and installing automated payroll systems.

(p)   Good project management is essential when developing and installing new systems.

Business and IT options

26.3   Much of the work in developing, maintaining and installing automated payroll systems is traditionally carried out by computer staff. Reference (1) in 26.27 below contains a fairly comprehensive description of the techniques used by these practitioners. But these days there is an emphasis on administrative staff doing a considerable amount of IT development and operations work for themselves. This is discussed further in 26.20 below.

Most of the material in this chapter assumes a large organisation using its own administrative and technical staff to develop new business systems. However, this approach is increasingly challenged in both the public and private sectors. Small organisations have no alternative but to make extensive use of outside services. Typical options when using external services would include the following.

(a)   The virtual elimination of the payroll function by using a payroll administration service, i.e outsourcing — most business IT is then the responsibility of the service supplier. (See 16.6(d) above.)

(b)   The use of a traditional computer bureau — bureaux have been updated by the use of computer telecommunications.

(c)   Electronic systems, e.g. internal telephones, installed by the supplier. Smaller computer systems are often installed by a systems or software house.

(d)   The purchase of packaged software with maintenance and support services.

(*e*)   The use of a software house to modify packaged software or to produce a bespoke system.

(*f*)   The use of management and computer consultancy services to help select and implement a new system.

It is possible for many options to co-exist, either by accident or design, within one organisation. For example a company may use an administrative service for its pension payroll. It may use personal computers or computer bureaux for employee payroll systems at some subsidiaries. A mainframe computer could then serve the employee payroll departments at the main location and remaining subsidiaries.

Technical evolution of office machines

26.4   Early office machines such as typewriters and calculators were cumbersome and mechanical. Gradually electric power and simple electro-mechanical 'intelligence' were added to office equipment increasing its capability and speed. The result was the production of popular equipment such as the 'accounting machine', a forerunner of today's personal computer. The accounting machine was a combination of a typewriter and a programmed calculator. Increasingly, from the 1950s these machines incorporated electronics to improve their scope, reliability and speed. The use of micro-chip electronics in the 1970s accelerated this trend leading to the development of the word processor, mini-computers and PCs (Personal Computers). Both mainframe computers and telecommunication systems were also able to exploit the enormous improvement in micro-electronics. In the late 1990s it is common to include a micro-chip computer in many business machines, for example time recorders.

Typically, electronics is about manipulating electrical currents often for processing messages of some kind. For example the handling of the electrical signals representing the software and characters in a word processor requires complex miniature circuits with millions of these held on a few silicon chips. Yet it should be remembered that the technical progress of computers and office equipment is based on more than electronics. Progress also depends on improvements in mechanical devices, for example for moving paper quickly through a copying machine, magnetic devices like personal computer disk drives which hold billions of characters of data or software, and optical devices, such as in a laser printer. Software is also very important in modern equipment. For instance, printer controls can be displayed on a personal computer screen replacing the traditional physical lights and switches built into the printer panel. The remarkable thing about this technical progress is not only the extra power, speed, flexibility, and convenience of modern office machines compared to 50 years ago, but also the major reductions in the real price and the superior reliability. Payroll staff can expect even more progress in the future, for instance optical devices may become more important for processing and storing data. See Reference (4) in Section 26.27 for the technical aspects of modern IT.

The pace of technological change has, if anything, intensified recently. Just a few of the more recent hardware and software developments which are relevant to payroll are listed below.

(*a*)   New conventional computer hardware offers significantly more speed and data storage with little change in the real price, e.g. the Pentium II micro-computer processor from Intel.

(*b*)   HCI (Human–Computer Interface) — an example is the popular Windows environment on personal computers which uses a mouse and Graphical User Interface (GUI).

(*c*)   Optical disks — these offer the scope to store huge amounts of information, e.g. payroll historical data.

(*d*)   New telecommunication systems, e.g. those based on optical fibres, or the Internet which is described in 26.25 below.

(*e*)   Miniature electronic systems, e.g. hand-held devices like the Psion organiser.

A more detailed discussion of new information technology is contained in the following sections.

Convergence

26.5   The ongoing process of technical evolution, which brings together micro-electronics and other technologies, is called 'convergence'. With convergence, what were once separate machines can now be combined together either physically or by telecommunication links. Figure 26A below illustrates how time and attendance terminals in different parts of a factory can be linked by cable to a local PC. The PC can then transfer data on employee working hours over a telephone line to a central payroll computer. This computer use of communication links is often called 'networking'.

Planning procedure for IT

26.6   The current era is one of rapid change in both business and information technology. The recent and impending changes in the use of administrative IT will change familiar ways of operating all business systems, including those used in payroll work. The general technical nature of the information technology of the near future is reasonably clear. However, it is difficult to foresee the detailed implications of its use in business and administration. For example, voice recognition systems are available quite cheaply and continually improving. An example is the IBM personal dictation system. This allows users to talk

Figure 26A

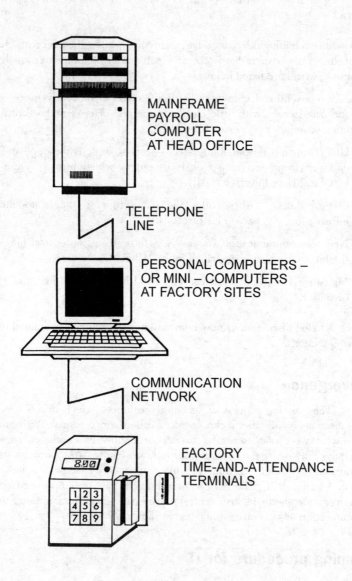

MAINFRAME
PAYROLL
COMPUTER
AT HEAD OFFICE

TELEPHONE
LINE

PERSONAL COMPUTERS –
OR MINI – COMPUTERS
AT FACTORY SITES

COMMUNICATION
NETWORK

FACTORY
TIME-AND-ATTENDANCE
TERMINALS

This is an illustration of a payroll computer network

Employees clock in and out by placing plastic identity cards into the terminals. The hours worked are stored by a personal computer and are automatically transmitted to the mainframe where the payroll calculations take place into their ordinary personal computer using a microphone. The software then converts the speech into text, usually for printing as some kind of report or letter. However, the role of such developments in mainstream administration is uncertain. Furthermore, there are commercial aspects to any new technology, like the standards adopted. This can be seen by looking at the recent past. It was not obvious in the early 1980s, for instance, that Microsoft would dominate the future personal computer market with Windows, its version of a Graphical User Interface. (The general trends in payroll administration and computer technology are discussed in Chapter 30 (Future Developments Affecting Payroll Administration) and in Reference (8) in 26.27 below.)

Like everyone else, both the developers and users of payroll systems must adopt new technology, as well as ensuring that systems are updated in line with new business requirements. This can be hazardous as new IT systems can cause serious problems. A series of adverse reports, mainly from the public sector, indicate problems such as late delivery, cost overruns, technical failures, and abandoning systems after considerable expenditure. The journal, *Computing*, reported a case where the problems with a payroll computer system for health service employees was assessed at millions of pounds. Sensible planning for IT systems can minimise the problems caused by a changing business and technical environment, and the risks of new projects.

In the past, extensive, detailed and long-term business and technical plans were produced for whole organisations. These plans purported to represent the future for several years ahead. This approach is, perhaps, less popular today for a variety of reasons. For instance, the business environment after the Year 2000 appears more turbulent and less predictable than today's (1998) e.g. will the UK join EMU (the proposed European Monetary Union), and if so, when? This makes detailed long-term planning more difficult and less useful. However, the long-term detailed approach to corporate planning is still influential, and in this context a payroll IT plan is often a small part of a set of interlocking plans for the business as a whole. This is illustrated in Figure 26B below and is explained in greater detail below.

(*a*)   ***The business or corporate plan*** — In the first instance, the technology of the payroll process is totally subservient to the needs of the organisation. Long-term business plans may stretch over five or more years. They cover the planned development of the whole organisation involving new products, new markets, new factories, etc. All other plans are subordinate to, and link with, the business plan.

(*b*)   ***The human resources plan*** — People are required to make the business plan work. Part of the human resources plan may include changing the number and type of employees. The HR plan could also require changes in the pay and benefit arrangements such as new incentive schemes, staff status and monthly pay for manual workers, or 'cafeteria' pay and benefit schemes. Clearly there is a 'knock-on' effect for the administrative and computer payroll systems.

Another aspect could be planned changes in the organisation of the human resource departments themselves, including the payroll function. For example, a move towards a centralised human resources department for all the divisions of a company might imply reliance on a centralised mainframe computer. Decentralised separate human resource departments could lead to each department choosing its own systems and equipment.

(c)   ***Planning administrative technology*** — To exploit new technology and to support the long-term business plan there needs to be an overall plan for business automation. These plans become an interrelated series of projects involving the installation of new equipment and new software. Some software may be developed 'in-house' by internal computer staff or software packages can be bought from external specialist suppliers. In computer circles this general approach is often called 'strategic information planning'. Because of technological convergence, the administrative IT may be part of a wider general automation strategy involving, for example, robots and automatic machine tools in a factory environment.

(d)   ***Payroll IT planning*** — This involves making choices within higher level plans and constraints. For instance, an extension of cashless pay must operate within an industrial relations framework and be supported by the necessary computer facilities. More importantly, there often business and information technology policies which encourage or discourage the buying of external products and services. Such policies can for instance result in a predisposition to use packaged software or bureau services. Figure 26B below is a diagram of a payroll IT plan in relation to the interlocking set of plans for the whole business.

As an alternative to the detailed approach to planning outlined above a more modern approach might be to empower both subsidiary organisations and departments to plan and organise the details of their own business and technical affairs. This might be done within a high-level strategy or set of policies. This kind of broad strategy is sometimes called a 'strategic vision'.

(See Reference (3) in 26.27 below for a management view of planning for new technology generally.)

Extent of choice in IT plans

26.7   Where there is no detailed planning for IT then subsidiary companies or even departments can make independent decisions. This can lead to incompatible systems used in isolation without benefits of commonality like supplier discounts for volume purchases. For instance a group of companies could eventually acquire a mixture of equipment from IBM, ICL, Digital, Dell, and smaller IT suppliers. The software used could be equally varied. Linking accounting, payroll, pensions, and personnel systems based on different hard-

Figure 26B

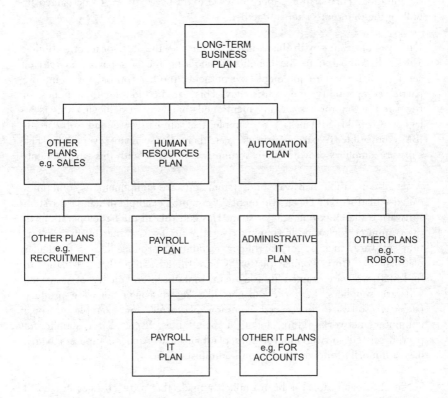

Illustration showing how the payroll IT plan is derived from a hierarchy of other business plans

ware and software is usually feasible in this situation. However, it might be expensive and awkward. Another major factor is the need for new systems to match the old, e.g. a new payroll might still have to feed employee contributions data to an old pensions system. Internal computer staff are usually sensitive to these problems and they attempt to minimise them, even in the absence of any policy directives. For instance, they tend to encourage user managers to share or extend existing equipment as well as promoting the purchase of compatible hardware and software. Thus, in effect, a *de facto* IT strategy can evolve.

These days internal computer staff may be less involved than in the past. Computer sales people are well aware that in many cases they can now sell directly to departmental managers rather than IT managers and their systems analysts. To external computer staff, say from a software house, a fragmented IT environment can be a business opportunity. It means that there is a prospect of selling new systems which are incompatible with others in the client organisation. Furthermore, there may be extra paying work to be gained by linking the different systems together.

One way of dealing with this is just to argue that the costs of incompatibility are small compared to the benefits of choosing the best payroll system or service whatever the equipment environment. Another approach is to impose partial compatibility and consistency. This can be done with a policy of regulated autonomy. As already mentioned, one way of achieving this is by laying down broad rules, for example that all hardware and software is IBM-compatible. A payroll manager can then choose from several specialist software suppliers provided their system is compatible with this environment.

A set of compatible hardware and system software components is sometimes called a 'platform' or IT 'environment'. A common example of standard system software is the Unix operating system. This controls all the basic operations of the computer, for example running several programs simultaneously. Application software, such as for payroll or accounts is produced for a particular platform like Unix. Popular platforms have the advantage that it is easier to find staff who are trained to use them, and there are plenty of packaged software suppliers. Larger companies like Peterborough Software produce packaged software for several common platforms, for example personal computers networks, Unix, and IBM mainframes. Even a large supplier of payroll-related software may ignore platforms like Apple computers which have a minority following in business administration.

So far the assumption has been implicitly made that most changes in payroll administration and its associated automation merely involve a modification or extension of whatever currently exists. Occasionally, of course, a few old office procedures or old equipment need simple replacement. These assumptions are, in fact, made throughout most of this book. As a simple example, a mainframe system can be replaced by a cheaper, more responsive PC network, but the job done by the new equipment is essentially the same. However, this view of continually making amendments to existing systems, with the occasional replacement of old equipment, is seen by some managers, business consultants and academics as a fundamentally conservative stance. It is seen by them as preserving the weaknesses inherent in the current business organisation.

The alternative strategy is to seek more dramatic improvements in factors like cost and service than can be achieved merely by adjusting office procedures or improving the technology. This radical approach to reviewing a business organisation and its supporting technology is called Business Re-engineering or BPR (Business Process Re-engineering). One slogan associated with Business Re-engineering is: 'Don't automate, obliterate'! This means that the old business organisation and supporting IT systems should be totally re-designed rather than improved. In this context this might mean a total re-organisation of payroll and associated functions such as personnel and accounts! Modern office technology is thus seen as supporting options for a major re-organisation of business processes and people's jobs. This is, of course, an old risky idea with a new name. But the prospects of major improvements in performance factors like productivity and service have made re-engineering fashionable in business circles.

Payroll-related systems and human resource databases

26.8 There is a whole series of manual or computer systems which are related to payroll. The main payroll-related systems cover the following business areas:

(*a*)   time and attendance, and flexitime;

(*b*)   holidays;

(*c*)   disability (including SSP and SMP);

(*d*)   personnel;

(*e*)   welfare;

(*f*)   pensions and employee benefits, e.g. free medical insurance;

(*g*)   employee expenses;

(*h*)   tax administration of employee expenses and benefits which is mainly Form P11D work;

(*j*)   financial and management accounts;

(*k*)   treasury management, e.g. for cashiers;

(*l*)   decision support;

(*m*)   executive information which combines payroll and personnel data with other business information, e.g. a display showing a graph of total sales value against total labour costs over the last ten years.

The IT systems that support the above business areas usually partly automate and support clerical functions. Besides their primary functions, payroll and related administrative systems produce management information as a by-product. Thus a primary function of a personnel system is to provide employee details, such as the full name and address of a particular member of staff. But a personnel system can also provide basic management statistics such as the age distribution of the workforce. Not all systems are primarily concerned with routine (but often complex) administration. Executive Information Systems and Decision Support Systems have the support of management functions as their primary role. These are discussed in 26.15 below as part of a more general computer-oriented classification of business systems.

PMR and similar journals often carry articles describing the current position with regard to IT systems which support payroll and allied business functions. For example, see References (7) and (12) in 26.27 below for a discussion on P11D systems together with a list of software suppliers. *PMR* also carries a regular 'Services Directory' which includes lists of software package suppliers and payroll service bureaux along with other useful information like details of payroll stationery suppliers. Articles in the 'Systems News' section of *PMR* contain brief descriptions of the decisions of various organisations with regard to payroll-related IT.

Many of the systems covering the business areas listed previously use data that is common to payroll systems. Thus personnel and pension systems also contain data like employee name, National Insurance number, and earnings data. This duplication of data can be seen as wasteful and leads to inconsistencies, for example, when data is updated on one system but not on the other. This suggests that from both a business and technical viewpoint it would be useful to combine all such data into one 'human resource database'. Computer software packages are available for this, for instance Uni 2000 from Peterborough Software. These packages can support many of the above administrative functions, particularly in the core areas of payroll and personnel administration.

When discussing the integration of human resources work it is important to distinguish between the management and technical approaches. These can be considered independently. The management concept of integrating all human resources administration, including payroll and related activities like pensions work, is not dependent on integrated computer systems. This management view is all about merging business departments and functions. By way of contrast, a human resource database is primarily a technical concept with some administrative advantages. Using a human resource database does not require merging the various administrative functions or departments. The technology of human resource databases can easily support either one integrated human resource department or separate administrative functions. For instance, the security features of a human resource database would allow separate personnel and payroll departments both to view basic employee details like name and employing department. But the security arrangements could exclude a personnel department from viewing or amending a tax code. (See also 16.8 above for a further discussion on human resource management.)

Justifying the costs of office technology

26.9   Perhaps the primary consideration relating to payroll IT is to ensure that the costs are justified by the benefits. Costs and benefits can be both tangible and intangible and should be considered in their widest sense. A tangible item is usually valued in cash terms, for example the cost of equipment or the benefit of using less manpower to run a new system resulting in a reduced salary bill. The intangible features are more uncertain and difficult to quantify. For instance, an intangible cost of payroll automation is a reduction in the commonsense checking of data which occurs in manual systems. An intangible benefit might be the rapid automatic production of analyses and reports, for example a departmental attendance analysis covering the whole of the previous year.

An administrator or systems analyst should prepare a feasibility study on any new payroll computer project. (See 26.22 below for details.) This would include a cost-benefit analysis of the various alternative approaches. An alternative approach (or 'option') may be to use a personal computer network rather than a computer bureau. However, the ultimate decision as to whether a project is worthwhile and which option to adopt lies with the management. Many projects, such as the introduction of cashless pay for manual workers, include several facets of which IT is only one. The feasibility study and cost-benefit analysis would then embrace the whole project not just the computer aspects.

The typical benefits and costs of an automated payroll system can be listed as follows.

(a) **Tangible benefits include:**

- manpower savings, which often exceed the costs of IT. New equipment and systems can also be cheaper in real terms than those they replace;

- reduced skill and training costs. Manual payrolls probably require more skilled staff. A general knowledge of the basic use of computers is more common than a thorough knowledge of PAYE calculations.

(b) **Intangible benefits include:**

- greater reliability and accuracy;

- faster service;

- greater data security;

- security copies of payroll data can be stored on magnetic media off-site;

- controlled access to data through password systems;

- the superior presentation of computer-printed stationery;

- better information;

- the rapid production of listings, control reports and statistics which is a major benefit of computer systems;

- better integration and linking with other systems;

- possible controlled sharing of data with other departments;

- greater job satisfaction. This may not always be the case, although in general, using a well-designed computer system is more satisfying than the drudgery of an old-fashioned manual payroll operation;

- maintaining a modern legally-compliant payroll system *may* be easier, especially with software packages.

(c) **Tangible costs include:**

- equipment and software;

- development and set-up work by payroll and IT staff;

- running costs.

(d) **Intangible costs include:**

- a loss of some payroll skills. Modern computer systems tend to convert everyone into computer operators. Some skills such as PAYE calculations are gradually forgotten as the relevant rules are part of the computer software;

- greater reliance on outsiders. An automated system cannot continue running, let alone be developed, without using computer staff or computer service engineers;

- a reduction in skilled personal supervision of payroll activities;

- because fewer people run computer systems the individual commonsense checks for errors and fraud are weaker.

Piecemeal approach to IT

26.10 In the payroll office of the past it was perfectly sensible to automate office functions on a piecemeal basis. So the old-fashioned time recorder which stamped factory clockcards could be introduced irrespective of the need to purchase a typewriter in the following year. Each machine was separate and was only indirectly linked to other equipment through human clerical operations. Today, with convergent technologies, office machines have to be electronically linked to each other and for this purpose they must be 'compatible'. This means that though piecemeal approaches are feasible, considerable care must be taken to ensure that all the various components of a system 'mesh' together.

Compatibility of office machines and equipment

26.11 Compatible machines can work together in co-operation with each other without human intervention. Compatibility exists at several levels.

(a) **The physical level** — For example, the numerous variants of plugs and sockets used in communications cabling must match each other.

(b) ***Electronic signalling*** — The same system of signalling must be used by both sending and receiving machines. This applies not only to telecommunications but also to the use of magnetic tapes and disks for transferring data between machines.

(c) ***The software and data*** — The computer programs operating the sending and receiving machines must be consistent and interpret data in the same way.

There are other aspects of integration, in particular the use of databases or collections of data shared between various users, such as the payroll and personnel departments. Bankers Automated Clearing Services (BACS) provides a familiar example of compatibility issues. BACS is an electronic payment transfer system which involves linking the computers of banks and business organisations. It is commonly used for crediting employees' accounts directly. (See 22.10 above for details on electronic funds transfer (EFT).) BACS used to provide a detailed specification for the use of magnetic tapes and disks before they were discontinued in 1998. BACS now uses telecommunication links for payments (the BACSTEL service). The following example is part of the specification for BACSTEL. It covers the link standards to be followed. It is quoted to illustrate the technical aspects which must be handled by IT staff working on for payroll systems:

(i) X.25 Dataline access into a Public X.25 Data Network.

(ii) PSTN access into an asynchronous port on a Public X.25 Data Network.

(iii) ISDN direct dial-up access using the X.25 protocol.

(iv) PSTN direct dial-up access using a V.32 or V.32bis modem and either 2780 or 3780 protocols.

It will be noticed that this specification refers to other telecommunication standards like X.25 or V.32 which are well-known to IT staff. The BACSTEL specification also covers matters like operational procedures for using the service, the security features, and the detailed format of the computer payment records to be transmitted. See Reference (16) in 26.27 for further details on BACSTEL.

The Inland Revenue is also developing EEC (Employer's Enhanced Communications). This involves transmitting standard PAYE forms like the P11D and the P45 and P6 electronically between the employer's computer systems and those of the Inland Revenue.

Note that the use of magnetic media for communicating between computer systems is declining and they are slowly being replaced, mainly by telecommunication methods. BACS discontinuing the use of magnetic media is just one important example of this.

Integrating payroll IT with other business systems

26.12   Figure 26A above clearly illustrates the problem. Often the equipment is also used for other purposes. For example, factory terminals may be used not only to collect information for production control but also for collecting incentive scheme data. The central payroll is just one computer system amongst many. As explained in 26.6 above, it is often desirable to have some overall policy or strategy on integration to ensure that the needs of the whole organisation as well as individual departments are met.

As mentioned in 26.8 above, one major form of integration in this context is the use of systems based on a human resources database. Such a database could serve personnel, payroll, pensions, and employee benefit applications. It would offer advantages like consistency, no duplication of data, and a reduced need to transfer data between systems. However, some information still needs to be transferred to other systems such as accounts.

Standardisation of equipment and software

26.13   So far business automation has been discussed in terms of the technical benefits of compatibility and integration. Standardisation of equipment and software offers further advantages where there are several subsidiary companies or divisions. These advantages can include bulk purchase discounts, reduced training requirements and mutual assistance between members of the group.

Categories of equipment for payroll departments

26.14   Most payroll systems, both manual and automated, evolve gradually in response to new requirements and in order to exploit new technology. In large organisations this evolution can be controlled by explicit long-term plans. Nearly all payroll departments today contain a mixture of automatic and manual systems and the decision to automate is a practical one mainly based on economics.

The equipment used today falls into four categories:

(*a*)   general purpose computer systems, e.g. office personal computers linked to each other and also to a server computer over a LAN (Local Area Network);

(*b*)   special purpose computer equipment, e.g. time and attendance terminals;

(*c*)   modern office automation, e.g. the word processor;

(*d*)   traditional office equipment, e.g. microfilm readers.

The essential technological concept of the first three categories is the use of computers. The main advantage of computer-based systems over traditional office equipment is that they are programmable. This allows computer-based systems to be easily adapted for many different purposes. For example, with appropriate programming (software), a personal computer can be used for a system in a chemical laboratory as well as for one in a payroll office. Another feature, which is almost essential these days, is the use of modern telecommunications to link computer equipment.

The four different types of equipment above can often be combined together in one department to provide an effective total system. However, at the present time the ideal of a totally integrated electronic paperless office still appears remote. Currently, there are numerous alternatives available in combining equipment from the four categories. This 'options overload' can be reduced by policy directives, for example use one common software supplier like Sage or Pegasus for all financial personal computer application areas like administering the sales ledger and payroll. As already discussed, one important policy is to use a standard 'platform' for all business IT systems. A platform is a set of compatible hardware and system software like personal computers and the operating system, 'Windows NT'. This approach considerably eases the problems of developing, maintaining, combining, and linking business IT systems, even if the software comes from different suppliers. This policy may sometimes be impractical, as already suggested, because of piecemeal development of IT in the past. However, consistency can be slowly imposed over a period of years and, even in a partial form, IT policies and standards are helpful.

General purpose computer systems

26.15   There are several ways of classifying the various types of computer information system. A common classification is given below. Though payroll-related examples are given, the classification scheme uses general categories that cover most areas of business administration.

(a)   *Transaction Processing Systems (TPSs)* — A TPS is a system which processes business transactions. Transaction processing in this general sense is probably the most fundamental and important area of business administration and applied IT. A payroll system is a good example as its prime purpose is to process transactions such as tax code changes, and perform calculations to generate new transactions such as employee payments. As discussed later most organisations use packaged software for processing payroll transactions.

(Transaction processing sometimes refers to large multi-terminal interactive systems using a central computer, i.e. purely to on-line systems.)

(b)   *Management Information Systems (MISs)* — An MIS provides summarised data for management. A statistical analysis of employee earnings is a good example. The details summarised by a MIS are usually collected at first by a transaction processing system.

(c)   ***Information Retrieval Systems (IRSs)*** — IRSs are often known loosely as viewdata systems or on-line databases. The idea is to make a central library of text (or pictorial data available to a remote terminal or a PC. IRSs are used for disseminating changing information like foreign exchange rates and share prices. IRSs are commonly available on a commercial basis. But special text databases, unique to a particular organisation, can be useful. For example, they can contain current pay rates and conditions of service such as holiday rules. The big advantage of all on-line databases is ready access to up-to-date reliable information. Also it is easier to distribute the information than with traditional methods, for instance by circulating paper documents.

(d)   ***Office Automation (OA)*** — Office automation in the modern sense implies systems like word processing and electronic mail. Some traditional forms of office automation, such as photocopiers, do not involve computers. OA is such an important area that it is discussed separately in 26.17 and 26.18 below.

(e)   ***Decision Support Systems (DSSs)*** — A DSS is an interactive system which helps decision-making. A simple example of a DSS is a system for planning a change to an employee bonus scheme. A DSS in this case is a software system that allows managers to explore the consequences of any changes in bonus calculations. It can analyse not only the effects on employee pay, but also additional pension and National Insurance costs to the employer.

(f)   ***Executive Information Systems (EISs)*** — EISs present business information in a convenient fashion, usually graphical, for senior managers. They are sometimes known as executive support systems (ESSs). The information comes from other internal computer systems such as personnel, payroll, accounting, and sales systems. External business data can also be included, such as government economic statistics.

(g)   ***Expert Systems (ESs)*** — Typically expert systems use artificial intelligence techniques to provide advice. They basically incorporate a set of rules and knowledge on a specific subject such as employee recruitment. The details of a particular case are fed into the computer which applies its rules and knowledge to reach a recommendation. In such situations the computer reaches a conclusion by using a combination of formal reasoning and rough intuitive logic like that used by a human expert.

(h)   ***Miscellaneous*** — There are many miscellaneous computer systems, IT facilities, or software 'tools' that are difficult to classify. These are often small scale, but they may be met in office administration. Some examples are CBT (Computer-Based Training), computer-based assessment (e.g. computerised tests for personnel selection) and what are effectively computerised brochures for products and services. Another example is a special purpose calculation program, such as one for estimating the level of AVCs (Additional Voluntary Contributions) that an employee should adopt for extra pension rights.

The main difference between the types of system above is conceptual. The concepts of each type of system are usually implemented via software. All types of system frequently use similar hardware technology.

In day-to-day payroll work the first three categories of system (transaction processing, management information, and office automation) are the most important. Decision support systems by their very nature are used only occasionally in pay work. Also they tend to be used in a simple form based on spreadsheet software. Executive information systems are senior management systems, and the payroll aspects are small. Expert systems have only been used in a very limited or experimental way in payroll-related administration.

Ordinary business systems frequently combine two or more of the above types of system. For instance, a computer payroll package is essentially a transaction processing system. But it also includes some MIS features such as printing employee overtime analyses. The classification above is rather rough and ready and IT is progressing rapidly. Thus any such classification scheme represents something that is useful for discussing most of yesterday's and todays IT applications, but not necessarily tomorrow's. There is also no doubt that the familiar forms of business IT will change, perhaps beyond recognition, over the next decade.

Recently there have been several important hybrid developments which combine OA (Office Automation) and IRSs (Information Retrieval Systems). The most well-known is the Internet which is a huge open and global system which allows access to anyone in the world for a small fee. It also allows organisations to offer on-line services, e.g. insurance quotes. Besides offering users global electronic mail the Internet can be used, amongst innumerable other things, for the retrieval of payroll data onto a personal computer screen. One example is the on-line National Insurance News provided by the Contributions Agency. The Internet is discussed more fully in 26.25 below. Proprietary systems offering electronic mail and information retrieval are set up by many organisations for closed groups of people, for instance their own staff and customers. One well-known example of the software used to do this is Lotus Notes which operates on personal computer networks. Thus Lotus Notes could support access by any approved person in a company to an up-to-date version of pay details like expense allowances, eliminating the need for distributing paper copies. It should be appreciated that these developments (combining OA and IRSs) are not conceptually new, and indeed they had predecessors over ten years ago. But, the modern design, low-cost, and widespread availability of the new systems makes them very attractive.

The above classification only covers the direct use of IT for business administration. It does not cover for instance technical IT, such as real-time manufacturing control systems. More relevantly some other types of IT may have an indirect effect on administration. Thus the 'tools' (special programs), used to help develop IT systems, can speed up the delivery of administrative computer software and reduce its cost. An example is Microsoft Access (an easy-to-use database and programming system). These development tools are employed by programmers, systems analysts, and increasingly administrative staff.

As already mentioned the main traditional area of interest in payroll administration is transaction processing and management information. Besides core payroll administration there are related areas like time and attendance recording which are listed in 26.8 above. When establishing business systems the two main factors are hardware and software. Software is usually the most difficult area.

(i)   *Hardware* — The hardware technology used in business administration may range from the large mainframe supporting hundreds of terminals to a small hand-held computer. Payroll bureaux, for instance, tend to use mainframes because of the large volume of work. Medium-sized organisations with a few thousand employees may use a mini- or mid-range computer or networked PCs. A small business may use a stand-alone PC. A very small business, say with ten employees, may use special stationery systems (with an electronic calculator).

Computer input is invariably provided by the ubiquitous keyboard and screen. Output is usually via printers, telecommunications links, or magnetic media. Special equipment (supported by special software routines) may sometimes be used to extend the range of input and output options. OCR (Optical Character Recognition) is one example. It can be useful for inputing the data on paper forms directly into payroll transaction processing systems.

In some organisations a mixture of different types of hardware is used to support payroll-related systems. Figure 26A above illustrates a typical combination of large and small computers with time and attendance terminals. The combination of hardware may not be ideal, but is a question of practical considerations like using spare capacity on old existing machines.

(ii)   *Software* — Specialist suppliers can provide some excellent payroll software. This is mainly available to establish transaction processing and management information systems. Different software products can often be linked together. Many payroll packages such as PS2000 from Peterborough Software or the Pegasus personal computer payroll system are flexible and can be adjusted to meet a variety of needs. The degree of flexibility does, of course, vary considerably between packages. In the case of a large organisation such as a County Council with, for example, 50,000 employees there is always the option of producing special 'bespoke' software to meet its own precise requirements. Surprisingly, bespoke payroll systems are sometimes produced by much smaller organisations. As software is such a major consideration this is discussed in depth in Chapter 27 (Computerising Your System).

Special purpose computer equipment

26.16 In a payroll context special purpose computer equipment consists mainly of time and attendance (T&A) equipment. T&A terminals are operated by an employee placing an identifying plastic card or key in the terminal. The terminal system records the employee number (which may be a barcode on the card) and the time. Arrival or departure is signalled by pressing a button or registering the plastic card. Some terminals include key pads and other features to allow more data to be entered, such as job numbers. T&A terminals provide a good illustration of the distribution problem which is deciding where the data processing is to be done. Some provide printed reports and displays of attendance from local devices, others rely on a mini- or mainframe computer. (See Reference (13) in 26.27 below for further details on T&A.)

Modern office automation

26.17 This concept involves linking terminals or PCs ('work stations') into an organisation-wide network. One of its main features is the use of electronic mail to transmit memos, forms and other documents between user work stations. Among the long-term objectives of such systems is the 'paperless office', although most systems are well provided with printers! Currently their main use is manipulating text. However, office automation is extending into the image and voice areas where pictures and voice messages can be transmitted between work stations. Also as discussed in 26.15 above, new developments like the Internet which is a global open system, have extended the scope of office automation. Although based on the same underlying computer and electronic technology the relationship between modern office automation and conventional computer data processing is not always clear. The use of CD-ROM disks is another development which is partly compatible and partly competitive with the OA developments already described. CD-ROM (Compact Disk-Read Only Memory) can be used to publish information traditionally held in books and manuals. An example is the huge amount of information on employment law published by Tolley's in CD-ROM form and which will be extended to include all areas of payroll in Spring 1999.

Newer IT facilities such as DIP (Document Image Processing) or more broadly DMSs (Document Management Systems) are becoming of considerable importance. With DIP, documents (for example hand-written correspondence) can be scanned into the computer and stored on disk. The images of the documents can easily be retrieved and displayed on a screen. A simple payroll use would be retrieving the image of a list of authorised signatures to check against signed overtime returns. A related development is workflow automation whereby electronic documents can be automatically routed to work stations for human action. (See Reference (3) in 26.27 below for further details.)

Traditional office equipment

26.18   This area has declined over the last 30 years as computers have taken over the functions of machines such as 'addressographs'. This obsolete equipment used stencils to print details on clock- and job-cards. The trend for traditional office equipment to be absorbed or replaced by computer-based systems continues. As explained in 26.5 above this process is sometimes called 'convergence'. Some types of traditional equipment are superficially similar to what they were 30 or 40 years ago. But traditional equipment, like the telephone and photocopier, has been continuously improved by exploiting new scientific and technical developments. In many cases traditional office machines exploit the same progress in fields like micro-electronics that have advanced computers so much. The technical potential for the complete integration of all office equipment, traditional and modern, already exists. This means that 'universal' computer-controlled workstations could handle all the voice, image, text, data, and telecommunications work of the office without the need for separate machines. However, it will probably be several years before this is commonplace. In the meantime, hybrid systems combining traditional approaches like microfilm with computers also exist.

A brief checklist of familiar traditional office equipment is given below. Careful selection and use of such equipment is likely to make a useful contribution to providing an efficient payroll service for several years to come.

(*a*)   *Ordinary equipment* — Mundane office equipment such as filing cabinets and date stamps still has a useful role.

(*b*)   *Communications devices* — Mobile telephones and fax are common examples.

(*c*)   *Paper-handling machines* — Two familiar examples are a binding machine and a paper shredder.

(*d*)   *Mechanical filing systems* —These are useful for situations involving extensive paper records. Via a control panel the automatic filing system rotates a large number of paper files into a position where the operator can manually retrieve or store the file of interest.

(*e*)   *Microfilm* — Microfilm or microfiche is useful for storing images of ordinary documents. COM (Computer Output on Microfilm) has often been used in payroll-related work to replace bulky computer printouts.

(*f*)   *Reprographic machines* — These days original versions of office documents are normally produced with word processors and DTP (DeskTop Publishing) systems. Photocopiers are ubiquitous for the quick reproduction of documents, and conventional printing is used for volume or quality work such as pension scheme booklets. The use of colour printers with word processors and DTP systems, together with the use of colour photocopiers, is a viable option in some cases. Colour is relatively expensive which restricts its use to small volumes of printing with this type of equipment.

(*g*) *Mailing machines* — Common examples are mail-opening machines, and franking machines which print postage 'stamp' impressions on envelopes.

(*h*) *Security systems* — Electronic access control systems and smoke detectors are good examples.

The role of special stationery should not be forgotten in either manual or automatic systems. For example, payslips are often computer printed inside their envelopes ready for mailing. An interesting recent development is the use of laser-printed payslips which can be pressure sealed by machine.

(See Reference (2) in 26.27 below for a general discussion of non-computer office equipment.)

Human and managerial aspects when installing a new system

26.19 Human considerations are vital when installing a new IT system. Some important factors are listed below.

(*a*) *Health and safety* — Although important, this is usually fairly minor in practice, for example, avoiding trailing power and signal cables in an office.

(*b*) *Ergonomics* — For example, systems (both hardware and software) should be designed to be easy and convenient to use. The newer display systems based on GUIs (Graphical User Interfaces) can make conventional administrative computer systems significantly more ergonomic. See Figures 27B to 27F below.

(*c*) *Staff attitudes* — Attitudes to new technology can range from a Luddite approach to enthusiastic co-operation. Sometimes administrative staff show an excessive interest in computer technology to the detriment of their main duties.

(*d*) *The effect on employment* — For example, redundancies still occur because of new systems, and jobs are frequently changed.

(*e*) *Participation* — When all parties participate in producing new systems, quality and commitment should be improved. Common sense suggests this is true provided there is judicious management. Academic research tends to confirm the value of participation.

(*f*)   ***Training*** — Staff require both classroom and hands-on training with new IT.

(*g*)   ***New-technology agreements*** — These agreements with trade unions lay down a general procedure for introducing new technology in an organisation. For example, they may deal with, *inter alia*, union negotiation procedures, employment re-structuring and retraining; other trade union agreements, such as those on redundancy, can also be involved. Some employers may have new technology policies. These are similar, but do not necessrily involve trade union agreement.

(*h*)   ***Disability*** — the *Disability Discrimination Act 1995* lays considerable responsibilities on employers to avoid discriminating against disabled job applicants or disabled existing employees. The employer must make 'reasonable' adjustments to the working environment, systems, and jobs to meet the needs of the disabled.

Managers and computer staff in large organisations are usually familiar with the above issues and the methods of overcoming any difficulties.

When evaluating new bought-in systems, especially software packages, the following matters must be considered.

(i)   ***The supplier*** — Two things are important when examining a potential supplier. The first is their financial stability. There is often a high cost in terms of time invested in setting up a new payroll system, and if a company fails and is unable to support the product, this time could be lost. Ideally, the financial stability of the particular product or service needs to be ascertained as companies do not support a loss-making product for long.

This leads on to questioning the supplier's commitment to the product or service. Payroll is particularly dependent on legislative updates as well as changes in business practice, for example the adoption of COMPs (Contracted-Out Money Purchase pension schemes). The supplier's commitment to service these needs must be established. Perhaps the existence of a user group or the proportion of revenue derived from payroll are indicators, but in the last analysis a judgement must be formed, preferably after talking to existing users.

The 'style' of the supplier is more important than it sounds. Clearly an aggressive approach to customers or an unresponsive attitude to errors is not desirable.

(ii)   ***The service*** — Whatever the IT option chosen, there is a need for an ongoing relationship with the supplier for the provision of maintenance and updates and training and help.

The support arrangements need to be clearly spelled out. What time of the day is there a staffed support desk as opposed to an answerphone?

Under what circumstances can somebody visit the payroll site? On what days, e.g. bank holidays, is the service withdrawn? Not only are the answers to these questions important, but the way they are answered reveals the supplier's attitude to supporting customers.

The implementation schedule should be examined in detail, and a timetable agreed. It should be clear from this how much work is required from the payroll department. It should also be possible to meet the supplier's project manager and assess how easy it is to work with him.

(iii)   ***The product*** — The new system needs to be examined for its technical aspects. However, care must be taken here. The question to be asked is whether it has a straightforward modern design, capable of being understood and updated, and not is it merely technically exciting and state of the art.

Documentation should be considered, with a view to answering the question – can it be understood even when working overtime at 8.00 p.m. on an urgent job? It should be clear, unambiguous and capable of taking a complete novice through the system. It should also be well indexed. It should be noted that modern computer systems incorporate a lot of documentation on-line, for example help screens.

How the data is input and held should reflect how your organisation works. Can the screens be made to follow your working documents, and is the data you will want available on the right reports and enquiries?

(iv)   ***The contract*** — Whatever the potential supplier says, the contract is negotiable and the purchaser should look closely at it. It defines the relationship between the two parties, and the way it is written again reveals how the supplier treats his customers. Certainly the contract should be intelligible, as it is necessary to consult its provisions from time to time.

As mentioned previously, the maintenance of payroll software in line with legislative changes is vital. Associated support services such as a help-line are also important. It is essential that all such matters are covered by a sensible contract or contracts.

The contents of any contracts can be negotiated, although clearly there can be points which the supplier could refuse to alter. Ensure that all promises and commitments made by the supplier are either referred to in the contract or are included in general terms by reference to a proposal made by him.

(See Reference (5) in 26.27 below and Chapter 28 (Selecting a Computer System) for further details.)

Responsibility for developing and operating IT systems

26.20   Broadly, systems development is producing or acquiring everything that is required for a new business system. This could include, for instance, producing new software and documentation, and ordering the relevant computer hardware. Implementation is installing the hardware and software. Maintenance is keeping the hardware and software working correctly, and ensuring that the software is kept up to date. Operations is running the IT equipment.

When people talk about systems development it is not always clear what is meant by a 'system'. Sometimes the word merely implies a collection of software to support a business function such as personnel work. When used in a much wider sense it can imply virtually everything necessary to perform a major business activity such as payroll work. The word 'system' can then include factors like hardware, software, special stationery, office procedures, and supporting services such as a security company collecting cash from the bank. It can, of course, imply something intermediate between these two cases. The meaning is important because it determines how much work is needed to develop or maintain a system. Any confusion over the meaning and scope of the word 'system' should be removed as early as possible. See also 26.22(i) below.

As mentioned in 26.3 above, modern approaches to business and IT provide a wide range of options with regard to the mix of staff, both internal and external, used to develop, implement, maintain and operate a payroll system. One extreme is to eliminate both the internal payroll and IT departments, and outsource the activities of both. The other extreme is to do as much as possible internally, using both in-house IT and payroll staff. When using internal staff one extreme is for the IT staff to write all the computer programs for a bespoke payroll system, and then operate the system centrally. At the other extreme, payroll staff do the bulk of the work. For example, they can install, adapt and operate a popular payroll software package in their own office. The options for developing a payroll system are further enriched by the variety of commerical services available, for example the use of a payroll bureau. As far as the employing business is concerned the options chosen to develop a payroll system are of secondary importance compared to receiving a good total payroll service. The options, or mixture of options chosen, are governed by practical factors like cost, timescale and the expertise available to an organisation. Also, historical arrangements within an organisation cannot usually be abandoned overnight.

Whatever mixture of staff and services is used to develop, modify and operate a payroll system there must always be somebody to declare that the final result is satisfactory. For example, employee gross pay calculations vary considerably between employers, and it is easy to make mistakes when they are computerised (or more likely when they are recomputerised). The people who can certify that a system is working correctly, particularly with regard to the fine details, are usually senior payroll staff. Auditors also have a role in this.

Once the division between external and internal work has been decided there is still the problem of dividing the internal work between various staff and departments. Traditionally in large organisations, internal computer staff did the bulk of the developing, maintaining and operating of mainstream business IT systems. Today, however, there is an emphasis on 'end-user computing' where administrative staff do a substantial amount of IT work for themselves. There is usually some central regulation to prevent anarchy. A regulatory framework limits incompatible and inconsistent computing emerging in different departments. One approach is to use an Information Centre. This is an internal computer department to help administrative staff select and use approved software, such as for word processing and spreadsheet work.

With regard to modern payroll systems, end-user computing can mean that the administrative staff operate a complete networked personal computer system in their own office. There is no need to rely on a central mainframe service with professional computer operators. Furthermore, the administrative staff can change the pay structure and produce new management reports easily without any help from computer staff. In the past, for instance, a new statistical report would have required the computer staff to write a new program, which might have taken a few days. Today, with the 'report generator', which is a part of any good payroll software package, the administrative user can produce a simple computer report for themselves in a few minutes.

End-user computing is a question of degree, and as implied so far, the wide range of options is not theoretical but practical. Today there are many intermediate situations between centralised computing and payroll independence in IT matters. The whole philosophy of end-user computing does of course imply greater responsibility and competence by administrative staff. It also implies extra work and probably greater risks. The benefits are a quicker response to IT needs and more flexibility. There may be cost savings, for instance, when 'downsizing' the payroll hardware from a central mainframe to networked PCs. As usual the validity of such arguments depends crucially on the circumstances.

Management services occupations

26.21   Historically, various advisory and technical occupations, such as systems analysis, have arisen to provide services to the management of an organisation. These 'management services' have often been delivered in an overlapping and fragmented way by several different departments and different specialists. In the past there were attempts to combine these various services into one management services department, though the expression today often implies a large central computer department. However, management services, at least in theory, is more than computer services. Some of the management services occupations that may have some relevance in a payroll department are briefly described below.

(a)   ***Work study*** — This is the 'scientific' approach to improving human and machine activities, particularly in factories. These ideas have been applied in many other areas including clerical work. There is often an emphasis on measuring and timing work operations. Of particular interest to payroll departments is the role of the work study officers in designing incentive schemes for manual workers.

(b)   ***Organisation and methods*** — O&M is a systematic attempt to improve the efficiency and effectiveness of office work partly through the application of work study techniques. Traditional O&M has now almost disappeared. However, the concept is still valid. Many people have commented that there is a tendency to rediscover and recreate this occupation in more modern forms. The mundane O&M work on office methods is now often split between user staff and computer systems analysts. The broader organisational work is frequently carried out by senior managers and business consultants. More recently O&M has returned in the form of small-scale business re-engineering and quality improvement in office administration.

(c)   ***Systems analysis*** — The systems analyst's job is concerned with the automation of business systems, usually through the application of computers. It involves identifying requirements, designing new or changed systems and implementing them. Where there is an emphasis on the user doing his own computing, systems analysts can become systems 'consultants' working in an information centre or software house. Their role is then, as a facilitator, helping the user develop and operate his own systems.

(d)   ***Computer operations*** — This involves not only the operating of computer equipment but also other activities such as data control and data preparation. Data control staff check all incoming data and progress it through the computer department. They check that all computer processing is correct and distribute all computer output such as print-outs and computer printed forms, e.g. labour cost reports and payslips. Specialist data preparation staff sitting at video terminals enter data on forms such as time sheets into the computer. One feature of current computer approaches is a marked decline in the operational role of computer personnel. As discussed elsewhere, the trend is to give users their own equipment and let them directly operate the hardware and software systems. This is particularly true with data entry work where direct entry of data by clerical staff using PCs or terminals is normal practice today. Indeed, the use of staff specialising in jobs like entering computer data, or operating computer equipment full-time, is seen as only being appropriate in unusual circumstances, typically with large IT systems. The general approach is to minimise the necessity for this.

However, on a larger scale new computer operational functions have emerged, for example, 'network management' which involves monitoring and controlling the operation of larger computer telecommunication networks.

(e)   *Other staff* — There are, of course, other staff involved in management services, such as computer programmers. However, their role is less apparent to the payroll computer user. Computer programmers write or amend software according to specifications produced by systems analysts and often have little direct contact with the payroll department.

(f)   *Auditors* — For reasons of history and their necessary independence, auditors are usually completely separate from management services staff. However, auditing is a key management service in the literal sense of the phrase. As IT is the basis of most modern financial systems, auditors have a considerable interest in the development, maintenance and operation of IT systems. This may go beyond the traditional areas like internal control and security. Internal auditors in particular may be interested in issues like efficiency, effectiveness and economy. See Chapter 24 (Payroll Audits) for further details.

All these jobs may have other titles, for instance a work study officer could be called an industrial engineer. Various hybrid jobs also exist, an example would be where an analyst-programmer combines the functions of a systems analyst with those of a computer programmer. These days most business and management consultants take a much more active interest in IT-based projects, and they have adopted or adapted many of the techniques of O&M and systems analysis.

The systems development life-cycle (SDLC)

26.22   A common approach to producing a conventional IT system, whether business or technical, is to follow the series of steps illustrated in Figure 26C below. This approach is called the systems development life-cycle (SDLC). It is a practical concept which can be adapted according to circumstances. The SDLC is best suited for developing IT systems in quite a formal documented way. It works well in its conventional form with medium-sized and large-scale transaction processing and management information systems. Payroll-related systems often fall into this category in larger organisations employing thousands of people. Much of the discussion below refers to this situation, or the development of payroll-related systems by a software house.

The formal SDLC allows the work of several people to be co-ordinated for the months, or even years, necessary to produce a large business system. An example is producing bespoke payroll software for an organisation employing 15,000 people. The detailed co-ordination of the various staff involved, like computer programmers, is achieved via careful procedures and documentation which specifies the system and any associated plans. The quality is better

Figure 26C

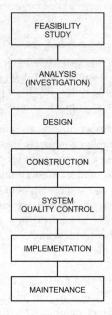

Illustration of the main stages of the systems development life cycle (SDLC)

This formal approach to developing a business IT system is particularly important with complex and critical systems such as payroll. A full explanation of the various stages is discussed in 26.22 below

because the documentation describing the system is checked before it is used to produce software, or order stationery like payslips, or carry out office procedures. It is also much easier to maintain a properly documented system and keep it in line with changing business and legal requirements.

In small organisations, interested in implementing a simple payroll software package for, say, 200 employees, the formal SDLC is often skimped or even omitted. However, even with small applications like this, a cut down but documented version of the SDLC is still recommended. For example, the payroll requirements can be analysed and specified in outline as a checklist. A software package can then be checked against the list to ensure that it can meet the requirements. For example, can it handle, say, six different voluntary deductions, and a money-purchase pension scheme?

Clearly there are some simple cases where the SDLC approach is virtually irrelevant. An example might be buying and installing a cheap, simple computer program for a personal computer.

The SDLC can be adapted to develop IT systems based on standard software packages, modifying packages, or fully bespoke systems designed and programmed precisely to the user's own requirements. Variants of the SDLC are common, for instance when a software house produces a payroll or pensions package, or a user organisation adapts such packages for its own use.

The basic idea behind the conventional SDLC is simple. It follows the general common-sense logic of most business and technical projects, whether it is developing a new factory production layout, bringing in a new pay scheme, or marketing a new software package. Crudely, the approach is to collect information on the problem, design and create a solution, check the details of the solution are correct, and then implement the solution. In the computer context, as elsewhere in business and technology, this simple concept can be extensively refined. Figure 26C above represents the first level of refinement and shows the main stages of the traditional SDLC which are outlined below. Reference (1) in 26.27 below contains further details.

(a) **Feasibility** — This is a study presented as a formal report as to whether the project (developing a new system) is worthwhile. It also identifies the best approach to developing a new system, for instance, to use a payroll bureau rather than a package.

(b) **Analysis** — All the relevant facts about the old business system and the future requirements are collected together. Interviewing is the most common fact-finding technique used by systems analysts with business systems generally. However, with payroll and pension systems many of the requirements are scattered through official literature. A commonplace example of a source of information for a payroll system is CWG1 (April 1998), the 'Employer's Quick Guide to PAYE and NICs'.

(c) **Design** — A new system is designed to exploit the technology available and incorporate all the requirements met by the old business system. Any new requirements are also included. The new system should be represented by a semi-formal specification which can be many pages in length. Semi-formal means no more than laying out the specification for the new system in the style of a business or technical textbook, for example with the text in paragraphs and lists, together with supporting diagrams. Further specifications are often produced describing how the various parts of the software work in detail, and defining the details of the data to be stored on a file or database.

(d) **Construction** — This is basically programming (writing software) according to the design specifications. Preparing user documentation and help screens for the new system is also part of the construction stage.

(e) **System quality control** — All the hardware, software, and documentation must be checked before releasing the system. This is done by both inspection and testing. The payroll users should always conduct a final acceptance test of the system after the IT staff have finished their own testing. This not only provides a final check for obvious errors, but ensures that any misunderstandings are identified and corrected.

(*f*) **Implementation** — This is a whole series of jobs, such as installing the hardware and software in the user's environment, training the user staff to operate the new system, setting up all the data on the new system, and so on. See Chapter 29 (Implementation of Your Computer System) for further details.

(*g*) **Maintenance** — Any minor faults in the software must be corrected as they are discovered. Regular changes to payroll software occur as legislation and business requirements change.

There are several comments on the SDLC given below.

(i) **The system** — The word 'system' is vague, and its precise meaning depends on circumstances. A 'system' may mean just a set of computer programs which help with a particular set of office jobs. It may also mean the software and hardware together. In its widest sense it could be the software, hardware, and the departmental organisation. One key job at the feasibility stage is to decide on the scope of a system or project, for example, does a payroll 'system' include time-and-attendance or not?

(ii) **Cycle** — The above stages form a 'cycle' because after years of maintenance a system is ultimately replaced with a new system created by repeating the above stages.

(iii) **Variants and methodologies** — As already implied, there are many variants of the SDLC which are common in business computing. Variants can include, for instance, a more detailed breakdown of the various stages. For example systems design can be split into business systems design (screens and print-outs) and technical systems design (programs, magnetic disk files, etc.).

The proliferation of variants of the SDLC long ago led to a call for standards. This is an unfulfilled dream, and a universal standard version of the SDLC is about as likely as one universal financial currency throughout the world. As with currency, however, local standards have been developed.

Standardised ways of working in IT are called 'methodologies'. For example, in a methodology all the symbols used on computer diagrams are pre-defined and used consistently. Methodologies also include best practice, for example the work must be checked at each stage before going on to the next. Methodologies attempt to detail and standardise part or all of the SDLC.

There is no one universal methodology, just a set of competing methodologies. One well-known and common methodology in the UK is

SSADM (Structural Systems Analysis and Design Method). The development of SSADM was sponsored by the Civil Service and it is also used in the private sector. SSADM is mainly meant for developing large one-off systems. Many companies adapt standard methodologies such as SSADM for their own circumstances, or devise their own methodologies. For example, payroll and pensions software houses often have their own special methodology for rapidly implementing their own systems on a customer's site.

There have been attempts to mitigate or abandon what is perceived as the rigidity and bureaucracy of the traditional SDLC with its emphasis on laboriously preparing specifications and documentation. One approach, really an alternative rather than a variant, is called 'prototyping'. This works by producing rough-and-ready computer software and then running it on a computer. The user then identifies errors and improvements which are rapidly included in a new version of the software. Thus the software can be continuously executed and modified until the user is satisfied. By implication, the software must be easy to amend allowing quick incorporation of the user's changes. 'Quick' usually means that an analyst-programmer can amend the software in minutes or hours. This implies using either modern 'fourth generation' computer languages or flexible software packages. With simple systems and easy-to-use fourth generation programming this works well up to a point. However, maintaining such software soon becomes a big problem as there is little documentation produced.

Prototyping works fine with the visual aspects of systems like screen displays, but it is of little help for the core of logically complex systems, where there is no alternative to specifying the details in some formal way. For example, payroll build-up-to-gross or NIC calculations must be specified with formulae, tables of rates, etc. However, there are current methodologies (ways of working) that attempt to develop quite extensive new business IT systems quickly (in a matter of weeks). These RAD (Rapid Application Development) methodologies use a series of rapid-progress techniques, like prototyping described above and intensive full-time user involvement. One of these RAD methodologies is DSDM (the Dynamic Systems Development Method) which has recently become popular in the UK.

In many smaller organisations (in the author's experience) there is only a token attempt to follow the SDLC in a formal, documented manner. Systems analysts and programmers with long experience of a particular system can rely on memory and being able to 'read' the computer program coding directly. This can work well until, of course, the staff move. Newcomers then find that it is impossible to maintain a system with little documentation and cryptic programming.

(iv)   ***Documentation*** — If followed properly, the traditional SDLC and modern variants like SSADM produce extensive documentation. The

most important early documents are the feasibility study and the design specification for the new system. The design specification for a new system may also be the basis for a formal contract with a software house. As already mentioned, future generations of IT staff find an undocumented system difficult to maintain or extend. Methodologies and standards often lay down the purpose, format, and style of the computer documents to be produced, thus ensuring consistency.

(v) *Construction* — This is essentially preparing programs and user manuals. Construction is the most expensive and time-consuming stage when producing software in conventional programming languages such as C or COBOL. There can be many person-years involved in programming a modest payroll system. Buying packages (pre-written software) is the conventional way of reducing this cost. This works well with payroll and related fields such as pensions. Well known examples of payroll packages are 'Open Door' from Peterborough Software and 'k-PAYE' from KCS.

(vi) *Quality* — The management of IT quality is much more than testing the software before releasing it for use. There are two particularly important areas. Quality control (QC) is the detailed testing and checking of work. Quality assurance (QA) is creating the general framework of procedures and standards and checking that the QC is actually done. The distinction between QA and QC is not always observed and the terms may be used interchangeably.

Compliance with business and technical policies and standards is important. As mentioned previously, these policies could, for instance, indicate a preference for the use of packages rather than bespoke systems, the use of a particular supplier's equipment, e.g. IBM AS/400 mid-range computers, or the use of a particular methodology like SSADM. They could also include a new technology agreement with a trade union.

The standardised quality management framework of British Standard BS EN ISO 9000 (previously BS5750) is frequently met these days. BS EN ISO 9000 lays down a general scheme for maintaining quality in any area of business and technology.

The system quality control stage of the SDLC is meant as a final check of the system before it is installed. Testing the software is the prime method. However, there should be detailed checking of work at all stages of developing a system, such as checking a specification of bonus calculations. The basic idea is 'right first time' and to prevent defects and mistakes seeping into a project as it progresses.

As already implied quality control does not just mean testing the software, but also checking documentation and pre-printed stationery such as payslips.

Another useful approach to quality is provided by IMIS which provides evaluation services for financial systems. IMIS is the Institute for the Management of Information Systems (formerly the IDPM, the Institute of Data Processing Management). Three levels of standards have been devised with organisations like the Inland Revenue for computerised payroll systems. These cover such matters as the correct processing of tax codes, SSP calculations, and payment methods. IMIS produces packs of payroll test data and also operates a scheme where suppliers can have their software independently accredited by IMIS. The supplier then has their system registered as complying with the scheme, and can use the IMIS logo when promoting their product. It should be noted that the IMIS scheme can, of course, only cover statutory matters like PAYE and good general IT and business practice, for example security features and the use of audit trails. The IMIS scheme cannot, by its very nature, cover local matters such as the employer's pay structure.

The Contributions Agency is developing a service to assist and evaluate the NIC aspects of software development.

(vii) *Time-scale* — The development and implementation time with traditional systems is invariably months and often years. This is the time from the authority going ahead with a feasibility study to completing the implementation of a fully operational new IT system. Using packaged software not only reduces the total amount of work and cost, but considerably reduces the time-scale. With a PC package, a simple payroll can probably be implemented in a day or so. But it may take months for a large complicated payroll to be fully implemented with a mainframe package. The life span of an implemented system, with maintenance, can be from five to 20 years.

(viii) *Maintenance* — Maintenance includes the correction of faults, the incorporation of minor improvements and the implementation of minor changes in the payroll requirements. Any major changes are, of course, treated as a new project. New major systems should always be monitored closely at the initial stages of their working life. Every change in an automated system means that there is a possibility of introducing faults (called 'bugs'). Minor faults may not be immediately apparent. Software is particularly vulnerable to bugs. The only solution to this problem is thorough testing after every change and continual vigilance.

Equipment often has a life span of five or more years. Software can survive longer, sometimes over 20 years. Administrative procedures can last for decades with modifications, for instance PAYE which was originally introduced in 1944. This means that the total cost of maintaining automatic business systems can become quite substantial over the years. One attraction of using software is the misleading ease with which it can be altered to meet changed requirements like new legislation such as SMP in 1987. Overall the costs of maintaining payroll systems (hardware, software and associated office procedures) can be over 20 per cent p.a. of the original capital costs. Most of the maintenance costs are those of the labour involved rather than spare parts, etc. With payroll work there is the severe pressure to pay people on time which demands quick repairs to hardware and software. System amendments can be complicated and they are often required at short notice by statutory and business changes. One of the big advantages of payroll software packages is that the statutory maintenance is handled by the supplier.

It is important to remember that IT maintenance activities can also include such matters as changes in the associated administration. For example, the introduction of optical storage of documents as an improvement in business efficiency, changes all the record filing and retrieval procedures. Other factors in systems maintenance are stationery, for example changes to computer-printed Forms P14/60 and staff training to handle a modified system. In practice, most payroll IT work is maintenance consisting of a series of modifications and minor extensions to existing systems. Developing entirely new systems or completely replacing old systems is relatively rare, say once every five to ten years. Thus cheap, quick and reliable systems maintenance is an important objective but it is difficult to achieve.

(ix)   *Reviews* — After a new system has been operating for a short while post-implementation reviews can identify any weaknesses, opportunities for improvement and general lessons for the future.

(x)   *Co-ordinating systems development* — The development of an extensive new payroll automation system requires many activities. It is the job of the systems analyst to co-ordinate them. He may have to organise the purchase of mainframe terminals and some special computer programming. He may, however, actually do some of this work himself or delegate it to others. On large projects the co-ordination activities are so numerous that a special 'project manager' is required. (See 26.23 below.) Maintenance activities require similar control.

Project management

26.23   All business automation projects and maintenance work require management. Fundamentally it is a question of detailed planning and ensuring that all the numerous jobs are done on time, within cost estimates and are of the required quality. The plan against which all progress is measured is normally produced in outline at the feasibility study stage. A final plan can then be produced when the detailed design is completed. Much of the day-to-day co-ordination of work can be handled by the systems analyst. However, the regular reporting of progress to both a project manager and a high level project committee is essential. Corrective action can then be identified and authorised if the project is in difficulty. For instance, when software is written internally and is not purchased from external sources the cost of programming can exceed the budgeted expenditure. The project committee usually consists of the payroll and other user managers, a senior manager and a computer executive. Regular monthly or more frequent meetings are usual in the case of large or important projects. Where a systems analyst is not used, or merely provides support services, then the payroll administrator must do much of the work discussed above himself. Formal standardised approaches to IT project management exist, for example, PRINCE (PRojects IN Controlled Environments). These may be useful for large payroll projects.

Recent developments in IT

26.24   There are many developments in information technology that are affecting business administration, and some of these are listed in 30.4 and discussed in Reference (8) in 26.27 below. Two of the more important recent developments, the Internet and the Year 2000 problem, are discussed in more depth below.

The Internet

26.25   The rapid and continuing growth in the use of the Internet over the last few years has justifiably attracted a lot of interest. The Internet has many domestic, technical, and business applications. These include its use in payroll administration and related fields like pensions or personnel management.

(a)   ***Introduction to the Internet*** — In simple terms, the Internet is a huge and open on-line system linking together thousands of organisations and millions of people. Internet users can send electronic mail to each other and access remote databases. A big business advantage of the Internet is the fact that users have access to the current version of changing information like product prices, share prices, tax details, and news announcements. The Internet may also be seen as a network of telecommunication networks where the networks of individual organisations are linked together. The main computer systems linked to the Internet are called 'servers'. These computers serve requests for services like the provision or storage of data. From the point of view of a user, the Internet is a collection of standardised computer facilities with rather odd names like Gopher or Usenet. One of the most important business facilities of the Internet is the World Wide Web which is described in (b) below.

The Internet is an 'open system' in the general sense that it provides common technical standards so that any one in the World can link to it cheaply. The minimum requirement for individuals or organisations is a personal computer, a modem (a telecommunication device), standard software like Netscape Navigator and Eudora, and an ordinary telephone line. A final requirement is a small subscription, say £10 per month, to an Internet service provider who offers some data storage space on a computer server and an electronic 'gateway' onto the Internet. Thus the Internet is within the technical and economic limits of domestic users as well as small businesses.

Besides electronic mail and database services there are other facilities like file transfer (moving a collection of data or software from one computer to another). Most of these facilities are easier to demonstrate than describe, and readers unfamiliar with the Internet are advised to seek a demonstration.

The Internet offers no new technology, as electronic mail and on-line databases have been available for many years. It merely offers a cheap and standardised version of old concepts. However, there are some subtle differences. One is that traditional computer telecommunication services are strictly controlled and regulated by large organisations for their own specific purposes, such as BACSTEL for electronic payments. The Internet is almost anarchic by comparison as virtually anybody can use it for any purpose, including payroll-related administration.

As discussed below, using the Internet can be made reasonably secure by using normal computer practices like passwords. One approach is to use an 'intranet'. An intranet is merely a special version of the Internet accessible only to authorised internal staff. The advantage is that familiar standard Internet facilities are used. An extranet is a similar idea. Again it involves having a special version of the Internet, but in this case it is accessible to authorised external organisations and individuals such as customers and suppliers. Again, the advantage is the use of familiar standard facilities for a restricted purpose. Combining open access to some Internet facilities with restricted access to others is useful. For example, a sales catalogue may be accessible via the Internet to anyone, but details of overtime authorisation procedures may be only available to internal managers on an Internet screen.

(b) ***Payroll-related use of the Internet*** — As a practical example, a central payroll administrator can use a personal computer which may be connected to the Internet via a telephone line or a local computer network. The administrator can send an electronic mail message regarding, say, the employment of casual workers, to a departmental manager in a subsidiary company a hundred miles away. The message takes minutes to arrive. The Internet can also interconnect a scattered workforce. As an illustration, a salesman could send an 'e-mail' pay query to his payroll department. This could be done in the evening using a laptop computer connected to the phone in his hotel room. He could collect the reply the following day, again using his laptop. As another example, e-mail or file transfer can be used to send out reports like departmental budgets.

One of the most important facilities on the Internet is the World Wide Web (WWW or just the Web). This is a hypertext system, i.e. by touching items on the screen with the cursor the user retrieves a new screen of data. Taking a simple example, the main screen display for a life assurance company may show 'investment products' and 'pensions'. On moving the cursor to 'pensions' and clicking the mouse button, the investment screen is displayed with a list of different types of pension plan, for example personal pension plans and an FSAVC plan (FSAVCs are Free Standing Additional Voluntary Contributions). By moving the cursor to FSAVCs the details of the FSAVC plan can be displayed. The word 'Web' implies a set of interconnected screens and data, not necessarily available from the same computer server. For payroll administrators the Inland Revenue Web site provides useful information, such as details of Inland Revenue leaflets and press releases. On-line recruitment is available on the Web from companies like Reed or the publishers of Computer Weekly. Job details, say, for an accountant or computer programmer, can be viewed on the screen and application details sent back over the Internet.

Organisations like the Contributions Agency and Peterborough Software place payroll-related magazines (called 'web-zincs') on the Internet. One web-zinc is National Insurance News from the Contributions Agency which, for instance, has carried an article on rebates for employers taking on the long-term unemployed. These can be read (rather uncomfortably) from the screen or printed by the Web user for easier reading. Departments within organisations, can set up their own Web pages for unrestricted internal access. For example these could include an internal telephone directory, an organisation chart, and an office procedures manual. Internal Web pages can include standard details for all employees such as information on a loan scheme for train season tickets or the employer's pension plan. Special notices can also be put on Web pages, such as announcements concerning Self-Assessment.

The vast size of the World Wide Web and its continuously changing nature can sometimes make it difficult to track down precisely what a particular user wants. Special services, for instance those from Yahoo, can be used to search for information of interest in areas like taxation and salary surveys.

A few World Wide Web facilities are listed in Table 1 (general business examples) and in Table 2 (payroll-related examples). The name of the organisation providing information is accompanied by the appropriate Web address (technically called a URL or Universal Resource Locator). There is no intention to recommend the products and services whose details are displayed from these Web sites.

Future uses of the Internet will include on-line banking by both organisations and individuals, which has already been achieved in the USA. Once the Internet becomes more widely available to individuals both at work and at home, one can foresee payslips being sent out on the Internet.

(c)   **Further details on the Internet** — The Internet offers access to a huge
and rather confusing collection of on-line services. After payment for
telecommunications link and access to the Internet, further services may
be free or incur extra charges. Some services are composed of a mixture
of free and chargeable elements, for example, the current share price of
a quoted company may be provided free, but further details on the
company are chargeable. The telephone time to the Internet service
provider is typically charged at local rates to a domestic or small business
user. A large organisation can use an ISDN link (ISDN = Integrated
Services Digital Network). This provides greater speed and economy for
large volumes of data transmission.

Organisations may reduce the volume and cost of their printed literature
by providing Web versions on-line. On-line literature almost eliminates
the costs of distribution and printing. Advertising via Web documents is
also a possible source of revenue.

Table 1: *A few internet web addresses of general business interest*

Organisation	Web address
American Government	www.whitehouse.gov
The BBC (British Broadcasting Corporation)	www.bbc.co.uk
Computer Weekly (Technical Magazine Publishing)	www.computerweekly.co.uk
The Financial Times	www.FT.com
The Ford Motor Company	www.ford.co.uk
IBM (Computers)	www.uk.ibm.com
Liverpool John Moores University	www.livjm.ac.uk
Liverpool City Council	www.liverpool.gov.uk
Paris (French Tourist Information)	www.paris.org
Reed-Elsevier (Publishing Group)	www.reed-elsevier.com
Royal and Sun Alliance (Insurance)	www.royal-group.co.uk
Sainsbury (the Retail Group)	www.j-sainsbury.co.uk
Yahoo (Web Searching)	www.yahoo.co.uk

*The Table above includes a very small sample of the general information available on the
World Wide Web and collectively give a good idea of how it can be used in business. The
Web sites of information providers like the BBC can also contain useful payroll
information e.g. Government budget details.*

Table 2: *Examples of internet web addresses for payroll-related administration*

Organisation	Web address
American Society for Payroll Management	www.aspm.org
The Association of British Insurers	www.abi.org.uk
Butterworths (Legal Publishing)	www.butterworths.co.uk
Barclays Bank	www.barclays.co.uk
Chartered Accountants	www.icaew.co.uk
Cyborg (Human Resource Software)	www.cyborg.com
The Data Protection Registry	www.dpr.gov.uk
Equitable Life (Pensions, AVCs, etc)	www.equitable.co.uk
Financial Times (Financial Information)	www.info.ft.com
Global time Systems (Time & Attendance Systems)	www.gtstime.com
Institute of Personnel Development	www.ipd.co.uk
Institute of Payroll and Pensions Management	business.infotrade.co.uk/ippm
Intex (Payroll Software)	www.intex.co.uk
Lexis-Nexis (On-Line Legal Information)	www.lexis-nexis.com
Link Group (Pay Modelling, etc)	www.linkg.co.uk
National Association of Pension Funds	www.napf.co.uk
Pegasus (Financial Software)	www.pegasus.co.uk
Peterborough Software (HR and Financial Software)	www.peterboroughsoftware.co.uk
Reed (On-Line Recruitment)	www.reed.co.uk
Smart Systems (Manpower Management Software)	www.smart-systems.co.uk
Tolley Publishing Company	www.tolley.co.uk
UK Government (e.g. N I and Tax)	www.open.gov.uk

The above Table is a sample of the information available on the World Wide Web for payroll work and related activities like pensions administration. The UK Government site is of particular importance as it contains a directory to many public sector Web sites e.g. the Benefits Agency, the Contributions Agency, the Inland Revenue, and the Employment Department.

Provided care is taken with the amount of time spent on the Internet, it can be very economical. For example, the cost of international electronic mail is the same as regional electronic mail and measured in pence per document. Employees wasting time by exploring interesting but irrelevant Internet facilities, such as sports news, might be the biggest cost!

Access to the Internet is typically via a service provider such as CompuServe, Demon, U-Net, or British Telecommunications, and these companies offer a range of services. There are consultancy services available for using the Internet, for instance Web authoring where data pages are designed and installed. Larger organisations can do much of the work for themselves by installing their own Web server rather than sharing that of the service provider.

Security is often mentioned as a problem with the Internet, but normal IT precautions like using passwords, data encryption, and 'firewalls' are likely to be adequate in many situations. The term 'firewall' is misleading. It is typically a computer facility which prevents unauthorised access to an internal IT network, for example by a malicious external 'hacker' using the Internet. The firewall does, however, allow authorised access. Another problem with the Internet can be poor response times. This may be partly improved by using faster equipment at the user end. However, the user only controls part of the network. Congested long-distance communication lines, and accessing data on popular over-used computer sites, can result in a very annoying slow response. This is particularly true where images and graphics are transmitted, or where the data comes from foreign sites, for example in America. Another problem with introducing the Internet may be that old proprietary systems, for purposes like electronic mail, cannot be replaced immediately. Thus two rival systems may have to co-exist for sometime.

The Year 2000 problem

26.26   One of the most publicised examples of IT systems maintenance is the need to change a large percentage of business systems to cope with the 'Year 2000' or 'millennium' problem. This occurs where dates used by a computer are currently, for instance, in the format 28/09/98 rather than 28/03/1998. Typically 'pre-millennium' business software cannot sensibly handle ambiguous two-figure year numbers for dates after the year 2000. For instance with software written for use in the 1980s or 1990s, a date written as 28/09/01 would be ambiguous and is usually treated as an error by a computer. Thus the date could be interpreted as 28/09/1901. This interpreted date would not, for instance, be a sensible date for an employee joining a company in 1993, hence the error condition. But the same pre-millennium software operating early in the next century would reject as erroneous the valid date 28/09/2001 expressed with the same figures i.e. 28/09/01. The situation is complicated by the various different methods that computer staff have devised to handle date information and time calculations such as the amount of pensionable service between two dates. Unfortunately, as in the example given previously, many of these date-handling methods, but not all, only work before the year 2000.

As date-handling is common in business computing, and occurs to a lesser extent in technical computing, some alarmist articles have been written in the business and technical press about the consequences of the Year 2000. These articles basically say that the cost of changing (maintaining) IT systems to cope with the millennium problem will be high, there is not enough time left to amend all the systems, and unchanged systems will cause havoc. The language used to describe the problem is sometimes a little extreme. Given the modern dependence on computer systems the situation has been viewed as a world-wide crisis. Thus there is the apocalyptic vision of most of the commercial and technical infra-structure of the modern world failing at midnight on the 31st December 1999!

The millennium crisis problem is usually presented as a software problem, but it affects other aspects of business systems like computer data storage and stationery. The high cost of rectifying the Year 2000 problem is caused by the need to examine, amend, and test many pieces of computer date logic, screen layouts, print-outs, database records, interfaces between computer systems, and business forms. The work is straightforward but potentially extensive, tedious, and error prone. There are two main ways of dealing with the millennium problem. One is for software to infer that high two-figure year numbers refer to the 20th Century and that low two-figure year numbers refer to the 21st Century. For instance 02/11/98 is regarded by the software (and human beings) as 2 November 1998, and 17/07/05 is regarded as 17 July 2005. The other way of solving the problem is for all dates to use four-figure year numbers e.g. 17/10/2007. The software can then decide whether a date is sensible or not according to the circumstances in the normal fashion. For example, a date of birth in a personnel system would be acceptable between, say, 70 years and 15 years prior to the current date.

How does the millennium problem affect payroll administration and related areas of business administration? This clearly depends on the business and IT systems used and their supplier. Typically, pension administration systems already handle dates in the 19th and 20th Centuries, such as for pensioner and employee dates of birth. Dates in the 21st Century are also handled, for example, for employee retirement dates. This may not be true, however, for payroll and accounting systems. Clearly a thorough study of business and IT systems is required, and those which are not millennium-compliant need to be amended quickly. This may or may not be covered by maintenance agreements with IT suppliers. Of course, all the millennium-compliant computer systems (and stationery) used in an office need to be compatible. For instance, can millennium-compliant systems using two-figure year numbers and four-figure year numbers be used side-by-side and linked? Also historical data, such as salary histories, may need re-formatting. See References (14) and (15) in 26.27 below for a discussion of the Millennium problem.

References

26.27   The following literature contains further information on topics mentioned in the chapter as well as reference details.

(1)   Moynihan E, 'Business Management and Systems Analysis', Alfred Waller, 1993. (This book covers the development, implementation, and project management of business IT systems. It has a UK approach and covers payroll and SSADM.)

(2)   Harrison J, 'Office Procedures', Third Edition, Pitman 1993. (A basic introduction to office methods and equipment. Both traditional and modern equipment are covered.)

(3)   Turban F, McClean E, and Wetherbe J, 'Information Technology for Management', Wiley, 1996. (This book relates IT to modern thinking on business, management, and organisations.)

(4)   Zorkoczy P, 'Information Technology: An Introduction', Pitman, Fourth Edition, 1995.

(5)   'Payroll & Personnel Systems Year Book 1998', IMIS Publications, 1997. (A catalogue of payroll and related software.)

(6)   'BACS to withdraw MM Submissions', PMR, August 1996

(7)   Kitson Impey, 'Form P11D Software to the Rescue'. PMR, February 1997

(8)   Moynihan E and Taylor M, 'Payroll Futures', PMR, February 1997

(9)   Capron H L, 'Computers: Tools for an Information Age', Addison-Wesley, Fifth Edition, 1997.

(10)   Kingsbury P, 'IT Answers to HR Questions', Institute of Personnel and Development, 1997.

(11)   Lucas H C Jr, 'Information Technology for Management', McGraw-Hill, 1997.

(12)   Richards H, 'P11D-Day Approaches', PMR, February 1998. (A discussion on software for managing Form P11D with a list of suppliers.)

(13)   Singleton J, 'Timed to Perfection', PMR, September 1997. (Article on time and attendance IT systems.)

(14)   Gandhi-Burnett K, 'Facing up to the Millennium', PMR, June 1997.

(15)   'Millennium Bug Campaign', PMR, March 1998.

(16)   'BACS User Manual: Telecommunication Link Transmission Specification', Twelfth Edition, February 1997.

27 Computerising Your System

Background and history

27.1   The Industrial Revolution required physical and mechanical expertise, therefore power sources, engines, motors, machines, etc. were developed to assist us with mass production. Payroll departments used the early office machines such as the typewriter and comptometer, both hand operated.

The Information Revolution produced computers from those early beginnings to assist us with our mental, as well as physical and mechanical expertise.

The computer is a machine that stores and works with data; data is interpreted and turned into information. It is the computer's ability to retrieve that information with speed, accuracy and attention to detail that assists us with our mental expertise. A computer does not rely on the mechanical moving parts, such as rods, pistons or wheels, found in conventional machines; it uses electrons as moving parts. Electrons are magnetised in some metals so that they will line up pointing in the same direction; it is this technology that is then used by the computer to store information permanently. The manipulation of that information by the computer requires a program to tell the computer what to do and in which sequence, to produce a desired result.

In the early days program writing was tedious and laborious, requiring a computer programmer to produce the special machine-code numbers that computer circuits could recognise. Programming languages were then developed so that programs were much easier to write; a translation program would then translate the language into the machine code understood by computers. These languages were given 'generation' designations and there are now third and fourth generation languages being used.

Payroll departments, because they work according to defined rules and regulations relating to statutory and contractual obligations, were among the first departments to take advantage of computerisation. As software systems became more sophisticated other departments also became computerised, but the early independent payroll computer systems could not communicate with the other independent software systems, so interfaces had to be written that would copy the information in one system and transfer it into another system. Similarly software written for one brand of computer would not work on another incompatible brand of computer.

The introduction of relational database management systems then revolutionised data processing. What took pages of programming could now be achieved with a single command. Open systems that are based on three fundamental principles – compatability with accepted industry standards, portability across a range of mainframes, minis and PCs, and connectability across different makes of computers and different locations – became available.

So today there are software systems that can be used on most brands of computers, and integrated systems that not only communicate with each other but can exist as one common store of data which can be accessed from all sizes of computer, situated in different geographic locations.

These advances have meant that many organisations now have Management Information System (MIS) departments, in order to manage the network of computerised processing procedures and computer-accessible databases used by the other management functions within the organisation. However, as the pace, complexity and competition in the marketplace affects organisations, the reliance on computer systems grows and Information Systems managers face the twin challenges of improving productivity and enhancing quality. To do this, they must keep abreast of the latest offering by hardware and software vendors, as the rapid technological pace plays havoc with the old classifications. 'Right-sizing', 'Down-sizing', and 'Multi-Media' are the latest discussion points.

The computer can now be used to produce computer software itself. Computer Aided System Engineering (CASE) and specialist application development tools will build high performance applications in a fraction of the time needed previously and with fewer errors. It allows systems development that is independent of hardware, software, network and user interfaces.

It is this powerful technology at our fingertips that is the driving force of our economy today and into the foreseeable future. The interaction between the human brain contributing creativity, judgement and intuition and the computer contributing accuracy, speed and attention to detail, produces a synergistic effect with unlimited potential.

Common computer terminology

27.2   Just as we do not need to know how a car engine works to drive a car, we do not need to know how a computer works to use it in our working environment. However, it does help to know some of the terminology. Listed below are some brief descriptions of these words, including both the earlier terminology and the newer terminology that is used on a daily basis.

(*a*)   *Hardware* — Physical equipment such as the computer, printers and other mechanical devices.

(*b*)   *Computer* — An electronic symbol manipulating system. Designed to accept and store input and to retrieve that input in a set format as output.

(*c*)   *Personal Computer (PC)* — A micro-computer general purpose processing system that can range in size from the small portable laptop computers, or even the palmtop computers now available, to the more familiar desktop computer. They are designed for use by one person at a time, but can be networked. The new PCs possess the processing power and storage capabilities of many of the older small mainframes. These powerful machines can be linked up with external databases to take advantage of huge repositories of data. With software that exploits graphic user interfaces the PC becomes a work station.

(*d*)   *Mini Computer* — A more powerful general purpose processing system that will serve multiple users. The size range is from desktop to small filing cabinet.

(*e*)   *Mainframe Computer* — An even more powerful general processing system that has greater storage capacity than minis. The size ranges from a small filing cabinet to a large filing cabinet.

(*f*)   *Network* — An interconnection between computer systems.

(*g*)   *Data* — This is the plural for datum, which means fact. Information consists of facts. Facts are recorded using symbols; alpha, numeric and special characters would be the common symbols used for human resource data.

(*h*)   *Record* — A set of related facts.

(*j*)   *Database* — This is data stored in a format which is then useful to the user. For example, a simple paper folder holding paper documents such as a starting form, P45 and bank details for one employee, filed in a cabinet with other similar folders for other employees, would be a database. This information held on computer would be a computerised database.

(*k*)   *File* — A collection of related records stored in the computer.

(*l*)   *Program* — A set of sequenced instructions for the computer to perform a particular operation.

(*m*) **Process** — The computer performing a program.

(*n*) **System** — An organised grouping of integrated methods and procedures needed to produce an end result.

(*p*) **Software System** — A collection of complex instructions designed to cause a computer to operate in a certain sequence.

(*q*) **File Management System (FMS)** — A software system that allows users to define data items and place them onto a file, for example the employee masterfile which contains all the information relating to a single employee. A FMS can only access records from one file at a time.

(*r*) **Database Management System** — A software system that can access records from two or more files at the same time.

(*s*) **Distributed Database System** — A system that stores data in more than one geographic location. This data can be accessed as if it were a single integrated system.

(*t*) **Relational Database Management System** — A software system that treats files as tables, with columns and rows, and can find the fastest way to manipulate and retrieve data.

(*u*) **Application Software** — Pre-written software designed for specialised tasks. For example a Payroll Application is designed to produce the gross-to-net payroll calculations and the output necessary for a payroll department.

(*v*) **Tools** — Application software that allows the user to easily write programs to create, store, modify, retrieve and manage information without needing to know complex computer programming languages.

(*w*) **Open Systems** — The ability to move data and applications across dissimilar computers, via local and wide-area networks.

(*x*) **Portable Systems** — Available on a variety of different hardware and operating system platforms.

(*y*) **Windows** — A software shell manages the exchange of data between separate applications that may be used by the end user. A typical package would include pull down menus, graphics, coloured screens and icons. The various open current screens are overlaid on top of each other, like pages of paper, and the mouse is used to navigate around.

Input requirements of a computerised system

27.3 The concepts behind the design of payroll application software are the ability to reflect the structure of the business information, people information and pay information. Depending on the size and requirements of an organisation these can be as simple or sophisticated as required. The employee's

Figure 27A

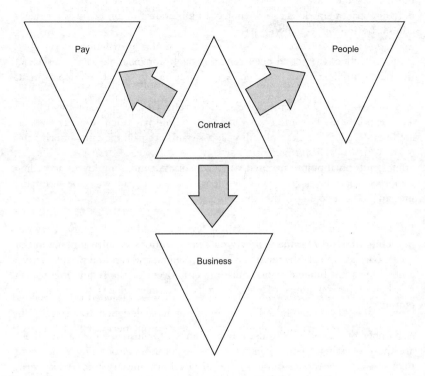

Illustration of input requirements

contract of employment is the link between these three areas. Figure 27A above shows this in a diagrammatic form. This chapter will cover a sophisticated requirement.

Structure of the business information

27.4   Internal organisations within a business may be thought of in terms of departments, sections, branches, divisions etc. These organisations can be placed into a reporting hierarchy structure, for example the payroll department may come within the finance division within one hierarchy, but in another it may come under Human Resources.

A business also has contacts with external organisations such as the Inland Revenue, Unions etc.

Locations are the physical locations of an organisation, for example the payroll department is located at the Head Office address, while the Farnham Branch is located at the High Street in Farnham.

621

Jobs reflect the type of work needed by the business, for example a retail business would have a job-type such as sales. Clerical job-types exist in a payroll department. Jobs can be subject to job evaluation procedures for salary administration and equality of pay.

Positions reflect the actual occurrence of a job, for example sales assistant at the Farnham High Street branch or a section leader in the payroll department.

Grades, or grading structures are used to reflect the responsibilities of jobs and/or positions. In some cases rates used within pay calculations are associated with grades. For example, all sales assistants are paid the same hourly rate.

Spines and spinal points are used when organisations pay employees according to agreed salary levels for grades and length of service, allowing for automatic increments to a ceiling within the spine.

Budgets are used to estimate the staffing levels needed for a business. They can be defined for organisations, jobs, grades or positions or any combination of these. For example, turnover at the Farnham High Street branch means there is a need for a head count of five full-time employees or the requirement for a number of person hours of 190. Payroll department needs seven full-time employees.

A number of 'calendars' are used by a business, for instance for payroll there are the processing calendars linked with the statutory processing year. There may also be calendars associated with the fiscal accounting year, holiday year, pension year and those which hold the regional bank holidays.

Money is the currency used within the business, the business's own bank details and the payment methods used to distribute net pay to employees and payments to third parties.

Status is the employment status types such as new starter, current employee, leaver, ex-employee, dormant employee etc. used to produce correct gross-to-net calculations as specified in the terms and conditions of employment and to provide management information.

People information

27.5   Basic personal information relating to employees consists of their full name and address, date of birth, date of start, marital status, sex, title etc. Further personal information consists of their next of kin, emergency contact, retirement date, bank details etc.

Time and attendance information relating to the employee is used to determine the direct and indirect costs to the organisation in employing that employee.

Absence reporting is becoming increasingly important, not only for its effect on payment entitlement, but because organisations need to monitor the reasons for the absence, in case of future legal action by the employee.

Shift scheduling has become increasingly important. In the Service Industries for example, new contracts of employment are issued which include as basic hours, hours that would previously have been classified as unsocial.

Appraisal information is being linked to performance payments.

Training information relating to courses attended, results and dates, may be a requirement by law or by contract of employment.

Pay information

27.6 'Elements' are the building blocks or items of pay that are then used to produce gross-to-net pay calculations.

Earnings elements will then be all those payment types that build up gross pay, such as basic pay, overtime payments, bonus payments etc.

Deduction elements will be all those deduction types that reduce gross pay:

(a) Pre-tax deductions are those that must be taken before PAYE is calculated. For example contributions to a charitable giving scheme are a deduction that can be made before PAYE is calculated.

(b) Statutory deductions are deductions the employer makes for PAYE, NIC and AEOs.

(c) Voluntary deductions are those deductions the employee has authorised the employer to make on their behalf and pay to a third party, for example trade union fees.

Employers also make payments on behalf of the employee which they pay to a third party direct, such as the employer's contribution to a pension scheme for the employee.

Direct payment elements are payments made through the payroll which are not classified as gross pay, for example expense reimbursements; these might have to be included for PAYE and/or NIC calculations.

'Balances' can be the positive or negative accumulation over time of one element, or of a number of elements either adding to, or subtracting from, the same balance. For example, gross pay balance would be the sum of all the earnings elements, pensionable pay balance may be the sum of selected earnings elements, pension paid balance would be the sum of all the employee's pension contributions only. Balances should be accessible over a number of time dimensions. Some are linked to the statutory processing calendar, such as run level, period level, quarter level and year-to-date level. Other balances may be linked to the other business calendars, such as fiscal year, holiday year etc; for example the processing year runs from 6 April to 5 April, the holiday year runs from 1 January to 31 December and the balance of holiday days taken is kept using the holiday year calendar.

Formulas can be written to perform calculations on data input in order to produce a required result. Formulas can be simple, for instance dividing an annual salary input by twelve to produce a monthly salary in pounds and pence; or a more sophisticated formula can be written based on data combinations, for examaple if the employee has started or is leaving part way through the month, or has been promoted part way through the month, the formula can be written to calculate the monthly salary according to which condition exists for each employee.

Management costings can be related to the accounting costs of gross-to-net pay production in the Nominal Ledger of a business. They can also be related to the labour costs; just as a budget projects estimated costs, labour costings can be used to produce actual costs. For example, gross pay for the Farnham Branch is a debit to one account and a credit to another account in the general nominal ledger. The gross pay and the employer's contribution to NIC is the cost to the business of employing the employees at the Farnham Branch.

Contract information

27.7   The terms and conditions of employment link the three areas together. For example, new employee, Mrs Mary Smith, living at 3 Green Lane, Farnham, works as a part-time sales assistant for 20 hours a week in the Farnham Branch and is to receive the relevant hourly rate for her grade as a monthly payment less statutory deductions. The 20 hours includes five hours to be worked on a Sunday.

Input requirements of a computerised system

27.8   Getting this information onto the database in the most efficient and user-friendly manner on line, means using screen layouts that allow the user to enter that information in the most logical and economical manner with the minimum of key strokes.

Graphic User Interfaces (GUIs) present much of their information to users in graphic form, generally on overlapping rectangular areas of the screen called windows. Users can manipulate windows using a pointing device known as the mouse to make them larger, or smaller, or to position them elsewhere on the overall screen. They can also select objects (files and documents) to work on by using the mouse to click on small pictorial representations called icons, or use the mouse to pull down menus to select the screen they wish to use. Graphic entities can be scrollbars, sliders, checkboxes, buttons and text edit fields.

This means screens with fields:

- may have on-line validation;

- offer a valid list of values to choose from, and by using the ability to click on a tool bar to open that list and to pick off the value;

- entry of values by a click on a single button;

- that can be entered in any sequence;

- that can be seen/entered by scrolling/sliding through existing records;

- that can open other work areas;

- that have on-line help and documentation;

- that can provide a view to historical data.

Access to those screens may be direct via a menu or by logically stringing screens together to emulate the workflow by picking the next screen to work on by clicking on a button.

Figures 27B to 27F below are examples of the type of on-line entry screens designed with Graphic User Interface tools.

Process requirements of a computerised system

27.9   The computer will accept, store, manipulate and retrieve data according to the instructions given to it via the programs. Processes take place when the computer is following those instructions. They can be summarised as follows.

(a) Validation process of data at time of input, that is the computer checking that the data input is in the required format and is a valid input value for storage.

(b) Audit Trail process produces the information needed to show all the transactions that have taken place on the database, who was responsible, the date and time of the transaction and the previous value if the transaction updated an existing value.

(c) Payroll process run identifies the employees and elements included in the run and the processing status of those employees and elements; processes the elements and produces the calculated results for those elements, maintaining the balances and producing messages to assist with payroll reconciliation.

(d) Rollback process run allows the removal of an incorrect payroll process run for the whole payroll or at employee level.

Figure 27B

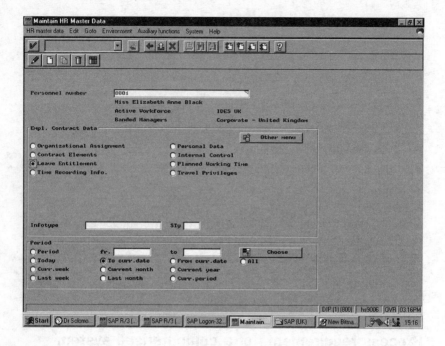

Illustration of a Windows screen

(Guidance: You will see that there is a menu printed along the top. By clicking on it with
the mouse, the menu will open. The same procedure allows you to move through the menu
to select the screen/action you want to work on. Below this is a set of icons. By selecting
any one of the icons you can perform a certain action with one click of the mouse. For
example, by clicking onto the icon with the 'tick' on it, you can validate your entries,
before continuing. Below these are a set of push butons that allow you to select which
action you wish to perform.

In the area 'Core Employee Info' there are a number of radio buttons. By clicking on one,
you open the screen that contains the data fields you want to use. The field at the bottom
allows you to enter a choice of your own or by clicking on the 'Other menu' button you
can select a whole new menu.

In the area 'Period' you can select the dates that you want associated with the action.)

Figure 27C

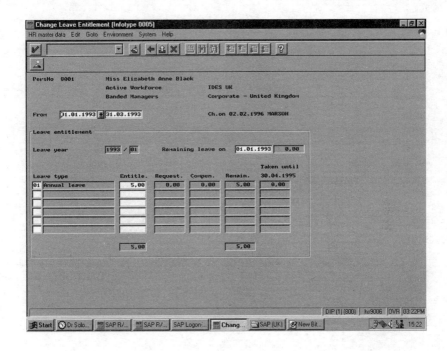

(Guidance: For example, by selecting 'Leave entitlement' you will be put through to this screen.)

Figure 27D

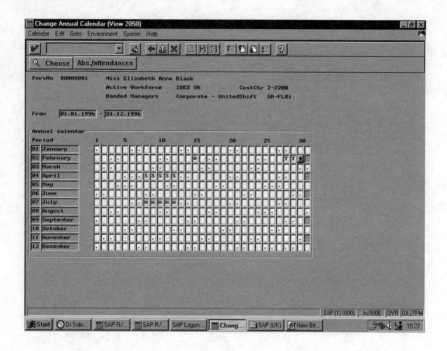

(Guidance: Or by selecting 'Annual calendar' you can see at a glance the attendance
history. On the right-hand side of this screen is a scroll bar. You can display more of the
calendar by using this.)

Figure 27E

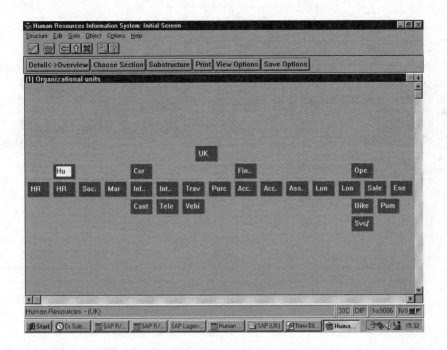

(Guidance: Using the graphical interface you can see at a glance existing structures. These
can be viewed as modified, or new structures can be created.)

Figure 27F

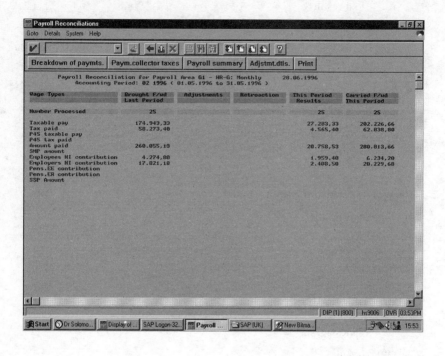

(Guidance: You can view report results on-line and then drill down to lower levels just by double-clicking with the mouse on the selected information you want to expand on.)

(*e*) Payments process allocates the disbursement of net pay and payments to third parties using the different payment methods available.

(*f*) Costing process produces accounting and costing information for each calculated result.

(*g*) Reversal process run where a payment was generated but withheld and a record needs to be maintained within the system to reverse costing and balances for reporting against.

Output requirements of a computerised system

27.10 The above sections featured the possible input requirements and the processes manipulating the data. The output is the retrieval of that data in a required format.

For payroll the standard output would be as follows:

- validation report;
- audit report;
- pay advice;
- payroll summary;
- payroll reconciliation report;
- payroll messages;
- BACS media;
- cheques;
- cash analysis;
- journal entries;
- costing analysis; and
- statutory year-end reports.

In addition the system should provide the tools to enable you to produce the following from your own output:

- management reports;
- *ad hoc* reports;
- on-line queries;
- event and exception reports;
- interface files.

See Figure 26G above for the standard symbols used in systems flowcharts.

References

27.11   The references listed in 26.25 above may also be relevant to this chapter.

(1)   'Through the Millennium Barrier', 'Exploring the Options', 'Making the Right Choice' are all articles which appeared under the 'Selecting a Payroll System' feature in PMR, July 1997.

(2)   'P11D-Day Approaches', PMR, February 1998. (An article on P11D software.)

(3)   'Facing up to the Millennium', PMR, June 1997.

(4)   'Form P11D Software Review', PMR, January and February 1997.

28 Selecting a Computer System

Scope of this chapter

28.1   Payroll departments have traditionally operated in isolation, but as organisations realise the importance of employees working in a computer-orientated structure of the business, the choice of a computerised system for payroll should also be made in conjunction with other computerisation needs.

Modern computer systems are designed, built and installed using structured techniques and software tools that make the installation of a new system a professional, well-controlled and predictable process. These systems can be capable of implementing high-performance, multi-user systems in a fraction of the time needed by traditional techniques. Specialist application software packages are available with an inbuilt flexibility that allows users to define their own business needs and customise the software without affecting the underlying database.

User-friendly software applications are available that allow users with limited computer experience to perform actions that previously required computer specialists.

Modern technologies allow data and application systems to be distributed both geographically and across computer hardware from different manufacturers. Sophisticated security access controls allow integrated systems to appear as a single separate system to the end-user.

This all means that the choice of a computer system should no longer be restricted because of a brand of computer, size of computer, single department requirement, physical location or costs.

Feasibility studies should be based on the required output from the system within the overall current and future information needs of the organisation.

Selection criteria

28.2   Therefore, the criteria for selecting a computer system should be based on the following:

- functional requirements;

- ease of use;

- ability to incorporate changes;

- security of access:

- support and services;

- ease of retrieval;

- integration with other systems; and

- technologies used.

See Figure 28A below for selection criteria in diagrammatic form.

Functional requirements

28.3   Ideally a computer system should perform all those functions that a payroll department would perform manually. This means considering both the routine and the non-routine functions. The answers to the questions set out below will have to be evaluated by reference to the size of the payroll population in making meaningful comparisons between the two systems.

(*a*)   **New starters** — Will it pro-rate payments if an employee joins part way through a processing period? Will it allow a new employee to be processed in a period after a payroll process run has already taken place?

(*b*)   **Changes and promotions** — Will it pro-rate payments if an employee has had contractual changes during a period?

(*c*)   **Leaving and left** — Will it process all leaving pay requirements? Does it handle all statutory requirements for paying people who have left?

(*d*)   **Supplementary process runs** — Will it allow an employee to be processed again during a period because of additional payments?

(*e*)   **Adjustments and overrides** — Will it allow adjustments to, or override completely, the expected calculated results of a payroll process?

(*f*)   **Balances** — Will it allow for additional balances? Will it allow entry of opening balances and direct balance adjustments?

(*g*)   **Reversals** — Will it allow the complete reversal of values created during a payroll process run for an employee in error?

(*h*)   **Rollback** — Will it allow for the removal of a test payroll process run or a run containing incorrect data?

(*j*)   **Formulas** — Will it allow complex formulas to be written?

(*k*)   **Costings** — Will it produce journal entries for General Ledgers? Will it produce detailed labour costs analysis?

Figure 28A

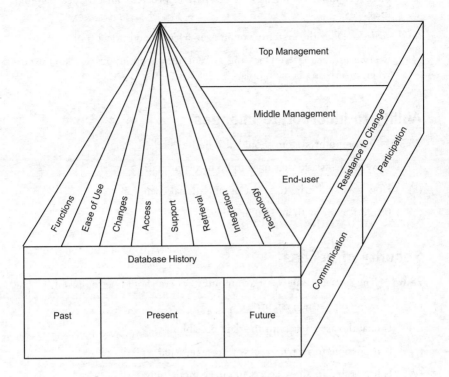

Illustration of criteria for selection of a suitable computer system

(*l*)   ***History*** — What sort of history is available? Is it possible to view the contents of a database as it existed at any period in time? Is it possible to enter data for a date in the past or future?

(*m*)   ***What if?*** — Will it allow you to produce on-line a payroll process run for one employee?

(*n*)   ***Year end*** — Can it hold data one year for reporting the next year, for example Class 1A national insurance contributions?

Ease of use

28.4   A computer system should also be judged for its user-friendliness.

(*a*)   *Training* — Will it take a lot of training before the system can be used?

(*b*)   *Documentation* — Does comprehensive, readable documentation exist?

(*c*)   *On-line help* — Does on-line help exist? Can it be added to in order to make it user-specific?

(d)   *Messages* — Does the system produce helpful, prompt messages for incorrect input on-line? Does the payroll process run produce helpful messages?

(e)   *Tools* — Does the system contain user-friendly additional tools?

(f)   *Continuous working* — Does the system allow continuous working even when processing is taking place?

Ability to incorporate changes

28.5   A computer system should also be flexible.

(a)   How are legislation changes to be incorporated?

(b)   How easy will it be to effect organisational changes?

(c)   Could it cope with a new currency?

Security of access

28.6   The security aspects of a computer system should be foolproof.

(a)   How secure is the system?

(b)   Is unauthorised access to the data possible?

(c)   Is it possible to restrict access to certain data?

(d)   Is it possible to allow access in query mode only?

Support and services

28.7   This aspect is one of the most important features of determining the suitability of a computer system.

(a)   If something goes wrong with the hardware or software, what support is available?

(b)   Is that support available for 24 hours?

(c)   Are documentation and software updates supplied on time?

(d)   How large are the development and support teams?

(e)   With the advent of the Global Market can the supplier support the legislation requirements of other countries?

Ease of retrieval

28.8   Retrieval and subsequent use of the data stored within the system can be time critical. Ease of retrieval is an important factor.

(*a*)   Can the data be accessed for spreadsheet use?

(*b*)   Can the data be accessed by a word processor?

(*c*)   Can the system alert to forthcoming events such as anniversaries or warn that required data are missing?

(*d*)   Can it send messages using electronic mail?

(*e*)   Can multiple search criteria be used to retrieve selected records?

(*f*)   Can it accept and produce interface files from other systems?

(*g*)   In addition to the retrieval of structured data, will the system allow the storage and retrieval of unstructured data, i.e. free format text?

Integration with other systems

28.9   Integration with other systems helps to reduce costs.

(*a*)   Will the system be truly integrated with one common store of data?

(*b*)   Will data be duplicated in other systems?

(*c*)   Is it an open system?

(*d*)   Will the system integrate seamlessly with other existing office automation?

(*e*)   Does the supplier offer a full system integration service, supplying both the hardware and software and continual maintenance and support?

Technologies used

28.10   A computer system can also be judged on efficacy of the technologies used.

(*a*)   Will the technology used mean that any future choices that will be needed are restricted because of hardware dependency?

(*b*)   Can the software be customised without affecting the underlying database?

(*c*)   Will the future requirements be easily catered for or are preparations being made such as for the Year 2000 millennium bug solution or the introduction of European Monetary Union (EMU)?

Choosing a computer system

28.11   The decision to change to a computerised system from a manual system or to change from one computerised system to another is usually based on the assumption that it will increase productivity, be more efficient and benefit the organisation as a whole. See Figure 28B below.

Figure 28B

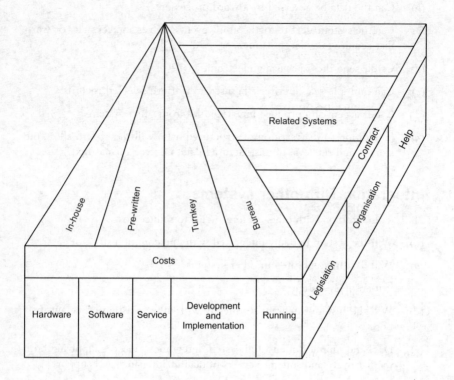

Illustration of factors determining suitability when choosing a new computer system

Effects on staff of a new system

28.12 The effects on staff who will use the new system should not be ignored; the resistance to system change is a very real factor and must be taken into account. Employee confidence is a critical factor in the success of any new computer system implementation.

Resistance by employees to change can be for a number of reasons:

(a)   *Fear of the unknown* — The hardware may be unfamiliar and they may feel that they will be unable to learn the skills necessary to use it on a regular basis.

(b)   *New working practices* — They are familiar with the working practices developed for their old system but the new system might require a new set of working practices calling for a further learning curve.

(c) **Loss of status** — Payroll, because of early computerisation and the confidential nature of the data, has usually worked in isolation. With a new, maybe integrated system, the responsibilities and authority of the users may diminish.

(d) **Reorganisation of departments** — New systems may mean that departments are merged, offices have new working layouts and friendly working groups may be separated.

(e) **Initial increase in workload** — Employees still need to be paid whilst the new system is being implemented and this will inevitably increase the amount of work in the short-term. Users may be worried how they will cope.

Minimising effects of change on staff

28.13 In order to minimise the effects of the change for staff and to build confidence in the new system, the resistance to change factor must be recognised and dealt with earlier rather than later. There are still people who will use a hand calculator to add up a list of values and then mentally add the figures to see if the calculator was right. They lack confidence that in the first instance they input the correct figures and secondly that the calculator is capable of giving a correct answer. However, it is always desirable to scan results manually to ascertain whether the results make sense, i.e. if you multiply a four digit sum by two digits, the answer should be a sum of five or six digits.

Communication and participation are the confidence builders. Staff who are made aware of the changes and the effects they will have on them, who are able to communicate their concerns and have them addressed, will not suffer a loss of self worth. They should be able to participate in some of the decision-making for the new system, so that they have had a hand in some of the changes and feel more responsible for making the changeover a success. They should understand that they will receive adequate training, will have good documentation and on-line help and will have back-up and support if something goes wrong, so that confidence in using the new system can be built. They should be involved in parallel running, that is using the identical input data for the new system as the old system and comparing the results, thereby building confidence in the ability of the new system to produce the required output.

Related management information systems

28.14 A payroll system, whether manual or computerised, exists within the total organisation's information system. It will receive data from other systems and produce data for other systems. There is a flow of data internally within the organisation. There will also be a flow of data from external organisations and third parties, i.e. statutory bodies, pension scheme administrators, unions etc. There is also a flow of data going to these third parties.

Corporate database

28.15   The ideal for internal related systems is a 'corporate database' that allows all of the data to be held once on the system and accessed by all the systems that require that data in their processing. For external systems and in the absence of a 'corporate database' for internal related systems, data transfer takes place using the following media.

(*a*)   ***Documentation:***

- original documentation, e.g. a contract of employment;

- printed forms, e.g. P45;

- computer print-outs, e.g. list of employees and their contributions to a particular union.

(*b*)   ***Computer electronic media:***

- magnetic tapes;

- floppy disks;

- cassettes;

- cartridges;

- magnetic disks.

(*c*)   ***Telecommunications:***

- commercial telephone lines;

- computer cable networks.

Internal systems subject to data flow

28.16   Internal systems subject to data flow to and from the payroll system are listed below.

(*a*)   ***Time and attendance systems (T & A)*** — These systems are designed to record the times an employee is at work.

(*b*)   ***Absence monitoring systems*** — These systems record the reasons for absence and the employee's use of the allocated holiday entitlement. Sickness absence can be used for occupational sick pay schemes and the records needed for statutory sick pay compliance. Maternity leave can be used for occupational maternity schemes and statutory maternity pay compliance.

(c) **Pension systems** — These systems are used by pension administrators to record the data relating to the beneficiaries of the scheme and to produce pension entitlements for pensioners.

(d) **Personnel systems** — These systems are used for managing the people side of the organisation, such as manpower planning, job evaluation, training, benefits and compensations, recruitment and applicant monitoring, etc.

(e) **General Ledger systems** — Financial accounting uses the payroll calculated results in the Nominal Ledger. Management accounts uses earnings and employer charge elements to monitor labour costs for budgeting and analysis purposes. The Payables Ledger may be used to reimburse expenses which in turn may be needed for the statutory deductions of PAYE and NICs and for P11D returns.

(f) **Group measured day work and similar systems** — These systems are used to measure productivity, which may be linked to bonus payment schemes.

(g) **P11D or expenses and benefits systems** — These systems are used for the recording of taxable benefits and the subsequent production of P9D and P11D reports for submission to the Inland Revenue. Increasingly, expenses and benefits are being paid through the payroll and recorded by the payroll office as opposed to finance or accounts departments.

External systems subject to data flow

28.17   External systems are subject to data flow to, and from, the payroll system.

(a) **Statutory bodies** — The Inland Revenue, Department of Social Security, the courts of the United Kingdom and other government departments.

(b) **Banking systems** — For distribution of net pay to employees' bank accounts and to third parties.

(c) **Other third parties** — Deductions from employees' gross pay for payment to third parties, for example, charities, unions, savings institutions.

In-house system

28.18   A custom-built or in-house system is designed and built for a specific organisation to reflect their exact needs. Developing software in-house will mean a major commitment of staff, money and time in the first instance, and an ongoing commitment of staff, money and time to incorporate the changes needed due to statutory legislation and organisational changes.

A detailed system analysis must take place to identify the required output, the processing procedures to produce that output and the input data required during processing to produce that output. Using a top-down analysis methodology it is then possible to identify top-level functions and sub-functions so as to produce a functional hierarchy of requirements.

System designers will then be able to decide the most effective and efficient methods of building the system that will produce the desired output requirements. These should include the long-range plans of the organisation's information needs and the need for flexibility to incorporate changes. The build of the system should incorporate rigorous testing, quality assurance routines and documentation at all stages.

Implementation of the system should consist of inputting data, running processes and viewing output. Training of end-users will be needed, end-user documentation and help information should be supplied.

Ongoing maintenance of the system will be needed to update the system to meet the changing needs of the organisation and to comply with new legislation.

Pre-written software application packages

28.19   Commercially written software applications have had to go through similar top-down methodology in order to produce off-the-shelf software. The software will be flexible enough to incorporate the individual requirements of the majority of its potential users. Popular packages will have developed the functionality and features needed to keep in line with their own competitors. The software would have been rigorously tested both before and after it became commercially available. Quality Assurance is of the utmost importance for commercially supplied software. Software suppliers must keep up-to-date with statutory changes and be able to supply their customers with updates to their application so that the package will always comply with statutory legislation.

(*a*)   ***Documentation and training*** — Documentation and training should be available to customers on an ongoing basis so that new staff may be trained and documentation is always kept up-to-date. Enhancements to the system should be available as new requirements are needed by the market and support should be available over 24 hours.

(*b*)   ***Implementation*** — Implementation of the software, i.e. entering the rules for the terms and conditions of employment, should be straightforward and the supplier should be able to supply consultants to advise and assist if necessary.

(*c*)   ***Customise the software*** — There should be the facility to customise the software without affecting the underlying database or programs. Other software tools should be available to produce the organisation-specific output from the system. Some users will want to tailor the software to their own specific requirements; if this tailoring affects the underlying database or programs then it will be up to the users to test, document and support their own work.

Turnkey solution

28.20   A commercially purchased software package still requires the end-user to implement the package for their own requirements, i.e. the package supplies all the necessary data input requirements, processes and standard output, but the end-user must define their own specific set-up data relating to their own business, people and pay requirements. The end-user must customise or tailor the system as required by him. A turnkey solution is used where the hardware is under the control of the end-user but the system software has been fully implemented and is available for immediate use. This means that the supplier of the software has also supplied the set-up data definitions, has customised or tailored the system for the organisation's specific use and has used the software tools to add to the list of standard reports, the additional reports necessary for the end-user. In other words the system has been implemented using the exact requirements of the end-user. All the end-user then needs to do is simply switch on the system and use it to produce the required output results.

Bureau option

28.21   In-house custom built systems, pre-written commercial payroll applications and turnkey solutions all require the end-user to supply the hardware and be responsible for generating the required output. Additionally, there is the burden of ensuring that systems are kept up to date with the constant changing statutory requirements and new technology options being introduced.

The bureau option is where as much of your payroll processing as you require is taken care of by an outside agency. From a past reputation of inflexibility, this option is becoming increasingly popular with services that provide as much, or as little, of the payroll function within a business, removing the worry of new statutory requirement needs for the payroll system and offering some of the latest facilities available with new technology. Bureaux may use custom-built software or commercial software, provide the documentation, supply the end-user training and customer support and maintain compliance with legislation and future issues such as the Year 2000 millennium bug and the move to European Monetary Union (EMU). For a basic service the end-user is responsible for supplying the input data and checking the output data. The bureau option may be chosen where security and confidentiality is required along with the need to keep up with modern-day technologies without incurring expensive development or upgrade costs, and ensuring minimised interruption to the core activity of a business.

Costs

28.22   Whilst cost-analysis may no longer be the first critical factor to be considered, it is still one of the major factors. Cost-analysis should take into account the tangible and intangible benefits of the system.

Cost comparisons must take into account the following factors.

(a)   *Hardware factors:*
- performance, reliability, capacity and price;
- reliability of supplier;
- effective life;
- compatibility with existing hardware;
- compliance with industry standards.

(b)   *Software factors:*
- performance, reliability, flexibility and price;
- ease of use;
- documentation;
- ease of change;
- support;
- portability across hardware;
- connectability and accessing of data stored in different computers.
- compatibility with accepted industry standards.

(c)   *Service factors:*
- training facilities;
- consultancy;
- maintenance terms;
- reputation of supplier.

(d)   *Development and implementation factors:*
- manpower costs;
- speed of implementation;
- learning curve;

- integration with other systems;

- new stationery costs.

(e) **Running cost factors:**

- manpower costs;

- management information;

- reliability and accuracy;

- security.

The contract

28.23 Irrespective of the source of the supplier of the system, the contract governs what the end-user can expect in terms of the continuing long-term commitment of the supplier to the successful operation of the system.

These would be some of the intangible benefits:

(a) **Changes due to changing legislation** — Payroll applications in recent years have had to incorporate a number of legislation requirements, for example the changes for statutory maternity pay. Application suppliers would need to be aware of this and have the necessary updates ready for the application, to give to their users well in advance of that date.

(b) **Changes due to organisational requirements** — The demands of the marketplace mean that organisations must move quickly to take advantage of the changes. Payroll applications as part of management information systems must also incorporate these changes. Enhancements to the application should be an ongoing commitment.

(c) **Support to be given by the supplier** — This support can be classified under the following headings.

  (i) Self-help, consisting of:

  - quality documentation that is well written, organised, indexed and kept up to date;

  - on-line help that provides clear and understandable system messages and prompts as error handling controls;

  - on-line help that can be customised.

  (ii) 24-hour support, consisting of:

  - a support desk;

  - site visits.

Year 2000 — Millennium

28.24   It is essential that implications of the Year 2000 are considered when selecting a new computer system. The 'millennium time-bomb' is not a virus or a bug. It is a design limitation widely dispersed throughout the world of IT products and services, including payroll software. Essentially, the problem occurs when the year within a date is held and manipulated as two digits rather than four. As a result, calculations, sorts and other operations that span the end of the century will generate errors, or cause systems failures. You must ensure that the computer systems and the payroll system you choose are ready for the Year 2000.

References

28.25   The references listed in 26.27 are also relevant to this chapter.

(1)   'Form P11D Software Review', PMR, January and February 1997.

(2)   'Facing up to the Millennium', PMR, June 1997.

(3)   'Selecting a Payroll System', PMR, July 1997. (This issue contains several useful and interesting articles offering guidance on selecting a payroll system.)

29 Implementation of Your Computer System

Scope of this chapter

29.1   Having searched for and found the ideal computer system for the organisation's needs, the next step is to establish an implementation plan. This plan should identify the critical factors in implementing the system with the key objectives and timescales agreed by all concerned. 'Critical factors' are the people involved, the purchase and installation of the hardware, software and stationery, data flow to and from related systems, data input, testing for the required output, conversion and the changeover. 'Timescales' are the anticipated implementation completion date and the interim sign-off dates. See Figure 29A below.

Implementation: planning people

29.2   Planning the key objectives for people will fall under the following headings: Current situation, Build team, Specialist team members, Suppliers of hardware, software and stationery, Communication and data flow requirements.

(a)   *Current situation* — Establish facts and figures relating to the proposed implementation, for example:

   (i)   Will the timescales needed for implementation be fixed due to immovable factors, e.g. must the system be in place by a certain date because the computer on which the current system operates will no longer be available?

   (ii)   Will the timescales needed for implementation be affected because key personnel will not be available?

   (iii)   Will the proposed timescales conflict with other peak work periods such as year end, company year end etc?

   (iv)   Who will be the internal staff responsible for the implementation and what will be the mix of personalities?

   (v)   Will there by any resistance to the change?

   (vi)   Can key personnel be replaced if necessary?

   (vii)   Will management decisions affect the plan?

Figure 29A

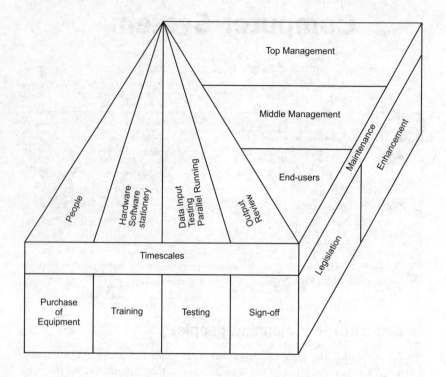

Illustration of implementation of computer system

    (viii) What sort of training will be needed for whom and when will this be required?

    (ix) Who are the external people involved? Will they be available as and when required?

    (x) Who are the suppliers of the hardware, software and stationery?

(b)   ***Build team*** — There should be a core team of dedicated people involved throughout the plan. This team can be augmented as and when necessary by other specialist contributors, but the importance of having a core team that exists throughout the life of the plan is to ensure continuity of knowledge and progress. The size of the core team will depend on the scale of the implementation, but should include both MIS and end-user staff. It should also include consultants provided by the suppliers of the software. The role of the Project Leader should be agreed. Existing staff levels may need to be reviewed; there may be the need to recruit, retrain or redeploy internal staff.

(c)   ***Specialist team members*** — Other specialist members of the team need to be identified from both internal and external sources. An example of an internal specialist would be a contributor from a related system. An example of an external specialist would be a training consultant.

(d)   ***Suppliers of hardware, software and stationery*** — Suppliers of hardware, software and stationery, the availability of the hardware, software and stationery and the people involved in the plan must be considered.

   (i)   Is the hardware required already available to the organisation or does it need to be purchased? If it needs to be purchased who has to approve the purchase order and in which fiscal period is it to be accounted for?

   (ii)   Will the delivery date for the hardware be guaranteed and is any involvement by the supplier required?

   (iii)   Where will the hardware be situated? Is any site preparation needed, and if so how long will it take and who will be involved?

   (iv)   Has the current hardware sufficient capacity for the new system or will additional storage capacity be required?

   (v)   Will interfaces to and from related systems need to be built, and who will be responsible for them?

   (vi)   Will existing stationery, such as pay advice forms, be suitable for the new system or will new stationery need to be designed and ordered, and who will be responsible for this?

   (vii)   When will the software be available? Will it be produced in-house or is it a commercially produced software application? If it is purchased software, can it be customised and will any tailoring be necessary? Who will be the people involved?

   (viii)   Will training be needed before the hardware/software can be used? Who will supply this training and when will it be done?

(e)   ***Communication and data flow requirements*** — Understanding of the communications channels and information flow paths and the involvement of the people concerned are critical factors.

   (i)   Reporting structures within the organisation need to be understood and complied with. For example, the signing-off of purchase orders may be time critical.

   (ii)   Data flow paths of input data for the new system need to be identified. Will any changes be needed? For example, will the current time and attendance monitoring system be changed by the introduction of a new computer system or the introduction of new stationery? What involvement will be needed from the people responsible for the supply of the data?

(iii)   Data flow paths for output data from the new system need to be identified. For example, will additional management information reports be required? The electronic media for payment of net pay through the banking systems will need to be approved. What involvement will be required from the people who will receive the output?

Implementation: hardware, software and stationery

29.3   Planning the key objectives for hardware, software and stationery requirements concerns the purchase, upgrading, installation, training requirements and design of stationery. Some of the considerations have been discussed in the previous section concerning the people involvement. Cost considerations were dealt with in Chapter 28 (Selecting a Computer System). It is assumed that at the implementation stage the choices of hardware and software for the new system have been made.

(*a*)   *Hardware purchase, installation and upgrading* — The following questions need consideration.

- What are the lead times for delivery of the hardware and installation after placing the order?

- If existing hardware needs to be upgraded, what are the lead times?

- Where is the hardware to be physically located? Does it involve any site preparation? What are the lead times?

(*b*)   *Software purchase, installation and upgrading* — The following questions need consideration.

- What are the lead times for purchase and installation of the software?

- What customisation is required?

- What tailoring is required?

- What consultancy is available from the supplier?

(*c*)   *Stationery purchase, design and delivery* — The following questions need consideration.

- What are the lead times for purchase of commercially designed stationery?

- What are the lead times for the design and production of custom designed stationery?

(*d*)   *Training* — The following questions need consideration.

- What training for all users of the system will be needed in order to use the hardware and the software?

- Who will supply that training?
- Will that training be on or off site?

Implementation plan stage

29.4 This phase of the implementation plan is a period of organisational and personnel strain, and the prior establishment of an harmonious, trained team will pay dividends.

(a) ***Data input*** — Data input to the system will be the set-up data and employee data. The actual method of data input might be direct entry via a terminal based on pre-written documentation or by transferring files of information from a current system. When transferring data electronically from one system to another, care should be taken that duplicate records and existing errors are not also transferred.

    (i) Set-up data will be required by the system based on the definitions needed by the organisation, i.e. structure of the business information, people information and pay information as outlined in Chapter 27 (Computerising Your System).

    (ii) Employee data for the business requirements as defined by the set-up data will be required.

    (iii) Payment data for employees will be needed so that the output from the new system can be compared to the old system for parallel running.

(b) ***Parallel running*** — Parallel running involves the processing of identical input data for both the old and the new systems and comparison of the output. Differences in expected output must be detected and the causes found and corrected if necessary, or understood if the old system produced the error.

(c) ***Condition testing*** — Condition testing is required where input data is in error or incomplete or of an unusual combination; the functionalities and features of the system are tested, first to understand the output and secondly to test the suitability of the resulting output.

(d) ***Output review*** — The output review must be undertaken by all the internal and external related system users in order to check the system's accuracy and acceptability for their requirements, as well as by the end-users in the payroll department.

Conversion, changeover and post-implementation review

29.5 Once the output has been reviewed and accepted, conversion and total changeover to the new system can take place. Depending on the size of the conversion in terms of numbers of employees and the organisational structure of the business, the changeover could be completed in one processing period for the whole organisation, or phased in over a number of periods using the organisational structure itself to convert sub-divisions of the organisation during different processing periods.

When the changeover to the new system is complete there should be a post-implementation review. The post-implementation review is usually conducted by personnel who have not been totally involved in the implementation of the system, but are beneficiaries of the output from the system.

This review should consider the following questions.

- Does the system comply with the original objectives for the system?
- If not, what are the reasons and could they have been foreseen?
- What needs to be done about the differences?
- Are the planned processing procedures taking place?
- Have obsolete procedures and working practices been dropped?
- If not, what are the reasons?
- Have further modifications or enhancements been indicated?
- If all the people concerned with the implementation have left at the same time, could continued use of the system be guaranteed, i.e. does full and complete documentation exist?

Sign-off

29.6   Sign-off of the successful implementation, conversion and changeover to a new computer system is only the beginning. The system will need to be continually maintained, enhanced or modified as new legislation, organisational changes, the changing needs of related systems and end-users are introduced as functional requirements.

References

29.7   The references in 26.25 above may also provide useful reading.

(1)   'Millennium Bug Campaign', PMR, March 1998.

(2)   'Facing up to the Millennium', PMR, June 1997.

30 Future Developments Affecting Payroll Administration

Scope of this chapter

30.1   The four major external factors which affect payroll administration are Government requirements, the economy, business practice and technology. Additional important factors are the often unique decisions of each individual business on matters such as employee pay and benefit schemes and the organisation of payroll and related functions. Of course, each factor is partially influenced by the others.

One example of a mixture of factors leading to significant changes in business administration is to be found in the pensions field. There have been numerous small changes and several fundamental alterations of pension arrangements over the past 20 years. Some of these changes have affected payroll administration as well as pensions work. The origins of these changes lie in a mixture of political, economic, social, and practical factors. For instance, many people had, and still have, inadequate financial provision for old age. Improved pension arrangements, both private and public, are one way to tackle this. This thinking led to both SERPS (the State Earnings-Related Pension Scheme) in 1978 and personal pensions in 1988, both enabled by the appropriate legislation. Pensions and related benefits were still not in a satisfactory state, and the changes introduced by the *Pensions Act 1995* were a further step in resolving this enigma. The new Government has undertaken a fundamental review of pensions since taking up office in May 1997. A concept of stakeholder pensions has been introduced and further changes and legislation can be expected in the next five years.

Thus, the pension fundamentals have changed significantly over the last 25 years, but the detailed administration has changed even more radically. This has also required changes in payroll practice, for example the collection of middle-band earnings as part of NIC procedures and differnt types of contracting-out. Furthermore, pensions and payroll software has had to be changed regularly to remain in line with legislation. There have also been continuing changes in other payroll-related areas such as employment rights. Again, the cumulative changes are significant.

Undoubtedly politics has the most dominant influence on payroll administration. A significant minority of political ideas are transformed into legislation affecting payroll. A dramatic recent example, familiar to payroll administrators, is the 'reform' of local authority taxation. Community Charge ('poll tax') was introduced by the *Local Government Finance Act 1988*. Where a person would not pay this tax his or her employer could be compelled to operate an attachment of earnings order and deduct poll tax payments from the employee's pay. Poll tax was extremely unpopular and it has been replaced by the more acceptable Council Tax. However, yet again where house owners default, their employer can be compelled to make deductions from wages via the payroll system. (See Chapter 13 (Attachment of Earnings Orders) for further details.)

The purpose of this chapter is merely to list some possible developments which could affect payroll administration over the next few years. The lists of possible changes given here do not attempt to be exhaustive. But if they do nothing else they should emphasise the instability and dynamic nature of the current payroll environment. As a familiar example annual government budgets can contain many changes in payroll-related legislation. The budgets in 1997 and 1998 were a good illustration of this.

Plenty of payroll-relevant changes are expected in the rest of the current Government's term of office, as well as other more remote developments. Some of the expected changes identified in this chapter will have a considerable impact. Payroll practitioners and software developers need to study and prepare for the administrative implications of the more predictable changes. This can be done by all the usual means such as reading journals like *Payroll Manager's Review* and attending conferences. Historically many legislative changes have been introduced with short notice. However, government departments, especially the Inland Revenue and the Contributions Agency, are consulting with employers, their software suppliers and related organisations to improve the efficiency of current and future legislation. This consultation does not materially affect primary legislation and the will of Parliament remains paramount but assists both the Government and employers in shaping workable regulations.

Government requirements

30.2   As already demonstrated with Community Charge, changes in different areas of Government interest may lead to 'knock-on' consequences for payroll administration. This is particularly true of taxation and social security with their links to payroll via PAYE, National Insurance, SSP and SMP. Also, changes in employment law are often significant in payroll terms. For example, the *Trade Union Reform and Employment Rights Act 1993* required that employers obtain written permission from employees every three years to deduct trade union subscriptions from pay. This requirement was removed in the summer of 1998.

Over the last decade there has been a spate of payroll-related proposals by the main political parties and other interested groups. These proposals suggest a great deal of dissatisfaction with the current employment, tax and social security systems in the UK. It is easy to point out defects in the existing arrangements but the proposed 'improvements' also have their critics. All this leads to the safe prediction of on-going turbulence in payroll administration as politicians introduce new legislation which is later found to be unsatisfactory. This results inevitably in the introduction of yet further changes.

Government-sponsored changes in payroll and related fields are, of course, primarily the result of political considerations. However, some changes may be imposed either by circumstance or by external factors, such as the European Community. Other changes may be of an administrative nature and politically neutral. The discussion below mainly refers to the recent past with a new Labour Government from May 1997. The Labour Party commissioned a book on 'social justice' which is Reference (2) in 30.6 below. This book contains many ideas concerning matters such as social security, taxation, and employment. If implemented, some of these ideas would affect payroll-related administration. Labour Government changes include a national minimum wage, social security reform and welfare to work initiatives.

Recent, proposed or possible changes due to government action are listed below.

(*a*)   ***Dramatic alterations*** — It is probable that there will be major changes in social security and taxation over the next decade. To some extent this has already happened. Social security in particular is under close political scrutiny at the moment by all political parties. It is also a serious issue for many foreign Governments. There is a feeling that social security is out of control. In the UK, social security expenditure is planned to be £98.4 billion in 1998/99 rising to £112.4 billion in 2001/02. This represents 29.4 per cent of total government expenditure in 1998/99 and 28.8 per cent in 2001/02. It is the largest item in government spending. Changes are being introduced over a period of years. There is a precedent with trade union and employment law, where the cumulative effect of legal changes over the last 15 years or so has had a major impact.

(*b*)   ***Increased taxation and reduced State benefits*** — This has been demonstrated by the Government budget of 1993. For instance, in November 1993 some budget increases in taxation were effected by: not raising income tax limits in line with inflation, reducing mortgage interest tax relief, and a one per cent increase in employee NICs. As regards cutting social security benefits, in 1996 there will be a reduction in the period for which unemployment benefit (renamed job seeker's allowance) can be claimed. A further example can be found from 1995 with the introduction of incapacity benefit. This replaces sickness benefit and invalidity benefit. The new benefit is less generous, involves stricter medical tests, and is taxable. This concept is not traditionally associated with a Labour Government but the new Chancellor of the Exchequer has promised not to raise taxes during the early years of government. The comprehensive spending review announced in July 1998 proposes some increase in government spending financed from increased government receipts flowing from increased employment.

(c)   ***Merging income tax and NICs*** — This proposition is quite old. NICs have become more like a form of employment tax. The NI system was, of course, originally envisaged as a basic but universal insurance system for the working population. However, the appeal of merging the two systems may be superficial as there would be many complications in the area of NI and social security benefit rights. But greater harmonisation of the two systems is a prospect. The merger of the Contributions Agency into the Inland Revenue will probably be the necessary catalyst.

(d)   ***Merging the tax and social security benefit systems*** — This is another old idea from the Liberal Party under which a benefit might become 'negative income tax'. The proposal to pay Family Credits and Disability Working Allowances as Working Families Tax Credits and Disabled Persons Tax Credits through the wage packet is a step in this direction. It will demonstrate current Government thinking by linking tax credits with work.

(e)   ***Detailed changes in tax and NIC rules*** — There have been many such changes during the last two decades. Examples include the introduction of contracted-out NICs in 1978 and the 20 per cent income tax band in 1992. This band has been progressively expanded from £2,500 to £4,300 from April 1998. There were also the recent changes in the taxation of company car benefits. [*FA 1993*]. Class 1A NICs has broken the contributor principle of the NI system. Class 1B NICs (on PAYE Settlement Agreements) will further erode the link between contributor and beneficiary.

The comprehensive changes in NICs from April 1999 abolish the 'entry fee' payable as earnings reach the lower earnings limits (and earnings threshold for employers). The changes include replacing the various banded rates for employers with a uniform rate of 12.2 per cent on all earnings over the threshold.

(f)   ***SSP and SMP*** — The limited rights for the employer to recover SSP were changed again in April 1995 and a single rate of SSP introduced at the same time. The latest changes in SSP include the right of an employer to opt out of SSP by providing equivalent or superior OSP benefits. Improved SMP rights were introduced in the middle of 1994/95. Paternity rights are now under discussion.

(*g*) ***Detailed changes in tax administration*** — Again, there have been many such changes over the last two decades. For example, prefix K codes were introduced in 1993, and there was a new reporting regime for company cars in 1994. It should also be noted that self-assessment was introduced in the 1996/97 tax year. There is some concern about its indirect consequences for payroll administration, for example the provision of P11D details to employees for their new tax returns. In essence, self-assessment allows individuals to calculate their own tax liability. It is mainly intended to simplify the assessment and collection of income tax and capital gains tax by individuals, including the employed, self-employed, and pensioners. It is a mjaor change in tax administration for individual tax payers with complicated tax affairs. The side-effects on employers with good payroll practices may be small and will be identifiable during 1997/98. It should be noted that there are some associated changes which affect the rules for calculating the amount of tax liability, such as for the self-employed.

(*h*) ***Levying tax and NICs more effectively on employee benefits*** — This can be done by limiting concessions, for example the restriction of tax relief on employee home relocation expenses and benefits. [*FA 1993*]. From April 1998, relocation expenses (except those enjoying tax relief) are included in the NICs definition of earnings. Benefits in kind have also been progressively brought into the tax and NIC system, for example Class 1A NICs introduced in 1991 and the proposed Class 1B.

(*j*) ***Reviewing self-employment*** — The new sub-contractor rules for the construction industry are now in place. This has already had effects on employment status and will probably be the demise of 'labour-only' contracts in the future.

(*k*) ***Less-likely changes in the tax system*** — A remote example which could affect employees and pensioners is local income tax. Collection of student loans through income tax was equally unlikely. However, from April 2000 employers will be involved in the recovery of student loans which will be done via the income tax system.

(*l*) ***Government pay policies*** — National pay freezes, like those of the 1970s, are unlikely in the near future. However, the last Government had introduced pay restrictions on public sector employees, for instance teachers, and this has led to some unrest. This illustrates the dilemma for any Government, which, as well as trying to manage the national economy, also has a conflicting role as a direct or indirect employer. Normal employers, of course, dislike the rigidity of general pay freezes almost as much as employees. The perceived high pay of some directors in private sector companies, particularly public utilities, is another area where pay controls have been demanded and are more likely given the new Government.

(*m*) **Minimum and 'fair' wage policies** — These have been proposed by the current Government and legislation for the minimum wage takes effect in April 1999.

(*n*) **Employment promotion** — Organisations have been provided with incentives to increase employment in the past, for example the old regional employment premium. A recent example is the NI Holiday scheme where an employer who takes on a new employee who was previously unemployed for two years, has a holiday from paying second-ary NICs. The new Government has produced a far more radical approach in its 'New Deal' initiatives where employers receive significant cash sums for employing long-term unemployed individuals as well as contributions to necessary training costs.

(*o*) **Training** — The poor training provided for employees in the UK has often been criticised. Schemes such as 'Investors in People' are meant to address this. There may be new schemes with incentives and penalties to encourage employers to invest in training.

(*p*) **Pay and benefits** — The Government is likely to continue promoting particular types of pay and benefit schemes. The most obvious current examples are those for pensions and employee shares (stakeholders).

(*q*) **Changes in the State pension age** — The *Pensions Act 1995* has raised the State pension age for women from 60 to 65. This will be introduced in a series of steps between the years 2010 and 2020.

(*r*) **Pensions** — The Maxwell scandal in 1991 led to calls for more secure pension arrangements. The Goode Committee in 1993 and the White Paper of 1994 both made a series of proposals for changes affecting occupational pensions. Many of these proposals are included in the *Pensions Act 1995*, such as member-nominated trustees and the abolition of GMPs in 1997. (See Chapter 10 (Pension Schemes) for a discussion of all this.) Personal pensions became subject to PAYE from April 1995.

(*s*) **Effect of the European Union** — The effect of the EU is illustrated by recent changes in the law which extend the rights of part-time staff, for example improvements in their rights to employment protection and access to pension schemes. The current UK Government is likely to be less opposed to EC employment initiatives than their predecessors and is committed to comply with the European *Working Time Directive*. The *Working Time Regulations 1998 (SI 1998 No 1833)* came into force 1 October 1998.

(*t*) **Deregulation** — The *Deregulation and Contracting Out Act 1994* is the latest attempt to reduce and simplify business regulation. Some deregu-lation initiatives should affect payroll and related business functions. However, many business executives are sceptical about deregulation. Regulations, even if sometimes incompetently drafted, exist for a reason. In areas like life insurance and pensions more regulation has been introduced. The new Government has retitled this 'Better Regulation' and aims to produce regulations that strike a good balance between State control and business operation.

(*u*) **Changing public administration** — This is revealed in many ways. For instance, there is the recent growth of semi-independent executive agencies like the Contributions Agency. Another example is the transfer of Inland Revenue computing to an external computer services company.

(*v*) **Devolution** — As well as the Parliament in Westminster we have an Assembly in Northern Ireland. A Welsh Assembly and a Scottish Parliament will come into being by the year 2000. The Scottish Parliament will have (minimal) tax raising powers (varying basic rate income tax by as much as three per cent in the pound). Social security policy and all other taxation remains with Westminster. Further devolution of powers will surely follow.

(*w*) **Competitive tendering** — Related to (*u*) above is the increased use of market testing and competitive tendering in the public sector. For instance, with local authorities, services, such as school meals and refuse collection, are being put out to tender. Public sector employees can usually bid to do their own work. Where such tenders are won by private sector contractors the employees can be transferred from a public sector payroll to a private sector one.

Economics and business trends

30.3 The state of the UK economy has a major effect on individual businesses. The level of imports, interest rates, exchange rates, oil prices etc. eventually affect the number employed in a business and their remuneration packages.

More directly relevant to the payroll practitioner is the response of an organisation to the general business environment.

Some trends which may affect payroll are listed below.

(*a*) **Turbulence** — A turbulent business environment can be expected well into the future. This turbulence leads to changes that can be major, and a good example is the British coal industry. This has been declining since the First World War. Of course, the industry has been criticised for being slow to adapt, when owned both privately and by the State. But there were progressive adverse changes in the energy market, for example competition from foreign coal suppliers, oil, gas, and finally nuclear energy. The number employed in 1923 was over 1.2 million people. On nationalisation in 1946 there were nearly 800,000 employed. The industry has almost disappeared in employment terms over the last 50 years, the period of a working life. By the early 1980s the number employed had fallen to about 200,000 with a further fall to 40,000 in 1992. In 1993 further market changes led to a rapid closure of pits, and only a few thousand are left employed in the industry today. It is ironic to note that the coal mining occupational pension fund is currently one of the largest in the country.

Other familiar cases of severe industrial decline include railway transport and the textile industry. Most examples of business change are less extensive, for instance the decline of naval shipbuilding which is partly attributed to reduced defence requirements. Some fields of business, like the IT industries, always seem to be changing. For example, technical developments over the last 20 years have adversely affected established computer companies, but helped new businesses such as Intel and Microsoft to grow astonishingly.

The change drivers vary from industry to industry, but are broadly a mixture of political, economic, social, and technical factors. From a payroll viewpoint, one important consequence of economic change is the effect on the number employed in an organisation, for instance staff reductions in high-street banks and public utilities. An extreme example is BT (British Telecommunications) which has reduced its staff by 100,000 over recent years. There is also an effect on conditions of employment; for example, there are fewer manual workers today. More details of the effects of business change on employment are given below.

There is, of course, a positive side to business and technical change. The history of IBM, founded over 100 years ago, demonstrates that established businesses, despite occasional setbacks, can adapt and prosper in a rapidly changing world. Technical change can create new businesses and new types of job. For example, computer payroll bureaux were first formed in the 1950s and 1960s. Looking to the future the business and employment effects of the proposed information superhighway can hardly be guessed at this point in time.

(b) **Staff status** — There may be a continuing tendency to offer manual workers salaried terms such as cashless pay and improved sick pay.

(c) **Deductions** — Employers may slowly extend the services offered through the payroll system such as 'give as you earn' charitable deductions, or season ticket loans.

(d) **Refining pay and benefits** — Employers will continue to seek improvements and changes in pay and benefit schemes. Some of these changes may be fashionable, some more fundamental. Cafeteria schemes where the employee chooses from a range of pay and benefits within an overall total is one idea that may become more popular. A review of performance-related pay, which suffers from many criticisms, is a safe prediction. Further developments can be expected in the financial services which provide employee benefits. An example is flexible annuities which provide some control over the level of pension payments and underlying investments, as compared to the fixed benefits of a conventional annuity. The effect of legislation will continue. For example, the insurance premium tax in 1994 increased the costs of medical insurance, and if further increases are levied, may deter employers from taking out medical insurance for their staff. A reverse trend is the perceived poor service and restricted availability of free National Health Service medical treatment. This may encourage employers to offer medical and other forms of insurance such as cover for dental care.

(e) ***Performance-related pay*** — This has become increasingly common over the last few years for ordinary salaried staff, and there is little sign of the trend slowing. Indeed it is now being considered for teachers in State schools.

(f) ***Refining service conditions*** — Along with changes in pay and benefit schemes, conditions of employment will continue to be revised. From the employee's viewpoint some of these changes will be beneficial, such as career breaks, and other adverse, for instance, evening and Sunday working. Other ideas include annualised hours and 'European Standard' conditions.

(g) ***A decline in national bargaining*** — For a multitude of reasons national pay bargaining has declined in favour of local determination of pay and may never return. .

(h) ***Polarisation of pay and benefits*** — The pay and benefits of the UK workforce may become increasingly polarised. Thus, an expanding number of employees may receive poor pay and benefits. Others, particularly those working for large, successful companies, should continue to receive good pay and benefits. Minimum wage policy will not rectify this for many years.

(j) ***The influence of the European Union*** — European views are bound to have both a legal and economic effect on UK business. One recent example of how the EU affects UK pay and benefits is the ***Barber*** cases. (See 5.8 above.) Economic and Monetary Union (EMU) and the introduction of the Euro will have an effect on payroll whether or not the UK joins.

(k) ***Work-induced changes*** — As the nature of work changes so there is a need to change employment and pay structures.

(l) ***Demographic changes*** — These manifest themselves in several ways. For example, an ageing workforce is more likely to be interested in pensions, younger people have spent more time in formal education, and so on. We now have people aged about 50 who have never worked because of unemployment levels and who may never do so before they retire.

(m) ***Pay restraint*** — Pay restrictions have been common in both the public and private sectors in the recent recession. Some restrictions will continue into the near future particularly in the public sector. In other cases employers may raise wages significantly in an attempt to recruit and retain scarce skills.

(*n*)   **Unrest** — There may be a small increase in industrial action. This could be attributed to a decline in living standards and working conditions, and less fear of unemployment under a Labour Government.

(*o*)   **Inflation** — This is not stable and some pundits predict more problems. As mentioned above, as the economy begins to improve more employers will be inclined to pay higher wages. The costs of industrial supplies and raw materials are also likely to rise. The rising costs will ultimately be passed on to customers.

(*p*)   **Reduced trade union influence** — Trade union membership has declined markedly over the last few years. The ties between the trade union movement and the new Government are unlikely to be as great as 20 years ago. This may restrict the likelihood of industrial unrest (see (*n*) above). Strikes in the early days of the new Labour Government have not been as disruptive as they were 20 years ago.

(*q*)   **Human resources management** — There will be a continuing interest in a more integrated approach to administering payroll and personnel matters. Criticisms of modern human resources management may lead to changes in personnel practices.

(*r*)   **Changing employment patterns** — Some of these changes are mentioned under other headings. For example, the paragraph below discusses the trend for businesses to employ smaller core workforces. Some other trends are the long-term shift away from employment in manufacturing towards services, an associated preference of the economy for employing female workers, and a greater use of part-time employees with some employees have two or more part-time jobs. The economic and social consequences of such changes are bound to be significant, for example high youth unemployment amongst males is linked to rising crime. Also from a government perspective two part-time jobs yield less income tax and NICs than one full-time job.

(*s*)   **Smaller core workforces** — There is a clear tendency for many businesses to reduce the number of employees, for example by automation, contracting out, and management 'delayering'. The reduced core of permanent employees can be supplemented on a flexible basis by more transient workers. The supplementary workforce may consist of part-time employees, traditional outworkers, networkers (people who work at home using computers and telecommunications), and contract staff. These extra workers may be technically either employed or self-employed.

(*t*)   **Payroll organisation** — Lack of uniformity in the various approaches to payroll organisation will continue. Some employers will continue with the traditional approach where payroll remains a financial function. Some will consider integrating payroll with personnel to form a human resources administration department. Outsourcing now extends to the payroll function. This is a growth area for the bureaux who take on the role of an employer's pay office.

(*u*) **Trade and professional organisations** — Organisations like the NAPF (National Association of Pension Funds), PMI (Pensions Management Institute) and the Payroll Specialist Group of the British Computer Society will continue to influence future developments, for example by commenting on government consultative documents. They will also influence practice, for instance via codes of practice such as those of the IPD (Institute of Personnel and Development) on redundancy and employee data.

(*v*) **Qualifiations in payroll** — The increasing professionalisation of payroll office work is demonstrated by the success of payroll qualifications such as those offered by Payroll Alliance and the IPPM (the Institute of Payroll and Pensions Management). There is also the prospect of payroll NVQs (National Vocational Qualifications) in the near future. Since 1997 it has been possible to study for a degree, at master's level, in payroll management.

(*w*) **Business services** — Those services devoted to payroll and related administration will continue to develop, such as consultancy and payroll administration services.

(*x*) **Entrepreneurial approaches** — Payroll (and other) managers can be encouraged to make efficiency improvements and develop new services. These new services, for example advertisements with payslips, will be expected to earn revenue in some cases.

(*y*) **Internationalism** — The growth of multi-national organisations functioning as businesses within many countries will increase the overseas posting of employees. In turn, payroll must address the needs of expatriate and in-patriate employees and become conversant with the tax and social insurance rules for many different countries.

The consequences of a smaller permanent workforce could mean the virtual disappearance of an independent payroll service as many trading and manufacturing businesses progress towards being large in terms of turnover and small in terms of the permanent workforce. The payroll function could then be administered on a 'small company' basis, i.e. as part of the cashier's or company secretary's function perhaps combined with the use of subcontract services. Even in organisations which still employ a significant number of people the long-term trend is towards factors like fewer staff, small employment units and monthly pay. The result is therefore reduced conventional payroll arrangements. This trend is exacerbated by factors like the contracting out of non-core business functions.

Technology

30.4   Some of the technical developments which may affect payroll administration are listed below.

(*a*)   ***Office automation*** — In all its various forms modern office equipment offers excellent opportunities to improve both the quality and cost of business services such as payroll. One common example is the rapid growth in the use of fax machines over the last decade. As discussed in Chapter 26 (Payroll Technology) new ideas like DIP (Document Image Processing) could radically change office work.

(*b*)   ***Advanced hardware*** — One of the distinguishing features of 20th century technology is the continuing and rapid progress of computing. This leads to reduced costs, better quality, and superior facilities. These advances offer business administration the scope for better IT systems, for instance the use of OCR (Optical Character Recognition) for payroll data input, and the use of optical disks to store payroll and pensions data. As the costs of computer power and storage continue to reduce, the scope for automation increases. April 1998 saw the introduction of OCR versions of tax year end Forms P14.

(*c*)   ***Telecommunications*** — The use of telecommunications in general will continue to expand, such as the use of mobile telephones. Another example is the rise of telephone-based insurance and banking services. Linking computer systems by telecommunications will also continue to develop. The impact of proposed information superhighways is bound to affect business administration significantly. (See also section (*w*) below on the Internet.)

(*d*)   ***Time and attendance*** — There should be a continuing interest in time-and-attendance systems, for example because of the responsibility of most employers to pay SSP without compensation.

(*e*)   ***EDI (Electronic Data Interchange)*** — As part of the MOSES project (Modernisation of Schedule E Systems), Enhanced Employer Communication is proposed. This will be by magnetic media and EDI which initially encompassed P45, P46 and P6 data. The pilot scheme started in October 1997. As the number of employers 'trading' with the Inland Revenue via EDI increases and large employers join the scheme, the pilot can be assumed to be permanent. More Inland Revenue forms will be 'traded' in the future.

(*f*)   ***GUIs (Graphic User Interfaces)*** — These computer displays, which make extensive use of colour and images, are steadily replacing dull text displays on computer screens. Many business computer systems have been upgraded to use the popular 'Windows' GUI. What is increasingly common at home is expected in the workplace.

(*g*)   ***Open systems*** — There is a steady trend towards using 'open systems', for example the use of a standard software environment which is common to many computer manufacturers.

(*h*)   ***New software development methods*** — Software development has traditionally been slow, tedious, and unreliable. It is not easy to design and write reliably the hundreds of thousands of lines of computer instructions that comprise payroll software. Worse still has been the problem of maintaining the software, i.e. keeping it up to date. Newer approaches should improve both the speed and quality of software production. One important development is CASE (Computer Aided Software Engineering). This uses a set of advanced software tools to improve software production. The software tools can, for instance, be used to prepare and edit at a computer screen all the diagrams used to design software. Some other important new approaches to systems development are discussed separately below.

(*j*)   ***Fourth generation languages*** — These make programming easier and cheaper for both computer and user staff. Their use should continue to develop because they are a convenient way for payroll staff to produce computer reports to their own specification.

(*k*)   ***Client-server*** — This modern approach to IT systems is becoming popular. The concept is one of co-operating computer processes, usually distributed over a network. For instance, a 'client' like a screen display can request data from a remote computer acting as a database 'server'. There is no obvious difference to the user between client-server systems and conventional approaches which treat the whole computer system as one process. However, the client-server separation of the processing makes the design of the IT system more flexible with indirect benefits to the user.

(*l*)   ***Object orientation*** — Like the term 'client-server', payroll administrators can expect to meet object orientation in the sales literature for new computer systems. Again, it is not something that is physically obvious like OCR. Object orientation is a new approach to developing computer systems, and a difficult concept. The basic idea is to intimately combine software routines with the data being processed. The claimed advantages include a more natural way of solving (some) software problems, and more convenient reuse and maintenance of existing software.

(*m*)   ***Multi-media systems*** — These combine text, sound, and images under computer control. The main current applications are educational, for example encyclopaedias like 'Encarta 98' where text and images are displayed on a screen with sound effects. Business applications are at present in areas like marketing. They will eventually reach administration, for instance computerised office manuals with special audio-visual effects.

(*n*)   **End-user computing** — As in other areas of business, payroll staff will continue to develop their computing skills and take more responsibility for their own IT. Fourth generation languages (see (*j*) above) and GUIs (see (*f*) above will encourage this.

(*o*)   **Human resource databases (HRDs)** — There should be a slow expansion of the use of HRDs in large organisations. So-called '2P' systems which combine personnel and payroll data are the most likely form.

(*p*)   **Decision support systems (DSSs)** — These offer considerable potential for planning pay and benefit schemes. These are widely used already, for instance for costing pay rises, and their use should develop further.

(*q*)   **Executive and management information** — This is using the ever increasing volume of computer-held data within an organisation to provide high level information on the organisation for strategic planning and control. The use of payroll data should increase and this will often be presented in an attractive graphical form.

(*r*)   **Fifth generation computing** — This is mainly the application of artificial intelligence to business and technical problems. Though it has been successfully used in some specialist areas it has not been applied to the extent that people originally expected. However, there is no doubt that it can make a contribution to ordinary business administration including payroll.

(*s*)   **Machine-readable information** — Data has been issued for many years on magnetic disks and tapes, and by telecommunication methods. In recent years this has progressed from computer data files and software to quite ordinary information that traditionally has been isssued in paper form. The increasing use of CD-ROMs (Compact Disks-Read Only Memory) to replace books is a current development. The most relevant example of this in the payroll arena is the guidance from the Inland Revenue and Contributions Agency available from 1997 on a single CD-ROM. On-line databases of business information are another illustration. As mentioned above the distribution of conventional text and image information can of course be supplemented with sound in 'multimedia' systems. Clearly 'electronic publishing' has a future as information in electronic form can have considerable advantages such as more vivid displays and more convenient access. Doubtless this will also affect the distribution of information in payroll administration. One can envisage a future where all the regulations and advice currently published in government booklets, journals, and books will be available in a convenient electronic form. (See also section (*w*) below on the Internet.)

(*t*)   **IT quality** — There is a continuing interest in methods of improving the quality of IT systems, such as via ISO 9000 (previously BS 5750) and the IMIS Software Evaluation Service.

(*u*) **Radically new systems** — As discussed above, the continuing advance of electronics, computing, telecommunications, etc, is normally used to improve existing equipment and systems. However, this technical progress may also be used to design radically new machines and systems for business use. A simple example is the use of laptop computers which has considerably improved the selling of life assurance. With on-line terminals (via the Internet (see (*w*) below)), kiosks are being provided by the Government for businesses to register with and report to government departments. Similarly, large employers are introducing kiosks to enable employees to notify changes of address, bank account and other static personal data.

(*v*) **Legal changes** — As IT progresses and becomes evermore important in modern society, further legal changes can be expected. This will reflect the changing technology, new use of the technology, and increasing demands for its regulation. The new *Data Protection Act 1998* will increase individuals' rights in respect of personal data held about them. It also includes structured manual files (see Reference (3) in 30.6 below).

(*w*) **The Internet** — This has already been discussed in Chapter 26 (Payroll Technology). In principle it is not new but a combination of many of the factors already mentioned above. It is an 'open' electronic communication and database system. It allows access to anyone in the world with a personal computer who is prepared to pay a small fee. It has a myriad of uses for both domestic and business purposes. One payroll example is obtaining on-line a summary of changes in taxation and NICs from the annual Government budget details. The Internet and some proprietary rivals will doubtless expand rapidly. One can foresee them contributing to the decline of all traditional approaches to business based on paper documents and postal services.

Whilst the progress of office technology needs to be watched it is an elementary observation that existing technology is not fully exploited. Thus, many computer systems, such as the popular 'Windows' system, offer quite sophisticated electronic diaries. Yet many of these routine facilities are not fully exploited.

Conclusions

30.5   It is evident to the most casual observer that this is a time of rapid political, economic, social, and technical change. Businesses and professions must adapt to survive. It is perhaps ironic that payroll administration, often considered to be 'routine' work, is at the centre of many of these changes. As a result the payroll administrator will be expected to be adaptive and make an effective contribution to absorb successfully the many changes to which both the department and organisation are subject. His or her role need not only be 'reactive', i.e. merely responding sensibly to change, but can also be 'proactive', i.e. anticipating change and seeking new ideas, new opportunities and new solutions to problems, which contribute to the overall goals of the business.

References

30.6 A long list of recommended reading is not appropriate as impending developments can only be found in current literature. Financial, payroll, computer and other related journals contain relevant material from time to time. Documentary programmes on television, business seminars and the meetings of professional bodies also provide indications as to future developments.

(1) Fishburn D, 'The World in 1996', The Economist Publications, 1995. (A readable summary of international, political, and economic developments.)

(2) The Commission on Social Justice, 'Social Justice: Strategies for National Renewal', Vintage, 1994.

(3) 'Data Protection – Everybody's Business', BCS, 1998.

(4) 'Towards the Paperless Office', PMR, August 1997.

(5) 'Getting Ready for EMU', PMR, February 1998.

(6) 'Counting the Costs to Employers', PMR, April 1998. (Student loan repayment.)

(7) 'Budget Break Out', PMR, April 1998.

(8) 'The Working Families Tax Credit', PMR, June 1998.

(9) 'Tax System Direct Payment', PMR, July 1998.

Appendix A

Table of Statutes

Table of Statutory Instruments

Appendix B

Table of Cases

Appendix C

List of Main PAYE Forms and Facsimiles of Selected Key Forms

PAYE form number	
P1	Tax return giving details of income and capital gains. Completed by the tax payer. (There are various versions with different form numbers.)
P2	Notice of tax coding sent to an employee.
P6*	Notice to employer of code or amended code. Used throughout the year.
P7X	Instructions to employer. Authority to amend suffix codes during tax year.
P8	Employer's Basic Guide To PAYE. (Instructions to employer on the operation of PAYE.)
P9	Notice to employer of changed code for coming tax year. Can be replaced with code lists or, exceptionally, by magnetic media by arrangement.
P9D*	*Return of expenses payments, and benefits for an employee to whom Form P11D is not applicable.
P9X	Instructions to employer. Authority to amend suffix codes at start of tax year.
P11	Deduction working sheet for recording PAYE calculations. Substitutes may be used.
P11D*	Return of expense payments and benefits for directors and employees who earn at the rate of £8,500 or more per year including expenses and benefits.
P11Db	Form which confirms that all P11D Forms, where needed, have been completed and sent to the tax office.
P14(OCR)*	End of year return of pay, tax, national insurance contributions, SSP and SMP.
P24	Covering form to be issued with P9 tax code notifications before the beginning of the year.
P30B	Payslip for employer's PAYE remittances.
P30BC	Payslip Booklet containing payslips.
P32	Record for keeping monthly totals of tax, NIC, SSP, SMP.
P34	Employer's requisition for ordering PAYE Forms.
P35*	Employer's annual statement, declaration and certificate.
P35(MT)	Version of P35 for employers who make their returns on magnetic tape.
P35(CS)	Continuation sheet for P35.
P35(TAS)	Returns of awards under a taxed award scheme.
P38 or P38A	Employer's supplementary return for employees who earned over £100 in total for the year but for whom a deduction working sheet was not completed or who were not entered on the P35.
P38(S)	Students employed during vacation: declaration by employer and statement by student.
P39	Return of persons employed by non-resident employers.
P45*	Tax details of an old employment in three parts.
	Part 1 – Sent to the tax office by the old employer.
	Part 1a – Retained by the employee
	Part 2 – Retained by the new employer.
	Part 3 – Sent to the tax office by the new employer.

PAYE form Number	
P45(W)	P45 (Part 2) notes to employee in Welsh.
P46*	For use when a new employee does not produce a P45.
P46–5	Notice of new or amended NI number.
P46(Car)*	*Advance particulars of car or fuel provided for directors and employees earning at a rate more than £8,500 p.a.
P46(Ent)	For use when certain theatrical performers/artists do not produce a P45.
P47	Employer's application for authority to refund tax exceeding £200 to new employee — now obsolete.
P48	Authority to refund tax exceeding £200 to new employee — now obsolete.
P60*	*Employer's certificate of pay and tax deductions to be given to employee at end of year.
P61	End of year notification to employee of tax refund withheld during a trade dispute.
P62	End of year advice to employee involved in a trade dispute.
P160	Notification of retirement of an employee to whom a pension is paid by the employer.
P403	For use by funds paying holiday pay to employees.
P440	Analysis of totals on P35(TAS).
P440(CS)	Continuation sheet for P440.
P443	Certificate to employee giving details of taxed incentive award.
TAS Payment Advice	Advice note sent out with P35(TAS).

* Facsimiles of these forms are reproduced below.

Note: Forms issued by the Inland Revenue computers are similar to the traditional ones but have a 'T' or 'Z' added to the form number. Tax forms other than those listed here are occasionally encountered in payroll practice.

Form P6

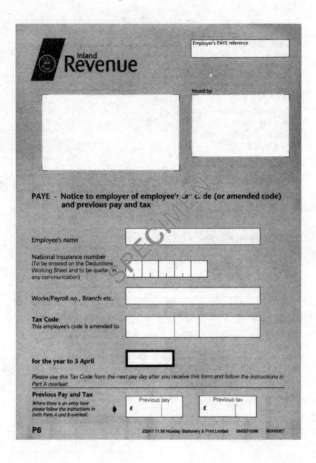

Illustration of a notice to an employer of an employee's code (or amended code) and previous pay and tax

Form P9D (1997–98)

Illustration of a Form P9D, return of expenses payments and income etc. to be used for the 1997/98 tax year

Appendix C

Form P9D (1997–98)

B • **Vouchers and credit cards**

Enter the expense of providing the vouchers and the goods and services for which they can be exchanged.
Exclude the value of any vouchers, such as cash vouchers, which have suffered tax under PAYE.

Travel and transport vouchers, including season tickets — `1.13` £

Gift vouchers, including National Savings Certificates and Premium Bonds — `1.13` £

Meal vouchers – *as requested by page 76 of booklet CWG2 "Employer's Further Guide to PAYE and NICs"* — `1.13` £

Any other vouchers exchangeable for goods and services — `1.13` £

Credit cards provided for the employee and his or her family – *enter the total amount of expenses met by credit card provided by you for the employee to use unless you have already entered these expenses under one of the above headings* — `1.13` £

C • **Accommodation**

Give the cash equivalent of accommodation provided for the employee and/or his or her family/household. Deduct any amounts paid by the employee towards the cost of providing the accommodation – for example, rent.

If the employee is provided with living accommodation give details of the rateable value. This is the gross value that applied before Community Charge was introduced. If the property does not have a gross value enter "No rateable value established" and give your estimate of what the gross value would have been if rates had continued. If the property costs more than £75,000 special rules apply see booklet 480, paragraphs 21.16 to 21.22.

If as well as providing the accommodation you paid some of the employee's bills (such as heat and light) show these in the appropriate box or boxes overleaf, whether or not the value of the accommodation itself is exempt from tax.

Enter property address

Enter rateable value of property — £

Enter rent and insurance borne by you — £

The cash value of accomodation provided is the greater of the above figures. Enter that figure here. — `1.14`

Where necessary use this box to describe the benefits mentioned above and overleaf

Illustration of a Form P9D (continued)

686

Form P11D (1997–98)

Inland Revenue

P11D EXPENSES AND BENEFITS 1997-98

Note to employer
Complete this return for a director, or an employee who earned at a rate of £8,500 a year or more during the year 6 April 1997 to 5 April 1998. Do not include expenses and benefits covered by a dispensation or PAYE settlement agreement. Read the P11D Guide and booklet 480, Chapter 24, before you complete the form. Send the completed P11D and form P11D(b) to the Tax Office by 6 July 1998. You must give a copy of this information to the director or employee by the same date. The term employee is used to cover both directors and employees throughout the rest of this form.

Note to employee
Your employer has filled in this form. Keep it in a safe place as you may not be able to get a duplicate. You will need it for your tax records and to complete your 1997-98 Tax Return if you get one. Your tax code may need to be adjusted to take account of the information given on this P11D. The box numbers on this P11D have the same numbering as the Employment Pages of the Tax Return, for example, 1.12. Include the total figures in the corresponding box on the Tax Return, unless you think some other figure is more appropriate.

Employer's details
Employer's name

PAYE tax reference

Employee's details
Employee's name

Tick here if a director

Works number or department

National Insurance number

A • Assets transferred (cars, property, goods or other assets)

Description of asset — Cost/ Market value £ – Amount made good or from which tax deducted £ = **1.12** Cash equivalent £

B • Payments made on behalf of employee

Description of payment — **1.12** £

Tax on notional payments not borne by employee within 30 days of receipt of each notional payment — **1.12** £

C • Vouchers or credit cards

Value of vouchers and payments made using credit cards or tokens — Gross amount £ – Amount made good or from which tax deducted £ = **1.13** Cash equivalent £

D • Living accommodation

Cash equivalent of accommodation provided for employee, or his/ her family or household — **1.14** Cash equivalent £

E • Mileage allowance

Car and mileage allowances paid for employee's car — Gross amount £ – Amount made good or from which tax deducted £ = **1.15** Taxable payment £

F • Cars and car fuel
If more than two cars were made available, either at the same time or in succession, please give details on a separate sheet

	Car 1	Car 2
Make and Model		
Dates first registered	/ /	/ /
Dates car was available	From / / To / /	From / / To / /
Business mileage used in calculation for this car. *Tick only one box for each car. If the car was not available for part of the year, the business mileage limits are reduced proportionately.*	2,499 or less ☐ 2,500 to 17,999 ☐ 18,000 or more ☐	2,499 or less ☐ 2,500 to 17,999 ☐ 18,000 or more ☐
Enter engine size and tick type of fuel *If there is a car fuel scale charge*	Engine size in cc ☐ cc Petrol ☐ Diesel ☐	Engine size in cc ☐ cc Petrol ☐ Diesel ☐
	Car 1	Car 2
List price of car *If there is no list price, or if it is a classic car, employers see booklet 480; employees see leaflet IR133*	£	£
Price of optional accessories fitted when car was first made available to the employee	£	£
Price of accessories added after the car was first made available to the employee	£	£
Capital contributions (maximum £5,000) the employee made towards the cost of car or accessories	£	£
Amount paid by employee for private use of the car	£	£
Cash equivalent of each car	£	£
Total cash equivalent of all cars available in 1997-98	**1.16**	£
Cash equivalent of fuel for each car	£	£
Total cash equivalent of fuel for all cars available in 1997-98	**1.17**	£

P11D(1998)   BMSD 11/97

SPECIMEN

Illustration of a Form P11D expenses and benefit return which will be used for the 1997/98 tax year. This form is subject to change

Form P11D (1997–98)

G • **Vans**

Cash equivalent of all vans made available for private use — **1.18** £

H • **Interest-free and low interest loans**
If the total amount outstanding on all loans does not exceed £5,000 at any time in the year, there is no need for details in this section.

	Loan 1	Loan 2
Purpose of loan(s) – *please use the code shown in P11D Guide for employers*		
Number of joint borrowers *(if applicable)*		
Tick the box if the loan is within MIRAS	☐	☐
Amount outstanding at 5 April 1997 or at date loan was made if later	£	£
Amount outstanding at 5 April 1998 or at date loan was discharged if earlier	£	£
Maximum amount outstanding at any time in the year	£	£
Total amount of interest paid by the borrower in the year to 5 April 1998 – *enter "NIL" if none was paid*	£	£
Date loan was made or discharged in the year to 5 April 1998 if applicable	/ /	/ /
Cash equivalent of loans after deducting any interest paid by the borrower	**1.19** £	**1.19** £

I • **Mobile telphones**

Cash equivalent of mobile telephones provided — **1.20** £

J • **Private medical treatment or insurance**

	Cost to you	Amount made good or from which tax deducted	Cash equivalent
Private medical treatment or insurance	£	– £	= **1.21** £

K • **Qualifying relocation expenses payments and benefits (non-qualifying expenses go in P below)**

Excess over £8,000 of all qualifying relocation expenses payments and benefits for each move — **1.22** £

L • **Services supplied**

	Cost to you	Amount made good or from which tax deducted	Cash equivalent
Services supplied to the employee	£	– £	= **1.22** £

M • **Assets placed at the employee's disposal**

	Annual value plus expenses incurred	Amount made good or from which tax deducted	Cash equivalent
Description of asset	£	– £	= **1.22** £

N • **Shares**
Tick the box if during the year there have been share-related benefits for the employee ☐

O • **Other items**

	Cost to you	Amount made good or from which tax deducted	Cash equivalent
Subscriptions and professional fees	£	– £	= **1.22** £
Description of other items	£	– £	= **1.22** £

		Tax paid
Income tax paid but not deducted from director's remuneration		**1.22** £

P • **Expenses payments made to, or on behalf of, the employee**

	Cost to you	Amount made good or from which tax deducted	Taxable payment
Travelling and subsistence payments	£	– £	= **1.23** £
Entertainment *(trading organisations read P11D Guide and then enter a tick or a cross as appropriate here)* ☐	£	– £	= **1.23** £
General expenses allowance for business travel	£	– £	= **1.23** £
Payments for use of home telephone	£	– £	= **1.23** £
Non-qualifying relocation expenses *(those not shown in section K)*	£	– £	= **1.23** £
Description of other expenses	£	– £	= **1.23** £

Illustration of a Form P11D (continued)

Working Sheet 1 (1997–98)

Inland Revenue | **P11D WORKING SHEET 1** | **LIVING ACCOMMODATION 1997-98**

Note to employer

You do not have to use this form but you may find it a useful way to calculate the cash equivalent if you provided living accommodation for a director or an employee during the year 1997-98 (that is 6 April 1997 to 5 April 1998).

Read the P11D Guide and Chapter 21 of booklet 480 before you complete this form. Sections 1 and 2 apply to a director or an employee whatever their rate of pay. If you provided any benefits associated with accommodation you may find the check list at Section 3 helpful.

If you use this form you must also fill in form P11D or P9D. You are advised to keep a copy of each completed working sheet as it could help you to deal with enquiries. You do not have to give a copy of the completed working sheet to the director or employee, or to the Tax Office.

The term employee is used to cover both directors and employees throughout the rest of this form.

The term accommodation refers to the living accommodation provided to the employee and the property consisting of that accommodation.

If the employee can choose between

• taking living accommodation

or

• giving up the accommodation and taking a higher cash wage

then the taxation value of the living accommodation may be greater than the cash equivalent calculated using this working sheet. That will be so if the extra wages the employee could have got (for the period the accommodation was provided) if he/she had given up the accommodation would have been more than the cash equivalent shown in box E or R, in which case enter that amount of extra wages in box 1.14 of the P11D or P9D.

Employer's details

Employer's name

PAYE tax reference

Employee's details

Employee's name

Works number or department

National Insurance number

The Accommodation

Give the address of the accommodation provided

SPECIMEN

Was the accommodation provided for a full tax year?   Yes ☐   No ☐

If the answer is No, then when you are asked for amounts, enter the part of the rent or annual value which relates to the period for which the accommodation was provided. Chapter 21 of Booklet 480 tells you how to work out the annual value.

1 • **The basic charge** *Complete this section in all cases*

Amount of rent paid for the year (or part of the year) by you or any other person at whose cost the accommodation is provided to the employee — **A** £

Enter the annual value (or part of the annual value) of the accommodation (see Chapter 21 of Booklet 480) — **B** £

Enter the greater of A and B here — **C** £

Enter any amount made good to you by the employee for the living accommodation. (If this amount is more than C, enter the amount at C here.) — **D** £

Take D away from C. The figure at E is the cash equivalent of the basic charge. — **E** £

Enter E at box 1.14 on form P11D or P9D unless there is an additional charge.

Please turn over to find out if you need to calculate the additional charge

P11D WS 1 (1998)   BMSD11/97

Illustration of the Living Accommodation P11D Working Sheet, which employers can choose to use to calculate the cash equivalent of the benefit in kind. This Working Sheet may be subject to change before issue to employers

Working Sheet 1 (1997–98)

2 • **The additional charge**

Complete this section if the cost of the accommodation was more than £75,000.
The cost of the accommodation is

• the cost of acquiring the accommodation
  plus
• the cost of improvements made to the accommodation
  less
• any payments made by the employee towards these costs or for the grant of a tenancy.
When considering the costs remember that they can be incurred by

• you as the employer
• the person providing the accommodation
  or
• any person connected with either of the above other than the employee.
There is a different rule if the employee first occupied the accommodation after 30 March 1983. If the person providing the accommodation held any interest in it throughout a period beginning **6 years before the employee first occupied** the accommodation, then the figure to enter at box F is the market value of the accommodation at that date plus the cost of subsequent improvements.

Cost of the accommodation (including the cost of improvements)	**F**	£
Payments made by the employee towards the cost or for the grant of tenancy	**G**	£
Take G away from F	**H**	£
Excess of cost over £75,000 is H minus £75,000	**J**	£
Multiply J by 6.75% (which is the official rate of interest at 6 April 1997)	**K**	£
If the accommodation was provided for part of the tax year only, enter the number of days it was provided here.		
Divide the number of days by 365 and multiply the result by K	**L**	£
Enter the rent paid by the employee for the accommodation	**M**	£
Less any rent which you have included in box D	**N**	£
Take N away from M	**P**	£

Take P away from K (if the accommodation was provided throughout the tax year)
or
take P away from L (if the accommodation was provided for only part of the tax year)

Enter the result here	**Q**	£
Enter the amount shown in box E on the front of this form	**E**	£
Total of Q and E	**R**	£

The figure at R is the amount to be entered in box 1.14 on form P11D or P9D.

3 • **Other benefits**
This section is a check list to help identify other benefits commonly associated with the provision of living accommodation.

Tick if appropriate

Expenses incurred by the provider of the accommodation on benefits or facilities connected with the accommodation	☐
Heating	☐
Lighting	☐
Repairs and Decoration	☐
Other *please describe in box below*	☐
The annual value of the use of furniture in the accommodation which is provided by reason of the employment	☐
The benefit from furniture given or transferred to the employee	☐

Paragraphs 6.5 to 6.7 and 21.7 to 21.12 of booklet 480 explain how to calculate these other benefits and give details of exemptions and limits to the charge. **Enter the benefits in the appropriate boxes on form P11D or P9D.**

Illustration of the Living Accommodation P11D Working Sheet (continued)

Working Sheet 2 (1997–98)

Revenue | **P11D WORKING SHEET 2 CAR BENEFIT AND CAR FUEL BENEFIT 1997-98**

Note to employer

You do not have to use this form but you may find it a useful way to calculate the cash equivalent for each car made available to a director or an employee who earned at a rate of £8,500 a year or more during the year 1997-98 (that is 6 April 1997 to 5 April 1998). A separate form is needed for each car.

Read the P11D Guide before you complete this form.

If you use this form you must also fill in form P11D. You are advised to keep a copy of each completed working sheet as it could help you to deal with enquiries. You do not have to give a copy of the completed working sheet to the director or employee, or to the Tax Office.

The term employee is used to cover both directors and employees throughout the rest of this form.

Employer's details
Employer's name

PAYE tax reference

Employee's details
Employee's name

Works number or department

National Insurance number

1 • The car
Make of car available to employee

Model

Date the car was first registered

Was the car available to the employee for the whole of 1997-98? Yes ☐ No ☐

If "No" state the period the car was made available to employee From

to

Enter the number of days the car was **unavailable**
(see paragraphs 12.32-12.33 of booklet 480). When apportioning the benefit on a time basis, you must use this figure in all calculations for

Was this the only car made available to the employee? Yes ☐ No ☐

If "No" please make sure that working sheets are completed for each car that was made available to the employee during 1997-98.

If more than one car and car fuel benefit working sheet is completed for this employee enter the number of working sheets here

The price of the car for tax purposes
In this section you are asked to give details of the list price of the car. If the car had no list price when it was first registered you need to enter the notional price in box A. The notional price is the price which might reasonably be expected to be its list price if the car's manufacturer, importer or distributor had published a list price for an equivalent car for a single retail sale in the UK.

Classic cars
A classic car is one which
• is more than 15 years old on 5 April 1998
• has a market value of more than £15,000
and
• has a market value which is higher than the original list or notional price – including accessories.

For these cars you enter at A the price that the car might reasonably be expected to fetch if you sold it on the open market on 5 April 1998. If the car was unavailable to the employee at 5 April 1998 then use the last day in the tax year 1997-98 that it was available to the employee. For this purpose, assume that all the qualifying accessories available on the car are included in the sale.

Calculating the price of the car
List price of the car (see note above if there is no list price) £

Price of optional accessories fitted when the car was first made available to the employee £

Total price of car and accessories **A** £

Price of accessories added after the car was first made available to employee **B** £

Add the price of these accessories to the total at A **(A + B) =** **C** £

Less capital contributions (maximum of £5,000) the employee made towards the cost of the car or accessories **D** £

The price of the car for 1997-98 (maximum £80,000) **(C - D) =** **E** £

P11D WS2 (1998)   BMSD2/98

Illustration of the Car Benefit and Car Fuel Benefit P11D Working Sheet, which employers can choose to use to calculate the cash equivalent of these benefits in kind. This Working Sheet may be subject to change before issue to employers

Working Sheet 2 (1997–98)

2 • The car benefit charge

The price of the car for 1997-98 (maximum £80,000)   **E** £ _____

Full benefit charge for 1997-98: 35% of price of car for year   (E x 35%)   = **F** £ _____

Less

any discount due for business mileage over 2,500 miles

This car is the employee's   **First car**   **Second car**

Tick the first car box except when the second car was made available concurrently with the first car.   ☐   ☐

Then calculate the discount based on the business miles in that car. If the car was unavailable for part of the year the business mileage limits for that car are reduced proportionately.

2,500 - 17,999 business miles – $^1/_3$ x benefit charge (F)   no discount   **G** £ _____

     or

18,000 business miles or more – $^2/_3$ x benefit charge (F) $^1/_3$ x benefit charge (F)   **G** £ _____

Car benefit after mileage discount   (F – G)   = **H** £ _____

Less

age discount only for cars registered before 6 April 1994 $^1/_3$ x H   = **J** £ _____

Car benefit after age discount   (H – J)   = **K** £ _____

Less

$\dfrac{\text{Number of days car was unavailable (if any)}}{365}$ x   K   = **L** £ _____

Car benefit after deduction for days car was unavailable   (K – L)   = **M** £ _____

Less

any payments made in the year for private use of the car   **N** £ _____

Car benefit charge for 1997-98 on this car is   (M – N)   = **P** £ _____

Enter P at box 1.16 on form P11D

If the employee has had more than one car available during 1997-98, add together the figures that appear at P on each working sheet. Then enter the total at box 1.16, Section F on form P11D.

3 • The car fuel benefit charge

Tick the type of fuel   Petrol ☐   Diesel ☐   Enter the engine capacity in cc _____

Car fuel scale charge from booklet 480, Appendix 2   **Q** £ _____

Less

$\dfrac{\text{Number of days car was unavailable (if any)}}{365}$ x Q   = **R** £ _____

Car fuel benefit charge for 1997-98 on this car is   (Q – R)   = **S** £ _____

Enter S at box 1.17 on form P11D

If the employee has had more than one car available during 1997-98, add together the figures that appear at S on each working sheet. Then enter the total at box 1.17, in Section F on form P11D.

Illustration of the Car Benefit and Car Fuel Benefit P11D Working Sheet (continued)

Working Sheet 3 (1997–98)

P11D WORKING SHEET 3   VANS AVAILABLE FOR PRIVATE USE 1997-98

Inland Revenue

Note to employer
You do not have to use this form but you may find it a useful way to calculate the cash equivalent if you provided a van which was available for private use by a director or employee who earned at a rate of £8,500 a year or more during the year 1997-98 (that is 6 April 1997 to 5 April 1998).

Read the P11D(Guide) before you complete this form.

If you use this form you must also fill in form P11D. You are advised to keep a copy of each completed working sheet as it could help you to deal with enquiries. You do not have to give a copy of the completed working sheet to the director or employee, or to the Tax Office.

The term employee is used to cover both directors and employees throughout the rest of this form.

Employer's details
Employer's name

PAYE tax reference

Employee's details
Employee's name

Works number or department   National Insurance number

1 • The van

Was the van available exclusively to the employee at any time in the year?   Yes   No

If "yes" complete boxes A to E below. If "no" do not complete boxes A to E below.
If "no" and one or more shared vans were made available to the employee and used for private purposes, use the shared vans working sheet on the back of this sheet to calculate how much of the charge relates to this employee.

Tick the appropriate box

When was the van first registered?   After 5 April 1994   enter 500 at A
on or before 5 April 1994   enter 350 at A

Amount of standard charge for van   **A** £

1. If the van was first made available to the employee exclusively after 5 April 1997, add up the number of days from 5 April 1997 to the day before the van was made so available and enter it here.

2. If the van ceased to be available to the employee exclusively before 6 April 1998, add up the number of days from the day after it was last so available to 6 April 1998 and enter it here.

3. If the van was shared for one or more periods between the first and last days in the year on which it was available to the employee exclusively, enter the total number of days here.

4. If between the first and last days in the year on which the van was available to the employee exclusively there were one or more continuous periods, each of 30 days or more, when the van was neither a shared van nor available to the employee exclusively enter the total number of days here.

5. Total number of days in 1997-98 when van was not available to the employee or was a shared van.   (1. + 2. + 3. + 4)

Number of days shown at 5. x A   **B**
                         365

Standard charge less reduction for days when van was not available or was a shared van (A – B)   = **C** £

Enter the amount of any contribution the employee was required to make for private use of this van and did in fact make   **D** £

(C – D)   = **E** £

Enter the figure for shared vans (maximum £500) here (see over)   **F** £

Enter the amount of any contribution the employee was required to make for private use of shared vans and did in fact make   **G** £

(F – G)   = **H** £

Add together the figures at E and H.   **J** £
If there is more than one working sheet for this employee add the figures in all the boxes E and box H.

Enter J, limited if necessary, at box 1.18 Section G, box on form P11D.
Limit J to £500 if at no time in the year did the employee have more than one van available for private use by him or her or any member of his or her family or household.

P11D WS3 (1998)   BMSD 10/97

Illustration of the Vans Available for Private Use P11D Working Sheet, which employers can choose to use to calculate the cash equivalent of the benefit in kind. This Working Sheet may be subject to change before issue to employers

Appendix C

Working Sheet 3 (1997–98)

2 • Shared vans

If more than one shared van was available you will need to repeat the steps down to M below for each van on separate working sheets. You can photocopy this form if necessary.

Tick the appropriate box

When was the van first registered?　　　After 5 April 1994　　　☐ enter 500 at A

　　　　　　　　　　　　　　　　on or before 5 April 1994　☐ enter 350 at A

Amount of standard charge for van　　　　　　　　　　　　**K** £ ▢

Was the van shared and capable of use by this employee for the whole of 1997-98?

Yes ☐　　　*Enter the figure at K in box M below.*

No ☐　　　*Complete 1. to 4. below.*

1. **If the van first became a shared van after 5 April 1997**, add up the number of days from 5 April 1997 to the day before the van became a shared van and enter it here. ▢

2. **If the van ceased to be a shared van before 6 April 1998**, add up the number of days from the day after it was last a shared van to 6 April 1998 and enter it here. ▢

3. **If the van was not capable of use for a continuous period** of 30 days or more not included in 1. or 2. above enter the number of days here. ▢

4. **If the van was available to one employee only** for a period exceeding 30 days not included in 1. or 2. above enter the number of days here ▢

5. **Total number of days** in 1997-98 when van was not a shared van. (1. + 2. + 3. + 4) ▢

$$\frac{\text{Number of days shown at 5.}}{365} \times K = \textbf{L} \; ▢$$

Standard charge less reduction for days when van was not a shared van or was incapable of use (K - L) = **M** £ ▢

Repeat the above steps for each shared van that was available during the year.

Add together the totals at M for each shared van and enter them here　　**N** £ ▢

Divide N by the number of employees who used any shared van made available for private purposes　　**P** £ ▢

Enter the figure at P in box F overleaf.

Illustration of the Vans Available for Private Use P11D Working Sheet (continued)

694

Working Sheet 4 (1997–98)

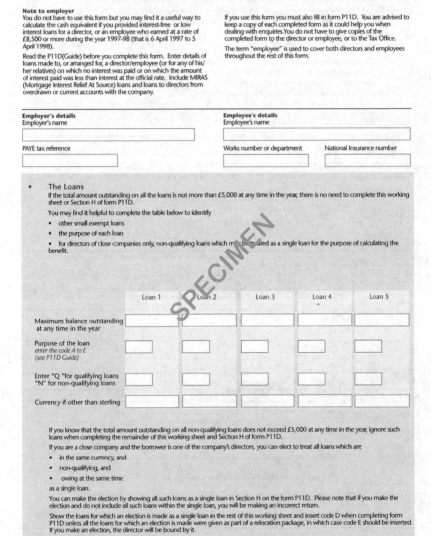

Illustration of the Interest Free and Low Interest Loans P11D Working Sheet, which employers can choose to use to calculate the cash equivalent of the benefit in kind. This Working Sheet may be subject to change before issue to employers

Working Sheet 4 (1997–98)

- **Official Rates of Interest**
  To calculate the cash equivalent of a loan you will need to know
  - the average official rate of interest for the year ended 5 April 1998 if the loan was outstanding throughout the tax year
  - the actual official rates and dates they applied where the loan was not outstanding throughout the year
  - the official rate for Japanese Yen or Swiss Francs where the loan was made in one of those currencies and the conditions in paragraph 17.5 of booklet 480 are met.

  The official interest rates up to early November 1997 are printed in Appendix 4 of booklet 480 but later changes and the average official rate of interest for the year are not known until near the end of the tax year.

  Form P11D(Int) is available through the Annual Pack Orderline (Phone 0345 646 646) and contains
  - details of the average official rates of interest for 1997-98 and the actual rates and dates they applied
  - a guide to calculating the average official rate of interest where a loan was owing for part of the year.

  Details of the official interest rates can also be obtained from your Tax Office.

- **Calculating the cash equivalent**
  Use the formula below for each loan separately (except where an election has been made to treat a director's loans as a single loan).

	Loan 1	Loan 2	Loan 3	Loan 4	Loan 5
A Maximum balance on later of • day loan was taken out or • 5 April 1997.					
B Maximum balance on earlier of • day loan was discharged or • 5 April 1998.					
C Total (A + B)					
D Divide C by 2					
E Official rate of interest	%	%	%	%	%
F Multiply D by appropriate official rate.					
G Number of complete tax months in tax year (6th of month to 5th of following month) throughout which loan was owing.					
H Multiply F by G					
J Divide H by 12					
K Enter interest paid in 1997-98					
L Cash equivalent of loans J minus K	L				

The figure at L is the amount to be entered in box 1.19 on forms P11D.

If the employee has more than 2 loans, you can write "see attached" in box 1.19 and attach a copy of this working sheet.

Employees may elect for a more complex but accurate method of calculating the benefit from interest free or low interest loans. Employers are not responsible for providing such a calculation.

Illustration of the Interest Free and Low Interest Loans P11D Working Sheet (continued)

Working Sheet 5 (1997–98)

Revenue Inland | **P11D WORKING SHEET 5** | RELOCATION EXPENSES PAYMENTS AND BENEFITS1997-98

Note to employer
You do not have to use this form but you may find it a useful way to calculate the cash equivalent if you provided relocation expenses payments and benefits for a director or an employee who earned at a rate of £8,500 a year or more during the year 1997-98 (that is 6 April 1997 to 5 April 1998).

Read the P11D(Guide) before you complete this form.

If you use this form you must also fill in form P11D or P9D. You are advised to keep a copy of each completed form as it could help you to deal with enquiries. You do not have to give copies of the forms to the director or employee, or to the Tax Office.

The term "employee" is used to cover both directors and employees throughout the rest of this form.

Employer's details
Employer's name

PAYE tax reference

Employee's details
Employee's name

Works number or department

National Insurance number

1 • Qualifying expenses payments

Any items from last year (1996-97) that were incurred in connection with this relocation where you did not give details on the P11D (for1996-97) because they were below the exemption limit should be included at item 4 below.

Enter the gross amount of all qualifying expenses payments **A £**

The cost to you as an employer of any qualifying benefits 1.

less anything paid towards the cost by the employee 2.

Enter the amount of qualifying benefits (1. less 2.) = **B £**

Enter the cost of qualifying living accommodation provided **C £**

Total of expenses and benefits (A + B + C) = **D £**

2 • Calculating the exempt amount

For each relocation a fixed amount of qualifying relocation expenses and benefits can be exempt. Qualifying expenses and benefits which
• were connected to this relocation
• were incurred in an earlier tax year
and
• were below the exemption limit.
have to be taken into account when working out the exempt amount for this employee for 1997-98.

Exempt amount for 1997- 98 (£8,000) 3. 8,000

Less amount of qualifying expenses and benefits incurred in 1996-97 or earlier years 4.

Exempt amount for this employee (3. less 4.) = **E £**

If 4. is more than 3., enter "NIL" in box E

Total of expenses and benefits (D - E) = **F £**
If E is more than D enter NIL in box F

Enter F at box 1.22, Section K on form P11D

P11D WS 5(1998) BMSD11/97

Illustration of the Relocation Expenses Payments and Benefits P11D Working Sheet, which employers can choose to use to calculate the cash equivalent of the benefit in kind and expenses payments. This Working Sheet may be subject to change before issue to employers

Appendix C

Information for Employee's Tax Return

Inland Revenue | **FIXED PROFIT CAR SCHEME** | *INFORMATION FOR EMPLOYEE'S TAX RETURN*

Note to employer

You do not have to use this form but if you have agreed a Fixed Profit Car Scheme with your Tax Office, you may find it a useful way of giving employees the information they need to complete their personal Tax Returns. You do not have to complete section 'A' if section 'B' is completed.

If you have agreed a Fixed Profit Car Scheme with your Tax Office do not put any of this information on form P11D or P9D. If a Fixed Profit Car Scheme has not been agreed with your Tax Office, car and mileage allowances must be entered on form P11D or P9D.

This form can be used for the year ended 5 April 1998 and later years. Forms are available from the Annual Pack Orderline (Phone 0345 646 646). You may find it helpful to keep a copy of each completed form as they could help you when dealing with any enquiries.

The term employee is used to cover both directors and employees throughout the rest of this form.

Employer's details

Employer's name

PAYE tax reference

Tax year

Employee's details

Employee's name

Works number or department

National Insurance number

Note for employee

A Fixed Profit Car Scheme is an arrangement which may be agreed between the employer and the Tax Office to establish any profit element in motor mileage allowances. It reduces record keeping for employers and employees. The taxable profit is the excess of the mileage allowances over the 'tax free' amount set by the Inland Revenue.

Please keep this form in a safe place as you may not be able to get a duplicate. You will need it for your personal records and to complete your Tax Return if you get one. Box 1.15 on this form corresponds to the one that should be completed in your Tax Return. Your employer may not have completed box 1.15 to show any taxable profit. If you

- need to work out the taxable profit from the other information provided
- require details of the 'tax free' mileage rates
- want further information.

Leaflet IR125: Using your own car for work, is available from any Tax Office or Enquiry Centre.

The Tax Office may need to adjust your tax code to take account of the information on this form.

A • **The car and mileage allowances paid for a car owned or hired by the employee**
Give details of the total amount paid to the employee and the number of business miles for which payments were made in the year.
Only include car and mileage allowances within a Fixed Profit Car Scheme. If the employee has opted out of the agreement between the employer and the Tax Office, the allowances paid should be included on the form P11D or P9D.

Car or mileage allowance paid for employee's car

Gross amount £

Business miles for which payments made in year

B • **Fixed Profit Car Scheme Profit**
Employers are asked to complete box 1.15 below to show the Fixed Profit Car Scheme profit from the profit tables

Fixed Profit Car Scheme profit from the tables

Taxable profit
1.15 £

FPCS 2

BMSD11/97

Illustration of a form which employers can choose to use to supply their employees with information regarding car mileage allowances paid for use of employees' cars on business, and the profit element under the Fixed Profit Car Scheme. This form is only to be used where the employer has agreed a Fixed Profit Car Scheme with the tax office, and may be subject to change before issue to employers

Note: *The Inland Revenue will be replacing the Form for reporting purposes at the end of the year*

Form P14(OCR)

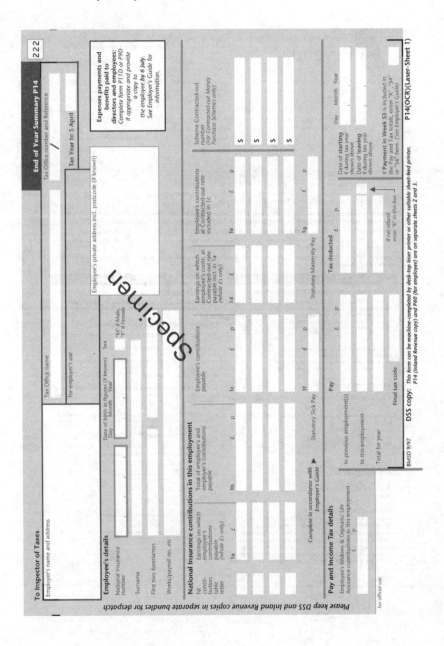

Illustration of an end of year return

Appendix C

Form P35

Inland Revenue

Employer's Annual Return

Year ended 5 April 19___

Your reference _____

Tax Office reference _____

Tax Office telephone number _____

Return to:

Accounts Office reference _____

PAYE Income Tax and National Insurance contributions

This form will help check that you have made the right PAYE payments during the year. Please see your *Employer's Quick Guide to PAYE and NICs* (CWG1 cards) for guidance, or contact your Tax Office if you need help. **You are required by law to:**

• complete and sign this form, and **send it in time to reach the Tax Office by 19 May** following the end of the tax year

• send with this form the DSS and Inland Revenue copies of the *End of Year Summary* (form P14) for each employee you were required to complete a *Deductions Working Sheet* (form P11) for during the year.

Penalties are chargeable where a return is late. We will charge these automatically if the return for the year ended 5 April 1997 is received after 23 May 1997.

Checklist

Tick the boxes – you must answer each question

1 Have you enclosed an *End of Year Summary* (form P14) or a form P38(S) for every person in your paid employment, either on a casual basis or otherwise, during the above tax year? No ☐ Yes ☐
If no, please submit an *Employer's Supplementary Return* (form P38A)

2 Did you make any "free of tax" payments to any employee? In other words, did you bear any of the tax yourself rather than deduct it from the employee? No ☐ Yes ☐

3 So far as you know, did anyone else pay expenses or provide benefits or vouchers exchangeable for money, goods or services to any of your employees because they were employed by you during the year? No ☐ Yes ☐

4 Did anyone employed by a person or company outside the UK work for you in the UK for 30 or more days in a row? No ☐ Yes ☐
If yes, have you included them in the list on the back of this form or on any continuation sheets? No ☐ Yes ☐

5 Have you paid any of an employee's pay to someone other than that employee (for example, to a school)? No ☐ Yes ☐
If yes, have you included it in the payments shown on that employee's *End of Year Summary* (form P14)? No ☐ Yes ☐

Remember - you are also required to

• Give a *Certificate of Pay, Income Tax and NIC* (form P60) to each relevant employee by 31 May following the end of the tax year.

• Give a copy of form P9D and / or P11D, or equivalent information, to each relevant employee by 6 July following the end of the tax year.

• Send any outstanding PAYE or NIC to the Inland Revenue Accounts Office. Interest is chargeable on amounts not received by 19 April. *Do not send payment with this form* - see your payslip booklet for instructions.

P35 (Man.)

Declaration and Certificate

Tick box for each item

This declaration and certificate covers any documents authorised by the Inland Revenue as substitutes for the forms mentioned below.

I declare and certify that for the above tax year

■ an *End of Year Summary* (form P14) is enclosed for each employee or director for whom I was required to complete a *Deductions Working Sheet* (form P11) during the year

■ completed *Employer's Supplementary Returns* (forms P38A)
are enclosed ☐ are not due ☐

■ completed *Returns of expenses payments and benefits* (forms P11D and P11D(b)) *
are enclosed ☐ will be sent later ☐ are not due ☐

■ completed *Returns of Expenses Payments and Income from which Tax Cannot be Deducted* (form P9D) for employees earning at a rate of less than £8,500 per annum *
are enclosed ☐ will be sent later ☐ are not due ☐

All the details on this form and any forms enclosed are fully and truly stated to the best of my knowledge and belief

Signature of employer

Capacity in which signed

Date

You may be penalised or prosecuted if you make false statements

* If you are a new employer we may not have sent you any forms P11D or P9D. If you are paying expenses or providing benefits please refer to the *Employer's Further Guide to PAYE and NICs* (booklet CWG2). Ask your Tax Office for these forms if you need them.

Please turn over

21239 2.97 Niceday Stationery & Print Limited   BMSD 1/97   W0K2231

Illustration of a P35 annual return

700

Form P35

Deductions Working Sheets

List here the individual *Deductions Working Sheets* (forms P11) which you have filled in during the year and which contain a figure under either of the headings shown.

If there is not enough space here to list all your employees please prepare continuation sheets.

Enter only the figures for 'this employment'

Employee's name Put an asterisk (*) beside the name if the person is a director	National Insurance contributions (NIC) Enter the total of employee's and employer's NIC †	Income tax deducted or refunded Write 'R' beside amount to show a net refund	† Include Class 1A contributions payable in the year, unless you paid these by the Alternative Payment Method.
	£	£	
	£	£	
	£	£	
	£	£	
	£	£	
	£	£	Note: the columns for **SSP and SMP paid** have been discontinued, but the figures may still appear on some computer-printed continuation sheets. If so, please ignore them.
	£	£	
	£	£	
	£	£	
	£	£	
	£	£	
	£	£	

Calculation of NIC and Income Tax now due

National Insurance contributions (NIC)

Total from this page	A	£
Totals from continuation sheets	B	£
Total NIC A + B.	C	£
Received from Inland Revenue to pay SSP / SMP	D	£
C + D	E	£
Statutory Sick Pay recovered	F	£
Statutory Maternity Pay recovered	G	£
NIC compensation on SMP see your payment record	H	£
NIC Holiday claimed	I	£
F + G + H + I	J	£
Total NIC payable to Accounts Office E − J	K	£
NIC already paid	L	£
NIC now due K − L	M	£

Remember to deduct amounts marked "R"

Income Tax

Total from this page	N	£
Totals from continuation sheets	O	£
Total tax N + O	P	£
Received from Inland Revenue to refund tax	Q	£
Tax deducted from sub-contractors see your *Contractor's Statement* (form SC35)	R	£
P + Q + R	S	£
Tax already paid	T	£
Tax now due S − T	U	£

Do not send payment with this form. Send it to the Inland Revenue Accounts Office immediately. See notes overleaf.

Contracted-out pension schemes

Enter here your employer's contracting-out number, where applicable:

(You will find the number on the Occupational Pensions Board's Certificate)

§ I claim payment under Section 7 of the Social Security Act 1986 for each employee on whose *End of Year Summary* (form P14) I have entered a scheme contracting-out number. So far as I know, none of these employees is in an employment which has been contracted-out by reference to any other scheme since 1 January 1986.

§ You can only claim if this form is used for 1992-93 or earlier

Illustration of a P35 annual return (continued)

Form P45

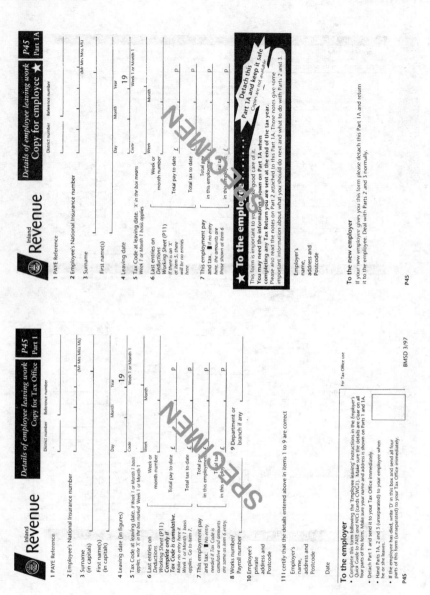

Illustration of the four parts of a Form P45 showing details of employee leaving — Parts 1 and 1A

Form P45

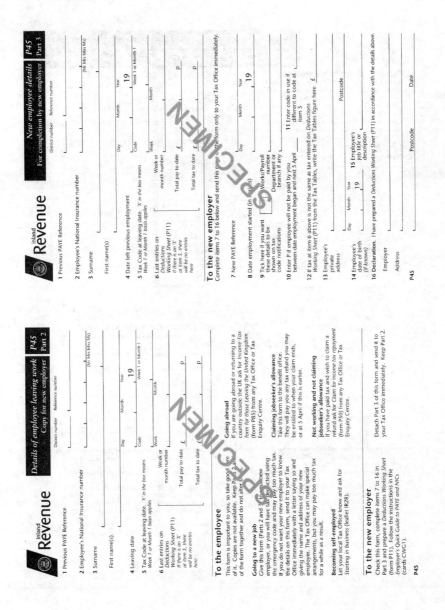

Illustration of the four parts of a Form P45 showing details of employee leaving — Parts 2 and 3

Form P46

PAYE Employer's notice to Tax Office   P46

Use this form to tell the Tax Office about
- employees who do not have a form P45 or
- employees previously paid below the PAYE threshold

To be completed by the employee

Read each statement below carefully. Tick **each one** that applies to you. If none of them apply, do not sign the statement. Complete the lower part of the form.

Statement A
This is my first regular job since leaving full-time education. I have not claimed Jobseekers Allowance, or income support paid because of unemployment since then.

Statement B
This is my only or main job.

Statement C
I receive a pension as well as the income from this job.

I confirm I have ticked the statements that apply to me.

Signed _____ Date _____

To be completed by the employer

Employer's name

Employer's address

Postcode

Employer's PAYE reference   District no.   Reference

Date this form was completed   Day   Month   Year

Your Employer's Quick Guide to PAYE and NICs (CWG1) tells you how to complete this form and what to do with it – *see Card 8.*

P46(1997)   BMSD1/97

Employee's details – *to be entered by employer*

National Insurance number   Letters Numbers Numbers Numbers Letter

Surname including title Mr/Mrs/Miss/Ms
Title   Surname

First name(s)

Home address

Postcode

Date of birth (in figures)   Day   Month   Year

Put 'M' for male or 'F' for female in box

Works or payroll number, *if any*

Branch or department, *if any*

Job title

Date employment started   Day   Month   Year

Coding information *to be completed by employer*

Existing employee now above PAYE threshold
enter X in box if this applies

New employee who has signed statement *enter letter here*

New employee who has not signed a statement

Code operated for this employee

Enter X in box if code operated on week1/month 1 basis

Employee *If you wish you can detach this part and send it to the Tax Office yourself. Ask your employer for the Tax Office's address.*

Your employer's PAYE reference

Completing this form will help your employer and the Tax Office to give you a correct PAYE code. Without it you may pay too much or too little tax.
Please list below in date order all the jobs you have had and any periods when you were out of work during the last **twelve months**. Please do not leave any gaps between the periods. If you were claiming benefit while you were out of work please show this in the space provided.

Your National Insurance number   Letters Numbers Numbers Numbers Letter

Under **Additional information** give the following details
- your employer's name and address if you were employed
- your business name and address if you were self-employed
- the type of benefit you claimed while out of work
- what you were doing if you were not working and not claiming benefit, for example, in full time education.
Use a separate sheet if there is not enough space on this slip.

| Dates | | Tick one box for each period | | | | |
From	To	Employed	Self employed	Claiming benefit	Not working	Additional information

P46(1997)

Illustration of a Form P46, employer's notice to tax office

Form P46(Car)

Inland Revenue

Notification of a car provided for the private use of an employee or a director

Employer's name _____ PAYE reference _____

Employee's/Director's name _____ NI number [| | | | |]

Part 1

You are required to make a return on this form for an employee earning at the rate of £8,500 a year or more or a director for whom a car is made available for private use. The completed form is required within 28 days of the end of the quarter to 5 July, 5 October, 5 January or 5 April in which any of the following takes place.

Tick whichever applies

1. The employee/director is first provided with a car which is available for private use ☐

2. A car provided to the employee/director is replaced by another car which is available for private use ☐

3. The employee/director is provided with a second or further car which is available for private use ☐

4. The employee starts to earn at the rate of £8,500 a year or more or becomes a director ☐

5. A car provided to the employee/director is withdrawn without replacement ☐

Part 2 Details of car provided

Make _____ Model _____ Date first registered _____

Price of car (normally the list price at date of first registration) £ _____

Price of accessories not included in price of car £ _____

Date car first made available to employee _____

Capital contribution (if any) made by employee to cost of the car and for accessories £ _____

Sum payable (if any) by employee for private use of the car £ _____ a week / a month / a quarter / a year

Is fuel for private use provided with this car ? yes ☐ no ☐ If so, is the employee required to make good the cost of all fuel used for private motoring **and** do you expect him/her to continue to do so? yes ☐ no ☐

If the answer to the previous question is 'no' please indicate the type of fuel petrol ☐ diesel ☐ and the cylinder capacity up to 1400cc ☐ 1401 - 2000cc ☐ 2001 or more ☐

If you have ticked box 1, 2, 3 or 4 in Part 1 please show the expected level of annual business mileage for this car less than 2500 ☐ 2500 - 17999 ☐ 18000 or more ☐

If you have ticked box 2 in Part 1 but the employee has more than one car available for private use please provide details of the car replaced } Make _____ Model _____

If you have ticked box 5 in Part 1 please provide details of the car withdrawn } Date withdrawn *(where appropriate)* _____

Declaration

I declare that all particulars required are fully and truly stated according to the best of my knowledge and belief

Signature _____

Capacity in which signed _____

Date _____

P46(Car)

22977 9.96 Niceday Stationery & Print Limited   CCO8/96   W0L2643

Illustration of a Form P46(Car), notification of details of a car provided for private use

Appendix C

Form P60

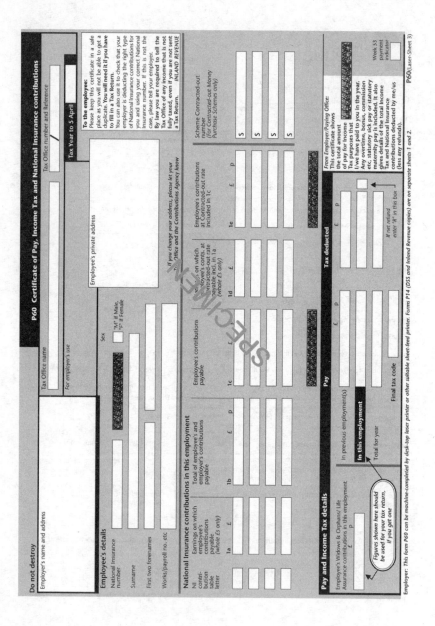

Illustration of a certificate of pay, income tax and NICs

706

Appendix D

Income Tax Details

Income tax rates

1997/98		1998/99	
Taxable Income	*Rate*	*Taxable Income*	*Rate*
£	%	£	%
0–4,100	20	0–4,300	20
4,101–26,100	23	4,301–27,100	23
Remainder	40	Remainder	40

Income tax reliefs

	1997/98	*1998/99*
	£	£
Personal allowance	4,045	4,195
Married couple's allowance	1,830*	1,900*
Single parent allowance or addition if claimant's wife ill	1,830*	1,900*
Persons aged 65 to 74		
— Personal allowance	5,220	5,410
— Married couple's allowance	3,185*	3,305*
Persons aged 75 and over		
— Personal allowance	5,400	5,600
— Married couple's allowance	3,225*	3,345*
— Income limit for age allowance	15,600	16,200
Widow's bereavement	1,830*	1,900*
Blind person's allowance	1,280	1,330

*Relief on these is given at 15% for 1998/1999 and 10% thereafter

707

Car and Van benefits

Cars and fuel, and vans, provided by the employer for private motoring are benefits in kind. They are valued for tax purposes as annual amounts which are shown in the following tables.

Cars: the regime from 6 April 1994

1994/95, 1995/96, 1996/97, 1997/98, 1998/99

The percentage of the price of the car used to determine the cash equivalent of the taxable benefit.	35%
The overall limit to the price.	£80,000
The maximum allowable capital contribution.	£5,000
The reductions of the cash equivalent, where:	
– at least 2,500 business miles travelled:	one-third
– at least 18,000 business miles travelled:	two-thirds
– the car is at least four years old:	one-third
Classic cars, and market value	£15,000

Note:

Pro rata calculations of the cash equivalents and business miles travelled are applicable where the car is unavailable in the year, according to certain criteria.

The reduction where the car is four or more years old at the end of the year of assessment in question, is applied to the net figure after reduction, if any, for business miles travelled.

Vans

1993/94, 1994/95, 1995/96, 1996/97, 1997/98, 1998/99

Age of vans on 5 April	*Vans under 4 years old* £	*Vans over 4 years old* £
Standard charge	500	350
Daily charge for alternative calculation method	5	5

Note:

Heavier commercial vehicles, being of a laden weight limit exceeding 3,500 kilograms, which would be treated as a van, are excluded from the scale charges if they are not used wholly or mainly for private use.

Car fuel benefit

	1997/98		1998/99	
	Petrol £	Diesel £	Petrol £	Diesel £
Cylinder capacity				
Up to 1,400 cc	800	740	1,010	1,280
1,401 cc to 2,000 cc	1,010	740	1,280	1,280
2,001 cc or more	1,490	940	1,890	1,890

Without cylinder capacity but original market value of

	£	£
Up to £5,999		
£6,000 to £8,499	} 1,490	} 1,890
£8,500 or more		

Notes:

(1)   The scale charges are reduced to nil if the employee is required to make good all fuel provided for private use and does so.

(2)   The scale charge does not apply to fuel provided for vans.

(3)   The scale charge applies to each company car, but is *pro rata* to the period the car is available.

Inland Revenue Authorised Mileage Rates

	1997/98			
	Cars up to 1,000 cc	Cars 1,001 −1,500 cc	Cars 1,501 −2,000 cc	Cars over 2,000 cc
First 4,000 miles	28p	35p	45p	63p
Excess over 4,000 miles	17p	20p	25p	36p

	1998/99			
	Cars up to 1,000 cc	Cars 1,001 −1,500 cc	Cars 1,501 −2,000 cc	Cars over 2,000 cc
First 4,000 miles	28p	35p	45p	63p
Excess over 4,000 miles	17p	20p	25p	36p

NIC details

Class 1 Not Contracted-out

1997/98

	Employee (%)				Employer (%)
	Up to LEL		Over LEL		
Total Earnings	Standard	*Reduced	Standard	*Reduced	
£62.00 to £109.99 weekly	2	3.85	10	3.85	3.0
(£269.00 to £476.99 monthly)					
£110.00 to £154.99 weekly	2	3.85	10	3.85	5.0
(£477.00 to £671.99 monthly)					
£155.00 to £209.99 weekly	2	3.85	10	3.85	7.0
(£672.00 to £909.99 monthly)					
£210.00 to £465.00 weekly	2	3.85	10	3.85	10.0
(£910.00 to £2,015.00 monthly)					
Over £465.00 weekly	2	3.85	10 to UEL thereafter Nil	3.85 to UEL thereafter Nil	10.0
(Over £2,015.00 monthly)					

*Reduced rate for married women and widow optants

1998/99

	Employee (%)				Employer (%)
	Up to LEL		Over LEL		
Total Earnings	Standard	*Reduced	Standard	*Reduced	
£64.00 to £109.99 weekly	2	3.85	10	3.85	3.0
(£278.00 to £476.99 monthly)					
£110.00 to £154.99 weekly	2	3.85	10	3.85	5.0
(£477.00 to £671.99 monthly)					
£155.00 to £209.99 weekly	2	3.85	10	3.85	7.0
(£672.00 to £909.99 monthly)					
£210.00 to £485.00 weekly	2	3.85	10	3.85	10.0
(£910.00 to £2,102.00 monthly)					
Over £485.00 weekly	2	3.85	10 to UEL thereafter Nil	3.85 to UEL thereafter Nil	10.0
(Over £2,102.00 monthly)					

*Reduced rate for married women and widow optants

Class 1 Contracted-out money purchase (COMP) scheme

1997/98

| | Employee (%) | | | | Employer (%) | |
	Up to LEL		Over LEL		Up to LEL	Over LEL
Total Earnings	Standard	*Reduced	Standard	*Reduced		
£62.00 to £109.99 weekly	2	3.85	8.4	3.85	3.0	1.5
(£269.00 to £476.99 monthly)						
£110.00 to £154.99 weekly	2	3.85	8.4	3.85	5.0	3.5
(£477.00 to £671.99 monthly)						
£155.00 to £209.99 weekly	2	3.85	8.4	3.85	7.0	5.5
(£672.00 to £909.99 monthly)						
£210.00 to £465.00 weekly	2	3.85	8.4	3.85	10.0	8.5
(£910.00 to £2,015.00 monthly)						
Over £465.00 weekly	2	3.85	8.4 to UEL thereafter Nil	3.85 to UEL thereafter Nil	10.0	8.5 to UEL there-after 10.0
(Over £2,015.00 monthly)						

*Reduced rate for married women and widow optants

1998/99

| | Employee (%) | | | | Employer (%) | |
	Up to LEL		Over LEL		Up to LEL	Over LEL
Total Earnings	Standard	*Reduced	Standard	*Reduced		
£64.00 to £109.99 weekly	2	3.85	8.4	3.85	3.0	1.5
(£278.00 to £476.99 monthly)						
£110.00 to £154.99 weekly	2	3.85	8.4	3.85	5.0	3.5
(£477.00 to £671.99 monthly)						
£155.00 to £209.99 weekly	2	3.85	8.4	3.85	7.0	5.5
(£672.00 to £909.99 monthly)						
£210.00 to £485.00 weekly	2	3.85	8.4	3.85	10.0	8.5
(£910.00 to £2,102.00 monthly)						
Over £485.00 weekly	2	3.85	8.4 to UEL thereafter Nil	3.85 to UEL thereafter Nil	10.0	8.5 to UEL there-after 10.0
(Over £2,102.00 monthly)						

*Reduced rate for married women and widow optants

Class 1 Contracted-out salary related (COSR) scheme

1997/98

	Employee (%)				Employer (%)	
	Up to LEL		Over LEL		Up to LEL	Over LEL
Total Earnings	Standard	*Reduced	Standard	*Reduced		
£62.00 to £109.99 weekly	2	3.85	8.4	3.85	3.0	Nil
(£269.00 to £476.99 monthly)						
£110.00 to £154.99 weekly	2	3.85	8.4	3.85	5.0	2.0
(£477.00 to £671.99 monthly)						
£155.00 to £209.99 weekly	2	3.85	8.4	3.85	7.0	4.0
(£672.00 to £909.99 monthly)						
£210.00 to £465.00 weekly	2	3.85	8.4	3.85	10.0	7.0
(£910.00 to £2,015.00 monthly)						
Over £465.00 weekly	2	3.85	8.4 to UEL thereafter Nil	3.85 to UEL thereafter Nil	10.0	7.0 to UEL there-after 10.0
(Over £2,015.00 monthly)						

*Reduced rate for married women and widow optants

1998/99

	Employee (%)				Employer (%)	
	Up to LEL		Over LEL		Up to LEL	Over LEL
Total Earnings	Standard	*Reduced	Standard	*Reduced		
£64.00 to £109.99 weekly	2	3.85	8.4	3.85	3.0	Nil
(£278.00 to £476.99 monthly)						
£110.00 to £154.99 weekly	2	3.85	8.4	3.85	5.0	2.0
(£477.00 to £671.99 monthly)						
£155.00 to £209.99 weekly	2	3.85	8.4	3.85	7.0	4.0
(£672.00 to £909.99 monthly)						
£210.00 to £485.00 weekly	2	3.85	8.4	3.85	10.0	7.0
(£910.00 to £2,102.00 monthly)						
Over £485.00 weekly	2	3.85	8.4 to UEL thereafter Nil	3.85 to UEL thereafter Nil	10.0	7.0 to UEL there-after 10.0
(Over £2,102.00 monthly)						

*Reduced rate for married women and widow optants

NIC Class 1 earnings limits

	1997/98			1998/99		
	Week £	*Month* £	*Year* £	*Week* £	*Month* £	*Year* £
Lower earnings limit (LEL)	62	269	3,224	64	278	3,328
Upper earnings limit (UEL)	465	2,015	24,180	485	2,102	25,220

Note:

There are no NICs payable if total earnings are below the LEL.

Class 1A Cars and car fuel

	Employer (%)	
	1997/98	*1998/99*
Cash equivalent of the benefit of a car or fuel	10.0	10.0

Note:

The cash equivalents of the benefits are ascertained, subject to certain modifications, as for tax purposes (including increases and decreases according to usage). The scale rates are reproduced earlier in this Appendix. There is no Class 1A liability on the tax scale charges for vans.

Class 2 Self-employed earnings

	1997/98 £	*1998/99* £
Flat rate contributions (weekly)	6.15	6.35
Small earnings exemption limit (per annum)	3,480	3,590

Class 3 Voluntary

	1997/98 £	*1998/99* £
Flat rate contributions (weekly)	6.05	6.25

Class 4 Self-employed

	1997/98	*1998/99*
Percentage of profits, on profits between	6.0%	6.0%
Earnings band	£7,010 to £24,180	£7,310 to £25,220

Appendix D

SSP and SMP

SSP

1997/98		1998/99	
Average weekly earnings	*Weekly rate of SSP*	*Average weekly earnings*	*Weekly rate of SSP*
Under £62.00	Nil	Under £64.00	Nil
Over £61.99	£55.70	Over £63.99	£57.70

SMP

	1997/98	1998/99
Higher weekly rate	9/10 of employee's average weekly earnings	9/10 of employee's average weekly earnings
Lower weekly rate	£55.70	£57.70

Employer's NIC compensation on SSP/SMP

1997/98

As at 6 April 1997, 92% of SMP paid by 'large employers' may be reclaimed by deduction from Class 1 NICs payable. 'Small employers' can recover 106.5% of SMP paid.

Where the SSP paid in a tax month exceeds 13% of the total NIC liability for that month, employers can recover the excess.

1998/99

As at 6 April 1998, 92% of SMP paid by 'large employers' may be reclaimed by deduction from Class 1 NICs payable. 'Small employers' can recover 107% of SMP paid.

Where the SSP paid in a tax month exceeds 13% of the total NIC liability for that month, employers can recover the excess.

Main national insurance benefits

	1997/98	1998/99
	£ per week	£ per week
Retirement pensions		
Basic State pension	62.45	64.70
Non-contributing wife	37.35	38.70
Extra for those over 80 years old	0.25	0.25
Payment to widows		
Lump sum payment	1,000.00*	1,000.00*
Widowed mother's allowance	62.45	64.70
Pension	62.45	64.70
Industrial injuries disablement benefit		
(Reduced according to degree of disablement) *Pension*		
(100% disablement)		
Over 18	101.10	104.70
Under 18	61.90	64.15
Incapacity benefit		
Long-term	62.45	64.70
higher increase for age	13.15	13.60
lower increase for age	6.60	6.80
Short-term (under pension age)		
lower rate	47.10	48.80
higher rate	55.70	57.70
Short-term (over pension age)	59.90	62.05
Maternity allowance		
Higher rate	55.70	57.70
Lower rate	48.35	50.10
Unemployment benefit		
Under State pensionable age	–	–
Over State pensionable age	–	–
Occupational pension abatement	–	–
Jobseekers allowance		
Single under 18	29.60	30.30
Between 18 and 24	38.90	39.85
Over 25	49.15	50.35
Miscellaneous	£ per day	£ per day
Employee's guarantee payment when laid-off	14.50	15.35

*This is a once and for all payment.

Age-related percentages for contracted-out money purchase schemes

Table 1

Appropriate age-related percentages of earnings exceeding the lower earnings limit but not the upper earnings limit

Age on last day of preceding tax year	Appropriate age-related percentages for the tax year				
	1997/98	1998/99	1999/2000	2000/2001	2001/2002
15	3.1	3.1	2.2	2.2	2.2
16	3.2	3.2	2.2	2.2	2.2
17	3.2	3.2	2.3	2.3	2.3
18	3.3	3.3	2.3	2.3	2.3
19	3.3	3.3	2.3	2.4	2.4
20	3.4	3.4	2.4	2.4	2.4
21	3.4	3.4	2.5	2.5	2.5
22	3.5	3.5	2.5	2.5	2.5
23	3.5	3.5	2.6	2.6	2.6
24	3.6	3.6	2.6	2.6	2.6
25	3.6	3.7	2.7	2.7	2.7
26	3.7	3.7	2.7	2.7	2.7
27	3.8	3.8	2.8	2.8	2.8
28	3.8	3.8	2.9	2.9	2.9
29	3.9	3.9	2.9	2.9	2.9
30	3.9	3.9	3.0	3.0	3.0
31	4.0	4.0	3.0	3.0	3.0
32	4.0	4.0	3.1	3.1	3.1
33	4.1	4.1	3.2	3.2	3.2
34	4.2	4.2	3.2	3.2	3.3
35	4.3	4.2	3.3	3.3	3.3
36	4.5	4.4	3.4	3.4	3.4
37	4.6	4.5	3.5	3.5	3.5
38	4.8	4.7	3.7	3.6	3.5
39	5.0	4.9	3.8	3.8	3.7
40	5.2	5.1	4.0	3.9	3.8
41	5.4	5.3	4.2	4.1	4.0
42	5.8	5.5	4.4	4.3	4.2
43	6.4	5.9	4.6	4.5	4.4
44	7.2	6.5	5.0	4.7	4.6
45	8.0	7.3	5.6	5.1	4.8
46	8.9	8.1	6.3	5.7	5.2
47	9.0	9.0	7.1	6.4	5.8
48	9.0	9.0	8.0	7.2	6.6
49	9.0	9.0	8.8	8.2	7.4
50	9.0	9.0	9.0	9.0	8.4
51-63	9.0	9.0	9.0	9.0	9.0

The Social Security (Reduced Rates of Class 1 Contributions and Rebates) (Money Purchase Contracted-out Schemes) Order 1996, [SI 1996 No 1055] as amended by The Social Security (Reduced Rates of Class 1 Contributions, and Rebates) (Money Purchase Contracted-out Schemes) Order 1998 [SI 1998 No 945].

Age-related percentages for appropriate personal pension schemes

Table 2

Appropriate age-related percentages of earnings exceeding the LEL but not the UEL

Age on last day of preceding tax year	Appropriate age-related percentages for the tax year				
	1997/98	*1998/99*	*1999/2000*	*2000/2001*	*2001/2002*
15	3.4	3.4	3.8	3.8	3.8
16	3.4	3.4	3.8	3.8	3.8
17	3.5	3.5	3.9	3.9	3.9
18	3.5	3.5	3.9	3.9	3.9
19	3.6	3.6	4.0	4.0	4.0
20	3.6	3.6	4.0	4.0	4.0
21	3.7	3.7	4.1	4.1	4.1
22	3.7	3.7	4.1	4.1	4.1
23	3.8	3.8	4.2	4.2	4.2
24	3.8	3.8	4.2	4.2	4.2
25	3.9	3.9	4.3	4.3	4.3
26	3.9	3.9	4.3	4.3	4.3
27	4.0	4.0	4.4	4.4	4.4
28	4.0	4.0	4.4	4.4	4.4
29	4.1	4.1	4.5	4.5	4.5
30	4.2	4.2	4.5	4.5	4.5
31	4.2	4.2	4.6	4.6	4.6
32	4.3	4.3	4.6	4.6	4.6
33	4.3	4.3	4.7	4.7	4.7
34	4.4	4.4	4.7	4.7	4.7
35	4.5	4.4	4.8	4.8	4.8
36	4.7	4.6	4.8	4.8	4.8
37	4.9	4.8	5.0	4.9	4.9
38	5.0	4.9	5.1	5.0	4.9
39	5.2	5.1	5.3	5.2	5.1
40	5.4	5.3	5.5	5.4	5.3
41	5.6	5.5	5.7	5.5	5.4
42	6.0	5.7	5.9	5.7	5.6
43	6.7	6.1	6.1	5.9	5.8
44	7.4	6.8	6.5	6.1	6.0
45	8.2	7.5	7.1	6.6	6.2
46	9.0	8.3	7.9	7.2	6.6
47	9.0	9.0	8.7	8.0	7.3
48	9.0	9.0	9.0	8.8	8.1
49	9.0	9.0	9.0	9.0	8.9
50-63	9.0	9.0	9.0	9.0	9.0

The Social Security (Minimum Contributions to Appropriate Personal Pension Schemes) Order 1996 [SI 1996 No 1056] as amended by The Social Security (Minimum Contributions to Appropriate Personal Pension Schemes) Order 1998 [SI 1998 No 944].

Appendix E

A Brief Checklist of Computer Payroll Requirements

Technical facilities

The following should be examined to see if they are adequate and compatible with any proposed software.

(*a*)   The computer processor and memory.

(*b*)   Magnetic disk space.

(*c*)   Video and time and attendance terminals.

(*d*)   Printers.

(*e*)   Additional devices such as magnetic tapes or communications equipment.

The amount, power and capacity of the equipment required depends primarily on the size of the payroll. Clearly some payrolls can make more demands than others of the same size. A weekly wages payroll with many overtime and bonus details creates more computer work than a monthly staff payroll.

The software regime has its own requirements. There must be compatibility between:

 (i)   the operating system;

 (ii)   the database management system or file handler;

(iii)   the communications software;

(iv)   the languages in which the payroll software is written;

 (v)   other system software, e.g. the report writer used;

(vi)   other application systems, e.g. time and attendance and accounts systems.

General features of payroll software

There is in practice no clear division between payroll and allied computer systems such as personnel records or sickness control. These systems may be separate, may overlap or be combined in one system. Some form of integration or linking is, however, highly desirable. (See Chapters 26 (Payroll Technology) and 28 (Selecting a Computer System).)

In an administrative context real time usually means updating a data file immediately via a video terminal. For instance, a computer payroll file can often be updated straightaway with an employee's tax code change via a video terminal. Some older 'batch' payroll systems can only store batches of changes and update the payroll file later when sufficient data has been entered. A good payroll system provides both batch and real time facilities in a sensible and convenient fashion.

The payroll system should allow the use of different peripheral devices according to convenience, e.g. a listing or report produced on different printers or on a video screen as desired. The ability to store a report in the computer until a printer is available is useful. This is called 'spooling'.

A good system of passwords to control terminal access is often vital. Some systems allow levels of access, e.g. one payroll clerk can view employee records while another can both view and update. Good data checking and cross-checking facilities, i.e. validation, is essential to a well set-up system.

Easy means of copying payroll files are vital. In the event of losing the payroll computer data, say due to a power failure, it should be a straightforward matter to restore the payroll file to its earlier condition. Special facilities can be provided to help restore the payroll file quickly and conveniently.

Audit trails, journals or logs are more or less the same thing and contain a record of all payroll changes. When printed out or displayed at the terminal they show everything that has altered the main payroll file. They are often combined with the update reports and show not only the old and new value of a payroll field, e.g. basic pay before a pay rise and after, but also the user's identification number and the number of the terminal used. This, together with the time and date, allows an auditor to check out the use of the payroll system. Also it often provides evidence for computer specialists when there are apparent faults.

Essential flexibility features are one or both of the following:

(*a*)   modifiable programs;

(*b*)   parameter driving.

Payroll facilities

Necessary payroll facilities are listed below.

(*a*)   *Amendment of master file*

(i)   Access to all the vital data held on the employee master file records is essential.

(*b*)   *Build-up to gross*

(i)   Comprehensive pay element and calculation facilities for the build-up to gross process. The computer system must distinguish between pay elements that are permanent or temporary, taxable and non-taxable, NICable or non-NICable, pensionable or non-pensionable etc.

(ii)   Sick pay, including SSP. All but the inclusion of sick pay in gross pay may be handled in a separate related system. Similar provision is required for OMP and SMP.

(*c*)   *Deductions*

(i)   Statutory deductions, i.e. income tax, NICs and attachments of earnings orders.

(ii)   Pension contributions allowing for the different types of scheme, e.g. COMPS and various calculation rules.

(iii)   Voluntary deductions including loans.

(*d*)   *Pay periods*

Weekly, two-weekly, four-weekly, monthly etc.

(*e*)   *Pay methods*

  (i)   Cash.

 (ii)   Manual cheque.

(iii)   Computer cheque.

(iv)   Paper credit transfer.

 (v)   EFT via magnetic tape, telecommunications etc. to BACS Ltd.

(vi)   Girobank credit transfers, paper or magnetic tape.

(vii)   Special, e.g. foreign, payments or proprietary systems such as Autopay.

(viii) The ability to split an employee payment between two methods, e.g. paying partly via cash and partly via EFT.

(All payments should be supported by all the necessary computer produced reports, e.g. a coinage analysis report for cash payments.)

(*f*)   *Payslips*

  (i)   Fixed or variable design.

 (ii)   Payslip messages.

(iii)   Mailing facilities, e.g. name and address printing, labels, use of proprietary ready enveloped payslips etc.

(*g*)   *Reports*

Because each organisation is different some payroll systems use either a special payroll report generator or a general-purpose report generator. Each user can then define his own reports. Some reports, however, are usually provided as standard. These reports are indicated below.

  (i)   Batch input validation report.

 (ii)   Full set of control reports, e.g. the payroll summary containing total net pay, total income tax etc.

(iii)   Record prints of the details for each payee.

(iv)   Update reports (combined with audit or journal facilities).

 (v)   Payment listings, i.e. reports listing the payees for each type of payment such as cash, cheque etc.

(vi)   Full set of payee listings showing various details.

(vii)   Deduction listings showing the payee identification and amount, e.g. for union subscriptions.

(viii) Exception reports, e.g. warnings for employees with very high or low gross pay, tax refunds exceeding £200 etc.

(ix)   Statistics.

 (x)   Labour cost analyses.

(*h*)   *Year-end reports*

(i)   Statutory documentation, e.g. Forms P14/60 and P35.

(ii)   A P35 (MT) magnetic tape or floppy disk substitute.

(iii) Method for resetting statutory fields for the new tax year.

(iv)   Special year-end reports, e.g. a list of employees and their pension contributions.

(*j*)   *Miscellaneous functions*

A system should have the following features.

(i)   Ability to uplift or decrease standard tax codes according to Inland Revenue instructions.

(ii)   Rapid manual input facility for amendments, e.g. Form P6 tax code changes, and variations, e.g. overtime.

(iii) Pay increase facility.

(iv)   Ability to handle special payments such as back pay.

(v)   Holiday facilities.

(vi)   Links to other systems such as accounts, pensions, personnel etc. (This includes automatic input from a system on the same computer or on a remote computer, e.g. magnetic tape input of P6 tax code changes.)

(vii) Ability to perform a trial set of payroll calculations and produce various reports, either without updating the payroll file or by an immediate and straightforward restoration of the earlier payroll files.

(*k*)   *Business requirements*

Besides meeting specific administrative and technical needs a computer payroll system must meet general business requirements. The main considerations can be briefly summarised as follows.

(i)   Compliance with the overall business and information technology strategies of the organisation.

(ii)   Relationship with other business functions, e.g. accounts.

(iii) Allowance for all human factors, e.g. training.

(iv)   Systems maintenance and support.

(v)   Reliable suppliers, including in-house computer staff.

(vi)   Over the lifetime of the system the benefits should justify the costs. All tangible and intangible benefits and costs must be identified.

(vii) Maintenance and development of the software is essential. A suitable software maintenance contract must be agreed.

Note:

See Chapters 26–29 for detailed information on payroll automation.

Appendix F

List of Organisations

The local offices of the Inland Revenue, Department of Social Security and Department of Employment are perhaps the most frequently used sources of information for the payroll administrator. Trade unions and employers' federations can sometimes be of assistance. In addition, of course, there is a whole series of other suppliers of information from financial consultancies to specialist publishers. Below are lists of organisations who have an interest in payroll administration and related areas such as employee benefits. The lists are not exhaustive.

Payroll associations

(1)   Institute of Payroll and Pensions Management (IPPM)
        Shelly House, Farmhouse Way, Monkspath, Solihull, West Midlands B90 4EH
        Tel: 0121 711 1341
        (Note: the IPPM aims to cover both the private and public sectors.)

(2)   Private Sector Payrolls Group
        Ms J Petherbridge, 67 High Street, Hampton Wick, Kingston Upon Thames, Surrey KT1 4DG
        Tel: 0181 943 9725

(3)   Public Services Payroll Forum
        Danelea, Laburnum Avenue, Robin Hood's Bay, Whitby YO22 4RR
        Tel: 01947 880534

Related professional associations

(1)   The Chartered Insurance Institute
        20 Aldermanbury, London EC2V 7HY
        Tel: 0171 606 3835

(2)   The Faculty of Actuaries
        Maclaurin House, 18 Dublis Street, Edinburgh EH1 3PP
        Tel: 0131 240 1300

(3)   The Institute of Actuaries
        Staple Inn Hall, High Holborn, London WC1V 7QJ
        Tel: 0171 632 2100

(4)   The Institute of Administrative Management
        40 Chatsworth Parade, Petts Wood, Orpington, Kent BR5 1RW
        Tel: 01689 875555

(5)   The Institute of Chartered Secretaries and Administrators
        16 Park Crescent, London W1N 4AH
        Tel: 0171 580 4741

(6)   The Institute of Personnel and Development
        IPD House, 35 Camp Road, Wimbledon, London SW19 4UX
        Tel: 0181 971 9000

(7)   The Chartered Institute of Taxation
       12 Upper Belgrave St, London SW1X 8BB
       Tel: 0171 235 9381

(8)   The Pensions Management Institute
       PMI House, 4–10 Artillery Lane, London E1 7LS
       Tel: 0171 247 1452

Management services and computing

(1)   British Computer Society (Payroll Specialist Group)
       1 Sanford Street, Swindon, SN1 1HJ
       Tel: 01793 417417

(2)   Computing Services and Software Association
       20 Redline Street, London WC1R 4QN
       Tel: 0171 395 6700

(3)   Data Protection Registrar
       Wycliffe House, Water Lane, Wilmslow, Cheshire SK9 5AF
       Tel: 01625 545745

(4)   The Institute of Management Services
       1 Cecil Court, London Road, Enfield, Middlesex EN2 6DD
       Tel: 0181 363 7452

(5)   The National Computing Centre Ltd
       Oxford House, Oxford Road, Manchester M1 7ED
       Tel: 0161 228 6333

(6)   The Institute for the Management of Information Systems
       IMIS House, Edginton Way, Ruxley Corner, Sidcup,
       Kent DA14 5HR
       Tel: 0181 308 0747

(7)   IDPM Software Evaluation Service
       The Business Centre, 6 Church Street, Twyford, Berks RG10 9DR
       Tel: 0118 934 5262

Accountancy

(1)   The Association of Accounting Technicians
       154 Clerkenwell Road, London EC1R 5AD
       Tel: 0171 837 8600

(2)   The Chartered Association of Certified Accountants
       29 Lincoln's Inn Fields, London WC2A 3EE
       Tel: 0171 242 6855

(3)   The Chartered Institute of Management Accountants
       63 Portland Place, London W1N 4AB
       Tel: 0171 637 2311

(4)   The Chartered Institute of Public Finance and Accountancy
       3 Robert Street, London WC2N 6BH
       Tel: 0171 543 5600

(5)   The Institute of Chartered Accountants in England and Wales
PO Box 433, Chartered Accountants' Hall, Moorgate Place,
London EC2P 2BJ
Tel: 0171 920 8100

(6)   The Institute of Chartered Accountants in Ireland
11 Donegall Square South, Belfast BT1 5JE
Tel: 01232 321600

(7)   The Institute of Chartered Accountants of Scotland
27 Queen Street, Edinburgh EH2 1LA
Tel: 0131 225 5673

(8)   The Institute of Internal Auditors
Unit 13, Abbeville Mews,
88 Clapham Park Road, London SW4 7BX
Tel: 0171 498 0101

Government organisations

(1)   Advisory, Conciliation and Arbitration Service (ACAS)
Brandon House, 180 Borough High Street, London SE1 1LW
Tel: 0171 210 3613

(2)   Commission for Racial Equality
Elliot House, 10–12 Allington Street, London SW1E 5EH
Tel: 0171 828 7022

(3)   Department for Education and Employment
Sanctuary Buildings, Great Smith Road, Westminster, London SW1P 3BT
Tel: 0171 925 5000

(4)   Department of Social Security
Richmond House, 79 Whitehall, London SW1A 2NS
Tel: 0171 210 3000

(5)   Equal Opportunities Commission
Overseas House, Quay Street, Manchester M3 3HN
Tel: 0161 833 9244

(6)   Health and Safety Executive
Rose Court, 2 Southwark Bridge, London SE1 9HS
Tel: 0171 717 6000

(7)   Her Majesty's Stationery Office (HMSO)
123 Kingsway, London WC2B 6PQ
Tel: 0171 242 6393
(Also at principal cities.)

(8)   Industrial Tribunals Central Office (England and Wales)
100 Southgate Street, Bury St. Edmunds, Suffolk IP33 2AQ
Tel: 0345 959775

(9)   Inland Revenue
Somerset House, Strand, London WC2A 1LB
Tel: 0171 438 6622

(10)   Pension Schemes Office, Inland Revenue
Yorke House, PO Box 62, Castle Meadow Road, Nottingham NG2 1BG
Tel: 0115 974 1600

(11)   Contracted-out Employment Group, DSS Longbenton
       Benton Park Road, Newcastle upon Tyne NE98 1YX
       Tel: 0191 225 0150

(12)   Occupational Regulatory Authority (OPRA)
       Invicta House, Trafalgar Place, Brighton, East Sussex BN1 4DW
       Tel: 01273 627600

(13)   Social Security Advice Line for Employers
       Tel: 0345 143143

(14)   The Court Services (CAPS)
       (Centralised Attachment of Earnings Payment System)
       PO Box 404, Northampton NN1 2ZY
       Tel: 01604 601555

Miscellaneous

(1)   Confederation of British Industry
       Centre Point, 103 New Oxford Street, London WC1A 1DU
       Tel: 0171 379 7400

(2)   The Industrial Society
       Peter Runge House, 3 Carlton House Terrace, London SW1Y 5DG
       Tel: 0171 839 4300

(3)   The National Association of Pension Funds
       12–18 Grosvenor Gardens, London SW1W 0DH
       Tel: 0171 730 0585

(4)   Trades Union Congress
       Congress House, 23–28 Great Russell Street, London WC1B 3LS
       Tel: 0171 636 4030

(5)   BACS Limited
       3 De Haviland Road, Edgware, Middlesex HA8 5QA
       Tel: 0181 952 2333

(6)   Payroll Alliance
       Tolley House, 2 Addiscombe Road, Croydon CR9 5AF
       Tel: 0181 686 9141

(7)   Cheques Credit Clearing Co Ltd, Mercury House, Triton Court,
       14 Finsbury Square, London EC2A 1BR
       Tel: 0171 711 6200

Appendix G

Redundancy Pay Ready Reckoner

Complete years of service

Age	2	3	4	5	6	7	8	9	10	11	12	13	14	15	16	17	18	19	20
20	1	1	1	1	—														
21	1	1½	1½	1½	1½	—													
22	1	1½	2	2	2	2	—												
23	1½	2	2½	3	3	3	3	—											
24	2	2½	3	3½	4	4	4	4	—										
25	2	3	3½	4	4½	5	5	5	5	—									
26	2	3	4	4½	5	5½	6	6	6	6	—								
27	2	3	4	5	5½	6	6½	7	7	7	7	—							
28	2	3	4	5	6	6½	7	7½	8	8	8	8	—						
29	2	3	4	5	6	7	7½	8	8½	9	9	9	9	—					
30	2	3	4	5	6	7	8	8½	9	9½	10	10	10	10	—				
31	2	3	4	5	6	7	8	9	9½	10	10½	11	11	11	11	—			
32	2	3	4	5	6	7	8	9	10	10½	11	11½	12	12	12	12	—		
33	2	3	4	5	6	7	8	9	10	11	11½	12	12½	13	13	13	13	—	
34	2	3	4	5	6	7	8	9	10	11	12	12½	13	13½	14	14	14	14	—
35	2	3	4	5	6	7	8	9	10	11	12	13	13½	14	14½	15	15	15	15
36	2	3	4	5	6	7	8	9	10	11	12	13	14	14½	15	15½	16	16	16
37	2	3	4	5	6	7	8	9	10	11	12	13	14	15	15½	16	16½	17	17

Age in years at date of redundancy

Age																			
38	2	3	4	5	6	7	8	9	10	11	12	13	14	15	16	16½	17	17½	18
39	2	3	4	5	6	7	8	9	10	11	12	13	14	15	16	17	17½	18	18½
40	2	3	4	5	6	7	8	9	10	11	12	13	14	15	16	17	18	18½	19
41	2	3	4	5	6	7	8	9	10	11	12	13	14	15	16	17	18	19	19½
42	2½	3½	4½	5½	6½	7½	8½	9½	10½	11½	12½	13½	14½	15½	16½	17½	18½	19½	20½
43	3	4	5	6	7	8	9	10	11	12	13	14	15	16	17	18	19	20	21
44	3	4½	5½	6½	7½	8½	9½	10½	11½	12½	13½	14½	15½	16½	17½	18½	19½	20½	21½
45	3	4½	6	7	8	9	10	11	12	13	14	15	16	17	18	19	20	21	22
46	3	4½	6	7½	8½	9½	10½	11½	12½	13½	14½	15½	16½	17½	18½	19½	20½	21½	22½
47	3	4½	6	7½	9	10	11	12	13	14	15	16	17	18	19	20	21	22	23
48	3	4½	6	7½	9	10½	11½	12½	13½	14½	15½	16½	17½	18½	19½	20½	21½	22½	23½
49	3	4½	6	7½	9	10½	12	13	14	15	16	17	18	19	20	21	22	23	24
50	3	4½	6	7½	9	10½	12	13½	14½	15½	16½	17½	18½	19½	20½	21½	22½	23½	24½
51	3	4½	6	7½	9	10½	12	13½	15	16	17	18	19	20	21	22	23	24	25
52	3	4½	6	7½	9	10½	12	13½	15	16½	17½	18½	19½	20½	21½	22½	23½	24½	25½
53	3	4½	6	7½	9	10½	12	13½	15	16½	18	19	20	21	22	23	24	25	26
54	3	4½	6	7½	9	10½	12	13½	15	16½	18	19½	20½	21½	22½	23½	24½	25½	26½
55	3	4½	6	7½	9	10½	12	13½	15	16½	18	19½	21	22	23	24	25	26	27
56	3	4½	6	7½	9	10½	12	13½	15	16½	18	19½	21	22½	23½	24½	25½	26½	27½
57	3	4½	6	7½	9	10½	12	13½	15	16½	18	19½	21	22½	24	25	26	27	28
58	3	4½	6	7½	9	10½	12	13½	15	16½	18	19½	21	22½	24	25½	26½	27½	28½
59	3	4½	6	7½	9	10½	12	13½	15	16½	18	19½	21	22½	24	25½	27	28	29
60	3	4½	6	7½	9	10½	12	13½	15	16½	18	19½	21	22½	24	25½	27	28½	29½
61	3	4½	6	7½	9	10½	12	13½	15	16½	18	19½	21	22½	24	25½	27	28½	30
62	3	4½	6	7½	9	10½	12	13½	15	16½	18	19½	21	22½	24	25½	27	28½	30
63	3	4½	6	7½	9	10½	12	13½	15	16½	18	19½	21	22½	24	25½	27	28½	30
64	3	4½	6	7½	9	10½	12	13½	15	16½	18	19½	21	22½	24	25½	27	28½	30

Age in years at date of redundancy

Appendix H

Community Charge and Council Tax Attachment of Earnings Orders

Deduction Tables

Table A: Deductions from Weekly Earnings for Orders made from 1 October 1998

Net earnings				Deductions rate %
Not exceeding	£55			0
Exceeding	£55	but not exceeding	£100	3%
Exceeding	£100	but not exceeding	£135	5%
Exceeding	£135	but not exceeding	£165	7%
Exceeding	£165	but not exceeding	£260	12%
Exceeding	£260	but not exceeding	£370	17%
Exceeding	£370			17% in respect of the first £370 and 50 per cent in respect of the remainder

Table B: Deductions from Monthly Earnings for Orders made from 1 October 1998

Net earnings				Deductions rate %
Not exceeding	£220			0
Exceeding	£220	but not exceeding	£400	3%
Exceeding	£400	but not exceeding	£540	5%
Exceeding	£540	but not exceeding	£660	7%
Exceeding	£660	but not exceeding	£1,040	12%
Exceeding	£1,040	but not exceeding	£480	17%
Exceeding	£1,480			17% in respect of the first £1,480 and 50 per cent in respect of the remainder

Table C: Deductions Based on Daily Earnings
for Orders made from 1 October 1998

Net earnings				Deductions rate %
Not exceeding	£8			0
Exceeding	£8	but not exceeding	£15	3%
Exceeding	£15	but not exceeding	£20	5%
Exceeding	£20	but not exceeding	£24	7%
Exceeding	£24	but not exceeding	£38	12%
Exceeding	£38	but not exceeding	£53	17%
Exceeding	£53			17% in respect of the first £53 and 50 per cent in respect of the remainder

Appendix J

Scottish Earnings Arrestment Orders Deduction Tables

Table A: Deductions from Weekly Earnings Applicable to Arrestments from 30 November 1995

Net earnings				Deduction
Not exceeding	£63			Nil
Exceeding	£63	but not exceeding	£75	£2.00
Exceeding	£75	but not exceeding	£80	£4.00
Exceeding	£80	but not exceeding	£85	£5.00
Exceeding	£85	but not exceeding	£95	£6.00
Exceeding	£95	but not exceeding	£105	£8.00
Exceeding	£105	but not exceeding	£115	£10.00
Exceeding	£115	but not exceeding	£125	£12.00
Exceeding	£125	but not exceeding	£135	£14.00
Exceeding	£135	but not exceeding	£145	£16.00
Exceeding	£145	but not exceeding	£155	£18.60
Exceeding	£155	but not exceeding	£165	£20.00
Exceeding	£165	but not exceeding	£175	£22.00
Exceeding	£175	but not exceeding	£185	£24.00
Exceeding	£185	but not exceeding	£195	£27.00
Exceeding	£195	but not exceeding	£210	£30.00
Exceeding	£210	but not exceeding	£230	£34.00
Exceeding	£230	but not exceeding	£250	£38.00
Exceeding	£250	but not exceeding	£270	£42.00
Exceeding	£270	but not exceeding	£290	£47.00
Exceeding	£290	but not exceeding	£310	£52.00
Exceeding	£310	but not exceeding	£330	£57.00
Exceeding	£330	but not exceeding	£350	£62.00
Exceeding	£350	but not exceeding	£370	£68.00
Exceeding	£370	but not exceeding	£400	£82.00
Exceeding	£400	but not exceeding	£430	£97.00
Exceeding	£430	but not exceeding	£460	£113.00
Exceeding	£460	but not exceeding	£500	£131.00
Exceeding	£500	but not exceeding	£540	£149.00
Exceeding	£540			£149.00 in respect of the first £540 plus 50 per cent of the remainder

Table B: Deductions from Monthly Earnings
Applicable to Arrestments from 30 November 1995

Net earnings				Deduction
Not exceeding	£273			Nil
Exceeding	£273	but not exceeding	£310	£9.00
Exceeding	£310	but not exceeding	£330	£14.00
Exceeding	£330	but not exceeding	£350	£19.00
Exceeding	£350	but not exceeding	£380	£26.00
Exceeding	£380	but not exceeding	£420	£33.00
Exceeding	£420	but not exceeding	£460	£40.00
Exceeding	£460	but not exceeding	£500	£47.00
Exceeding	£500	but not exceeding	£540	£54.00
Exceeding	£540	but not exceeding	£580	£61.00
Exceeding	£580	but not exceeding	£620	£68.00
Exceeding	£620	but not exceeding	£660	£75.00
Exceeding	£660	but not exceeding	£700	£82.00
Exceeding	£700	but not exceeding	£740	£90.00
Exceeding	£740	but not exceeding	£800	£104.00
Exceeding	£800	but not exceeding	£860	£118.00
Exceeding	£860	but not exceeding	£930	£132.00
Exceeding	£930	but not exceeding	£1000	£147.00
Exceeding	£1000	but not exceeding	£1070	£162.00
Exceeding	£1070	but not exceeding	£1140	£177.00
Exceeding	£1140	but not exceeding	£1220	£196.00
Exceeding	£1220	but not exceeding	£1300	£217.00
Exceeding	£1300	but not exceeding	£1400	£239.00
Exceeding	£1400	but not exceeding	£1500	£261.00
Exceeding	£1500	but not exceeding	£1600	£324.00
Exceeding	£1600	but not exceeding	£1800	£396.00
Exceeding	£1800	but not exceeding	£2000	£472.00
Exceeding	£2000	but not exceeding	£2200	£562.00
Exceeding	£2200	but not exceeding	£2400	£652.00
Exceeding	£2400			£652.00 in respect of the first £2400 plus 50 per cent of the remainder

Table C: Deductions Based on Daily Earnings
Applicable to Arrestments from 30 November 1995

Net earnings				Deduction	
Not exceeding	£9			Nil	
Exceeding	£9	but not exceeding	£11	£0.25	
Exceeding	£11	but not exceeding	£12	£0.50	
Exceeding	£12	but not exceeding	£14	£0.80	
Exceeding	£14	but not exceeding	£16	£1.10	
Exceeding	£16	but not exceeding	£18	£1.80	
Exceeding	£18	but not exceeding	£20	£2.15	
Exceeding	£20	but not exceeding	£22	£2.50	
Exceeding	£22	but not exceeding	£24	£2.85	
Exceeding	£24	but not exceeding	£26	£3.20	
Exceeding	£26	but not exceeding	£28	£3.60	
Exceeding	£28	but not exceeding	£31	£4.20	
Exceeding	£31	but not exceeding	£34	£4.90	
Exceeding	£34	but not exceeding	£37	£5.80	
Exceeding	£37	but not exceeding	£41	£6.70	
Exceeding	£41	but not exceeding	£45	£7.70	
Exceeding	£45	but not exceeding	£49	£9.00	
Exceeding	£49	but not exceeding	£54	£10.80	
Exceeding	£54	but not exceeding	£59	£12.60	
Exceeding	£59	but not exceeding	£64	£15.30	
Exceeding	£64	but not exceeding	£70	£18.00	
Exceeding	£70	but not exceeding	£75	£20.70	
Exceeding	£75			£20.70	in respect of the first £75 plus 50 per cent of the remainder

Appendix K

Scottish Current Maintenance Arrestment Daily Rate of Protected Earnings

Pre 30 November 1995	£5.00
From 30 November 1995	£9.00

Index